MW01492838

"What stands out about this book in that it is n̶[...] rather about the process of becoming a researcher. There is a strong focus on develop[...] one's identity, attitudes, and values as a scholar. I've had the good fortune to "try out" draft chapters from this book in my Research Methods in Industrial and Organizational Psychology course for the last few years. I've taught this for decades, and this text really adds value to the course. It is very favorably received by students. Landers and Behrend have provided a great service to the field with this project."

Paul Sackett, *Richard Fink Distinguished Professor of Liberal Arts, Department of Psychology, University of Minnesota, USA*

"Landers and Behrend have provided an indispensable guide to research methods in I-O psychology, driven by an underlying principle that similar books often forget, namely that research is a human enterprise at its essence. In fact, the leading chapter explores a philosophical question that is as unique as it is important: How might one's beliefs, assumptions, and practices influence the conduct of research? Through their social and scientific explanations, the authors make the strong case for diverse research and researchers in I-O psychology.

This philosophical perspective then drives its subsequent chapters: creating a compelling case for conducting a study, conducting a solid literature review, stating your research hypotheses clearly, choosing a research method judiciously, deciding on a research sample appropriate to the study, cleaning and analyzing your data in a principled manner, and identifying a journal and target audience. Landers and Behrend emphasize that careful planning underlies all the above components of one's research strategy (e.g., preregistration, IRB approval, pilot testing, revising a paper). The concluding chapter, in fact, provides a checklist of these components, so that all I-O psychologists can take a systematic approach to their research (and to avoid common pitfalls). The book chapters contain other checklists that I hope readers will find to be as valuable as I did (e.g., developing a survey, cleaning data, conducting a meta-analysis).

Overall, Landers and Behrend convey their deep knowledge and experience in a highly accessible, informative—and yes, humorous—manner. You will greatly benefit from reading this book if you are a graduate student, faculty member, or practitioner who wants to improve how they conduct, interpret, use, and critically discuss research in I-O psychology. It is not a stretch to say this book is a tool for I-O psychologists to provide greater benefit to workers, teams, organizations—and by no large stretch, society."

Fred Oswald, *PhD, Professor and Herbert S. Autrey Chair in Social Sciences, Department of Psychological Sciences, Rice University, USA*

Research Methods for Industrial and Organizational Psychology

This important and useful book offers a clear and comprehensive foundation for research methods in industrial and organizational (I-O) psychology. The text provides readers with a key understanding of the research, theory, and practice needed towards becoming a research methods expert.

The use of trustworthy and rigorous research methods is foundational to advancing the science of industrial and organizational psychology and its practice in the field. Understanding this, the authors have paired straightforward, plainly written explanations in a conversational tone with illuminating diagrams and illustrations. Many descriptions are followed by in-depth demonstrations and examples from relevant software, including SPSS, R, and even Excel when it's the best option available. Insightful and accessible, the text covers the full gamut of I-O research methods, from theory to practice and everywhere between.

Paired with a detailed instructor's manual, this book serves as a gentle but thorough introduction to the complex world of research methods in I-O psychology for both master's and Ph.D. students, as well as researchers, academics, and practitioners.

Richard N. Landers, Ph.D., is the John P. Campbell Distinguished Professor of Industrial-Organizational Psychology at the University of Minnesota and Principal Investigator of Testing New Technologies in Learning, Assessment, and Behavior (TNTLAB).

Tara S. Behrend, Ph.D., is the John Richard Butler II Endowed Professor of Human Resources and Labor Relations at Michigan State University. She directs the Workplaces and Virtual Environments Lab, which focuses on the psychological and policy implications of emerging workplace technologies.

Research Methods for Industrial and Organizational Psychology

Science and Practice

Richard N. Landers and Tara S. Behrend

Routledge
Taylor & Francis Group

NEW YORK AND LONDON

Cover Image: © Getty Images

First published 2024
by Routledge
605 Third Avenue, New York, NY 10158

and by Routledge
4 Park Square, Milton Park, Abingdon, Oxon, OX14 4RN

Routledge is an imprint of the Taylor & Francis Group, an informa business

© 2024 Richard N. Landers and Tara S. Behrend

The right of Richard N. Landers and Tara S. Behrend to be identified as authors
of this work has been asserted in accordance with sections 77 and 78 of the
Copyright, Designs and Patents Act 1988.

All rights reserved. No part of this book may be reprinted or reproduced or
utilised in any form or by any electronic, mechanical, or other means, now known
or hereafter invented, including photocopying and recording, or in any information
storage or retrieval system, without permission in writing from the publishers.

Trademark notice: Product or corporate names may be trademarks or registered
trademarks, and are used only for identification and explanation without intent to
infringe.

Library of Congress Cataloging-in-Publication Data
Names: Landers, Richard N., author. | Behrend, Tara S., author.
Title: Research methods for industrial and organizational psychology : science and
    practice / Richard N. Landers and Tara S. Behrend.
Description: New York, NY : Routledge, 2024. | Includes bibliographical references
    and index.
Identifiers: LCCN 2023047600 (print) | LCCN 2023047601 (ebook) |
    ISBN 9781138052925 (hardback) | ISBN 9781138052932 (paperback) |
    ISBN 9781315167473 (ebook)
Subjects: LCSH: Psychology, Industrial—Research—Methodology. |
    Organizational behavior—Research—Methodology.
Classification: LCC HF5548.8 .L246 2024 (print) | LCC HF5548.8 (ebook) |
    DDC 158.7—dc23/eng/20231011
LC record available at https://lccn.loc.gov/2023047600
LC ebook record available at https://lccn.loc.gov/2023047601

ISBN: 978-1-138-05292-5 (hbk)
ISBN: 978-1-138-05293-2 (pbk)
ISBN: 978-1-315-16747-3 (ebk)

DOI: 10.4324/9781315167473

Typeset in Optima
by Apex CoVantage, LLC

Access the Instructor resources: www.routledge.com/9781138052932

For Amy and Owen,
who inspire me every day,

for Paul and Deniz,
who taught me to care about the why,

and for Larry,
who first inspired and later took a chance on a certain young
methodologist.

– Richard

For my mentors:
For Lori, who taught me that research is supposed to be fun,
For Eric, who showed me that our research can make people's
lives better,
For Adam, who was always the voice of reason (and who made me
do IRT by hand),

And for my students, who give my work meaning and joy.

– Tara

Contents

Acknowledgments   *xi*
About the Authors   *xii*
Foreword   *xiii*

PART I
Foundations   **1**

1   Becoming a Researcher, Becoming an I-O Psychologist   3

2   Reviewing Research Literature with a Goal in Mind   27

3   Selecting the Best Research Strategy From Your Literature Review   53

4   Selecting a Research Population and Identifying a Sample   76

PART II
Qualitative Methods   **97**

5   Approaches for Investigating and Respecting Complexity   99

6   Data Collection, Analytic Strategies, and Minimizing Bias   121

PART III
Quantitative Methods   **147**

7   Measuring Psychological Constructs   149

8   Research Design in Pursuit of Trustworthy Conclusions   181

9   Building and Administering a Questionnaire   211

10 Creating a Rating Scale That Reflects a Construct   236

11 Cleaning Data Without Hacking Them   262

PART IV
Advanced Topics   **297**

12 Null Hypothesis Significance Testing and Reasonable Alternatives   299

13 Understanding and Executing Meta-Analyses   326

14 Strategies for Openly Sharing Research, Materials, and Data   358

15 From Start to Finish: Guidelines and a Checklist for Conducting
    Research   391

    Glossary   *421*
    Index   *452*

Acknowledgments

The authors wish to acknowledge and thank the many individuals who contributed to making this book possible, especially Jerod White for his extensive research and editing support; Zach Roper for providing his perspective and input; members of the WAVE Lab and TNTLAB for being trial subjects for the ideas presented here; and Paul Sackett, Melissa Robertson, Louis Tay, Chelsea Song, Sang Woo, and Frankie Kung for their feedback and pilot testing with students on early drafts.

About the Authors

Richard N. Landers, Ph.D., is the John P. Campbell Distinguished Professor of Industrial-Organizational Psychology at the University of Minnesota and Principal Investigator of Testing New Technologies in Learning, Assessment, and Behavior (TNTLAB). His research concerns the use of innovative technologies like games, artificial intelligence, and virtual reality to improve assessment, hiring, learning, and research methods. He is a Fellow of the Society for Industrial and Organizational Psychology, American Psychological Association, and Association for Psychology Science. He currently serves in editorial roles for various academic journals and is author of two textbooks and editor of two scholarly volumes. He has been featured in outlets like *Forbes, Business Insider*, and *Popular Science*, and he consults in industry via Landers Workforce Science LLC (https://landers.tech).

Tara S. Behrend, Ph.D., is the John Richard Butler II Endowed Professor of Human Resources and Labor Relations at Michigan State University. She directs the Workplaces and Virtual Environments Lab, which focuses on the psychological and policy implications of emerging workplace technologies. She is a former program director for the National Science Foundation, overseeing the Science of Organizations and Future of Work programs, and is currently serving on the National Academies Board on Human-Systems Integration. She is President (2023–2024) of the Society for Industrial and Organizational Psychology.

Foreword

"It is tempting, if the only tool you have is a hammer, to treat everything as if it were a nail." – Maslow (1966), also called the "Law of the Instrument" or "Maslow's hammer"

Most research methodologists, myself (Richard) included, did not originally intend to become methodologists. In fact, most graduate advisors in I-O psychology quite explicitly recommended *against* it. The most commonly expressed bias is that methodology is a tool to be used in service of "real" research questions, like why some human trait is related to some other human trait.

During my graduate training, I was struck, however, by the sheer volume of "real" research that was published despite their methods not really supporting their stated conclusions. I started to wonder how so much poor-quality research, whether in terms of research design or real-world applicability, managed to get through peer review and into print. This perception was crystallized while writing my dissertation, which incorporated a series of meta-analyses about the effectiveness of web-based instruction. Those meta-analyses pulled sources mostly from the education literature, where this problem was even worse than in psychology – the *majority* of the research designs I read about did not really support the conclusions that were drawn, and there were seemingly field-wide misconceptions about how statistics can be used to support research conclusions, some of which you'll read about in this book.

Over my pre-tenure years, my annoyance at the state of methods in our journals intensified. I began to think about the thousands of hours of wasted researcher time, wasted participant effort, wasted pages of journals that surely could be used for more reliable, more valid, and more important insights. I was troubled when I realized how many research hours within my own lab had been wasted, because we'd built research studies on top of what turned out to be flimsy, non-replicable foundations. As this interest in methods grew, I found myself fascinated with what was a new method to psychology at the time – web scraping and the analysis of web scraped data – and published my first large-scale methods-oriented research paper, diving headfirst into the world of methodology to help others draw better conclusions.

After publishing that paper, I began to be invited to give more frequent methods workshops. And in conducting those, I began to better understand and appreciate just how lost many researchers felt. Across all the workshops and talks I've given, I have never once detected malicious intent from an attendee. Instead, I saw quite clearly that most researchers learned research methods by osmosis, absorbing spoken and unspoken lessons from their advisors and mentors in graduate school, many of which were not good lessons. They frequently crafted for themselves a set of internalized "best practices" built primarily on habit rather than thoughtful consideration of the issues surrounding those methods.

In the last few years, as demand for I-O psychology education has increased, primary methods education through osmosis has become even more common. An increasing number of I-O osmosis-trained faculty are being asked to teach methods, which is creating a big game of methods telephone, fracturing and diluting expertise in a field that has historically deeply invested in methods. So, hoping to put a dent in that problem is what motivated me to approach Tara about writing this book, which is aimed primarily at first-year graduate students and early career researchers but hopefully contains lessons for all.

With that in mind, I hope you approach this book not as an instruction manual to slog through but instead as a tool for understanding how you can conduct high-quality research that helps make the world a better place. I further hope you use it to reflect on your own goals, values, and beliefs in research. If you disagree with our reflections and recommendations here, great! – as long as you have done so thoughtfully, with purpose and intent, and with knowledge of all those who have come before you trying to do exactly the same. That's how we continue to grow, both individually and as a field.

– Richard N. Landers

When Richard approached me about writing this book, I was skeptical. I thought, there are already so many methods books. Does the world really need another one? And why should we be the ones to write it, if so? Richard tried to persuade me by promising that I could put all my dorkiest stories and research metaphors in the book. Unfortunately for the reader, that promise was realized– this book is full of truly corny jokes, and I apologize in advance for that. But the thing that ultimately convinced me that Richard was right was that no existing book sufficiently explained the "why" of research. Why do we make one choice over another? What are the consequences of our choices, over the span of a project or the span of a career? It's so easy to forget that research is conducted by human beings, with values, beliefs, and habits, and who are subject to external incentives and influences. This book does the job of reminding us about the human element in research. You can find formulas elsewhere. Here, you can explore the social, historical, and scientific context that is relevant to using the formula.

Our conversations about this book began in late 2016. Since that time, we have had many, many discussions about the ideas we wanted to include– and we had to make some difficult choices. We couldn't fit everything, but we wanted to make sure we gave space to the kinds of ideas that other methods books leave out. I didn't want this to be a book about "you must do this" and "definitely don't do this" – instead, I wanted to help connect the dots between research decisions and outcomes and set people up to be better thinkers and evaluators of research not because they have learned a set of rules but because they understand the consequences of a researchers' decisions and can follow and critique the set of logical inferences a researcher makes in their study.

I am decidedly not "a methodologist," in that I don't publish papers very often that are explicitly *about* methodological topics. On the other hand, I truly love designing and executing research projects, and I hope that the sense of joy I feel comes through in these pages.

– Tara S. Behrend

Reference

Maslow, A. H. (1966). *The psychology of science: A reconnaissance.* Harper & Row.

Part I

Foundations

## Chapter 1

Becoming a Researcher, Becoming an I-O Psychologist

Learning Objectives

After reading this chapter, you will be able to:

1. Describe the philosophy of science that drives I-O psychology research.
2. Identify and contrast ontological and epistemological frameworks.
3. Start to define your own identity as an I-O psychology researcher.
4. Describe ethical standards that drive I-O psychology research.
5. Identify similarities and differences between individual research identities.

"It was the best of times. . . . And then you went to graduate school."

– Charles Dickens (sort of)

If you're reading this book, you're probably fairly new to the world of research, within the first few years of the adventure. As an early career researcher, you are probably still trying to figure out who you are and what your place will be. What will it mean for you to be a researcher in I-O psychology? What *is* **research**, anyway?

First, you'll need to understand the "big picture." What is research and what's it *for*? What's the point of all this effort to learn about so many tiny, picky details? How do we know we are drawing meaningful conclusions? This requires understanding the philosophical foundations of not just research in general but your research area in particular. This will lead you to eventually ask: Why does my advisor do what they do? What have I taken for granted by conducting research the same way as them? You may be surprised at just how long this list is.

Second, you'll need to determine what role research will play in your professional life. Will you be running a research lab of your own at a university, mentoring graduate students on their own career paths? Will you be using your research skills to answer questions for an organization? Or will you be a consumer of research, reading the newest papers to inform your decision-making on the job? What are your goals for work–life balance, research application, and the people surrounding you?

Third, you'll develop a set of values about research. Why are *you* doing research? This is not a question of why research is "good" or "useful" but rather why you personally are involved in it. People answer this question in many different ways. We (Tara and Richard)

DOI: 10.4324/9781315167473-2

conduct research because we genuinely believe that we are generating new knowledge that will help solve important societal problems and improve human wellbeing. This is grandiose, we know. But this core belief is essential to our identities as researchers. You might be driven by different goals and different values. Even the people in your graduate program or your office may not share your values. But that makes it all the more important to figure out what your values are and then ensure you stick to them.

Answering these questions form the very foundation of who you are as a researcher, so it's important to think about them before finding yourself deeply in a research program and career that you neither understand nor value. Later in this chapter, you'll see some reflections from working I-O psychologists about how they have shaped their identities. You'll see that they are quite varied but also quite clear in establishing their values and priorities.

Step 1: Developing a Firm Philosophical Foundation

The most fundamental values in research come from your philosophical orientation toward the nature of reality and the nature of knowledge-building itself. Where does knowledge come from? How do I create it? This is not something you've probably spent much time thinking about so far, but you likely already have an implicit philosophy based on the classes you've taken, the perspectives you've found resonate with you, and also the ones that didn't. Alternatively, you might just be coasting along without critically evaluating why you're doing what you're doing. In either case, it's time to focus and make these decisions with purpose.

Understanding the philosophical basis of your research is essential. Many researchers, over the course of their careers, stop paying attention to the philosophical assumptions they are making and begin to take them for granted. The result can be understood with an old expression adapted from Maslow (1966), "When all you have is a hammer, everything looks like a nail." If all you know is one approach, soon you will only ask questions that can fit into that approach, or worse, you will distort the questions you are asking.

To avoid that, we must ask: *how do we know what we know?* Philosophers, who presumably stroke their long white hair while pondering this question, have developed elaborate systems to think about **knowledge**, which can be defined as a collection of justified true beliefs, and how knowledge is generated. The meaning of *justified* differs depending upon your assumptions about knowledge, and giving structure and shape to those assumptions is the role of philosophy.

As we explore this further, consider the following statement about something we might say we "know": The sun will come up tomorrow. What must you assume to confidently say this statement is true, to justify this statement as your authentic belief?

Ontology

One possible justification is probabilistic. The sun has come up every day for the last 1000 days. A predictable pattern has been established. The most probable outcome is that it will come up again on the 1001th day. The foundation on which such logic can be applied is a researcher's **ontological stance**, which refers to your belief system regarding the nature of reality (the term "**ontology**" refers to the philosophical field that studies the nature of ontological stances, although you will often see the word "ontology" used to refer to "ontological stances," including in this very chapter). There are many different ontological stances, far more than you really need to know about. But many of these ontological stances, and the

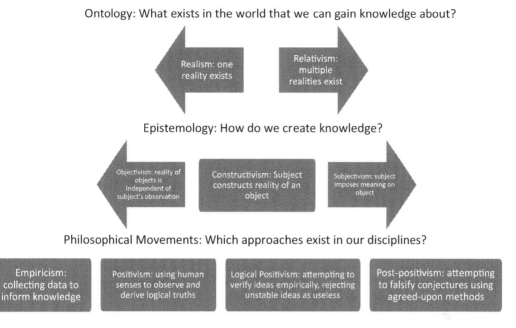

Figure 1.1 Ontology, epistemology, and philosophical movements relevant to I-O psychology.

one reflected in this justification, can be considered branches of **realism** (see Figure 1.1), named so because realism asserts that there is a single reality. In this case, that reality is that the sun either objectively exists or it doesn't, and its rising either will occur or it won't – and in this case, the available evidence suggests that the sun exists and will rise again.

It is important to realize that even from a realist perspective, different observers may have dramatically different perspectives and draw different conclusions regarding that reality. A common example of this is in determining the causes of a plane crash. Consider the following perspectives:

1. Federal investigators conclude that the cause of the crash is faulty equipment.
2. The airline concludes that although the equipment was faulty, the cause of the crash was that the pilot failed to conduct all the required safety checks before takeoff.
3. The pilot's union concludes that although safety checks were not conducted, the cause of the crash was insufficient training in safety protocols.
4. Federal regulators conclude that poorly written personnel policies led to the pilot being overworked and fatigued, and thus the policies caused the accident.

All of these conclusions regarding reality may appear "true" from the observer's point of view. But regardless of these multiple perspectives, all parties must first agree that *the plane did indeed crash and that a single true cause or set of causes exist*. Thus, for realists, there is some true external reality that is *not* subject to interpretation that serves as a foundation from which to ask meaningful questions, even when different people come to different conclusions about that reality.

Realism is considered in contrast to **relativism**, which is also a full family of ontologies, as shown in Figure 1.1. Relativists assume that reality exists for each person observing it. Relativists don't necessarily deny the existence of any objective reality – although some do – but generally agree that pondering whether an objective reality exists underneath all of these individual realities is a waste of time, because such a singular reality would be unknowable anyway.

Let's return to our belief that the sun will rise tomorrow. In my reality, the sun has historically always come up, and I have no reason to believe that will change, so in my reality, the sun will come up tomorrow. For a person that has lived their entire life underground, without sunlight, the sun does not even exist. In that person's reality, the sun is a non-entity; there is no "truth" about the sun's patterns, because the sun does not exist for that person at all. In relativism, there is no inherent conflict to the differences between my reality and this underground-person's reality; these realities can coexist, each unique for each of us.

Epistemologies

In addition to ontological differences, there are **epistemological** differences between researchers that concern the way knowledge is best created (and as you might expect, the term "**epistemology**" refers to the study of this idea and is often used synonymously with **epistemological framework**). There are three common epistemological frameworks, shown in Figure 1.1. Hardcore realists most likely endorse an **objectivist** epistemology, which is one assuming that knowledge of reality comes from reality itself; for example, because the sun has properties that objectively exist, it is through research that we can add to our knowledge of the sun by discovering those properties. Hardcore relativists most likely endorse a **subjectivist** epistemology, which assumes that knowledge of each person's reality comes through exploration of that reality by the person that created it. From a relativist perspective, because each person has their own reality regarding the sun rising, the only way to learn about that reality is by asking that person to explore it – and even then, your understanding as a researcher will be clouded by your own reality. (You can easily see how deep down the philosophical rabbit hole relativism can lead you!). An orientation that combines objectivist and subjectivist elements is **constructivism**, which is the most common epistemological stance in modern psychology. From this perspective, knowledge is both individually and socially constructed. This knowledge could be created in pursuit of either objective truths (i.e., realism) or knowledge of multiple shared realities (i.e., relativism). In either case, our own **biases** (whether expressed as objectively existing or as personal truths) are barriers to building knowledge about what we want to build knowledge about.

The implications of epistemology are important, so let's consider a contemporary example. How do researchers know personality exists?

For objectivists, the existence of personality would begin as an assertion about an emergent property of humans. Then, data would need to be collected to either confirm or disprove the idea of this emergent property. Within this perspective, if personality exists as a set of universal human traits, it will emerge for everyone, so evidence collected should be used to test this emergence.

For subjectivists, the existence of personality is unique to each person, in terms of both its expression and perception of others. A person's personality may be expressed or it may not; other people may have personalities or they may not. Each person constructs their own meaning surrounding personality. (Something you may be realizing around now: it is difficult to follow the scientific method as a pure subjectivist!).

For constructivists, the existence of personality is socially constructed. Personality may or may not objectively exist in the sense of areas of the brain, or neurochemical processes, or some other process. What matters is that the idea of personality has been generally agreed upon for many centuries, that people differ from one another in terms of their behavior in predictable ways, and understanding those patterns is what's important.

This highlights a few tensions you see in modern discourse regarding personality. For example:

- A researcher who complains, "personality doesn't exist until I can see it in a brain scan," or "personality is just a social construction, so it's not worth my time," is really asserting their realist ontology and objectivist epistemology.
- A researcher who states, "I only care about each individual and their unique expression of their true self as they experience and understand it," is really asserting their relativistic ontology and subjectivist epistemology.
- A researcher who reasons, "personality may be socially constructed or it may not, but for now, it's a useful framework to understand differences between people," is asserting a blended-but-leaning-realistic ontology and a constructivist epistemology.
- A researcher who considers, "personality is a different idea for different people, but studying it can still provide a useful framework to understand differences between people," is promoting a blended-but-leaning-relativistic ontology and a constructivist epistemology.

Mixing and Matching

An important point to realize is that ontologies and epistemologies are not necessarily fixed by an individual. Although we use a lot of shorthand in this chapter, the "reality" is that each person can vary in terms of both depending upon the subject. For example, your authors believe in an objective reality in general (i.e., realism) but also that in certain domains, like research methods, there are few clearly and objectively "better" and "worse" methods. Because research methods often involve trade-offs, like sacrificing generalizability to increase experimental purity, a "good" study has certain characteristics as agreed upon by the overall research community but also is defined in part by each researcher's personal goals, values, and beliefs (i.e., their own reality). In that sense, we are realists in regard to most domain knowledge but more relativistic (although not completely so!) in terms of methodological superiority.

The point of all of this is not to force you to pick a single philosophical orientation and force you to stick to it. Instead, we want to encourage you to think carefully and purposefully about why you think the way you do and how that translates into the research you find interesting, valuable, and worthwhile.

Philosophical Movements

Up to this point, we've really focused on the underlying assumptions and beliefs regarding how you think about the world around you. The topic of **philosophical movement** is more specific; it refers to how groups of researchers in the past took their ontologies and epistemologies and used them to create standard, agreed-upon approaches to understanding topics within specific disciplines. Understanding philosophical movements will help you understand the context of the specific research practices you see valued (and unvalued) in modern published research.

There are hundreds of philosophical movements, and once again, you would likely not benefit (at least at this point) from learning about all of them. Instead, we're going to focus on the most prominent philosophical movements that led to modern **philosophy of science**, which defines what science is, what qualifies as scientific research, and the purpose of science as a whole. We're also going to spend relatively more time on **philosophy of social science**, since that's what guides modern I-O psychology.

Modern philosophy of social science emerged from philosophy of science. To understand why they are different, realize first that the natural sciences have historically been biased toward a realist and objectivist approach to discovery. When those methods were applied to understanding psychology (and other social sciences), problems in approach and interpretation became increasingly obvious over time. For example, in chemistry, it's very easy to apply a realist objectivist orientation to chemical reactions: one can simply mix two chemicals together many times and observe the reactions, and the consistency of the reactions, to gain insight about the chemicals involved. For humans, that doesn't work so well. If you want to draw conclusions about personality, you are forced to contend with a lot of external problems: people don't express their personalities consistently and often change their behavior due to stimuli outside of research control, personality cannot be measured directly, some people don't even agree that personality exists, and so on. In contrast, chemicals are remarkably consistent in terms of their reactions with other chemicals under carefully controlled conditions, tools with field-wide acceptance are commonly used in chemistry, and you will find few chemists arguing against the very existence of molecules.

A prominent long-term battle of philosophies of science, which led directly to the schism between natural and social sciences we see today, started with **positivism**, a 19th-century philosophical movement associated with philosopher Auguste Comte. Roughly speaking, positivism asserted that all knowledge stems from what we can experience with our human senses, as understood through human reason. To understand the world and build knowledge, one needed to smell and look and touch it, reasoning through what you experience. This borrowed heavily from the much older philosophical school of thought that appears called **empiricism**, which originated centuries earlier, at least as far back as Aristotle. Where empiricism describes the general idea that carefully collected data can inform knowledge, positivism advocated a specific method of conducting empirical research with the purpose of finding evidence supporting ideas. For example, if you wanted to show that the movement of the stars and behavior were related, you would need to observe the movement of the stars and people's behaviors, and then draw conclusions about the relationship based upon what you observed. This was in contrast to earlier approaches that focused more heavily on human reason alone. Thus, positivism promoted an early form of the modern **scientific method** as the sole method for creating meaningful knowledge. It was highly dismissive of any speculation regarding things that could not be directly observed.

A response to positivism, **logical positivism**, started with a philosophical movement of the 1920s and 1930s. It was created largely to integrate advances in the theories of logic and mathematics into positivism, and it was associated with philosophers like David Hume (who argued against it in favor of positivism) and Immanuel Kant. A key idea in logical positivism was the **verification principle**, which asserted that unless a statement can be empirically tested, it is a "truth of logic" (i.e., "**tautological**") and therefore cannot contribute to the creation of meaningful knowledge. Logical positivism thus placed supreme value upon empirical testing of ideas and the rejection of anything else as useless for knowledge creation. Thus, logical positivism, like positivism before it, was a realist and objectivist approach to research. Many natural scientists today still use logical positivism as the philosophical foundation to their work, although whether or not they can articulate that reasoning is a different question.

Significant criticism of logical positivism followed in the 1930s and 1940s, most commonly associated with Sir Karl Popper and Thomas Kuhn. Their ideas came to be known as **post-positivism**, which still reflects realist assumptions but is constructivist in epistemology, unlike logical positivism. If you've heard of Popper before, it's probably because of his critique of verificationism, where he argued that it is impossible to verify things one believes to be true, that observing a single instance of something does not prove a general rule. Instead, he argued for **falsification**, the idea that the only logically consistent way to build knowledge is to present **conjectures**, which are simply proposed statements about reality, like our sun-rising example before, and then seek to falsify them through the collection of compelling evidence. For example, if you want to test the idea that the stars influence human behavior, you conjecture that they do and then set out to meaningfully disprove (falsify) that conjecture. If you fail to disprove it despite using generally agreed-upon meaningful methods to do so, you can only conclude that you failed to disprove its truth; you cannot conclude that you proved it to be true.

The logic of falsification is one you likely recognize if you have completed a statistics course that included null hypothesis significance testing; one does not seek to confirm a conjectural hypothesis but instead establishes a null hypothesis and collects data with the goal of falsifying it. Chapter 12 will explore this idea in depth as it applies to our typical models of building truth in I-O psychology.

Those influenced by the post-positivism movement generally believe that although there is an objective reality, it cannot be known perfectly due to imperfections in measurement, variations in probability, human error, and other forces.

Post-positivism is the current dominant framework by which social scientific research methods, including those described in the remainder of this book, are organized. It triggered a **paradigm shift**, a term popularized by Kuhn, a fundamental change in the way social scientists and some natural scientists approached the questions they wished to assess via research. Kuhn also introduced a few related concepts useful in understanding paradigm shifts. Specifically, he argued that scientists vary between periods of **normal science**, where the methods and tools used are generally accepted throughout the scientific community, making those times highly productive and consequential, with interspersed periods of **revolutionary science**, in which the foundations of the field are shaken as challenges to the field's status quo make creating new agreed-upon knowledge very difficult. Arguably, psychology has been in a period of revolutionary science since its inception, as a single set of "standard methods and tools" have never really been agreed upon fieldwide at any time in our history, although things have certainly varied between "unstable" and "extremely unstable," as most recently seen during the replication crisis of the 2010s (which we will return to in Chapter 14).

Post-positivism recognizes the many human failings that can threaten the **validity** of the claims made by I-O psychology while simultaneously endorsing the idea of "right answers," somewhere out there. Most I-O psychologists today endorse the philosophical stances labeled post-positivism. Having said that, you don't need to agree with us that post-positivism is currently the best framework for conducting I-O psychology. In fact, it's more interesting if you don't agree with us. But before you make such a challenge, either to us or to the field in general, you must understand both the history presented here and the sheer scope of what you're challenging.

Defining Validity

You're going to see the term "validity" a lot in this book, and that's because validity is at the very heart of why we do research. Validity is, generally speaking, a property of inference that refers to its truthfulness or usefulness (depending on your philosophy of science). In other words, we make an observation and then draw a conclusion based on that observation, and the truth of that conclusion is its validity. Because this is such a basic concept in science, you will see dozens of specific "types" of validity that refer to different ways this concept is applied.

For example, "construct validity" refers to the truthfulness of how well the measures we use, like questionnaires, reflect the traits we claim them to reflect. "Internal validity" usually refers to how well the way a research study is design so as to support causal conclusions.

Importantly, all types of validity only share the basic characteristic mentioned previously: truth or usefulness. The specific way this is interpreted in a particular context depends on the context. So it's important to always be vigilant about the specific way the word validity is being used and how it applies in the specific context you're studying at the moment.

Defining Research

Something you might have noticed at this point is that despite talking extensively about how a person interprets research, how philosophy underlies research, and so on, we have not yet *defined* research. The reason for this is simple: the term "research" means different things to different people, varying not only upon your ontological and epistemological stances, but also upon your personal values and interests. This makes defining the term research particularly difficult.

That is not to say that people haven't tried. One attempt that we find particularly informative is one stated in the Frascati Manual, a set of research standards published by the intergovernmental Organisation for Economic Co-operation and Development (OECD, 2015) and adopted by several US government agencies:

> Research and experimental development (R&D) comprise creative and systematic work undertaken in order to increase the stock of knowledge – including knowledge of humankind, culture and society – and to devise new applications of available knowledge.

Thus, in this definition, the key defining feature of research is its *purpose*, and not so centrally the specific **research methods** used. It is about doing something new, to improve societal understanding of a phenomenon or increase our capabilities, to enable us to do things we couldn't do before. According to the US National Center for Science and Engineering Statistics (2018), many kinds of activities can be classified as research, including the following particularly relevant to I-O (adapted slightly from the NCSES list):

- Laboratory research aimed at discovery of new knowledge
- Searching for applications of new research findings or other knowledge
- Conceptual formulation and design of possible product or process alternatives
- Testing in search or evaluation of product or process alternatives
- Modification of the formulation or design of a product or process
- Design, construction, and testing of preproduction prototypes and models
- Design of tools involving new technology
- Design and development of tools used to facilitate research and development or components of a product or process that are undergoing research and development activities
- Software development or improvement activities that expand scientific or technological knowledge

It's also useful here to contrast this list with activities that NCSES listed as "not research" that we think are particularly relevant to I-O:

- Routine, ongoing efforts to refine, enrich, or otherwise improve upon the qualities of an existing product
- Adaptation of an existing capability to a particular requirement or customer's need as part of a continuing commercial activity
- Legal work in connection with litigation
- Software development or improvement activities that do not depend on a scientific or technological advance, are created based upon known methods and applications, involve only the conversion and translation of existing software, or adapt existing products to specific clients

As you can see, the lines can sometimes be a bit fuzzy. While reading the remainder of this chapter, consider how your research activities might or might not be considered "research" to different people with different perspectives.

Step 2: Defining the Role of Research in Your Professional Life

A significant challenge for new researchers, when defining themselves in relation to their field, is figuring out what exactly their cognitive and affective relationship should be with their own research. It's very common, and we would argue unhealthy, for researchers to actually build their entire self-concept around their careers. When such people hit stumbling blocks in their research, as they inevitably will, it becomes a threat that shakes them to their very core. As you might expect, there are many such mistakes one can make when navigating this minefield, and missteps have derailed the careers of many graduate students and young faculty. We don't want you to have the same experience, so we have collected here a number of recommendations for how to navigate this. A key theme you'll notice among all of them, though: you are not alone.

Defining Your Research Orientation

Our first recommendation is to think about whether basic or applied research appeals to you. Generally speaking, research activities can be grouped into four types, as highlighted in Table 1.1

Pure basic research is not concerned with practical application at all and is only focused on basic understanding of the world for its own sake. Practical application is a problem left entirely to others. In the natural sciences, Niels Bohr is a prominent example of a pure basic research scientist. In the world of I-O psychology, research that is truly basic is uncommon, but a great deal of management literature could be assigned to this category. If you are primarily interested in creating knowledge for the sake of creating knowledge, you are probably a pure basic researcher.

Pure applied research is not concerned with generating generalizable or fundamental knowledge but instead focuses on solving a practical problem. Thomas Edison, whose primary goal was to invent lots of stuff, is a classic example of a pure applied research scientist. Research that is conducted within organizations for the purpose of solving a particular problem belongs in this category. If you are primarily interested in going into an organization and solving specific problems, you are probably a pure applied researcher.

Use-inspired basic research in the 2 × 2 framework depicted in Table 1.1 is sometimes called "Pasteur's Quadrant" after Louis Pasteur, whose research perfectly embodied this approach. In use-inspired basic research, a researcher will keep in mind the practical problems that can be informed by the research, but it is still conducted in such a way as to generate broadly significant knowledge. Teaching and practicing I-O psychology this way is sometimes called the **scientist-practitioner model**, which describes an active and purposeful effort to integrate methods, goals, and perspectives of those conducting the research with those applying research in the field in all aspects of our science. This model is viewed by many I-Os, your authors included, as an ideal to strive for.

Tinkering is concerned with neither knowledge nor practice. Instead, curiosity and improvisation are all that drive the research practices that a tinkerer engages in. Tinkering can be a lot of fun but is not generally considered scientific research, because it lacks formal structures for discovering knowledge. However, tinkering can lead to scientific research. For example, in I-O psychology, a practitioner within an organization might, based upon their own intuition, constantly try out new kinds of training program without basing their decisions on prior research and without any specific goal for systematically making their organization better. Tinkerers approach problems with the question, "I wonder what will happen if . . ." and then try it. Such discoveries can be a great starting point for both basic and applied research.

Table 1.1 Cross-tabulation

Quest for Fundamental Understanding?		*Consideration of Practical Application?*	
		YES	NO
	YES	Use-Inspired Basic Research	Pure Basic Research
	NO	Pure Applied Research	Tinkering

Battling Imposter Syndrome

Another challenge in shaping your identity is a battle with your own self-confidence. You might have early-career peers who seem to navigate this new world effortlessly. Meanwhile, you're wracked with anxiety. What if you aren't good enough? What if the people who admitted you into this graduate program made a huge mistake? And, maybe you think that you're the only one with these worries. If so, congratulations. You are the owner of a fine case of **imposter syndrome**, which refers to the belief that you are in over your head and that you're the only one who knows it. That you are somehow fooling everyone into appearing competent while being secretly incompetent. Some people experience this feeling for their entire career. No matter how successful they become, they always harbor the fear that they will eventually be "found out" as less deserving, less skilled, or less capable than people believe them to be.

We can't tell you to just get over your imposter syndrome – but we can promise you that every successful person has dealt with it in the past and that many are still dealing with it. In fact, Chapman (2017) discusses how academia is particularly triggering. Feeling like you are incompetent can drive you to learn more, do more, accomplish more, in an attempt to prove yourself, as long as you don't let the fear take over.

Symptoms of imposter syndrome might include:

• Reluctance to take on tasks that put you in the spotlight
• Anxiety
• Lack of enjoyment in work
• Perfectionism
• Inability to accept compliments
• Unwillingness to ask for better opportunities or special consideration

What should you do if you are feeling symptoms of imposter syndrome? Research suggests that **embeddedness** can help. Embeddedness is a sense of being connected to a community. If you don't feel like your immediate colleagues are people you can relate to, then find people who do. Join campus organizations, community organizations, seek out a mentor, or look for online groups of people who understand you.

End of the Road

If you're not careful, imposter syndrome can gradually turn into **burnout**. When burned out, you are filled with anxiety and dread about your work and an overwhelming desire to escape your own life. This psychological condition has severe consequences for your happiness. Here are common symptoms of burnout:

• dehumanization of the people around you
• sense of dread
• lack of purpose
• feeling like you are just going through the motions
• feeling emotionally drained

If you think you might be feeling this way, you might be interested in the Maslach Burnout Inventory by Maslach et al. (1996) or speaking with a professional counselor.

The Dunning-Kruger Effect

Here's the really unfair thing. At the same time you might be experiencing imposter syndrome, you could also be falling for what has been called the **Dunning-Kruger effect**, the general idea of which is demonstrated in Figure 1.2. Justin Kruger and David Dunning (1999) conducted empirical research suggesting that many students (and people more generally) are not able to accurately estimate their knowledge level relative to others. Specifically, incompetent people tend to overestimate their ability, and competent people tend to underestimate their ability when asked. In their study, they asked psychology students to estimate their skill in logic and grammar, among other skills. The students who were in the bottom quartile were the most inaccurate in estimating their skill, as they grossly overestimated how good they were. From additional research in much more recent years, it has become apparent that the Dunning-Kruger effect is nowhere near as severe as Figure 1.2 suggests. Nevertheless, it's a useful illustration of the general idea.

Why does this misestimation happen? The explanation for people on the lower end is a lack of **metacognitive skill**. Metacognition is "thinking about thinking," and it's an important skill to develop in your career. The students who lack specific technical skills also tend to lack the ability to notice when they make errors. A bad speller has no idea that they are a bad speller because they don't see the misspelled words they write – everything looks fine to them.

What happens, then, when you learn about proper spelling? Your ability to spell goes up. You start to have a pretty good grasp of your own abilities and can more accurately compare yourself to others. But what happens if you make spelling a focus, something that you want to absolutely excel at? Your ability to spell continues to go up, but so does your ability to notice when you make an error. Suddenly, you start noticing all the misspelled words in your writing, all the time. It's all you can focus on. If you are asked to estimate your spelling skill again, you might now think of yourself as worse, not better. You have more knowledge about your true skill level, which has improved in an absolute sense but has declined in your own eyes.

This happens to almost everyone in graduate school. You start off at a place where you don't know what you don't know. Your job is to learn about all the things you don't know. You have to build your own mental model of the frontiers of human knowledge so that you

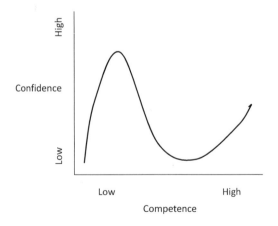

Figure 1.2 Dunning-Kruger effect.

can determine where the boundary is and where you can make a meaningful contribution to it. As soon as you start getting better doing this, though, you will start feeling like you don't really know anything at all. You'll feel like a sham, an imposter, and you will question your competence.

The common solution to both imposter syndrome and overconfidence is to shift the way you think about the world and how you define success. Carol Dweck (2008) has become famous for the concept of the **growth mindset**, an idea largely described by an older and larger research literature on **mastery orientation**. People who have a growth mindset/mastery orientation aren't focused on how their performance stacks up to someone else's. Instead, their motivation is driven by targeting skill development as a goal and seeing improvements in those skills each day, one day at a time. "Success" doesn't mean getting an A in a class. It means building upon a skill, learning something you didn't know before.

Growth is difficult and painful. Doing what you're already good at is easy. Avoiding negative feedback is a good way to protect your self-image, but it is a bad way to get better. Becoming a good researcher means becoming comfortable with the discomfort of growth. But as you grow, and as you struggle, you must try to remember that everyone else is facing exactly the same struggle that you are, whether they show it or not.

Understanding, Anticipating, and Responding in a Healthy Way to Stress

We are arguing that you should put yourself into a situation that will be inherently stressful, so it is important to add a caveat here. A little bit of stress is both necessary and valuable, but too much stress will cause your health and wellbeing to suffer. This fact has been established since the 1920s based on Yerkes and Dodson's (1908) observation that soldiers performed best when they had medium amounts of stress – not too much, not too little – a concept now referred to as the **Yerkes-Dodson law**, demonstrated in Figure 1.3. You're not a soldier, but the same general principle applies to you too. Too little stress means that you are not pushing yourself enough to grow. Too much stress, though, means that you are on the path to burnout and a crash. Besides the effect on our wellbeing, your memory and attention will suffer, which means the quality of your work will suffer too.

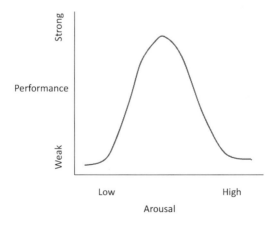

Figure 1.3 Yerkes-Dodson law.

Monitor yourself carefully to make sure this doesn't happen. Unfortunately, a little bit of trial and error might be needed in order to find that sweet spot. Ultimately, you want to train yourself to refuse or bow out of projects and commitments when your stress level is too high, but also seek to add commitments when your stress is a little too low, to push yourself to a healthy balance point.

Acting Ethically

Ethics is something we often don't talk about except in a very detached way, but it is an essential part of your identity as a researcher. If you have done any sort of research at a university, you have probably taken some sort of online course in research ethics which has dryly described various rules and regulations regarding what you can and can't do in a research study. We will talk about that, too, in later chapters where relevant, but for now, there's a more important and foundational dimension to ethics: yours. Conducting ethical research is just one dimension of a broader question regarding your ethical system, how well you define ethical behavior for yourself, and how consistently you follow the ethical system you've created. In this section, we'll discuss this in two dimensions: your professional and personal ethics surrounding your research.

PROFESSIONAL ETHICS

The first and more straightforward dimension of ethical considerations is **professional ethics**. Professional ethics have been refined over generations of researchers, and as an undergraduate in a research methods class, you likely read about many "early lessons" in research ethics that led to our current professional ethics systems, like the Stanford Prison Experiment, Milgram's obedience studies, and the Tuskegee Syphilis Study. We won't rehash those here other than to say that knowledge of history is essential if we wish to avoid repeating it. Most modern ethical guidelines have been shaped by ethical missteps of the past.

Your professional ethical code should be first based upon current national and international ethical standards that apply to your particular subfield. In the United States, for I-O psychologists, the two main sources of ethical guidance come from the American Psychological Association (APA) and the Society for Industrial and Organizational Psychology (SIOP).

All psychologists are bound by a code of ethics that comes from both government regulations about human subjects research and professional codes of ethics from the APA. The US Department of Health and Human Services' Code of Federal Regulations Title 45 Part 46 (typically referred to as the **Common Rule**) dictates the protections that must be followed by federal agencies and academic institutions in human subjects research. Developed in 1981 and refined in 1991 and 2018, its foundation was the 1964 **Declaration of Helsinki**, which was developed in a different era in response to the then-outdated **Nuremberg Code**, the set of research ethics developed out of the atrocities committed in the name of science in World War II.

These days, most large institutions, both in academia and in practice, have independent **institutional review boards** (IRBs) that interpret the Common Rule to provide ethical oversight and approval for proposed studies, but due to the age and vagueness of the Common Rule, vary a bit in the specifics of their interpretations. What might be approved by one IRB might not be approved by another IRB. Also, because the Common Rule is a generic framework for research ethics to be applied to all **human subjects research**, it's obviously not specific to research of the type we conduct as I-O psychologists.

A prominent ethics code a bit closer to home is the APA's (2017) *Ethical Principles of Psychologists and Code of Conduct*, commonly referred to as the **APA Code**. The APA Code is itself an evolution and expansion of another human subjects research ethics document written in 1978, the **Belmont Report**, which offered core principles of **respect for persons**, **beneficence**, and **justice**. Although we recommend you read the full APA Code yourself, we briefly summarize its principles in the following:

- Principle A, Beneficence and Nonmaleficence, requires us to do what we can to maximize benefits and minimize harm in all our professional actions.
- Principle B, Fidelity and Responsibility, requires us to behave in a way that honors the trust that is placed in us by others.
- Principle C, Integrity, requires us to behave honestly and truthfully.
- Principle D, Justice, requires us to treat others fairly.
- Principle E, Respect for People's Rights and Dignity, requires us to respect others regardless of their identities and behave in a way that is free from prejudice.

Most specific to I-O psychology is the Society for Industrial and Organizational Psychology's **Committee for The Advancement of Professional Ethics** (CAPE), which you should spend time reviewing in detail: www.siop.org/Career-Center/Professional-Ethics. CAPE offers some guidance on specific ethical dilemmas you might experience, with resources and advice about how to handle those situations. Example resources include flowcharts for dealing with suspected unethical behavior, case studies, and excerpts from the APA's ethical principles that are most relevant for I-O psychologists.

Ultimately, though, even these many sets of guidelines are not comprehensive enough to give you clear direction about every situation you might find yourself in. Conducting ethical research involves seeking out the advice of trusted mentors, as well as consulting these sources for advice. Ignorance of ethical requirements is no excuse.

We have focused here on issues that affect I-O psychologists working in the US. Many international organizations also publish ethical guidelines for their members. For example, you might consult the ethical guidelines of the European Federation of Psychologists' Associations (http://ethics.efpa.eu/metaand-model-code/meta-code/) or the General Principles of the Code of Ethics by the Australian Psychological Society (www.psychology.org.au/About-Us/What-we-do/ethics-and-practice-standards).

For more on international dimensions of ethics more broadly, see this paper and the special issue it introduces:

Leach, M. M., & Leong, F. T. L. (2010). International dimensions of psychological ethics. *Ethics & Behavior, 20*(3–4), 175–178. https://doi.org/10.1080/10508421003798851

Why Do I Need to Waste Time on IRB Applications?

A common research complaint is the time required to submit an application to the IRB for a research project and then wait for changes or approval. After all, if a researcher is well versed in the Belmont report and their disciplinary code of ethics, why involve more evaluators? Don't the increased oversight and regulation just waste a lot of time? The short answer is: sometimes, but it's still necessary. The good side of IRBs is that they prevent you from hurting someone, infringing on their rights, or breaking laws both intentionally and unintentionally. For example, you might think that it doesn't hurt anything to grab all the grade data from students in your classes for use in a research project without realizing the legal trouble you could get into for doing so. But the IRB knows, so when they read your intent to take grade data, they will make sure you don't run afoul of the law. The bad side of IRBs is that the list of rules they need to follow is extensive, and they have no way to know which rules might apply to your project until you send your application in for approval. That means your experience with the IRB, in most cases, will be to send an application into the void, wait an indeterminate number of weeks or months, and then get back a form letter. So in most cases, you will find the IRB an unpleasant and seemingly unnecessary hurdle to getting your research started. But every once in a while, they might save your job, your educational opportunities, your wallet, or even the basic human rights of your participants.

PERSONAL ETHICS

Beyond your commitment to ethical behavior in your research, your personal conduct should be driven by your **personal ethics**. This means much more than "don't lie, don't steal" and "follow the golden rule." Becoming a professional means that you will build a reputation, and that reputation is as much a part of your legacy as your research products. In the following we list a few common challenges that test people's personal ethical boundaries in a way that influences their professional decision-making, career, and reputation. You may experience these exact problems or different ones.

1. *Overcommitment.* In graduate school and beyond, there will always be more opportunities than hours in the day. This is especially the case when you are good at what you do. Agreeing to do something and not doing it, though, is an ethical failure. Aim to under-promise and overdeliver, not the other way around.
2. *Agreeing to projects that raise your ethical flags without adequate reflection.* A client or colleague may approach you with a project idea that gives you pause. There may be money involved, or prestige. If you cannot conduct the study with a clear conscience, walk away. Maybe the results of the study will be used to fire people. Maybe the participants are being exploited somehow. Or maybe the data were obtained unethically.
3. *Conducting frivolous research.* Frivolous research is unethical because it wastes people's time. It wastes participants' time. It wastes your colleagues' time, in reading the draft and reviewing it. It wastes your time. And all this time could have been used to work on a problem that actually matters.
4. *Careerism.* An important concept in I-O psychology research is the **dark side of goal-setting**, which refers to unintended consequences of creating highly motivating goals. In short, people tend to optimize their behavior to achieve their goals without considering costs that don't have goals associated with them. One illustration of this problem is **careerism**, which refers to actions researchers take in their research to optimize on career outcomes, like salary and promotion opportunities, instead of conducting high-quality

work. For example, imagine if a researcher conducted two data collection efforts within a single project, but only one effort produced the expected results. The researcher then has a choice. The honest thing to do would be to combine the results of the two projects into a single, comprehensive paper that fairly lays out the discrepant results, offers possible explanations, and explains decisions made along the way. The careerist thing to do would be to ignore the half of the project that didn't work and only publish the results of the half that did. They would do this because of a perception that it is "easier" to publish "good" results than the whole truth when the whole truth is complicated. This kind of career-optimized decision-making harms the quality of the research conclusions produced and ultimately reduces everyone's trust in the value of science. We urge you not to be a careerist.

5. *Keeping silent.* It is possible, though hopefully unlikely, that you will see someone do something that is clearly in violation of an ethical code. It could be research related, or have to do with some other aspect of professional conduct. Maybe you see a senior researcher bullying a junior researcher. Maybe you overhear two people discussing data fabrication. Maybe you see that the statistics in a paper have been altered. No matter what the issue is, it is your *responsibility* to speak up. We know that there are costs associated with doing so. But the cost of staying silent is much greater. In addition to the bigger-picture costs of allowing the behavior to continue, there is a good chance that if a research paper is published with your name on it, and it is later discovered to have an ethical issue, your name and reputation will be associated with the unethical act.

Blending Worlds

Author Reflection: "Perhaps one of the most surprising lessons to me about ethics in my entire career was how personal and professional ethics blend, and how behavior outside of professional contexts can influence people's perceptions of you. Many years ago, I attended the funeral of a prominent colleague, who died after a long, successful, and admirable career. At one point in the funeral, there was what amounted to an open mic of friends, family, and colleagues making teary comments on the deceased. Some of these people were his children. They described – not intending to disparage the dead, mind you – how during their childhoods they most often saw their father through the door of his office, where he was always sitting, writing at a desk, and how it was often because he was writing that he rarely had time to play with them. The story was intended by the children to say "now I understand why" after seeing so many colleagues give heartfelt stories of his impact on their lives. But to me, as an early career researcher at the time, I only heard the story of a man who didn't spend enough time with his kids. And despite his long career, and his many accomplishments, that's now the very first thing I think whenever I hear his name." – Richard

---

Step 3: What Are Your Values? Who Will You Become?

We have handed out a lot of advice in this chapter. We hereby give you permission to chart your own course. To shape your own career. To enthusiastically ignore advice from people that doesn't ring true for you – even the advice we are giving you right now. The only responsibility you can't ignore is doing the work to figure out that course.

To illustrate how complicated this is, here's a list of some advice your authors have received about how to be good researchers:

1. Get famous for doing "one thing" and write a lot of papers about that thing
2. Look for "least publishable units" so you can get more papers out of a single dataset
3. Don't do experiments – they take too long
4. Don't do field research – it's too messy
5. Don't study technology – it's not "I-O" enough
6. Go to more conferences
7. Go to fewer conferences
8. Go to different conferences
9. Spend less time on teaching
10. Spend less time trying to get grants
11. Spend more time trying to get grants
12. Publications aren't as important as grants
13. Only publish in "A" journals or it doesn't count
14. Do more "theory-building"
15. Use more structural equation modeling (SEM)
16. Use cross-lagged panel models
17. Don't publish with your advisor
18. Seek out collaborators and big teams with lots of co-authors to boost your vita
19. Focus on the big picture
20. Be more specific
21. Make your dissertation big enough to be a publication engine
22. Publishing is all that matters. Don't teach, don't do service. You are your vita
23. Don't write books
24. Don't waste time getting into the weeds of methods. Nobody loves a methodologist.

(To be fair, the last half of #24 might be true. At a minimum, nobody loves a methodologist as much as another methodologist does.)

We are not the kinds of people who like to be told what to do, so luckily (for us) we ignored a lot of this advice. Some of it is universally bad. Some of it is only sometimes bad. Some of it is outdated, and some of it is still pretty OK. But in order to sort through it all, we needed to engage in **identity formation**, and so do you. Having a clear set of values and goals will allow you to determine if any particular piece of advice is worth listening to.

Specific to the topic of this book, we meet a lot of students who do not identify as methodologists at first. They tell us things like, "I'm just not good at statistics." This is hard for us to hear because we know that methodology skills are not innate – everyone has to learn them (recall the growth mindset discussion previously). We hate to hear that students are giving up before they have even begun because they don't see methodology as a part of their identity.

We also meet students who tell us that they love methods (yay) but that they are getting bad advice from their peers about the value of methods. Like we heard ourselves in Bad Advice #24, they are told that learning methods is a waste of time and that they need to focus on a "content area" to make a real contribution.

One of your authors, Tara, recently met with some computer scientists who were, on any given day, building tools for researchers as diverse as cancer scientists, the forestry service, an architect, and a biochemist. They weren't worried that they lacked focus. They were thrilled to be facilitating new discoveries in such diverse fields. They loved that they got to build tools and give them away to scientists who were thinking about a particular hard problem. Our hope for this book is that you start to see yourself as having similar power in your hands. The tools of I-O psychology methodology are incredibly useful and can facilitate new discovery for diverse societal problems and questions. As a trained methodologist, you will be able to solve problems not just in your own research but in the research of other fields. This is itself a good outcome worth pursuing.

Perspectives on Identity

Different kinds of researchers are like different kinds of musicians. Some are like star singer-songwriters, deciding what to sing, when to sing it, and with whom. Such might switch from country to pop to folk and still retain their identities, just as some researchers change from topic to topic. Other researchers are like players in an orchestra – they follow the lead of the conductor, work closely with others, and play similar pieces throughout their career. No two musicians or researchers think about their identities in exactly the same way. To this point, we asked a diverse set of researchers to tell us about their research identity. Their responses follow.

Alex Casillas, Ph.D., research manager

"I'm not an I-O psychologist but I play one on TV." That's how I introduce myself at I-O conferences, where I often share my story that I graduated with a Ph.D. in clinical science with a specialty in personality and behavioral assessment and became very interested in doing applied research (instead of pursuing academic or clinical paths). As part of the applied research that I do, I have led the development of assessment and training solutions for K–12, postsecondary, and workforce settings. The I-O perspective has allowed me to make connections about how selection and training issues manifest themselves in a variety of settings. More importantly, I have been able to leverage what we know about important workplace issues (e.g., climate, discrimination, high potentials) in order to develop solutions for education settings that are better aligned to the workplace. Furthermore, as I have become better informed about the critical importance of creating a diverse and innovative workforce, I have focused my work to address issues of diversity, equity, and inclusion (DEI) across the education-to-work pipeline. As an immigrant and first-generation college graduate, I am passionate about this work and my ability to contribute to solutions that can assist underserved learners.

Ines Meyer, Ph.D., academic

Fairness has been a strong driver for me from when I was a teenager, and it has transcended into my research identity. I think my own life experiences have shaped how I see my role as an I-O psychology researcher. After obtaining my first degree, I moved from Germany, where I grew up in a rural environment with little visible differences in wealth, a country which provided a strong social safety net to its residents (e.g. in terms of healthcare, child support, and unemployment grants), to South Africa. Here, I daily see people struggling to survive. It is as if I have to use my expertise to contribute to a more just society, as I have experienced the contrast between what life can look like and what it is like for most. To me, this requires not just making a choice about research topics but also remaining conscious about how I conduct research. For example, some of my research focuses on the benefits of living wages for employees, employers, and society. Since it serves to advocate for poverty alleviation through fair pay, I believe I have to adopt fair pay in the research process, too. In this case, I have trained unemployed youth living in financially deprived areas as research assistants. They work alongside student researchers, but regardless of educational background, all of them get paid the same amount; equal work requires equal pay, and this amount is based on what our research has identified as an appropriate living wage.

Larissa K. Barber, Ph.D., academic

My professional identity as an I-O researcher has been strongly shaped by early experiences in health psychology and social psychology labs. However, exploring what makes people healthy and happy in the workplace is most exciting to me given my background (first-generation college student from a working-class background). I've experienced a wide range of jobs that convinced me work isn't just something we do. Instead, work is how we find meaning in life and connect with others. My research is guided by the belief that science should be used to improve workers' lives, and I-O psychologists have a social responsibility to help organizations see the implications of their work practices on human experiences – not just objective productivity outcomes. I've adopted the scientist-practitioner-humanist model in my professional identity, including how I educate and mentor my students. To me, helping organizations make evidence-based decisions isn't only about following scientific principles for a smarter, productive workplace; it's critical to value the human experience of work (a humane workplace) above all else. This has led me to center my research on how to create a psychologically healthy workplace that promotes employee involvement, work–life balance, employee growth and development, health and safety, and employee recognition.

Leaetta Hough, Ph.D., independent practitioner

Several years ago I was an expert witness for plaintiffs in an employment discrimination law suit. At the conclusion of the case, the judge said: "This is a profoundly important case, one that evokes the finest of our nation's aspirations to give everyone equal opportunity and a fair shot." What led me to be a participant in that case? It was apparent to me and others from the beginning of my career that I delighted in challenging "received wisdom." That led me to question the then-prevailing view that the use of personality measures did not add much if anything to employment selection decisions. I persevered and became a leader in utilizing personality measures to predict important job-related outcomes while reducing adverse impact against minorities. Given my success in developing and researching personality measures, I was often called upon to describe in court the research supporting their use. Given my strong belief in providing all with equal opportunity, I was pleased to hear the summary provided by the judge in the case I noted previously. My participation in the case captures the essence of my career – challenging the science and practice of I-O psychology to address and resolve real-world problems.

Macy Cheeks, M.S., government analyst

I walk a less-traveled path for an I-O psychology researcher. I answer tough questions for organizations using data analytics. I employ qualitative and quantitative evidence to paint vivid pictures helping organizations ensure underrepresented groups are treated as equal. To engage in this type of work, I have to remain curious and vigilant. My research is the perfect marriage between equal employment opportunity and social justice – serving as the foundation for diversity, equity, and inclusion initiatives. I am also the co-founder of Blacks in I-O Psychology, a professional networking and learning association for Black I-O psychologists, practitioners, students, and allies. On a daily basis, I plant seeds and take measured steps to uplift Black voices in a space that was built by white men. Blacks in I-O strive to make the field more accessible to minority scholars. Through historically Black colleges and universities (HBCU) outreach, community seminars and mentorship, we epitomize the core value of what it means to be an I-O psychologist: one who identifies problems and solves them. My greatest joy as an I-O researcher is my ability to make an impact and inspire change, supported by facts and data.

Marisa Bossen, Ph.D., independent practitioner
I leverage my I-O psychology background as a **leadership and career development coach for women** through my own company, Brava Coaching & Consulting. My graduate school research focused on what factors predict on-the-job career success and leadership emergence/effectiveness (particularly for introverts). The height of the #MeToo movement occurred the year after I graduated while I was job-hunting, and I realized it was important to see an equal number of women in leadership positions. But that was not enough: I wanted those women to be such great leaders that in time, when someone heard the word "leader," they didn't automatically envision a man, nor would we have to qualify the word "leader" with the adjective "female" any longer. I started my own business because I wanted to be, and effect, the change I wanted to see in the world. My background in I-O psychology gives me a comprehensive toolkit to help my clients overcome their obstacles to being great leaders by using: (1) a whole-person approach (i.e., addressing their emotions, beliefs, unique contexts, behaviors, and goals), (2) a levels of analysis approach within their workplace (i.e., addressing their role, their place on a team, and the entire organization and external system in which their organization exists), and (3) the skills to reliably predict and measure their progress over time. Furthermore, I feel my I-O psychology education and training provides me with a deep research-based knowledge bank with which to help my clients, so that their coaching is effectively tailored to them and they feel valued both as humans and as significant contributors to the work they are dedicating a third of their life to.

"Me-Search"

An important part of your identity will come from the kinds of research questions you choose to answer. It is also true that your identity will shape the kinds of research questions you think are interesting. Your personal experience and unique view of the world will make certain topics more personally interesting and engaging. This isn't always a bad thing – introspection can lead to novel insights. But, it really should not be the only source of your research ideas. Many psychology researchers over the years have been accused of pursuing research agendas only to solve their own problems or figure out their own personal mysteries. This kind of research agenda is pejoratively described as **"me-search."** So much of the world lies outside of your immediate personal experience. You can use your talents and tools to solve problems that you haven't even learned about yet. Keep an open mind about what you find "interesting."

References

American Psychological Association. (2017). *Ethical principles of psychologists and code of conduct (2002, amended effective June 1, 2010, and January 1, 2017)*. www.apa.org/ethics/code/index.html

Chapman, A. (2017). Using the assessment process to overcome Imposter Syndrome in mature students. *Journal of Further and Higher Education, 41*(2), 112–119. https://doi.org/10.1080/0309877X.2015.1062851

Dweck, C. S. (2008). *Mindset: The new psychology of success*. Ballantine Books.

Kruger, J., & Dunning, D. (1999). Unskilled and unaware of it: How difficulties in recognizing one's own incompetence lead to inflated self-assessments. *Journal of Personality and Social Psychology, 77*(6), 1121–1134. https://doi.org/10.1037//0022-3514.77.6.1121

Maslach, C., Jackson, S. E., & Leiter, M. P. (1996). Maslach Burnout inventory: Third edition. In C. P. Zalaquett & R. J. Wood (Eds.), *Evaluating stress: A book of resources* (pp. 191–218). Scarecrow Education.

Maslow, A. H. (1966). *The psychology of science: A reconnaissance*. Harper & Row.

OECD. (2015). *Frascati manual 2015: Guidelines for collecting and reporting data on research and experimental development, the measurement of scientific, technological and innovation activities*. OECD Publishing. https://doi.org/10.1787/9789264239012-en

US National Center for Science and Engineering Statistics. (2018). https://www.nsf.gov/statistics/randdef/rd-definitions.pdf

Yerkes, R. M., & Dodson, J. D. (1908). The relation of strength of stimulus to rapidity of habit-formation. *Journal of Comparative Neurology and Psychology, 18*(5), 459–482. https://doi.org/10.1002/cne.920180503

Further Reading

Brossoit, R. M., Wong, J. R., Robles-Saenz, F., Barber, L. K., Allen, T. D., & Britt, T. W. (2021). Is that ethical? The current state of industrial-organizational psychology graduate training in ethics. *The Industrial Organizational Psychologist, 583*. www.siop.org/Research-Publications/Items-of-Interest/ArtMID/19366/ArticleID/4888

• Brossoit and colleagues explore the methods and extent of ethics training in I-O graduate programs, finding that fewer than half of I-O graduate programs offer a course on ethics. Still, almost all I-O program directors perceive that their program values graduate training in ethics in research. Most of this training is incorporated in other courses and/or in lab/advising meetings.

Lefkowitz, J. (2017). *Ethics and values in industrial-organizational psychology*. Taylor & Francis.

• In this book, Lefkowitz integrates work from moral philosophy, moral psychology, I-O psychology, and business to create a "framework for moral action." Lefkowitz provides readers with practical models for ethical decision making in organizational contexts.

Lowman, R. L. (2006). *The ethical practice of psychology in organizations*. American Psychological Association. https://doi.org/10.1037/11386-000

• Drawing from his experience in practice, Lowman provides real-life case examples to engage readers in ethical thinking about situations related to personnel selection, organizational interventions, consulting relationships, research and academic issues, training and certification, and more.

Rousseau, D. M. (2020). Becoming an organizational scholar. *Annual Review of Organizational Psychology and Organizational Behavior, 7*, 1–23. https://doi.org/10.1146/annurev-orgpsych-012119-045314

• Rousseau is a prominent I-O psychologist who reflects on the lessons she has learned in her more than 40 years in the field. Among other useful tips, she notes the importance of building relationships to develop your scholarly career and how to develop the "superpower" of asking good questions. Stories are provided about how Rousseau developed her major contributions to the field, including her work on psychological contracts and evidence-based management.

Sackett, P. R. (2020). Reflections on a career studying individual differences in the workplace. *Annual Review of Organizational Psychology and Organizational Behavior, 8,* 2.1–2.18. https://doi.org/10.1146/annurev-orgpsych-012420-061939

- Sackett is also a prominent I-O psychologist who reflects on changes in the field over the past 45 years and shares his views on changes the field is currently experiencing. A special focus of this article is on developments relevant to Sackett's research interests, such as meta-analytic thinking (see Chapter 13), personality, and fairness in personnel selection.

Questions to Think About

1. What is research?
2. How do we know if the conclusions we draw from our research are meaningful?
3. What are your research interests? What are your research values?
4. What is the difference between ontology and epistemology? Provide an example for each in the context of your own research interests.
5. Are non-falsifiable research questions useful for building knowledge? Explain why or why not.
6. Think about the last time you performed poorly on some task. Describe your experience in terms of mastery orientations. How can a growth mindset help you grow and develop new skills?
7. Refer to the perspectives on identity included in this chapter. Describe the researchers' interests and values. How do their interests and values compare to yours? What resources are available to you to develop your interests, values, and skills as a researcher?

Key Terms

- APA code
- Belmont Report
- beneficence
- bias, epistemologically
- burnout
- careerism
- Committee for the Advancement of Professional Ethics (CAPE)
- Common Rule
- conjecture
- constructivism
- dark side of goal-setting
- Declaration of Helsinki
- Dunning-Kruger effect
- embeddedness
- empiricism
- epistemology
- epistemological framework
- falsification
- growth mindset
- identity formation
- imposter syndrome
- institutional review board
- justice
- knowledge
- logical positivism
- mastery orientation
- metacognitive skill
- model, scientist-practitioner
- normal science
- Nuremburg Code
- objectivism
- ontological stance
- ontology
- paradigm shift
- personal ethics
- philosophical movement
- philosophy of science

- philosophy of social science
- positivism
- post-positivism
- professional ethics
- pure applied research
- pure basic research
- realism
- relativism
- research
- research methods
- respect for persons
- revolutionary science
- subjectivism
- tautology
- tinkering
- use-inspired basic research
- validity
- verification principle
- Yerkes-Dodson law

Chapter 2

Reviewing Research Literature with a Goal in Mind

Learning Objectives

After reading this chapter, you will be able to:

1. Set appropriate goals for a literature review.
2. Create meaningful research questions.
3. Identify gaps in the research literature related to a research question.
4. Evaluate the quality of published research.
5. Create a strategy for a literature review.
6. Identify the most important details of a published research paper.
7. Create an outline for a research paper.

One of the first big, challenging tasks you face as a researcher is to "review and synthesize the research literature." That's an intimidating statement that implies a lot in a few words. On its face, it sounds like you need to understand *everything* that might be relevant to a project, everything that has ever been done even vaguely related to what you're working on. It sounds like a lot of work with an ambiguous payoff and a lack of clearly defined boundaries, which is just about the worst sort of goal to strive for.

Fortunately, it doesn't need to be that way. This is really a problem of mindset and of toolkit. If you approach a literature review as a *gigantic impossible task*, that's just what you'll turn it into. But if instead you set a series of smaller, manageable goals and work toward achieving them one after the other, you'll be able to put together all the information you need in a format that you'll benefit from not only in your current project but in any future project that calls on that same literature. Yes, it's a big task, but it's a manageable one.

Imagine you are heading to a fancy party. On the way, you hear a really interesting story on the radio about bees. You are so excited to learn about bees and everything they can do, and you can't wait to talk to the party guests about what you have learned! Once you arrive, you see that the guests are standing in circles of 4–6 people, having conversations and enjoying themselves.

You have two options:

1. Stand in the middle of the room and shout, "Who wants to talk about bees? I just think they are so fascinating!"

DOI: 10.4324/9781315167473-3

2. Join a group of people. Listen to what they are talking about. Show that you understand their conversation. Maybe they aren't talking about bees, but they are talking about climate change, and you can find a way to connect the ideas together and segue gracefully.

The second approach is much more likely to be successful connecting you to other people who care about bees. Maybe the first group you join is talking about something utterly unconnected to bees, so you leave that group and find one that is more closely aligned to your interests. But you must first listen before you speak. This is the way that research works, too. You must *listen to the scientific conversations* that are happening. You have to think about how your interests fit into the larger conversations going on in the research literature. You should use your experience conducting the review to identify a specific audience that will be interested in what you have to say, and frame your contributions in a way that adds meaningfully to the conversation that this audience is already having.

With that in mind, the purpose of this chapter is to provide you with both the mindset and toolkit to approach a research literature synthesize without tearing your hair out. It will be most useful to you if you read it while thinking about a research literature review looming in your own near future.

Goal Orientation in Literature Searches

Students without a plan trying to review a research literature often do something we could call a "brute force" approach, one that focuses on simply passing their eyes over as much text as possible that is in any way connected to a focal topic.

Let's explore an example. Jill has been assigned by her advisor to synthesize the current literature on goal setting interventions. In response, she opens Google Scholar and searches for "goal setting interventions." She clicks on the first article that pops up and reads the title and abstract. They look relevant to goal setting interventions, so she sits down and starts reading the article. Jill struggles quite a great deal because she has no context for what she's reading, and at some point, she starts browsing social media to distract herself from how difficult and boring the article is. Eventually, she goes back to Scholar, goes to the second entry on the list and repeats the process. After four hours of struggling this way, she realizes that she doesn't remember anything she read. Whoops.

This happened in part because Jill approached the literature review like a *task to be completed*, which in psychology we often refer to as a **performance goal orientation**. But what Jill didn't know yet is that we have a sizable research literature on the downsides of this orientation in isolation. When you focus on only your performance, you tend to ignore what you should really be doing in a literature review: learning.

The purpose of a literature review should not simply be to *get through* the literature. Instead, the purpose of your literature review should be for you to learn everything you need to know to address a **research question** you want to answer. This means that you'll get a lot more traction out of a mastery orientation, where the goal you're trying to accomplish is *to learn from* instead of *to get through* the literature. We introduced mastery orientation in the last chapter when talking about forming your identity, but it applies in different ways at every step in the research process.

Given this, there were four major problems with Jill's approach:

1. Jill was trying to "finish" instead of trying to "learn."
2. Jill approached her research topic as if it were a single, enormous mountain standing in her way.

3. Jill did not have a core research problem to learn about, just the name of a general topic area.
4. Jill did not have a structured process to follow.

To adopt a learning orientation, the biggest challenge is that you need to stop worrying about efficiency. For a graduate student or early-career faculty member, that's a big ask. But worrying about efficiency – for example, trying to "get through two articles in an hour" – is your biggest enemy. Worrying about efficiency will distract you away from learning, and without learning, reading through research articles is an enormous waste of time. So, to avoid Jill's Mistake #1, you need to stop worrying about time.

The easiest way to do this is to set aside time for learning. For example, you might tell yourself "between 10am and 12pm, I'm just going to spend time learning about my research question." Turn off your email reminders. Close your social media. Turn off your phone notifications. Set an alarm for 12pm, but don't look at it. Just let yourself be immersed, on task, in the literature.

And what do you do for those two hours? A lot of things; your task at any moment depends on which goal you're pursuing at the time, so we'll explore that next.

Effective Goals for Literature Review

Literature review has many purposes, but the on-the-ground goals are always the same: to understand current theory, to identify evidence in support of theory, and to reveal gaps in the literature that could be filled with new theory and evidence. We'll tackle these one at a time.

Understanding Theory

Theory,[1] as the term is commonly used in psychology, can be defined as the current general scientific understanding of a phenomenon of interest. In the I-O literature, it includes many different dimensions of understanding. Most commonly, theory includes four types of information, each supported by a body of **evidence**:

1. Conceptual definitions of key **constructs** in the literature (see inset)
2. Generally acceptable **operational definitions** (also called **operationalizations**) of key constructs in the literature
3. Descriptive interrelationships between constructs as measured by their operational definitions
4. Causal effects of constructs on other constructs: directly, indirectly, and interactively.

Using theory, you should be able to describe a phenomenon completely and also predict what will happen in the future given changes to the constructs in that theory. If you can't, that theory is either incomplete or flawed. For example, in Figure 2.1, we can see a visualization

---

[1] This word has different meanings in different fields. If you learned about "theory" in high school physics, you probably think of theory as something much more formalized, like the "Newtonian theory of gravity." In psychology, for better or (mostly) worse, we work with a much looser definition of "theory." In the interest of you being able to hold a conversation with another psychology researcher, we'll use the definition operationalized in mainstream psychology in this book, but it's important to realize that this is a minority view, especially when compared to the natural (e.g., physics, chemistry) or formal (e.g., mathematics, logic, computer science) sciences. For more on this issue, see Cucina and McDaniel (2016) and Robinaugh et al. (2021).

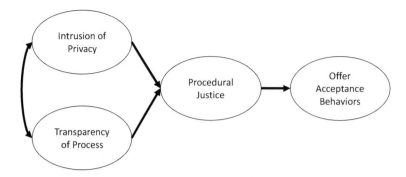

Figure 2.1 A path diagram illustrating causal relationships from Hausknecht et al. (2004).

of part of a theory of applicant reactions. This type of figure is called a **path diagram**, and it typically shows three aspects of a theory: the names of key constructs (although no definitions), non-causal interrelationships, and causal effects.

First, we can see interrelationships with the use of double-ended arrows. In this path diagram, the theory represented suggests a *non-causal* relationship between perceptions of intrusion of privacy and transparency of the hiring process. This means that intrusion of privacy and transparency are related but are not theorized to affect each other directly. Second, it proposes that intrusions of privacy *cause* changes in applicants' perceived procedural justice, and that those changes in procedural justice in turn affect how likely they are to accept an offer of employment.

Theories depicted this way make no claims about constructs that are not depicted. Although that might seem obvious on the surface, it can play out in peculiar ways. For example, this figure is perfectly consistent with the idea that perceptions of intrusion of privacy and transparency of the hiring process could have a shared cause that is not depicted. If this shared cause were added, the non-causal relationship between those two variables might need to be removed. In this sense, theories are sometimes called **useful abstractions of reality**. They are not generally intended to comprehensively describe all possible causes, effects, and other relationships related to a topic of interest.

Importantly, path diagrams like the one in Figure 2.1 do not depict the other two aspects of theory. Although we can see the names of constructs (i.e., intrusion of privacy, transparency, procedural justice, and offer acceptance behaviors), we have neither definitions of these constructs nor common ways to operationally define them. To learn this information, we'd need to look beyond the path diagram and actually read the articles that contain them.

Constructs and Operational Definitions

Constructs are unmeasurable phenomena that we are interested in theorizing about. In the I-O literature, most constructs are psychological. For example, job satisfaction is a construct; it cannot be measured directly (for example, with a ruler) but instead must be measured indirectly via a proxy behavior, such as responses to a

10-item questionnaire. No one believes that responses on a questionnaire *are the same as* job satisfaction, but a questionnaire may be the best we can do. This is why we would say that the 10-item survey measure is an *operational* definition of job satisfaction. We aren't *literally* defining job satisfaction as questionnaire responses; we are doing it *operationally*, to enable our research study. We'll cover operational definitions in much greater detail in Chapter 7, so for now, just remember that constructs cannot be measured directly and must instead be assessed via operational definitions that can be measured. Sometimes this process is mathematical; sometimes, it isn't.

Considering Evidence

Theory should ideally be based on prior empirical research supporting that theory, which is broadly what most people mean by the term "evidence." For example, for me to call the path diagram in Figure 2.1 a "theory," the relationship between transparency of process and procedural justice, and all other arrows depicted, should have at least been empirically tested at some point in the past (or perhaps in the same paper where this theory appeared). In that way, we can say that the relationships depicted in that path diagram are in fact "current scientific understanding of applicant reactions" and thus part of the current scientific conversation about these constructs.

Unfortunately, in practice, many theories are never tested or are proposed on a weak foundation. Kurt Lewin (1951), father of social psychology and an early researcher in organizational psychology, famously said, "There's nothing so practical as good theory," yet many I-O psychology theories are not good, often because they are based purely upon reason and not upon evidence. In I-O psychology, and more specifically its close cousin organizational behavior, there are even entire academic journals devoted to allowing researchers to propose new theories without ever collecting any data to create evidence in support of those theories. Assuming such theories describe real phenomena can be harmful to your research career because they may lead you down an unproductive research path if you assume that relationships actually exist when they in fact have never been tested and may not actually exist.

To combat this problem, a successful literature review will simultaneously build an understanding of current theory but will also weigh current evidence supporting theory. To support the theoretical relationships in Figure 2.1, there are many types of evidence we'd need to look for, one for each type of information contained within a theory:

1. Are these constructs well defined, based upon prior empirical research? Do these definitions make sense?
2. Have these constructs been measured consistently, with operational definitions that I trust?
3. Have these relationships been empirically observed?
4. Have causal relationships been supported with methodology that will successfully support causal conclusions?

At this point in your research career, you may find the idea of answering these questions intimidating. But as you gain more experience, and after you read this book, you will begin to find that asking these questions of everything you ever read becomes second nature. For each of these questions, there are literally hundreds of considerations that could affect whether or not you believe the theory. With the approach described in this book, you are, in a sense, training to become a professional skeptic, refusing to believe anything until there's evidence to support it, and evaluating all evidence reported on a case-by-case basis.

Using Evidence to Create Theory

Although the goal of all I-O psychological methods is to **inform theory**, which is to say, to make theory better, there are three major approaches you can take to do so. Any one research method, with few exceptions, is built upon a foundation of **deductive**, **inductive**, or **abductive** reasoning. The three differ in a few key ways:

- In deductive methods, a tentative theory is presented first, and evidence is collected to support or falsify that theory second. The theory to be tested is driven by the results of past research.
- In inductive methods, evidence is collected first, and patterns are observed in collected evidence second. Observed patterns are interpreted to develop a theory about the nature of those patterns and why they exist.
- In abductive methods, both theory and evidence already exist but are suspected to incompletely explain a particular phenomenon. This is most common when there are multiple theories describing the same problem that disagree in their implications.

Most I-O psychology research, at least right now, is deductive in nature. In fact, a particular framework, called the **hypothetico-deductive model**, is the dominant decision-making framework field-wide. Using this model, researchers develop **hypotheses** from theory, which are specific testable propositions, then test them. Based upon how well the hypotheses predicted the observed outcome, the proposed theory is either supported or not.

For example, let's imagine that there is an existing theory, already supported with evidence, about the significant benefits of reading I-O methods textbooks on personal enlightenment. Aha, you say. I bet that theory is incomplete. There is another theory that indicates textbooks only help people who are open to learning. I will **integrate** these theories into a single new theory that more comprehensively describes these ideas. Then I will **hypothesize** the specific effect directly: when people are open to learning, the effect of reading I-O methods textbooks on personal enlightenment will be greater than when they are not. I will then collect data to see if my prediction is true; if so, my theory is supported; if not, I will need to try something else.

In this way, I have used two existing theories to **deduce** a specific hypothesis. I then collected data to test my deduction hypothesis. Inductive methods work in the opposite order.

For example, let's say I'm interested in the relationships between reading I-O methods textbooks and personal enlightenment – and more specifically, I'm interested in why that relationship might exist. To investigate, I decide to interview a bunch of people about their relationship with I-O psychology methods textbooks and ask them about their experiences. After I talk to enough people, I believe I've worked out what's really going on, and

I interpret those data, the process most directly called **induction**, to develop a theory which I present.

Although they represent diametrically opposed assumptions about the best way to create knowledge, both approaches are potentially valid ways to develop theory. In selecting any specific research methodology for a project, you will be implicitly stating your own beliefs about which approach makes the most sense to you, as well as promoting your ontological and epistemological views, as we discussed in Chapter 1. Just be sure you've decided this with purpose before you commit. Don't default to the hypothetico-deductive hammer just because it's the only tool you've used before now.

Inductive Integration of the Flux Capacitor and Dominant Fleenor

A major challenge when revising a research literature you were previously unfamiliar with is parsing **jargon**, the high-complexity and uncommon words frequently seen in formal research reports. The term is often used disparagingly, to imply that the people using it are **gatekeeping**. In this way, a researcher might use specific words and phrases as a way to create in-groups and out-groups, as if to say: if you don't understand the words I'm using, you must not belong here. Although jargon *can be and often is* used for gatekeeping, correctly used jargon serves a practical purpose by conveying a lot of complex information in a very small space. For example, when you read the word "hypothesis" in a research report, you should think of it in the sense described in this chapter and not in the general layperson sense of "an idea someone had." The creation of useful jargon in this way allows for more clear and efficient discussion between experts who already agree on the fundamentals.

When used for gatekeeping, jargon is for in-group signaling. Using the word "extant" (more on this later and again in Chapter 15) communicates that the writer is a serious scientist who uses serious science words. Often, the use of those serious science words does not actually add anything meaningful to the writing. Another common bit of science gatekeeping is using the plural data instead of the singular data, as illustrated in Figure 2.2. The implication is that serious scientists say "data are" and the outgroup (everyone else) says "data is." The reality is that whether you use singular or plural, everyone knows what you're talking about anyway, which makes it a silly issue to care about.

As with many aspects of research and writing, the correct approach to jargon is to maintain balance. First, do not assume that jargon is impenetrable, something that "only an expert" and therefore "not you" could master. All jargon was created by someone trying to summarize a complicated idea in a word or two, so encountering new jargon just signals that you need to learn about the complicated idea before proceeding. When reviewing a literature, don't skip over it assuming it will become clear from context; it usually doesn't. Second, when writing, don't use jargon unless it actually serves the purpose of efficiency and clarity. Don't make things more complicated than they need to be.

Figure 2.2 Gatekeeping made real. Courtesy Zach Weinersmith, smbc-comics.com.

Filling Gaps

The purpose of a new research project, whether deductive or inductive, is to fill in **gaps** in the research literature. Gaps can be defined as missing evidence or unconsidered perspectives given current theory. For example, if our literature review revealed that all of the questions named in the previous section were answered *except* that the research methodology used in prior studies does not actually support causal conclusions, we've found a gap, and that gap could be the focus of a new project, such as a master's thesis or doctoral dissertation, depending on how big the gap is.

As a practical matter, gaps are much easier to fill when they're smaller. To understand why, it's useful to think of theory and the evidence supporting theory as a table supported by many legs. Your goal with research is generally to add legs to the table. The more gaps there are, the fewer legs your table has to stand on, and the less stable it will be. If there are too many gaps, it's going to take more than one leg (i.e., many studies providing lots of different types of evidence) to stabilize it, which means it is generally a waste of time even to try – no matter how nice your new table leg is, the table's still going to crash later. In these cases, you may want to choose a smaller table.

For example, in the case described previously, the *only* place where this theory lacked evidence was in the lack of research methodology supporting causality. Given that, there are a lot of legs already. We know the constructs exist, we know they are measured well, and we know that they have predictable interrelationships. Thus, the gap is fairly small. Now, let's imagine an alternative version: there's a lack of research supporting causality, but we also don't really understand what procedural justice is, and there's actually no research that has ever measured transparency before. Suddenly, our table became a lot more iffy. When this happens, it's usually best to tackle a smaller, more foundational gap first instead of tackling the big gap head on. In this case, you'd probably want to fill the smaller gap of "how do you measure transparency?" before tackling the causality problem. If you don't, you run the risk of someone criticizing your work later, saying, "But how do you know that you actually measured transparency? If I can't trust your transparency measure, how can I trust your theory?" This threatens the value of your entire project.

In I-O psychology, there are a lot of gaps just about everywhere. They tend to be larger among the topics that are traditionally defined as "organizational" (e.g., leadership, teamwork) versus the topics traditionally considered "industrial" (e.g., selection, performance appraisal). This is in part because the industrial side of the field is much older, so they've had more time to fill gaps. But you can find plenty of gaps in both.

Additionally, although theory is defined as "current scientific understanding," it's also important to remember that *groups* of scientists can have competing theories. In such situations, the difference between them is itself a gap. The ideal resolution to this sort of situation is for the two groups of scientists to work together to build a common understanding of their topic area toward a shared resolution and unification of their disparate theories. In practice, this rarely happens, because it's a very difficult problem to solve with many dead ends and, relatedly, because the academic system in which most people conduct and publish research generally only rewards success. You will more often see two somewhat parallel threads of research on the same topic but citing different papers that may or may not eventually combine (e.g., see the research literatures on *organizational climate* and *organizational culture*). In such cases, you must make an informed decision: do you adopt one theory and ignore the other, or do you try to fill the gap?

This sort of problem also commonly occurs with interdisciplinary research areas; you may find researchers in psychology and researchers in sociology studying the same problem but using completely different constructs, research methods, and even assumptions about measurement and causality. In such cases, the gaps are so big that they often are never filled despite the potential value to the world it would bring in doing so.

Making Decisions About "Extant" Research

Although the basic goals are always the same, a literature review is conducted for a larger, practical purpose that guides how you go about it. For example, you may be reviewing the literature because you need a project for your master's thesis. In that case, you'll specifically be looking for small gaps, and you may abandon a path of investigation if you discover fundamental, difficult-to-address roadblocks that would take a full career to solve. If you are planning out a doctoral dissertation, you will want to find a somewhat larger gap – but still not too big (a piece of advice you will likely hear at some point: "the best dissertation is a done dissertation"). When reviewing research to plan a particular project, you'll want to follow theory threads. For example, if you had identified applicant reactions theory as a base from which you wanted to conduct a research project, you would use that as a starting point to track back further, exploring both what prior theory led to this theory being proposed and also to track sideways, exploring alternative theories that contain the same or similar constructs.

Alternatively, you may be conducting a literature review in an exploratory manner to develop a "current understanding of **extant research**." This is a particularly frustrating goal if you have a performance orientation because you don't have and will never have a well-defined end-point. Instead, your overarching goal is to constantly make judgments about whether or not the papers you're reading are in fact relevant to a modern interpretation of theory in your target area of interest. At some point, you must make a judgment of "good enough" where you decide that the signal-to-noise ratio has become too low. More specifically, you reach this point when you decide that reading additional research papers is no longer giving you much new information to inform your current understanding of theory.

This sort of judgment will come more naturally to you over time, but here are a few pointers to get you started:

1. Journal prestige is correlated with quality, but it's nowhere close to a perfect relationship. In general, you're going to on average find higher-quality work in high-profile journals, like *Psychological Bulletin* or *Proceedings of the National Academies of Science*, but some really shoddy research still gets published in "top-tier" journals, and you shouldn't trust research by default just because it's published in a high-profile outlet. The inverse is also true; low-tier journals on average contain lower-quality work, but some excellent work also appears in them, so don't count them out automatically. Evaluate each paper on its own merits.
2. Citation rates are similarly correlated with quality. Although more highly cited works are *probably* of higher quality, this is not guaranteed. Additionally, papers are sometimes highly cited because they are great examples of what not to do or because they are highly controversial. Don't assume that just because a paper is highly cited that you can automatically trust it; always check out the evidence both within that paper and surrounding it.
3. Academic research operates on a much slower timescale than human thinking, but old papers are still more likely to be outdated than newer ones. In general, don't assume age means anything for papers less than 10 years old, but beyond that, be careful to explore which claims no longer hold up. Some research areas also move faster than others. In the study of machine learning in computer science, research more than 6 months old is probably already outdated. I-O doesn't generally move nearly so fast, but this is something to evaluate on a case-by-case basis.
4. Abstracts are often less carefully peer-reviewed than other parts of articles. In some cases, abstracts contain very misleading conclusions. Sometimes these conclusions aren't even stated in the article itself! (Side note: this is an easy way to tell if someone has not actually read certain papers they are citing.)
5. Remember that the people that wrote the articles you're reading are in fact people. They brought their own biases to their research that may have influenced the approach they took or the conclusions they drew. Having said that, you should assume good faith; unless presented evidence to the contrary, assume that researchers are not saying anything that is outright false. But even with that assumption, researchers may have left out relevant information, selectively reported results, or done a variety of other questionable research practices. We'll come back to this point in much more detail in Chapters 5 and 14.

Why Is This Research Extant?

Extant research is a jargonistic phrase used to refer to existing research that is relevant to a particular problem. It is used in contrast to *all* research, which includes research that has not yet been conducted or is otherwise not yet available. "Extant" is, in practice, a bit of a weasel word, overused to make a research paper sound more authoritative than it otherwise might. For example, in the phrase, "we reviewed the extant research," there is no reason to use the word extant; it is a bit like claiming, "we only reviewed the research that currently exists and not the research that doesn't." Try not to use it in your own writing unless you specifically need to distinguish between existing research and research that has not yet been completed.

A Practical Strategy for Literature Review

OK – let's get down to brass tacks. How do you actually go about conducting a literature review? An effective literature search can be best conceptualized as an eight-step process where you frequently return to previous steps, as shown in Figure 2.3. We'll discuss each in the following.

(Re)define a Research Question

All good literature reviews start with a question of interest. Good research questions have several characteristics:

1. With enough information, the question could one day be answered.
2. There is not yet widespread consensus on the answer to the question.
3. The question has well-defined boundaries with a realistic scope.
4. The question is ethical.
5. Answering the question could result in a practical outcome benefiting someone, either immediately or after the investigation of subsequent questions.

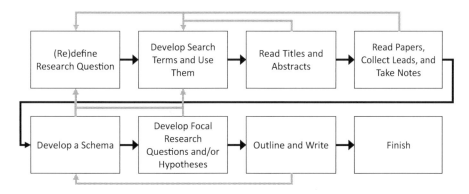

Figure 2.3 A process for developing and writing literature reviews.

Your assessment of these characteristics will change as you read, so on your first pass, you will write a "starter" research question; something that fulfills these requirements to the best of your knowledge. Let's consider a few examples, one for each of these characteristics.

Answerability. This refers to the likelihood that an answer exists to your question. Eventually, all research questions should be tested, so if the research question cannot ever be tested, it is not a good research question.

Research Question 1: Do people need to work?
Assessment: The question is too vague to even know how to answer it.
Possible Revision: Do people need to work to have high life satisfaction?

Consensus. If an issue is "settled" in the literature, your investigation of it is unlikely to add to knowledge. But importantly, you can (and should) still ask research questions closely related to issues of widespread **scientific consensus**, a term used to describe how a substantial majority of researchers currently understand a particular phenomenon. Be careful in precisely determining where the "consensus" lies; for example, if your research question puts boundary conditions on something well explored, there may not be widespread consensus on those boundary conditions. Importantly, challenging an existing consensus can be worthwhile and important; just know up front that it will take more time and effort than something **incremental**. Challenging consensus requires a lot more time, effort, and confidence and comes with much greater risk.

Research Question 2: Is individual job performance important to organizational performance?
Assessment: There is widespread consensus that "the people make the place." Without employees, there is no organizational performance.
Possible Revision: How does diversity of an organization's employees influence how individual job performance impacts organizational performance?

Scope. Scope has more to do with the overall purpose of your literature review than your research question. If you are writing a master's thesis, you need a thesis-sized question. As you investigate the literature, you may find that the problem you thought you were investigating is actually much larger than it appeared. In such cases, you will need to revise your question to examine a smaller area.

Research Question 3: What is job satisfaction correlated with?
Assessment: This question does not have well-defined boundaries; job satisfaction is correlated with hundreds of other constructs, and reviewing all of them would take years.
Possible Revision: Does job satisfaction correlate with turnover intentions, and if so, why?

Ethics. In science, no question should be forbidden just because it turns over stones that some people believe are better left unturned. But having said that, research questions can be posed in such a way that it is clear you are bringing an agenda to the table that will affect your objectivity. You should not ask such questions, or more technically, you should endeavor to debias your research questions (and your perspective, and later, your methods) before pursuing them further. It's also worth noting that even debiased, ethically posed research questions cannot necessarily be studied using ethical research methods (a concept we will explore further in Chapter 8).

Research Question 4: How can leaders manipulate an underperforming employee to get them to quit voluntarily?

Assessment: Although some leaders may do this already, it is not ethical to conduct research with the purpose of creating a roadmap for manipulation. You might also delight a bit in human suffering; maybe see a therapist first.

Possible Revision: What actions do leaders engage in that encourage voluntary turnover?

Practicality. Although research does not need to make an immediate practical outcome for organizations, it needs to be targeted somewhere that will eventually – perhaps after asking several subsequent questions – lead to a practical outcome. If you can't imagine why anyone would ever need to know the answer to your question, or if you know that the phenomenon you're investigating is unlikely to ever happen in a real organization, or if you find evidence that the effect you're interested in is always tiny and non-influential, look for a new research question.

Research Question 5: Should organizations require employees to smile at each other?

Assessment: Realistically, no organization would ever do this. Just . . . no.

Possible Revision: Does the expression of employee emotions affect how other employees experience their workday?

After you progress through the literature review process, you will likely return to this step several times. You probably don't know enough when you start reviewing to write a great research question, so it is expected that you will redefine your research question several times. Just be sure that every time, your revised question is better than the one it replaced in terms of these five dimensions.

Develop Search Terms and Use Them

Once you have a good (starter) research question to investigate, you need to figure out what to search for. Search term selection is important, because it affects your signal-to-noise ratio. In other words, high-quality search terms will result in most of your search results being relevant, whereas low-quality search terms will result in you sifting through huge lists of irrelevant research. Thus, a key reason that you will return to this stage often is that you will need to revise your search terms as you build a better understanding of the concepts you're reviewing.

The best search terms tend to be multi-word constructs that people don't usually use in casual conversation – such as "goal orientation." This is because such words are not generally used outside of research studying those constructs. In contrast, constructs like "job performance" have very common usage because people refer to job performance even if they aren't studying job performance. As a result, it's generally better to search for the exact phrase "job performance" including surrounding quotation marks (which would return only results that have "job performance") instead of a general keyword search for job performance (which would likely return any paper containing the word job and the word performance anywhere within).

As for where to search, this depends on your research question. For most core I/O research questions, the American Psychological Association's **PsycINFO** (www.apa.org/pubs/data bases/psycinfo/index.aspx) will contain all the information you need. It is a **curated database**, which means that the APA ensures that anything in PsycINFO is in fact a psychology-relevant paper. They won't necessarily be related to *your research question*, but you won't get papers that are completely unrelated to I/O as you will with other databases. The primary downside to PsycINFO is that you are charged an access fee to use it. If you are affiliated with a university, you most likely get this access for free as part of your university's library subscriptions. If you aren't sure if you have this or how to access it, ask your reference librarian. If you aren't affiliated with a university, you can purchase access to PsycINFO for a fee that is added onto membership fees in the APA.

The most common (free) alternative to PsycINFO is **Google Scholar** (http://scholar.google.com). Unlike PsycINFO, Google Scholar is not curated; it's a search engine. Google's search algorithm includes anything that *looks like* a scholarly paper. The upside to this approach is that Google's search algorithms cast a wide net, so if you want literally every scholarly-ish paper ever written about a topic, you can probably find it there. The downside is that their algorithm can be, and often is, gamed by people who make work that looks like peer-reviewed scholarship but is in fact a position piece without any evidence. Google is continually improving their algorithms to avoid this, but the lack of hand-curation regardless means that you have much greater personal responsibility for evaluating what you find there.

Two other popular databases that cast a wider net than PsycINFO but are curated are **Web of Science**, which is maintained by the mass media conglomerate Reuters, and **Scopus**, which is maintained by the scholarly publishing giant Elsevier. Like PsycINFO, these are subscription based, and most universities will have a subscription to at least one of the two. The quality of citation information does not differ considerably between them, although the software used to access them does. If you use both, you will likely develop a preference for one or the other, but in general, it doesn't matter much in terms of what you get out. You don't need to search both.

Once you decide which database(s) to use, be sure to learn their search term quirks. For example, Google Scholar will allow you to specify anything as a phrase by surrounding it in double quotes: a search for *"job satisfaction"* versus *job satisfaction* will turn up quite different results. But if you try to use quotes in EBSCOhost, which is a particular software platform commonly used to access databases, it will most likely look for *actual quotes* in the text and return nothing. Instead, ESBSCOhost expects you to specify your search field as "entire phrase".

For more detail on Google Scholar search query terms, see https://scholar.google.com/intl/en/scholar/help.html.

For more on PsycINFO, see: whttps://www.apa.org/support/psycinfo.

Another option for literature search is the use of an **artificial intelligence**. Importantly, artificial intelligences as they current exist are really just highly complex predictive models, taking your input terms (i.e., predictors) to produce predictions of the kinds of words that usually follow the words you searched for. For example, if you open an artificial intelligence and ask it, "What's the most recent research on leadership?", it does not actually answer that question; instead, it predicts what the most likely text to follow the words you typed would be and then provides it to you. In this way, artificial intelligence does not actually reason through your question and thus can lead to highly misleading answers if you aren't careful to verify everything it says through a curated database search.

As a practical note, as you run searches, it will be useful later to keep a running record of all the search terms you use, where you use them, and how many records come back using each approach.

Understanding Publishers

This isn't the last time you'll see the name Elsevier. It is one of a handful of publishing companies responsible for a wide array of scholarly journals. A publisher theoretically does several things useful for scholarly publishing:

1. It provides technology to support them, such as printing (if the journals are still on paper) and maintenance of journal websites.
2. It connects directly with university libraries to integrate journal titles, abstracts, and keywords into their systems for easier searching within library websites.
3. It connects directly with university IT infrastructure to make access easier for university community members.
4. It builds and maintains peer review web software to make the review process simpler (many years ago, you submitted to a journal for publication by making a dozen copies on paper and mailing the packet to an editor!).
5. It curates journal content by seeking new journals that will be of legitimate interest to the scholarly community and shutting down journals that are misleading or engaging in unethical practices.
6. It employs copy-editors and layout editors to create the physical appearance and branding of the journal.

The degree to which a publisher is successful at these things varies quite a lot. Some publishers don't even do some of these things, for example, by requiring authors to hire copy-editors for their own submitted articles. For now, just keep in mind that the fact that a journal or book is published by a publisher whose name you've heard of (e.g., Elsevier, Routledge, Springer, Sage, Wiley) or is associated with a university (e.g., Cambridge University Press, University of Chicago Press, MIT Press) makes it more likely that the article you're reading is legitimate and trustworthy but that such endorsement is *absolutely* not a guarantee.

You still need to evaluate the quality of the article on its contents, based upon your own judgment as a professional researcher, as there's a lot of junk science that still makes it into such journals. We will revisit this topic in much greater detail in Chapter 14 when discussing how to identify a journal for your own manuscripts.

Read Titles and Abstracts

Each time you conduct a search, you will be given a high-level summary of the articles your search terms reveal in the form of titles and, in some databases, abstracts. Your task at this point in the literature review process is to determine if the articles you're seeing are likely to be relevant to the research question you've asked.

For maximum efficiency, you want to do this so that you can read both titles and abstracts simultaneously. Your database software may or may not have a way to do this, but if you can find one, it will save a lot of time. When you are going through summaries of 500 articles, an extra 5 seconds to click and wait for each page to load in your web browser adds 41.7 minutes to your task. Try to streamline wherever possible; load the maximum number of entries per page, and try to get all of the information in front of you at once.

As you read, you'll want to copy article references into a personal database of citations and links to the article themselves. For this purpose, we strongly recommend using citation management software, like Zotero (www.zotero.org/) or Mendeley (www.mendeley.com/), both of which are free. In both cases, the software you install can automatically detect when you're looking at a scholarly article webpage, harvest key information about it, and then save it all into a local database on your computer. You can even attach the PDFs later. This will speed up your review time substantially.

As you go through titles and abstracts, you may discover that the search terms you chose are not producing the sorts of papers you thought they would. In general, if you find your "relevant article" rate is less than about 50%, you should go back to the previous step, revise your search terms, and conduct a new title and abstract search. If the first few pages were highly relevant but later became less relevant, you might push this as low as 10%.

Read Papers, Collect Leads, and Take Notes

Finally we arrive at the meat of a literature review. After you have curated a good starter set of readings – at least 10 or so – you need to actually read them. Unlike reading for pleasure, reading an academic journal article is a very active process; you need to read thinking about your research question and try to understand how what you're reading helps you develop an answer to that question.

To do this, you will develop an **annotated bibliography**, which is a list of citations organized by subtopic that addresses aspects of your research question, with each citation accompanied by a text description. To create an annotated bibliography, simply write down the citation you are investigating, followed by its abstract. Afterward, summarize in your own words key pieces of information relevant to the theory and evidence contained within it. In general, this will include this sort of information (although this may differ a little based upon your research question):

1. Core theoretical framework (from the paper's introduction)
2. Research questions and hypotheses (from the introduction)
3. Methodology, including sample and research design (from the Methods)
4. Statistical analyses employed (from the Results)
5. Summary of findings in relation to research questions and hypotheses (from the Results)
6. Theoretical implications (from the Discussion)

This generally means writing one or two paragraphs about each paper you read. When you're done, the last step is to *collect leads*, which means going back to find the specific arguments made in the article that are *most closely related* to your topic and then hunting down the citations associated with those points. If you're using Zotero or Mendeley, you can simply find these articles by title on Google Scholar and save them to your local database immediately.

Also remember that you may find, as you read, that a particular article isn't very informative to your research question. In these cases, don't be afraid of discarding it. Remember, this is not time wasted; this is you learning more about what's relevant and what's not to your research question.

After you read your current batch of articles, you have a decision to make. You can at this point:

1. Collect a new batch of 5 to 10 using your current search terms and repeat. This is most appropriate if you still have unanswered questions related to the specifics of your current search.
2. Identify key citations within the articles you've already read, locate those papers, and read them for more context about or to evaluate claims being made in the articles you found by searching.
3. Revise your search terms. This might be done if you are not finding relevant information in your current search or if the information you are finding tends to address a much more specific question than the one you were asking.
4. Revise your overall research question. This is done if you realize at this stage you are not really searching for what you're asking for.
5. Move on to the next phase. Once you feel you have a good grasp of the basic issues at play in relation to your research question, it's time to move on. Importantly, this doesn't mean you have *exhaustively* explored every nook and cranny of your research question.

Develop a Schema

This stage of the process is where you do your hardcore *thinking*. Once you have read the first 5 to 10 articles on your core research question, perhaps after revising your core research question a few times to get to closer to a *good* question, and after visiting key citations to be sure you fully understand the cores of the various arguments being made, you should have an idea what the major related concerns, issues, and focal topics are within the boundaries of your research question. This will help you create a **schema**, which refers to the mental organizational system you'll use to keep all of this information organized into meaningful pieces.

For example, let's go back to research question from earlier in this chapter:

How does diversity of an organization's employees influence how individual job performance impacts organizational performance?

After reading your first 10 articles on this topic, you'd want to convert this question into a **mind map**, which is a visualization of the schema you are creating that illustrates how ideas and concepts fit together. When you create a mind map about your research question, you'll want to frame it in terms of both the four aspects of theory described previously plus methodology. An example mind map for this research question appears in Figure 2.4.

We recommend starting with five major dimensions: constructs, context, methodology, statistics, and theory. Within constructs, you'll also want to explore three additional aspects: definitions, measurement (operational definitions), and correlates. As you continue your literature review, you may revise this to add or remove dimensions, depending upon your

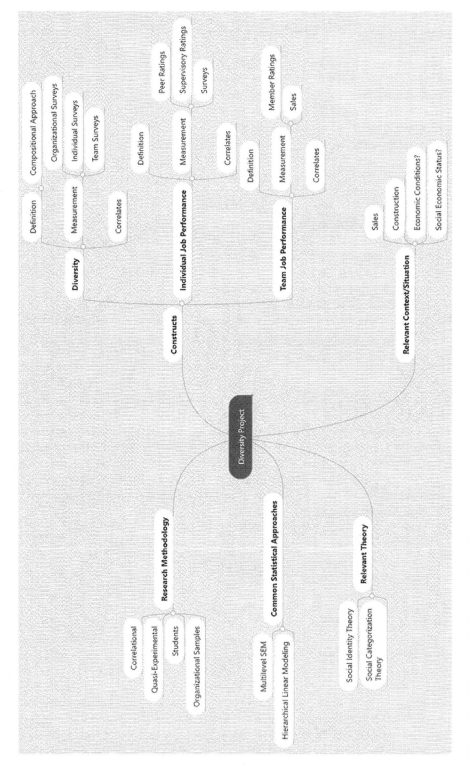

Figure 2.4 Mind map depicting initial schema.

research question. Don't worry too much about getting things "perfect" until you've revisited this stage a few times, and feel free to add sublevels at any time.

Once you are confident your mind map depicts your schema, your next goal is to figure out where the gaps in your schema are. From the schema in Figure 2.4, we can make a few conclusions:

1. Our initial search didn't turn up anything about the definitions or correlates of individual or team job performance. We'll need to find something on these, if not in the diversity context, then elsewhere.
2. We didn't find anyone using experimental methods. Since our research question is about causality (it uses the word "influence"), how are researchers addressing causality, if at all? Perhaps we should try a set of search terms adding the word "experiment" or "causality" next.
3. We found two relevant theories that were cited consistently across all of the literature. We should look into those two theories further to see where they come from and what they say.
4. Most papers didn't define diversity, but of the ones that did, they used the term "compositional approach." We didn't find any other approaches, but the mere fact that they called it "compositional approach" suggests there are alternatives. We should search for alternatives to be sure this is truly the best option.
5. Both students and organizational samples were used as sources of data; are there any tradeoffs to that?

Every time you return to this stage of the process, you should revise your schema to reflect your current understanding of your research question. But after revising your schema, you have a few options:

1. If it becomes clear that the schema that arises from your research question is not at all the project you had wanted to do, toss it all out and go back to defining your research question.
2. If the schema is generally on track but has any gaps in it, develop new search terms for the most important gap and repeat the search process. *Once you have a basic schema you're happy with, only conduct research on one gap at a time.*
3. If you're confident your schema covers all of the major issues related to your research question, move on to the next phase.

Develop Focal Research Questions and/or Hypotheses

With a schema developed, it's finally time to actually develop your "final" research questions to investigate or specific hypotheses to test. Up to this point, you've been getting narrower and narrower within the many dimensions of the problem you've been investigating, developing narrower and narrower research questions. Now, it's time to direct all of that mental energy into the tip of a needle: a specific testable idea. For some types of research, this endpoint may still ultimately be a research question, just a very specific one that you can't find an answer to in existing literature. For other types of research, this might be a research question plus a specific testable proposition called a hypothesis, a statement of what you believe to be true but need to collect data to verify. Because the process of developing research questions and hypotheses define the remainder of your project, we'll cover them in much greater detail as the bulk of Chapter 3, and then again later in this book as relevant to different, specific research approaches. For now, we'll stay big picture.

There is good reason to be cautious at this stage. It is very easy to jump straight to writing focal research questions and hypotheses. Put another way, it's tempting to skip over all of the hard work really deeply understanding a research literature. It's also difficult, at the beginning of your career, to know precisely when you've done "enough" background research to reasonably support any particular research question or hypothesis. Yet jumping ahead can not only set you back on your personal goals, it can have much broader harms on science itself. Do your homework.

For more on this idea, see:

Scheel, A. M., Tiokhin, L., Isager, P. M., & Lakens, D. (2020). Why hypothesis testers should spend less time testing hypotheses. *Perspectives on Psychological Science, 16.* https://doi.org/10.1177/1745691620966795

Once you are happy with your research questions and hypotheses, it's time to start writing. If you aren't, you may need to go back to develop new search terms to fill in remaining gaps you didn't realize you'd left open or even redefine your research question entirely.

Once again, this reveals why it's so important to take a mastery orientation to literature reviews. Regardless of how "good" you are, regardless of how much effort you put in, regardless of how careful you were, *you will absolutely, frequently go down the wrong path.* The key to pushing forward despite this is to realize that every wrong turn is a new learning opportunity, a way for you to be able to articulate later, "No, we didn't investigate that path, *and here's why.*"

Outline and Write an Introduction

If you've done everything as recommended to this point, which means you have a fully gap-free schema, outlining and writing should be the easy part. You're simply recording all the ideas you've already had and already worked through. You've even already organized most of them via your mind map. This is not writing the way you might write in a humanities course; this is **technical writing**. In technical writing, there is a defined path from start to finish, specific information that you must include, and expectations from readers that you will have adequately covered all the topics you were supposed to cover in a generally accepted order. In a literature review in I/O psychology, that path is always the same: it starts with a general organizational problem that needs solving, and it ends with specific research questions or hypotheses that will help solve that problem.

So how do you actually go about writing? The key is to understand your **process**, the set and order of mental steps you take in order to actually put words to the page. A person's process is really about two things: it is about motivation and technique. If you're an actor, you must motivate yourself to throw yourself entirely into the emotional and behavioral state of a character. You must also do so well.

When writing, recommendations about process focus largely on **writer's block**. As a person engaging in technical writing, with a decent process, you should never have writer's block. The reason is that scientific writing is a highly technical, by-the-books sort of task. You don't need to be inspired, and you shouldn't wait to be inspired. In fact, writing scientific articles while inspired is the leading cause of bad scientific articles. Instead, you need to be methodical. With sufficient technique, motivation becomes less relevant.

Each person's process is a little different, so the following process is not one you should adhere to rigidly if it doesn't work for you. Having said that, don't abandon or ignore it without trying. You may be pleasantly surprised with the results. Following this process step by step helps to avoid extensive re-writing, which is the worst nightmare of many graduate students and early-career faculty with limited time to write.

STEP 1: PICK AN AUDIENCE, INCLUDING PUBLISHING VENUE, AND PLAN TO WRITE FOR THEM

If this is your thesis or dissertation, write for the committee who will be reviewing it. If this is for a journal, write for the people who typically read that journal. For example, if you want to publish in the *International Journal of Selection and Assessment*, can you imagine the paper you're writing on its pages? If not, you need to revisit this step. In the case of journals, you're not writing for casual consumers of the journal but instead for typical *reviewers* of the journal, which is a crucial distinction. We'll return to the idea of writing for a particular audience of reviewers in more detail in Chapter 14.

Regardless of audience, there is an expected format of literature reviews. Each paragraph starts with a **topic sentence**. You make the major points you are trying to get across to support your argument in the topic sentence of each paragraph. The sentences that come after that point only serve to support that topic sentence *and nothing more*. In scientific writing, you should not make callbacks to previous points unless absolutely necessary, and you (usually) should not use transition sentences between paragraphs. Each paragraph should be a self-contained little island of information – a major point, followed by information to support that point.

If this sounds different than what you learned in English class, you're right. Narratives rely on a poetic flow of ideas expressed eloquently, although not necessarily clearly (depending upon the author's intent). For maximum rhetorical impact, the author of a narrative may leave out important details to encourage you to think a certain way, only revealing them later to maximize the impact on the reader. In contrast, scientific writing relies on predictability and fully supported points. You must always make your points up front and then provide supporting details. This takes a dramatically different approach than writing a story – which is what we'll get to next in Step 2.

STEP 2: WRITE A SKELETON OUTLINE THAT MATCHES YOUR FINAL VENUE'S EXPECTED STRUCTURE

Once you've identified the expectations of your reviewers, you'll want to start to meet those expectations. The first step in this process is laying out an outline that matches the required format of your intended publication target. These vary widely. In I-O psychology, you might need to write a paper in APA, or you might not. Check the journal's website and find out. For our example here, I'm going to assume that you're writing a manuscript for a journal requiring APA style. That means the next step is creating this outline:

TITLE: TBD

I.   (Introduction)

    a. (Introduction to the Introduction – less than 4 pages)
    b. **Heading 1**
    c. **Heading 2**
    d. **Heading 3**

II.   **Method**

    a. **Participants**
    b. **Materials**
    c. **Procedure**

III. **Results**
IV. **Discussion**

    a. (Introduction to the Discussion)
    b. **Limitations**
    c. **Practical and Theoretical Recommendations**
    d. **Conclusion**

That's it – an entire APA-style paper. Although we'll only be writing an introduction for now, it's good to keep your entire plan in mind from the beginning. Note that a few sections are surrounded by parentheses. That is because these headings are not "real" headings – they will not go into your paper. Instead, they are implied by the structure of your paper. All other headings (the bolded ones) will eventually appear, word for word, in your actual paper.

One section of particular note is the **introduction to the introduction**, which is the 4 or fewer pages that come immediately after your title but before any other headings. *The intro to the intro is the most important part of your paper.* It should introduce the practical context of your paper, set up all major arguments you plan to make and terms you plan to use in your paper, and end with a precise statement about the overall research question you will be addressing, sometimes with a summary of the methods you'll be using to address it. If a reviewer or committee member can't figure out *exactly* what you're researching and why by the end of this section, they are unlikely to understand the potential of your paper. If they don't understand the paper's potential, they will judge everything else you wrote through the lens of "I don't understand why this matters." Do everything you can to prevent that from happening.

That's it at this stage – ensure your skeleton outline matches the audience's expected format, and you're ready to move to Step 3.

STEP 3: CREATE A *SUMMARY OUTLINE* BY FILLING IN THE OUTLINE OF THE
INTRODUCTION WITH VERBATIM HEADINGS, SUMMARIES OF MAJOR POINTS, AND
TARGET PAGE COUNTS

This outline is, at this point, pretty fluid. You want to keep the overall structure of the skeleton outline, but you may add or remove headings as needed, and at this stage, before a research study has been completed, you'll want to stick to only building out the introduction. This is the time to make decisions about the flow of arguments you need to make to support your research question as a compelling one to ask. Here's an example:

TITLE: *An Amazing Exploration of Writing Scientific Papers*

I.   (Introduction)

    a. (Introduction to the Introduction – less than 4 pages)

        1. Discuss how popular paper writing is

    2. Discuss how more research is needed on paper writing training

    3. Describe how we'll be testing paper writing training

II. **Paper Writing Theory** (2 pages)

    a. Paper writing theory is complicated

    b. Paper writing requires training

III. **Paper Writing Training** (2 pages)

    a. Training is very important to improve paper writing

    b. Training delivers paper writing theory to those in need

    c. Past research has supported the use of training to improve paper writing

        1. H1. Being trained in paper writing will improve paper writing.

    d. There may be additional individual difference and situational moderators

    e. Writing climate appears important to paper writing effectiveness training

        1. H2. Writing climate will moderate the effect of paper writing training on paper writing.

By the end of this stage, you should be able to see that the flow of major ideas supports the points being made. Additionally, each hypothesis or research question that you are trying to **motivate** will come right after a paragraph in which you summarize the most direct, clear, and compelling arguments possible for why that hypothesis or research question is an important one to address, worthy of the effort and resources you are going to expend studying it. In this way, your summary-outlined introduction should follow a predictable flow: an overall introduction to your research in the intro to the intro, followed by some theoretical stage-setting (section ii previously), followed by a series of arguments each ending with a testable proposition or question to be asked. If you can see this flow in your own outline, and if your advisor or a cowriting friend can see it when they look at your outline, you're ready to move on to Step 4.

STEP 4: CREATE A *DETAILED OUTLINE* BY REPLACING MAJOR POINT SUMMARIES WITH VERBATIM TOPIC SENTENCES

In the next stage, update the summary outline by replacing general concepts with actual topic sentences. For example, the intro to the intro might be changed to this:

I. (Introduction to the Introduction – less than 4 pages)

    a. One of the most common plagues of the modern era of science is poor writing.

    b. Despite its popularity, research on how to train people to produce high-quality scientific writing is sparse.

    c. In the present study, we explore the implications of paper writing theory for the creation of high-quality paper writing training.

When creating a detailed outline, you should try not to add or remove any paragraphs that you've already set in the previous step. Sometimes it is necessary, but if you completed the previous step correctly, it will be minimal. It happens most often when writing topic sentences – you realize that something you summarized before is more complicated than you initially believed and now needs to be split into two distinct points.

Topic sentences are the only point at which there should be "transitions" in your paper. A topic sentence can refer to a previous topic sentence if two points are closely tied together. However, you should avoid this unless absolutely necessary so that the paper is easier to reorganize later, if necessary (for example, by reviewer request in a revise and resubmit).

Because the topic sentences are where the "story" of your paper is told, you should be able to read your entire outline of topic sentences and come away with a complete picture of everything you argued, everything you did, and everything you contributed. If a reviewer were to take everything in this version of your outline at face value (i.e., if they didn't care about previous research supporting your points), your outline alone should form a compelling argument for what you did. If you can't do that, you need to revise your outline before proceeding to Step 5.

STEP 5: CONVERT YOUR OUTLINE INTO A PAPER BY ADDING SUPPORTING POINTS TO EACH TOPIC SENTENCE. TRY NOT TO CHANGE ANY TOPIC SENTENCES AT THIS POINT

In scientific writing, actually writing your paper is the easiest step! At this point, you have created a very specific and precise blueprint. You've finished all the hefty thinking work already! Thus, the final step is simply to add supporting details, with plenty of citations, for each of your points. The key in this stage is that every sentence you write – every word – should be written to support the topic sentence of the paragraph you are currently writing. Don't worry about additional planning or additional points, and remember to ensure that each paragraph is self contained.

If you discover that you've left something big out, you may need to leave the "Writing" stage and return to previous stages of preparing a literature review to correct that problem. If you've done your due diligence, you shouldn't need to go too far back – such as to the "redefine your research question" stage – but it does happen occasionally. Don't be afraid to throw out writing or even entire developed outlines if you discover this kind of problem. If you don't, you will often spend much more time trying to "fix" the problem than if you'd just started over again.

If you're on track at this point, you should already have a carefully curated and designed framework of information about a relevant, appropriately scoped, practical question of interest. And with that done, you're ready to design a study.

References

Cucina, J. M., & McDaniel, M. A. (2016). Pseudotheory proliferation is damaging the organizational sciences. *Journal of Organizational Behavior, 37*(8), 1116–1125. https://doi.org/10.1002/job.2117

Hausknecht, J. P., Day, D. V., & Thomas, S. C. (2004). Applicant reactions to selection procedures: An updated model and meta-analysis. *Personnel Psychology, 57*(3), 639–683. https://doi.org/10.1111/j.1744-6570.2004.00003.x

Lewin, K. (1951). Problems of research in social psychology. In D. Cartwright (Ed.), *Field theory in social science: Selected theoretical papers* (pp. 155–169). Harper & Row.

Robinaugh, D. J., Haslbeck, J. M. B., Ryan, O., Fried, E. I., & Waldorp, L. J. (2021). Invisible hands and fine calipers: A call to use formal theory as a toolkit for theory construction. *Perspectives on Psychological Science, 16*. https://doi.org/10.1177/1745691620974697

Further Reading

Gervais, W. M. (2021). Practical methodological reform needs good theory. *Perspectives on Psychological Science, 16*. https://doi.org/10.1177/1745691620977471
  • Gervais describes how the psychological sciences are changing in response to issues such as the limited replicability of past findings. Gervais argues that those who wish to change scientific culture should step back and consider how theory (particularly about how culture evolves) can inform the norms, incentives, institutions, beliefs, and practices of psychological scientists.

Grahek, I., Schaller, M., & Tackett, J. L. (2021). Anatomy of a psychological theory: Integrating construct-validation and computational-modeling methods to advance theorizing. *Perspectives on Psychological Science, 16*. https://doi.org/10.1177/1745691620966794
  • Grahek and colleagues describe how psychological theories often provide weak explanations and overly broad predictions. The authors propose integrating two processes, construct validation (which primarily emphasizes psychological characteristics) and computational modeling (which primarily emphasizes processes) as a means of generating stronger explanations and more precise explanations in psychology.

Meehl, P. E. (1990). Why summaries of research on psychological theories are often uninterpretable. *Psychological Reports, 66*(1), 195–244. https://doi.org/10.2466/pr0.1990.66.1.195
  • Meehl provides a scathing critique of the ways scholars typically evaluate psychological theories. Meehl made several noteworthy contributions to psychological theory during the latter half of the 20th century and has more recently been recognized as a guiding light for the reform of psychological methods. Although the content of this paper is complex, it inspired a great deal of content in this book.

Pickett, C. (2017, April 12). *Let's look at the big picture: A system-level approach to assessing scholarly merit*. https://osf.io/tv6nb
  • Pickett argues that scholars should be evaluated on whether and to what extent they have advanced their scientific discipline, rather than the number of citations or awards they have received. Potential methods for assessing a scientist's influence on the scientific system include increasing the supply of new researchers, increasing the productivity of other scientists, increasing the transmission of information, and making the field a better and more productive place.

Spellman, B. A. (2015). A short (personal) future history of revolution 2.0. *Perspectives on Psychological Science, 10*, 886–899. https://doi.org/10.1177/1745691615609918
  • Spellman reviews methodological crises within psychological science from the early 21st century (e.g., failures to replicate, questionable research practices) and argues that this signifies revolution. Spellman notes that changes in technology and researcher demographics, limited resources, and misaligned incentives are all prompting scholars to reform their science.

Sutton, R. I., & Staw, B. M. (1995). What theory is not. *Administrative Science Quarterly, 40*(3), 371–384. https://doi.org/10.2307/2393788
  • Sutton and Staw outline five characteristics that differentiate papers with some theory from papers with no theory. They emphasize that "theory" is not the same as providing references, data, lists of variables/constructs, diagrams, or hypotheses, no matter how comprehensive.

Questions to Think About

1. What scientific conversations (research areas) would you listen to (read about) if you wanted to conduct research on the following topics?

   a. How do Uber drivers manage their stress?
   b. Which employees are most likely to drop out of an online mindset training program?
   c. Which organizations are most likely to survive in an economic recession?

2. What is a theory?
3. Explain the criteria you would look for to judge the quality of a research article.
4. Why might someone redefine their research question while conducting a literature review?
5. Do a keyword search for "counterproductive work behaviors" on a curated database of your choosing and Google Scholar. Compare your search results for each. Why might these results not be equivalent?
6. What are the most important pieces of information to include in an annotated bibliography?

Key Terms

- evidence
- gap
- gatekeeping
- Google Scholar
- hypothesis
- hypothesize
- incremental research
- induce
- induction
- inform theory
- integration
- introduction to the introduction
- jargon
- mind map
- model, hypothetic-deductive
- motivate
- operational definitions
- operationalization
- path diagram
- performance goal orientation
- process
- PsycINFO
- research question
- research, extant
- schema
- schemata
- scientific consensus
- Scopus
- technical writing
- theory
- topic sentence
- useful abstraction of reality
- Web of Science
- writer's block

Chapter 3

Selecting the Best Research Strategy From Your Literature Review

Learning Objectives

After reading this chapter, you will be able to:

1. Contrast exploratory and confirmatory research approaches.
2. Develop an appropriate research question.
3. Interpret a path diagram.
4. Understand the difference between primary and secondary research.

So you've successfully reviewed the literature and identified a general research question of interest. Let's imagine that question is: Does "method-mindedness" (MM) influence research performance? We believe MM is a previously unmeasured individual difference defined as the degree to which a person seeks to deeply understand the research methods they use in their research.

Let's further imagine that you went ahead and ran a study, asking two questions: (1) What is your MM on a scale from 1–5? and (2) What is your research performance on a scale from 1–5? (This may seem a little silly on the surface, but we actually measure many variables in a similar way, so it will serve as a useful example.)

Some time later, after investing time, energy, and perhaps even some cash, your study is complete! And look – the MM 1–5 score is correlated with Research Performance 1–5 score! Huzzah! Contribution to the literature done, right?

But wait – how do you know that it was in fact method-mindedness that caused the effect? What if your MM score is a proxy for statsiness? What if MM is multidimensional and really made up of three MM subfactors, and only MM-type-3 caused the effect? In fact – how do you even know MM exists in the first place?

Without previous studies that have already asked meaningful questions about the nature of MM, you can only speculate about all of these things, yet different answers to these questions than yours could frame your results very differently. And different frames could make it difficult for your ideas to be understood and appreciated by the scientists you're trying to convince you are correct.

All of this uncertainty marks a poor research question, one you should not have wasted your limited time trying to investigate. Instead, you should have picked a smaller (although

DOI: 10.4324/9781315167473-4

still quite large), more central question: what is the validity of method-mindedness? How do we know it is actually what previous researchers have claimed it to be?

Understanding when additional questions need to be asked and how to ask them is one of the first skills you should work on when learning research methods. It's also one of the most difficult skills to master, because it's not clear until you're knee-deep in a literature what questions have and have not actually been answered and how precisely they are interrelated.

As described in Chapter 2, these unanswered research questions are also called "gaps." But what kind of question can be used to fill a gap, and how does the nature of that question drive your research design? Answering that question is the purpose of this chapter.

Conducting Empirical Research

In the process of conducting a literature review, you will have created, explored, and moved on from countless little research questions. These little research questions are for a very particular purpose: to ensure that you have completely explored all boundary issues that need exploring related to your focal research question. But these little research questions are different from your *focal* research question, the one you will build a research study to investigate. The key difference between those little research questions and your focal research question is that your focal research question truly meets all of the requirements specified in Chapter 2 for "good" research questions: it's answerable, there is lack of consensus, it is well defined, it is ethical to ask, and it will either immediately or eventually produce a practical benefit.

As soon as you encounter a question that meets all of these criteria, you potentially have a research question on which to base an **empirical study**. Although we introduced empiricism as a general philosophical movement in Chapter 1, we use the term slightly differently here: to describe a research study designed with that philosophical movement as a foundation for decision-making. In this slightly different sense, an empirical study refers to research that involves the collection and interpretation of data and appropriate effort to be as objective as possible about how you go about it. By conducting empirical research, you generally are trying to contribute to *theory*, the current general scientific understanding of a concept that we introduced in Chapter 2. Empirical research can be conducted with a wide range of more practical research frameworks, the most common of which we'll discuss later in this chapter.

While preparing for theses and dissertations, the most common problems graduate students typically have are related to scope. If you need the answer to a *different* research question first in order to have a firm foundation of the research question you're actually interested in, your project is *too big*. You can think of this like **fighting a war on two fronts**, a reference to the strategy used by Allied Forces in World War II to force Germany to split its military resources across thousands of kilometers, toward Western Europe in the west and toward Russia in the east, simultaneously. Because Germany only has one military, each front was only half as strong as it would have been if united. Similarly, it's very difficult to conceptually defend a research question as meaningful when you need to provide a complete, well-supported defense of more than one meaningful gap, especially when the arguments and support needed to defend those gaps are quite different. In practice, you are forced to split the number of pages you have to explain something into two (or more!) parts.

Using our chapter-opening example, let's say we wanted to research the impact of a personality trait we believe exists, MM, on task performance. The impact of one variable on another is, without any other information, a reasonable thing to want to know. But if there is no existing research on MM, the project has now become too big, because in order to research the impact of MM on task performance, you need to define, measure, and understand MM first. If you skip those steps, you are not building your research on a firm foundation, and that's risky to not only the quality of your results but also to your mental health. To fix that, you need to **rescope** the project to something more manageable by asking a better, more focused research question.

Types of Questions You Can Address Empirically

There is no single right or wrong way to organize the types of research questions that you can ask of a literature in the search for gaps, but we find it useful to distinguish three different general categories of question: ones that address what, ones that address which, and ones that address how. "What" questions are descriptive and generally involve explorations of a phenomenon of interest, such as constructs or the interrelationships between constructs. "Which" questions describe boundary conditions, such as the situational context or interactive forces that affect how a phenomenon occurs. "How" questions describe processes, the intermediate causal steps between a cause and effect of interest. These questions are depicted in Table 3.1.

Table 3.1 Types of research questions

Type of question	Subtype	Purpose	Example
What?	Description	To determine what constructs exist	A focus group study in which subject matter experts are asked for their views on a construct
	Measurement	To determine how to operationally define a construct	A series of studies with the goal of developing a trustworthy survey
	Causal Effect Estimation	To determine what the effect is of X on Y (or the difference in Y when X is at different levels)	An experiment in which people are randomly assigned to two different conditions to determine if outcomes differ
	Relationship (Noncausal) Estimation	To determine what the relationship is between X and Y (or the difference in Y when X is at different levels)	A survey in which two constructs are measured and their relationship examined
Which?	Moderation by Situation	To determine which situational influences impact a causal effect	An experiment in which people are randomly assigned to two different conditions, and also to two different situational contexts, to determine if condition and situation interact
	Moderation by Person	To determine which individual differences impact a causal effect	An experiment in which people are randomly assigned to two different conditions, and also complete a survey about their personalities, to see if condition and personality interact
How?	Mediation	To determine how the effect of X on Y occurs via the intermediate effects of X on Z and Z on Y	A survey study in which data on three variables are collected to determine if the data collected are consistent with that expected when mediation occurs

Broadly speaking, questions higher in this table must be answered before questions lower in this table should be asked. For example, if the impact of X on Y is not yet known (What?), it is a bit early to investigate moderators (Which?) or mediators (How?), at least without a degree of risk.

Questions That Ask: What?

There are two broad categories of research study that may be used to investigate *what* questions. The first type, **qualitative research**, focuses on deep understanding and narrative description. Qualitative research studies typically involve the collection of unstructured information, like text, videos, or audio, followed by a thoughtful process of converting that information into theory that relies heavily on human interpretation. In this research paradigm, data generally guide decisions about theory, and such research tends to be considered more **exploratory** in nature. The second type, **quantitative research**, involves the use of carefully designed measurement instruments to capture information about constructs and the use of statistics to interpret that information. In this research paradigm, data may guide decisions about theory (i.e., exploratory), or theory may guide decisions about data (i.e., **confirmatory**). However, the key difference is the focus on statistical analysis. As we explore the types of research questions that can be asked, we'll also provide visualizations using the language of path diagrams briefly introduced in Chapter 1. Path diagrams are extremely common in modern I-O psychology, so it is important to start becoming comfortable with what they represent as soon as possible. Each will be explained as we get to them.

The first type of *what* research question is **description**. Its purpose is to answer the most foundational question in all of science: what is this? When a researcher utilizes a qualitative research approach to description, they typically take an exploratory approach in which they make few assumptions about what the construct is, allowing data to guide their judgments until they are confident in their developed conclusions about it. When a researcher utilizes a quantitative research approach to description, they usually take a confirmatory approach in which they develop some ideas about what a construct is and what it means, followed by making a variety of assumptions about what they're looking for and then calculating statistics according to those assumptions to *confirm* their ideas. When quantitative researchers take an exploratory approach, they generally ask a broad range of questions to cast a wide net and then allow the data to guide their course of action. In Figure 3.1, you can see a construct represented in path diagram notation as an oval.

For example, consider the I-O area of job analysis, which involves the use of scientific method to describe a job. A qualitative job analyst would likely conduct focus groups, interviews, and observations of **subject matter experts** (SMEs), people with expertise in the thing you want to develop a theory about, to create a holistic picture of the job. From SME data, they would develop a theory of the job's components, demands, resources required, and

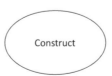

Figure 3.1 A construct depicted with path diagram notation.

any other information of interest. A quantitative job analyst would likely use a previously validated job analytic measure, like McCormick, Jeanneret, and Mecham's (1972) Position Analysis Questionnaire, and administer this to SMEs, using the scores on that measure to create a numerical summary of various position characteristics. In I-O, many people asking descriptive research questions utilize qualitative and quantitative research approaches together to address the same question; in this way, a researcher can combine the precision of a quantitative approach with the depth of a qualitative approach. You will learn much more about qualitative research design in Part 2 of this text and quantitative designs in Part 3.

The second type of *what* research question, **measurement**, is usually a quantitative question. It concerns the creation of operational definitions from known constructs. Thus, to ask a measurement question, someone must have already conducted a descriptive study on which to base the measurement research. In practice, description and measurement studies are often presented in sequence within one paper; the first study introduces the construct and explores it, often qualitatively, whereas the second study develops a quantitative measurement instrument. For example, Landers and Callan (2014) developed a measure that quantifies the beneficial and harmful behaviors that people engage in while using social media at work. In their Study 1, a qualitative study was conducted to create a theory of these behaviors. In Study 2, a measurement instrument was developed, tested, and revised. In Study 3, this final measurement instrument was tested. You will learn much more about trustworthy practices for the development of good quantitative operational definitions in Chapter 7.

In Figure 3.2, you will see a measurement research question represented as a path diagram. Note that the construct, MM, is an oval, whereas its operational definition, a 5-point survey question ranging from strongly disagree to strongly agree, is a rectangle. Rectangles are used to represent anything that is an objectively defined number, such as responses to a survey. Additionally, there is an arrow pointing from the construct to the operational definition; this is used to state the assumption that the construct *causes* the operational definition. In this case, it's theorized that a person's MM causes them to respond to that question in different ways – presumably a person high in MM should agree more strongly with the question "Are you methodsy?" than a person low in MM.

The third type of *what* research question is **causal effect estimation**. In a quantitative approach, it concerns the use of high-quality measures to create a numerical estimate of how strong a causal relationship is, most often using statistics like Cohen's d, Hedges' g, and

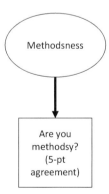

Figure 3.2 A construct and its operational definition in path diagram notation.

eta-squared (η^2). In qualitative research, estimation is usually limited to a general description of negative, zero, or positive effects. Thus, both descriptive and measurement studies must have already occurred to meaningfully investigate causal relationships. The most common type of quantitative causal effect study involves experimentation, the random assignment of people or organizations to different conditions. Causal effect estimation is also a core purpose of a complex statistical technique called *structural equation modeling*, although it is not reasonable to infer causality just because someone used SEM. Strategies for quantitatively supporting causal relationships will be covered in more detail in Chapter 8.

It's All Greek to Me

One skill that you'll find strangely useful when trying to understand statistics and research methods is the ability to name Greek letters. In the olden days of highfalutin education, learning a bit of Greek and a bit of Latin was more commonly taught as part of a "liberal arts education" than it is now, so many students of the past learning about statistics had already been exposed to a little Greek by the time they got to statistics. We are not so (un)lucky. You don't need to learn the entire Greek alphabet to get by these days (although it doesn't hurt), but memorizing the following characters and their pronunciations will probably help you out:

- α – lowercase alpha
- β – lowercase beta
- γ – lowercase gamma
- Δ – capital delta
- ε – lowercase epsilon
- ζ – lowercase zeta ("zay-tuh")
- η – lowercase eta ("ay-tuh," rhymes with zeta)
- θ – lowercase theta ("thay-tuh," rhymes with zeta, starts like "thin")
- κ – lowercase kappa
- λ – lowercase lambda (sometimes spelled "lamda")
- μ – lowercase mu ("myu")
- ξ – lowercase xi ("k-zye" as one sound, but you can get away with "zye")
- ρ – lowercase rho ("roe," rhymes with "toe")
- σ – lowercase sigma
- Σ – capital sigma
- τ – lowercase tau (rhymes with "cow")
- φ – lowercase phi ("fee")
- χ – lowercase chi ("kye")
- ψ – lowercase psi ("sye")

Additionally, here's a little trick that can save you a few clicks. If you need to write a Greek character in Microsoft Word on Windows (warning: this doesn't work in Google Docs or on a Mac), just type the roughly-equivalent English letter, then highlight the letter and press Ctrl+Shift-q. For example, try it with *m* to see it transform into a *mu*.

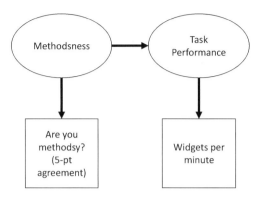

Figure 3.3 A causal effect between constructs and their operational definitions in path diagram notation.

A theory of causal relationships between MM and task performance appears in Figure 3.3. One-sided arrows are used to indicate the direction of causal impact, so in this case, MM is theorized to impact task performance. In comparison to Figure 3.2, a task performance construct has been added, which it itself operationalized with a new measure, widgets per minute. Importantly, there is no causal arrow between the two operational definitions. This is because there should be no relationship between a person's response to "Are you methodsy?" and widgets per minute *except* through the impact of the constructs that in turn caused them. Thus, MM is theorized to impact both task performance and responses to "Are you methodsy?" Task performance, although caused by MM, is theorized to itself only cause a widgets per minute score.

The fourth type of *what* research question, **relationship estimation**, is the most common type of research question found in I-O psychology. Providing support for causal relationships is complex, so many researchers instead pull back and say, "I just want to show that these variables are *related*." Relatedness is much easier to support, since it simply involves creating operational definitions of each construct of interest and then using them both on the same group of people. Relationships are commonly summarized with statistics like Pearson's *r* or multiple *R*. The difficulty bar is much lower to support relationships versus causal effects.

A path diagram depicting a theory of relationships is shown in Figure 3.4. The only difference between this diagram and the one appearing in Figure 3.3 is the use of a double-sided arrow. This suggests only that MM and task performance **share variance** (or **covary**) but not that one causes the other. Importantly, we must still assume that each construct causes its operational definition; otherwise, we cannot measure constructs at all.

Questions That Ask: Which?

Once the basic *what* questions have been sufficiently addressed in the literature, researchers begin to ask *which* questions that explore the boundary conditions under which the observed causal and noncausal effects actually occur. These boundary conditions can be split into two causes: situational influences and person influences.

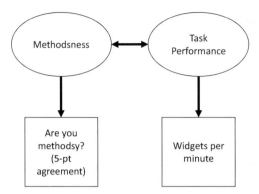

Figure 3.4 A relationship between constructs and their operational definitions in path diagram notation.

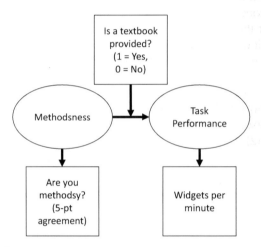

Figure 3.5 Moderation by situation in path diagram notation.

The first type of *which* question is **moderation by situation**. In I-O psychology, this type of research question is most directly inspired by social psychology, where situations are often manipulated in experiments and their effects observed. In moderation by situation, the magnitude of a relationship changes as a result of a situational state. You might also hear this referred to as a *two-way interaction* or more simply, an **interaction**. For example, the impact of MM on task performance might be theorized to be *moderated* by the provision of a methods textbook like this one. More specifically, we might theorize that MM impacts task performance, but only when a textbook is provided. When a textbook is not provided, we might theorize no impact at all. In this example, we would therefore call the presence of a textbook a **moderator**, sometimes called a **conditional effect**.

When theorizing moderation, it's important to be specific about how you suspect the effect being moderated to change. It's not enough to simply say, "There's moderation!" You need to be specific. Is the relationship negative in some situations and positive in others? Is the relationship zero in some situations but positive or negative in others? If you can't make that prediction, then you probably don't have enough theory to form a good research question.

In Figure 3.5, we can see the new moderating effect depicted as an arrow pointing to the middle of a causal arrow. Moderation cannot occur in relationship estimation, so you need a good reason ahead of time to believe that a relationship is causal to propose it is also moderated. In this example, the moderator is measured and not a construct (as indicated by the use of a rectangle), but a construct could be used for moderation instead, as we will see in the next example.

Moderation of Moderation of Moderation of Moderation . . .

Beyond simple moderation, you can also have moderation of moderation. For example, we might propose that a positive methods climate and provision of a textbook *together* are required to produce positive increases in task performance when MM is high. This is more commonly referred to as a *three-way interaction* because it involves the combination of three causes. In fact, you can have any number of moderations you want: moderation of moderation of moderation is called a *four-way interaction*), moderation of moderation of moderation of moderation is called a *five-way interaction*, and so on. In the real world, when modeling psychological variables, anything beyond a two-way interaction is extremely uncommon at an effect size that will be practically useful. So if you want to propose one, you'd better have a phenomenally good theoretical reason to do so and understand (1) you're taking a bit of a risk in terms of practicality, and (2) you're likely going to need an enormous sample size.

The second type of *which* question is **moderation by person**. In I-O psychology, this type of research question is most directly inspired by personality psychology, where the characteristics of people are often considered to interact with each other to produce behavior. Thus, this type of research question is similar in structure to moderation by situation but with a different type of moderator. In our previous example and in Figure 3.5, we might replace the provision of a textbook (a factual situation) with *work climate for methods*, defined as the degree to which your supervisor, coworkers, and others provide physical and non-physical resources to support research methods (if you're reading this book, hopefully your methods climate is pretty good!). This is depicted in Figure 3.6, and as you can see, the only change from Figure 3.5 is that the measured variable has been replaced by a construct and operational definition pair.

Questions That Ask: How?

There is one major type of *how* question, which, like *which* questions, can be asked as soon as *what* questions have been answered. This question is one of **mediation**, the process by which one variable influences another through an intermediate variable. Instead of X affecting Y directly, X instead affects Z and Z in turn affects Y. For example, we might theorize that the reason MM affects task performance is because people with high MM will be more motivated to work on methods-related tasks. In this case, motivation is a **mediator** of the

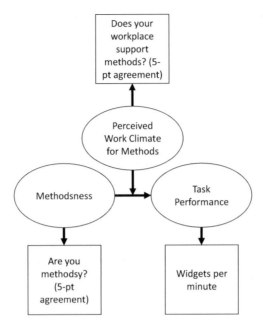

Figure 3.6 Moderation by person in path diagram notation.

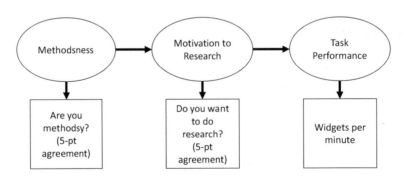

Figure 3.7 Mediation (indirect effect only) in path diagram notation.

relationship between MM and performance. We might also say that MM has an **indirect effect** on performance through the pathway of its **direct effect** on motivation and motivation's later direct effect on performance.

In Figure 3.7, you can see mediation represented as a chain of causal arrows. An important realization about path diagrams in regard to mediation is what arrows are *not* depicted. In this figure, there is no direct arrow between MM and performance. This means that our theory says MM affects performance through no mediator *except* motivation. More succinctly, the theory in Figure 3.7 presents only an indirect effect. If we believe that MM affects performance through motivation *and directly or through other unspecified mediators*, then we should also draw that arrow directly from MM to performance, as shown in Figure 3.8.

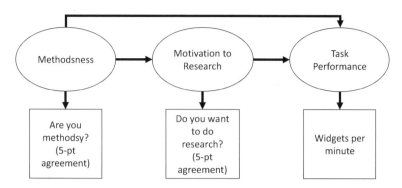

Figure 3.8 Mediation (both direct and indirect effects) in path diagram notation.

In this case, the theory contains both indirect and direct effects, so we would conclude that MM affects performance through both motivation and other intermediate causal forces.

Confusing Moderation and Mediation

One of the most common points of confusion for people just learning about more advanced research questions beyond basic relationships and direct causal effects is the differences between moderation and mediation. Here are some succinct descriptions that might help in a pinch:

Moderation occurs when one variable affects how strong the relationship is between two others. It is also called an interaction. It is depicted in path diagrams as an arrow pointing at the middle of another arrow.

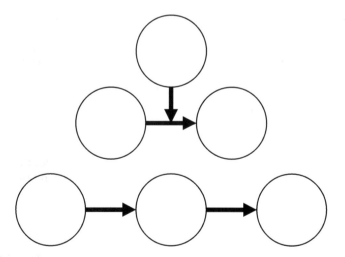

Mediation occurs when one variable affects a second variable through a third variable. It is depicted in path diagrams as a chain of causal arrows in sequence.

Asking Multiple Questions Simultaneously

In I-O psychology, published papers typically do not test one individual research question at a time. There are a lot of trade-offs in this approach to research, and this isn't the way things are done in many other fields, including other disciplines within psychology. Instead, I-O psychologists typically propose a broader, grander theory that contains multiple smaller research questions. Sometimes these become **named theories**, which is, as the term implies, a theory that has coalesced into something people recognize with a single term. For example, goal-setting theory, leader-member exchange theory, and applicant reactions theory are all named theories; if you said these phrases out loud to I-Os with advanced degrees, they would all likely think of roughly the same constructs, operational definitions, and path diagrams.

For example, when someone says "goal-setting theory," one of your authors (Richard) immediately associates that with Ed Locke and Gary Latham, who have done a lot of work on this theory over the years. Richard thinks of how goal-setting research is typically conducted as an experimental intervention, so much of the literature asks causal questions. Richard thinks of the conditions under which goal-setting is effective, its moderators, such as goal intensity (typically operationalized as do-your-best goals versus easy, difficult, and impossible goals), the use of feedback, the match between the ability of the target and the goals they are being provided, the resources the target is being provided to achieve the goal, and the use of learning versus performance goals. Richard thinks about why goal-setting works and its mediators, such as by increasing self-efficacy, by directing goal choice, by encouraging persistence towards specified goals, and by encouraging the development of goal achievement strategies.

Given all of that, if Richard wanted to see if goal-setting theory was accurate, he could potentially do so by testing all of these relationships at the same time. This is probably a waste of time, however, because "Does goal-setting theory work?" is a bad research question for many of the reasons we've already discussed: given the complexity of goal-setting theory, simply asking "does it work" is of inappropriate scope. It's too big.

The balance between big and small research questions is a difficult one when you're learning and one with which you will likely struggle many times. But there are occasions where testing multiple research questions simultaneously is appropriate and gives more information than cutting it up.

For example, let's explore the path diagram depicted in Figure 3.9, which comes from a study of goal orientation when a person initially fails to achieve a goal. What can we infer about the research questions being asked in this study? What research questions are being

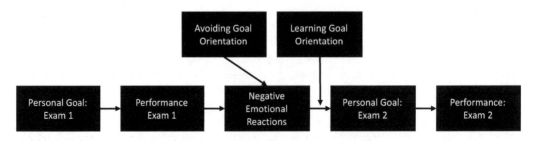

Figure 3.9 Path diagram adapted from Cron et al. (2005).

asked and what could be asked? It is useful to go through all of the items in Table 3.1 as you do this.

First, *what* are the constructs and *what* is used to measure them? In this case, there aren't any, and you can tell because there are no ovals. Assuming the path diagram was created correctly (it was, mostly), this implies that the researchers are not testing constructs – instead, they're testing observed variables only. If you look at the details of this study's method, you'll find that's true – for example, although "negative emotional reactions" looks like the name of a construct, it is only statistically tested as the average of 10 survey items ranging from 1 (not at all) to 11 (very much). Thus, this theory contains no information about constructs. If the researchers draw conclusions about constructs (they do), we'll need to consider carefully if we believe that conclusions about constructs can be justified.

Among the rectangles, two should stick out as odd: why are two indicators (*Personal Goal: Exam 1* and *Performance: Exam 1*) inside another indicator? This is non-standard path diagram notation, so we'll need to dig into the paper to figure out what this means. If you do that, you'll discover the reason: they want to know about the *difference* between goal and performance, but they don't want to calculate a difference *score*, because that approach discards a lot of information. Thus, they will use specialized statistical methods to examine the two simultaneously.

Second, now that we're clear on the variables themselves, *what* causal and noncausal effects are proposed? There are six causal effects here and no relationships. *Personal Goal: Exam 1* and *Performance: Exam 1* are theorized to impact *Personal Goal: Exam 2*. *Personal Goal: Exam 1* and *Performance: Exam 1* in combination as *Goal-Performance Congruency* are theorized to impact *Negative Emotional Reactions*. *Negative Emotional Reactions* is in turn theorized to affect *Personal Goal: Exam 2*. *Avoiding Goal Orientation* is theorized to affect *Negative Emotional Reactions*, and *Personal Goal: Exam 2* is theorized to impact *Performance: Exam 2*. In fact, that's the only variable that is supposed to affect *Performance: Exam 2*. Since that's a strong claim, we'll return to the implications of this later.

Third, look for moderating effects. In this diagram, there is only one: the relationship between *Negative Emotional Reactions* and *Personal Goal: Exam 2* is moderated by *Learning Goal Orientation*. We'll need to check the text again for the precise nature of this moderation. In this case, the researchers propose that the relationship should be negative, but that high learning goal orientation will change the moderated relationship to zero.

Fourth, look for mediating effects. There are many. For example, the difference between *Personal Goal: Exam 1* and *Performance: Exam 1* (i.e., *Goal-Performance Congruency*) is theorized to affect *Personal Goal: Exam 2* both directly and indirectly (through *Negative Emotional Reactions*). The effect of literally every other variable in the model on *Performance: Exam 2* is mediated by *Personal Goal: Exam 2*. That's quite a bold claim, but one that can only be tested in a model this complex.

With all of that said, let's take a step back to reconsider the big picture. You just read several paragraphs' worth of information that can be inferred simply by looking at a single path diagram. These are the thoughts that will run through the head of a methodologist simply by looking at that one picture, and those judgments will happen in the space of a few seconds. That is the power of path diagrams in summarizing complex theoretical relationships, and that should signal to you just how important it is that you understand them. Otherwise, you'll miss out on a lot of little details.

To illustrate why this is particularly important in this study, consider that the researchers did not actually test the bold mediational claim implied by their diagram, that all of these forces impact later performance through goal setting effects. You might infer that from the path diagram, but you should not given the statistical tests they actually conducted. Thus, we need to consider the theory implied by this path diagram with some skepticism; it could reflect reality, but without a direct test of all of these paths simultaneously, their precise arrangement is ultimately only an assertion. Instead, we only have empirical support for the two hypothesized direct effects and one indirect effect actually tested in their paper.

Most critically for you, this means that if you based a master's thesis or dissertation on extending this study's results, if you assumed, for example, that learning orientation only impacts performance via goal-setting – if you did not realize this was a gap in the literature – you might not obtain the results you were expecting for your own research. This also highlights the importance of understanding precisely what research questions are being asked in a study and precisely which of those questions are actually tested. It's frequently not the same list.

Path Diagram Cheat Sheet

We'll return to path diagrams in much greater detail in later chapters, but for now, you might find the cheat sheet in Figure 3.10 handy.

Diagram Feature	Meaning
⟶	Causal effect
⟷	Noncausal relationship (correlation/covariance)
◯	Construct
▢	Measured variable

Figure 3.10 Standard path diagram features and associated interpretations.

Picking a Research Approach for a Research Question

Once you've decided on a specific research question to ask, you must decide which research framework to apply to studying it. As noted earlier, certain types of questions imply specific approaches whereas there is some flexibility in others. There are two broad categories of research approaches: **primary research**, in which you collect and interpret data on the subjects of your research questions yourself, and **secondary research**, in which you collect and interpret previously gathered primary research data and results. Primary research in psychology is motivated by initial secondary research in the form of a literature review, so secondary and primary research are commonly published together in the same papers. However, some secondary research is published without any new primary research. We'll describe each set next.

Primary Research

Qualitative research, which commonly involves focus groups, interviews, and the human analysis of content, focuses primarily but not exclusively on *what* questions of description. The purpose of qualitative research is to generate theory by delving deeply into complex, unstructured data and using human judgment to draw insights in an exploratory fashion. Bryman (2004) describes how qualitative research has been used to understand the role of leaders in organizational change. Specifically, the way large-scale change occurs in an organization is typically slow and expressed in a way that appears unique to the specific organization in which it is occurring. Attempting confirmatory quantitative research in this context – for example, through the use of survey methodology – would require the researcher to identify ahead of time constructs of interest, specific operationalizations, and even theoretically link them together in order to test that theory, all in an environment in flux where each of these decisions is likely itself a research gap. Even exploratory quantitative research would be difficult, because it's unclear ahead of time what specific questions and possible answers would shed light on the research question. With so many unknowns, qualitative research becomes an attractive way to develop theory.

For example, Kahn (1990) collected data on 16 people employed as architects in a high-profile architecture firm in the northeastern United States and 22 summer camp counselors in the West Indies. His purpose was to investigate common themes in terms of engagement and disengagement between the two samples in order to develop a theoretical model of causes of work engagement. Ultimately, using a qualitative approach called grounded theory, Kahn proposed a complex theory of the psychological conditions of engagement, including definition, experiential components, types of influence, and specific influences. One of Kahn's key findings was the creation of a concept called *psychological safety*, which refers to the degree to which workers believe their work environment is safe and meaningful.

In contrast, quantitative research involves the careful specification of constructs of interest ahead of data collection, the careful measurement of those constructs under specific conditions and then the application of statistical analysis to understand the relationships between variables observed. When this research is exploratory in nature, questions may be asked that are not tied to a specific construct, and patterns in the data may be used to identify patterns that appear to be the influence of constructs. When this research is confirmatory, which is much more common in psychology, questions are only asked if they are believed to reflect a specific construct of interest and can be theoretically tied to other constructs with high-quality measures. Then, collected data are compared to a set of (hopefully) reasonable assumptions.

A few years after Kahn's work described previously, Brown and Leigh (1996) conducted a quantitative study with two major purposes: (1) to develop a high-quality operational definition of psychological climate based upon Kahn's study of psychological safety and (2) to see how this measure was related to job involvement, effort, and performance quantitatively. They thus addressed questions of measurement, effect estimation, and mediation. Using the foundation of Kahn's work to support the more basic *what* questions, they were thus able to go a step further in developing new theory.

Mixed-methods research like this is most commonly seen split across multiple studies, for a few reasons. First, authors don't often train deeply in both qualitative and quantitative research strategies, so many researchers do not have sufficient expertise to investigate research questions from such different perspectives. Second, sometimes sufficient theory is available that additional qualitative research would not yield many new insights, so new qualitative studies are not needed in some areas. Third, qualitative and quantitative research often require very different data collection strategies, making the time and resource investment much higher, which may not be worthwhile from a career standpoint. For example, if a researcher conducts both a qualitative study and a quantitative study and considers each independently "publishable," they may feel it is a better return on their time investment to publish them as two studies, even if they are closely related. We'll discuss this troubling concept of "least publishable units" in much more detail in Chapter 14 and mixed methods more broadly in Chapter 15.

For now, in I-O research, just know that the most common mixed designs involve quantitative research being used to build upon qualitative research or qualitative research being used to provide additional nuance and detail for quantitative research. In a much smaller number of studies, these approaches are used in combination. For example, Landers and Callan (2014), discussed earlier, present a three-study series in which the first study utilized a qualitative research design to gather information in an unstructured way about how people use social media while they're at work. Using human interpretation, they sorted that information into categories, which they then used to develop a survey as an operational definition of those categories. Then, in the second study, which was quantitative, they refined the developed surveys to improve their psychometric properties. In the third study, they tested the refined measure's ability to predict a variety of outcomes of interest. Thus, their opening qualitative study answered questions of *description*, the following quantitative study questions of *measurement*, and the final quantitative study questions of *relationship estimation*.

Secondary Research

Narrative review is a common type of secondary research method in which literature previously collected is gathered and re-interpreted in aggregate. Narrative review is most useful in situations where there is a research gap in terms of the "big picture." In this situation, new research is needed to frame existing research in terms of larger scale problems. For example, Brown and Vaughn (2011) collected all research conducted on social networking sites, like Facebook, that could be relevant to employee hiring and summarized them in terms familiar to I-O psychologists: construct definitions, legal and ethical risks, and construct validity. Most of the literature they reviewed and interpreted was not located within the I-O psychology research literature, so this review served as a sort of "translation" of this work. As an example of this translation, within their review, the researchers presented a definition of social network sites written by Danah Boyd and Nicole Ellison (2007), themselves researchers in communications and information systems, fields several steps away from psychology. Brown and Vaughn filled a gap with a literature review by saying "here's how social network sites fit into employee hiring research," which had not previously been done.

Importantly, narrative review is primarily useful in situations like this, where basic *what* questions of description and measurement have been answered in other fields but not within I-O psychology (or sometimes not within your specific focal area within I-O psychology). Narrative reviews related to the more complex *what* questions, effect and relationship estimation, are more difficult to justify because it is often unclear to what extent effect and relationship estimates from other fields would in fact generalize to the I-O context. In these cases, primary research is more common and easier to justify.

Where narrative review is generally inappropriate is when trying to draw conclusions about effect and relationship estimates based upon existing literature. For example, if a researcher wanted to know if a study design characteristic, like type of sample, moderated the magnitude of effects across studies, it might seem like narrative review could accomplish that. Specifically, a common intuition here is that if you wanted to know if sampling students versus employees mattered, you could simply count the number of studies that were statistically significant for each group and compare them. For reasons that we will discuss in much greater detail in Chapter 13, this is not a valid approach. In these situations, you will need to conduct a **meta-analysis**.

Meta-analysis is what the name implies: the analysis of previous analyses. More specifically, meta-analysis is a quantitative approach of both causal effect and relationship estimation that is done by mathematically summarizing the causal effects and observed relationships, respectively, found in other studies. Meta-analysis allows an entire research literature to be summarized in an **unbiased** way; here, we use the term *unbiased* to mean that your personal beliefs and values related to your research do not (or rather should not) influence the substance of your research results (if you've been paying attention, you will recognize this value as implied by our prior discussion in Chapter 1 on *post-positivism*). Recognizing the potential for bias is important, because human literature reviewers often have a troubling tendency to insert their own agenda into literature reviews, with or without realizing it. For example, findings that are contrary to your own personal ideas may be ignored or discarded, whereas findings that confirm your ideas are retained and explained in depth. Modern meta-analytic methods are designed to remove a great deal of this bias.

Meta-analysis also allows for the development and testing of theory that cannot be tested within a single study. For example, Blacksmith et al. (2016) conducted a meta-analysis to summarize the effects of the type of technology used to conduct interviews – between telephone, videoconferencing, computer mediation, interactive voice response and face-to-face interviewing – on applicant reactions. This is a valuable outcome of meta-analysis, because realistically, a study randomly assigning people to experience one of these technologies would be resource intensive. More importantly, it is unnecessary when previous studies examining pieces of this research question already exist and can be summarized this way.

Although meta-analysis is a powerful tool, it's important to remember that it is limited by the quality of the primary research it summarizes; if a flawed research literature is meta-analyzed, it's likely that those flaws will remain in the meta-analysis in some way – and, more problematically, such persistent flawed claims can become even more credible after appearing in a meta-analysis. We dedicate all of Chapter 13 to meta-analysis, so we will revisit such limitations in much greater detail there.

Selecting a Research Question and Approach

So, now that you have a general understanding of research approaches and research questions, how do you match the two? Answering this question requires you evaluate four things:

1. Contribution
2. Application
3. Feasibility
4. Ethics

Contribution refers to how much impact your study results could have on the thinking of scholars in your area of study. Contribution is generally framed as either **transformational** or incremental (which we introduced in Chapter 2). Transformational research has the potential to change researchers' minds, to create new paradigms, or to radically shift thinking. Thus, justifiable transformational research tends to be high-risk/high-resource/high-reward. In other words, you would not want to invest 5 years of your life in a project that no one will really care about. Incremental research helps us understand something just a little bit better. It improves theory just a little bit – but it does improve it. Thus, the size of your contribution should be matched carefully to the scope of your project. Investigating qualitative research questions, for example, often takes a great deal more of your own time to do well than investigating quantitative research questions. Even within quantitative research questions, rigorous experimental designs where participants must be run one person at a time can take years to achieve an adequate sample size. Thus, there is no simple answer to this question except to say that if you don't know how big a contribution you might be making, you should talk to a researcher in that area to get a sense of it before you try. If they think what you're doing is very important, perhaps it is worth investing your career to understand it.

Many graduate students, full of passion for their chosen field, want to jump right into doing transformational research; almost all of us want to have big, important ideas that people sit up and pay attention to. We should not devalue incremental research, though. And even more importantly, you should remember that the size and grandiosity of your claims should match the quality of your evidence for those claims. That means that if you tackle the biggest questions, it will take you several years, or more, to get sufficient evidence to make a compelling claim. You might want to start with something more manageable than asking, "what is the secret to being happy at work?"

Application is a consideration of how your findings can inform practical problems faced by society. We visited this concept at the very beginning of this book, in Chapter 1, when we discussed the scientist-practitioner model. It is our view that all I-O psychology projects must have the potential for practical application to organizational success and that all high-quality I-O research blends basic and applied approach within its overall purpose of building practical, accurate knowledge. This doesn't need to be true for an individual study, but you, as a researcher, must have a path in mind for how that study will eventually lead to practice. Because if you don't, who will?

Why Some People Say Science Is Broken

Right now, in psychology and management in particular but also in science more broadly, it is much more difficult to publish results that are incremental than those that are transformational. There is an unhealthy obsession with researchers who have made a "name" for themselves, such that those who have made the flashiest and highest-profile transformational results tend to be the most respected (Vazire, 2017). Over time, this has encouraged researchers to seek out fame and glory, sometimes at the expense of good science. Such practices result in damage to our science's replicability, its validity, and ultimately its reputation with the broader public. As an I-O psychology researcher, you will at some point need to make a decision for yourself about many of the ethical issues presented in this book – for example, in this case, should you do incremental research you know would be good science or transformational research that is flashy and will get press attention but is based upon shaky statistical analyses? We will unabashedly encourage you toward the path of good science, but ultimately, this decision is something you will need to personally grapple with in quiet moments of reflection. Where do you draw the ethics line for yourself? We visit this issue in many other chapters of this book but in the greatest depth in our discussions of data cleaning (Chapter 11), mixed methods research (Chapter 15), and publication strategies (Chapter 14).

Feasibility is a bit more straightforward. In practice, we often have external constraints on our research methods. For example, a qualitative study can generally only be done when you can get access to the people you want to do the study on for long periods of time. If you can't realistically get the number of people you need to sit down for an hour with you to interview, you will be unlikely to get enough information to trust your results. In a quantitative study, your particular chosen research approach may require one-on-one study administration. If it does, do you have time to actually collect the number of people your power analysis says you need? Thesis defense and journal submission deadlines come up faster than you think they will, so feasibility should always be an issue you consider when planning a study.

Ethics is the most critical, because if there are ethical challenges with your research study, contribution, application, and feasibility do not matter. In qualitative research, ethical issues most involve privacy and researcher bias. Because you are sometimes getting deep into people's lives, as a qualitative researcher, you may have access to people's deep, dark secrets. If you don't have the constitution to keep such information to yourself, you should not conduct a study where you might have access to it.

In terms of bias, qualitative research provides the opportunity to shape the direction of empirical investigation quite explicitly. For example, if you feel you don't have enough information on a topic of interest, you can change the way you are interviewing or conducting focus groups to target that new topic mid-stream. This is a simple part of qualitative research, but it can be easily abused if you make such changes in pursuit of an agenda, whether that agenda is one you realize you have or not. Thus, you should carefully consider *why* you want to do a qualitative research study and ensure it's not for the wrong reasons. If it's because *EVERYONE IS WRONG ABOUT THIS*, that's a bad reason.

Ethical issues in quantitative research mostly involve manipulation/deception and, again, bias. Experimentation in particular can be dangerous if you don't carefully consider the impacts of your manipulations on the people you're experimenting on. For example, in an organizational context, you might naively assume that you could randomly assign employees to either receive training or not to receive training. But within this assignment lurks an ethical problem – what if your training is useful to promotion or future job opportunities? Suddenly, you are no longer providing extra training – you're withholding opportunities from those who did not receive the training. In real organizations, it's critical to always remember that you are dealing with real people and their real lives, and you shouldn't do anything to them that you wouldn't mind being done to you in the same situation.

Bias is more subtle in quantitative research, which in many ways makes it more dangerous. When you want to find particular results – for example, if you want the result of a hypothesis test to be statistically significant – you may make a myriad of small, seemingly inconsequential decisions that ultimately make a difference in terms of whether that happens. For example, you might clean the data *just a little extra* or you might drop a couple of analyses that didn't work out. These sorts of decisions are called **questionable research practices**, or **QRPs**. As your motivation to fudge the numbers increases, so typically do QRPs. There are a number of techniques you can use to insulate yourself from QRPs, which we cover in much more detail in our explorations of data cleaning (Chapter 11) and publication strategies (Chapter 14).

Positionality and Reflexivity

One of the biggest challenges related to ethics is understanding your **positionality** – the social and political context that informs your identity and, in turn, how your identity affects your understanding and interactions with the subject matter you are researching. For example, if you grew up in poverty, you probably have strong opinions about poverty. That's natural! It is very human. But that means if you were to conduct a research project related to how poverty affects job performance, you would likely struggle trying to compartmentalize your pre-existing opinions about poverty so as to be more "objective" in your research. That's also natural, and it is certainly not your fault. However, you do have a responsibility to identify how your positionality influences your research and try to honestly assess if that influence is problematic. Sometimes it might even be beneficial.

For an example of the complexities of positionality in the context of studying race, explore this paper:

Bourke, B. (2014). Positionality: Reflecting on the research process. *The Qualitative Report*, *19*(33), 1–9. https://doi.org/10.46743/2160-3715/2014.1026

Replication as a Research Strategy

In addition to conducting novel gap-filling research, another method of growing popularity within psychology is **replication**, in which you re-create someone else's research to provide additional data or context for the generalizability of that research. Replication studies are currently most common when researchers suspect there were QRPs involved in the original research, but this is not a requirement. Replication research is regardless a vital part of the scientific process.

Broadly speaking, replication comes in two general forms:

1. **Direct replication** involves a point-by-point re-creation, to the extent possible, of the precise research design, materials, and other approaches taken by the original authors of the study you are replicating. Even in direct replication, it's impossible to replicate absolutely everything about the original study. Most obviously, it's now later in time, you're in a different research setting, and technology has advanced since the original study was conducted. Despite such differences, conducting a direct replication means trying to re-create the study *as much as you possibly can*, which might include steps like contacting

the original researchers for exact copies of their materials. There are some possible exceptions, however. If the original study was underpowered, for example, you might try to replicate everything *except* the sample size in an effort to get a more precise estimate of that effect than the original authors did. The similarity required to reasonably conduct a "direct replication" is currently a matter of some debate.

2. **Conceptual replication** involves a new test of an existing finding from past research. Instead of replicating every detail as much as possible, some details may vary as a way to test the boundary conditions of the original finding. All that must remain the same is the core hypothesis or research question. For example, if the hypothesis-to-be-replicated in the original research read: "Extraversion is associated with emergent leadership behaviors," you might conceptually replicate that analysis by testing with a different measure of extraversion, different leadership behaviors, in different leadership contexts, or with other key varying details.

Either of these can be part of a highly desirable type of gap-filling research called **replicate-and-extend**. Using a replicate-and-extend research strategy, you might conduct either a direct or conceptual replication as the foundation of your own study but then ask your own novel research questions beyond the replication. In this way, you still conduct a replication (good for science) but also get to test some of your own new ideas. It also lends some support to the quality of your own research study if replication was successful, as you can argue that successful replication of a well-established finding provides some evidence that your own research study was built on solid ground, a prime staging area for testing new ideas.

Importantly, successful replication of either type does not automatically support the findings of the original research, nor does a failed replication automatically refute it. Instead, each study must be viewed as unique evidence, contributing to an understanding of the underlying phenomenon of interest, in service of building accurate theory across studies. Each study should be judged on its own merits and weaknesses, and even the differences between a direct replication and its inspiration may be larger than they first appear. Even after replication, you may find that the two studies in combination still don't provide enough evidence for clarity, necessitating further replications or other study designs altogether to meaningfully build theory. In this way, replication is just another (powerful) tool in your research toolkit.

To go deeper in your understanding of what replication can and can't do, compare and contrast these papers:

Feest, U. (2019). Why replication is overrated. *Philosophy of Science, 86*(5), 895–905.

Simons, D. J. (2014). The value of direct replication. *Perspectives on Psychological Science, 9*(1), 76–80. https://doi.org/10.1177/1745691613514755

References

Blacksmith, N., Willford, J. C., & Behrend, T. S. (2016). Technology in the employment interview: A meta-analysis and future research agenda. *Personnel Assessment and Decisions, 2*(1), 2.

Boyd, D., & Ellison, N. B. (2007). Social network sites: Definition, history, and scholarship. *Journal of Computer-Mediated Communication, 13*, 210–230.

Brown, S. P., & Leigh, T. W. (1996). A new look at psychological climate and its relationship to job involvement, effort, and performance. *Journal of Applied Psychology, 81*, 358–368. https://doi.org/10.1037/0021-9010.81.4.358

Brown, V. R., & Vaughn, E. D. (2011). The writing on the (Facebook) wall: The use of social networking sites in hiring decisions. *Journal of Business and Psychology, 26,* 219–225.

Bryman, A. (2004). Qualitative research on leadership: A critical but appreciative review. *The Leadership Quarterly, 15*(6), 729–769.

Cron, W. L., Slocum, J. W., VandeWalle, D., & Fu, Q. (2005). The role of goal orientation on negative emotions and goal setting when initial performance falls short of one's performance goal. *Human Performance, 18,* 55–80. https://doi.org/10.1207/s15327043hup1801_3

Kahn, W. A. (1990). Psychological conditions of personal engagement and disengagement at work. *Academy of Management Journal, 33,* 692–724. https://doi.org/10.2307/256287

Landers, R. N., & Callan, R. C. (2014). Validation of the beneficial and harmful work-related social media behavioral taxonomies: Development of the work-related social media questionnaire (WSMQ). *Social Science Computer Review, 32,* 628–646. https://doi.org/10.1177/0894439314524891

McCormick, E. J., Jeanneret, P. R., & Mecham, R. C. (1972). A study of job characteristics and job dimensions as based on the position analysis questionnaire (PAQ). *Journal of Applied Psychology, 56,* 347–368. https://doi.org/10.1037/h0033099

Vazire, S. (2017). Our obsession with eminence warps research. *Nature, 547*(7661). https://doi.org/10.1038/547007a

Further Reading

Banks, G. C., Field, J. G., Oswald, F. L., O'Boyle, E. H., Landis, R. S., Rupp, D. E., & Rogelberg, S. G. (2019). Answers to 18 questions about open science practices. *Journal of Business and Psychology, 34*(3), 257–270. https://doi.org/10.1007/s10869-018-9547-8

- Banks and colleagues define open science, discuss its benefits for organizational sciences, and provide readers with actionable recommendations to inform decisions throughout the research process.

Bourke, B. (2014). Positionality: Reflecting on the research process. *The Qualitative Report, 19*(33), 1–9. https://doi.org/10.46743/2160-3715/2014.1026

- Bourke is a white researcher studying the experiences of students of color in a predominantly white university. In his article, Bourke reflects on how his identity affected or could have affected his research, including how he felt it influenced his actions and understanding. In general, this is an excellent example of the kind of reflection on positionality that will help you understand your biases in relation to any research project.

Feest, U. (2019). Why replication is overrated. *Philosophy of Science, 86*(5), 895–905. https://doi.org/10.1086/705451

- Feest presents most psychological research as definitionally exploring uncertain and conceptually complex phenomena. Because of this, Feest suggests that researchers should approach replication with the expectation that studies will not replicate, challenging the notion that a failure to replicate implies that researchers have engaged in questionable research practices.

Murphy, K. R., & Aguinis, H. (2019). HARKing: How badly can cherry-picking and question trolling produce bias in published results? *Journal of Business and Psychology, 34*(1), 1–17. https://doi.org/10.1007/s10869-017-9524-7

- Murphy and Aguinis explore a specific questionable research practice called HARKing, which refers to hypothesizing after results are known. Murphy and Aguinis conducted simulations to compare the effects of two different kinds of HARKing – cherry-picking and question trolling – and find that searching through data involving several constructs, measures of those constructs, interventions, or relationships to find seemingly notable results produces upwardly biased estimates.

Simmons, J. P., Nelson, L. D., & Simonsohn, U. (2011). False-positive psychology: Undisclosed flexibility in data collection and analysis allows presenting anything as significant. *Psychological Science, 22*(11), 1359–1366. https://doi.org/10.1177/0956797611417632

- Simmons and colleagues argue that researchers are motivated to use flexibility in research decision-making to find ways to argue in support of their hypotheses even when the majority of evidence suggests those hypotheses are false. Simmons and colleagues conduct simulations and present a pair of experiments to demonstrate this, and they conclude by offering readers and journal reviewers guidelines to deal with this issue.

Questions to Think About

1. What are the three primary types of research questions?
2. Describe the main differences between moderation and mediation.
3. Draw a path diagram for the following research study: Extraversion predicts workers' satisfaction with videoconference meetings, and this effect is mediated by time spent talking with colleagues. The relationship between extraversion and time spent talking with colleagues is moderated by the quality of the workers' internet connection.
4. When might a researcher be interested in conducting a narrative review? Provide an example.
5. How might the feasibility of a given research approach differ for an I-O psychologist conducting laboratory experiments at a university and an I-O psychologist conducting applied research within an organization?
6. How does engaging in questionable research practices hinder the accumulation of knowledge in science?

Key Terms

- ethics
- exploratory research
- feasibility
- fighting a war on two fronts
- indirect effect
- interaction
- measurement
- mediation
- mediator
- meta-analysis
- mixed-methods research
- moderation by person
- moderation by situation
- moderator
- named theories

- narrative review
- positionality
- primary research
- qualitative research
- quantitative research
- questionable research practices (QRPs)
- relationship estimation
- replicate-and-extend
- replication
- rescope
- secondary research
- share variance
- subject matter experts (SMEs)
- transformational research
- unbiased, epistemologically

Chapter 4

Selecting a Research Population and Identifying a Sample

Learning Objectives

After reading this chapter, you will be able to:

1. Explain why the lab versus field debate is misleading when considering real-world sampling.
2. Identify the advantages and disadvantages of probability versus convenience sampling.
3. Quantify the effects of direct range restriction and omitted variables on estimated effects.
4. Identify the most appropriate among common convenience sampling approaches for your research questions.

The first step in designing a research study is to figure out what group your research question concerns. Are you interested in predicting employee behavior in general or in some unique context? Are you trying to create recommendations for astronauts traveling to Mars or any generic white-collar workplace? These are the fundamental questions of identifying a **population** of interest. When you try to find people that represent a population, you face the problem of **sampling**.

Sampling is an area of often surprising controversy in I-O psychology, and this is driven by the unique application domain of I-O. In social psychology, the population of interest is typically "humans in general." Because it's extremely costly to randomly pick people from the world population, social psychologists have historically relied upon easy-to-obtain samples, like college students, and use these samples to draw conclusions about humans in general. Social psychologists generally recognize that college students (particularly those in the United States) are not perfectly representative of humanity in general, yet such samples are often the best they can get access to with zero or near-zero budgets. These days, generally accepted-but-weaknesses-acknowledged sampling has expanded a bit to include crowdsourced research participants, like those working on Amazon Mechanical Turk, but the driving motivational force for these sampling strategies is still one of convenience.

Things are a bit different in I-O. Most research questions in I-O focus upon people who are working, and many college students, especially in "traditional" 4-year universities, have either never held a job or have only held entry-level service jobs, often as a cashier, restaurant server, salesperson, or retail associate. It is also well documented in I-O that different jobs have different expectations and also that tenure in the workforce tends to change

DOI: 10.4324/9781315167473-5

attitudes and expectations regarding work. So researchers in I-O often more quickly assume that college students do not appear to be very representative of employees, worldwide or otherwise.

Given that, there have been a variety of power struggles and mindset shifts over the years about what appropriate sampling strategies for I-O psychology research looks like. To be clear, this has shifted *several times*. At times, college students have been reasonable or even ideal sample sources, and other times, they have been absolutely forbidden if you had any hope of publication. Sometimes organizational samples have been absolutely required, and other times, organizations have been viewed as chaotic, uncontrolled environments absolutely unsuited for serious science. All of this controversy is now commonly referred to as the problem of **lab versus field**, where "lab" generally refers to college student research (or more recently, research with crowdsourced samples), and "field" generally refers to research in organizational settings.

But as you will learn in this chapter, things are not nearly so straightforward as they appear with such a simple comparison. The labels "lab" and "field" tend to mean different things to different people and are used as proxy terms for a wide range of specific research design decisions that sometimes have very different implications for the interpretability of your research. So as you read, keep an open mind, and most importantly, remember that the answer to "is lab or field better for my research?" is universally "it depends."

Samples and Populations

The most fundamental distinction when learning about sampling is the differences between **samples** and **populations**.

Populations refer to the groups of people you want to draw conclusions about in pursuit of answers to your research questions. Most I-O research, even if it doesn't say so outright, is targeting a broad population of "employees in organizations." Some research will target more tightly defined populations, like "doctors" or "machinists" or "first-generation college graduates," but this is relatively uncommon. In quantitative research, numbers you want to know about populations, like means and correlations, are called **parameters**.

The key to making a decision about the population you care about and the parameters you are trying to assess should be driven entirely by your research questions. Are you asking a question about workers in general, or is it more specific than that? What specific situational contexts or psychological processes are you interested in, and where do they happen?

Usually, you will not have access to the populations you are interested in. For example, it's not possible to give a survey to every worker on Earth. Even if that were possible, it would not be possible to give a survey to every worker that ever worked or ever will work. In this context, you always need a sample instead. So how do you get one?

Fundamentally, high-quality sampling is about identifying a group that is **representative** of the population you are interested in. Technically speaking, representativeness refers to the degree to which the sample you have identified differs only at random from the population across all possible variables on which they could be assessed.

For example, let's say you were interested in a population of "workers of the world." If you *were* able to collect that entire population and conduct whatever study you wanted to conduct, you'd be able to collect a lot of parameters about that population: means, standard deviations, correlations, covariances, and so on. When you collect a sample, you want some assurance that the statistics you collect on it are essentially the same as the parameters you *would have* collected from the population. Research design in regard to sampling thus focuses on selecting a sample in such a way that sample statistics are similar to population parameters.

What If I Have Population Access?

On rare occasions, you may have access to the entire population you are interested in. For example, a person conducting research on an organization from within that organization might have access to all personnel records of all current employees. If that person's research question concerns personnel record data, she might have access to the entire population she's interested in. In this situation, sampling is not needed – at all. When you have data from 100% of a population of interest, meaning you can measure all of its parameters directly, a lot of things change about how you draw conclusions from it. For example, while we might normally draw a sample from a population and use inferential statistics (like ANOVA, regression, and such) to draw conclusions, the conceptual basis of inferential statistics is entirely based around the idea of drawing conclusions about populations from samples. If your research question is "did more men get promoted than women last year?" and you have access to 100% of the personnel records in your company about promotions, you can just calculate the relevant parameters (promotion rates for men, women, perhaps other groups of interest) and see which numbers are bigger – no ANOVA required. But if you want to ask "do men get promoted in this company more often than women?", your research question now suggests a broader population of interest – all of the people in your organization. Be careful to pay attention to distinctions like this, since they should drive a great deal of your decision-making.

Sampling Lab Versus Field

The "lab versus field debate" is a classic argument appearing within the I-O psychology research methods literature. The conflict can be briefly summarized in terms of two often seemingly opposed viewpoints:

1. Lab settings enable greater control over the research environment, and greater control enables stronger and more definitive conclusions regarding research questions.
2. Field settings are more authentic representations of workplace behavior, and authentic representation increases confidence in successful application of research results in other field settings.

One can immediately see the endless chain of follow-up arguments. Even if lab settings enable greater control, that doesn't matter if those results don't replicate in real organizations. Even if organizations can replicate field research better, that doesn't matter if you can't run the particular experiment that you need to test your research question in the first place. Even if you run the perfect lab experiment, the contextual factors affecting the success of that in the real world don't exist in the lab. And on, and on, and on.

All of this type of argument largely misses two key points:

1. **Both sample sources are flawed, and neither should be relied upon exclusively.** It is tempting to want to conclude that one of these approaches is simply "superior" to the other, since that is cognitively simpler. It's much easier to claim "lab is better" or "field is better" than "it depends on the context, purpose, and research question." Yet this is the true state of affairs – you must consider this on a case-by-case basis. For example, if you are studying the relationship between the personality trait agreeableness and job satisfaction, does it matter if you sample college students instead of employees? To determine the answer to this question, we need to break it down into its component parts. First, the core parameter of interest is a correlation parameter (rho) summarizing the relationship between two variables: agreeableness and job satisfaction. Is there any reason to believe that college students are atypical or unlike the general population of employees in relation to their agreeableness? Probably not; there's a lot of evidence that personality is normally distributed and does not vary dramatically by age or by time. But is the same true of job satisfaction? Does job satisfaction vary by age, by job family, by experience? If so, college students might not be a wise choice, as our correlation could become inaccurate. But conversely, if we can't identify an organization where we expect employees to be honest when reporting their job satisfaction, perhaps college students emerge as a superior option due to that higher level of control alone. And, of course, perhaps the best option is to try multiple sampling techniques and assess convergence between results in each of them. The correct response to such trade-offs are not always clear, but you must make the decision willfully and purposefully.

2. **"Lab" and "field" are meaningless proxy labels collapsing across more meaningful, specific differences that actually do matter.** Although it's easy to assume "lab" means "college students" or "Mechanical Turk workers" and "field" means "employees," this isn't necessarily true. Both lab and field research take many different forms, and different researchers mean different things by these terms. As J. P. Campbell (1986) described in a landmark piece, "Labs, Fields, and Straw Issues," there are numerous distinctions of much greater usefulness, such as methodology (experiment versus quasi-experiment versus non-experiment), sample source (college students, employees at a convenient organization, employees in general, MTurk workers with work experience, etc.), and others. The remainder of this chapter will be largely devoted to helping you identify which sampling decisions are most likely to affect the quality of conclusions you draw and how you can better tie your decision-making about sampling to those conclusions. Don't simplify to "lab versus field." Your research will be better for it.

Thus, when it comes to selecting a "lab" or "field" sample for your own research, you should be making more specific and cautious decisions, based upon the particular needs of your research design. We will return to this concept in greater detail in Chapter 11.

For Further Reading:

Locke, E. A. (1986). *Generalizing from laboratory to field settings: Research findings from industrial-organizational psychology, organizational behavior, and human resource management.* Lexington Books.

Probability Sampling

The most trustworthy and also most uncommon sampling approach in I-O psychology is **probability sampling**. Probability sampling refers to the careful specification of a population of interest and then the selection of a subset of that population based upon meaningful probabilities. For example, if your population of interest consisted of all current employees in the organization you worked for, you might decide that it wasn't worth the company's time to ask every single employee a particular set of questions. Instead, you might want to send your questionnaire to only a useful subset of those people – one from which you could still draw accurate conclusions about the organization's employees in general. There are several general approaches to probability sampling, each with different purposes and specific approaches.

(Completely) Random Sampling

The most common and easiest to understand probability sampling technique is **random sampling**, which is sometimes called **random selection.** Random sampling is just what it sounds like; each person in the population is given an equal probability of being selected for inclusion in a sample.

One of the easiest ways to do this currently is with a spreadsheet program like Google Sheets, Microsoft Excel, or Apple Numbers:

1. Create a list of everyone in your population in Column A.
2. Next, put =RAND() into each cell in Column B next to someone in Column A.
3. Sort on Column B.
4. Select people into your sample from the top of the list until you run out of spots.

Because the =RAND() function generates a random number from a uniform distribution, every number it generates has an equal probability of occurring. When you sort on those random numbers, you have reordered your population into a completely random order. When you select from the top of that list, you have therefore selected people into your sample completely at random.

Note that this approach relies upon the concepts explained in classical test theory (see Chapter 7). A sample correlation should consist of a combination of a population correlation and error: $r = \rho + error$. By collecting a sampling at random, error should be random, and when error is random, the mean of error = 0. Thus, with random sampling, r should approximately equal ρ.

Stratified Random Sampling

One potential downside to completely random sampling is that you are assuming that complete randomness "works," as in it gives you a representation of the population. In some cases, you may be skeptical about that process.

For example, let's continue imagining you are working in an organization, interested in drawing conclusions about all current employees, but don't want to actually send a survey to all of them. Now imagine you were interested in the differences in job satisfaction across racial groups in your population and that your organization is currently made up of 700 white employees, 200 Black employees, and 100 neither white nor Black. You don't want to waste company time by administering 1000 surveys if you don't need to, so you want to create a sample, and let's say in this case you are hoping to administer only 50 surveys. (We will discuss specific rationales for numbers like these in later chapters where we discuss power analysis.)

Do you see the problem yet? Fifty surveys of 1000 people means that each person has a 5% chance of being included in the sample. But random really is random, so there will likely be random fluctuations in that percentage for each group of interest, and smaller groups will be affected more by this. Even if your random selection works out exactly as you might hope, you'll end up with 5% of 100 neither white nor Black people – which is only 5. What happens if that number is off by even 2 people? Suddenly, the representation of this group in your overall estimates, which is already quite bad, becomes completely unusable.

Addressing concerns like this is the purpose of **stratified random sampling**. In this case, if we were concerned about racial representation, we could specify race as a **stratum** of interest and then conduct completely random sampling within each group within that stratum. If we were also interested in differences by age, we could even specify two strata – both age and race – and then conduct random sampling within each combination of group memberships.

This effectively guarantees a certain level of representation of each group you want to ensure is represented. By splitting the sample into three racial groups and then selecting 5% of each racial group, you know ahead of time you will end up with a sample balanced along this label you have identified as meaningful.

The downside of stratification is that if you have larger sample sizes, this is generally a lot of extra work for relatively little reward. Randomness works very well with larger sample sizes. If instead of 1000 employees, you had 100,000 with the same racial balance and 5% sampling goal (i.e., 5000 surveys), stratification by race would be unlikely to give you different results from random sampling alone. Thus, stratification is specifically for situations where you are concerned that a particular group could be underrepresented if random sampling alone had been used.

You can try stratified random sampling yourself in your spreadsheet program of choice:

1. Create a list of everyone in your population in Column A.
2. Create a list of characteristics of interest in Column B. For example, "F" for Female and "M" for Male.
3. Calculate the number of "F" cases and "M" cases in proportion to the total number of cases, and record this somewhere out of the way. For example, you might use the following formulas in cells E1 and E2:
   =COUNTIF(B:B, "M")/COUNT(B:B)
   =COUNTIF(B:B, "F")/COUNT(B:B)
4. Next, put =RAND() into each cell in Column C next to someone in Column B.
5. Sort on two columns sequentially: Column B, then Column C. You will need to use the Sort pop-out in your spreadsheet program. In Google Sheets, for example, this is accessed using "Sort range" in the Data menu.
6. Next, calculate the number of "F" cases and "M" cases you want to sample based upon these proportions. For example, if your population was 75% Male cases and 25% Female cases, and you wanted to end up with a sample of 20, you would sample .75 × 20 = 15 Male cases and .25 × 20 = 5 Female cases.

7. Your two-step sort will have created two lists of people nested within your overall spread-sheet; you should see a randomly ordered list of Female cases followed by a randomly ordered list of Male cases. Select the number that you need from each list separately given the calculation you just completed.

Cluster Sampling

A concept similar to stratified random sampling is **cluster sampling**, which is used in situations where meaningful groups exist within other meaningful groups and you want to sample at both levels separately as a way to control costs.

For example, let's assume you work in a manufacturing organization with 200 plants and varying numbers of employees per plant, but 100,000 employees system-wide. There is a certain cost associated with rolling out your survey at a plant, as you'll need to shut part of the line down, train supervisors to administer it, allocate space for survey-taking in the plant breakrooms, and otherwise ring up a number of costs. Thus, you want a representative sample, but you also don't want to randomly pick employees from just any plant. To do this, you might instead randomly select *among plants* and then randomly select employees from within the plants you have randomly selected. Thus, you end up with two levels of randomness, and representativeness of your sample to your population now relies upon two assumptions: that the employees selected from each plant are representative of all employees in their plant and that the plants selected are representative of all plants in general.

Cluster sampling is never used *except* to increase the practicality of data collection. If you had randomly selected employees system-wide in this scenario instead, you might have ended up with a higher-quality sample, but you would have incurred much higher costs at the plant level.

Is There a "Best" Approach to Sampling?

For most research questions in I-O psychology, you will be unable to use any of these types of probability sampling. To understand why, consider the common element of all of these strategies: the population is known. You can list it. You can put everyone's name in a list, and those people are the only people you want to know about.

Although this type of research question *can* come up in certain contexts – particularly of the type described previously, where you are working in an organization and are tasked with understanding something about the organization at the present time – most questions are more general. They ask questions about some group of employees, in general. Whenever you can't at least theoretically include data from every single person in the population, probability sampling is unobtainable.

You might ask at this point – so why do I need to know about probability sampling? The answer is that in I-O psychology, there are few gold standards, but probability sampling is definitively the gold standard for sampling. You need to understand it so that you understand exactly what is lost and why when you inevitably switch instead to I-O psychology's default approach: convenience sampling.

Convenience Sampling

Almost every sample in I-O psychology is a **convenience sample**, which means it has been identified instead of a probability sample because of convenience factors, such as the researcher's ability to access the sample or cost. College students are the most prototypical convenience sample. They are so common because they are so very convenient, often requiring psychology researchers not to even leave their building, and because they are cheap, as they are often compensated with course credit.

Representativeness Concerns

Does convenience automatically result in poorer quality conclusions? Absolutely not. Remember that the goal of probability sampling is to maximize the chances that all sample parameters are similar to population parameters. Probability sampling does this by relying upon an assumption a lot like classical test theory: although individuals in a sample will vary, the statistics calculated upon them should still match parameters from the population they were sampled from as long as the mean of error across persons in the sample is zero. In convenience sampling, the goal hasn't changed, but the assumption has. We can no longer assume that the mean of error is zero; so instead, we must either make a reasoned argument that mean error differs from zero in non-meaningfully, or we must identify specific meaningful differences and take steps to address them.

Here's another way to think about it. There is a population you want to draw conclusions about, perhaps a population of "all workers everywhere." There is also a population you have access to, perhaps a population of "college students completing psychology courses for credit." The core problem, then, is that you can only sample from the college student population but want to draw conclusions about the worker population. That means that any differences between the two populations as well as between your sample and the sample you would have collected if you'd had access to all the world's workers threaten the representativeness of your sample. Fortunately, this problem manifests itself in the real world in two fairly straightforward ways.

RANGE RESTRICTION

The first problem to address in convenience sampling is **range restriction**. Range restriction refers to reductions in ranges of values observed in a sample due to external constraints placed upon that sample relative to the population you want to know about. For example, if you were interested in the correlation between cognitive ability and job performance in an organizational sample, you'd need to first worry about range restriction in cognitive ability if people had been hired on the basis of cognitive ability (i.e., people with high cognitive ability people were previously hired, whereas people with low cognitive ability were not) and second about range restriction in job performance if people had been fired on the basis of job performance (i.e., people with low performance were previously fired, whereas people with high job performance were not).

Both of these are examples of **direct range restriction** because one of the two variables involved has been restricted directly. For example, imagine a standard employee selection situation: some people were not hired because of low scores on their personality tests. If

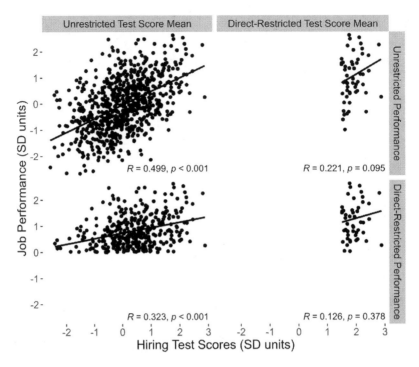

Figure 4.1 Scatterplot displaying original and directly range restricted relationship between simulated performance ratings (restricted at the mean) and simulated interview scores
(restricted at +1.5 SDs).

everyone who received a performance rating below the mean, that directly influences the
resulting correlation, as demonstrated in Figure 4.1. Most critically, direct range restriction
leads to **attenuation**, which refers to a reduction in observed covariance. Any statistics calculated upon range restricted data will be smaller in magnitude than they would have been
if calculated from an unrestricted sample. In the displayed figure, the correlation observed
in the dataset on the top left (unrestricted) is $r = .513$, and the correlation observed in the
dataset on the bottom right (restricted on both x and y) is $r = .118$, despite that dataset containing a subset of the cases from the original dataset.

If you were interested in the true relationship between these two variables (at top left) yet
had access to a range restricted dataset (any of the other three), you would need to mathematically estimate the true correlation from the observed correlation for its level of restriction to get an estimate of the true relationship. Or, in other words, if you were interested in
the population relationship between hiring test scores and job performance, looking naively
at that correlation in an organization that had already been using that test for hiring would
mislead you.

Correcting for direct range restriction is relatively simple mathematically, developed by
Thorndike (1949). To do so, you need to know the standard deviation of both the *original* and
restricted samples, which you don't always have, and it also assumes there was no chance

variation in your restricted sample that makes it systematically differ from your unrestricted one. To illustrate, here is the formula to correct for direct range restriction in one variable:

$$R = (r \times S/s)/1 - r^2 + r^2(S/s)^2$$

where s is the uncorrected standard deviation, S is the corrected standard deviation, r is the uncorrected correlation, and R is the corrected correlation.

We can walk through the example if you have two additional pieces of information: for the top-left graph, the SD of the hiring test was .985, and in the top-right graph, it was .320. Using that, we can calculate the estimated unrestricted correlation from the top right correlation:

$$R = (.221 \times .985/.320)/1 - .2212 + .2212(.985/.320)^2 = .572$$

This can also be demonstrated easily in R, using the following code:

```
library(psych)
rangeCorrection(.221, .985, .320)
```

Although .572 is an overestimate of the correct value (.499), it is certainly much closer to the true value than the original, .221. Importantly, range restriction corrections like this are rarely completely accurate and can be biased in either direction, because they rely upon assumptions that cannot be tested in any particular dataset. As such, they should generally be considered a tool of last resort; *it is preferred to sample such that range restriction won't be present, if at all possible.*

Although direct restriction is relatively straightforward, range restriction can also be quite subtle. In the case of **indirect range restriction**, direct range restriction has occurred on a variable not under study that is nevertheless correlated with a focal variable. For example, if people were hired on the basis of an interview with a hard cutoff score, there would be direct range restriction of the relationship between interview scores and job performance. But if interview scores were correlated with cognitive ability, there would also be indirect range restriction in the relationship between cognitive ability and job performance, which would attenuate the observed correlation,

In Figure 4.2, we can see a demonstration of this concept. Importantly, *this is the same dataset with the same restrictions as in* Figure 4.1. Although there is still direct range restriction on both test score and job performance, what's changed is that we're now looking at the correlation between *cognitive ability* and job performance, which, as you can see in the unrestricted dataset, is equal to .595. What you cannot see in the figure is that the correlation between cognitive ability and hiring test has been simulated at .600. Thus, although the direct range restriction occurs on the hiring test, there is a subsequent attenuation on relationships with cognitive ability. This is what makes the range restriction *indirect.*

The insidiousness of this effect is that if you went into this organization to determine the relationship between cognitive ability and job performance, the correlation you'd calculate would be .465 – which is quite a bit smaller than the .595 true score correlation – yet your figures would show few or no obvious "cut offs" where cases simply don't exist. The direct range restriction you see in Figure 4.1 is obvious from a scatterplot; the indirect range restriction you see in Figure 4.2 is not.

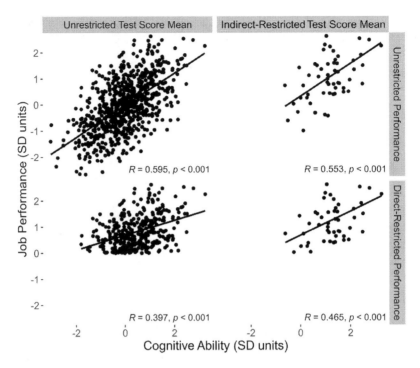

Figure 4.2 Original and indirect range-restricted relationship between performance ratings and cognitive ability when directly restricted on interview scores and performance.

Indirect range restriction can hypothetically be corrected just like direct range restriction, but you need a lot more information about the unrestricted sample, and in most organizational settings, you probably won't have authentic estimates of those effects. Thus, once again, it's best to avoid range restricted samples entirely if you can, but if you can't, it's best to identify estimates that you can use to do the corrections you need to do.

Thus, understanding if the particular conveniences of a convenience sample affects the quality of your conclusions first requires a careful analysis of potential sources of range restriction. Are there any reasons to think that the range of values you would observe in your convenience sample would be smaller than if you had access to the population, either directly or indirectly?

The most straightforward and easiest-to-detect examples of range restriction are reflected in the examples provided previously: processes that selected people into that population and processes that selected people out. For each major type of convenience sample observed today, we'll discuss each of these sorts of processes a little later in this chapter.

For a much more complete treatment of range restriction in I-O psychology, along with all the formulas you'll ever need, see Sackett and Yang (2000). We'll also revisit this concept in a later chapter in this book, on meta-analysis, where corrections are critically important.

OMITTED VARIABLES BIAS (OR: ENDOGENEITY)

The second and more difficult-to-address challenge in convenience samples is omitted variables bias, which refers to uncontrolled causal effects of unmeasured variables in models.

Although we will discuss the many challenges associated with drawing causal conclusions from research in Chapter 8, it's useful to consider this question a little early: how can unmodeled and unmeasured causal effects correlated with sample characteristics influence the accuracy of your research conclusions?

Consider this example. Let's say you're a researcher interested in the effects of diversity training on interaction quality between coworkers. In the convenient organization you have access to, the distribution of participation in diversity training is non-random, because employees volunteer to complete it. This isn't necessarily a problem if the choice to participate is not correlated with any variables you are interested in measuring. But that raises two questions.

First, how do you know if volunteerism was correlated with something you measured? The short answer is: you don't. Much like when designing research studies for the purpose of supporting causal relationships, the absence of confounding omitted variables is ultimately a point you need to argue and not the result of a statistical test.

One possible exception to this is if you *also* had access to a second sample without that omitted variable bias to use for comparison. To continue our example, let's imagine that before you implemented voluntary diversity training to examine relationships between training and outcomes (your "main study"), you conducted a pilot study first. In this pilot study, you identified a random subset of your employees and asked them if they would like to volunteer for diversity training, just as you will do in your main study. Then, *regardless of their response*, you assigned them *mandatory* diversity training and also gave them all the same measures you plan to use in your main study. Within this pilot study population, you would now be able to measure the "true" correlation between volunteerism and your main study variables. If you found no relationships in your pilot study data, you would then have some confidence that omitted variables correlated with volunteerism would not bias observed correlations in your main study.

In this way, arguments that your study is not biased due to either range restriction or omitted variable bias are arguments about the validity of your sampling approach. And as we learned about both validity and convenience samples, we can never conclusively declare that our sampling approach is or is not valid; it is always a matter of the quality of evidence we have available to support the argument that our sampling approach was valid.

Second, if omitted variables bias was present, how do you address it? Is there a formula we can use to correct our biased effects to estimate unbiased effects, just as we did with range restriction? Yes – sort of. Simple endogeneity problems often resemble indirect range restriction, and the same corrections can be used, if you can collect sufficient data to make the correction. However, doing so would require identifying all omitted variables, with confidence, and that is quite unlikely.

So why is this called "omitted variables bias"? The short answer is that we can understand what happens by literally omitting variables in a regression equation. For example, consider the following regression equation, which simply regresses one criterion on two predictors:

$$y' = \beta_0 + \beta_1 x_1 + \beta_2 x_2 + e$$

In regression, this has a relatively simple explanation: a predicted y score is equal to the sum of the intercepts, the cross-products of each weight and each score, and the residuals. It also conceptually implies what it should: for example, if x_1 equals exactly zero, then a 1-point increase in x_2 is associated with a β_2-point increase in y', which is why we might refer to β_2 as "the effect of x_2 controlling for x_1".

The reason that interpretation is possible is because of e, the residual/error term – specifically, across the entire dataset, e is supposed to equal zero on average. Now let's imagine we "omit" the x_1 term, moving the missing term so that it becomes part of error:

$$y' = \beta_0 + \beta_2 x_2 + E$$
$$E = e + \beta_1 x_1$$

Although running a regression analysis (or calculating a correlation) in this situation would still produce a value for β_0 and β_2, the effect of the misplaced variable inside the error term will now bias both of those estimates – in other words, β_0 and β_2 are now **confounded** with β_1, which is to say: interpretations of both the effect β_2 and the intercept β_0 are now inaccurate in relation to the population values they are intended to represent.

Thus, if you collect any sort of convenience sample without identifying and avoiding or eliminating or explicitly measuring omitted variables, you run the risk of confounding every effect you're interested in measuring with the variables you *didn't* measure. In this way, convenience sampling potentially threatens the accuracy of *every statistic you calculate* using that sample. This is why it's so important to identify these threats and deal with them directly rather than assuming (for example), "well everyone uses MTurk, so I might as well too."

Common Types of Convenience Samples

In I-O psychology, there are three particularly common convenience samples: organizations, college students, and **online panels**. Each has advantages and disadvantages in different scenarios. The effects of convenience change dramatically depending upon your defined population of interest, as these choices influence the types of range restriction and omitted variables bias that are likely to occur.

For comparison with these three types of convenience samples, let's first consider the simplest case – what happens when your population is a particular organization and your sample is conveniently drawn from that organization? This is a fairly common situation for I-O practitioners conducting research on one organization; for example, you might be an internal I-O or an external consultant who has been given access to a complete email address database of every employee in the company, and the only population you are interested in is that company. As in our earlier example, let's imagine you create a "volunteer" opportunity and then conduct your study among the volunteers. In this case, you need only worry about potential confounding effects of volunteerism. Because your effects may be biased because of volunteerism, you should work, either through data collection or logical argument, to build a reasonable case for why volunteerism at your organization leads to neither range restriction nor omitted variables bias.

This example is relatively simple in terms of these confounds, though, because our population and sample only differed in terms of volunteerism. More commonly, we want to generalize our results from a convenient sample within a convenient organization to *employees in general*. This is a much more complex problem.

Although organizational samples are intuitively the "best" kind of convenience sample, it's important to remember that organizations are almost universally convenient and sometimes in very peculiar ways. The first issues to be concerned about are selection, training, and attrition processes. Employees are hired, so whatever process used to hire them could have created confounds in comparison to a population of "employees in general." Employees are also trained, which changes their knowledge, skill, abilities, and other characteristics (KSAO) profiles depending upon which training programs they've taken. Employees also attrit out of the organization, and the reason they attrited may furthermore create confounds. For example, if employees mostly leave because they get better job offers versus if they leave because they're fired for poor work performance, you will end up with dramatically different remaining employee populations. All of these forces potentially influence the particular soup of confounds you end up with.

Organizational samples are also historically difficult to access, especially for graduate students and early career scholars. As a result, college student samples are also very common in I-O, as most psychology departments have access to psychology department research participant pools made up of students in introductory and other undergraduate psychology courses. The concerns with college student samples are fundamentally no different from convenient organizations: you need to carefully consider potential causes of range restriction and omitted variables bias. Do you think that work tenure is correlated with variables you're interested in measuring? Well then, college students are probably not a great source – not because they are "nonrepresentative" in some vague way but because range restriction in tenure is likely to attenuate the effects you observe using such a sample to an unknown, uncorrectable degree. Be specific!

Problems with college student samples have led to the rapid rise in popularity of online panels, which refers to a group of potential research participants that have signed up for an internet-based employment service in order to complete job opportunities. The most well-known panels today are probably Amazon Mechanical Turk and Prolific. An important realization about online panels like these is that they are made up of gig workers looking for short-term employment. They are not college students being nudged into a better grade or employees being commanded to participate by their boss. As such, they tend to be more representative (i.e., less range restricted and fewer omitted variables to worry about) when compared to college students samples, as they are all working adults. They also tend to be more flexible to run powerful research designs than organizational samples but less so than college students. But most problematically, because they are all gig workers, if any of your variables are correlated with a person's willingness to work as a gig worker taking $2 jobs on the internet, you may not want to pick "online panel" as your convenient source of choice without suffering some significant confounds due to sampling.

As you can tell from this discussion, there are many trade-offs, some obvious and some not so much, between these convenience sample types. We have summarized some of the most prominent potential sources of confounds due to sampling in Table 4.1.

Single-Subject Designs and Samples

Although convenience samples are the most common samples in I-O psychology, there are several other types used in particular types of studies. Beyond the types we've talked about so far, we'll only briefly discuss one other type which appears infrequently in the I-O literature but frequently enough that you should be aware of it: the single-subject study.

Single-subject (or single-N) research refers to a class of research designs in which samples consist of only a single person. They generally involve applying multiple treatments to that personal in succession, observing the effects of each treatment. For example, in what might be called an *ABABAB design*, a single research participant would be exposed to an

Table 4.1 Potential sources of confounds due to sampling strategy between convenience sample types

Category	Convenient organizations	Convenient college students	Convenient online panels
Entry "Job" Interests	Employee selection processes; Job titles/domain	College/university selection criteria; Major/minor fields	Self-selection rationale to join panel; "Gig" as primary job? Outside employment? Multiple employers?
Learning	Employee training received	Prior coursework completed	—
Volunteerism	Coercion to participate, choice to participate, and sometimes pay motivation	Coercion to participate, choice to participate, and sometimes pay motivation	Pay motivation, and sometimes choice to participate
Tenure & Past Experience	Organizational and team tenure	Student status (freshman, sophomore, etc.)	Prior experience on online panel
Prior Exposure	Overexposure to organizational research and survey fatigue	Prior exposure to similar experimental paradigms and survey fatigue	Prior exposure to similar experimental paradigms and survey fatigue
Attrition	Voluntary and involuntary turnover causes	College dropouts or changing majors away from participant pools	Reasons for quitting online panel membership
Higher-Order Influences	Influence of supervisory buy-in on participation	Self-selection into studies on the basis of titles and descriptions	Incentivization strategies (e.g., online panels may incentivize with virtual points or game rewards in addition to cash incentives)
Economic Conditions	Poor economy = fewer employees	Poor economy = more people seeking education	Poor economy = more people seeking gig work
Age	Range typical to the work conditions in the organization (e.g., manual labor jobs favor the young)	Range typical to the institution, either "traditional" 18–22 or non-traditional	Age range of typical gig workers, which varies by platform
Gender	Disparities created by work role or nature of company (e.g., manual labor jobs favor males)	Disparities created by major (e.g., neuroscience and neuropsych favor males)	Gender disparities created by gig platform advertising strategies
Socioeconomic Status	Correlates of particular job types or classes (e.g., manual labor favor lower SES)	Limited range of socioeconomic status and education depending upon school status (e.g., elite institutions favor the wealthy)	Socioeconomic correlations of gig economy participation (e.g., gig work favors the poor)
Race and Ethnicity	Composition of the organization, potentially covarying with job title	Composition of college, potentially covarying with major	Composition of gig worker populations
Nation and Language	Nation of operations and its primary language	Nation of residence and its primary language	Nation in which platform legally operates and its primary language
Culture	Cultural correlates of organizational tenure (e.g., a poor organizational climate for diversity)	Cultural correlates of staying in college (e.g., a dominant narrative for behaviors of a "good student")	Cultural correlates of gig work opportunities and pursuit (e.g., online communities that influence platform participation)

experimental treatment in each B condition and then measured without that treatment in each A condition, perhaps over 6 days of data collection. If a strong change in outcome is observed consistently as expected from those changes (i.e., there is a "low" outcome score on all A days and a "high" outcome score on all B days), we have some evidence that the treatment successfully elicits an effect increasing the outcome.

Although the gut reaction of many I-Os to single-subject designs is "insufficient sample size to draw valid conclusions," single-subject research can be informative to a particular class of research question, especially those considering very small populations of interest. For example, if an I-O researcher was interested in conducting research on "people who have committed violent acts in the workplace," it would be very difficult to collect a large, representative sample of such people. Facing a decision between "single-subject or nothing," single-subject research can be a desirable approach for some research questions. However, supporting the validity of a single-subject design in generalizing to any population beyond the single subject themself is difficult, as the evidential value of a single person to a larger group cannot be estimated in such a study.

Given this difficulty, and because such designs are uncommon in I-O, we will consider them no further in this book; however, we urge you not to automatically discredit them as valid sampling approaches under some circumstances or to learn more about them if you have a research question that is not better addressed with another design.

Can I Be a Single-Sample Study?

One fun result from learning about research methods is that you build a diverse set of skills for asking and getting trustworthy answers to complex questions. One of the best illustrations of this is your newfound ability to conduct a single-sample study on yourself, with the intent of generalizing the results to future you. For example, imagine you're considering adopting a new artificial intelligence–driven email management system that prioritizes your email for you. How will you know if it's really better? Easy. Use it for a week and record measures of the outcomes you care about – perhaps your total number of minutes using email that week. Then turn it off for a week and repeat. If you do this for 2 months, you've created an *ABABABAB* single-subject design, and you can compare the total number of minutes using email on A weeks with B weeks to make a final, empirically informed decision.

Sampling Concerns When Summarizing Existing Studies

Up to this point, we've been focusing upon sampling in primary research. Secondary research requires a bit of a different approach. Secondary research takes many forms, but there are three approaches that are particularly common in I-O, each with their own sampling requirements: systematic review, meta-analysis, and archival research.

Systematic review is a synthesis of existing research using a formal strategy to ensure unbiased summary. They are in this sense a specific type of literature review. In ordinary literature review, as we discussed in Chapter 2, you must develop research questions and hypotheses on the basis of your own personal understanding of a research literature, then write up your understanding of that research literature to support the particular points and arguments that need to be made to motivate the specific research questions and hypotheses that you developed. It is an iterative process in which you increase your understanding of a phenomenon by reading the literature, attempt to put together your understanding of the literature on paper, and then return to the literature to refine that understanding until you've developed a reasonable argument to support your research study.

The problem with a personal-learning approach to literature review is that despite its reliance upon published research, it is still heavily opinion driven in terms of what to include and what not to include, and we have very clear evidence now that two literature reviews by two researchers with opposing motivations can research opposing conclusions. Systematic review as a research design and sampling strategy is intended to address this bias by formalizing the strategy used to identify and write about research. Generally speaking, systematic reviews accomplish this by enforcing a very specific sequence of decision-making, starting with carefully defining the research question, setting data sources in advance, setting firm inclusionary and exclusionary criteria, defining specific data extraction and interpretation procedures, and performing some kind of summary analysis.

In I-O, because quantitative research is so much more common than qualitative, the specific type of systematic review called meta-analysis is far more common. Meta-analysis extends the use of systematic review procedures to develop population estimates of effects across collected studies. The foundation is the same – a lot of advance planning goes into all systematic reviews – but meta-analysis takes this a step further by enabling the statistical modeling of effects across an entire population of studies. We'll return to meta-analysis in much more detail in Chapter 13.

In both cases, sampling concerns aren't exactly the same as we've discussed so far; the explicit purpose of both systematic review and meta-analysis is to collect as close to a *population* of current research as possible, that is, every manuscript ever written, whether published or not, that contains the information you are looking for. Importantly, this is conceptually still a *convenience sample*, because your meta-analytic or review sample will still consist only of the manuscripts that you've managed to locate, that were made available to you, and that were conducted in the first place; that is, a researcher decided that study was worth conducting. If there are range restriction or omitted variables problems, that sample of studies will still not represent the population you are really trying to reflect: every research study that ever has *or ever will be* conducted studying the effect you're studying.

To understand the impact of convenience sampling as the sole possible strategy for conducting systematic reviews and meta-analyses, we'll briefly discuss a problem which we'll dive much deeper into in Chapter 13 when discussing meta-analysis: **publication bias**. As noted earlier in this chapter, one of the key assumptions in sampling is that your sample reflects your population, with no range restriction or omitted variables problems. Unfortunately, when considering an entire research literature, most effects do have an omitted variable: *researcher interest*. You see, researchers are fickle creatures and tend to be more interested in results that are "impactful" or "meaningful," which leads to the review process more often rejecting research that is not statistically significant and accepting research that is than would be expected by chance alone, if statistical significance didn't influence their opinions in terms of study quality (as it shouldn't). This usually has the net effect of inflating effect estimates, making mean effects seem larger and more important than they really are.

As a result, avoiding, identifying, and correcting for publication bias is a key consideration in the conduct of both systematic reviews and meta-analysis, so we will return to it in much greater detail in that discussion (Chapter 13).

Sampling Concerns With Existing Secondary Data

Archival research refers to the use of primary research data that someone else collected. If you find your data in an online data repository (like http://data.gov) or collect an existing dataset from an organization, your research is archival in nature. I-O archival research is conceptually similar to primary research in that it generally contains data about people, unlike systematic reviews and meta-analysis, which contain data about study results. But archival research is quite different in that the specific data generating features, analytics, data cleaning, and other processes run on the data before you got your hands on it may be unknown, which creates many risks, including but not limited to range restriction and omitted variables bias. Beyond these potential confounds, you also run more human risks, such as not fully understanding what the original researchers did in terms of sampling or design, or more worryingly, that the researchers did something that they did not disclose in documents shared with the archival dataset. Regardless, the same general confounding threats remain and should be addressed in the same general way – through careful consideration and considered argument.

Why do the archival data that you located and analyzed reflect the population you're interested in drawing conclusions about? Are there range restriction issues to worry about in terms of how the dataset was originally collected or in terms of any subset you have access to? Are there omitted variables to worry about? These issues are at the core of high-quality sampling, regardless of the specific method used.

Ethics in Sampling

As discussed in Chapter 1, adherence to professional ethics is central to all decision making related to research. Sampling is no different. There are populations that are very difficult to ethically sample from. For example, one of the most popular ethics training platforms, required at many research universities, are those created for the **Collaborative Institutional Training Initiative** (CITI). CITI training emphasizes certain populations that are "sensitive," such as current inmates in jail or prison. These populations are difficult to ethically sample from, because prisoners have been stripped of certain human rights as a component of their sentencing. Prisoners might not feel that participating in your research is optional, even if it is technically optional. In this way, when populations are vulnerable, we have greater personal responsibility to be absolutely sure that their rights are respected.

A similar, although less severe, challenge occurs in organizational contexts. Employees often feel pressured into participating in research initiatives from their own companies, whether directly, such as by a supervisor, or indirectly, simply due to the power structures related to their job. It is your professional responsibility as a researcher to ensure that your participants know that their effort is optional. If your research is being overseen by an IRB, you may also need to obtain and manage informed consent, which formalizes the agreement between researcher and participant, a concept we will discuss in more detail in Chapter 5.

References

Campbell, J. P. (1986). Labs, fields, and straw issues. In E. A. Locke (Ed.), *Generalizing from laboratory to field settings* (pp. 269–279). Lexington, MA: Lexington Books.

Locke, E. A. (1986). *Generalizing from laboratory to field settings: Research findings from industrial-organizational psychology, organizational behavior, and human resource management.* Lexington Books.

Sackett, P. R., & Yang, H. (2000). Correction for range restriction: An expanded typology. *Journal of Applied Psychology, 85*(1), 112–118. https://doi.org/10.1037/0021-9010.85.1.112

Thorndike, R. L. (1949). *Personnel selection; test and measurement techniques.* Wiley.

Further Reading

Landers, R. N., & Behrend, T. S. (2015). An inconvenient truth: Arbitrary distinctions between organizations, mechanical Turk, and other convenience samples. *Industrial and Organizational Psychology, 8,* 142–164. http://dx.doi.org/10.1017/iop.2015.13

- Landers and Behrend, geniuses that they are, challenge the notions that certain sampling strategies are universally "good" or "bad" and that organizational samples are a gold standard. Instead, they argue that sampling is better thought of in terms of concrete measurement and validity implications (i.e., range restriction, omitted variables bias).

Levay, K. E., Freese, J., & Druckman, J. N. (2016). The demographic and political composition of mechanical Turk samples. *SAGE Open, 6*(1), 2158244016636433. https://doi.org/10.1177/215824 4016636433

- Levay and colleagues explored the extent to which samples drawn from Amazon's Mechanical Turk (MTurk) differ from population samples and the underlying nature of the differences. They found that although there were differences between the two samples, many of these differences could be reduced when researchers controlled for political beliefs and demographic attributes of participants.

Peer, E., Vosgerau, J., & Acquisti, A. (2014). Reputation as a sufficient condition for data quality on Amazon mechanical Turk. *Behavior Research Methods, 46*(4), 1023–1031. https://doi.org/10.3758/s13428-013-0434-y

- Peer and colleagues addressed concerns about data quality when using crowdsourcing websites such as Amazon Mechanical Turk by comparing two methods for ensuring data quality. They found that sampling high-reputation workers (those with at least 95% approval ratings) produced the highest-quality data.

Wanous, J. P., Sullivan, S. E., & Malinak, J. (1989). The role of judgment calls in meta-analysis. *Journal of Applied Psychology, 74*(2), 259–264. https://doi.org/10.1037/0021-9010.74.2.259

- Wanous and colleagues describe how researcher judgment calls can influence conclusions at every stage of the meta-analysis process, including sampling. They demonstrated this by comparing several pairs of meta-analyses on the same topics.

Walter, S. L., Seibert, S. E., Goering, D., & O'Boyle, E. H. (2019). A tale of two sample sources: Do results from online panel data and conventional data converge? *Journal of Business and Psychology, 34*(4), 425–452. https://doi.org/10.1007/s10869-018-9552-y

- Walter and colleagues meta-analytically compared the internal reliability estimates and effect size estimates for studies with samples drawn from online panels and conventional sources. They concluded that, with some caveats, online panels generate similar psychometric properties as conventional samples and are generally appropriate for many exploratory research questions in psychology.

Questions to Think About

1. What is sampling? Why is sampling not needed if you have access to a population?
2. Describe the lab versus field debate. How is this debate potentially oversimplified?
3. Compare and contrast probability sampling and convenience sampling.
4. Under what circumstances might a single-subject design and sample be useful in I-O psychology?
5. What are omitted variables, and how can their effects be demonstrated using regression?

6. Assume you are interested in the relationship between scores on a pre-hire situational judgment test and post-hire job performance. You calculate a correlation of $r = 0.18$. Based on our discussion of range restriction in this chapter, what kinds of conclusions would you draw about this correlation?

Key Terms

- indirect range restriction
- lab versus field
- online panels
- parameters
- population
- probability sampling
- random sampling
- random selection
- range restriction
- representativeness
- sample
- sampling
- single-N research
- single-subject research
- stratified random sampling
- stratum
- systematic review

Part II

Qualitative Methods

Approaches for Investigating and Respecting Complexity

Learning Objectives

After reading this chapter, you will be able to:

1. Explain the assumptions associated with qualitative research traditions.
2. Compare and contrast qualitative research approaches.
3. Define and identify grounded theory, case study, and ethnography.
4. Identify ethical issues unique to qualitative research.

Amber wants to know what it is like to work at a Silicon Valley startup. What does it *feel* like? What is the day-to-day experience of a person in this unique setting? Amber thinks that theories of organizations might not apply to this kind of new workplace, but she isn't sure exactly how they might be different. She spends a few weeks at a startup, absorbing her surroundings, paying close attention, asking questions, and taking notes. Over time, she notices things – and asks people about the themes she has noticed. For example, she notices that the atmosphere in a startup is more experimental and exciting. She feels a sort of thrill herself in being a part of this environment. She asks people who work there if they feel that sense of excitement, and she asks them about how it affects their experience of working there. Amber turns these stories into rich, detailed written descriptions that paint a picture of the phenomenon of this firm, in this time and place. Amber is engaging in qualitative research.

In Chapter 3, we showed how selecting the best approach to research depends on the sort of research question you want to address. Questions that take the form "does X exist?" or "how many kinds of X exist?" or "what is the experience of X like?" might be best approached with qualitative methods. Qualitative means "understanding the qualities of" and has a long history in the fields of sociology and anthropology. Despite being largely associated with these fields, qualitative research can be extremely useful in I-O psychology research, especially when combined with other methods that allow for generalized knowledge claims (see Chapter 15).

A minority of I-O research studies use qualitative approaches. According to an analysis by David and Bitektine (2009) of the highest-ranked management journals, only between 8% and 10% of papers published were qualitative. This reflects a preference of many editors and reviewers for what they believe are more scientifically **rigorous** methods. Many

DOI: 10.4324/9781315167473-7

quantitative researchers assume that their methods are rigorous, because they rely on numbers and statistics.

We caution against this kind of thinking. The best way to think about rigor is that rigorous methods adhere completely to currently accepted professional standards for a particular approach at the time research is completed. Just as with any topic of scientific interest, research methods have their own theory (see Chapter 1). At any time, the existing community of qualitative methodologists endorse particular methodological approaches as ideal for a given type of research question. Thus, this community collectively determines the standards for rigor, and these standards change over time. Rigor involves adhering to those standards as best we can.

Can Qualitative Research Be Rigorous?

Some quantitative researchers criticize qualitative methods by using the phrase "lacking rigor," equating high-quality research with numbers and complex analyses. Yet both quantitative and qualitative approaches can be relatively more or less rigorous. Any approach is more rigorous when it adheres more closely to current methodological theory. Unfortunately, this phrase is used carelessly and thoughtlessly by many researchers as a weapon against methods they don't use or perhaps even understand.

A relevant, famous quote from sociology is "not everything that can be counted counts, and not everything that counts can be counted" (Cameron, 1963). It is true that the best research approach depends on the research question. It is also true that most of the questions we ask in I-O psychology are better suited to quantitative methods, because we are often interested in generating generalizable knowledge for the purposes of **prediction**. The field of I-O psychology is fairly mature, at least as far as domains of psychology go, which means the kind of exploratory work that qualitative work excels at is not always needed or helpful. In fact, it is sometimes counterproductive. Science moves forward by accumulating evidence. If prior evidence is rejected in favor of seeking out "new and shiny" things, it becomes much more difficult to make sense of what we already know. So, *qualitative research can be powerful, but it can also be used or misused in situations when quantitative approaches would be more appropriate.* (The reverse is true as well.)

This is a point worth emphasizing. There are forces at work in the field of psychology and management (especially management) that encourage researchers to make *new* things – new constructs, new theories, new methods. Making up a new construct and putting your name on it can be a fast track to building a reputation in the field, and with a reputation come prestige, grant money, and power. But these forces are anti-scientific. Building on what others have done is how science progresses. You should aim to **stand on the shoulders of giants** – not to kick the giants in the kneecaps, and not to ignore them completely. We hope you will resist the temptation to make up new words for old ideas just to make a quick buck. If it's a quick buck you want, we promise there are easier careers to pursue than academic research. This concern is not unique to qualitative research, yet qualitative research is perhaps more prone to "reimagining," "reconceptualizing," or "discovering" ideas that don't need to be reimagined, reconceptualized, or discovered.

History of Qualitative Research in Psychology

The earliest research in psychology could be considered qualitative. This is not surprising, because qualitative research is often most useful when a field of inquiry is new. Consider, for example, the early work of Triplett (1898). Triplett observed professional cyclists who were training for races. He noticed that they tended to cycle faster when competing with others compared to practicing solo. He did not take measurements or manipulate the environment in any way. He simply observed something new and surprising. He used his own expert judgment to determine that the relevant feature of the environment was the other cyclists, and not the wind, or the sun, or the time of day. By putting forth his observations and, in effect, presenting a theory, other researchers could later test his theory by exploring alternative explanations and determining the magnitude of the effects he observed. These methods are simplistic by modern standards. But this study was the foundation of social facilitation theory, which is still used now to explain team dynamics.

Examples of Modern Qualitative Research in I-O

The *Journal of Applied Psychology (JAP)*, one of our oldest and most well-known journals, publishes far fewer qualitative papers than quantitative ones. This was not always the case; in the journal's earliest years, it emphasized case studies of unusual or exceptional phenomena. For example, Gates (1918) conducted an in-depth case study of a person who demonstrated exceptional skill in marksmanship. This was an attempt to figure out which qualities he might have had that contributed to his exceptional skill. Cortina et al. (2017), writing on the occasion of the 100th anniversary of *JAP*, speculated about why qualitative research has declined in prevalence. They write,

> The case study method was a frequent approach for increasing our understanding of the exceptional. This sort of case study approach has been seen very rarely in *JAP* over the last 70 years or so . . . we might gain important insights about organizations by applying rigorous case study and other qualitative methods in order to understand the exceptional.
>
> (p. 276)

As our field moved away from trying to understand the exceptional, toward developing robust models to predict the typical, we relied less on qualitative methods. In the long run, this might not be wise, and we may see the balance shift again in the future. Cortina et al. (2017) speculate that a shift like this might happen sooner rather than later (see Table 5.1).

Definition of Qualitative Research

Qualitative *research* is difficult to separate from the *researcher*; this is by design. We can define qualitative research with the words from Denzin and Lincoln (2005):

> a situated activity that locates the observer in the world. It consists of a set of interpretive, material practices that make the world visible. They turn the world into a set of representations that include field notes, interviews, conversations, photographs, and recordings.
>
> (p. 3)

Table 5.1 A chronology of methodological topics in the *Journal of Applied Psychology* (1917–present), adapted from Cortina et al. (2017)

Era	Methods
Who Are You? (1917–1925)	• Objectivity and methods to solve important problems • Cognitive ability testing • Interest in the exceptional • Beginning of statistical significance and prediction models • Sources of rating errors (e.g., halo, guessing) • Focus on psychometric properties, classification, and test equivalence
The Roaring 20s, the Depression, and WWII (1925–1945)	• Test scoring methods, test form equivalence, and cross-validation • Assessment of non-cognitive testing (e.g., social/emotional intelligence, values, interests) • Limitations of self report measures • Shift to hypothetico-deductive model • Properties of distributions (e.g., growth curves, Poisson) • Reflections on the past: Too much survey work, need to expand samples of interest
The Baby Boom and Beyond (1946–1969)	• Predictive power of personality measures, especially MMPI • Social desirability and faking • Development of new measures • Literature reviews become common • Science of job attitudes • Statistical significance over effect size • Smaller font for "Method" section • Reflections on the past: stop studying the exceptional, decline in practitioner authorship, shortened time perspective for the field
Measurement and Its Discontents (1970–1989)	• Focus on measure development (e.g., job characteristics, work values, job involvement) • Item response theory, self- versus supervisor reports, number of points and anchors in a rating scale • Increased focus on methods-specific papers • Data-analytic innovations of meta-analysis and structural equation modeling
From One to Many (1990–2014)	• Methodological plurality • Broadening of methodological choices • Introduction of methods-oriented journals • Publication of reactive and prescriptive reviews of methodological practices • Realization that data-analytic approaches do not offer a panacea to solve research issues • Subgroup differences • Levels of analysis, aggregation, and multilevel modeling • Importance of effect sizes • Restoration of "Method" section font size
2017 and Beyond	• Replication of research • Understanding the exceptional, both good and bad • Identifying inappropriate methods in the review process • Better research design and measurement • More specific theories

It is inherently interpretive and naturalistic – this means that drawing from personal experience and introspection is considered within bounds, and even valuable, in interpreting the subject matter at hand. It means that the **context** of the research is of the utmost importance. A qualitative study that did not devote extensive attention to describing the context of the research would not make any sense.

In a quantitative study, a discussion of context typically includes the age, race, and sex of the participants and the geographic region they live in. Sometimes additional factors like the occupations or job tenure of the participants will be included. Perhaps the industry of the organization, or its size, will be mentioned (e.g., "a large financial services organization in the southeast United States"). In a qualitative study, however, brief summaries of contextual details like this are generally insufficient. You should describe every aspect of the organization. How is their parking lot shaped and organized? Was it sunny when you arrived? Did you pass through a security gate to get there? What was the person wearing when he spoke with you? Was he sweating? What is the town like where the organization is located? How many Starbucks are within walking distance? All of this information helps paint a vivid picture in the reader's mind about the context of your analysis and may ultimately be relevant.

For example, the shape and organization of a parking lot might imply power relationships within the organization. The weather might influence people's general affect when responding to interview prompts. Security gates might signal distrust from management. Such influences are not always clear either when data are collected, analyzed, or even read in a journal by future researchers.

Because undergraduate education in psychology tends to focus on quantitative methods, these concerns might feel a bit bizarre to you. In quantitative approaches, any interpretation done outside of existing rules is viewed as bias that should be removed from the research process. Such extreme methodological polarization, in our view, does a disservice to both quantitative and qualitative research. *Absent context, neither qualitative nor quantitative is inherently "better,"* and you should be careful to remember this fact before commenting on the value of either approach. Both can be used effectively to generate knowledge and insight, and each should be used only with a full understanding of its limits relative to the other. In fact, it can be argued that both qualitative and quantitative research are subject to moral and political biases but that qualitative researchers are more self-aware about these influences and attempts to integrate them into their research more transparently.

In organizational psychology contexts, qualitative research is often met with skepticism about its rigor compared with quantitative methods. They might describe qualitative research as "soft" or "touchy-feely." These criticisms often reflect differences in ontology and epistemology, as first discussed in Chapter 1.

For science to progress, triangulation of multiple perspectives is needed. Qualitative research can help add rich information about the perspectives of individuals, but it still must be combined with other approaches to completely understand something, as no one perspective is sufficient. Although we'll explore the specifics of how mixed methods can be used to combine qualitative and quantitative methods in Chapter 15, the point can be clearly illustrated by a famous Buddhist parable:

Three blind men encounter an elephant for the first time.
The first man grabs the elephant's tail, and says, "An elephant is like a snake!"
The second man grabs the elephant's ear and says, "An elephant is like a big fan!"

The third man grabs the elephant's leg and says, "An elephant is like a tree trunk!"

The men get very angry with each other, because for each man, his perspective of the elephant is correct but limited, for none of them understand the whole elephant.

Qualitative and quantitative approaches also differ in their approach to **axioms**, which refer to the values and assumptions that researchers hold as self-evident. Quantitative approaches are generally designed to minimize the impact of axioms on all aspects of the research process. Specifically, the aim in most quantitative approaches is that any researcher carrying out the analysis should be able to reach exactly the same result, regardless of the researcher's beliefs or point of view. In fact, quantitative research can be critiqued or faulted wherever it is evident that decisions about research were personally motivated; for example, if a person is studying sexism, they must be extra careful to ensure that their axioms created by past experiences with sexism do not affect the research in any way. In contrast, many qualitative approaches encourage exploration of axioms as a dimension of the research. A person studying sexism would be expected to reflect on their own experiences and beliefs about sexism and to acknowledge them in the manuscript.

An Author Accused of Bias

"Once, a few years into my first academic job, I was working on a paper with a team of qualitative researchers. We had conducted an intensive case study of a high school in Texas, where a majority of the students were first-generation Americans and spoke Spanish as a first language. Many were low-income and few had parents who had attended college. We spent a week in the school, talking with students and teachers and trying to find out what made the school successful under difficult circumstances. We wrote the paper, sent it to a qualitative research journal, and waited for reviews. When the reviews came back, I was totally shocked. The reviewers wanted to know more about me, the author. They wanted to know what race I was! Whether my parents went to college! I was pretty offended. I felt like the reviewers were saying that I wasn't credible based on who I was as a person. My colleagues had to explain to me that in the qualitative tradition, my personal experience was relevant because it affected how I perceived the events I saw at the school. I was part of the story and I had to make that salient to readers. I confess that I took a while to come around; I was pretty resistant to the idea, because I like to see myself as unbiased and rational. But, I now have a better appreciation for why the reviewers made this request." – Tara (one of your authors)

Subjectivity and Objectivity

You might notice that we have avoided using the words "objective" or "subjective" in describing the differences between approaches. The reason is that qualitative researchers argue that both approaches are in fact subjective but that quantitative researchers fail to acknowledge the subjectivity in their approach. Rather than getting into a semantic argument here, we focus on the substantive ways that the approaches differ.

What Is "Good" Qualitative Research?

Researchers who are unfamiliar with qualitative methods will often reject it by claiming that it is not "valid." We will define and discuss these terms much more as they apply to quantitative methods in future chapters. When qualitative researchers say that a research study is **valid**, they mean that it is coherent and carefully crafted. You can think of validity in this case as being able to articulate and defend the theoretical assumptions that underlie your conclusions. To be valid, good qualitative research must therefore be **transparent**, which means that a reader has enough information to assess with some confidence whether the analyses were carried out honestly and whether they support the conclusions. Modern qualitative research does not value theory-testing and cannot be judged by the same standards of validity as approaches that use quantitative epistemologies. The very idea that there is generalizable truth to be discovered is not consistent with qualitative approaches. As you will see in the following, qualitative approaches are highly diverse and will differ in the ways they think about validity and transparency, but ultimately these two criteria matter regardless of the approach you choose.

What Kinds of Qualitative Approaches Exist?

A wide variety of approaches and methodologies exist (see Table 5.2). Not all approaches are common in I-O psychology, for reasons of precedent and trendiness as well as because the approaches are not well suited to studying psychological phenomena. Of these approaches, case studies and grounded theory are by far the most popular in psychology. Content analysis is also a very popular approach, which can be executed within either a fully qualitative approach, as described later in this chapter, or as a combination of quantitative and qualitative approaches. Each approach to qualitative research differs slightly in its philosophical assumptions and intellectual traditions. At the end of this chapter, we recommend a variety of resources for students who wish to learn more about these traditions.

Case Studies

A **case study** is an in-depth exploration of some phenomenon – a person, and organization, or an event, for example. The goal of a case study is to describe every aspect of the phenomenon, telling a story in rich detail for the purpose of identifying important features of the phenomenon.

Case studies are useful in describing highly unusual phenomena – if there's just one thing you want to study, a case study might be your best option. More often, though, the phenomenon you want to study is just one example of a more general class of similar phenomena. Asking if your case study is truly unique or not is the best way to make sure that you don't waste time conducting a case study when other methods might be more appropriate. For example, imagine that you want to study Elon Musk, a highly successful technology CEO and investor. You believe that Elon Musk is so unusual that no other person on Earth is comparable. If studying Elon Musk is of interest, it is important to identify the reason why he is of interest. Is he a member of the set "highly successful CEOs?" Or perhaps "immigrants who are entrepreneurs?" Or is there some other set that you wish to represent with your study of Mr. Musk? Depending on which phenomenon you wish to describe, a case study might not be the right choice. Unfortunately, people often choose case studies when the phenomena

Table 5.2 Summary of qualitative approaches described in texts, adapted from Creswell and Poth (2016)

Authors	Qualitative Approaches		Disciplines/Fields
Jacob (1987)	• Ecological Psychology • Holistic Ethnography • Cognitive Anthropology	• Ethnography of Communication • Symbolic Interactionism	Education
Lancy (1993)	• Anthropological Perspectives • Sociological Perspectives • Biological Perspectives	• Case Studies • Personal Accounts • Cognitive Studies • Historical Inquiries	Education
Strauss and Corbin (1990)	• Grounded Theory • Ethnography • Phenomenology	• Life Histories • Conversational Analysis	Sociology and Nursing
Moustakas (1994)	• Ethnography • Grounded Theory • Hermeneutics • Empirical Phenomenological Research	• Heuristic Research • Transcendental Phenomenology	Psychology
Denzin and Lincoln (1995)	• Case Studies • Ethnography • Phenomenology • Ethnomethodology • Interpretative Practices	• Grounded Theory • Biographical • Historical • Clinical Research	Social Sciences
Miles and Huberman (1994)	• Interpretivism • Social Anthropology	• Collaborative Social Research	Social Sciences
Slife and Williams (1995)	• Ethnography • Phenomenology	• Studies of Artifacts	Psychology
Denzin and Lincoln (2005)	• Performance, Critical, and Public Ethnography • Interpretive Practices • Case Studies • Grounded Theory	• Life History • Narrative Authority • Participatory Action Research • Clinical Research	Social Sciences
Marshall and Rossman (2014)	• Ethnographic Approaches • Phenomenological Approaches	• Sociolinguistic Approaches (i.e., critical genres, such as critical race theory, queer theory, etc.)	Education
Denzin and Lincoln (2011)	• Case Study • Ethnography • Phenomenology • Ethnomethodology • Grounded Theory	• Historical Method • Action and Applied Research • Clinical Research	Social Sciences
Mertens (2015)	• Ethnographic Research • Grounded Theory • Case Study	• Participatory Action Research • Phenomenological Research	Psychology

they care about are not actually unique but are instead difficult to access. It would be a mistake to do a case study of Elon Musk if you were interested in generalizing to all CEOs, or even to technology CEOs, simply because Elon Musk was the only CEO you had enough information about in order to write a case study.

As described earlier, *JAP's* earliest history included many case studies, such as studies of professionals who displayed exceptional skill. The goals of these early studies was to document everything about a particular case so that others could pick it apart. A logical extension of this approach was that if everything about this particular expert could be documented and understood, others of his skills could be created by replicating those circumstances. For instance – imagine stumbling across a very dynamic and charismatic leader. We'll call her "Moprah." Moprah is captivating. She is able to sway public opinion with ease. She can motivate her employees to go to extraordinary lengths to meet the goals she sets. How does she do it? By studying Moprah in detail, imagine that you discover her background is extremely unusual, or even unique. She grew up in extreme poverty and draws from those experiences to relate to others. She is warm and genuine. She is honest about her own failings.

Does any of this make Moprah's approach or experiences uniquely powerful or informative, to justify a case study of her leadership style? Not necessarily. Many other people with similar personalities and backgrounds do not enjoy the kind of success that Moprah does. It would be a mistake to assume that you have uncovered the magic formula that describes good leadership by learning about Moprah. You must ask yourself honestly if there is anything *truly* unique, in your **professional judgment** as a researcher, about Moprah. If you cannot emphatically say "yes," you should probably use another method.

A strength of the case study approach is in its compelling communicative ability. Everyone who has taken an Introduction to Psychology course, for example, remembers the story of Phineas Gage, the railroad worker who suffered a brain injury after an explosion shot a railroad tie into his skull. From his case, we learned a great deal about the function of the brain. But this memorability can also be the downfall of case study. Details from cases often turn out to be untrue yet difficult to debunk. For example, Phineas Gage recovered from his injuries (Griggs, 2015), but nobody remembers that part of the story because it wasn't reported in the original case study. Because our goal in I-O psychology is to create generalizable knowledge, we should be cautious, extremely cautious, when attempting to draw conclusions from case studies. Phineas Gage may have led researchers to ask questions about the brain that they hadn't previously considered – but to answer those questions, they followed the case with years of careful testing and additional research.

The business world loves to glorify successful companies and recommend their practices in other companies. They are often surprised and dismayed when this approach doesn't work. Such failures perfectly demonstrate the danger of extrapolating and generalizing from a single case. For example, in the early 2000s, open-space office designs were hailed as innovative ways to support collaboration. Why keep everyone cooped up in offices? Let them interact so they can innovate together! Many organizations played follow-the-leader and adopted open offices in an attempt to capture the innovative magic they saw at work in high-tech firms.

Yet this model turned out not to work very well for anyone (Kim & De Dear, 2013). Open offices make it very difficult to have meetings or phone calls without disturbing others. Handling confidential material is also a hassle. Even the high-tech firms who initially created this trend soon discovered its impracticalities. "It worked at that other organization" is not sufficient to think it will work at your organization. Somewhat ironically, a better understanding of context would make this faulty logic obvious. *One cannot generalize from a case study.* Asking the question, "what is this case an example of?" is critical to making sure you don't make the same kinds of mistakes the business world is prone to making.

One final note on case studies: Case studies aren't always qualitative. You can collect quantitative data and conduct analyses on a single case – for example, by following a single person around for a long time and tracking many aspects of their behavior. These studies are referred to as "N=1" studies since they focus intensely on one single participant. A very famous study, "One Boy's Day" (Barker & Wright, 1951), used this kind of approach, simply recording everything a boy did during one day and presenting the data for other researchers to analyze. The availability of new technologies has increased interest in this sort of quantitative case study. See Chapter 15 for more details on this and other novel and mixed methods.

Grounded Theory

Grounded theory is a prescribed set of procedures for the inductive generation of theory from data originally proposed in the mid-20th century by Glaser and Strauss (2017). It is not always qualitative, but it is often at least partially qualitative. Its core characteristic is its inductive approach: for example, starting from data and then building an explanatory theory through an iterative process. It is also the most generally accepted qualitative approach currently used in I-O psychology, probably in part due to its highly systematic nature, a characteristic typically valued in quantitative research.

The iterative process at the core of grounded theory starts with observation, which is described in detailed notes. The notes are organized with **codes**, which refers to classifications made by the observer based upon what was observed that relate to themes. As themes are identified, new data may be collected, or the previous notes may be re-analyzed in light of these new themes. As a simple example, consider the question, "what makes good ice cream?" Let's say I interview three people to find out what they think, and they say the following:

A. "My favorite ice cream is from Joe's, because it is all organic and they make it right there in the store. They always have interesting flavors and I can always find something new I haven't tried before."
B. "I like buying local so I go to Moe's. The owner is a good friend of mine. She makes really creative flavors, too, and my son loves the "weird" ice cream like sesame seed flavor.

From these two excerpts, I might notice that several people mentioned *novelty* as a quality they appreciated. I also notice *local* as a theme right away. I can code the interviews as reflecting these themes and then determine which themes are related to each other based on how often they show up together. I can also continue my interviews:

C. "Bo's Cones on 5th is my favorite because it is very comfortable in there and I can go and hang out with my family and enjoy a summer afternoon there."

After reading interview C, the theme of *family-friendliness* becomes more apparent. I can go back to interview B and code it with this theme. Or perhaps, I could revise the theme to be about *community* more generally. These decisions are difficult and reflect the nuance and careful thought that is required to do proper grounded theory research. This is, of course, a dramatically oversimplified example. Real grounded theory is much more involved, although it follows these general steps.

Annika Wilhelmy and her colleagues used a grounded theory approach to understand how and why interviewers try to make impressions on applicants (Wilhelmy et al., 2016). In their study, they observed interviewers while they were engaged in interviews, and they analyzed memos and other artifacts from the organization. Their goal was to look for the

Table 5.1 How interviewers apply impression management (IM): structure of interviewer 1M intentions

Higher-level categories	Lower-level categories
Primary IM intentions: What do interviewers intend to signal to applicants with regard to representing the organization, the job. and themselves?	
1. Attractiveness	
2. Authenticity	
Secondary IM intentions: What do interviewers intend to signal to applicants with regard to their personal interaction with the applicant?	
3. Closeness	3a. Building rapport
	3b. *Individuality and appreciation*
	3c. *Trustworthiness*
4. Distance in terms of professionalism	4a. *Fairness*
	4b. *Selection complexity and effort*
	4c. *Straightforwardness*
5. Distance in terms of superiority	5a. Status and power of decision
	5b. *Performance expectations*
	5c. *Suspense*

Note. Categories of interviewer IM intentions that are printed in italics are new in comparison to Barrick et al. (2009) and Jones and Pittman (1982).

Figure 5.1 Impression management categories discovered via grounded theory by Wilhelmy and colleagues. (Table 1 from Wilhelmy et al., 2016.)

different kinds of impressions an interviewer might try to make on an applicant, instead of assuming that they were all trying to create a single kind of positive impression. In their observations, they noticed various kinds of behaviors that were not covered by existing impression management theory. Figure 5.1 shows, in italics, the kinds of behaviors they discovered. Using grounded theory procedures for meaning-making, they then generated a new, expanded theory that incorporated their observations, as shown in Figure 5.2

For an authoritative exploration of grounded theory, see Corbin and Strauss (1994).

Ethnography

The goal of **ethnography** is to provide a very detailed, very rich account of a cultural phenomenon. It is most popular in anthropology and sociology but is used with increasing frequency in fields such as education and communication. In I-O psychology, an ethnography might be used to richly describe a single organization's culture or even the culture of a particularly interesting work group. A core goal when using ethnography is to generate a particularly rich example, much like a case study, but then to use that example to learn something about the general phenomenon that created the example. Moving from the specific to the general in this way allows for a particular kind of knowledge to be created.

Unlike the case study method, ethnographic methods require researchers to establish and maintain long-term relationships with the subjects of their research. Some ethnographers go so far as to live or work alongside their research subjects. Immersion within a research domain to such a high degree can help ethnographers understand what is happening at a deeper level than the case study method typically allows. However, this also increases the

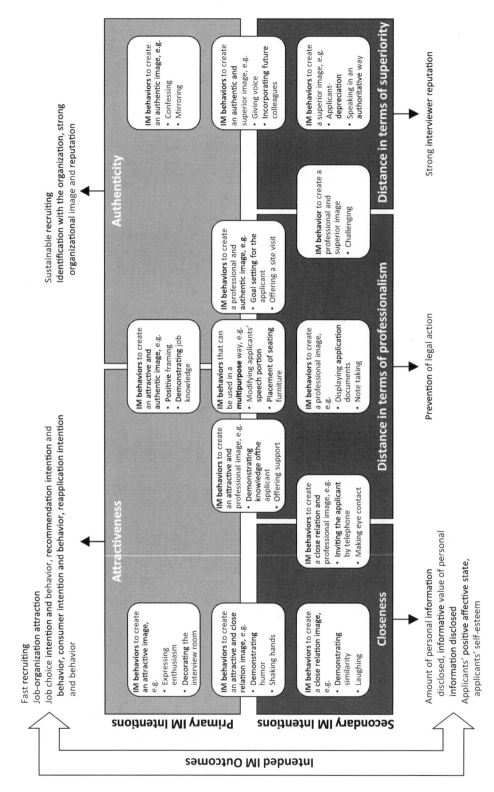

Figure 5.2 Interviewer impressions theory developed from grounded theory methods by Wilhelmy and colleagues. (Table from Wilhelmy et al., 2016.)

demand for a high degree of skill at ethnographic methods; an inexperienced ethnographer is more likely to be swept up in the culture of their research subject, which can make it difficult to disentangle their personal values and beliefs with the phenomenon they are researching.

Ethnography can be a powerful way to describe atypical or rare phenomena that do not lend themselves well to other approaches. For example, sociologist Matthew Desmond conducted an ethnography of wildland firefighters – the people who fight forest fires. Having been a member of the wildland himself, he incorporated his own emotional and physical experiences into his account. Ethnography differs from non-research methods of storytelling (e.g., journalism, documentary filmmaking) in its ties to theory building. Desmond described his work as follows:

> Why do individuals seek out high-risk occupations when safer ways of earning a living are available? How do they become acclimated to the dangers of their profession? This article addresses these questions by examining how individuals become wildland firefighters. Drawing on in-depth ethnographic data I collected while serving as a wildland firefighter employed by the US Forest Service, I explore how individual competences and dispositions acquired from a certain family and class background pre-condition rural working-class men for the rigors of firefighting. In Bourdieu's terms, I investigate how the primary habitus of self-described 'country boys' transforms into the specific habitus of wildland firefighters. Answers pertaining to why young men join firecrews and how they become seasoned to the hazards of wildfire are found not by examining processes of organizational socialization alone but by analyzing how processes of organizational socialization are specified extensions of earlier processes of socialization that take place during firefighters' childhood and adolescence.

The theory in this example is sociological and so draws from different thinkers and different terminology that psychologists draw from. Nonetheless, we can get a sense of how the intense, rich experience of ethnography leads to new insights that can be used to connect individual, organizational, and social levels of analysis. The explanations cannot be "proven" in a way that would be satisfactory to quantitative researchers. But within the epistemological bounds of qualitative approaches, this set of claims is justified.

Phenomenology

Phenomenology is the explicit study of subjective experience. It has a long history in psychology, starting with philosophers like Jean-Paul Sartre who were interested in the study of consciousness. The fundamental goal of phenomenology is to describe the ways that people engage in **meaning-making** – that is, how do they make sense of their experiences? These experiences include life events, relationships, and their understanding of their selves and identities.

Meaning-making shows up in the management literature under the label of **sensemaking**, a concept most commonly associated with Karl Weick. The study of sensemaking is meant to uncover the ways that people make sense of events and tell themselves stories about the explanations for those events through **introspection**. It has been applied to a wide range of contexts, from the military to organizations recovering from natural disasters.

In both I-O psychology and psychology more broadly, phenomenology is very rare, and our exposure to it is mostly because of work completed by management researchers.

Most modern psychological science starts from the assumption that deep introspection, the method at the core of phenomenology, is inherently faulty. Decades of research have shown us that we are not generally good judges of why we do the things we do. We attribute (i.e., explain) our behavior in ways that make our lives simpler and easier, often relying upon heuristics and habits, but not in ways that are necessarily the most accurate. As a result, phenomenology is not a broadly trusted research method.

Action Research

The fundamental assumption of action research is that the people who are affected by research should be active participants in that research. **Action research** is not a single method but rather a collection of methods, all grouped together based on this stance. Some of the most famous names in management and applied psychology are associated with action research, including Kurt Lewin, who first popularized the term. Kurt Lewin was one of the founders of applied psychology, active in the 1920s through 1940s. In his version of action research, each step of the research process is accompanied by a pause, during which the researcher investigates how their actions have affected the community they are studying. The **Lewinian spiral** depicts this process, as shown in Figure 5.3.

We don't see the term "action research" used much in I-O psychology these days, but the assumption is one we think deserves consideration. The approach is similar to grounded theory, and the broader world of inductive research, in which we allow theory to be shaped by new information as we obtain it. In action research, participants are "active" instead of "passive" in shaping the information that is conveyed to the researcher. Instead of conducting research to answer research questions, researchers work iteratively to ask new questions, answer those questions, solve problems, and potentially continue this cycle indefinitely.

Echoes of action research can be seen in the newer and trendier **design thinking** movement. Design thinking comes from the world of technology and is meant to help non-social scientists adopt a social science perspective in the design process by making sure the things they design work for actual people rather than hypothetical people. Popularized by organizations such as Stanford's Design School, the basic model for design thinking is depicted in Figure 5.4.

You can see from this model that the first step is to "empathize." This is conceptually similar to the fact-finding stage of action research. The goal is to learn about the problem you are trying to solve before you jump into solving it. What is the problem? How do people experience this problem? What is it like to have this problem? What solutions have been

Planning   Action

Fact-finding
about results
of action

Figure 5.3 Lewinian spiral.

Figure 5.4 Design thinking model from the Stanford Design School.

tried before? Next is to define the problem more specifically by identifying barriers to solving the problem and identifying key actors. After that, brainstorming of possible solutions. These two steps together are similar to the planning stage of action research. Finally, the design thinking process ends with building prototypes and testing them to see if they work, and under what conditions. This is the "action" phase of action research.

Design thinking and action research share in common the idea that researchers know less about a problem than the people who are actually experiencing the problem. They also share the idea that you can't know if something works until you get out there and actually try it. And, by trying it, you learn more that will allow you to refine your ideas and improve them on the next iteration.

Crafting a Qualitative Paper: Some Resources

Many excellent resources exist with advice about the craft of qualitative research: see Cunliffe (2011) and Gephart (2004) for a few examples of how to craft qualitative research for management journals. Norms about reporting vary dramatically between journals and between disciplines, so we recommend starting by identifying the researchers working in your area and observing the conventions they follow.

Ethics of Qualitative Research

As discussed in Chapter 1, ethics refers to the moral principles and professional guidelines you must follow when conducting, reporting, and communicating your research. Ethics must always be the first consideration for a researcher. The federal government, in its guidelines for human subjects research, notes,

> Research in humans differs from other research in that the subject has decision-making power and must be treated with respect. The long history, even in the name of science of one group of humans exploiting another has made it necessary to establish elaborate rules and procedures to protect human participants in research.
>
> (Korenman, n.d.)

Qualitative research has some unique ethical challenges. When you have an ethical dilemma, you should seek out the professional published resources we described in Chapter 1 or ask trusted colleagues for advice. The nature of these dilemmas is that the "correct" course of action might not always be obvious, so turning to professional guidelines can be beneficial. Part of being an ethical researcher is considering all the parties that can be potentially affected by your work and thinking about what the consequences of your research might be for them. It means thinking about your role as a researcher and representative of the profession, instead of just your personal everyday identity.

Consider the following example in the context of qualitative methods: Joanna is an Uber driver who decided to conduct a qualitative investigation of her fellow drivers and how they experience motivation during their work. She first had the idea after Uber sent her a message suggesting that she would get a $100 bonus if she picked up 25 passengers before the end of the week. She noticed herself feeling a lot more motivated after getting that message but also a little bit cynical. She wanted to know how other people felt about the ways that Uber tried to motivate them.

There are a number of ethical considerations that Joanna should mind. First, her participants are her friends, and they trust her. They may have shared things with Joanna in the past that affect her beliefs as she begins the study. Second, Joanna has to think about which entities have a say in approving her research. Should she seek approval from Uber? Joanna also needs to consider the potential power differentials between her and her participants. She drives Uber part-time for fun, but her friends do so to make a living.

Joanna can plan to conduct her study ethically by taking a number of steps, listed chronologically in the following. A summary of these steps more generally appears in Table 5.4.

First, as discussed in Chapter 1, she should clear her research plan with her institution's institutional review board (IRB). The IRB is made up of faculty and administrators who evaluate research plans to ensure that they protect the rights of participants. In the US, the primary set of rules that govern IRB decisions come from the federal government, as described by the Common Rule also discussed in Chapter 1. In addition to obtaining approval from IRB, site permissions should be obtained from any location in which research will be conducted. This, too, can present a challenge. Organizations that are aware of being observed may change the way they present themselves to create a more positive impression. They may attempt to interfere with data collection out of a misguided desire to be helpful – for example, by suggesting people for you to speak with or offering to give you "the grand tour" and managing the places and experiences you have access to.

Second, Joanna should plan to educate her participants about the purpose of the study and engage them in the **informed consent** process, a process that when followed implies that participants in a research study know exactly what they will be asked to do before they are asked to do it; what information they will be asked to provide; what will happen to their responses; who will have access to their responses; who will know their identity; how they will be compensated, if at all; and that they have the right to refuse to participate at any time without any negative consequences. Importantly, the consent process never stops. Although you may hear phrases like "obtain informed consent," a signature on a **consent form** is really just the first step, especially considering most participants do not read consent forms (Douglas et al., 2021). We have an ethical responsibility to ensure that participants are informed at all stages of the research process, from start to finish, which any many qualitative approaches, especially ethnography, can be lengthy. Informed consent reflects the general principle of Fidelity and Responsibility in the APA Code (see Chapter 1): research participants are likely to trust us because we represent trustworthy institutions, like the APA, our universities, and our organizations, and we must honor that trust. Participants should have an opportunity to ask questions. They should have access to additional information about the study whenever they want to see it.

Third, Joanna should plan to collect the data ethically, which varies a bit depending upon the specific qualitative method chosen. Guidelines for this will be discussed in Chapter 6, alongside the practical issues faced when attempting to conduct research using various qualitative methods.

Fourth, she must analyze her data ethically. There are many opportunities to misrepresent the data when engaging in qualitative analysis. Planning ahead is important if these errors are to be avoided. These analytic challenges will also be discussed in Chapter 6.

Fifth, she must think about how to communicate her results: to the scientific community, to her participants, and to the general public. Each of these audiences has particular needs. There are many issues relating to communication that can present challenges (see Creswell & Poth, 2016 for useful guidance on this topic, as well as the discussion of sharing research results in Chapter 14).

Within these stages, some issues are particularly salient in qualitative research. Although confidentiality, bias, and completeness are important in all research, they have special importance in qualitative studies.

Confidentiality means that the informants for the research are not personally identifiable to anyone except the researcher. This creates an inherent conflict between protecting participants and sharing data for the purposes of verifiability and transparency. It is especially challenging, and often impossible, to ensure confidentiality in case studies and ethnographies, when the very premise is to study someone or something that is unusual and thus easily identifiable. Imagine a case study about an I-O psychology professor who, in the year 2020, moved from an urban east coast university to a midwest land grant university. That probably only describes a few people. Add in other details, like gender and age, and it can only be one person (one of your authors). Some qualitative researchers address this issue by altering non-important details or omitting them. But how do they know which details will end up being important? As discussed earlier, this is one of the most challenging aspects of qualitative research already. **Anonymity**, which requires even the researcher being unable to identify participants after the fact, is often impossible in qualitative research.

Bias, in the context of qualitative research, refers to any instance of personal values or ideas being inserted into research findings without being acknowledged as such. The most common sources of bias for a qualitative researcher are your personal worldviews, moral beliefs, personal identities, and prior experiences, all of which can affect both how you see the world and how it sees you. For example, participants might interpret your questions differently or understand them differently depending on who is asking them. It's impossible to be completely unbiased or to remove all sources of bias from data, but it is possible and necessary to rely on procedures that will minimize bias, some of which we'll explore in Chapter 6. Remember, too, that one person's "bias" is another's "personal experience" and valuable source of information. Although clearly articulating your point of view helps address this issue, you may not even understand your own point of view well enough to understand how it might bias you.

Completeness refers to the extent of reporting by qualitative researchers. Because qualitative researchers make many decisions about what to include and not include in a research report, as reporting literally every detail would be overwhelming and not very useful, a cautious balance is necessary in the interpretative process to decide what is and is not relevant. This process, however, can introduce ethical challenges. For example, imagine that in the

Table 5.3 Ethical issues in qualitative research, adapted from Creswell and Poth (2016)

Timing During Research Process	Type of Ethical Issue	How to Address the Issue
Prior to conducting the study	• Seek college or university approval. • Examine professional association standards. • Gain local access permissions. • Select a site without a vested interest in the outcome of the study. • Negotiate authorship for publication. • Seek permission for use of unpublished instruments or procedures that other researchers might consider theirs.	• Submit for institutional review board approval. • Consult types of professional ethical standards. • Identify and go through local approvals for the site and participant's find a gatekeeper to help. • Select a site that will not raise power issues with researchers. • Give credit for work done on the project; decide on author order. • Obtain permission for use of any material that may be considered proprietary and give credit.
Beginning to conduct the study	• Disclose the purpose of the study. • Refrain from pressuring participants into signing consent forms. • Respect norms and charters of indigenous societies. • Have sensitivity to the needs of vulnerable populations (e.g., children).	• Contact participants and inform them of the general purpose of the study. • Assure participants that their participation is voluntary. • Find out about cultural, religious, gender, and other differences that need to be respected. • Obtain appropriate consent (e.g., parents as well as children).
Collecting data	• Respect the study site and minimize disruptions. • Avoid deceiving participants. • Respect potential power imbalances and exploitation of participants. • Do not "use" participants by gathering data and leaving the site without giving back. • Store data and materials (e.g., raw data and protocols) using appropriate security measures.	• Build trust and convey the extent of anticipated disruption in gaining access. • Discuss the purpose and use of the study. • Avoid leading questions, withhold sharing personal impressions, and avoid disclosing sensitive information. • Provide rewards for participating and attend to opportunities for reciprocity. • Store data and materials in secure locations for 5 years (APA, 2010).
Analyzing the data	• Avoid siding with participants and disclosing only positive results. • Respect the privacy of participants. • Avoid falsifying authorship, evidence, data, findings, and conclusions. • Avoid disclosing information that would harm participants. • Communicate in clear, straightforward, appropriate language. • Do not plagiarize.	• Report honestly. • Use composite stories so that individuals cannot be identified. • Use language appropriate for audiences of the research. • See APA (2010) guidelines for permissions needed to reprint or adapt the work of others.
Publishing the study	• Share reports with others. • Tailor the reporting to diverse audience(s). • Do not duplicate or piecemeal publications. • Complete proof of compliance with ethical issues and lack of conflict of interest.	• Provide copies of the report to participants and stakeholders. • Share practical results, consider website distribution, and consider publishing in different languages. • Refrain from using the same material for more than one publication. • Disclose funders for research and who will profit from the research.

process of your data collection, you observe one of your participants committing a minor crime. You must now decide whether to include this observation in your report. Including it means subjecting the participant to legal, professional, and social consequences. Not including it, however, means painting a picture of reality that is not quite accurate. Ultimately this sort of question does not have an easy answer.

Weiner-Levy and Popper-Giveon wrote about this challenge, calling the left-out data "dark matter" (2013), writing:

> Qualitative research literature generally ignores the voids that are created and the materials that are suppressed during data analysis and the writing phase. Qualitative studies are usually based on observations and interviews that hold an immense amount of data. These are transformed to a few condensed papers at the final stage. During this process, many of the findings and insights are omitted. . . . We maintain that these suppressed and obscured materials, the "dark matter" of qualitative research, have a marked effect on the research and significantly affect the findings and their structure even if they are not included in the final report.

They focus on two forms of dark matter: (1) **reflexivity**, which refers to the extent to which unexamined assumptions about the researcher's own beliefs and biases that might have ultimately suppressed and concealed more than they presented and revealed, a concept closely related to positionality as discussed in Chapter 3, and (2) relevant findings omitted from final reports despite their effect on research, for whatever reason.

Because qualitative psychology research focuses on capturing the richness of human experience, the researcher's judgment is fully on display and open to evaluation by others. Do not assume, however, that turning to quantitative research methods instead somehow makes researchers more objective and unbiased. As you will see in subsequent chapters, nearly every decision you make and every piece of information you perceive will affect the conclusions you make, regardless of your approach. Being aware of those influences is the key to becoming a good researcher.

Archival Qualitative Data Sources

Now that you have the basic tools of qualitative research design, where can you find qualitative data? Although it has an initial emphasis on political science, the Qualitative Data Repository (QDR) provides a useful archive for accessing data produced via qualitative methods in the social sciences. This online resource, funded by the National Science Foundation, is hosted by the Center for Qualitative and Multimethod Inquiry at Syracuse University. Users can easily search QDR for keywords pertaining to a specific research question. QDR aims to provide trustworthy data to its users by ensuring that data are *usable, discoverable, meaningful, citable, secure, non-discriminatory, and durable.*

Should you conduct your own qualitative study, you may wish to share it on QDR to encourage additional research on a topic. The QDR website includes a variety of resources to facilitate the appropriate storing and sharing of qualitative data, such as methods of informed consent and de-identification. These resources are intended to make both the processes and products of qualitative research more transparent, which can help future researchers better assess the empirical quality of a study. Those who deposit their data on QDR are given user-access controls to ensure that all human subjects requirements can be met. To search the QDR archive or for more information about storing your own qualitative data, see https://qdr.syr.edu/about.

References

American Psychological Association. (2010). *Publication manual of the American psychological association*. American Psychological Association.

Barker, R. G., & Wright, H. F. (1951). *One boy's day; a specimen record of behavior*. Harper.

Barrick, M. R., Shaffer, J. A., & DeGrassi, S. W. (2009). What you see may not be what you get: relationships among self-presentation tactics and ratings of interview and job performance. *Journal of Applied Psychology, 94*(6), 1394.

Cameron, W. B. (1963). *Informal sociology: A casual introduction to sociological thinking*. Random House.

Corbin, J., & Strauss, A. (1994). Grounded theory methodology. In Norman K Denzin and Yvonna S. Lincoln (Eds.), *Handbook of qualitative research* (pp. 273–285). Sage.

Cortina, J. M., Aguinis, H., & DeShon, R. P. (2017). Twilight of dawn or of evening: A century of research methods in journal of applied psychology. *Journal of Applied Psychology, 102*(3), 274–290. https://doi.org/10.1037/apl0000163

Creswell, J. W., & Poth, C. N. (2016). *Qualitative inquiry and research design: Choosing among five approaches*. Sage.

Cunliffe, A. L. (2011). Crafting qualitative research Morgan and Smircich 30 years on. *Organizational Research Methods, 14*(4), 647–673. https://doi.org/10.1177/1094428110373658

David, R. J., & Bitektine, A. B. (2009). The deinstitutionalization of institutional theory? Exploring divergent agendas in institutional research. In D. A. Buchanan & A. Bryman (Eds.), *The Sage handbook of organizational research methods* (pp. 160–175). Sage.

Denzin, N. K., & Lincoln, Y. S. (1995). Transforming qualitative research methods: Is it a revolution? *Journal of Contemporary Ethnography, 24*(3), 349–358.

Denzin, N. K., & Lincoln, Y. S. (Eds.). (2011). *The Sage handbook of qualitative research*. Sage.

Douglas, B. D., McGorray, E. L., & Ewell, P. J. (2021). Some researchers wear yellow pants, but even fewer participants read consent forms: Exploring and improving consent form reading in human subjects research. *Psychological Methods, 26*(1), 61. https://doi.org/10.1037/met0000267

Gates, A. I. (1918). The abilities of an expert marksman tested in the psychological laboratories. *Journal of Applied Psychology, 2*(1), 1–14. https://doi.org/10.1037/h0074646

Gephart, R. P. (2004). Qualitative research and the academy of management journal. *Academy of Management Journal, 47*(4), 454–462. https://doi.org/10.5465/AMJ.2004.14438580

Glaser, B. G., & Strauss, A. L. (2017). *Discovery of grounded theory: Strategies for qualitative research*. Routledge.

Griggs, R. (2015). Coverage of the Phineas Gage story in introductory psychology textbooks: Was Gage no longer Gage? *Teaching of Psychology, 42*(3), 195–202. https://doi.org/10.1177/0098628315587614

Jacob, E. (1987). Qualitative research traditions: A review. *Review of Educational Research, 57*(1), 1–50.

Jones, E. E., & Pittman, T. S. (1982). Toward a general theory of strategic self-presentation. In *Psychological perspectives on the self*. Lawrence Erlbaum.

Kim, J., & De Dear, R. (2013). Workspace satisfaction: The privacy-communication trade-off in open-plan offices. *Journal of Environmental Psychology, 36*, 18–26. https://doi.org/10.1016/j.jenvp.2013.06.007

Korenman, S. G. (n.d.). *Teaching the responsible conduct of research in humans: Chapter 2: Common rule*. US Department of Health and Human Services, Office of Research Integrity. https://ori.hhs.gov/education/products/ucla/chapter2/default.htm

Lancy, D. F. (1993). *Qualitative research in education: An introduction to the major traditions*.

Marshall, C., & Rossman, G. B. (2014). *Designing qualitative research*. Sage publications.

Mertens, D. M. (2015). Mixed methods and wicked problems. *Journal of Mixed Methods Research*, 9(1), 3–6.

Miles, M. B., & Huberman, A. M. (1994). *Qualitative data analysis: An expanded sourcebook*. Sage.

Slife, B. D., & Williams, R. N. (1995). *What's behind the research?: Discovering hidden assumptions in the behavioral sciences*. Sage.

Strauss, A., & Corbin, J. (1990). *Basics of qualitative research*. Sage Publications.

Triplett, N. (1898). The dynamogenic factors in pacemaking and competition. *The American Journal of Psychology*, 9(4), 507–533.

Weiner-Levy, N., & Popper-Giveon, A. (2013). The absent, the hidden and the obscured: Reflections on "dark matter" in qualitative research. *Quality & Quantity*, 47(4), 2177–2190. https://doi.org/10.1007/s11135-011-9650-7

Wilhelmy, A., Kleinmann, M., König, C. J., Melchers, K. G., & Truxillo, D. M. (2016). How and why do interviewers try to make impressions on applicants? A qualitative study. *Journal of Applied Psychology*, 101(3), 313–332. https://doi.org/10.1037/apl0000046

Further Reading

Glaser, B., & Strauss, A. (1967). *The discovery of grounded theory strategies for qualitative research*. Sociology Press.

- Glaser and Strauss's classic book discusses the methodology of grounded theory, which is often described as a recursive, process-oriented procedure in which data can inform theories. This work increased the acceptability of qualitative studies during a time when they were not widely accepted.

Stake, R. E. (1995). *The art of case study research*. Sage.

- Stake's book provides readers with a practical case study to demonstrate how the case study approach can be used to answer questions related to selecting a case, gathering data, and interpreting what is learned.

Pratt, M. G., & Bonaccio, S. (2016). Qualitative research in IO psychology: Maps, myths, and moving forward. *Industrial and Organizational Psychology*, 9(4), 693–715. https://doi.org/10.1017/iop.2016.92

- Pratt and Bonaccio showed that qualitative research is published in top I-O journals much less frequently than quantitative research and suggest that the blame may lie with common researcher misconceptions about what qualitative research is. They address these misconceptions directly and suggest how to better integrate qualitative research into I-O.

Cornelissen, J. P. (2017). Preserving theoretical divergence in management research: Why the explanatory potential of qualitative research should be harnessed rather than suppressed. *Journal of Management Studies*, 54(3), 368–383. https://doi.org/10.1111/joms.12210

- Cornelissen notes that despite the recent increase in qualitative studies being published in leading business and management journals, there is still a pressure for researchers to present their work in a quantitative fashion. Cornelissen argues that there is much to be gained by appreciating the intrinsic value of qualitative methods and the theorizing it allows.

Wright, P. M. (2017). Making great theories. *Journal of Management Studies*, 54(3), 384–390. https://doi.org/10.1111/joms.12240

- In response to Cornelissen (2017), Wright puts forth several recommendations aimed at better integrating quantitative and qualitative methods, with the ultimate goal of building better theories in business and management research.

Questions to Think About

1. What is qualitative research?
2. How is the quality of a qualitative research study assessed?
3. Consider your own research interests. What role can qualitative research play in exploring these topics?
4. Identify situations in which a researcher would benefit from conducting each of the qualitative approaches discussed in this chapter.
5. Assume you are interested in studying the experiences of workers who are employed in a newly created occupation for which there is little research. One of your colleagues tells you that a quantitative study of these workers will provide you with the most rigorous information. Do you agree with your colleague? What kind of study would you conduct?
6. What ethical issues are unique to qualitative research? What actions can you, as a researcher, take to address these issues?

Key Terms

- ethnography
- grounded theory
- informed consent
- introspection
- Lewinian spiral
- meaning-making
- phenomenology
- prediction
- professional judgment
- reflexivity
- rigor
- sensemaking
- standing on the shoulders of giants
- transparency (in qualitative research)
- validity (in qualitative research)

## Chapter 6

Data Collection, Analytic Strategies, and Minimizing Bias

DOI: 10.4324/9781315167473-8

Learning Objectives

After reading this chapter, you will be able to:

1. Identify strengths and weaknesses of interviews, focus groups, and other qualitative data collection strategies.
2. Choose a qualitative analytic strategy.
3. Collect and analyze qualitative data.
4. Acknowledge sources of bias during qualitative research.
5. Compare and contrast various qualitative data analysis techniques.
6. Report qualitative research in a transparent way.

If you have decided that a qualitative design might be appropriate for you, then you next need to decide exactly how to obtain your qualitative data. If your method section states, "I went to an organization and just hung out there for a while," you will give the editor a good laugh, but otherwise you will not accomplish very much. Even in qualitative designs, adherence to a set of rigorous methods that *can be described clearly to others* is necessary. In fact, the way you choose and describe your procedures is essential to its credibility.

This chapter is an introduction to some of the options you have: interviews, focus groups, observations, and artifact analysis. You may decide to combine these methods or stick with just one. Ultimately, you should choose based on what makes the most sense for your research question, and what is practically feasible. We will also get into some details about how to choose people to compose your group of participants and how to build instruments for data collection. Best practices exist to save you the heartache of trial and error.

The method you choose will affect the kind of information you get; this is a fact of life. You should be mindful of possible ways that this is occurring, and try to minimize the damage as much as possible. The second half of this chapter elaborates on what you should be careful of.

Types of Qualitative Methods

All qualitative methods that we will discuss have strengths and weaknesses. The section that follows offers descriptions plus a few decision points you can use to choose. In your own research, you will have to balance practical needs with theoretical needs to arrive at a strategy. Thinking about practical issues is of the utmost importance. In fact, when you are choosing a research question, practicality should be at the top of the list when deciding whether you can answer the question. So, considering the time, cost, and logistics associated with different qualitative strategies should be your first step.

Interviews

An **interview** is a dialogue between two people. Interviews can range dramatically in their structure, formality, scope, and length. The value of an interview is in its flexibility. When an interview subject says something interesting, the interviewer can follow up, **probe** for more information, ask for clarification, and get more details. An interview may end up in a totally different place than you intended it to at the beginning, and this is the point.

Here is an example of an interview snippet from a study about job searching:

[I]:   Okay. Alright, so when did you start looking for a job?

[S]:   When did I start? I would say about half a year ago. I mean I pretty much knew that I wanted to do something else probably even before then, but I actively really started looking for a job and putting in the time probably, you know, 6 months or so.

[I]:   You said that you knew for a while. What made you start just 6 months ago?

[S]:   Well, I was pretty happy with what I was doing probably for the first 2 years or so. After that I sort of, you know, realized that it's not really something that I want to do in the long term. But it took another, you know, year or so to really get to the point where I had the will and the motivation to really start looking at other stuff and put in the time. But what made me realize that I wanted to do something else? Basically it was really an overall lack of satisfaction with the nature of the work and what it deals with.

[I]:   What gave you the motivation ultimately to like, go online and start searching?

[S]:   To find something that basically I would enjoy more on a daily basis.

You can observe here that the respondent's answers led the interview in a particular direction – when they say that they knew for a while that they were unhappy but weren't searching for something new, the interviewer was able to probe on this point, ultimately getting useful information about the ways that job searching motivation can change and develop over time. Nonetheless, the subject is not providing the interviewer useful information. The interviewer is trying to determine whether there was an instigating event of some kind that led the subject to start searching, but the subject is being vague about what exactly led to their beginning the search.

If an interviewer isn't highly skilled, they can let an opportunity like this slip by without getting the information they need. Thus, there is some on-the-fly thinking required to conduct a good interview. Based on the previous snippet, what would make a good next question?

1. Change the subject: Ask, "where do you usually go to find job openings?"
2. Be direct: Ask, "Was there a specific event that made you take action?"
3. Be psychoanalytical: Ask, "Is there something you're trying to hide?"
4. Be coy: Say, "It's funny how life can just keep going on in a single direction and then suddenly, it changes."

Deciding on the next question can end up like a choose-your-own adventure plot twist. The interview might go in a very different direction, depending on how you choose. And some of those plot twists can lead to dead ends or, perhaps worse, long diversions. Importantly, some of these questions would not be a good choice regardless of your goals. We will present much more detail about writing appropriate, effective questions later in this chapter. For now, Option 4 would be a poor choice, because it is a **leading question:** the question gives the respondent a cue about how you want them to respond. You should never put words into your subject's mouth.

Another factor to think about when deciding whether to use interviews is the protection and use of any personal information the subject might disclose. Compared to focus groups, interviews are more intimate. Subjects might reveal personal details that the interviewer doesn't want or know what to do with. This information might or might not be related to the interview topic! People are often flattered and grateful that their opinion is being taken seriously and take the opportunity to share details that are not relevant to the question being asked and therefore to the research being conducted.

Specialized Interview Techniques

Some specialized interview techniques are used to obtain certain kinds of information. For example, cognitive interviews are used to understand routinized cognitive processes. This information is traditionally used in job analysis, a standardized approach to collecting detailed information about a given job. The information generated from job analyses can be used for selection, training, and performance management. Here is an example of the output of a cognitive interview with a firefighter:

Interviewer:	Walk me through your thought process when you arrive on the scene. What do you do first?
Firefighter:	First I see if there are any open windows anywhere.
Interviewer:	Why?
Firefighter:	The fire makes a vacuum. If the house is sealed and I open the door, I'm going to be toast. So if the house looks sealed, I look for a way to create a vent – break a window, tear a hole in the roof if I have to. Then I try to assess whether it's safe to enter.
Interviewer:	Then what?
Firefighter:	Once I'm inside I am immediately doing a search for people who might be inside. If it's nighttime I start by looking in bedrooms. Kids hide, so I look under beds and in closets. I'm always monitoring my equipment to make sure I have enough oxygen and that the fire isn't too hot.
Interviewer:	Then what?
Firefighter:	I am also looking for items that might explode, such as gas tanks or chemicals. If we see any of those items we evacuate immediately.
Firefighter:	After clearing the house of people the next step is to stop the fire from spreading to other structures and to put the fire out as safely as possible. Ideally the rest of my team is working on this while I'm inside so I join them when I can.
Interviewer:	Do you take breaks? How do you know when to take a break?
Firefighter:	Safety is very important; we all make sure to monitor our oxygen and maintain hydration. If we pass out we create more work for the rest of the team, and put ourselves in a potentially fatal situation.

From this interview, I might discern that an impulsive and hotheaded firefighter would create a dangerous situation for their entire team. I could follow up on this hunch by asking additional questions about **critical incidents** involving patience and logical thinking. A critical incident is an especially salient episode of good or bad performance that reveals an underlying assumption about what causes success or failure. You can solicit critical incidents by asking questions like: "Can you think of a time when a firefighter caused a mistake that was very costly? What was the situation and why do you think the firefighter was to blame?" Or, you could ask "What was the last time you remember a firefighter accomplishing something extraordinary? What qualities did the firefighter have that led to that success?" Or, "When you reflect on the last year, what event or action are you most proud of? What happened as a result of your action? What would have occurred if you hadn't taken that action?" Using critical incidents is a way of getting people to think about specific actions instead of offering vague generalities.

In this way, think about the specific questions you ask as part of a broader strategic choice: how can you phrase and order questions so that people respond with the most relevant and useful information related to the specific research questions you are asking?

Focus Groups

A **focus group** involves asking questions to multiple interviewees in a group where interviewees can react to one another. Focus groups have several advantages over one-on-one interviews. The first and most obvious advantage is that you can save time and avoid redundancy by allowing participants to hear each other's answers. Instead of asking 10 people the same question, you can ask it once and get 10 answers in quick succession. By allowing participants to hear each other, they may remember details they would have otherwise forgotten, which can lead to better, richer data.

A disadvantage to a focus group is that more introverted or less confident members of the group may be motivated to stay quiet if they believe that what they want to say has already been said or if they don't want others to hear what they think.

Composing a focus group might be a good idea if:

1. You want your participants to hear and build on each other's ideas
2. You think many people will have similar answers and you can save time by combining interviews
3. Some aspect of the question is controversial and you think the discussion will yield important insight.

A focus group might not be a good idea, though, if any of the following conditions are true:

1. The group is composed of people who have status and power differences, such as boss and subordinates, or a powerful ingroup and less-powerful outgroup.
2. The group is composed of two subgroups that have dramatically different backgrounds or perspectives on an issue (though you might not know this in advance – and it could lead to some useful insight if the group is able to discuss constructively without arguing).
3. The questions you want to ask are very straightforward and probably don't have nuances that are worth discussing in a group: for example, questions about what the official HR policies of a department are can be answered by one person.
4. The topics are sensitive or private enough that people will not want to share their perspective in front of others.

Artifact Analysis

In qualitative research, an **artifact** is any physical object related to a research participant that gives information about a psychological or cultural phenomenon of interest. A common reason to analyze artifacts is if you think people might not respond honestly to direct questioning. For example, someone wishing to understand smoking habits could count the number of cigarette butts left behind in various locations.

Another common motivation for artifact analysis is when you are interested in people who are not accessible for other methods, such as historical figures or public figures that you don't have personal access to. For example, Costanza and his colleagues (2016) wanted to study the cultures of highly successful organizations from the past century. Since many of those organizations no longer exist or have changed dramatically, he relied on magazine articles that were written about each company's founder. The articles, collected from *Forbes*, served as artifacts that he could use to discover clues about culture.

Observation

Broadly, **observation** refers to any method in which a researcher watches behaviors of interest as they naturally occur in some context and interprets what they observe. Direct in-person observation, also called **naturalistic observation**, is a common qualitative method. The benefit of observation is the assumption that the observer is minimally interfering with the phenomenon they wish to observe, and thus is capturing a more realistic picture of the phenomenon. For example, a researcher wishing to study crowd behavior at football games could easily do so by attending and observing the crowd at actual football games. A major challenge in naturalistic observation is finding a way to capture relevant details while remaining a natural part of the environment. A person taking notes on a tablet, looking at the audience and not the players, is not a normal part of a football audience. In a workplace, remaining unobtrusive while documenting worker behavior is much more challenging.

Video Observation

Especially in workplace observational studies, video capture is a common method for observing behavior without interfering. Analysis of video footage can be quantitative – like counting the number of times participants smile – or qualitative – like identifying broad emotional themes exhibited by participants. This kind of observation has become much more feasible due to the growing popularity of video recording technology in work settings. Many organizations use video cameras to monitor employees, and some occupations even require workers to wear body cameras on the job. Video footage from these sources can provide rich information about employee behavior, but not all video footage is of equal quality. LeBaron et al. (2018) provide a list of technical decisions that researchers must make when using video observations that can influence the quality of information obtainable from the eventual video:

1. How should you frame the shot?
2. Should you use more than one camera?
3. When should you turn the recording on and off?
4. Should you stay with the camera or leave the room?

A researcher's answers to these questions will depend on their research question. Studying worker behavior in a complex office environment with many rooms and cubicles might require more than one camera to capture human behavior from multiple perspectives. Perhaps several cameras will be set up around each room where worker interactions of interest might take place, or a researcher with a camera might simply stand in a particular location of importance during key times. It is important to note that a researcher's answers to these questions will influence the kind of data collected – workers may behave differently in the presence of camera-clad researchers than they would otherwise.

A major advantage of video observation is that videos can be saved for future reference and analysis. A researcher can slow, replay, or zoom in on a video to carefully analyze its contents. LeBaron et al. (2016) used video methods to study how physicians hand off patients at the change of their shifts. During recording, they chose to stay out of the hospital room, instead leaving their camera in the corner so as to not disrupt the workers. They then conducted interviews with the physicians they recorded. To analyze their data, they first watched the handoff footage to code for initial patterns of behavior. Then, they analyzed the interviews to identify themes. Finally, they reanalyzed the handoff footage based on the themes they observed in the interviews. Following this inductive approach, the researchers found that transitions from one handoff to the next were signaled through subtle shifts in eye gaze that might otherwise be overlooked with in-person observations.

For other explorations of video observation, see Mengis et al.'s (2018) examination of emergency room observation or Jarret and Liu's (2018) study of participants watching their own videos.

Internet Observation

Of all observational techniques, internet-based observation has become one of the most common. In internet observation, online behaviors in some authentic behavioral context are observed. A common type of internet observation occurs when researchers identify and collect information from target communities on online social media. For example, in an ethnographic field study, Salehi et al. (2015) examined online social media used by Amazon Mechanical Turk workers to understand their motivation related to collective action, in a similar fashion as earlier research on labor unions.

Thanks to the proliferation of written communication records from email, text, and chat, it is possible to learn about conversations and events in a highly naturalistic way. Imagine if I wanted to know how a particular conflict with your supervisor was resolved. Your memory of the event will be affected by all the usual factors inherent to self-report. But I can also find out about the resolution of the conflict by obtaining your emails and tracking the steps myself. As a researcher, however, I assume in doing so that 1) you have kept all the relevant emails and 2) that no in-person communication (or communication using a different medium or app) took place that was not recorded.

Thus, an advantage to internet observation versus other types of observation is that it is much easier for a researcher to avoid interfering with the existing community that they are studying. Unlike holding a camera in a union organization meeting, downloading text discussions from an online labor discussion is much less disruptive and may even be undetectable by members of that community. A disadvantage to internet observation is that the behaviors people engage in online may not accurately reflect their likely in-person behaviors.

Differences between people's online behavior and in-person behavior should be considered carefully, as relevant to target research questions.

Online and Offline Behavioral Traces

An emerging area of internet observation is the analysis of **digital traces** (also called **footprints**). Quantitative researchers have recently begun to harvest this kind of data to build complex predictive models in the realms of marketing, politics, health, education, and social science. Chapter 15 covers some of the issues that arise when we use digital footprints to understand behavior. For now, we simply note that this kind of data can also be described and analyzed qualitatively. For example, consider Figure 6.1.

The original data collection is quantitative: moment by moment, a measurement is taken of a person's eye position to calculate where they are looking on a webpage. The map is created by color-coding based on density: the brightest (and usually red, when in color) highlighted areas mean that a person looked at that area a lot. But, now, to interpret the data, a qualitative approach is needed. What does it *mean* that a person looked at the top left area of the page the most?

A lot of the more popular big data analyses, upon closer inspection, can also be described as qualitative in this way. For example, imagine that you wanted to study the relationship between well-being and the weather. To do so, you collect all the tweets that people post

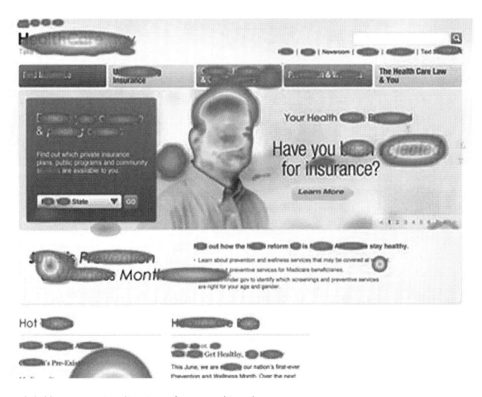

Figure 6.1 Heat map visualization of eye tracking data.

on sunny days and on cloudy days in their local area. You then generate a word cloud of the most common words on each kind of day.

Up until this point, the analysis is quantitative. Each word cloud is simply a visualization of quantitative data. Next, though, you compare the word clouds and interpret them for signs of emotional tone. Now you have shifted into an interpretative, qualitative framework, blending some of the advantages and disadvantages of qualitative and quantitative approaches. Mixed methods like this one are discussed in more detail in Chapter 15.

Other Types of Qualitative Research

Asking people for information is the oldest, and often the first, method a researcher thinks of. Given the many changes in technology over the past 20 years, though, there are plenty of creative ways to gather qualitative data that do not rely on asking people to provide their thoughts. When choosing one of these methods, you should first think very carefully about the following questions:

1. Is this the *best* way to get the information I want?
2. Am I being distracted by a potentially "cool" method and letting a better method slip by? This is a common distraction. Always remember: researchers are never cool. If you think your method is cool, it means you're probably doing something wrong.
3. Does this method of information-gathering actually tell me what I think it is telling me? This is a question of validity. The further away your information-gathering technique is from the actual phenomenon of interest, the more logical jumps you have to make to get from A to B, the more careful you have to be. Validity is discussed more in Chapter 7, but it is always something you have to think about, whether your approach is qualitative or quantitative.

Managing Bias

Empirical research of all types requires researchers to actively manage bias, although the techniques for doing so differ quite a bit across qualitative versus quantitative approaches. In the research design context, the term *bias* broadly refers to misrepresentation of true effects, contexts, or observations. In short, bias leads researchers to incorrect conclusions, whether the source of that bias is the researcher or the research participant. For example, in qualitative research, we generally want to avoid leading participants into responding in an unnatural way due to the way we ask questions or the way we impose ourselves upon their lives to observe them. We also want to avoid fooling ourselves by leaning towards interpretations that are favorable to interpretations we want, not because the data support them, but simply because we *want* the data to support them. It can be helpful to consider and label distinct sources of bias, as we do in the following, but it's also important to remember that this list is not exhaustive. Avoiding bias of any sort is something that must be considered carefully and completely at every stage of research design, execution, and interpretation.

Cognitive Biases

How many times did you browse a news website in the last year? What were you doing last Tuesday at 10 am? What was the last traffic sign you encountered?

I'm guessing that you are struggling to answer these questions. Maybe you can give an estimate for the first question. And maybe you can extrapolate for the second question, based on your typical morning routine. But your answers will still be estimates at best and guesses at worst. It is highly unlikely that you can give accurate answers for any of these questions. And there is a good reason for that, too. Our brains are built to optimize efficiency. There is no reason to record this sort of information, so we don't.

This means, though, that we are also susceptible to suggestion and reconstruction when it comes to memory. Such errors are types of **cognitive biases**. Because cognitive biases affect all humans, anyone can be affected by them, whether researcher or participant. There are dozens of cognitive biases; we will focus on just a few that are particularly common in qualitative research.

Anchoring Effects

Anchoring effects happen when we use information in the environment as a conceptual starting place for making a guess about something we don't know. Anchoring effects can create problems in focus groups and interviews in several ways. For example, the way a question is asked can act as an anchor. If I were doing marketing research, I could start by asking, "Does this office chair seem like it is worth more or less than $500?" and then ask "How much does it seem like it is worth?" You would use $500 as an anchor and set your price accordingly. Maybe you'd estimate it is worth $450. But if I asked first, "Does this chair seem like it is worth more or less than $1000?" You might set your subsequent estimate much higher – maybe $850.

Anchors don't have to be dollar values. For example, I might ask, "Do you read the news every day?" This sets "every day" as the baseline. If you read the news once a week, that now feels like a very infrequent habit. Subsequent conversation about your news habits will be affected by the baseline I inadvertently set.

The interviewer is only one source of anchoring. Other participants in a focus group can also act as anchors. The first person who speaks can set the tone and scope for other people's comments. Considering whether this is a concern for your research questions is very important and might be a good reason to choose interviews or observation instead of focus groups.

Expectation Bias

Expectation bias can best be summed up as "you see what you want to see." If I tell you that the following picture is a duck, you will see a duck.

But if I had told you it was a rabbit, you would have seen a rabbit. The truth is that the picture is ambiguous and can be "seen" in multiple ways. When you expect to see a duck, you see a duck. When you expect to see a rabbit, you see a rabbit. In both cases, the details that "make sense" will stand out to you, because your expectations bias your judgment.

Once you form an idea of what you expect to see, you may then seek out details that confirm your expectations, a related concept called **confirmation bias**. In the context of qualitative research, allowing your expectations to drive your decision-making can begin to drive the kinds of questions you ask. Confirmation bias is especially problematic when you begin to interpret data in favor of your pet theories and ignore or minimize the importance of contrary information. Be careful to let the data speak for themselves.

Figure 6.2 Expectation bias in action.

Bias in the Interview Context

Cognitive biases influence people in different ways in different contexts. There is no comprehensive list of the ways that bias influences how we act across all possible situations. Instead, you must learn potential sources of bias and actively monitor their potential effects. To illustrate how you might think about this in your own research, let's consider the interview context specifically.

Even worse than paying more attention to expected details, your expectations can create the details entirely. Imagine that you believe one of your participants should be angry about their unfair parental leave policies. You start by mentioning another company you visited recently. That company has 10 weeks of paid leave for all new parents. Isn't it unfair, you wonder, that this company has such a relatively stingy amount of leave? Your participants agree that the policy is unfair after hearing your description. They respond to our questions with increasing levels of frustration about not just the parental leave policy but other policies as well. You are pleased with your foresight and write a report that describes how the unfair policy leads to bitterness and resentment amongst the staff.

But, how much does that reflect reality? Did the staff feel bitterness before speaking with you? How likely is it that their performance at work was affected by this supposed bitterness? In this case, it is very likely that your leading questions, a consequence of your own confirmation bias, created a reality that did not exist previously.

Situations like this can be referred to as **self-fulfilling prophecies**. In essence, belief creates reality. Telling a young student that they are brilliant, and that you think they will become very successful, could cause them to work harder, making your initial beliefs become true. It is all too easy to allow the self fulfilling prophecy to affect your qualitative research. Every aspect of your interaction with the participant sends **signals** – subtle cues – about what you expect to be true. These signals can come from your questions, your body language, your tone of voice, or even your appearance itself. The same question means something different depending on whom it is coming from. And importantly, this occurs in reverse as well; the participants have expectations about what you will do and why, and you can find yourself in situations where your own questions are being led by what your participant wants to happen. In this way, researchers often create self-fulfilling prophecies when they only pay attention to information that supports their ideas, even if unintentionally.

Imagine Rachel, a upper-middle-class woman in her 40s from the midwest US, who grew up in a very conservative household. She has always believed that success in life is due to seizing the opportunities that life presents to you, working hard, and persisting through difficulties. She has become interested in the experiences of young job-seekers in Chicago, and has arranged to visit an unemployment office to interview some of the clients there.

She begins by interviewing Jesse, a 22-year old who has recently been laid off from a construction job. She first asks him, "How long have you been collecting unemployment checks?" The question strikes Jesse as a bit confrontational, but he replies, "Three months." Rachel follows up, wondering "Why haven't you found a job in that time? How many jobs have you applied to?" Jesse is now defensive and replies that he had been trying to find work, but there aren't any opportunities. Rachel records in her field notes that Jesse seems unmotivated. She asks him next, in an attempt to get him more excited, "What is your passion? What would be your dream job?" Jesse finds this question absurd; he would be happy with any job that paid well. Rachel notes that he "doesn't have clear goals."

Rachel's background and expectations affected her interaction with Jesse and also affected her interpretation of his responses. Any written product that comes out of this interview will be severely limited by the fact that Rachel's perspective distorted what she heard from Jesse. Unless Rachel is explicit about her own perspective, the reader will not be aware of this bias. But, for the reader to be aware of it, Rachel must be aware of her own **cultural biases**, and true self-awareness is a very difficult thing for *anyone* to achieve.

Mitigating Bias

As you have seen, there are many types of human biases, and we have only covered a few of the most prominent. As you conduct more qualitative research, be sure not to ever assume that you have fully managed your own biases. This is impossible. What you can and should do is continuously learn about bias, reflecting on how your opinions and behaviors might be or become biased. It is not uncommon for researchers to only realize, after years of research, the effects of biases they did not realize they had. This is normal; this is human. The important thing is to keep learning about yourself and actively trying to minimize those effects.

As a practical tool for reducing this kind of bias, consider job interviews. Although the research literatures on job interviews and research interviews are almost totally distinct, there are many commonalities related to bias mitigation. From the job interview literature, we know that **structure** is valuable in ensuring that various kinds of bias don't affect your conclusions about a candidate. For instance, imagine a hiring manager sitting down to interview Richard and Tara for the position of classroom assistant for a third grade teacher. He sees that Tara volunteers at her local public library. Richard happens to be from the same small town as the manager, and they went to the same high school! This is how each interview goes:

Tara's Interview:

Manager:	I see that you volunteer at the public library. Did you start that so you would have something to do when your kids were in school?
Tara:	No, I just love reading and wanted to share that with the community.
Manager:	Okay, okay, sorry, not trying to offend you. It's just unusual for someone your age to be entering the job market.
Tara:	What?

Manager: Don't get upset.
Richard's Interview:
Manager: I see that you are from Murphysville! Me too! Go Murphysville High! What year
               did you graduate?
Richard: Class of 07!
Manager: Oh, my wife is class of '07! Do you know her?
Richard: I think I do!
Manager: Small world! Great town, Murphysville. What was your sport? Basketball?
Richard: Yes, power forward!
Manager: Takes a lot of leadership skill and patience to play that position. Classroom assis-
               tants need those skills!

Structure in the interview questions could have eliminated some of what went wrong in these interviews. But structure might also limit the chance to discover something you weren't looking for. The logic of conducting interviews is that the back-and-forth dynamic allows the interviewer to pursue interesting surprises. If there is no room for improvisation because the interview is overly structured, the interview loses some of that power.

Planning a Qualitative Study

Sample Size

There isn't a single right answer to the question of sample size. If you are studying something exotic and weird, like psychology professors who fly airplanes on the weekends, you might have a very small population from which to draw participants. Also, if the population is very **homogeneous**, meaning people in the population are fairly similar to each other, you might not need a lot of participants to fully understand the phenomenon you care about. Ultimately, sampling for qualitative studies is a judgment call. A popular strategy is to continue adding participants to your sample until you stop hearing new things. At that point, you would say you have reached **saturation** – and you can stop.

No Really, What Should My Sample Size Be?

Especially for researchers coming from quantitative traditions, the lack of clear guidance on sample size for qualitative research projects can be frustrating. Instead of deciding ahead of time what sample will be necessary to meaningfully assess a difference or effect of interest, sample size in qualitative research is driven by the data themselves. You react to new data as you collect them by making decisions about the next step in your research based on what you have uncovered so far.

For example, you might initially approach a project thinking you will need just one focus group, only to discover that the phenomenon you're studying is far more complex than you initially thought, requiring you to increase your sample size by 10-fold. This active consideration and reaction to newly collected data is central to qualitative research and very much the point; if you stop collecting data before you reach the saturation point due to some expectation about sample size or time spent or whatever

---

other factor, you have sacrificed the very richness and depth that qualitative research is designed to uncover. Exploring richness and depth is why you chose qualitative research to begin with. Don't forget that.

Writing Good Questions

Questions absolutely drive answers. If you ask good questions, you will learn something new about your participants. If you ask bad questions, you risk offending or confusing your participants, wasting their time and yours. It is also likely that you will elicit "information" that is problematic: biased, vague, incomplete, off-topic, or all of these.

Before we look at how to write good questions, let's look at some bad ones and think about why they are bad.

1. Hi. I'm Tara. I'm doing a study about meso-micro-mediational dynamics at work. Have you experienced any of those?
2. Your boss told me that you are a bad performer. Why is that?
3. Isn't it frustrating that nobody around here ever gets a raise?

These questions are unlikely to get you anywhere. Instead, try to revise them so they follow the principles in the following:

1. Be simple. Ask one question at a time.
2. Use appropriate language. Avoid jargon . . . if jargon must be used, define it clearly.
3. Allow for honest responses. Avoid leading questions.
4. Allow for complete responses. Do not ask a lot of "yes or no" questions.
5. Frame questions in a way that allows respondents to provide full information. For example, you could start a question with "how" instead of "why" to learn about a person's thought processes . . . for example, "how did you decide to leave the organization?" instead of "why did you leave the organization?" Asking "why" can make a participant feel like they need to justify themselves and their actions.
6. Use follow-up questions, or probes, to encourage participants to elaborate on their responses.
7. Think about flow. Decide which questions naturally come first. Start with a warm-up question to build rapport. Put difficult or embarrassing questions near the end, after rapport is established. End with a question that provides closure.

If we use these principles to revise my example questions, we might end up with a script that looks like:

1. Hi, I'm Tara. Thanks for speaking with me today. I want to spend the next 30 minutes or so chatting about your experiences at work. Do you have any questions before I get started?
2. My first question is about your experience at Target. What is your job title? [probe: has your job title changed over time? How have your responsibilities shifted during that time?]
3. Next I'd like to learn more about your manager. How would you characterize their leadership style?

4. Does your manager express appreciation for good performance? [probe: how?]
5. Does your manager address incidences of poor performance? [probe: how?]
6. How is pay determined? How do you feel about the way pay is determined?
7. I'm curious about whether there are things you wish your manager would do differently.
8. This has been a very informative conversation! I appreciate your time. Last I want to ask whether there are other important features of your relationship with your manager that I didn't ask about.
9. Here is my contact information in case you would like to follow up. Thanks again.

Interview questions share some similarities with survey items in that they should be clear, simple, grammatically correct, and easily understood by respondents. For a more detailed list of survey item writing guidelines, see Chapter 9. Interview questions are different from survey items, though, in that you don't always know what kind of responses to expect, and you need to structure the questions in a way that allows for the unexpected.

Creating a Script

In addition to the questions themselves, you need to create an environment that will be conducive to getting useful information. It helps to write out a script to set the tone, set expectations, and collect informed consent from participants before you begin. An example focus group script that could be modified for an individual interview follows.

1. Hi everyone. Thank you for spending this time with us. We expect this session to take about 50 minutes. My name is Tara, and I'm a researcher at George Washington University. I'm here speaking with groups of people to learn more about their experiences at work.
2. I have a set of seven questions, but I don't mind if the conversation takes a different turn. I'll pose each question to the group and ask follow-up questions as needed.
3. I'm hoping to hear from everyone today. I won't call on anyone, but I do hope that everyone will share. You don't have to answer every question, of course.
4. Before we start I want to make sure to emphasize that I won't be sharing individual responses with anyone outside my research group. I won't use quotes that can be traced back to you. It is also very important that you treat what is said in here as confidential and do not discuss it with others outside this room.
5. Finally, please respect each other. Disagreement is great but it's important not to attack each other or discount what they say. Each of you has a different experience which is why you're all here together. Opinions will differ – this isn't a competition to be right.
6. I've passed out a consent form; please read it over carefully and sign if you agree to the terms. If you'd rather not participate you are welcome to leave at this point.
7. Does anyone have any questions before we begin?

Structuring the Interaction

A straightforward question-and-answer session is one option for participant interactions. Given the limits discussed previously, though, you might wish to impose additional structure on the interaction to elicit higher quality information. We'll explore two common structures: the Q-sort method and the Delphi technique.

Q-Sort Method

The **Q-sort method**, sometimes called **Q-methodology**, has been called a "systematic study of subjectivity" (Brown, 1993). It asks participants to rank-order opinion statements, called a **Q set** or **Q sample**, about some topic by placing those opinions on a continuum, such as between those they believe least important and those they believe most important. This sorting is done using a pyramid-shaped visual aid called a **Q grid** and was historically completed by asking a participant to place a college of small paper cards, roughly the size of a credit card, into appropriate locations on the Q grid. Once all participants have completed their grids, factor analytic methods are then used to identify participant clusters, and those clusters are then interpreted. These days, Q-sorts are frequently completed online. Q grids can be both created and the results analyzed using the R package *qmethod* (Zabala, 2014).

An example of a Q-sort with a 16-item Q set appears in Figure 6.3, which comes from a study by Cable and Judge (1997) who assessed the desirability of organizations using Q-methodology. Respondents were asked to place characteristics into the Q grid based on their beliefs about the characteristics of their dream organization. Characteristics in a column are considered tied, and the pyramid shape is chosen to approximate a normal distribution.

Delphi Studies

A **Delphi study** is one of the oldest techniques for qualitative research. It is designed to allow each participant's voice to contribute to the discussion and prevent a single powerful voice

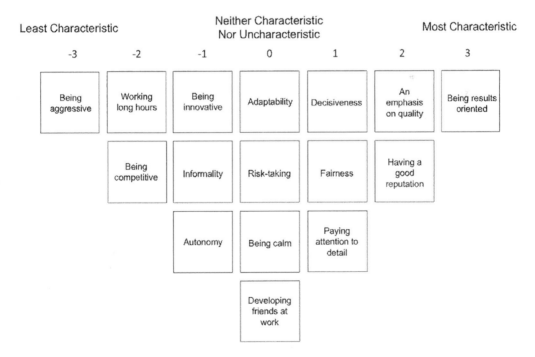

Figure 6.3 Q grid from Cable and Judge (1997).

or perspective from dominating conclusions. It's very easy for this to happen in organizations when there are power differentials between members of a focus group, for example.

A Delphi study proceeds in three stages.

1. In stage 1, a group of participants answers a set of survey questions individually and submits their answers anonymously.
2. In stage 2, the facilitator shares the collected information back to the group and leads a discussion about how and why answers may be different from one another.
3. In stage 3, the participants complete the questions a second time, but this time they have the benefit of hearing the group discussion and may end up changing their answers.

At the end, the goal is to have a set of answers to the questions that have converged with each other to capture something closer to the "truth." Because the goal is convergence, Delphi studies don't make much sense when your goal is to understand individual perspectives. But for measuring organizational culture, for example, this technique can be very useful.

Transcribing Recordings

If the data you've collected include voice recordings or other audio, you'll need to transform those to writing before analysis. The two primary approaches to doing so are manually (with a foot pedal) or automatically (with a cloud-based software program or service). Each approach has pros and cons: Transcription decisions will ultimately depend on the nature of your research – is it ethical to send recordings off to a cloud-based service? How many hours worth of recordings do you have? Languages/accents/jargon? Multiple speakers? Audio quality? How important is accuracy?

In **manual transcription**, a person transcribes using a keyboard. Since few people can type as fast as people speak, additional equipment is needed to pause or slow down recordings. Many popular foot pedals exist from companies including Olympus and Philips.

- Pros

    - Quicker, easier than transcribing by hand
    - Can keep recordings within the research team (fewer privacy concerns)
    - Fewer IRB clearances required

- Cons

    - Time consuming to set up and transcribe (especially when there is jargon, audio quality issues, multiple speakers)
    - High-effort on part of researcher
    - Compatibility issues: must make sure foot pedal works with software

If you don't want to do manual transcription, you can hire a service. Most charge by the minute/hour or by the number of pages transcribed. Many will transcribe recordings with multiple speakers. You will receive the word/text file relatively quickly (e.g., within hours). Many include timestamps and verbatim records (so you can decide whether you want to exclude or capture filler words like "um"). Transcription services may be AI based (Temi, Otter, Trint) or human/transcriptionist based (Rev, GoTranscript, Scribie).

- Pros

  - Quick
  - Low-effort on part of researcher
  - Many services can account for jargon, audio quality issues, multiple speakers

- Cons

  - Expensive – most charge by page or minute
  - Additional IRB clearances required
  - Accuracy (depends on service . . . often lower for AI based than transcriptionist based)

Analyzing Qualitative Data

Many helpful tools and resources exist to help you process the data you collect from a qualitative inquiry. There are also many approaches to analysis, and each makes its own set of assumptions about the world. The bottom line in choosing an analytic approach is that the right kind of analysis depends on *the research question and the kind of data* you have. Sure, "natural language processing" sounds cool. And it is. But it might not get you where you need to go if you really wanted to build grounded theory.

For traditional text analysis techniques explained from the perspective of I-O world, check out the following article, which includes links to a public domain application written in R: Banks, G. C., Woznyj, H. M., Wesslen, R. S., & Ross, R. L. (2018). A review of best practice recommendations for text analysis in R (and a user-friendly app). *Journal of Business and Psychology, 33,* 445–459. https://doi.org/10.1007/s10869-017-9528-3

Thematic Analysis

Thematic analysis is best for building grounded theory. This means you probably have a deep knowledge of the subject domain and you are hoping to add richness and interpretation. You want to describe sensemaking and everyday experience through the eyes of the people experiencing it. Your data, then, probably takes the form of interviews and observation notes.

Here's a snippet of interview we can use to start:

A: Why did you decide to start looking for a job?

B: I was feeling unappreciated, I guess. My boss was always ignoring me. I was the top performer but I felt like I had to announce it or nobody would notice.

A: Did you try raising these concerns with your boss?

B: I wanted to but I didn't know how – it seemed like being arrogant or bragging.

A: What happened after you started looking for a new job?

B: Well at first it was scary. I didn't know how to do it. But the more I sent out my resume and the more people started calling me back, the more I realized that my current job was a bad fit and I needed to go.

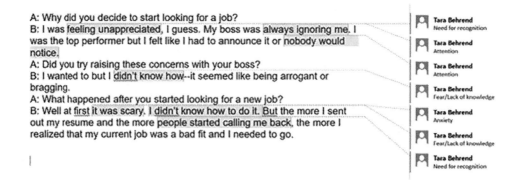

Figure 6.4 Open coding of research data.

The first step in a thematic analysis is **open coding**. Here, you scan the transcript for themes and mark them, using a software program or even in Microsoft Word (software options are discussed in the following). I might mark the snippet as shown in Figure 6.4.

The second step is to collect the codes and try to organize them further; this process is called **axial coding**. From the snippet in Figure 6.4, you can see the following codes: Need for recognition, attention, fear, lack of knowledge, and anxiety. Roughly, I could organize these codes into Negative Emotions and Need for Attention. I might want to add subcategories, or not, depending on how specific I want to be. I could then go back through the transcript and recode using my new coding scheme.

Ultimately the process of open coding and axial coding require many, many judgment calls. You might look at this snippet and see it as a story about an anxious, needy person who is unhappy at work. I might see it as a story of bad leadership letting a good employee's talents go to waste. We could each find justification for our view in the language of the transcript. Does this mean that thematic analysis is untrustworthy? No, but it does mean that the need for transparency is very high, so other researchers can observe the decisions you made and decide for themselves whether those decisions affected the conclusions.

What about content analysis?

Content analysis is a term that can be applied to many types of procedures. In qualitative research, it could be as simple as "a researcher read some text and decided what they thought it meant." In a machine learning context, content analysis refers to text analysis methods that seek to determine the presence of certain words, themes, or concepts. This method is used to quantify and analyze the presence, meanings and relationships of certain words, themes, or concepts. Content analysis can also refer to simple descriptive analyses such as word clouds or counts of particular key words. We have attempted to avoid the term given its ambiguous meaning. In practice, if you use some kind of content analysis, you should always explain what you mean by the term by presenting it within a more well-defined qualitative methods framework, such as grounded theory.

Natural Language Processing (Artificial Intelligence)

You have probably heard somebody talk about **natural language processing** (NLP), artificial intelligence, and/or machine learning at some point recently. In the context of qualitative data analysis, NLP refers to computer automated methods that analyze text data to help researchers understand how language is being used. We can offer the organization of text analytic techniques in Figure 6.4, and Table 6.1 as a great place to start. Importantly, as suggested by Figure 6.4, these newer techniques are best understood as evolutions of existing tools with greater power and precision, and not as altogether new techniques.

The goal and many of the challenges remain the same. In all cases, the purpose of text analysis is to extract meaning from unstructured text and create meaning. The challenge is human judgment; even the most advanced NLP techniques still require human interpretation at several points in their application.

The term NLP really refers to an entire family of analytic techniques used to interpret and meaningfully act upon text data. It is mostly directly the subject of research in the field of **computational linguistics**, an interdisciplinary domain combining perspectives from linguistics (part of the humanities) and computer science (a formal science). As such, understanding NLP requires blending expertise from these very different fields. NLP can also be combined with machine learning practices to categorize text or make predictions of criteria using text. For I-O, NLP is most commonly used to convert unstructured text into meaningful predictors for use in regression-family machine learning, such as to predict job performance from resumes or interviews.

NLP in its simplest form, called **bag-of-words tokenization**, is quite easy to understand even without a background in these fields. Bag-of-words modeling involves the conversion of text into **tokens**, often in the form of **word counts**, which are then used in subsequent

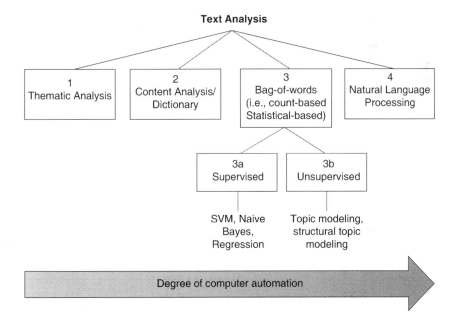

Figure 6.5 Overview of text analysis strategies, from Banks et al. (2018).

Table 6.1 Text analysis strategies in detail, from Banks et al. (2018)

	Thematic Analysis	Content Analysis/ Dictionary Analyses	Bag-of-Words (Count-Based)	Supervised Models (e.g., SVM, Naive Bayes, Logistic Regression)	Unsupervised Models (e.g., k-Means Clustering, Topic Models)	Natural Language Processing
Description	An iterative process where researchers develop a series of codes and categories based on operational definitions	Creates word/ phrase frequency counts of text	A group of techniques that are used to reduce and simplify text; ignores word order, which allows for statistical properties	Researcher knows input and output; system creates an algorithm to map the connection between the two variables	Clusters/factors/ topics are automatically and empirically created	Models how humans understand and process language (e.g., sentiment analysis, part-of-speech tagging, translation); word order is important
Strengths	Uses participants' own words or constructs from the extant literature; provides insight into phenomena that are not well understood	Allows for testing of quantitative research questions	Simple, statistical properties, scalable	Allows for a priori specifications; can produce marginal effects (e.g., rank words by most likely to predict outcome)	Facilitates the analysis of large amounts of data without manual annotations (labels or dictionaries)	Computer automated; attempt to analyze semantic meaning
Weaknesses	Time and labor intensive, particularly with large amounts of data; subject to researcher biases and errors; does not allow for theory testing	Requires subject matter expert validation when using a priori word lists	Omits word order leading to poor semantic meaning	Requires substantial preexisting knowledge; Potential overfitting due to many factors (words)	Require interpretation; tuning parameters;	Many tasks have high error rates; low level programming (Java, Python); some tasks are "black boxes"
Commonly Used Disciplines	Communication studies; sociology, management	Management		Computer science; political science	Computer science; political science	Computer science; marketing; psychology
Most Common Software	None; NVivo; ATLAS.ti	LIWC; DICTION; NVivo; ATLAS.ti		R. Scikit-Learn in Python	Java (Mallet). SAS; Python (gensim), R (topicmodels, stm)	Java; Python (nltk)

Table 6.2 Bag of words tokenization of "2. I think I have constructed a new measure of a research methods construct"

2.	I	think	have	constructed	a	new	measure	of	research	methods	construct
1	2	1	1	1		2	1	1	1	1	1

analyses. For example, the expression "2. I think I have constructed a new measure of a research methods construct." could be converted into what you see in Table 6.2.

The variables created this way can then be used as predictors in a predictive model, such as regression or a machine learning algorithm, using each word count as a distinct feature. If you think this seems a little too simple to possibly capture all the subtleties of language, you are absolutely correct. NLP research on bag-of-words tokenization mostly concerns how to engineer more useful features for any machine learning algorithms that use this token matrix as input. This precise form of NLP, where every unique word becomes tokenized, should only be considered the basis for more advanced, more accurate forms.

To illustrate the complexities, consider these issues:

- There's a lot of research that in English and similar languages, some words reflect the content of your speech whereas others are more functional. Functional words have been shown to generally not reflect a person's opinions or state of mind – they instead serve as a tool to make a sentence grammatically correct by formally relating concepts to one another. In Table 6.2, I, have, a, and of are all functional words. In bag-of-words tokenization, functional words are often deleted, because they won't likely contribute meaningful covariance with criteria and essentially just add noise to modeling.
- In the table, constructed and construct are considered different tokens. But these two words share the same **lemma**, sometimes referred to as the **dictionary form** of the word. Both are variations on "construct." Thus, **lemmatization** is often used to convert all words to their lemmas before tokenizing. In this example, both would become "construct." A related technique called **stemming** simply cuts the endings off words, but this is a less accurate (although much faster) version of lemmatization.
- Even after changing to lemmas, you might reason that the way that the "construct" token is being used is very different between uses. If you have this worry, you might use **part-of-speech tagging**, in which lemmas are marked with their part of speech, such as noun, verb, adjective, and adverb.
- The phrase "research methods" is uniquely meaningful in a way that its two component words don't express. Treating these two words together, they can be tokenized as a **bigram**, meaning both words together are used as a single feature. **Trigrams** can be created for word phrases with three component parts, and both bigrams and trigrams are more specific cases of **n-grams**.
- It's probably not meaningful to include the "2." and the dash, despite them being written by the person who created the text. This kind of information is frequently deleted before tokenization, including numbers, punctuation, and symbols. A unique problem in the digital age but common to social media data is what to do with emoji – should they be tokenized or deleted?

These changes are referred to as **preprocessing**, because they involve making changes to the original text to be used as the basis for creating tokens. After pre-processing with the steps described previously, tokenization might create the dataset in Table 6.3.

Table 6.3 Bag of words tokenization of "2. I think I have constructed a new measure of a research methods construct" after some preprocessing

think	*construct (verb)*	*new*	*measure*	*research*	*methods*	*research methods*	*construct (noun)*
1	1	1	1	1	1	1	1

This is a very different dataset! It only loosely resembles the one we started with in Table 6.2. Recall also that this would only be a single sentence within a much larger source; NLP projects can create tens of thousands of features, and these preprocessing decisions apply across the entirety of your dataset. Any minor decision can have massive impact.

All of this is to say that NLP shares many of the same strengths and weaknesses as trace data research when you intend to use regression-family techniques or machine learning for analysis. Project success is dependent on the specific engineering process used and researcher skill in creating, testing, and refining that process. A model is only as informative as the engineering process used to create it.

NLP also brings many unique challenges:

1. Almost all decisions should be informed by past research but decided based upon iterative development processes in your unique project. These decisions can dramatically affect your success, so it's critical to engage in transparent reporting (a concept we will revisit in our discussion of sharing results in Chapter 14).
2. Each language must be modelled separately, and there are no generally accepted methods for meaningfully interpreting data across languages.
3. There are no generally accepted preprocessing rules.
4. There are no generally accepted machine learning models to be used with NLP.
5. There are *many* more approaches to NLP, some of which only vaguely resemble bag-of-words tokenization. These may be more useful and valuable for your particular project. For example, a common approach is **sentiment analysis**, which involves the re-coding of tokens into scores reflecting their emotional content. Such scores may be even more valuable for predicting criteria than the tokens themselves.

Despite these challenges and complexities, NLP has been used successfully, although infrequently, in I-O research. For example, Campion et al. (2016) used the NLP tools in the statistical software SPSS to score applicant resumes with some success. Although they relied upon SPSS, which likely involved some unknown degree of non-optimal preprocessing and other feature engineering steps, they were still able to generally predict human ratings with convergent correlations in the .60s. Further, Speer (2018) found positive correlations between sentiment scores developed from narrative performance appraisals and numeric ratings.

We believe that these studies signify only the very beginning of significant value to be found for NLP across domains within I-O. However, as with trace data, we urge caution in their interpretation. Modern algorithms, no matter how sophisticated, cannot accurately simulate human understanding of text. They can only mimic it. Fortunately, mimicking it appears to be sufficient to investigate many interesting research questions, but we should never forget that NLP has such limits.

How Can We Know a Word's "Emotional Content"?

Sentiment analysis is one of the most popular NLP techniques due to a combination of features that make it attractive to researchers. Most critically, unlike many forms of NLP, it does not require large samples. It is able to do this because it relies upon **dictionaries**, which are datasets containing lists of lemmas or stems and scores representing their emotional content. Dictionaries can be developed in many ways, but consider this approach as prototypical:

1. A researcher collects a dataset that requires NLP for the analyses they want to run.
2. The researcher extracts a list of all common lemmas or stems from that dataset.
3. The researcher creates a one-question questionnaire on Mechanical Turk: "To what degree does this word seem angry?" on a scale from Not at All Angry to Extremely Angry.
4. The researcher collects enough ratings of all of these lemmas to get sufficiently stable estimates of the angriness of each word.
5. The researcher goes back to their original dataset, replaces each lemma with its angriness value, and then calculates the average angriness for each case in the dataset.

The use of pre-existing dictionaries makes this process even simpler, as it doesn't even require the researcher to collect their own emotion data. One of the most popular approaches for doing this currently is a system called **Linguistic Inquiry and Word Count (LIWC)**, an approach initially developed by Pennebaker et al. (2001). Although newer versions of LIWC incorporate machine learning to create predicted trait scores for a subset of LIWC traits, the core of LIWC remains the same: calculating word counts using dictionaries. Whether LIWC or other sentiment scores can accurately reflect a person's standing on the traits or even the emotional states it claims remains a matter of debate.

References

Banks, G. C., Woznyj, H. M., Wesslen, R. S., & Ross, R. L. (2018). A review of best practice recommendations for text analysis in R (and a user-friendly app). *Journal of Business and Psychology, 33*, 445–459. https://doi.org/10.1007/s10869-017-9528-3

Brown, S. R. (1993). www.researchgate.net/profile/Steven-R-Brown/publication/244998835_A_Primer_on_Q_Methodology/links/54749d440cf2778985abeb8e/A-Primer-on-Q-Methodology.pdf

Cable, D. M., & Judge, T. A. (1997). Interviewers' perceptions of person-organization fit and organizational selection decisions. *Journal of Applied Psychology, 82*, 546–581.

Campion, M. C., Campion, M. A., Campion, E. D., & Reider, M. H. (2016). Initial investigation into computer scoring of candidate essays for personnel selection. *Journal of Applied Psychology, 101*(7), 958.

Costanza, D. P., Blacksmith, N., Coats, M. R., Severt, J. B., & DeCostanza, A. H. (2016). The effect of adaptive organizational culture on long-term survival. *Journal of Business and Psychology, 31*(3), 361–381.

Jarrett, M., & Liu, F. (2018). "Zooming with": A participatory approach to the use of video ethnography in organizational studies. *Organizational Research Methods, 21*(2), 366–385.

LeBaron, C., Christianson, M. K., Garrett, L., & Ilan, R. (2016). Coordinating flexible performance during everyday work: An ethnomethodological study of handoff routines. *Organization Science, 27*(3), 514–534.

LeBaron, C., Jarzabkowski, P., Pratt, M. G., & Fetzer, G. (2018). An introduction to video methods in organizational research. *Organizational Research Methods, 21*(2), 239–260.

Mengis, J., Nicolini, D., & Gorli, M. (2018). The video production of space: How different recording practices matter. *Organizational Research Methods, 21*(2), 288–315.

Pennebaker, J. W., Francis, M. E., & Booth, R. J. (2001). *Linguistic inquiry and word count: LIWC 2001.* Lawrence Erlbaum Associates.

Salehi, N., Irani, L. C., Bernstein, M. S., Alkhatib, A., Ogbe, E., Milland, K., & Clickhappier. (2015, April). We are dynamo: Overcoming stalling and friction in collective action for crowd workers. In *Proceedings of the 33rd annual ACM conference on human factors in computing systems* (pp. 1621–1630).

Speer, A. B. (2018). Quantifying with words: An investigation of the validity of narrative-derived performance scores. *Personnel Psychology, 71*(3), 299–333.

Zabala, A. (2014). Qmethod: A package to explore human perspectives using Q Methodology. *The R Journal, 6*(2). https://doi.org/10.32614/RJ-2014-032

Further Reading

Banks, G. C., Woznyj, H. M., Wesslen, R. S., & Ross, R. L. (2018). A review of best practice recommendations for text analysis in R (and a user-friendly app). *Journal of Business and Psychology, 33,* 445–459. https://doi.org/10.1007/s10869-017-9528-3

• Banks and colleagues provide an overview of common text analysis techniques and explain how they can be used in I-O psychology. They also provide an open source interactive topic modeling tool to help extract meaningful topics from unstructured text.

Hickman, L., Thapa, S., Tay, L., Cao, M., & Srinivasan, P. (2020). Text preprocessing for text mining in organizational research: Review and recommendations. *Organizational Research Methods, 25,* 1094428120971683. https://doi.org/10.1177/1094428120971683

• Hickman and colleagues review organizational text mining research to provide recommendations that account for the type of text mining conducted, the research question being investigated, and the data set's characteristics. Hickman and colleagues provide recommendations with the aim of promoting transparency and reproducibility of research using text mining.

Short, J. C., McKenny, A. F., & Reid, S. W. (2018). More than words? Computer-aided text analysis in organizational behavior and psychology research. *Annual Review of Organizational Psychology and Organizational Behavior, 5,* 415–435. https://doi.org/10.1146/annurev-orgpsych-032117-104622

• Short and colleagues review recent advancements in computer-aided text analysis, focusing on how this technique can build knowledge in the fields of organizational psychology and organization behavior, including a review of specific software.

Ray, J. L., & Smith, A. D. (2012). Using photographs to research organizations: Evidence, considerations, and application in a field study. *Organizational Research Methods, 15*(2), 288–315. https://doi.org/10.1177/1094428111431110

• Ray and Smith present photographs as valuable artifacts for research within the organizational sciences, with several benefits such as capturing change processes over time and incorporating diverse voices within organizations. They discuss how the use of photographs in one of their studies influenced research design and the conclusions they ultimately drew.

Peticca-Harris, A., deGama, N., & Elias, S. R. (2016). A dynamic process model for finding informants and gaining access in qualitative research. *Organizational Research Methods, 19*(3), 376–401. https://doi.org/10.1177/1094428116629218

• Peticca-Harris and colleagues explore the challenges of trying to gain access to quality informants in qualitative research, with a particular focus on four elements: study formulation with plans to move forward, identifying potential informants, contacting informants, and interacting with informants during data collection.

LeBaron, C., Jarzabkowski, P., Pratt, M. G., & Fetzer, G. (2018). An introduction to video methods in organizational research. *Organizational Research Methods*, *21*(2), 239–260. https://doi.org/10.1177/1094428117745649

- LeBaron and colleagues present videos as valuable artifacts with the potential to replace other approaches, such as observational studies, interviews, and surveys. They present a variety of questions researchers must answer when using video methods, with a particular focus on the ontological assumptions that researchers may bring to their research design.

Boren, T., & Ramey, J. (2000). Thinking aloud: Reconciling theory and practice. *IEEE Transactions on Professional Communication*, *43*(3), 261–278. http://dx.doi.org/10.1109/47.867942

- Boren and Ramey review the think aloud protocol, a common method for collecting data about cognition and affect that is not normally verbalized and which participants may not even realize they engage in when asked retrospectively.

Questions to Think About

1. How should you decide which qualitative methods to use in your own research?
2. List the strengths and weaknesses of interviews and focus groups.
3. Pick one of the biases discussed in this chapter, provide an example of it in the context of your own research interests, and describe methods of alleviating it.
4. Describe a situation in which foot pedal transcription is ideal, then describe another situation in which cloud-based transcription is ideal.
5. Compare and contrast the following qualitative data analysis techniques: content analysis, bag of words, and natural language processing.
6. You and a group of colleagues want to learn more about the experiences of workers in family-run businesses. Develop a research question on this topic, choose methods of qualitative data collection, and describe how you would analyze this data. How can you report your findings in a transparent way?

Key Terms

- focus group
- homogeneous
- interview
- leading question
- lemma
- lemmatization
- Linguistic Inquiry and Word Count (LIWC)
- manual transcription
- n-gram
- natural language processing
- naturalistic observation
- observation
- part-of-speech tagging
- preprocessing
- probing

- Q-grid
- Q-methodology
- Q-sample
- Q-set
- Q-sort method
- saturation
- self-fulfilling prophecy
- sentiment analysis
- signals
- stemming
- structure
- token
- trigram
- word counts

Part III

Quantitative Methods

Chapter 7

Measuring Psychological Constructs

Learning Objectives

After reading this chapter, you will be able to:

1. Explain how I-O psychologists quantify abstract concepts.
2. Determine when to use various measures of reliability and construct validity.
3. Describe the three major components of the classical test theory equation.
4. Contrast classical test theory and modern test theory approaches to measurement.
5. Interpret item characteristic curves (ICCs), item information curves (IICs), and test information curves (TICs).

Courtesy xkcd.com.

A famous quote attributed to famed British mathematician Lord Kelvin claimed that,

> When you can measure what you are speaking about, and express it in numbers, you know something about it; when you cannot measure it, when you cannot express it in numbers, your knowledge is of a meager and unsatisfactory kind; it may be the beginning of knowledge, but you have scarcely, in your thoughts, advanced to the stage of science.

This is the essence of measurement, a concept deeply embedded in quantitative methods. This word refers to the application of numbers to some idea in order to speak about that idea in terms of precise quantity. If something exists, it must exist in some amount. And that amount must be describable using some kind of number. Numbers are useful for comparing observations to each other, for describing changes, for predicting the future . . . for all kinds of things we want to do as scientists. Without numbers, our knowledge is meager and unsatisfactory. This idea is a bit controversial to some – the very idea that we can measure

DOI: 10.4324/9781315167473-10

psychological traits with numbers is bizarre to some members of the public. They reject the idea that they can be "summed up by a number." You may have expressed this sentiment yourself when receiving unfavorable news about how you scored on a test. "My test score doesn't represent what I know! That test didn't do a good job reflecting my knowledge!" you might have said. If so, you were making a claim about the quality of that test as a measure of your knowledge.

If measurement is simply the use of a number to quantify an idea, there are many potential ways to measure something. A **measure** could be a test, or survey, or interview, or another tool. When we use methods like these to measure psychological characteristics in a trustworthy way, we are using practices from a discipline crossing psychology with statistics called **psychometrics**.

In the remainder of this chapter, we will lay out the conceptual foundations of psychometrics by exploring common conceptual frameworks used to understand the measurement of psychological characteristics. We must do this because the limitations and assumptions of those frameworks dictate what specific kinds of evidence are needed to reasonably argue that a particular measure is a "good" measure. If we don't agree on a framework first, we'll never agree on the quality of a particular measure. In fact, we might not even agree that the characteristic we are trying to measure exists in the first place!

Quantifying Abstract Concepts

I-O psychologists refer to abstract human characteristics as constructs. Constructs in psychology are qualities of a human that we wish to describe yet are not directly observable with our five human senses. Instead, we must "construct" them by making inferences about whether the quality exists from other information that we can observe. Put another way, we claim constructs exist by observing the consequences of those constructs and making logical conclusions about the connection between what we observe and what we believe exists. Intelligence is an example of a construct. You can't see or smell intelligence. But, by observing a person's behavior, particularly behaviors that you believe were caused by their intelligence, you can draw conclusions about how intelligent they probably are. You can listen to their speech, see the number of books in their office, feel the leather on their elbow patches, and conclude that you are dealing with an intelligent person. The correctness of your inferences is subject to scrutiny, of course; elbow patches don't make you smarter (despite what many professors seem to think). The number of books in a person's office is a function of many other factors besides intelligence. So, the inference that a person has greater intelligence because they have many books is probably faulty. Thinking about *the quality of the inferences we make* about constructs is the essence of measurement. Good measurement means that we are making good inferences about latent constructs.

This example about intelligence captures many of the pervasive challenges we deal with when it comes to measuring abstract concepts. We want to do measurement so we can make inferences about a person's traits and characteristics. Why? Because we want to predict, explain, and change their behavior based on those traits and characteristics. But I-O psychologists struggle in our pursuit of good measurement because:

1. No single approach to measurement is universally accepted.

Psychologists might use the same word to refer to very different ideas, and then they might use different words to refer to the same idea. Harold Kelley, a social psychologist, called this problem the **jingle-jangle fallacy**. As it applies to measurement, the jingle-jangle problem means that studying a concept like intelligence is difficult because not everyone agrees about what is meant by the word "intelligence" and that we cannot generally come to 100% consensus in theory development. These differences can happen because language is imprecise – we call our appliances "smart" when they can automate various decisions for us, and we also call people "smart" when they know lots of facts. Neither of these uses is really aligned with the scientific way that most researchers discuss intelligence.

When two construct labels sound the same, they **jingle**, and people may incorrectly assume they must be the same construct just because they have similar names. When two construct labels sound different, they **jangle**, and people may incorrectly assume they must be different constructs just because they have different names. Neither is necessarily true; it's the construct itself that matters and not its label.

In addition to the imprecise language problem, there are also incentives for researchers to make up new terms when they embark on a new line of research. Nobody will become famous for being the 10,000th researcher to study conscientiousness. But if I can make up a new term, and use this word to describe conscientiousness, then I can build a reputation as the first person to study this new thing. This incentive in the way that academic researchers are rewarded leads to a lot of unnecessary jangling, which has only become worse since Kelley first described it.

Every area within I-O deals with this issue. For example, the term *learning agility* has recently become popular in practice circles. Learning agility has been defined as a person's ability to learn new things to adapt to new circumstances and handle complex situations. At first glance, this sounds like a useful construct. It can be hard to know, though, whether learning agility should be treated as something other than intelligence without good measurement. Most definitions of intelligence would cover the ideas that are supposed to be part of learning agility; in other words, the theories do not appear to be distinct even if the labels jangle. When a researcher can become rich and famous (literally) by inventing a new word for something, the incentives for good measurement are misaligned.

2. Our measurements are based on limited samples of behavior.

As will be discussed in Chapter 4, we can think of the process of measurement as one of taking *samples* of behavior in order to make inferences about the *population* of behavior, using small groups of things to draw conclusions about those things in general. Any sample we collect is limited and flawed. Measurement as a sample of behavior is true even when the "behavior" is responding to items on a **questionnaire**. It is reasonable to ask whether that sample is of sufficient breadth and scope to describe the person's behavior in other contexts. Like any sample, it must be both big and representative enough to support valid inferences.

New technologies make it possible to take much larger samples of behavior – for instance, I can track a person's web activity for two weeks and then make conclusions about their overall habits. If the sample gets big enough, I am no longer making inferences at all – I'm just describing the behavior I observed for this individual. But, this kind of extreme and comprehensive data collection is still the exception. Most of the time, our goal is to make inferences about a population of behavior that goes beyond what we have directly observed.

Sometimes we can make big inferences based on small samples of behavior. A well-known test for narcissistic personality contains a single question: "Are you a narcissist?"

It turns out that a person's tendency to say "yes" to this question (which is a small sample of possible narcissistic behaviors) can be used to predict a wide range of behavioral outcomes (Konrath et al., 2014). The same kind of measure won't work for other traits. Extraversion, for example, is a broad, multifaceted trait. To predict whether someone will behave in an extraverted way, you want to ask lots of questions that tap into the various aspects of the trait. Only asking "do you like parties?" won't help you understand whether a person will enjoy a particular social situation on a particular day in the future. Although it will be related to their extraversion, it probably won't contain enough information about extraversion itself to be useful in isolation.

3. Measurements are subject to error.

We know that our measurements are imperfect, because they are based on limited samples, because we have imperfect ideas about the true nature of our constructs, and because the measurement tools themselves introduce some errors. We don't always know, however, how to estimate the error in our measurements. A number of strategies exist, described in later sections of this chapter, which each require careful thought and planning, plus a deep understanding of the construct domain.

Thinking clearly about errors is difficult. But, error is not solely a property of psychological measurement, and a more practical example will help you understand it. If you're training for a marathon, your mile time is unlikely to be exactly the same on every run. There are random fluctuations that determine whether you have a good day or a bad day on top of random errors in the precision of the stopwatch timing used. Yet regardless of such errors, your overall trajectory over time will still tell a story about whether you are meaningfully improving. Knowing the right level of precision to aim for can be challenging when concepts are abstract; psychological measurement in particular is often unclear. A big part of doing quantitative measurement properly is thinking about error – where it might be coming from, and how to minimize it. But, just like a mile time on a single day isn't the true measure of your running ability, any psychological measurement will deviate a little bit from perfect. The **classical test theory** framework, described in the following, is built on this idea.

4. Units of measurement may not translate to psychological research.

Because our measures refer to abstract qualities, the numbers we generate don't always work the way that numbers referring to physical objects work. If I count the number of people in this room and say there are zero people, I mean there are no people. But if I say a person wears size zero clothes, I don't mean they are naked. I mean their clothing is on the very lowest end of an arbitrary scale. Ounces and clothing sizes both refer to weight, in a way, but only one of those scales has a meaningful zero. The challenge in psychological measurement is that very few of our measurements have meaningful zeroes. Scoring a zero on a test doesn't mean you have zero knowledge. It means that your knowledge didn't make it to the next score threshold, but you still might know something about the subject.

5. It is challenging to connect measurements of one construct to other constructs of interest.

Constructs, by definition, are *constructed* – that means that on some level, we made them up. They are the product of human interpretation. The difference between a useful construct and a useless one is whether it relates to something else we care about as a society. As discussed, there is a lot of pressure on young researchers to identify new and exciting constructs; we hope you will resist that pressure and instead focus on better understanding constructs that have societal value. Imagine that I propose a new construct, "Sassitude," which I argue is important in predicting a person's success in administering sass to people who disrespect them. While it might be a little bit interesting to better understand this kind of interpersonal interaction, it is my job to first show why this is *important*. The trick is that when we think about the kinds of outcomes we find important, they are generally complex and difficult to predict. It makes measurement difficult as a result. The temptation is to predict easy things, like outcomes that are very proximal to the predictor. But, you must resist that temptation and instead tackle the problems that really matter.

The Standards: History and Purpose

The professional community of measurement specialists recognized the need for standardization in the way that measurement quality was determined. Standardization is necessary for test publishers, in order for them to communicate and establish the quality of their product, and it is also necessary for scientists to demonstrate the soundness of their evidence. In order to have a meaningful conversation about constructs, everyone needed to be speaking the same language. So, representatives from the fields of education, psychology, and psychometrics worked together to establish a set of standards, helpfully called. . . . **the Standards** (the full name of the book in which the Standards are written is *The Standards for Educational and Psychological Testing*).

In the next few sections, the basic tenets of the Standards are laid out. It's important for you to know that although these rules are not perfect, they are referred to by every serious scientist. Further, the Standards are sometimes used to argue court cases concerning the use of selection tests in employment discrimination lawsuits, and are part of the basis of federal rules in the US regarding fair employment testing practices. The Standards are revised as new knowledge is generated; the most recent version was published in 2014. The basics have stayed the same, but each version tends to reflect changing societal values and wisdom regarding testing.

If you are interested in reading *The Standards* in its entirety, the digital version of the entire book is available for free: www.testingstandards.net/open-access-files.html.

Classical Test Theory Fundamentals

Assumptions About Latent Variables

The core of classical test theory (CTT) is the assumption that a test score is a **random variable**. Random in this context means that the variable is measured imperfectly, with error, and that the error follows certain rules. Put another way, the value of the variable is determined based on a set of probabilities.

Consider the example of a series of 10 coin flips. How many heads do you expect to get?

I hope you were able to correctly estimate that you would expect five heads. The expected value, 5, is in the middle of a distribution of possible values. You would not be very surprised if you ended up with four heads, or six. There is a certain amount of imperfection, or error, that comes with each flip. But it's not completely random – for example, you would be surprised if you saw 10 heads or 10 tails in a row.

You should think of a test score in the same way. The expected value of a test score is what you would expect to happen on average. But there is also some amount of error in the measurement. Let's think of a midterm exam. You scored a 90%. That number, 90%, is the professor's best estimate of your knowledge. But maybe a few of the test questions were written badly. Maybe you had an off day. If you were to take the test over and over again, maybe the average of your scores would be somewhere around 93%. 93% is your expected value. We can also call 93% your **true score**. The actual test was attempting to estimate this true score, and it came up with an estimate of 90%. Not too far off, but not exactly right, either. 90% is called your **observed score**.

We can formally describe the relationship between these scores with the following equation:

$$X = T + e$$

where X = your observed score (90%)

T = your true score (93%)

And e = the error that is present in all measurement (–3%).

Error is the deviation between a true score and observed score. Observed scores will always deviate from true scores, which are more like idealized concepts than attainable goals. But we want e to be as small as possible. We also make some assumptions about e, in order for this to work out properly. Specifically, we assume that:

1. First, we assume that the mean of e for a population of test takers is 0. This means that the true score for some test takers will be overestimated and the true score for some test takers will be underestimated, but over repeated measurements, the average error will be 0. Any systematic over or under estimation would indicate a type of **measurement bias**, which is a different kind of problem (described later).
2. Second, e is normally distributed. In addition to the mean of e being zero, e is on average very predictable. Most e are small – in fact, we assume roughly 68% of e to be small (within +/– 1 standard deviation). 95% of e fall within +/– 2 standard deviations, and 99% of e fall within +/– 3 standard deviations. (These numbers should be familiar if you remember z-scores and/or sampling distributions.)
3. Third, e is uncorrelated with T. If e and T were correlated, this would mean that the accuracy of the test changes depending on a test taker's true score. This would mean that the equation doesn't hold up equally for all test takers, which means assumptions based on the equation are probably not a good idea.

A CTT-Based Approach to Good Measurement

Scale of Measurement

One of the most basic concepts of measurement is the assumed mathematical relationship between the response the numbers used to represent various answers to a question and construct standing, commonly referred to as **scale of measurement**. There are four scales of measurement:

1. **Nominal**, which implies that meaningful labels exist. For example, the question "Who is your favorite manager?" might have options "Sheila," "Jim," and "Someone else."

2. **Ordinal**, which implies that there is an order to labels that reflects order in the construct. For example, the prompt "Provide a rank order for how much you like each of your managers?" would result in numbers reflecting 1st, 2nd, and 3rd place.
3. **Interval**, which implies that the distance between ordered labels is consistent. For example, the question, "Rate how much you like your manager on a scale of –1 to +1, where –1 is dislike, 0 is neither, and +1 is like" implies that the difference between "Dislike" and "Neither" is the same, in terms of strength of "liking" as the distance between "Neither" and "Like."
4. **Ratio**, which implies that an interval scale has a zero point that represents the *absence* of the construct. For example, the question, "How many hours would you be willing to spend alone on a boat with your manager?" implies the absence of time (0) versus more time. The advantage to ratio scales is that proportions become meaningful; in this case, a person that answers 2 is willing to spend *twice* as many hours as a person who answers 1.

Scale of measurement is hierarchical in that scales later in this list also must meet all of the assumptions of scales of measurement earlier in the list. A ratio-level measure is by definition also an interval, ordinal, and nominal measure. An ordinal-level measure is also nominal but is not necessarily an interval or ratio measure. Think of each scale of measurement in this list as requiring more precise, and often more questionable, assumptions than the one before it.

Furthermore, the absence of scale of measurement is what defines qualitative data. For example, consider the question, "How do you feel about your manager?" Because there is no imposed structure to the potential answers to this question, it has no scale of measurement.

Scale of measurement must be decided before writing a question, because it influences which kinds of analyses can be applied to obtained scores. Nominal questions, for example, are non-numeric, which severely limits what approaches can be used to study them. Generally, the most common analyses seen in I-O psychology are enabled by assuming interval or ratio measurement. We will revisit this concept in more detail in Chapter 10.

Reliability

Starting from $X = T + e$, we can see that if we want X to be a good estimate of T, then e should be small. The relative contribution of T and e to X is called **reliability**. Another way to say this is that reliability is the proportion of true score variance contained within observed variables; for example, if reliability is .7, it implies that $T/(T + e) = .7$. Higher reliability means smaller amounts of error. For example, assume:

X = SAT score
T = intelligence (a latent construct)
e = error

By applying the CTT formula, this translates to: SAT scores (X) represent some combination of intelligence (T) and things that are not intelligence (e). A reliability of .5 here would suggest that 50% of the variance in SAT scores reflects variance in intelligence.

The purpose of assessing reliability is to help figure out the following two things:

1. The factors that contribute to consistency: stable characteristics of the individual or the attribute that one is trying to measure (T).

2. The factors that contribute to inconsistency: features of the individual or the situation that can affect test scores but have nothing to do with the attribute being measured (e).

We can answer these questions by designing experiments that vary the factors we think might contribute to T and e. This requires creative and careful thinking about all the factors that might affect your measurement. For example, I might hypothesize that changes in weather affect SAT scores. Weather in this case might be a source of error, in that it changes test scores but is unrelated to ability. To find out if this is true, I should design an experiment in which test takers complete the SAT in various weather conditions. If I see that scores go up in nice weather and down in bad weather, I've got evidence that weather is contributing to instability in measurement.

There is something important to realize here about the way we define reliability that might be surprising. Any factor can be viewed as contributing to consistency or inconsistency, depending on the way the experiment is designed, and thus can increase or decrease an estimate of reliability. Imagine that we magically know that bad weather decreases test scores by 10 points. If I administer the SAT twice, once on a sunny day and once on a cloudy day, weather would contribute to inconsistency across those two measurements and thus decrease reliability. But! If I administer the SAT twice, both on cloudy days, weather actually contributes to consistency and would increase our reliability estimate! In this way, reliability calculations depend on the way consistency is conceptualized. You as the researcher must carefully think about potential types and sources of inconsistency and actively look for them. Otherwise, they won't show up in your calculations, biasing your reliability estimates.

Luckily you don't have to start from scratch. There are several common methods to assess common sources of inconsistency that you can begin with when you start to think about estimating reliability:

1. Test-retest
2. Alternate forms
3. Internal consistency
4. Multiple raters

These four ways of assessing reliability are generally not interchangeable; they are used for different reasons, described in the following.

Test-retest reliability is assessed by administering a measure at two times. The time period will vary according to the concept you are interested in. If you want to argue that a personality trait remains stable over a person's life span, for example, you would probably try to space your measurements at least a few years apart. If you are more concerned with daily fluctuations in mood, perhaps a span of a week or so would be appropriate. The key here is that anything that changes from time 1 to time 2 would contribute to inconsistency and thus decrease the reliability of the scores. Some of these things might be random noise in the data, or **practice effects** – meaning that a person's score on the test improves as a function of having seen the test before. This would be relevant in any kind of ability testing.

Alternate forms reliability is assessed by creating two or more versions of a measure that are intended to measure the same construct but that vary in their wording, question order, or structure. If you've ever been in a large lecture hall in which multiple versions of an exam were given, you have seen this idea before. Hopefully, Version A and Version B measured the same material, or you would have something to complain about. Our measurements can differ across tests that have identical items. If students score more poorly on a test that orders all the hard items first compared to a test that orders those same hard items last, this would be concerning from a measurement perspective. Or, two tests may have the same item content and order yet differ only in how the questions are worded. If one of these tests has more advanced vocabulary than the other, we cannot treat them as equivalent measurement tools. As researchers, we worry that small things about the wording or ordering of questions can affect our measurement in ways we aren't anticipating.

Internal consistency is assessed by calculating the degree to which a group of items measure the same construct. There are two commonly computed forms of internal consistency reliability. One is **split-half reliability**. After giving a single measure to a group of respondents, you can calculate split-half reliability by dividing responses to items for each person into two halves. For example, you could split the measure into its odd- and even-numbered items, thus creating two sets of responses for each person. If the measure is internally consistent, there should be a high degree of similarity between the two sets of items.

Another form of internal consistency is represented in a statistic known as **Cronbach's alpha (α),** which is the most commonly reported index of reliability in I-O psychology. Conceptually, Cronbach's alpha is the average of all possible split half reliabilities. Conventionally, alpha values greater than .70 are acceptable for scientific publications; high-stakes tests generally have alphas above .95. The equation for Cronbach's alpha is as follows:

$$\alpha = \frac{N \cdot \overline{C}}{\overline{v} + (N-1) \cdot \overline{\overline{C}}}$$

Where:
   N = the number of items.
   $\overline{c}$ = average covariance between item pairs.
   $\overline{v}$ = average variance.

By looking at this equation, you might notice that alpha always becomes larger when adding items of equal quality to existing items. In this way, longer measures will generally reveal higher alphas than shorter measures.

For this reason, a higher alpha doesn't necessarily imply that the measure is of better quality. More specifically, a high level of internal consistency does not imply that a measure is unidimensional; it only implies that the items are consistent with each other. A measure can assess multiple constructs and still produce a high alpha with a sufficient number of interrelated items. For more information about how alpha is computed and interpreted, see this foundational article by Cortina (1993):

Cortina, J. M. (1993). What is coefficient alpha? An examination of theory and applications. *Journal of Applied Psychology, 78*(1), 98–104.

One last common form of reliability that you might come across in the literature is **multiple rater (or inter-rater) reliability,** which is assessed by calculating the degree to which raters agree in their judgments about some target. An example is multiple interviewers assigning a performance score to a candidate interviewing for a position. The section on G-theory later in this chapter elaborates on how to think about multiple rater reliability.

Validity

In psychology, *validity* generally refers to how well claims we make as researchers map onto some kind of truth. In the psychometric measurement context, discussion of validity usually refers to a more specific concept, **construct validity**, sometimes called **test validity**, and is all about what the meaning of X really is in our $X = T + e$ equation. When measuring, we are making claims that after taking e (error) into consideration, the remaining X (scores) only represent T (true score on a latent construct). In other words, we are making inferences about what X means. Validity evidence is what we collect to establish the soundness of our reasoning in assigning a *meaning* to X.

We've made a number of references to the idea of **inferences** so far. An inference is a logical conclusion based on evidence. Construct validity, in this sense, is the quality of our inferences about the construct we believe our observed scores measure. The goal of **validity** (or **validation**) **studies** is to collect evidence that supports inferences you want to make about construct validity. There are plenty of kinds of evidence you can collect and present. The key is to make sure the evidence aligns with the claims being made. The *right* kind of evidence, then, must always match the kind of claims you are making. This should remind you of the research process as a whole – the right methods are the ones that match the research question.

Importantly, conceptualizations of test validity have changed a lot in the last few decades, and you may still see references to older approaches. The oldest common approach conceptualized validity in three major types called "construct validity," "criterion validity," and "content validity." In this approach, a test either had or did not have each of these three kinds of validity. Further, if another kind of validity was relevant to a researcher, they might claim a test had that kind of validity too, like "ecological validity." Using this approach, a researcher might make a claim that a test was "content valid but not criterion valid." If you see these terms and this kind of phrasing while reading articles, it's important to recognize that they implicitly embrace this antiquated and historical view of validity, referred to as the **trinitarian view of test validity**, an approach associated with a foundational research paper on measurement by Cronbach and Meehl (1955). Although this paper essentially set the groundwork for all future work on the measurement of psychological constructs, this specific approach is no longer generally accepted.

Instead, this "types of validity" approach was replaced with what came to be called the **unitary view of test validity.** This approach proposes that instead of a test possessing multiple "kinds" or "types" of validity, it only has one validity, which is its construct validity. What we previously considered evidence of "criterion validity" is instead conceptualized as a type of evidence supporting a claim of validity based upon observed criterion relationships. Put another way, in the historical, trinitarian view, an observed correlation between a conscientiousness measure and job performance would support the "criterion validity" of that measure. In the unitary approach, that observed correlation is just one piece of evidence supporting an argument for the overall construct validity of the measure. Landy (1986) described test validity as necessitating hypothesis testing – in other words, you have an implicit hypothesis that your measure reflects the construct you believe it reflects, and this hypothesis should be tested with evidence.

This change in approach led to the rephrasing of the historical "types" of validity. "Criterion validity" became *criterion-related validity evidence*, "content validity" became *content-related validity evidence*, and so on. The specific names for these types of evidence, however, are unimportant. The critical change was that instead of claiming a test has or does not have various kinds of validity, a test instead has a single, overall **evidential basis** for a claim of construct validity, supported (or not) by multiple types of research evidence.

The unitary approach has continued to evolve. In the most recent edition of the Standards (2014), the "something-related" terms have been largely abandoned and replaced with five broad categories of evidence:

1. **Evidence based on test content** provided by research studies examining systematic and unbiased evaluation by subject matter experts concluding that the constructs being measured are indeed the constructs claimed. This category closely maps onto the older idea of "content-related validity evidence." A study assessing this kind of evidence might ask experts on a construct to evaluate a test of that construct and write a written report on how well they believe it does so. For example, if an expert on conscientiousness looks at your new conscientiousness measure and says, "That doesn't look like conscientiousness to me," there may be something wrong with your measure.

2. **Evidence based on response processes** provided by research studies showing that while people complete a measure, they are engaging in the cognitive, affective, and other mental processes that research on the construct suggests they should be engaging in. A study assessing this kind of evidence might ask people completing a measure to "think aloud," and what they say would then be analyzed to look for indicators of the construct. For example, if people play a game-based assessment of cognitive ability and say aloud, "I feel like this action is the more ethical choice," there may be something wrong with your measure.

3. **Evidence based on internal structure** provided by research studies showing that the statistical relationships between items, subscales, and other measure characteristics are what would be expected of the construct. This category closely maps onto the older idea of "construct-related validity evidence." A study assessing this kind of evidence might collect a large and diverse sample and then conduct statistical tests appropriate to the measure and construct's internal structure, such as confirmatory factor analysis and measurement invariance testing. For example, if prior theory suggests three subfactors but you only observe two, there may be something wrong with your measure.

4. **Evidence based on relations to other variables** provided by research studies showing that the interrelationships between the measure and other theoretically related measures match what prior theory on the constructs suggests. This includes theoretical antecedents, covariates, and consequences. This category envelops several kinds of evidence previously considered separately, including "convergence-related" (i.e., do items correlate highly with other items they should correlate highly with?), "discrimination-related" (i.e., do items correlate weakly with other items they should theoretically correlate weakly with?), and "criterion-related" (i.e., do items correlate with outcomes they should correlate with?) types of evidence. Studies assessing this kind of evidence are likely to simply assess many different constructs at once. For example, if you have designed what you think is a new conscientiousness measure but it correlates .95 with a Machiavellianism measure and .05 with an existing, well-respected conscientiousness measure, you are probably not really measuring conscientiousness, and thus there may be something wrong with your measure.

5. **Evidence based on the consequences of test use** provided by research studies showing that when the measure is used for decision-making, the outcomes of that use are what would be predicted by theoretical construct relationships. Studies assessing this kind of evidence often incorporate powerful research methods to support causal relationships.

For example, imagine you have designed a cognitive ability test and randomly hire half of applicants on the basis of that test and the other half on an unstructured interview. Cognitive ability tests have a well-documented, strong, positive relationship with job performance, whereas unstructured interviews do not. Thus, if you found that the average job performance of those hired on your new cognitive test was 2 standard deviations lower than those you hired on the interview, there may be something wrong with your measure.

All of these types of evidence, if collected with a well-designed research study, provide information that helps either support or undermine claims that a particular test is construct valid. It is not necessary to collect them all, but all could be informative. It is ultimately up to the people using the test to decide when the evidential basis collected is "good enough" to support the developer's claims.

Criterion Deficiency and Contamination

An important part of establishing content-related validity evidence for a construct is making a determination that the measure of your construct captures only the construct, nothing more, nothing less. When the measure is missing something important, it is **deficient**. When it is capturing something else beyond the construct, it is **contaminated**. As an example, consider the following three-item measure of extraversion:

1. I like to go to parties
2. I have a lot of friends
3. I get angry easily.

This measure has several issues with both contamination and deficiency. First, notice that the third item is about something else that is not quite extraversion. It's closer to agreeableness. Item 3 is a source of contamination. Second, notice that there are many elements of extraversion missing– this measure doesn't capture anything about ambition, for example, which is an important deficiency in the measure.

Statistical tests (e.g., factor analysis, which we discuss in Chapter 10) and expert judgment are both used to identify contamination in measurement. But only a strong expert understanding of the construct, based on theory, can identify deficiencies. There isn't a statistical test in existence that can tell you if you forgot to measure something.

Fairness

The last aspect of measurement quality according to the Standards is **test fairness**. The words "fairness" and "bias" are heavily culturally loaded, so it's worth over-explaining exactly what these words mean in the context of measurement. Fairness is a social concept and reflects the goals and values of a society. There are many approaches to defining fairness but two of the most common are:

1. **Equality of outcomes**: for example, on average, people from different socially defined groups receive the same scores.

2. **Equality of opportunity to succeed**: for example, people from different groups have the same access to preparation, resources, and feedback.

There is no "correct" definition of fairness, and a person who says "this is unfair" can mean any number of things (including "I didn't get what I wanted!" – just ask any toddler.) Bias, on the other hand, has a precise definition in the context of measurement. As a feature of a psychological measure, bias means that the assumption of random error centered on zero is not reasonable. When error is nonrandom, we can try to identify what caused it. This concept applies in two major ways in the testing context.

First, measurement bias means that some irrelevant source of information has been captured in a measure, and this irrelevant information leads some groups to score systematically higher or lower than they should. For example, the earliest cognitive ability tests asked questions like "Who plays third base for the Yankees?" or "What is a schooner?" These items are meant to measure general knowledge and vocabulary, but they are measure other things. People who live near New York, and near the ocean, are much more likely to have knowledge of these items. So they measure two things: "vocabulary" and "place of residence." Place of residence is a source of measurement error. Because this error is *nonrandom*, and varies systematically as a function of where someone lives, we refer to it as bias.

Second, **predictive bias** is relevant only when scores are being used to predict an outcome of some kind. Personnel selection is the most common context relevant to predictive bias in I-O psychology, but predictive bias could also turn up in any other predictive or decision task. You can think about predictive bias as systematically over-predicting or under-predicting a person's outcome as a function of their subgroup membership. The regression line for that subgroup is not correct. The slope or intercept or both do not apply equally well to all people in the sample. This means that using that regression line to predict performance will disadvantage people depending on their group membership. This approach, commonly called the **Cleary model**, is a common method for the assessment of predictive bias (Cleary, 1968), although there are several alternative approaches.

Why Study Fairness?

We believe fairness is one of the most important topics in measurement. Without high-quality measurement, we cannot draw meaningful conclusions about anything we have measured, and if measures are unfair, we could be creating policies or making decisions that harm a group without reasonable cause. For example, when a test discriminates against people who don't have job-required skills, it is probably a fair test. But when a test discriminates on the basis of race or gender, we end up with both less qualified employees and a more unjust society.

When we asked I-O professors Ann Marie Ryan and Christopher Nye why they continue to study measure fairness in the age of artificial intelligence, they told us this:

> We both have had interests our entire careers in working to make hiring processes fair for all that apply. With the changing nature of how organizations select employees, there is an opportunity to remind people that a lot of what we already know

about how to design valid and fair selection methods applies regardless of any new technology in use. While technology can make hiring processes more engaging, convenient, and accessible for applicants and more efficient for organizations, issues of fairness still need to be considered when designing and implementing an assessment. For example, multimedia assessments are more engaging for test takers and may simulate a work environment in more realistic ways, but they also potentially introduce a lot of irrelevant content into measures of a specific construct. Another example is that when applicants can take a test anytime and anywhere, the testing environment can influence how well individuals perform. Fairness in assessment is something that should be considered in every step of developing and implementing employee assessments.

Formative Versus Reflective Constructs

Until now, we have discussed constructs while making a key assumption, namely that the various items that make the construct are related to each other because they are caused by a common latent construct. In other words, the items are a reflection of the construct. The formal name for these constructs is **reflective constructs**. The vast majority of constructs you encounter should be modeled this way.

There is, however, an alternative. Consider the construct of job satisfaction, for example. Does it make more sense to say that there is an overall job satisfaction factor that then causes your satisfaction with your boss, your pay, and your work (the model on the left in Figure 7.1)? Or does it make more sense to say that you have different levels of satisfaction with your boss, your pay, and your work, and that you average them together to form an overall job satisfaction attitude (the model on the right in Figure 7.1)?

The difference between these models is that the second one makes no assumptions about whether the items are related to each other or what causes a person to respond in the way they do.

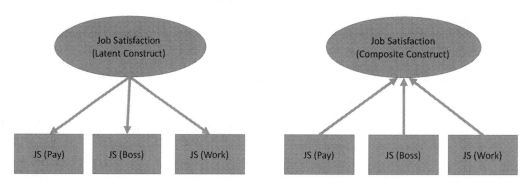

Figure 7.1 A reflective model of job satisfaction (left) and a formative model of job satisfaction (right).

Not everyone thinks that formative constructs should be considered constructs at all. And it isn't always appropriate to treat constructs this way. You can use the following guide, created by MacKenzie et al. (2005), to figure out if formative modeling is appropriate:

1. Are the indicators defining characteristics of the construct or manifestations of it?
2. Do the indicators appear to be conceptually interchangeable?
3. Are the indicators expected to covary with one another?
4. Are all of the indicators expected to have the same consequences?

Let's walk through an example of how this might work using the construct of person-environment (P-E) fit. P-E fit refers to the alignment between you and your job and has a number of dimensions. There can be a fit between your cultural preferences and the culture of an organization: this is culture fit. There is also demands-abilities fit; this is the alignment between what you can do and what the job demands of you. And there is needs-supplies fit, the alignment between what you need from a job and what that job provides. So, the question is, are these three kinds of fit part of a single whole? Or are they separate perceptions? We can walk through MacKenzie's rules to make this determination: The indicators of P-E fit (culture, needs-supplies, and demands-abilities) can be combined to create an overall perception of fit. But they don't come from the same place, and it is very possible to have strong fit on one dimension and weak fit on another. Imagine that you worked in a very collaborative place that fit well with your personal values. But it was two hours away from your house, making child care very challenging, and beyond that, the responsibilities of the job were way more than you were ready for. You'd be high on culture fit but not much else. There is no reason to expect that one kind of fit is related to another kind, and in fact they might be negatively related. And finally, these kinds of fit probably have different effects on your behavior and outcomes. You might quit over poor needs-supplies fit but have low motivation based on culture fit. For all these reasons, it sounds like person-environment fit is a formative construct. In fact, Darrow and Behrend (2017) compared formative and reflective models of fit and confirmed that a formative model was indeed a better approach for this construct.

G-Theory: An Elaboration on CTT

Consider that you and a friend are applying for the same job. As part of the selection process, each of you gives a presentation and organizes files while being rated by two current employees. Thus, your scores consist of four parts:

1. a rating from Employee 1 on the presentation task
2. a rating from Employee 1 on the organization task
3. a rating from Employee 2 on the presentation task
4. a rating from Employee 2 on the organization task

There are many sources that can affect the ratings you receive. Employee 1 may be a lenient rater who gives applicants high scores regardless of their task performance. The presentation task may be associated with lower scores because it is more challenging than the organization task. Employee 2 may dislike your friend's shoes and decide to give him low ratings. How do we account for all of these sources of variation? Recall that classical test theory explains observed scores with two components: systematic true scores and random sources of error. In our example, CTT does little to describe the specific effects of raters, tasks, or rater-applicant interactions on observed ratings.

Generalizability theory (G-theory) is a useful framework for investigating the reliability of measurements while keeping in mind potential sources of variation, referred to as **facets**. G-theory gives us a new way of thinking about reliability by asking the question, "Under what conditions can observed scores be reproduced?" To answer this question, we need to consider the components of an observed score.

In our example, an observed score X_{pr} represents a rating for applicant p given by employee r.

Now imagine that every employee at the company rated every applicant's performance on the two tasks. Calculating the average (μ) of these ratings helps us determine the extent to which ratings from Employee 1 and Employee 2 can be *generalized* to the population of all other employee raters. Using this information, we are able to decompose observed scores into several parts with the following equation:

$$X_{pr} = \mu + \left(\mu_p - \mu\right) + \left(\mu_r - \mu\right) + e_{pr}$$

where μ is the grand mean, $(\mu_p - \mu)$ is the person or applicant effect, $(\mu_r - \mu)$ is the rater or employee effect, and e_{pr} is an error term. This equation shows that an applicant's observed score is characterized as a departure from the grand mean in terms of the applicant's performance and the rater's evaluation, in addition to the unique interaction between the applicant and the rater.

This equation helps us answer the original question posed by G-theory as it relates to our example. If the rater effect associated with Employee 1 and Employee 2 is substantially greater than the person effect, we cannot generalize their ratings to the population of all other employee raters. This is because an applicant's observed score is affected more by characteristics or biases of the two employee raters than it is by his or her performance.

In this sense, G-theory also helps us think about validity. G-theory's detailed organization of error helps us determine the conditions under which our observations can – and cannot – be generalizable. When we know that our peripheral facets have small effects, we can be confident that our generalizations or inferences are accurate.

For example, suppose that the power went out minutes before you and your friend arrived to complete the job tasks. As a result, the employees who rated you were in a terrible mood because they had just lost important computer files. You and your friend received similarly low ratings across both tasks. CTT would consider these ratings reliable since the outage systematically affected the employees' ratings. However, such ratings could hardly be considered valid for differentiating between you and your friend's presentation skills.

G-theory instead helps us identify that the occasion facet – the timing and circumstances of the ratings – cannot be generalized to the other occasions that you and your friend could be rated. To correct for this source of unreliability, we need to collect ratings at a different time or on another day. In doing so, the observed ratings will allow for more valid inferences to be drawn regarding applicants' job-related skills.

You may be wondering how researchers determine which facets should be included when using G-theory. As you can see, making generalizability conclusions about raters and occasions requires us to collect ratings from multiple raters on multiple occasions. In order for G-theory to be effective, researchers must collect their data with their generalized populations in mind. These collection decisions can be challenging, which might explain why G-theory is sometimes overlooked in discussions of reliability and validity. Still, G-theory provides some clear advantages over classical test theory in that it identifies the specific conditions that our measurements can generalize to much larger sets of measurements.

Expanding the Way We Think About Measurement

Classical test theory has been the dominant player in I-O for a long time – the 800-pound gorilla, squashing all rivals who try to offer alternatives. But alternatives do exist, and they are often superior to CTT. A simple examination of the assumptions of CTT can show us that the assumptions are often unreasonable in that they don't describe reality. How sure can we really be, for example, that true score and error are uncorrelated in real situations? That would mean the test is equally precise for everyone we give it to, regardless of all other factors. It's not hard to imagine that there are sources of error in an ability test that are unique to people with either high or low ability. For example, maybe the test uses the word "affect." The word affect has two meanings: *to influence*, as a verb, and *emotion*, as a noun. Imagine a test item for verbal ability that looked like this:

*LIKE:LOVE::AFFECT:*_____

A. Change
B. Book
C. Mood
D. Hat

The answer the test writer imagined was A. Loving is a more intense version of liking, and changing something is a more intense version of affecting it. People of average verbal ability should be able to pick the right answer. But! Imagine you are high in verbal ability, and you know that affect has a second meaning. Now, you could think that like and love are synonyms, and so are affect and mood. You might choose C. This item is confusing for you *because of* your higher verbal ability and larger vocabulary than average.

Some of the assumptions of classical test theory, such as the idea that errors are normally distributed around zero, are often not very reasonable. This classical approach to measurement, which relies on the assumption of independent errors, is just one way to approach things. Luckily, there are alternatives. The primary alternative is **item response theory (IRT)**, also called **modern test theory**.

IRT Basics

For the following section, we'll refer to the following example math test, which has four items:

1. $8+8 = X$
2. $X + 7 = 12$
3. $5x = x + 8$
4. $e\char`^X = 1$

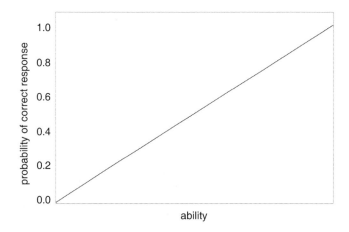

Figure 7.2 A classical test theory model for the probability of correctly responding to an item.

Classical models of measurement assume that the probability of responding correctly to an item increases linearly as ability increases. We can draw this assumption like this (Figure 7.2):

The probability of responding correctly, called the **difficulty** of the item, is simply the percentage of the sample that gets the item right, which means that if you give a test to a smart group of people, you'll get a different estimate of difficulty than if you gave it to a less-smart group of people. This is not great news. Consider two exams:

Exam A: GRE math test: you score 80% correct
Exam B: third-grade math test: your friend scores 100% correct

Is your friend better at math than you? There's no way to know!. In classical models of measurement, any estimates about a person's ability (math knowledge) will depend on the specific test items used. If you instead took the third-grade math test, our estimate of your math knowledge would be much larger. Ideally the estimate we come up with for math ability should be independent of the test items we use. With IRT, we are able to draw conclusions about you and your friend's math ability without being restricted to the items on a specific test.

The same logic can be applied to describe characteristics of test items. With classical measurement approaches, any estimates about an item's level of difficulty will depend on the specific sample of people who take the same test. A bunch of third graders responding to an advanced calculus item will yield a different item difficulty than would a bunch of college engineering students responding to the same item. With IRT, however, item statistics are independent of test-takers; a calculus item will have the same level of difficulty whether it is administered to a third grader or a college student.

The foregoing example alludes to a key advantage of IRT over classical models: With IRT, latent traits can be compared even if they are estimated using different tests, and item parameters should apply to any population of test takers.

You may be wondering how IRT provides person and item estimates that are independent of items and samples, respectively. This is largely because IRT models operate under an assumption that a single latent trait is responsible for how people respond to test items. Unlike classical approaches, IRT places people and items on the same scale, and this scale is on the metric of the latent trait, **theta** (θ).

Placing people and items on the same scale allows for some useful comparisons. Imagine that your friend is lower in latent math ability (θ) than you. Because items are on the same scale as people, we can also consider that the item $5x = x + 8$ is higher than your friend's math ability but lower than your math ability. Because all three of these estimates are on the scale, it makes sense to predict that you are more likely to answer the item correctly than your friend is, because your math ability exceeds the math ability required of the item.

IRT assumes that the relationship between a person's latent trait level and their responses to items follows a probabilistic, but not linear, relationship, that looks like this:

$$p_i(\theta) = c_i + \frac{1 - c_i}{1 + e^{-a_i(\theta - b_i)}}$$

This function is defined by three parameters:

a parameter = equivalent of discrimination. How well does the item discriminate between people with high and low θ?
b parameter = equivalent of item difficulty.
c parameter = guessing parameter; probability of getting the item right by guessing alone.

Graphing this function results in a curve, called the **item characteristic curve**, which looks like this (Figure 7.3):

The interpretation of this function is that at low levels of ability, a person has a very low probability of answering this item correctly. At around theta = –1, their probability of answering correctly begins to increase rapidly. People with ability at around theta = 2 or higher have a very high probability of scoring correctly.

A Demonstration of IRT Parameters

Let's look at how the three IRT parameters affect the shape of the ICC. For this example, we created a 40-item multiple choice test covering fundamental theories and principles of

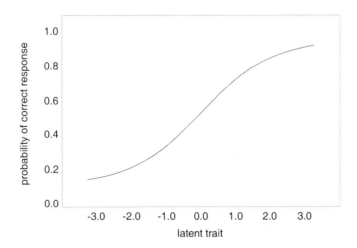

Figure 7.3 An item response theory model for the probability of correctly responding to an item.

psychology. Our latent trait is psychology knowledge, and we are interested in the probability that a respondent will answer each of the 40 items correctly.

Consider the following item:

1. Psychology is the study of

    1. *the mind and behavior.*
    2. matter and energy.
    3. outerspace.
    4. elephants.

This item seems pretty easy, and we would expect that even people without a background in psychology might answer it correctly. The ICC for this item is provided in Figure 7.4. The steepness of the curve tells us how well the item discriminates between people with high and low ability: this is the *a* parameter. As you can see, this item has an ICC that is relatively flat. It does not discriminate between people with little psychology knowledge and people with a lot of psychology knowledge. The probability of someone with a theta score of 2 answering this item correctly is not much higher than the probability of someone with a theta score of –2 answering it correctly.

Now let's consider an item with higher discrimination:

2. The father of behaviorism is

    1. Sigmund Freud.
    2. *John Watson.*
    3. Abraham Lincoln.
    4. Jean Piaget.

The ICC in Figure 7.5 corresponds to the behaviorism item. Here, we see that the probability of someone with a theta score of 2 answering this item correctly *is* much higher than the

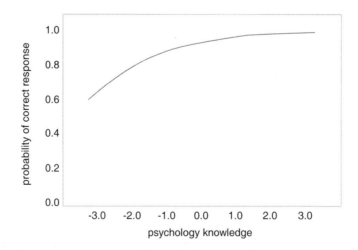

Figure 7.4 An item characteristic curve with low discrimination (associated with Item #1).

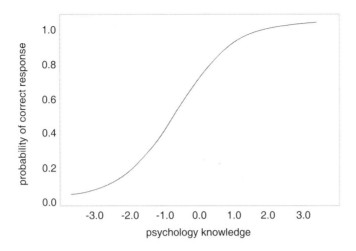

Figure 7.5 An item characteristic curve with high discrimination (associated with Item #2).

probability of someone with a theta score of –2 answering it correctly. This ICC has a relatively steep slope between theta = –2 and theta = 1.5, meaning that it discriminates between people at those levels of psychology knowledge quite well.

ICCs can also differ with regard to their points of inflection. For the traditional S-shape of most ICCs, the point of inflection is the point on the latent trait axis where the ICC switches from curving upwards to curving downwards (i.e., convex to concave). This point is referred to as the *b* parameter, the item's difficulty, or the item's location. More formally, an item's difficulty is the point on the latent trait axis where a person needs to be in order to have a .50 probability of answering an item correctly. It is also the point at which the ICC's slope is at its steepest.

Let's say we have two students, Alice, who is at theta = –1 for psychology knowledge, and Margaret, who is at theta = 2. The probability that Alice will respond to a specific item correctly will differ from Margaret's probability as a function of the item's difficulty. Consider the following two items:

1. The variable that is manipulated in an experiment is the

   a. *independent variable*.
   b. dependent variable.
   c. confounding variable.
   d. all of the above.

2. The variable that explains the relationship between two other variables is the

   a. moderating variable.
   b. *mediating variable*.
   c. independent variable.
   d. dependent variable.

Figure 7.6 depicts the ICCs for the two items. The first item is represented with a thick dashed line, and the second item is represented with a solid line. Here, the dashed ICC shows that the

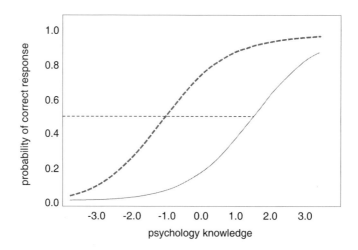

Figure 7.6 Item characteristics curves for Item #3 (in red) and Item #4 (in blue).

first item has a lower difficulty than the second item depicted with the solid ICC. The dashed curve has a difficulty of about theta = –1, whereas the solid line has a difficulty of about theta = 2. Thus, the probability that Alice will respond correctly to the first item (0.50) is equal to the probability that Margaret will respond correctly to the second item (0.50). Alice has a much lower probability of responding correctly to the second item (about .10), and Margaret has a much higher probability of responding correctly to the first item (about .90). As such, an item's difficulty is independent from a person's ability. An item will have the same difficulty regardless of who responds to it; only the probabilities associated with the item will change.

Putting the two parameters together, now refer to Figure 7.7 which depicts the ICCs for three new items. The dotted curve that starts at the bottom and ends above the other two curves depicts the item with the largest *a* (discrimination) parameter because it has the steepest slope. The dashed curve that starts at the top and ends at the bottom has the smallest *a* because it has the flattest slope; this item does not discriminate between people quite as well as the dotted item does. All three of these items have the same *b* (difficulty) parameter because a person with theta = 0 has a 0.50 probability of answering the items correctly.

It may seem that the dotted item is the "best" item, but the "best" item will depend on the unique purpose and goals of a test. If we wanted to discriminate between high schoolers who have never taken a psychology class, we would want items with ICCs that are steep (high *a*s) near the left side of the latent ability axis (low *b*s). In that case, the item depicted by the middle ICC might be our best choice given its steeper slope between theta = –2.5 and –1.5.

In an ideal world, having discrimination and difficulty parameters would be sufficient for researchers to accurately measure latent constructs. Sometimes when people fill out surveys or answer test questions, however, they respond for reasons that are not reflective of the latent trait being measured. People guess or respond correctly to items just by chance alone. The third parameter of IRT models, the pseudo-guessing parameter, is depicted by *c*.

In a basic sense, the pseudo-guessing parameter "bumps up" some ICCs; it introduces a lower asymptote to an ICC to reflect for the possibility that examinees, especially those low in ability, may answer the item correctly by chance. Figure 7.8 depicts two different ICCs for

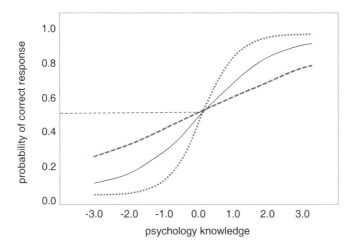

Figure 7.7 Demonstration of *a* and *b* parameters with three ICCs.

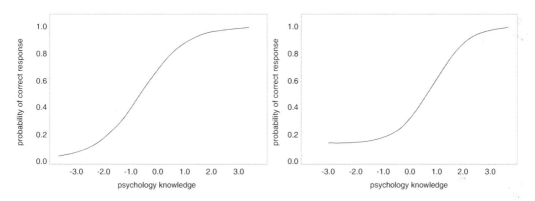

Figure 7.8 Item characteristic curves associated with Item #2, one without a guessing parameter (left) and one with a guessing parameter (right).

the behaviorism item mentioned earlier (Item 2). The ICC on the left shows the item in an IRT model that does not account for guessing, while the ICC on the right shows the same item in an IRT model that does account for guessing.

As you can see, when we account for the chance that anyone can get an item correct merely by guessing, it greatly affects the probabilities associated with those low in psychology knowledge. With the ICC on the left, we would expect a person with a theta of –4 to have almost no chance of answering it correctly; however, when accounting for guessing on the right, we expect that this same person has about a .20 probability of answering it correctly.

A pseudo-guessing parameter is useful for someone building a multiple choice test with items that only have a few options to choose from. In such cases, it is helpful to understand how plausible the *incorrect* options (i.e., distractors) are for an item. In our example, Item 2 had one distractor that most respondents would identify as being incorrect (Abraham

Lincoln). Thus, even someone with little psychology knowledge would be able to increase their likelihood of guessing the answer correctly by eliminating that option and leaving only three options to guess from. An IRT model with a pseudo-guessing parameter is well suited for accounting for these chance responses.

Polytomous IRT Models

Thus far, we've introduced **monotonic** IRT models; that is, all of the prior ICCs follow an "S"-shaped pattern such that a person with high theta values will have a higher probability of correctly endorsing an item. It is assumed that most IRT models are monotonic, but is this probability pattern always appropriate? If we think back to our opening example in which knowing that the word *affect* has two meanings, we see that being highly intelligent might actually lead someone to have a lower probability of choosing what we believe is the correct answer. In this case, we might expect to see a different pattern: a negatively skewed ICC, as shown in Figure 7.9.

We can do a better job of describing responses to this item by using a **polytomous** IRT model. Polytomous IRT models help researchers study a variety of items that do have a single correct answer. In our opening example, we could argue that the *most* correct answer was actually "affect," while "change" represented a partially correct answer. That is, there are degrees of "correctness" for the four response options to this item. We would expect that people high in intelligence would be most likely to endorse "affect," people with medium intelligence would be most likely to endorse "change," and people with low intelligence would be most likely to endorse "book" or "hat." If we were to score this item, there may be three scores a person receives: 2 points for selecting "affect," 1 point for selecting "change," and 0 points for selecting "book" or "hat."

The **partial credit model** is one type of polytomous IRT model that identifies the probabilities associated with responses varying in their degrees of correctness. Recall from our earlier dichotomous examples that each ICC corresponded with one response option, often the "correct" response. Polytomous models operate similarly, such that each response

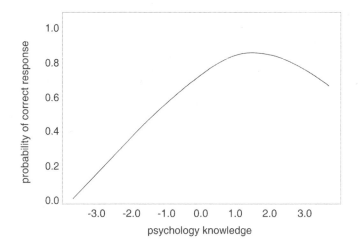

Figure 7.9 A negatively skewed item characteristic curve.

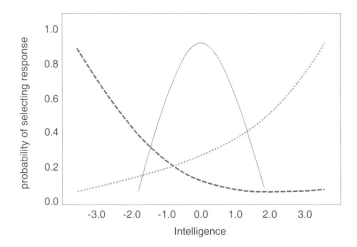

Figure 7.10 Item characteristic curves depicting the probability of endorsing the correct response (dotted line), the partially correct response (solid line), and an incorrect response (dashed line).

option gets its own ICC. A primary difference is that polytomous models often portray several ICCs at the same time, each representing the probability associated with selecting a certain response option. See Figure 7.10 for a plot of the probability associated with scoring a 2 (dotted line), 1 (solid line), and 0 (dashed line) in our example. As you can see, when a person's intelligence is around –2, there is an equal probability of scoring a 0 or 1, but as we approach intelligence levels around 0, it is highly likely that an individual will endorse the partially correct answer and score 1. It is when intelligence levels are around 2 that we would expect a person to endorse the most correct response.

Reliability in IRT

Reliability is established slightly differently in an IRT framework. In classical test theory, reliability is the amount of error or inconsistency that is reflected in a test's observed score. With IRT, reliability is no longer restricted to a test-level measure of precision, but instead a measure that can be estimated at both the test level and the item level. IRT views the concept of reliability through the lens of item information and test information.

In everyday terms, having information implies that we know something about a specific subject. In IRT, having information has a similar, yet somewhat more technical meaning. **Item information** refers to the amount of precision an item has when discriminating between people, and it varies across the latent trait (i.e., across difficulties). It is a measure of the variability in our estimates around an observed IRT parameter for a specific item. Items that have a lot of variability in their estimates will have large standard errors that suggest imprecise measurement. Items with more consistent estimates and smaller standard errors are said to provide more information than items with less consistent estimates. This is similar to CTT's concept of reliability, with the major difference that now each item can vary in its consistency of estimates under IRT.

We can graphically represent item information across the latent ability continuum. Most item information curves (IICs) will follow a bell-shaped distribution. The highest point on the

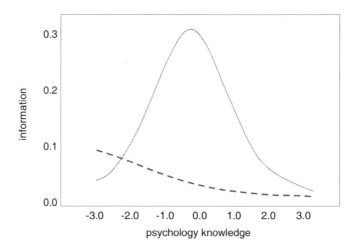

Figure 7.11 Item information curves for Item #1 (dashed line) and Item #2 (solid line).

IIC will be the same as the item's difficulty; it is the point at which information is maximized. Similarly, the height of an IIC at a certain point along the curve corresponds to its discrimination at that point. Items with large discrimination will produce tall and narrow IICs, while items with low discriminations will produce short and wide IICs. Tall and narrow IICs are indicative of more precise measurement around the narrow range of latent abilities. Flatter IICs are indicative of less precise measurement.

Figure 7.11 depicts the IICs for Question 1 (dashed line) and Question 2 (solid line) referred to earlier. As we can see, Item 1 hardly follows the normal bell-shaped distribution of most IICs. This is not surprising, given that the item's ICC showed it lacks discrimination. We can see that while this item provides little information overall across the latent continuum, it provides the most information for people with very little psychology knowledge (theta > –4). On the other hand, Item 2 has a more normally distributed IIC. It provides the most information between theta = –1 and theta = 1. That is, it provides a more precise measure that better discriminates between people at those levels of psychology knowledge. In comparing the two IICs, we see that neither Item 1 nor Item 2 provides a very precise measure to discriminate between people with very high theta values. Further, Item 1 actually provides a more precise measure of those with very low psychology knowledge.

IRT also provides a test-level measure of reliability in the form of test information. A test's total information accounts for the possibility that each of its items will contribute some information to discriminate between people across the latent ability, regardless of any other items on the test. In this sense, there is independence of items that allows us to combine their information in an overall test-level measure of information. Figure 7.12 is the test information curve (TIC) of our psychology assessment, which represents the sum of the 40 individual IICs. We can see that our test can reliably discriminate between people between around theta = –1 and theta = 1. However, our measurements are quite imprecise for discriminating between people who have a lot of psychology knowledge or very little psychology knowledge.

Item and test information also help us evaluate the validity of generalizations drawn from our assessment, serving as a type of validity evidence related to internal structure. Reliability

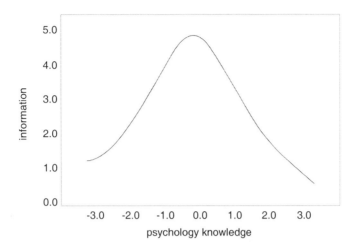

Figure 7.12 A test information curve.

is a necessary but not sufficient precursor to establishing valid conclusions. Our test information curve suggests that we lack information at extreme values of theta, which automatically limits the validity of generalizations we can draw when discriminating between people with those theta values.

The same logic applies at the item level. Item 1 had very low discrimination for people above theta = –4. Does this mean that we cannot draw valid conclusions using this item? Maybe, but assessing validity requires us to consider the overall goals of our test. If we are using the test to discriminate among a group of master's level psychology students, this item would not provide us with very strong validity evidence. However, it may provide us with stronger validity evidence for discriminating within populations of college freshmen or high school students.

One major advantage of IRT over classical measurement approaches is that its several parameters can be adjusted, allowing researchers to select a specific model that *best* fits their test data. In this sense, IRT models are falsifiable in that they can be proven wrong and rejected in favor of a better-fitting model. This comparative approach to measurement is not possible with CTT. Selecting the best fitting model is desirable from a validity perspective, but it is not always easy from a practical perspective. Some IRT models require large sample sizes (i.e., 2000+) in order to appropriately estimate all parameters of interest. Thus, researchers must carefully weigh the goals of their assessment (e.g., validity) with their available resources (e.g., sample composition and size) when using IRT as a measurement method.

Applied Polytomous Example: Vocational Interests Survey

Polytomous IRT models can also be used for survey or questionnaire data that have no correct or incorrect answers. To demonstrate how this is so, we used a publicly available dataset from the Open Science Framework (https://osf.io/be5ja/). This dataset contains over 80,000 respondents' answers to 20 questions regarding how much they would enjoy doing various work-related tasks. Response options to these items ranged from "Strongly Dislike" to "Strongly Like." For illustrative purposes, we are focusing only on a subset of the items related to a latent construct of "Interest in Working with Data," each of which has five response options.

When using IRT to analyze data, one of the first steps is to select an appropriate model. Doing so requires us to examine the quality of fit (discussed in more detail in future chapters) associated with any models that show potential for explaining our data. Our comparison of fit indices showed that the graded response model fit the data best. Like the partial credit model, this model also provides several ICCs associated with each possible response option. Interested readers are encouraged to read Tang (1996) for an explanation of the graded response model and how it differs from other polytomous IRT models.

After selecting our model, we were able to create IICS and ICCs associated with the various data-related items. In Figure 7.13, we show the IICS (on the left) and ICCs (on the right) of two of these items, "Oversee a hotel" (on the top) and "Maintain office financial records" (on the bottom).

If we were to administer this survey to another set of respondents, would we want to keep both of these items? These figures suggest that only one of the items, "Maintain office financial records," provides us with noteworthy information across the continuum of "Interest in Working with Data" (the IIC on the bottom left). The IIC on the top left shows that the item related to overseeing a hotel provides almost no information across the entire continuum,

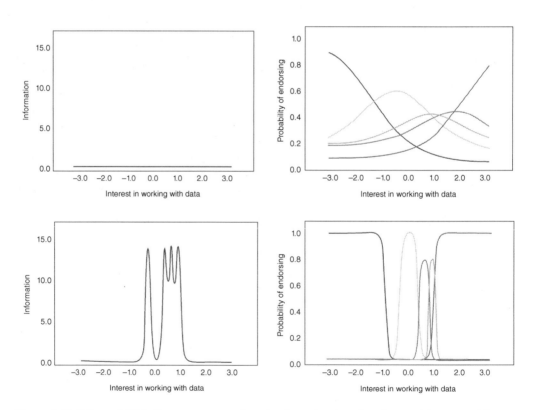

Figure 7.13 IICs and ICCs for a poorly performing item (top) and an item with acceptable performance (bottom).

suggesting that our measurement of the latent construct is less reliable with this item. This notion is further supported when we compare the ICCs associated with both items. With the office example, we see in the ICC in the bottom right that each of the five response options (e.g., "Strongly Dislike") is associated with the highest probability of endorsement at various points across the latent continuum. The hotel item in the top right, on the other hand, has ICCs that overlap a great deal. For example, among individuals around 1.5 on the latent continuum, the probabilities of endorsing four of the response options are almost equal. This evidence collectively suggests that the hotel item may not be a good measure for our latent construct and could be removed for future administrations of the survey, assuming our aim is to measure only an interest in working with data.

Other Uses of IRT

IRT has both theoretical and practical applications. From a theoretical perspective, IRT has helped advance the way researchers conceptualize and measure various personality and attitude surveys. For years, researchers analyzed responses to many of these measures by taking a sum of individuals' responses. This approach assumes a **dominance** response process, which argues that there is a linear relationship between the trait and the response to a measure. The more of the trait, the stronger the agreement you should have to a question that is meant to measure the trait. This assumption might seem obvious but the truth is that it might not always be correct. An alternative framework, the **ideal point** response process, could also be used to describe the relationship between traits and measures. Instead of a linear relationship, ideal point models use a **curvilinear** relationship. This means that the relationship between a trait and a positive response to a measure increases *up to a point*, and then decreases. Consider a personality question like "I like to go to dinner parties." A dominance model would assume that the more extraversion you have the more you will agree with this item. Very extraverted people will have the strongest agreement. An ideal point model, on the other hand, would say that as you increase in extraversion, you would be more likely to agree with this item. But at some point, people who are very very high in extraversion might start to disagree with this item. Maybe small dinner parties are too boring for the extremely extroverted, and they would disagree that they like dinner parties because they only like huge, epic parties. An ideal point model would reflect this probability of a positive response as follows in Figure 7.14:

Understanding the difference between dominance and ideal point response processes is important when we realize that it is possible for a person to have "too much of a good thing." Consider conscientiousness, which is generally perceived as a desirable trait predictive of job performance. However, it is possible that a worker could be so conscientious that he gets lost in the details of his job or takes too long perfecting his work. That is, there may be a curvilinear relationship between conscientiousness and job performance, such that the optimal levels of conscientiousness would be somewhere in the middle on the latent continuum. If we were to rely only on an individual's summed score across a couple conscientiousness items, it may be difficult for us to detect such relationships. One group of researchers explored this scenario by conducting a simulation study investigating curvilinear relationships and response processes (Carter et al., 2017). Their findings led them to conclude that IRT methods are crucial in identifying curvilinear relationships such as these.

IRT has also been used to identify potential sources of unfairness in employment assessments. **Differential item functioning (DIF)** means that item parameters vary as a function of

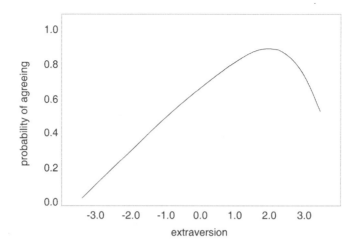

Figure 7.14 Ideal point model for "I like to go to dinner parties" item.

something other than a person's theta score. For example, an item might function differently for men and women, such that the item underpredicts theta for women. A variety of methods have been proposed to identify items that have DIF, and many of these methods rely on IRT.

These uses of IRT are just examples of the many possible applications of this analytic framework. The suggested readings at the end of the chapter provide much more in-depth information if you want to dig deeper and use IRT in your own research.

References

American Educational Research Association, American Psychological Association, National Council on Measurement in Education, & Joint Committee on Standards for Educational and Psychological Testing (US). (2014). *Standards for educational and psychological testing*. AERA.

Cleary, T. A. (1968). Test bias: Prediction of grades of Negro and White students in integrated colleges. *Journal of Educational Measurement, 5*, 115–124.

Cronbach, L. J., & Meehl, P. E. (1955). Construct validity in psychological tests. *Psychological Bulletin, 52*(4), 281–302.

Darrow, J. B., & Behrend, T. S. (2017). Person-environment fit is a formative construct. *Journal of Vocational Behavior, 103*, 117–131.

Konrath, S., Meier, B. P., & Bushman, B. J. (2014). Development and validation of the single item narcissism scale (SINS). *PLOS One, 9*(8), e103469. https://doi.org/10.1371/journal.pone.0103469

Landy, F. J. (1986). Stamp collecting versus science: Validation as hypothesis testing. *American Psychologist, 41*(11), 1183–1192.

MacKenzie, S. B., Podsakoff, P. M., & Jarvis, C. B. (2005). The problem of measurement model misspecification in behavioral and organizational research and some recommended solutions. *Journal of Applied Psychology, 90*(4), 710–730.

Tang, K. L. (1996). *Polytomous item response theory models and their application in large-scale testing programs: Review of the literature* (ETS Report No. RM-96-08). www.ets.org/research/policy_research_reports/publications/report/1996/ibtw

Further Reading

Carter, N. T., Dalal, D. K., Guan, L., LoPilato, A. C., & Withrow, S. A. (2017). Item response theory scoring and the detection of curvilinear relationships. *Psychological Methods*, *22*(1), 191–203. https://doi.org/10.1037/met0000101

* Caret and colleagues explore curvilinear relationships between psychological characteristics and outcomes by conducting two simulation studies, finding that IRT methods are well-suited to assess ideal point response data. They encourage researchers to think carefully about whether responses to their measures will follow dominance versus ideal point processes.

Cortina, J. M., Sheng, Z., Keener, S. K., Keeler, K. R., Grubb, L. K., Schmitt, N., Tonidandel, S., Summerville, K. M., Heggestad, E. D., & Banks, G. C. (2020). From alpha to omega and beyond! A look at the past, present, and (possible) future of psychometric soundness in the journal of applied psychology. *Journal of Applied Psychology*, *105*(12), 1351–1381. https://doi.org/10.1037/apl0000815

* Cortina and colleagues reviewed the psychometric practices of researchers publishing in one of I-O psychology's top journals and compared them to recommended practices, previous practices, and practices in other journals.

Hambleton, R. K., & Jones, R. W. (1993). An NCME instructional module on: Comparison of classical test theory and item response theory and their applications to test development. *Educational Measurement: Issues and Practice*, *12*(3), 38–47.

* Hambleton and Jones provide a broad overview of the major similarities and differences between classical test theory and item response theory. They explain how each theory addresses common measurement issues and contrast the two approaches in terms of assumptions, item-ability relationships, item and person statistics, and sample size requirements.

Lang, J. W., & Tay, L. (2021). The science and practice of item response theory in organizations. *Annual Review of Organizational Psychology and Organizational Behavior*, *8*, 311–338. https://doi.org/10.1146/annurev-orgpsych-012420-061705

* Lang and Tay describe how item response theory approaches can be used for testing, questionnaire responding, construct validation, and measurement equivalence of scores. They also provide examples with data and R code for readers interested in learning and applying IRT methods in their own research.

Society for Industrial and Organizational Psychology. (2018). *Principles for the validation and use of personnel selection procedures* (5th ed.). Society for Industrial and Organizational Psychology. https://doi.org/10.1017/iop.2018.195

* This document, produced by the Society of Industrial and Organizational Psychology, provides I-O psychologists with evidence-based principles related to conducting test validation research. In line with recommendations in The Standards, the Principles cover key issues related to reliability, validity and fairness, but in the context of employee selection.

Questions to Think About

1. What is measurement?
2. How does the jingle-jangle fallacy affect I-O psychologists' ability to accumulate new knowledge?
3. What do we mean when we say, "the validity of an inference"? Why is it not appropriate to say, "the validity of a test"?
4. What is the difference between a formative construct and a reflective construct?
5. Compare and contrast classical test theory, generalizability theory, and item response theory. Consider their practical differences (e.g., feasibility, required sample sizes) as well

as their conceptual differences (e.g., how each theory treats the concepts of reliability and validity).

6. One of your colleagues is interested in using the vocational interests scale mentioned in this chapter to select new employees at your organization. You are concerned about whether using the test for this purpose would be reliable, valid, and fair. How can classical test theory, generalizability theory, and item response theory methods help you address these concerns?

7. Imagine you just discovered a new measure in the research literature for a construct you want to study. What types of evidence would you need to feel confident in using it?

Key Terms

- alternate forms reliability
- bias, evidential
- bias, measurement
- bias, predictive
- classical test theory
- construct contamination
- construct deficiency
- construct validity
- construct, formative
- construct, reflective
- contamination
- Cronbach's alpha
- curvilinearity
- deficiency
- differential item functioning (DIF)
- difficulty
- dominance response process
- equality of opportunity to succeed
- equality of outcomes
- error
- evidence based on internal structure
- evidence based on relations to other variables
- evidence based on response processes
- evidence based on test content
- evidence based on the consequences of test use
- facet
- fairness, test
- generalizability theory (G-theory)
- ideal point response process
- inference
- inter-rater reliability
- internal consistency reliability
- interval
- item characteristic curve
- item information
- item response theory (IRT)
- jangle
- jingle
- jingle-jangle fallacy
- measure
- model, partial credit
- model, polytomous
- modern test theory
- monotonicity
- multiple rater reliability
- nominal
- observed score
- ordinal
- practice effect
- psychometrics
- questionnaire
- random variable
- ratio
- reliability
- scale of measurement
- split-half reliability
- Standards, The
- test validity
- test-retest reliability
- theta
- trinitarian view of test validity
- true score
- unitary view of test validity
- validation study
- validity study

Chapter 8

Research Design in Pursuit of Trustworthy Conclusions

Learning Objectives

After reading this chapter, you will be able to:

1. Explain different types of common experimental and quasi-experimental designs and their relative advantages.
2. Apply causal reasoning to psychological research questions.
3. Identify and minimize threats to validity that are associated with various designs.
4. Explain the logic of moderation and mediation.

Correlation doesn't imply causation.

– Everyone

But sometimes it does.

– Something we imagine Judea Pearl might say

Correlation doesn't imply causation, but it does waggle its eyebrows while mouthing "look over there."

– Randall Monroe (see Figure 8.1)

Doing research is about collecting data, to generate knowledge, to make claims about the world. This chapter is about how to do the collecting of information in a way that will best facilitate the kind of knowledge you want to generate. Remember that the "best" research design will always, always depend on the kind of question you want to answer.

When Can I Say "Causes"?

On some level, we all want to talk about causes and effects when we do research. From the earliest mammals, we have been driven to understand the world around us by linking causes and effects so we could predict the future. Imagine a bunch of monkeys in the jungle. They see a strong wind rustling the trees, and then moments later, coconuts that were previously unreachable come tumbling down. The monkeys learn that the wind "caused" the coconuts. Next time they notice that it's a windy day, they run to the coconut trees and await their free

DOI: 10.4324/9781315167473-11

Figure 8.1 Correlation versus causation (courtesy xkcd.com).

lunch. This temporal association was highly adaptive for them – the smarter monkeys, the ones who were first to notice a chain of causal events, would get the coconuts first, while the other monkeys, the ones who were muttering "correlation doesn't imply causation" under their breath . . . well, they didn't get any coconuts.

Humans, like our ancestors, have always relied on causal inferences for survival. How will rain affect the crops? What effect will fermentation have on this milk? We are strongly oriented towards looking for patterns in the environment and then connecting them into chains of events. The problem, and one that leads researchers astray so many times, is that we over-apply this pattern and ascribe causality to other kinds of patterns.

Thinking about causality is a difficult, abstract endeavor taken up by philosophers, computer scientists, mathematicians, and others who have offered formal definitions. For example, John Stuart Mill wrote in the 19th century that a causal relationship exists when "(1) the cause preceded the effect, (2) the cause was related to the effect, and (3) we can find no plausible alternative explanation for the effect other than the cause." In mathematics, causes are defined as factors that are both necessary and sufficient to produce an effect. Judea Pearl, a 21st-century philosopher and computer scientist, offered a three-level "ladder of causation" in which level one, the weakest, is observing ("what is?"); level two is doing ("what if?"); and the strongest form of causation, level three, is **counterfactuals** ("why?"). These differences reflect differences in these thinkers' philosophies of science (review Chapter 1 for a refresher).

In this book, a **cause** is a stimulus that comes first in a chain of events and can be linked to subsequent events as an explanation for those events. We use "cause" and "explanation" interchangeably. An effect, then, is the outcome of a cause. Research designs differ in their ability to support inferences about causality, as we will show in this chapter.

Thinking in terms of counterfactuals can help you think clearly when trying to understand causality. For anything you think to be causal, ask yourself this question: "Would an outcome be different now if *this* had been different in the past?" For example, imagine you had at some point chosen a career path into I-O psychology because you felt you'd been inspired by a particularly enthusiastic I-O psychology professor in your first-ever I-O psychology course. One counterfactual question to ask is: If a different professor had taught that class, would you have still pursued I-O? If no, then your career path may have been in part caused by that professor. But if yes, then some other cause was at play.

That is a simple example, and a silly story will demonstrate why causal inference is even tougher in the complexities of the real world. The story is about a linguistics researcher who visited New York City for the first time and went to Little Italy. She met with a group of older residents who had been living there for 50 years. They all had very strong Italian accents. Then she met with a group of people who were a little younger – their accents weren't very strong, but there were a few words they pronounced with an accent. Then, the researcher met with some younger people – and they didn't have any accent at all! Wow, thought the researcher. It must be the case that aging causes your accent to get stronger! The researcher observed a pattern (age and accent strength were related) but assigned it the wrong explanation. In fact, of course, the older residents had stronger accents because they had moved to NYC from Italy, whereas their kids grew up in NYC and thus did not have the same accent as their parents. The researcher's error was not in the observation of the pattern, but in the assignment of an explanation.

We can diagram the major reasons that these sorts of patterns occur as shown in Figure 8.2.

In Scenario 1, Variable X causes the outcome Y, which is often what we assume to be true. In Scenario 2, the "outcome" Y actually causes Variable X. When researchers claim or assume the relationship in Scenario 1 has occurred, but Scenario 2 is really what happened, this is referred to as **reverse causality**. In Scenario 3, there is a third variable that actually causes both X and Y. This common cause creates a relationship between X and Y, but not a causal one. We call this kind of relationship **spurious** because it isn't causally meaningful. It just looks casually meaningful because we mis-specified our model. Good research design is making sure that you have ruled out Scenario 2 and Scenario 3 when you want to make a causal claim.

Which scenario best describes what happened to our linguistics researcher? She observed that age (X) and accent (Y) were related. This is not a false or incorrect finding, by itself. But then she concluded that age caused accent, and that was the mistake. There was a third variable, Z, that itself caused the observed relationship between age and accent. In this case, place of birth is Z. People who were born in Italy have a stronger Italian accent, and people

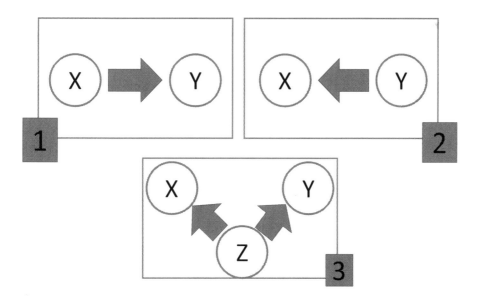

Figure 8.2 Possible explanations for an observed relationship between X and Y.

who were born in the US have a weaker Italian accent, and the relationship with year of birth occurred because of the way that US immigration patterns occurred – yet another Z in the real causal equation – and not because of any individual-level changes. By sampling people at one particular moment in time, the true underlying pattern was obscured.

This kind of mistake in attributing cause is so common that it has a name: the **third variable problem**. In I-O psychology, people commit this error all the time. We want to describe causes of behavior in organizations, but we don't always have access to the kind of data that allows us to do this. For example, how would you answer the following questions?

- What makes a leader effective?
- How do teams learn to trust each other over time?
- Was this training program effective?
- How can burnout be prevented?

Each of these is a causal question in disguise. Researchers often phrase their research questions this way so that they look "less" causal. But that does not change the reality of the claim being made. These questions can be rephrased to make the causal claims more obvious:

- What traits or behaviors cause a leader to improve organizational outcomes?
- Which events cause teams to trust each other?
- Did this training program cause participants to learn anything or change their behavior at work?
- What actions cause burnout, and what interventions can cause it to decrease?

Because these are all causal questions, regardless of the way they are phrased, data need to be collected and analyzed in a way that removes Scenarios 2 and 3 from the set of reasonable explanations.

Let's take the first question, about leader effectiveness, and think about possible alternative explanations that could get in the way of proper causal inference. Imagine that you collect data from both leaders and followers. You ask the leaders about their personality, their intelligence, and their height. Then, you measure each follower's performance by collecting their annual performance ratings (which their supervisor generated), and you also ask the followers how satisfied they are with their leader. You discover the pattern of correlations shown in Table 8.1.

Table 8.1 Observed correlations between leaders and followers

Leader Traits	Follower Performance	Follower Satisfaction
Agreeableness	0.70	0.50
Extraversion	0.60	0.40
Conscientiousness	−0.20	0.20
Openness	0.00	0.30
Neuroticism	0.00	−0.30
Intelligence	0.20	0.60
Height	0.00	0.60

What might you conclude? One interesting relationship is that Agreeable leaders have higher-performing and more satisfied followers. Should you conclude that agreeableness is a factor that makes teams more satisfied, which causes them to perform better? Or, is it more likely that agreeable leaders give their team higher ratings, so the team merely appears happier and more satisfied because they have high ratings?

The data in Table 8.1 will not help you figure out which of these explanations is correct. They also won't help you figure out if a third variable is causing the relationships. The third variable, in this case, could be participation in a leadership development program. Maybe agreeable leaders are more likely to agree to participate in those programs, and the program causes more satisfied and productive followers.

There are two major ways that a researcher can go about removing these alternative explanations. The first is through **research design**, especially by using **experimentation**, and the second is a particular kind of statistical analysis. Between the two, research design is the safer and simpler choice; there are far more assumptions needed to infer causality from statistical analysis than from design. Further, designing research to support causal conclusions is a much older and more established approach, and therefore one that researchers tend to trust more, so we'll spend the majority of this chapter discussing it.

Regardless of the specific approach you adopt, you should remember that no amount of fancy analysis will fix a bad design or sloppy thinking.

Balancing Control and Generalizability Through Design

Research design is as its core making a series of decisions about control and generalizability. **Control** refers to ruling out other explanations for the patterns you see, whereas **generalizability** is about determining whether the same patterns would be expected to hold across other situations. Ideally you would want your design to have both control and generalizability, but unfortunately, this typically isn't possible.

Control and generalizability are inversely related, but not in a straightforward, predictable way; generally speaking, the more you attempt to rule out alternative explanations by creating a tightly controlled environment, the less that environment looks like other environments you might wish to describe with your research. For example, in the leadership example previously, let's imagine that you want to better understand the effect of height on leadership success. But you know that height might also be related to other factors (e.g., ethnicity or sex), and you want to eliminate those as possible explanations. One option would be to ask all the leaders in your sample to wear different-height shoes (i.e., randomly assign them to a particular height) so you can rule out those explanations. This would be successful in ruling our sex or ethnicity in explaining height-leadership relationships. But is this scenario you've created useful? Are there any real organizations in which you could imagine dictating leaders' footwear? Do you really think that a leader on little stilts would be taken seriously? Although this approach would tightly control alternative explanations related to height and height alone, it also creates problems related to generalizability, since rated leader effectiveness may decrease due to stilt-wearing and not due to height itself.

Thus, when designing research, you should always think about this balance. When trying to increase control, how is generalizability harmed? When trying to increase generalizability, how is control harmed? Are there alternative balances you are not thinking about?

In seeking balance, you are ultimately trying to make valid claims. Recall that validity is a property of an inference and refers to truthfulness or usefulness. In this context, validity refers to the truthfulness or usefulness of our research design in drawing the kind of conclusions we want to draw. This means that the best or "correct" research design for a given research problem is the one that allows you to make the kinds of useful and truthful claims you want to make. The various threats to the usefulness and truthfulness of your research conclusions and inferences related to research design, which we can roughly group into threats to **internal validity** and threats to generalizability.

Internal Validity Threats

Maximizing internal validity is about ruling out alternative explanations for the effects you observe. This is often referred to as "minimizing **internal validity threats**" or "minimizing confounds." A good experimental design will minimize, but can never totally eliminate, alternative explanations. Cook and Campbell (1976) creates a typology of "threats to internal validity" (or put another way, common design-related confounds), which serves as a convenient mental checklist to consider when designing a study. Despite their age, this typology has held up remarkably well since then. Treat this list as an *incomplete* but good starting place when designing your own studies.

Demand characteristics. Demand characteristics are the clues that an experimenter might give off that hint to participants about what is expected of them. Sometimes these clues are subtle, and sometimes they are surprisingly obvious. Imagine a marketing study in which two products, A and B, are being compared. As the experimenter offers a shopper a sample of each product, she asks, "do you see a difference between A and B?" The shopper is probably aware that conducting an experiment in which two identical things are compared would be strange. He might agree that A and B seem different because he understands that they must be different – that's how experiments work, so why else would she have asked that question? He might even convince himself that he does in fact detect a difference. If A and B represent the "original" and "new and improved" versions of the product, the marketer might then wrongly conclude that the improvement made a difference in the product. One fun example of demand characteristics are taste test comparisons between the two dominant cola brands: Pepsi and Coca-Cola. When asked "which is better" based on taste, research participants often have strong opinions about which *should* be better and try to identify which is which based on that opinion and not based on their taste buds.

History. History, though a bit awkwardly named, means that while an experiment is going on, various other things are happening in the world and those external events affect the participants in the study. The events might be big and noticeable or small and subtle. Imagine that I designed a study to understand the effect of a wellbeing intervention on job satisfaction. I administer a pre-test of wellbeing in January. I deploy my intervention, and then I administer a post-test in April. In comparing pre-test and post-test scores, I conclude that the intervention worked, because scores were higher in April. In this example, I have failed to account for history. First, it is known that wellbeing changes seasonally, and these seasonal changes co-occurred with the timing of my measurements. People are generally happier in spring than winter. Other seasonal events might also confound the experiment – for instance, accountants are probably less happy in April because their workload (in the US) increases dramatically at that time. Second, it is unlikely that absolutely nothing else occurred within the organization, such as shifts in managerial habits and practices or organizational policy, that might have affected wellbeing over the same time period. These are all internal validity threats attributable to history.

Maturation. Maturation can be thought of as a specific case of history having to do with the passage of time. Maturation is especially of concern when designing longitudinal research. People change over time – they grow and learn and develop. If this change isn't accounted for in your experimental design, it is a confound. This is a common problem in training research. The most important question in training research is "did the training work?" and often a longitudinal design is ideal for answering this question. Are people better at their jobs after the training? The issue, here, is that people naturally get better at their jobs over time. A researcher must rule out the effect of natural practice and learning opportunities that improve job performance if they are trying to understand and isolate the effect of the training.

Regression to the mean. Recall from Chapter 7 that measurement error is generally assumed to be normally and randomly distributed around the true score of whatever it is you're trying to measure. In a given sample, scores that are very far away from the true score are unlikely, and scores that are closer to the mean are more likely. This pattern can affect internal validity in an often unexpected way. Consider the example of wanting to study pretest-posttest effects for a growth mindset intervention. At time 1, you take a measurement of growth mindset, and these measurements are normally distributed around a low number. At time 2, you measure the same thing, only to discover that the people who scored lowest at time 1 have improved dramatically. Although this might be in part attributable to your thoughtful intervention, it's also likely that a fair number of low scorers at time 1 scored low due to chance factors, and at time 2, this unluckiness was reduced, pushing their scores toward the mean.

This tendency is called regression to the mean, a term that often confuses methods students because of the word "regression." In this specific context, "regression" only refers to the ordinary English language definition of regression, as in "reduces apparent differences," such as in the sentence "we made some progress, but then regressed." It does not refer to the statistical test called "regression."

Testing. One of the most common complaints raised about standardized tests is that students who have had prior exposure to the test will do better by virtue of having some familiarity with how the test works. In any research design where participants complete a test more than once, your participants will have some knowledge about the later test by virtue of having taken the earlier test. This is a problem because if you want to understand the effect of an intervention, it becomes difficult to separate out the effect of the pre-test from that of the intervention. Put another way, the casual effect of completing the pre-test is confounded with the causal effect of the intervention.

This issue is more severe in the case of knowledge, skill, and ability testing – any test where there is a "correct" answer – due to the **retrieval-practice effect**. This effect is well-explored in educational psychology in a body of research that suggests people learn quite effectively through the act of test-taking. In short, when a person completes a test, they are practicing remembering test material, and that practice causes them to remember more on later tests. In this way, repeated exposure to the same or similar tests is not just a confound – it may be a causal intervention that changes what your participants remember about what they are being tested on! It also implies that using slightly different versions of the same tests at different time points doesn't necessarily help avoid the effect.

For more on the retrieval-practice effect, see:

Roediger, H. L., III, & Karpicke, J. D. (2006). Test-enhanced learning: Taking memory tests improves long-term retention. *Psychological Science, 17*(3), 249–255.

Selection. Selection effects refer to the ways that participants in your sample might be different than other people specifically because they were selected for your study. For example, most studies of relationships between job performance and personality are conducted with people who are employed. People who had certain extreme personality characteristics were not hired, and so they do not have an opportunity to be selected for the study. It's probably the case that including them would change your conclusions about how personality affects performance.

Diffusion of treatment. In certain research designs, people are placed into groups that are treated differently – and people in one group sometimes aren't very happy when they discover the specific way they were being treated differently from others. This is a particularly common threat to internal validity when we provide optional opportunities to subsets of employees, such as special leadership training. It is unlikely that people in a study are completely independent from one another; people often have friends at work. Perhaps some groups of these friends start talking about the tips and tricks about getting into better-paying positions in the company based on the training they're getting. This can lead to people in one group getting some of the "treatment" intended only for another group. This can also lead to hurt feelings, resentment, and other negative outcomes that further change how people behave at work, which in turns muddies the conclusions from your research even further.

Picking a Design

Different experimental designs will be differentially able to address these threats. There is no perfect design, only the design that is most useful for your particular research question. We'll say that again: There. Is. No. Perfect. Design. The skill of designing a research study is determining which approach is best for eliminating the alternative explanations (confounds) that are most important and relevant to your study. A diversity of designs is necessary for research to progress. If everything we know about job performance comes from observation, our understanding is limited. If all we have are experiments, we are similarly limited. You might notice that some areas of research, or individual researchers, lean toward choosing one design most of the time. That is not something to aspire to.

Generalizability Threats

Generalizability refers to the extent to which the results of a study can be applied to other situations, populations, times, or contexts that were not studied. In other words, it is the extent to which the findings of a study can be generalized beyond the specific sample and context in which the study was conducted. The generalizability of a study depends in part on the similarity between the sample and the population to which the findings are intended to be applied.

A concept closely related to generalizability, but a bit narrower, is **external validity**. In practice, people often use these terms interchangeably, as the difference is subtle. External validity is the older concept, credited to Campbell and Stanley (1963), used then to refer to how well a treatment effect (i.e., the result of an intervention) observed in a study would replicate either in the population from which the sample was drawn from ("generalizing to") or in related populations ("generalizing across"). For example, imagine we ran a training intervention study to improve diversity climate in an organization by randomly selecting employees to experience it and found an increase of 1 standard deviation on an outcome measure. We might ask two questions related to external validity:

- To what degree do we expect these results to replicate in our entire organization? (generalizing to)
- To what degree do we expect these results to replicate in other organizations? (generalizing across)

These are not straightforward questions to answer. For the first question, because we randomly selected employees from our organization, we have reason to believe the results would generalize to all employees from our organization. If we had instead only recruited volunteers for our intervention, we would not be so confident, since that would have created a selection effect (i.e., an internal validity threat) that would also create an external validity threat in terms of population correspondence – our volunteer sample might be systematically different from the organizational population. Trying to generalize across, rather than to, adds even more potential confounds as the differences between your sample and target population become more difficult to precisely describe. Here is a partial list of ways our sample in this case might differ from the intended populations:

- Occupation/work design: Is the nature of the job or work your participants engage in different from those in the target population?
- Demographic characteristics: Do the demographic characteristics, like race, gender, age, religion, work experience, personality, lifestyle, culture, etc., differ from the target population?
- Time: When was the sample collected and how might people or work be different now?
- Economic context: Are the kinds of jobs and social class of people in your sample different from the target population?
- Situation: What was happening while data were being collected?

Another way to think about external validity this way is that differences caused by factors like these reflect unmeasured moderators (see Chapter 3 and also later in this chapter) of the effects you observed. There is no way to know if your training would have been effective for non-volunteers without measuring the effect among non-volunteers. Without that, you must make assumptions and inferences about external validity.

Generalizability is an even broader concept than external validity as it includes not just differences between samples and populations in terms of representation of individuals but in terms of specific decisions made in experimental design. For example, even if *our* training that *we* designed affects outcomes as expected, the same training program administered by different facilitators might not. Cook and Campbell offered the acronym "**UTOS**" to help think about types of generalizability threats.

- **U: Units**. Units in psychological research are most often people or time periods. Generalizability of units means: do your findings apply to all the people in your sample and all the people *not* in your sample?

- **T: Treatments**. Treatments refers to the experimental design and stimuli you use in the study. Generalizability of treatments means: would your findings look the same if you used a different design or experimental procedure?
- **O: Observations**. Observations refers to measurements or outcomes used in the study. Generalizability of observations means: would you reach the same conclusions if you used different measures of your constructs?
- **S: Settings**. Settings refers to the time and place the study was conducted. Variables like culture and economic context can affect generalizability of setting.

There is a very famous historical experiment in psychology by Stanley Milgram about the effects of power, and we can use UTOS to identify some of the generalizability threats in the study. In the study, Milgram asked volunteers who responded to a newspaper ad to come to his lab at Harvard University to participate in an experiment. He claimed that the experiment was meant to study the ways that people learn. He asked volunteers to administer electric shocks to a "learner" when the learner made mistakes. Hidden from the participant was that the learner was not a real person – it was a series of faked audio recordings. The true purpose of the study was to understand whether the volunteers would comply with Milgram's orders to hurt an innocent person. He concluded that indeed, people would comply with orders from a powerful person and go against their best judgment and morals.

Let's pick this design apart from a UTOS perspective:

- **Units:** The people in the experiment were all white men living in the Boston area who read and replied to a newspaper ad. People with demanding jobs do not have time to come visit psychology labs in the middle of the day. And not everyone reads the newspaper. If any of these characteristics influence participant behavior in the experiment, generalizability to non-Bostonian-newspaper-readers-with-a-lot-of-free-time is threatened.
- **Treatment:** Milgram studied the effects of power and obedience using a highly contrived simulation that does not resemble most real-world situations. There is no reason to expect that administering shocks to an unseen stranger is psychologically similar to, say, punching your next-door neighbor in the face or complying with other kinds of requests. Thus, generalizability to real-world displays of obedience and power is questionable.
- **Observations:** The primary measure of compliance in this study was the number of volts of electricity the participant was willing to administer. A highly publicized finding from the study is that some percentage of the participants were willing to administer the maximum voltage, presumably causing great harm to the learner. There is no way to know if anyone in the study took that action seriously. Some may have even understood it to be an experiment. Thus, generalizability to other kinds of compliance may be limited.
- **Settings:** The study was conducted in Harvard University by a serious-looking scientist wearing a white lab coat. This is a very particular setting and may not generalize to other everyday settings in life and work. Generalizability to non-Harvard settings lacking lab coated experiments may also be limited.

None of these external validity threats by itself necessarily condemns a study. But the total weight of the threats is severe and important to consider before drawing any firm conclusions.

How to Study UTOS

Meta-analysis, which will be discussed in Chapter 13, is one of the most useful ways to discover possible effects of UTOS or other factors. It is impossible for a single study to include people from every job, background, time, and place. But if 20 researchers conduct 20 studies in 20 contexts, those results can be compared to identify possible patterns that might affect the conclusions of the study across their studies. For example, early meta-analyses were conducted to understand the effects of various predictors (intelligence, personality, job interview scores) on future job performance. Meta-analyses were conducted to show that the relationships between predictors and performance were consistent regardless of the job type where each particular test was used, because different research studies had used samples that varied in those characteristics. Those meta-analyses could not answer questions about potential gender or nationality effects, however, because the individual studies available at that time did not contain any variation in gender or nationality to examine those characteristics. In this way, meta-analyses are very powerful tools that can be used to understand factors influencing generalizability but are limited to whatever research designs have already been used to study that relationship.

When I-O psychology researchers talk about generalizability, they are often a little vague about whom exactly they want to generalize to, and there is sometimes an implied desire to generalize to "all workers at all times and all places."

Our advice is to move away from this habit, and to be more precise about who exactly you intend to generalize to with your research conclusions. Including a section on "Context" in your manuscripts can help you be clear on this point (see Chapter 14 for more details on writing this part of a manuscript). Some editors are under the mistaken belief that a study cannot make a strong contribution to theory unless it makes universal claims. Although universal claims are more impressive to laypeople (e.g., "Improve job satisfaction with this one simple trick!"), they are often not very scientific.

One of my (Tara's) favorite papers, by Gary Johns, makes a strong argument for why we should care more about context. He points out that phenomena at a higher **level**, which refers to the **nesting** of units within other units, than the one being observed are often essential to make sense of observations. For example, people may be nested within teams, which are nested within organizations, which are nested within industries, which are nested with nations and cultures. Although we will revisit this concept in greater depth later in this chapter, an example of this kind of thinking is shown in Figure 8.3.

Although this is a chapter about quantitative research design, qualitative methods like those described in Chapter 6 can help you determine the aspects of context that may be pertinent to your study.

Isolating Causal Effects with Experiments

The essence of an **experiment** is that the researcher creates a situation that holds as many variables constant as possible so as to better understand the effect of specific variables of interest. Generally, participants in an experiment are assigned to one or more groups that

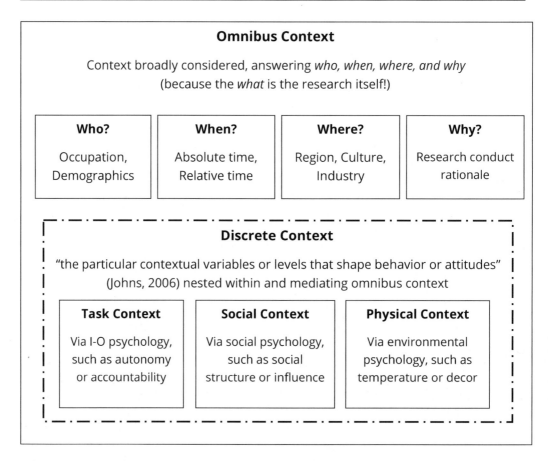

Figure 8.3 Aspects of context, adapted from Johns (2006).

differ only on variables of interest. In order to study a variable experimentally, you must be able to change its value at will, which is referred to as **manipulation**. Plenty of variables we care about in I/O psychology cannot be manipulated, including age, gender, personality, intelligence, and many others. Such variables will never show up as the focus of an experimental study. There are also variables that are plausibly manipulable but extremely difficult to do so in practice, like income or country of residence. You probably wouldn't choose an experimental design for those variables either.

All experimental designs have **controls** and **treatments**. Treatments are variables that you manipulate, and controls are variables whose values are held constant by virtue of the design of the experiment. To experimentally control for a variable is to specify that you think the variable might act as a third variable (review Figure 8.2!) that would affect your ability to draw accurate conclusions about causality and take steps to prevent it from influencing the results of your study.

Imagine an experimental study about the effects of virtual reality on learning. Your goal would likely be to control everything about the learning experience except for whether it took place in virtual reality or not. This approach would minimize alternative explanations

Manipulation Strength

An important issue in treatment design is **manipulation strength**, which refers to the intensity of the causal effect of the treatment. For example, imagine two different research teams who decide to study the effects of "diversity training." Team A randomly assigns people to a two-week-long intensive training program versus a control group with no training. Team B randomly assigns people to view a 60-second video about diversity from a popular social media platform versus a control group with training. Although in both cases the teams are (arguably) studying "diversity training," the strength of Team A's manipulation is much greater and therefore much more likely to result in an observable effect. In the UTOS framework, this is a "T" problem. Although experiments are great for minimizing threats to internal validity, generalizability remains an important consideration.

for differences between virtual reality and non-virtual reality groups. Ideally, the learning content, length of time, time of day, incentives, costs, and all other aspects of the experience would be held constant across groups as experimental controls. In practice, controlling everything you should control can be difficult. For example, if the virtual reality training took three hours and traditional learning took 30 minutes, time and anything associated with time, like fatigue, would become third variables confounding your ability to draw causal conclusions.

Since treatments are the variables you intentionally vary to as to observe their effects, the goal of experimental design is to hold everything that isn't a treatment constant as a control across groups. In the previous example, people in both group A (VR) and group B (no-VR) would ideally have identical learning experiences *except* that people in group A would get those experiences in VR. Because group B would experience only the held-constant controls, it would be referred to as the **control group**. Because group A would experience the held-constant controls *plus* the VR treatment, it would be referred to as the **treatment group**. Each of these groups is commonly referred to as a **condition**. Thus, a study with one treatment group and one control group has two conditions.

An important clarifying note: in some contexts, you'll see conditions called "levels," but we'd caution you against doing that, because "levels" has another meaning more common in I/O psychology that we will discuss later in this chapter.

Two other common terms you will find in the context of experimental design are **independent variables (IVs)** and **dependent variables (DVs)**. These terms are used to refer to manipulated and observed/measured variables, respectively. The IV is called "independent" because in an experiment, the researcher makes the choice of which group gets which version of the manipulation *independently* of other variables. In the VR study example, the use of VR cannot be affected by learning (i.e., reverse causality), because we manipulated VR independently of learning. Learning, in contrast, is *dependent* on whether VR was used or not. Sometimes researchers use the terms IV and DV in non-experimental research to describe assumed theoretical differences between predictors, correlates, and outcomes, but we urge you not to make this same mistake.

It isn't logistically possible to identify and control every possible confound. There is no way, for example, for you to know all of the possible individual differences, work contexts, and so on that might influence the outcomes in the treatment and control groups differently.

To deal with this problem, **random assignment** is used to place each individual within the sample into either the control group or treatment group using chance alone. Using random assignment means that any third variables that could affect your conclusions, even if you don't know what those third variables are, become controls, because they are unrelated to group membership. When variables cannot be controlled in your design, it is important that they be randomly assigned.

This works because of the same logic we saw with classical test theory in Chapter 7. Specifically, when people are randomly assigned to different groups, the mean of individual-level error within a group should be zero. The resulting data can be described with the same classical test theory formula we used before:

$$X = T + e$$

Where X = the observed outcome of the experiment

   T = the true causal effect of the intervention when it is present

And e = random error due to chance

Because random error is minimized when using random assignment, on average, for people in the control group, $X = 0$, and on average, for people in the treatment group, $X = T$. Thus, the differences in scores between the treatment and control groups can be plausibly considered the magnitude of the causal effect of the treatment, and this is exactly how we draw conclusions about causal effects in experiments – by 1) comparing the means between treatments and controls to estimate effects and 2) using the results of t-tests, ANOVAs, or other simple general linear models to draw inferences.

A quick aside here: methods learners frequently mix up random *assignment* with random *sampling* and random *selection*. Random selection and random sampling refer to the same thing – identifying cases from a population for inclusion in a sample – and were described in Chapter 4. Random selection/sampling is a completely different concept from random assignment. Keep them distinct in your mind!

Technical Approaches to Random Assignment

There are many specific ways to perform random assignment. One of the easiest is to generate a column of random numbers in Google Sheets Excel using the *=rand()* formula, and then list participant IDs in the next column. Then, sort by the random number column. Because the participants will now be listed in a random order, you can simply count out the first half of IDs in your spreadsheet and assign them to your treatment group, and then assign the second half to your control group. If you have more than two groups, adjust the split according to however many groups you need to populate.

Test Your Understanding

To test your understanding so far, consider the following study published in the *Journal of Applied Psychology* (Watson et al., 2013). In this study, researchers wanted to understand the effect of tracking during training. All participants were instructed to complete a training task using Microsoft Excel. Each participant arrived at a computer station and was given one of three sets of instructions based upon a random assignment chart made beforehand. In the first group, participants were told that everything they did on the computer would be observed by the experimenter in real time from a second computer station. In the second group, participants were told that their computer activity would be saved and reviewed later. In the third group, participants were told that their computer activity would not be tracked. Participants were not aware of the purpose of the study or aware of what the other conditions were. After completing the training activity, all participants completed an attitudes and reactions questionnaire and took a test measuring their Excel skills.

Because random assignment was used to assign people to groups, this is an experiment. The manipulated independent variable in this study was the tracking method, and participants were assigned to one of three conditions. Because the goal was to examine tracking, and one condition contained no tracking, we can conclude that condition was the control group. The other two groups had different types of tracking, which means they were both treatment groups. The dependent variables were Excel skills and attitudes about the training. Finally, participants being unaware of the purpose of study or the nature of other conditions was likely a choice made to minimize demand characteristics, that is, an internal validity threat.

If these are the same conclusions you drew when reading the example, you are well on your way to understanding experimental design.

Choosing a Specific Experimental Design

The most common experimental designs involve two or more groups of people who receive different treatments. There are many variations on this basic concept, some of which are much less commonly used in I-O psychology research.

For example, a less common experimental design is the **waitlist control design.** In this kind of design, everyone receives the treatment, but some people receive it right away and some receive it later. The main reason to use this design is if the treatment is desirable and withholding it from some people would be seen as unfair. The opportunity to participate in a leadership development program, for example, might be something that everyone in a company wants. In this case, rolling the program out in waves will still allow you to get good information about the effects of the program without excluding anyone.

In this way, choosing the ideal research design is a thoughtful process of balancing the various advantages and disadvantages that every design brings. For simple research questions, such as the comparison of two groups, there are often clearly preferred approaches. But for real, complex research questions, there is more often a group of designs that offer various trade-offs, none of which are ideal. Learning to navigate this complexity is what will make you a competent designer of research.

Picking a Level of Analysis

An early and essential step in designing a study is determining the appropriate **level of analysis**. Level of analysis refers to the approach you take to addressing nested data. In some cases, nesting is a goal. For example, in the experiment described previously, all cases receiving treatment are nested within the treatment group, and all cases not receiving treatment are nested within the control group. In this context, we have created **multilevel data** with the explicit purpose of comparing outcomes across groups at the higher level of analysis, such as by comparing a treatment group mean versus a control group mean using a t-test. This is an example of **aggregation**, the process by which you analyze data at the group level (in this case, using means and standard deviations) despite collecting data at the individual level.

Levels in observed data can be very complex. For example, individuals can be grouped into departments in an organization, and organizations can be grouped into regions or industries; analyzing at any level higher than the one at which you collected data required aggregation. On the lower levels, data can be collected from each person multiple times, requiring aggregation *up to* the individual level from the time level.

It is up to you to determine the appropriate level of analysis for your study. This choice has major implications for the conclusions you will be able to draw. One well-known issue created by improper level of analysis specification is called **Simpson's paradox**, which is also called the **Yule-Simpson effect**. Simpson's paradox is that the direction of an observed relationship at one level may be reversed at higher levels, leading to opposite conclusions depending on which level you're observing. Here's an example of how Simpson's paradox can affect conclusions in organizational research. Let's imagine that you are concerned about gender bias in selection. You have observed the data shown in Table 8.2.

You conclude that there is indeed gender bias at work! Women are clearly being selected at lower rates. But in your next step, you disaggregate the data into the department level of analysis. You observe the data shown in Table 8.3.

Here, the data suggest that either men or women have an advantage depending on the department being examined. But since larger numbers of women applied in more competitive programs, aggregating all the data created the appearance of an overall gender disadvantage. Visually, a case of Simpson's paradox might look like the scatterplot shown in Figure 8.4.

Table 8.2 Higher-level observations in a study of gender and selection

	Applied	Selected	%
Men	8442	3714	44%
Women	4321	1512	35%
Total	12763	5233	41%

Table 8.3 Lower-level observations in a study of gender and selection

Applicants	A	B	C	D	E	F
Men	825	560	325	417	191	373
Women	108	25	593	375	393	341
Total	933	585	918	792	584	714
Percent Accepted						
Men	62%	63%	37%	33%	28%	6%
Women	82%	68%	34%	35%	24%	7%
Total	64%	63%	35%	34%	25%	6%

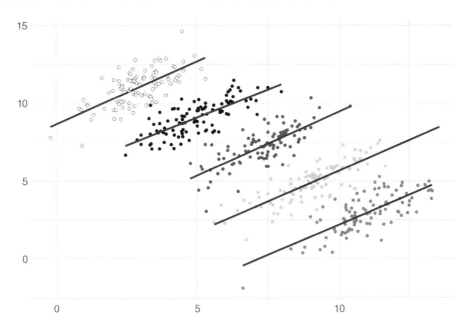

Figure 8.4 Scatterplot depicting Simpson's paradox.

Within each group, there is a positive relationship between X and Y (red lines). But over-all, there is a negative relationship between X and Y (black line).

A real-life psychology example of level-of-analysis confusion fueled decades of debate on self-efficacy. Motivation theorists had strongly opposing viewpoints about whether self-efficacy is positively or negatively related to performance. Each side had evidence to sup-port their argument. Thanks to the work of Vancouver et al. (2001), this disagreement was shown to be a result of level-of-analysis misspecification. At the between-person level, some people have higher self-efficacy and higher performance, and some have lower self-efficacy and lower performance, so overall there is a positive relationship between self-efficacy and performance. However! For any given individual, there is a negative relationship between self-efficacy and performance when observing their self-efficacy over time. Understanding the theory of this relationship can be a bit mind-boggling, so we will leave the psychological explanation to the motivation theorists. But we can nevertheless see the pattern of effects clearly in Figure 8.5.

Given all this, we can say with certainty that specifying a level of analysis properly is essential to drawing valid conclusions. Many of the phenomena we are interested in occur at multiple levels, and they may behave differently at each level. Choosing the "best" level for your study, like almost everything else in research methods, is a matter of weighing various advantages and disadvantages between the different approaches, and the first major decision is among the following three general strategies:

Between-persons designs are fundamentally about comparing people to each other. The claim "conscientiousness is related to performance" usually means "conscientious people have higher performance than non-conscientious people." Another example is "Positive

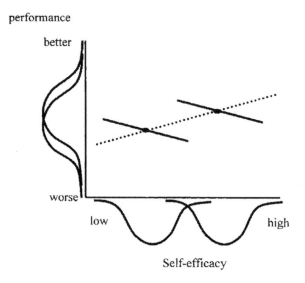

Figure 8.5 Simpson's paradox in the relationship between self-efficacy and performance, from Vancouver et al. (2001)

affect is related to organizational citizenship behavior (OCB)" – this implies that some people are higher in positive affect, and those people also perform more OCBs. In many I-O psychology scenarios, our task is to make distinctions between people for some purpose. In conducting between-person studies, you need to pay a lot of attention to third variables that can affect your conclusions. Control is essential.

Within-person designs do not compare people to each other. Rather, comparisons are made between time points or occasions that a single person experiences. In a within-person design, each person serves as their own control, making many person-level third variables less relevant. A within-person question about conscientiousness and performance might be, "Do people perform better in settings that bring out their conscientiousness?" Another example is "Do people engage in more OCBs on the days they feel more positive affect?" Because we can never randomly assign a person to a person that is not themselves, within-person designs are by nature non-experimental, which creates different internal validity threats.

Cross-level designs involve variables at multiple levels that interact with each other. For example, you might be interested in the relationship between training and organizational citizenship behavior – is a person more likely to engage in OCB after training than before? – which is a within-person question. You could change this to a cross-level question by asking, "Are people more likely to improve from training if their supervisors encourage them beforehand?" In this design, we are giving everyone training and measuring them twice (within-subject), but we're also randomly assigning half of participants to get extra supervisor support (between-subject). To understand the resulting design, it's helpful to visually map the variables you hope to measure at each level to keep them organized. You could model this example cross-level research question as shown in Figure 8.6. Here, there is a both a between-person component (the effect of training) and a within-person component (the effect of supervisor intervention).

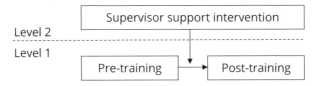

Figure 8.6 Cross-level study design.

Describing Experimental Designs

Cell-based research designs, like experiments, can take many specific configurations of between- and within-person factors, so there are a few common ways to refer to complex designs. Both between-person and within-person designs are commonly described using a shorthand notation based upon the number of conditions within each manipulated variable. For example, if you manipulated three between-person *or* within-person variables, each with two levels, this would likely be referred to as a 2 × 2 × 2 ("two-by-two-by-two") design. It might also be referred to as a three-way design, referring to the number of variables being manipulated or crossed; the more general case of this is called an **n-way design** or **factorial design**.

In cross-level designs, it may not be clear as to which variables are between and which are within, so additional notation is common to indicate which are which, as in "a 2B × 2B × 4W design," which implies a 4-cell (probably time points) within-subjects design nested within a 2 × 2 between-subjects design. However, this *might* also be referred to as a "mixed 3-way design" due to the mixing of between- and within-subjects factors across three variables.

As you might be noticing, although there are common conventions, this notation is *not* totally standardized. You'll always still need to read methods sections carefully to be sure of what any particular researcher actually means by the notation and terms they use.

Using Cross-Level Designs to Reduce Internal Validity Threats

One of the most well-known special cases of a cross-level design is the **Solomon 4-group design**, a particular configuration of control groups designed to uncover testing effects, shown in Figure 8.7. In this design, the first group of participants experiences both the pre-test and the intervention. The second group gets only the pre-test. The third group gets only the intervention. And the fourth group gets neither. By comparing scores on the post-test between all four groups, you can determine whether a testing effect exists, an important threat to internal validity. In doing so, you've also created a within-person design (conditions 1 and 2) nested within a between-person design (all conditions); half of participants complete two tests, and the other half complete one. Despite the investigative value that this design brings in relation to the effects of pre-testing, it is not very common because it is not practical. Most obviously, it requires a lot of people, since only half of participants participate in the within-subjects part of

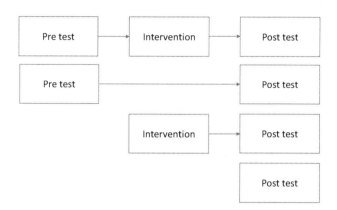

Figure 8.7 The four conditions in a Solomon 4-group design.

the study. It can also create challenges for fairness when deployed in field settings, as participants, especially those in the second condition, often wonder why they have to take a bunch of tests with no training or other intervention between them.

The Incredible Complexity of Multilevel Data

A complete treatment of the myriad challenges created when trying to analyze complex multilevel data is more than we can provide in this book, but it is important to be able to recognize when you are facing challenging multilevel data and to understand the complexity it adds. The most common kind of multilevel data I-O psychologists face is time points, nested within people, nested within organizational structures like departments or teams, nested within local organizations like specific stores or plants, all nested within the overall organization to which all of those levels belong. I-O psychologists in industry also frequently encounter a more complex type of multilevel data called **cross-classified data**, in which cases can belong to multiple overlapping groups. For example, if you were interested in studying leadership within a matrix organization where each employee was supervised by both a unit manager and a project manager, you would need to disentangle the effects of two distinct sources of leadership behaviors.

For a much deeper exploration of multilevel designs and the complex analyses needed to understand their results, try starting with:

Klein, K. J., & Kozlowski, S. W. J. (2000). *Multilevel theory, research, and methods in organizations: Foundations, extensions, and new directions.* Jossey-Bass.

Seeing Things as They Really Are: Field Studies

In many cases and for many reasons, an experiment might not be feasible. One major issue is that the goal of an experiment is to tightly control all aspects of the environment so as to isolate the effect of your chosen variables. As discussed in Chapter 4, this is a common approach in laboratory research. But the more you control the environment, the less it resembles the real world. In the real world, people have agency and autonomy and choose environments that they prefer. They aren't assigned at random. And some variables are not well suited to being isolated or controlled. A researcher studying gender differences, for example, cannot assign participants to gender roles and ask them to describe their experiences. In the real world, the relationship a person has with their gender is something that develops over a long period of time, and it is a function of many environmental and biological factors.

Imagine that you wanted to understand the effects of pay raises on work motivation. You could create an experimental scenario in which some people were assigned to receive pay raises after performing a task. But in the real world, the effect of a pay raise depends on so many other factors: did your coworkers get pay raises too? Is the raise in line with what you expected? How does it compare to your raise from last year? In the real world, a person's salary has major effects on their lifestyle and habits. None of these things can be meaningfully replicated in a lab setting. The more of this context that is lost, more concerns about generalizability arise.

So if you want to study pay raises, and you also want your findings to be as relevant as possible to the "real world," then you need to bring your work outside of the lab and into the field. In Chapter 4, we discussed how I-O psychologists typically use the term "field" to refer to organizational samples. But **field research** generically refers to any setting other than a controlled setting that you create. It may be a single organization, or a group of organizations. It might be an entire city or country, a type of study that is becoming more feasible with advances in big data methods. In any case, the setting in field research doesn't have to try to resemble the real world, because it is the real world.

In relation to research design, an important and common misconception is that field studies are superior to lab studies in their generalizability. Do not make this mistake. It is essential, regardless of everything else, that you always consider the context of your study and limit your claims accordingly. For example, would you think that a leadership study conducted with military cadets generalized to elementary school principals? Probably not, at least without qualifying the results with a lot of "it depends." The military context is highly structured, hierarchical, and rigid. There are life-and-death stakes to errors in judgment. There is an extensive training period. And so forth. The variables that relate to leadership in the military do not necessarily apply to all leaders everywhere, although some might. When you design a field study, it is thus your responsibility to fully describe the context in detail so that judgments about generalizability by consumers of your research will be as accurate as possible.

Earlier, we discussed a study of computer-based tracking. How would this be different if it were conducted in a field setting? First, the researcher would need to find an organization that was already using tracking to observe their trainees or interested in creating such a program. If the organization wouldn't let them run an experiment – and they usually won't – the researcher would then need to hope that maybe one department was using real-time tracking and another department downloaded the data for later, while a third department didn't use tracking at all. From this example, you can see why field research can be challenging. The likelihood that these departments are otherwise perfectly equivalent, aside from their use of tracking, is small. Maybe the decision to use tracking depends on the resources available to that department, and maybe high-resource departments attract the best trainees. Or maybe the supervisor who trusts her trainees the most chooses not to track, and the trainees respond to that trust by performing well. There is necessarily less control over these variables in a field setting. Yet the tradeoff in generalizability related to contextual factors like the stakes, the population, and so on, might be worth it in your informed opinion as a researcher. You need to decide on a study-by-study basis what is best for your research question.

Which Contextual Variables Matter to Me?

There is no standard checklist to help you decide which contextual variables might be important to your field study. This is always an exercise in difficult, critical thinking. You need to use your theoretical understanding of the subject matter to think about context and your familiarity with similar studies conducted already to understand common limitations of existing research. That said, you should use the UTOS framework described previously as a start. Consider how variables such as participant demographics, organizational culture, industry, national culture, current events, and particulars of the work or task might be relevant to the relationships you identify. This is just one of the many decisions you need to make based on your professional judgment, and not a standardized checklist.

Field Methods: Archival, Observational and Survey-based

Three major field methods are archival, observational, and survey-based methods. All are **non-experimental**, meaning that when running them, you do not directly control any variables. Of the three, surveys are the most common and appear throughout all kinds of organizational research. All three are design choices you might make when it is not possible to manipulate the variables you're interested in. Even when you can't manipulate a variable, you can still measure it using these methods.

Survey is the generic term we use to refer to the administration of questionnaires to a sample drawn from a population of interest in which respondents are asked to produce measurements on the variables we want to measure, typically on a paper or web-based questionnaire. Personality measures, demographic questionnaires, measures of work attitudes and other constructs, self-reports of performance, or anything else that could be administered on a form can be delivered to respondents using a survey method. Historically, the terms *questionnaire* and *survey* were not considered synonyms. Instead, *questionnaire* specifically referred to the paper or web-based form given to respondents and *survey* was used to refer to the research design in which that form was delivered, usually using random sampling (recall Chapter 4). These days, many people use the terms interchangeably, referring to the form respondents complete as either a questionnaire or a survey. Somewhat confusingly, when the term is used as a verb, as in "let's survey our employees," the word "questionnaire" is never used in its place.

Observational methods, sometimes called **naturalistic research** when the observation occurs in a research participant's natural environment, involve capturing and interpreting information of interest about a research participant directly, but without asking that person to provide anything in particular. This can reduce certain response biases that threaten internal validity, like social desirability or self-enhancement bias (see Chapter 10). Observation is classically done with your eyes, such as by sitting unobtrusively in the corner of an office while writing down everything you see. But observation can also be done with cameras, smartphones, or any other digital capture device and interpreted later, which can reduce rater biases that also threaten internal validity. A key advantage to observational methods over others is that you are able to directly observe behavior instead of relying upon memory, as is necessary when using retrospective questionnaires. Unfortunately, it is very difficult to directly observe many of the variables we care about as I-O psychologists, so observation is limited in published I-O psychology research. However, it may be becoming more common with the increasing popularity of **digital observation** methods, such as the analysis of social media data or digital trace records.

Archival methods refer to making use of data that have already been collected for some other purpose. Public records, personnel records, pre-existing datasets shared online, and any other data available second-hand may be used as archival sources. The primary limitation of archival methods is that the only things you know about your data are what you've been told about them, because you didn't design the study or research context that created or recorded those data originally. This means you need to be careful to question if the information is trustworthy and reliable, and it requires you to explore how faulty assumptions about data quality might affect your conclusions. Meta-analysis, the process of re-analyzing quantitative results from pre-existing primary research that we will cover in much greater detail in Chapter 13, is a prominent example of an archival method. Meta-analysts, much like other archival researchers, rely upon the quality of existing research in order to draw valid conclusions by comparing results across those studies.

Importantly, none of these three methods have IVs or DVs. Instead, we generally refer to variables in these studies based upon the kinds of statistical analysis we may eventually subject them to. For example, if we wanted to know about differences in job satisfaction associated with gender, we would more correctly refer to gender as a **predictor** and job satisfaction as a **criterion**. But the choice of those terms is a function of our analysis, not any assumed causal relationship. Because gender cannot be manipulated independently of job satisfaction, as in an experiment, it cannot be considered an "independent" variable.

Importantly, these labels – archival, observational, and survey – are best thought of as convenient shorthand for referring to common sets of threats to internal validity and generalizability. In authentic data collection scenarios, these threats can and do vary widely even within a particular approach. Always consider threats directly; don't stop with the label.

Combining Control and Realism: Quasi-Experiments and Field Experiments

In some truly wonderful situations, the world presents you with a scenario that allows you to combine aspects of control from experimental research and aspects of generalizability from non-experimental studies. For instance, an organization may make a major policy change. If you collected data before the change, and you collected data after the change, this could enable you to answer some interesting questions about the causal effect of the policy even without having conducted an experiment.

Another scenario, quite common in organizations, is that natural groupings that are theoretically similar already exist, allowing an intervention to be applied to one group or set of groups and not others, such as across departments, branches, locations, course sections, teams, and so on. For example, if an organization had branch offices in 12 US states, you might be able to convince the organization to apply your intervention in 6 of them. If you randomly assign teams to conditions but are studying people within teams, this isn't considered random assignment, since people are not randomly assigned – their teams are. Yet it functions similarly *if* you can reasonably make the argument that the offices found in those 12 US states were all essentially the same at the person-level relative to the variables you are studying.

This approach is called **quasi-experimentation** because it has some elements of experimentation but without random assignment of cases to experimental groups – this is the aspect that makes it "quasi." There is no way to be sure that the groups in a quasi-experiment are functionally the same as each other relative to whatever you're trying to study, as an experimental design does. However, it does offer increased control relative to completely non-experimental research designs, and there are dozens of specific quasi-experimental designs to add controls in specific desirable ways.

Quasi-experiments are very popular in I-O psychology research given that so many of the things we study are not ethical or possible to manipulate. A few specific types of quasi-experimental designs are discussed in the following, although you should remember that a complete list would contain dozens:

Interrupted Time Series. An interrupted time-series design involves collecting data on a variable of interest over an extended period of time, both before and after the introduction of an intervention or treatment (the "interruption"). This design allows researchers to examine the impact of the intervention on the variable of interest by comparing the trends in the data before and after the intervention. In this way, time is used as a control. This design is particularly useful for evaluating the effectiveness of interventions that are implemented over a long period of time, such as public health campaigns or educational programs. In organizations, a great many policy or other business changes can be studied using this design, assuming that you can anticipate the change and begin collecting data beforehand (or find archival data that has been collected beforehand).

Regression Discontinuity. Imagine the following scenario. You are Mark Wilson, the administrator for a leadership development program for a company that has 100 junior managers. A year ago, all managers participated in a 360-degree feedback data collection and received scores from 0 to 100. Six months ago, the top 20 managers based on those data were enrolled in the development program. You are now in charge of evaluating the program to see if it improved the participants' performance. Your data lead to Figure 8.8.

In a regression discontinuity design, the researcher selects a threshold or cutoff point that determines who is eligible to receive the treatment or intervention and compares change across groups. For example, the cut-off point might be a certain test score or grade point average. Individuals who score just above the cut-off point are eligible to receive the treatment, while those who score just below are not. By comparing the trajectories of individuals who just meet versus just do not meet the cut-off point, the researcher can estimate the effects of the treatment on the outcome of interest.

In Figure 8.8, the regression line predicting the second 360 from the first shows a strong linear relationship among all managers. This makes sense – no matter what we did in our training, we'd expect managers who were doing poorly a year ago to still be doing fairly poorly now, and managers who were doing great are likely to still be doing fairly great. The managers placed in the training program, however, have a small vertical bump – their line has a smidge higher intercept than the untrained managers. The vertical difference between the line you can imagine extending from the non-trained manager group up to the trained manager group is the effect of our intervention. In this way, we have added a control for a

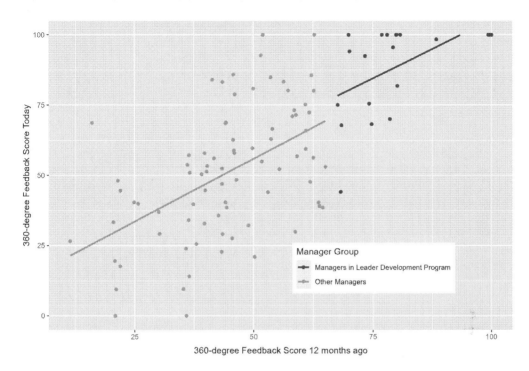

Figure 8.8 Example of regression discontinuity.

selection-related threat to internal validity and therefore have a little more confidence that our training actually made a difference than if we only looked at the post-training scores alone. (Importantly, if we were doing this *for real*, we'd want to also conduct a statistical test of the effect and an examination of practical effect size rather than just eyeballing a pretty figure!)

Unequal Control Group Field Experiments. Remember that the essence of a true experiment is random assignment to conditions. This implies that extraneous variables and their effect on your conclusions have been minimized; you can reasonably assume that people in each group are similar in the ways that matter. In an unequal-groups field experiment, people are not randomly assigned to groups. Rather, you make use of naturally occurring groups, and administer a different treatment to each natural group. Different branches or departments of an organization are frequently used this way: you might introduce a new policy or tool to one department and then compare it with a department that did not receive the new tool. A limitation of this design is that the groups may have other differences that interfere with your ability to draw trustworthy conclusions. They may be higher in baseline performance, or workload, or be located in areas that are more demanding. Still, the potential to do some experimental manipulation while benefiting from the realism of working in a real organization may be worth it. Imagine that you wanted to understand the effects of work-from-home policies. You could permit one department to work from home but not another, and then measure satisfaction, turnover, or performance.

Quasi-experimentation is a vast topic and worth exploring on its own if you think you might ever conduct research within a real organization. The undisputed foundational authors for quasi-experimental design are Cook and Campbell, although over the years, there have been many derivative book chapters, empirical articles, and new editions of their most fundamental book:

Cook, T. D., & Campbell, D. T. (1976). *Quasi-experimentation: Design and analysis issues for field settings*. Rand McNally.

Testing Causal Theories

Design should always be considered simultaneously with your plan to model and analyze the resulting data. As described in Chapter 3, I-O psychology researchers usually study three types of causal relationships: direct effects, mediation (indirect effects), and moderation (conditional effects). Different research designs are more appropriate for some questions than others, a concept we will revisit in more detail in Chapter 15. In the remainder of this chapter, we will expand on these ideas enough for you to get the basis of how theory and design related to each other. If you've forgotten the general differences between these concepts, a brief review of Chapter 3 is a good idea.

Direct Effects and Moderation

Most fundamentally, direct effects of manipulable variables are the easiest to causally support. This is because if you can manipulate it, and you're only worried about one variable, you can easily create an experimental design to test the effects of it on some outcome of interest. As described earlier in this chapter, this is commonly called a "factorial" or "n-way" experimental design.

This becomes more complicated when adding non-manipulable variables as moderators. Say, for example, that you believe the direct effect you are studying is moderated by gender. You cannot, to my knowledge, safely or ethically randomly assign people to different genders. As a result, this aspect of your study cannot be experimental and must be quasi-experimental, meaning that internal validity threats somewhat weaken your ability to make causal conclusions about gender. Given that, you would need to justify with citations to other research or make good arguments that it would in fact be gender causing any effects observed in your data and not, instead, something correlated with gender.

As a practical example, consider a development research study in which people are randomly selected among your organization's front-line managers to receive a special leadership development program that you have designed. You have a theory that the program will improve participants' leadership skills, that is, that your leader development program will *cause* an increase in skill. This is a direct, causal effect, and you can cleanly find support for this effect with your experimental design with minimal internal validity threats. But you also want to see if gender matters in terms of program success. You run the study and sure enough – the program is less effective for women! Their scores are lower at the end, so you conclude that the leadership program must have some hidden sexist elements that you didn't realize were there.

But there is also a reasonable alternative explanation. Across most American organizations, women are less likely to be placed in leadership roles in the first place, and we know from prior theory that people with more leadership experience are likely to be more effective leaders. Thus, causally speaking, your training may be *equally effective* for men and women – instead, what you have uncovered is systematic bias in leadership opportunities long before these women joined your organization. In this case, trying to reduce sexism in your program will accomplish nothing, because the training wasn't the cause of the problem in the first place.

As you can see, misattributing causes when testing moderators is a very easy trap to fall into and can lead you to incorrect conclusions that have real consequences, whether in industry or in academic research. Any time you are not using a strictly defined true experiment, this risk is present. You must constantly throughout the design process make a dedicated effort to identify and minimize internal and external validity threats. To do anything less will lead to the wrong answers.

Mediation and Indirect Effects

If you thought moderation was tricky, mediation is much worse. Because mediation involves a sequential chain of causal effects, it is not possible in a single experiment to test all aspects of a mediating relationship causally. At best, you can test the causal effect of the earliest/outermost variable *if* you manipulated it experimentally on the mediator and outcome variables. For example, Figure 8.9 shows a mediating relationship between an experimentally-manipulated technology intervention (e.g., perhaps you randomly assigned half of your company to start using some new AI software to get their work done) and job performance as mediated via motivation.

Although there are only two arrows, four separate effects are hinted at in Figure 8.9, each with different quality of evidence. They are:

1. *The direct effect of the intervention on motivation.* We have some trust in this relationship being causal, because an experiment was used to control the most common internal validity threats.
2. *The direct effect of the intervention on job performance.* Although we theorized that this relationship was indirect via motivation, we regardless have some trust in its relationship being causal for the same reason.
3. *The direct effect of motivation on job performance.* We *do not* have causal evidence to support this relationship. Both motivation and performance are observed, meaning we did not manipulate anything. This means that there could be omitted variables or issues at play that we are not currently controlling.
4. *The indirect effect of the intervention on performance via motivation.* Since direct effect #3 is not necessarily causal, the indirect effect is not necessarily causal either. We need causal evidence for *all* steps within a mediation to be confident in the particular sequencing we've theorized.

Since mediation is such a common goal of I-O research, what do you do in this situation? What most researchers due – and this isn't a recommendation – is simply *assume* the second

Figure 8.9 Mediation with an experimental antecedent.

relationship is causal. If you read a research paper where causality is not discussed explicitly, this is probably what the researchers are doing.

Is assuming causality a good idea? It depends. In some mediational theories, it's difficult to make an argument for an alternative order. For example, the alternative ordering of this theory would be that the intervention causes motivation via job performance, that is, the second and third boxes are switched. Is it plausible that job performance could cause motivation? If you think the answer is a clear "no," then you might not need or want to see evidence of effect #3 previously. If you think the answer is "maybe" or "yes," then you probably do.

At this point, you might be thinking to yourself, "of course job performance can't cause motivation – a person must be motivated to perform, not the other way around." But think about this – have you ever had such a bad day at work, one where no matter how hard you tried, things didn't go well? Did your performance affect your motivation that day?

Always question causal order, whether implied or explicit. Things are rarely as simple as they initially appear. That's why we need research!

U-Shaped Relationships: A Special Kind of Moderation

In moderating relationships, two variables interact with each other such that the effect of one variable depends on the value, or level, of the other variable. The U shaped relationship may not seem like an example of moderation, since there is only one predictor involved. But, it is actually the case that one variable, X, is interacting with . . . itself! You can think about this as saying, when X is low, the relationship between X and Y is positive. But when X is high, the relationship between X and Y is negative. The Yerkes-Dodson law, which you learned about in a past chapter, is the most famous U-shaped relationship. It argues that when stress is low, there is a positive effect of stress on performance. But when there is too much stress, more stress will harm performance. These are also called quadratic effects, because the regression equation for a U shaped effect contains a term for X and one for X^2.

Getting Started with Mediation Analyses

One of the most common starting points for modeling complex models mixing moderation and mediation is the PROCESS macro created by Andrew Hayes, which is available for R, SAS, and SPSS: https://processmacro.org/index.html.

If PROCESS is too limited for what you want to do with it, and especially if you want to examine latent variables like the ones discussed in Chapter 8, you probably will need to use a proprietary piece of software called Mplus or the open source *lavaan* library for R. Mplus is generally regarded as the most up-to-date and technically rigorous tool for this kind of analysis but is significantly more expensive than any other options. Having said that, if R and lavaan will run the analysis you need, you can safely stick with those.

References

Campbell, D. T., & Stanley, J. C. (1963). Experimental and quasi-experimental designs for research on teaching. In N. L. Gage (Ed.), *Handbook of research on teaching* (pp. 171–246). Rand McNally.

Johns, G. (2006). The essential impact of context on organizational behavior. *Academy of Management Review, 31*(2), 386–408.

Vancouver, J. B., Thompson, C. M., & Williams, A. A. (2001). The changing signs in the relationships among self-efficacy, personal goals, and performance. *Journal of Applied Psychology, 86*(4), 605.

Watson, A. M., Foster Thompson, L., Rudolph, J. V., Whelan, T. J., Behrend, T. S., & Gissel, A. L. (2013). When big brother is watching: Goal orientation shapes reactions to electronic monitoring during online training. *Journal of Applied Psychology, 98*(4), 642.

Further Reading

Antonakis, J., Bendahan, S., Jacquart, P., & Lalive, R. (2010). On making causal claims: A review and recommendations. *The Leadership Quarterly, 21*(6), 1086–1120. https://doi.org/10.1016/j.leaqua.2010.10.010

- Antonakis and colleagues present one of the most comprehensive treatments of causality within our field, describing how methodological decisions affect a researcher's ability to say that one variable causes another. They do so in three parts, by (1) showing how factors such as omitted variables can obscure causal claims, (2) presenting methods to test for causation in a variety of situations, and (3) reviewing the methodological rigor of causal claims made in top-tier journals.

Cook, T. D., & Campbell, D. T. (1976). *Quasi-experimentation: Design and analysis issues for field settings*. Rand McNally.

- The writings of Cook and Campbell are generally regarded as the most influential and fundamental explorations of quasi-experimental design. If you see yourself needing quasi-experiments, especially if you are planning a career as an applied researcher within an organization, you should read up on their work. However, you might not start with this particular book, which is one of the earliest they wrote. They also have several new editions of this book, plus other articles and book chapters at various levels of digestibility. But you should know going in that this is an absolutely massive area of research with tons to learn. It's worth it, but it will take you some time.

Klein, K. J., & Kozlowski, S. W. J. (2000). *Multilevel theory, research, and methods in organizations: Foundations, extensions, and new directions*. Jossey-Bass.

- Klein and Kozwloski's text is considered by many the definitive foundational textbook for understanding the importance of levels in organizational research. This book also presents the complexity of multilevel design and analysis fairly and comprehensively, making it an obvious first read if you need to take multilevel problems.

Questions to Think About

1. Can you identify which design is most susceptible to each kind of validity threat or generalizability threat?
2. Which designs might be most useful for the research questions you are interested in and why?
3. How will you consider external factors, like feasibility, cost, ethical concerns, and the current state of the literature in your area when designing your research?
4. When would you adopt experimental versus quasi-experiment designs? If an experiment is possible, is there any reason to use quasi-experimental methods?
5. Is there a limit to the number of plausible mediators between any two constructs?
6. How many layers deep can a moderation analysis become (e.g., a five-way interaction) before that finding is no longer useful?

Key Terms

- experiment
- experimentation
- external validity
- factorial design
- field research
- generalizability (in research design)
- history
- independent variable (IV)
- internal validity threat
- interrupted time-series design
- level
- level of analysis
- manipulation
- manipulation strength
- maturation
- multilevel data
- n-way design
- naturalistic research
- nesting
- non-experimental
- observational methods
- predictor
- quasi-experimentation
- random assignment
- regression discontinuity design
- regression to the mean
- research design
- retrieval-practice effect
- reverse causality
- selection
- Simpson's paradox
- Soloman 4-group design
- spurious
- survey
- testing
- third variable problem
- treatment
- treatment group
- unequal control groups design
- units, treatments, observations, settings (UTOS)
- validity, internal
- waitlist control design
- within-person design
- Yule-Simpson effect

Chapter 9

Building and Administering a Questionnaire

Learning Objectives

After reading this chapter, you will be able to:

1. Write effective questions.
2. Describe and contrast the four levels of measurement.
3. Describe and contrast various item types.
4. Sequence questions to avoid unwanted order effects.
5. Identify ways to ensure an appropriate response rate.
6. Identify various forms of unwanted responses.

In Chapter 7, we introduced the foundations of measurement. One of the most common and widely accepted methods of collecting data for measurement involves questionnaires. That said, we have found that advice about the craft of actually building a questionnaire is sparse. In this chapter, we begin with an introduction to writing effective questions. We then walk through the mechanical, logistical, and stylistic choices you will need to make when building a questionnaire to contain your carefully validated rating scales and other questions you want to ask of your participants. The next chapter will describe the creation of rating scales in more detail.

Before we dive in, let's note an important vocabulary decision that we have made regarding the word "survey." This word is used to describe any of the following: a methodology for collecting information from many people, the act of administering questionnaires, or the instruments used in that process (the questionnaires themselves). So for example, a person might write "We surveyed 100 people to determine the most popular I-O psychology podcast." Or they might write, "We used a survey method to learn about the preferences of I-O psychologists." Or, "Participants completed a survey about their preferences." This ambiguity leads to confusion. You will meet researchers who have strong opinions about which usage is correct. We typically tend to use "survey" to mean the method, and "questionnaire" to mean the materials that respondents are responding to, which is how you'll see them used here.

Writing Effective Questions

The first step to developing a high-quality questionnaire is writing good initial questions. There is both a science and an art to writing effective questions. Even questions that seem

DOI: 10.4324/9781315167473-12

clear to us may be perceived differently by our respondents than what we intended. It is generally safest to assume that respondents won't interpret your questions the way you expected them to until you have collected data that suggests otherwise.

Before actually writing the questions themselves, we find it helpful to ask ourselves three questions.

Question 1: "Does the Question Require an Answer?"

In his many years of conducting research on survey designs, Don Dillman argued the first question a researcher should ask is, "Does the question require an answer?" Perhaps this seems like an obvious question to ask, but it cannot be overstated. Survey respondents are busy people, and asking them irrelevant questions benefits neither you nor them. Consider the following example:

If you work in a virtual team, how often do you email your coworkers?

- Never
- Monthly
- Weekly
- Daily
- Hourly

Including the word "if" in the stem of the item automatically discourages some respondents from providing an answer. Anyone who doesn't work in a virtual team is not required to answer. This is an issue because we cannot decipher whether the absence of a response indicates glancing over the question or whether the question was simply irrelevant for the respondent. Even worse, some particularly conscientious respondents may feel inclined to respond to *all* items on a survey, leading them to provide a misleading answer to this item.

You might think that adding a "Does not apply" option to this question would solve our problem. However, words like "if" send a strong, "this question is optional" message to respondents looking to complete your survey in a reasonable amount of time. For this reason, we err on the side of caution and refrain from using words or phrases that make questions appear optional to respondents. A better approach is to use advanced logic here. First, ask participants "Do you work in a virtual team?" and then only ask those who respond "Yes" about the frequency of their email communication. We will discuss this method in greater depth later in the chapter.

It can be helpful to ask ourselves two additional questions while writing survey items, originally posed to us by the world's most authoritative expert on surveys, Don Dillman: "*Can* people respond?" and "*Will* people respond?" These questions help us think about our respondents' ability and motivation to answer our questions, respectively.

Question 2: "Can People Respond?"

To answer the first question regarding whether respondents *can* accurately respond to your items, we can rely on classic cognitive psychology research. In many ways, humans are quite poor at introspectively describing their higher-order cognitive processes. That is, sometimes we don't know *why* we think or behave as we do. For example, people in a study by Nisbett and Wilson (1977) were told to retroactively report their own past thoughts and behaviors. Instead, they instead listed what they believed were plausible explanations of their past mental processes. This naturally presents some concern for survey researchers expecting to gather valid information about mental processes.

Are reflective questionnaires a lost cause, then? Thankfully not. There are plenty of item-writing guidelines to increase the chances that you'll gather accurate responses. Let's say you want to know how many emails virtual employees send to their coworkers. You could ask how many of these emails they've sent in the past 6 months, but your respondents probably don't have a precise answer for that question. Alternatively, you could ask how many emails they've sent in the past month, week, or day. As the length of the recall time shrinks, so too do the memory-related errors that bias your survey responses.

But what if you want to know about your respondents' longer-term behaviors? Consider the following example, which is followed by a revised item that encourages more accurate responses from participants.

Initial Item: In the past 6 months, how many emails have you sent to coworkers?
Revised Item: On average, how many emails do you send to coworkers in a typical week?

The revised item takes some cognitive burden off the respondent while allowing you to gather information related to their longer-term email behavior. For example, you could multiply their answer by 26 (52 weeks/2) to get an estimate of their 6-month email behavior.

Question 3: "Will People Respond?"

Writing questions that encourage accurate responses is useless if participants aren't motivated to answer the questions at all. Motivating your respondents starts early on, when you introduce your survey to them and provide them with instructions. The tone of your introductory language should be appreciative, clear, and simple. Do not use any jargon. Explain the point of the study, explain what kinds of questions you will ask, and how long it will take. The Informed Consent language may be prescribed by your institution, but you have control over how you translate the study to your respondents and ask for their participation.

Following is a sample introduction:

The questions that follow will help us understand your feelings about electronic surveillance.

Your careful attention to each question will improve the accuracy of our research and make our findings more relevant to real-world surveillance practices. We know some of the questions are worded similarly to each other, but this is necessary for us to scientifically understand why people respond the way they do.

For each question, please read all the text carefully before responding. Thank you for your care and attention!

It is helpful to think about your own motivation while writing your survey content. Would you be more inclined to help a person who speaks to you in a demeaning or respectful way? Your motivation is likely higher when you are treated with respect. Completing a survey is no different. Because of this, many respondents approach the research they take part in as a transaction between themselves and the researcher. They may think to themselves, "What's in it for me?" As much as possible, your survey should be constructed in a way that resolves this thought within them.

Psychologist Robert Cialdini has conducted many studies on the persuasive tactics that make people feel inclined to help others. Many of these tactics apply to the written information conveyed in survey instructions and items. For example, individuals are often more inclined to help others when they *like* them or when they are simply given a reason to help. Compare the two instruction/item pairs in the following, keeping in mind these two elements of persuasion.

Example 1:

Instructions: Answer the question below. We need as many responses as we can get for this study.
Question: Write about your experience working in a virtual team at your organization.

Example 2:

Instructions: Thank you for your interest in this survey! Your participation in this study will help improve teamwork amongst virtual workers in your organization.
Question: Please share your experience working in a virtual team at your organization.

Which researcher would you feel more motivated to help? We suspect the second: They use friendly words to promote liking ("thank you" and "please"), and they give a concrete reason *why* answering the question is important (to "improve teamwork"). Interestingly, Cialdini's research has found that individuals are more likely to help others when a requestor gives *any* reason for the request. When it comes to writing survey content, giving respondents some information about why the survey is being administered is better than telling them nothing – but this information should be truthful, of course.

For some practical recommendations about persuasion tactics from a popular press exploration of the implications of Cialdini's research, see:

Cialdini, R. B. (2006). *Influence: The psychology of persuasion* (revised ed.). Harper Business.

Identifying the Appropriate Scale of Measurement

Now that we've covered the fundamental questions to ask when writing survey items, one important consideration is deciding *how* to measure what it is we care about. We have a wide variety of item types at our disposal when measuring psychological characteristics of respondents. That said, some item types are better suited to assess specific characteristics than other item types. The kind of rating scale we select will also determine the kinds of analyses we can do with our data, so it is very important to think about our measurements early on in the research process. One key step toward selecting an item type is determining an appropriate scale of measurement, a concept we introduced in Chapter 7.

Table 9.1 Appropriate analyses for each level of measurement

	Nominal	Ordinal	Interval	Ratio
Frequency distribution	Yes	Yes	Yes	Yes
Median and percentiles	No	Yes	Yes	Yes
Addition and subtraction	No	No	Yes	Yes
Means and standard deviations	No	No	Yes	Yes
Ratios	No	No	No	Yes

All four levels of measurement are relevant and common in psychological research. Table 9.1 depicts what kinds of mathematical operations are possible with data collected at each level.

Scale of measurement can sometimes be a bit ambiguous. One of the oldest disagreements in social science is whether "Likert-type scales" (more on this in Chapter 10), such as 5-point scales ranging from Strongly Disagree to Strongly Agree, should be considered ordinal or interval. You can appreciate both arguments.

On one side, when we have mean scores from long Likert-type questionnaires, they act like interval-level measures, most obviously in that the scores tend to fall in a normal distribution.

On the other side, to claim that these questions are truly interval level measurement, we'd also need to make the conceptual argument that the distance between "Agree" and "Strongly Agree" is the same distances as between "Disagree" and "Neither." Yet we have a lot of empirical evidence that this is not true for two reasons. One, people view "Neither" very differently than the other options. Two, the difference between Strongly and not-Strongly seems to vary by person. Some people see that as a big difference, and some people don't.

This distinction has *big* implications. A lot of the statistical tests common in I-O psychology, like ordinary least squares regression, factor analysis, and structural equation models, require interval or ratio level measurement for their mathematics to be possible. There are variations of many tests to adapt them to ordinal data, but this often creates sacrifices in interpretability.

As a result, many I-O researchers treat Likert-type scales as "close enough" to interval-level measurement for practical purposes. But that's a decision you should make explicitly, for yourself.

Selecting the Appropriate Item Type

Demographic Items

To assess demographics in samples drawn from the United States, our recommendation is to default to US Census designations where possible. Most critically, race and ethnicity are highly complex, and if you don't have specific hypotheses or research questions about them, stick to existing, well-understood options, and always allow respondents to choose multiple options. If your particular research necessitates it, you can add or split options, but be sure you have a specific reason to do so. Some survey tools also have built-in demographics items, but they may or may not be sufficient or appropriate.

The 2020 Census first asks about **ethnicity** using the following item:

- Is this person of Hispanic, Latino or Spanish origin?
  - No, not of Hispanic, Latino, or Spanish origin
  - Yes, Mexican, Mexican American, Chicano
  - Yes, Puerto Rican
  - Yes, Cuban
  - Yes, another Hispanic, Latino, or Spanish origin

And second about **race** using the following:

- What is this person's race?
  - White
  - Black or African American
  - American Indian or Alaska Native
  - Chinese
  - Filipino
  - Asian Indian
  - Vietnamese
  - Korean
  - Japanese
  - Other Asian
  - Native Hawaiian
  - Samoan
  - Chamorro
  - Other Pacific Islander
  - Some other race

Note that the 2020 US Census did not ask about **gender** and used a single binary question to assess **sex**. Since then, the Census Bureau updated the language in its pulse survey to the following:

- What sex were you assigned at birth on your original birth certificate?
  - Male
  - Female

- Do you currently describe yourself as male, female or transgender?
  - Male
  - Female
  - Transgender
  - None of these

- Which of the following best represents how you think of yourself?
  - Gay or lesbian
  - Straight, that is not gay or lesbian

- Bisexual
- Something else
- I don't know

Because gender and sexuality are evolving concepts in modern society, you might consider alternatives to this approach. For example, the Human Rights Campaign suggests the following language:

- Do you consider yourself a member of the Lesbian, Gay, Bisexual and/or Transgender (LGBT) community?

  - Yes
  - No
  - No, but I identify as an Ally
  - Prefer not to say

- What is your gender?

  - Female
  - Male
  - Non-binary/third gender
  - Prefer to self describe
  - Prefer not to say

- Transgender is an umbrella term that refers to people whose gender identity, expression or behavior is different from those typically associated with their assigned sex at birth. Other identities considered to fall under this umbrella can include non-binary, gender fluid, and genderqueer – as well as many more. Do you identify as transgender?

  - Yes
  - No
  - Prefer not to say

- What is your sexual orientation?

  - Straight/Heterosexual
  - Gay or Lesbian
  - Bisexual
  - Prefer to self-describe
  - Prefer not to say

Our recommendation for assessing demographics is to do so only if it is pertinent to your research questions or specific external validity concerns. Asking about demographic characteristics can be perceived as overly invasive, and with good reason. If a survey is conducted by an organization, the respondent might fear that their responses will be used to identify them even if the survey is anonymous. For example, there might be only one 37-year old openly bisexual Hispanic woman at a company. In that case, it would be quite easy to link this person to her responses.

Optimal Performance Items

Optimal performance tests are those that assess an individuals' aptitude or achievement in a given domain. These items are quite common in educational settings, and they typically include the following types:

1. Alternate choice: Presents a statement with two response options, generally True/False or Yes/No.
2. Multiple choice: Poses a question, followed by one correct answer and two or more incorrect answers for respondents to select from.
3. Matching: Presents two columns of words or phrases and asks participants to link them across columns based upon some specified principle.
4. Fill-in-the-blank: Includes a factual statement with a missing word or phrase for respondents to fill in.
5. Essay or short answer: Poses a question for which respondents must generate a written response, typically a paragraph or longer.

In each of these cases, scores reflect the number of questions answered correctly or on a continuum from completely incorrect to completely correct. In this way, optimal performance items are often scored as percentages and therefore on a ratio level of measurement, from 0% correct to 100% correct.

You probably have plenty of personal experience with optimal performance items in educational contexts. Organizations also use these items, particularly in the stages of employee selection and training. In fact, employers have used tests of general mental ability to select high-performing workers since as early as World War 1 (Yerkes, 1921). Perhaps you have taken such a test yourself: among the one most commonly used today is the Wonderlic Personnel Test, which takes only 10 minutes to administer and includes 50 items of varying types. Organizations also use optimal performance tests to assess change in employee knowledge – for example, assessing how much a worker knows about a company's core values before and after a training intervention.

High-quality optimal performance items, unlike Likert-type scale prompts, require writing multiple independent lines of stimulus text. Not only must you write the question prompt but also all possible responses. This makes question-writing both more complicated and more difficult, as you need to consider each question in terms of its prompt and all possible answers simultaneously, or you'll measure things you don't intend to measure. For example, consider this item on I-O history:

1. Which of the following foundational I-O research occurred around 1930?

   a. Hawthorne Electric
   b. Army Alpha and Army Beta
   c. Frederick's Taylor's Scientific Management

What does this question assess? Is it general I-O history knowledge or something different? Let's explore it from the perspective of a test-taker, the kind of data that might be collected in a study to produce "evidence related to response processes" (see Chapter 7). Let's say that in a think-aloud, a respondent says this:

"I sort of remember the name Hawthorne Electric but not much more than that. Army Alpha and Beta probably happened around wartime – probably WWI or WWII, which would be the 1910s or 1940s. . . . I remember Scientific Management is really old, like maybe 1900–1910? I guess that leaves Hawthorne Electric as the only possible answer?"

That answer is correct. But does that reasoning process really represent knowledge of I-O history, or does it instead reflect knowledge of wartime research practices, remembering the rough time period of Frederick Taylor, a dash of general cognitive ability, and a little luck? In this way, getting a correct answer to "Which of the following occurred around 1930" does not even give confidence that the respondent knows what happened in 1930!

This example illustrates two general challenges in writing optimal performance items, both of which we first introduced in Chapter 7. The first is deficiency, which refers to questions that only address a portion of the domain they are intended to assess. In this case, the question is intended to assess I-O knowledge about Hawthorne Electric – and it sort of does that, but not particularly well. It misses a lot. Thus it is deficient. The second is contamination, which refers to questions measuring *more* content than they are intended to assess. In this case, the question partially assesses knowledge of the timeline of World Wars! Thus it is also contaminated. In sum, given the response processes evidence we have collected, and given our interpretation of the results, we should rewrite this question!

Item Construction

A handful of relatively simple rules will help you write more good items than bad, whether optimal performance or otherwise. When first writing items, think of this as a checklist for every item. Once you become accustomed to thinking about these issues, you'll find writing items this way increasingly intuitive:

1. *Cover the exact scope of the variable you want to assess – no more, no less.* When writing items, ask yourself throughout the process, "does this item precisely match up to the definition of what I want to assess?" Does the question cover issues broader than your definition, narrower than your definition, or match it perfectly? It it's not perfect, toss it out and revise. And if you aren't sure, you might need to revisit your definition.
2. *Don't write **double-barreled items**.* "Double-barreled" refers to items that are phrased in such a way that a participant might have more than one answer to it. For example, "I like to go to parties and sporting events" could be answered negatively by people that don't go to parties, people that don't like sporting events, or only people that don't like both. You should rewrite the item to avoid this problem.
3. *Avoid unnecessarily ambiguous items.* If your items can be phrased in a factual way, there will be less "noise," and you will need fewer of them to get high-quality measurement. For example, there's a "right" answer to, "How many parties did you go to last week? Please provide a number." There is not a right answer to, "How many parties do you usually attend: none, a few, some, or many?" On the other hand, sometimes in writing items, you might embrace ambiguity with purpose. This is a common approach with personality items, because such items are usually intended to cover a wide range of situations, such as the International Personality Item Pool item, "I accomplish a lot of work."
4. *Write to the reading level of your population.* Don't use words or phrases that your respondents aren't likely to know. They will most likely guess as to what you meant.

If you aren't sure what words your respondents will know or not know, you may want to include methods in a pilot study to evaluate this before using your questionnaire for decision-making. There are also several common methods for assessing reading level, including the Flesch-Kincaid Readability Test, the Gunning Fod Index, the Coleman-Liau Index, and the SMOG Index. No reading level test is perfect, so we suggest using multiple tests and comparing the results when consulting any. If using R, you can find assessments of several of these using the *koRpus* package.

5. *Minimize the questionnaire's cognitive burden.* If there are 10 items in a row with the same response items, like strongly agree to strongly disagree, presenting them in a matrix, with items as rows and response options as columns, will usually minimize respondent frustration. However, too many matrices or matrices with too many rows will also cause problems, because from a respondent's perspective, they will all start to blend together. Try to simplify the experience as much as possible; you want to measure what you want to measure; you don't want to measure how fatigued your respondents are.

6. *Whenever possible, write more items than you think you need and use a pilot study to winnow them down.* One of the advantages of "doing scale development right," the way described in this book, is that you can develop a very large number of initial items and then be very selective in choosing which ones make it to your final measure based upon pilot study research. This is important, because you need to remember our rule to live by: don't assume any item you've written is a good one. We will revisit this concept in much greater detail in Chapter 10 when discussing scale development.

7. *Write questions that maximize useful variance.* The goal of questionnaires is to accurately reflect true differences among the people that respond to your questionnaire. If everyone was the same, you would not need to ask them about it. This is the concept of "useful" variance, that is, that people are free to respond in different ways, and that those different ways they respond reflect real differences between people. There are a few techniques you can use to maximize useful variance. If you ask questions about something that falls on a range but only allow two answers, called **dichotomous** scoring (e.g., true-false, yes-no), you throw away a lot of useful information. For example, responses to the question, "How much did you enjoy this managerial workshop?" will be more useful with seven options, written with an attempt at equal intervals, ranging from "I have never hated anything more" to "this was the best workshop I've ever taken" will give you a lot more useful information than a two-option scale of "I didn't" and "I did." In the next chapter, we'll discuss one of the most useful ways to maximize useful variance, the use of Likert-type scales.

There are also a few risk areas and pitfalls to consider that are not quite rules:

1. *You should probably avoid negatively worded items. Or maybe you shouldn't.* Negatively worded items are reverse-scored. For example, to measure satisfaction with managers, you might ask "Do you dislike your manager?" The problem is that the cognitive processes that a person engages in for a negatively worded item are not necessarily the same as the ones they would engage in if positively worded. The nature of the thing you're trying to measure appears to affect how much this matters. For example, a positive integrity item, like "I always do the right thing," is almost certainly not going to be responded to precisely the opposite way as "I never do the right thing" or "I always do the wrong thing." Precise phrasing can matter a *lot* in item development, and negative wording makes this much more difficult, so many writers don't write negatively worded items at all.

However, a potential problem with this approach is that by avoiding negative wording, you are biasing responses to be answered similarly even if they aren't really related. For example, positive integrity items may be highly correlated because of positive self-regard, a quality that leads people to view themselves positively regardless of the truth. From a technical perspective, this is referred to as **common method bias**, and it biases intercorrelations between items upwards – variables appear more strongly correlated than they really should be. All of this is to say that you'll see recommendations both for and against writing negatively worded items. Think about this carefully in your particular context; if you think people will respond *very* differently based upon positive or negative phrasing, then you need to figure out why first.

2. *Item writing is a craft, with both skill and art components, so meta-cognition is key.* One of the first discoveries students have when developing questionnaires, after they realize the sort of diagnostics that need to be done to claim a questionnaire appears reasonably valid, is that they are bad at it. Writing high-quality items is very difficult. Balancing all of these issues to create interesting, psychometrically sound items that respondents don't get bored by is a complicated task, and there is no one right way to do it. Fundamentally, you are crafting a stimulus, and you are hoping that the thing you actually want to measure causes people to respond to that question in different ways. It's very difficult to think in reverse like this. This is why meta-cognition – reflection on how you are creating items – is critical to improving your item writing skill. If you find you're writing bad items, you need to stop and think carefully about why that's happening so that you can fix it. Are you following your definitions closely? Are you bringing personal biases to your items? Are you consistently having trouble with one of the areas listed previously?

3. *Sometimes, items are just bad.* On many occasions, your authors have written items that they thought were great that did not perform well statistically, and we just could not figure out what was wrong with them. The correct response to this? Cut and run. There are always more items out there to be written. Don't waste your time on a bad one.

Drafting Items and Designing Surveys

For more details on the design of questionnaire items and the design of surveys to contain them, see:

Dillman, D. A., Smyth, J. D., & Christian, L. M. (2014). *Internet, phone, mail, and mixed-mode surveys: The tailored design method.* Wiley.

Ordering Your Items

As we mentioned in Chapter 8, the order that we present questions to participants may influence their responses to those questions. We should consider whether the questions we ask early on are structured in a way that keeps respondents engaged. There are a variety of **order effects** to consider when building a survey. Some effects cause **assimilation**, which happens when a respondent's answers across questions become more similar. The opposite of assimilation is contrast. **Contrast** happens when a respondent's answers across questions become more different.

Assimilation occurs for many reasons. For example, **carryover effects** occur when respondents perceive that two questions are related and therefore use similar considerations to answer both. Consider the following two questions: "How would you describe your relationship with your supervisor?" and "How are things at work going lately?" Despite measuring different constructs, carryover effects would occur if responses differed based on the order the questions were presented, such as if the supervisor question was asked first, respondents' considerations of their supervisor satisfaction blend over into their judgments about their general job satisfaction.

Another example of assimilation is the **priming effect**, which occurs when early questions make certain material more accessible for participants as they respond to later questions. Consider a survey about workers' perceptions about being monitored, which includes a checklist of various kinds of monitoring such as e-mail monitoring, video surveillance, and location tracking. If the final set of questions in this survey asked participants to list the five most common ways that their organization monitors their behavior, priming may occur if respondents list monitoring practices included in the initial checklist that are not necessarily common at their organization.

Turning now to contrast, a respondent's answers can become more different as a function of question order. One example is the **anchoring effect**, which happens when participants rely on early questions to set a standard for which later questions are presented. This may occur when we start a survey with questions about extreme or sensitive topics and follow those with questions about lighter topics. For example, consider that we ask participants to disclose their thoughts regarding sexual harassment before they disclose their thoughts about workplace gossiping. Respondents may purposely be lenient in thinking about gossiping due to the extreme standard set by the sexual harassment item.

Another example of contrast is **appearing moderate**, which occurs when respondents try to come across as neutral on a topic by endorsing some items but rejecting others. This effect is most likely when respondents have reason to believe that they will be judged for having an extreme opinion about something. It is also likely when they perceive that we will evaluate a series of items collectively, rather than individually. For example, job applicants might be tempted to appear moderate in an applicant experience survey if they are not quite sure whether the organization values their honest opinion. Even if they were generally unhappy with the application process, they might rate a few aspects of the process highly in order to appear less critical.

An easy way to reduce the likelihood of the appearing moderate effect is to present the questions so that respondents view them independently, rather than collectively. One option is to present each item individually, but respondents may tire of clicking through them one at a time. Another approach is to provide clear instructions that honest responses are valued and that every item should be answered truthfully. If we *do* want to understand respondents' general opinion about something, we can simply ask them a single general question. One study found that respondents are more likely to give higher ratings to a general item when it was asked after, rather than before, a set of specific items on the same topic (Willits & Saltiel, 1995). Respondents may be more likely to think about the general question as separate from the specific questions if it comes first.

A few concluding remarks are worth noting regarding order effects. First, some effects can cause both assimilation *and* contrast effects. For example, anchoring can also make responses more similar across items. If our respondents were completely unfamiliar with a topic in the last set of questions on your survey, how do you think they would respond? One possibility is that they would use context cues and respond as if the topic was similar to the preceding topics. If our survey began with questions about turnover intentions and ended with questions about dejobification, we might expect similar responses to both sets of questions, even though dejobification is not a real thing. It is nearly impossible to eliminate *all* order effects, but it is our job as researchers to reduce the effects that are within our control and relevant to our research questions. If we suspect, for example, that respondents won't know what dejobification is, we can reduce anchoring effects by defining the term for them. We encourage interested readers to refer to Dillman et al. (2014) for more information about order effects.

Guidelines Related to Ordering Effects

1. *Choose the first questions carefully.*

   - These questions set the tone for the rest of the questionnaire. Make sure that they are salient and relevant for all respondents.

2. *Group similar questions together.*

   - Respondents can evaluate items more quickly and precisely if they don't have to think about several different subjects at once. Grouping common items together can help reduce contrast effects that may occur when diverse items are next to one another.

3. *Use visual survey features to emphasize question grouping.*

   - Both paper and web-based surveys allow for question grouping via visual features. Grouped items may be printed or displayed on separate pages, in different columns, or in individual boxes.

4. *Place sensitive questions near the end of the survey.*

   - Establishing rapport with respondents early on increases the likelihood of respondents completing the entire survey. Respondents are less likely to quit in response to sensitive questions if they've already invested time in the survey.

*Guidelines adopted from Dillman et al. (2014)

A Note on Ethics in Survey Design

Although we encourage sensitive questions to go near the end of your survey, there may be some questions that you should never ask participants. For example, **personal identifiable information (PII)**, such as social security numbers, are both unlikely to be important to your research questions and also very likely to be perceived as invasive by your respondents. But not all cases are so obvious. Sometimes it can be difficult to determine whether or not a question is appropriate, and this is where IRB oversight of your research becomes most valuable.

As mentioned in Chapter 1, the IRB aims to ensure your research practices are appropriate by weighing the benefits of your research with the risks it poses to respondents. Among other guidelines, the Common Rule outlines if and how to obtain and document informed consent. Even if consent is not required, a survey study should generally begin with a description of the study, the potential risks it poses, and the rights of the respondents. The IRB and the Common Rule ensure that scientists adhere to ethical values and principles that underlie sound survey research, all while promoting the safety of participants.

Choosing Your Survey's Look and Feel

Think about your experiences being surveyed. Chances are, each questionnaire you've taken has looked a little different. While there is no one "correct" way to design a questionnaire, there are certainly some guidelines we can follow to design an *effective* questionnaire after you have written your items.

One of the first things to consider is how respondents will view your survey. Will they fill out a printed version of your survey, or will they answer questions electronically? Naturally, some survey design features are restricted to the delivery mode you choose. The two major modes of survey delivery are paper-and-pencil and electronic.

You might choose to administer a printed, paper-and-pencil version of your survey if you suspect your respondents are unable to access or use computers. This might be the appropriate mode for reaching an underprivileged sample without internet access or a sample without computer experience, for example.

In most situations, you will choose to deliver an electronic survey due to the convenience and functionality of using technology to survey individuals. Perhaps the biggest benefit is that administering a survey online saves time and money for both you and your respondents. If you need to reach hundreds of respondents, it can be quite costly to format, print, and physically mail your survey to so many people, not to mention the effort involved in opening and coding responses to your survey. Web-based surveys overcome these weaknesses, allowing you to reach a large sample of respondents in a shorter amount of time.

Sometimes researchers benefit from making use of more than one survey mode for a single questionnaire, which is referred to as a **mixed methods survey** (not to be confused with other "mixed methods"!). There are several reasons why multiple modes would be desirable. It may be that different subsets of a target population have access to different kinds of technology (for example, using web-based and paper-and-pencil surveys for people of higher and lower socioeconomic status, respectively). Or, an entire population may undergo a change that alters the way that a researcher can reach them (e.g., citizens with lower socioeconomic status gain Internet access). In either case, researchers must be careful to note the potential for measurement effects; that is, differences in which populations have access to which devices could explain response differences over time, rather than hypothesized effects.

Electronic Surveying

There are several types of electronic surveys, including email, web-based, mobile, telephone, and mixed-mode surveys. Email and web-based surveys are quite similar, with the major distinction being where on the Internet the survey itself is housed. With an email survey, the researcher sends the survey directly to respondents in the body of an email or as a downloadable attachment. With web-based surveys, researchers instead invite respondents (often, but not always, via email) to complete a survey housed in an online survey hosting platform. Common web-based survey platforms include Qualtrics, SurveyMonkey, and

SurveyGizmo, though many other options with similar functionalities exist. Each of these platforms allow users to create, house, and administer surveys online. Electronic surveys have some functionalities that are simply not possible with paper-based surveys, such as embedding audio, video, or even interactive virtual worlds into their electronic surveys.

Mobile surveys are those that respondents can complete from the convenience of their mobile smartphone or tablet device. Such surveys share many similarities with web-based surveys, but researchers should ensure a user-friendly survey experience on these smaller devices. Squeezing a bunch of items and response bubbles on a tiny screen would make for a tedious, frustrating survey experience. Most web-based platforms will ensure that a survey is optimized for mobile devices, but in cases where optimization is under question, there are a variety of web design and readability principles that researchers can consider.

Font size and color are both important when designing mobile surveys. One rule of thumb among mobile website design is that font sizes should be 16 pixels. Font sizes smaller than this may be difficult to read for visually impaired respondents. On the other hand, font sizes much larger than this would become cumbersome and require a lot of scrolling to read individual words. Finding an appropriate size may take some trial and error.

You can find a set of standards for high-quality web-based content in the **Web Content Accessibility Guidelines (WCAG)**, a document managed by the World Wide Web Consortium (W3C). For example, WCAG 1.4 specifies an overall goal to "make it easier for users to see and hear content including separating foreground from background." This means that your written questions should be distinct from the survey background. Generally, a white or off-white background with black text is undistracting and distinguishable enough for a pleasant survey experience. Light blue on dark blue is not.

The WCAG contains several dozen specific guidelines for making web content pleasant, predictable, and accessible to those with different ability levels, such as low vision. If you find the idea of combing through technical standards for web presentations, here's some good news: the default visual options on most survey hosting sites already meet these requirements! However, you should still be aware of the kinds of issues WCAG covers, because if you ever decide for a specific project to start changing fonts, colors, navigational structure, or other technical features of a website, you need to remember to check if you are making a change that will make the page non-WCAG-compliant without realizing it.

An important consideration that WCAG does not cover is the difference in display between desktop, laptop, tablet, smartphone, and everything else that might display web content. Just because a survey is formatted to display appropriately on a 15″ monitor does not imply that it will transfer well to a 4″ smartphone display. Unless enforced otherwise, researchers should expect that at least some of their respondents will use a mobile device to complete their survey, regardless of their sample or survey content. We thus recommend doing a test run of your questionnaires on a wide range of device types to ensure that no issues with formatting occur uniquely in some formats.

Telephone surveys are also classified as electronic. These may involve a researcher or research assistant verbally asking questions to a respondent over the phone, or they may involve prerecorded messages to which a respondent answers verbally or via their keypad. This latter method, known as **interactive voice response** (IVR) surveying, has been used to gauge customer satisfaction by many businesses and also in the Current Employment Statistics Survey conducted by the US Bureau of Labor Statistics.

One advantage of electronic surveys, whether web-based or telephone, is **branching**. Also known as **skip logic** or **advanced logic**, branching allows a researcher to channel respondents toward specific questions based on their responses to prior questions. For example, if a respondent indicates that they are employed, they may be asked to specify how many hours per week they work. It would not make sense for unemployed respondents to be presented with a question about their work hours. Electronic branching is generally seamless compared to paper-and-pencil branching, wherein researchers need to specify in words whether a respondent should answer a specific question.

Using Your Respondents' Time Wisely

Presenting your survey respondents with a sea of bubbles to click is inconsiderate and will probably lead to low-effort responding and survey attrition. The keys to building an attractive and engaging survey are to manage your respondent's **cognitive load** and to make the experience meaningful. That means making your requests clear, simple, non-distracting, and respectful.

Length

Some rules of thumb regarding length are outdated or misleading, such as recommendations to keep overall survey length to 20 items or less. As you will learn in the next chapter, it is not usually possible to measure psychological constructs in a trustworthy manner using so few items. Most surveys from authors that care about measurement quality will be quite a bit longer than 20 items. Our advice to you is to keep any questionnaire as short as you can while measuring what you need to measure at the level of rigor you need to address the questions you are asking. The exact number of items will vary by context, by purpose, and by audience. If you are surveying busy managers, don't expect them to click through a survey for 10 minutes. You'll be lucky to get three.

Converting Items to Time Estimates.

There are several techniques you can use to estimate completion time:

1. As a starting point, take the survey yourself and then triple the amount of time you take. Remember that you are very familiar with how surveys work, and what the questions are asking: you have a mental model already. Most people do not. So you will be able to answer your own survey faster than other people will be able to.
2. The best and most conclusive approach at this point is pilot testing; administer your questionnaire to at least a dozen people from the same population you ultimately want to sample and time their completion. If you will only have access to that population once, such as for an annual company-wide survey effort, try to find a comparable group to estimate on instead. For example, in our research, we often ask graduate students and undergraduate research assistants *not* working on the project to complete our final questionnaires, to get an estimate of time.
3. If you can't do any pilot testing, there are a few backup rules of thumb. Of course, "rule of thumb" means "don't trust this too much." One common strategy here is to count the number of items and multiply by 5–30 to estimate the number of seconds

---

that participants will take, depending on the complexity of the items. Another common strategy is to count the number of words each participant must read and divide by 100–150. If we imagine a 50-question personality inventory, 8 words each on average, we might estimate fast items (5 seconds each) and quick reading (150 wpm), which would result in $50 \times 5 = 250$ seconds = 4 minutes 10 seconds by the first calculation, or $8 \times 50/150 = 2$ minutes 40 seconds by the second. As you can see, one of these numbers is almost double the other, which is why this is never a perfect substitute for pilot testing. You must simply make too many assumptions.

Question Spacing

The division of items per page can have a big effect on respondents' survey experiences. Splitting your questions into a manageable number per page makes things less overwhelming for respondents, but is there an ideal number per page? One option is to include a single item per page, an approach that some argue makes respondents consider each item more carefully and reduce common method variance (Tourangeau et al., 2004). However, this requires respondents to do a great deal of clicking or tapping, especially if your survey has many questions.

Another option is to use a **matrix** which places a group of items into a grid using a common rating scale as shown in the following using actual I-promise-they're-real IPIP items shown in Table 9.2.

A study by Liu and Cernat (2018) directly compared single-item-per-page and matrix survey presentations. They found that although response times were similar in both formats, individuals were less likely to skip questions in the single-item conditions. This effect was stronger among individuals completing the survey on mobile devices. Another study (Toepoel et al., 2009) manipulated the number of items in a matrix, finding that 40 items per page was associated with shorter response times, more question skipping, and poorer perceptions of survey quality than was the equivalent survey with 4 items per page.

This research largely suggests that fewer items per page is better for data quality and respondent satisfaction. However, an important caveat is that administering a survey question-by-question is simply not ideal for most surveys in the real world. Imagine having to click through 150 questions one at a time! Such a format makes a survey very tedious for

Table 9.2 Actual IPIP items in a matrix presentation format

	Very inaccurate	Inaccurate	Accurate	Very accurate
Rule with an iron fist.	o	o	o	o
Can control objects with my mind.	o	o	o	o
Yell at inanimate objects.	o	o	o	o
Get nauseous when I see or think of spoiled food.	o	o	o	o
Have occasionally had the feeling that a TV or radio broadcaster knew I was listening to him.	o	o	o	o

participants. Our recommendation is to use fewer items per page when possible, but also to use matrix formats whenever including questions with identical rating scales.

There is no clear-cut rulebook for the maximum number of questions you should include per matrix, but somewhere around 10 is a good rule of thumb. A more important consideration is making sure that participants can view the headers of the matrix (the rating scale) without scrolling. It's always a good idea to preview a web-based or mobile survey on multiple devices before sending it out. This will ensure that respondents don't have to do unnecessary scrolling back and forth just to make sure they are selecting the right bubbles.

Visual Elements

When working on a big project, it's probably pretty motivating when you reach the half-way mark. Completing a survey is a similar experience, so it is usually a good idea to keep your respondents informed about their progress. Most survey hosting sites allow you to present a progress bar on the bottom of the respondents screen to indicate what percentage of the survey they've completed. In one study, respondents who had progress bars dropped out of the survey less frequently than those who did not have them (Heerwegh & Loosveldt, 2006). Although these differences were not statistically different, the study showed that progress bars were a generally desirable feature that most survey respondents prefer to have.

Contrary to common stereotypes that questionnaires are primarily text based, you should not be afraid to use visuals. However, these visuals should not be distracting and they should only be included within good reason. One misguided argument is that adding lots of pictures will make the survey more enjoyable for respondents, but this has not been supported by prior research (see Couper et al., 2004). Visuals can change the way that respondents interpret written questions, for better or worse. A good use of visuals would be to clarify the meanings of otherwise ambiguous questions. For example, if you are asking a question about the frequency that individuals engage in counterproductive work behaviors (CWBs), including images of the various forms of CWBs may help participants remember behaviors they would have otherwise overlooked or forgotten.

Ensuring a Good Response Rate

You've written effective questions, designed your survey, and received IRB approval. At this point, you expect that all of this effort should result in plenty of responses to help you answer your research questions. Unfortunately, response rates are typically quite low in organizational samples. This doesn't mean that you should settle with responses from a tiny fraction of your sample, though. Following are a few considerations to help ensure that you acquire a reasonable response rate for your survey.

Increase Saliency

Saliency is a quality that describes how relevant or important a survey is for a respondent. Highly salient surveys are those that ask about current behaviors or interests. To increase saliency and therefore your response rate, it is helpful to have a general idea of your sample's interests and behaviors. For example, a survey asking detailed questions about human anatomy is much more salient for a sample of doctors than it is for accountants. If your sample gets the impression that their voice doesn't matter regarding your questions, they will likely quit your survey.

Give Rewards and Reduce Punishments

As most psychologists will tell you, positive reinforcements are motivating. There are many rewards to incentivize survey responses, and these will vary across settings and samples. One of the most common rewards in the social sciences is university course credits. Most college students enrolled in introductory psychology courses are required to participate in a certain number of research studies throughout the course of the semester. By doing so, they are rewarded by meeting the research requirements of the course.

Financial rewards are often viewed as a good motivator. Some individuals complete surveys for a living through services such as Prolific or Amazon's Mechanical Turk. Researchers posting their survey to such platforms can select how much they will pay each respondent for completing the survey. Another financial reward that is cheaper is to host a cash or gift-card drawing for anyone who completes your survey. This is particularly effective if the reward – much like the survey itself – is salient to your sample. This approach can also be used to encourage more timely survey responses. For example, you can specify that only the first 25 respondents will be entered into the drawing. Even if timeliness is not a concern for you, this tactic is quite effective in getting respondents who would have otherwise ignored and forgotten your survey to complete it when they first learn about it.

Negative reinforcement is also very motivating. If there is one thing that respondents are worried about going into most surveys, it's the amount of time they need to dedicate to it. To increase response rates, it is helpful to remind your respondents that your survey will not take away too much of their time. A time estimate during the introduction of your survey, in addition to a progress bar, can go a long way in keeping your respondents engaged throughout the questionnaire.

Encourage Liking

As we discussed in the *Writing Effective Questions* section, people are more likely to help others whom they like. A simple "Thank you" message lets respondents know that their time is appreciated. These messages are not restricted to the beginning or end of the survey, either. If you are administering a particularly long survey, an effective technique is to include a separate page in the middle of the survey reminding them that you value the time they've invested in your research.

Stress the Importance of Their Participation

Sometimes being honest is the best way to get an acceptable response rate. Tell your respondents why you are conducting your research and why their responses matter. Scarcity is quite motivating, so let your sample know if you are experiencing a low response rate when appropriate. Respondents often presume that there are plenty of other people filling out your survey, or that there will be plenty of opportunities to respond to your survey in the future. If either of these are untrue, specify that when you introduce your survey.

Send Reminders

When all else has failed, follow-up messages can help motivate respondents to complete your survey. Don't be afraid to send multiple follow-ups, but do so in a strategic way. When you are about to send your last follow-up message, make the deadline clear to respondents. This tactic is quite effective coupled with the prior one; let your sample know if your response rate is much lower than you were expecting.

Screening Out Bad Responses

Even when we carefully construct our questionnaires to keep respondents engaged, we will still encounter responses we do not want to analyze for a variety of reasons. Fortunately, there are many methods researchers can use to screen out undesirable responses. Not all of these screening procedures follow the same guidelines. Be careful not to select a screening procedure just because it is popular; instead, identify what the potential threats to validity are for your study in particular, and *then* select a screening procedure. Each screening procedure helps to address unique data quality issues. As such, we organize this section by the three major types of cases that can be addressed using screening procedures.

We will revisit these techniques and expand on them significantly in Chapter 11.

Unrepresentative Respondents

Sometimes researchers get responses from individuals who do not represent the populations they are interested in studying. These unrepresentative responses can occur for a number of reasons. For example, if we wanted to understand how young adults react to various organizational diversity initiatives, it may seem appropriate to survey college students. However, it is entirely possible that we will get responses from college students who do not represent our population of interest. Some students may be older adult learners, for example, and we may wish to remove their responses from our analyses. A second example might be responses that are not from human subjects at all, but by **bots** – computer programs that impersonate humans and complete a variety of online tasks, such as filling out surveys. Either case poses threats to the quality of inferences we can draw from our data.

Fortunately, there are procedures that help us prevent and identify unrepresentative responses. In our first example, we might want to clearly indicate the age criteria of our study when we make it available to the college students. Even in the case that we obtain responses outside of this criteria, we can easily flag these responses for removal post-hoc. In our second example, we should be careful when selecting our surveying host. Some hosting services have their own procedures to block bots, but researchers should exercise their own caution as well. Some potential pieces of evidence for identifying bot responses include quality of open-ended responses, IP addresses, and time signatures. Multiple surveys submitted from the same IP address are a good, but not conclusive, sign that a bot completed your survey. In such cases, it is helpful to pair this evidence with open-ended responses or time signatures; when written responses are very off-topic or if the surveys were completed in a short time frame, it is more likely that a bot did so.

Careless Respondents

"Have you been to the moon?" – how many people could truthfully respond "Yes" to that question? Maybe two dozen? And chances are, none of them are in your study. Including **attention check questions** like this can help identify people who are not paying attention. We refer to these individuals as **careless respondents** or **low effort respondents**. Careless respondents are individuals who do not take your survey seriously while completing it. The survey can be designed so that if you say "Yes" to this question, a warning is displayed that says "Hey! Pay more attention!" Tara likes to put a picture of a baby elephant on one of the pages of a longer survey, with a message that says "You're doing great – keep going!" Then, later on, a question pops up that says "what kind of animal was in the photo on page 5?" This is a great way to introduce some fun into the survey but also helps to screen out careless respondents and bots.

A common check for people paying attention in experimental and quasi-experimental studies is the **manipulation check**, which refers to questions asking participants to provide information about which condition they were in. Importantly, to be useful, these questions cannot be leading. For example, in one prior study, Richard asked participants, "What were the instructions you received before the last task?" with five options – only two of which were real conditions. This decreases the chances that a participant will guess the right answer when they really don't remember at all.

There are many ways to identify careless responders even when there was no specific condition assignment to remember. One option to worry about during the study design phase is **instructed responding**, also called **directed responding**, in which an item is included that tells respondents to select a specific option (Select "Strongly Agree" for this item). If the respondent selects something else, they probably did not read the item.

We can summarize our recommendations here by saying the following:

- If you used an experimental or quasi-experimental manipulation, include a well-written manipulation check that does not telegraph the correct answer.
- Include at least one instructed response item on roughly every page of the questionnaire or every 50 items, whichever is later.
- There are also many statistical methods for detecting careless responding post-hoc, but we'll discuss those in Chapter 11.

Carelessness in the Wild

I-O psychologist Adam Meade has conducted a great deal of research on psychological measurement, and to date his favorite project dealt with creating a unique set of items for detecting careless respondents:

> My favorite paper is probably Meade and Craig (2012) on careless responding. It started with a conversation. My memory may be faulty but I believe it was at the NCIO conference and I was talking with Scott Tonidandel. We were talking about

sources of data, specifically student data and he asked about the quality of data we were getting at NC State from the undergrad participant pool. Without hesitating, I told him it was good. Of course it was good. I and others had been working with undergraduate participants at NC State forever. It was fine. It had to be. Then he mentioned that some of his friends at UNC-Charlotte were finding not so great data quality. He didn't elaborate and I didn't ask him what he meant by this. At the time, I felt grateful that we didn't have the data quality issues that Scott had mentioned. However, after the conversation, it really stuck with me. I'd never really questioned it before, but now I was interested. . . . Was my data any good and how would I know?

I was aware of a few different things that seemed related to this question, for instance the lie scales on the MMPI to detect malingering and social desirability scales, although this seemed a bit different. I knew my colleague Bart Craig knew quite a lot about assessments, especially a lot more about clinical assessments than I did, so I asked him what he knew about these types of scales to detect lying, faking, data quality, etc. We were both also aware of instructed response items from different surveys we had seen, though I had not seen the term "instructed response" before. Bart was very interested in something along the lines of an "unlikely virtue" scale similar to what you see on social desirability scales but with the idea of making the items impossible to be true rather than just unlikely. One day we met over beer, and brainstormed up some items, which was the most fun I've ever had writing items. Bart gets all of the credit for the more creative ones such as "I am paid biweekly by leprechauns" which is easily the single best scale item ever written. At a conference once, a researcher asked me about these items assuming we had carefully researched, tested, and vetted these items into a scale and was shocked to learn we just had fun writing these over beers one afternoon.

We are also both fans of 80s hard rock and had heard of the famous Van Halen brown M&M approach. If you aren't familiar with it, a rider among many, many, many in Van Halen's contract to perform was that the backstage area must have M&Ms but NOT brown M&Ms. At the time, the media reported on this as rock stars being impossibly difficult divas, but actually it was really an "instructed response" type of item. The contract apparently contained a lot of details about safety procedures such as the wiring and power supply and the brown M&Ms was an easy way for the band to tell if the venue had actually read the contract or not. If not, then they knew they had to carefully check compliance on all of the safety procedures. One of my biggest regrets as an author is letting the editor at *Psyc Methods* talk me into removing a lengthy footnote that included a quote about the brown M&Ms from David Lee Roth's book as the editor felt it wasn't essential and wasn't dignified enough for an academic journal.

We originally sent the paper to the *Journal of Applied Psychology* where it was rejected without revision. This could have been the end of it, but we knew we were onto something so we sent it off to *Psyc Methods*. In both cases, the original paper was quite a bit different from what was eventually published as there were three revisions before it was finally accepted. The original version only examined a sample of undergraduates with no simulation study and no mixture modeling – those were things that reviewers and editor suggested adding so this paper is a great example of how a journal and editor can really shape a paper into something quite different (and hopefully better) than the original submission. I think it also speaks to how reviewers shouldn't be so eager to recommend rejecting a paper that has a good idea at its core. Reviewers are far too eager to find a reason to reject a paper sometimes.

This paper is also a great example of being in the right place at the right time. Unbeknownst to me, there were several people working on exactly the same issue at the same time (e.g., Nathan Bowling, Paul Curran, Jason Huang to name a few). We managed to get our paper out to a widely read journal early on and it became one of those papers that you had to cite if you were working in this area. I think it's a great example of the notion of "multiple discovery" where an idea has a time that has come and multiple people will stumble upon it independently and simultaneously (such as with calculus, etc.). Had we been months slower in publishing the paper, the paper would probably have never have gotten the attention that it has. Tara and I have been on the other end of that with our M-Turk data quality paper not getting as much attention as other papers despite being better in most ways."

Fakers

A third kind of respondent we sometimes want to screen out is fakers. These are individuals who identify the goals of the survey administrator and purposefully respond to the survey in a socially desirable way. Faking is especially common in the realm of personnel selection, where there is an incentive to impress the hiring manager evaluating questionnaire responses (that is, getting a job). This type of response behavior is not restricted to evaluative contexts, however. They may also occur if respondents suspect that their responses are not anonymous. In such situations, respondents may feel uncomfortable disclosing their true thoughts.

One approach for identifying fake responders is the **overclaiming technique**. Overclaiming is a tendency of fakers to claim that they have knowledge about something that does not exist. While some researchers argue that including such items can help identify fakers (Paulhus et al., 2003), others say that it has little validity (Kam et al., 2015). We encourage the use of this technique if you have reason to suspect faking, but we should also make an important point about faking in general: In some situations, faking itself is a behavior that we might be interested in, as opposed to screening out for. In personnel selection contexts, for example, knowing what an organization wants is an important precursor to being an effective performer. That is, the person who fakes well on the pre-employment survey may fake just as well on the job. The extent to which faking in surveys is problematic will depend on the nature of your research.

Making the Most of Organizational Surveys

Properly designed surveys help researchers answer a wide variety of questions about organizations. As we've discussed, employees are busy people who are probably not interested in spending a lot of time filling out surveys. There is both a science and an art to building a survey – the guidelines outlined in this chapter are intended to help you not only create surveys that measure things in a scientifically rigorous way but also create an enjoyable experience for respondents.

References

Couper, M. P., Tourangeau, R., & Kenyon, K. (2004). Picture this! Exploring visual effects in web surveys. *Public Opinion Quarterly, 68*(2), 255–266.

Dillman, D. A., Smyth, J. D., & Christian, L. M. (2014). *Internet, phone, mail, and mixed-mode surveys: The tailored design method.* John Wiley & Sons.

Heerwegh, D., & Loosveldt, G. (2006). An experimental study on the effects of personalization, survey length statements, progress indicators, and survey sponsor logos in web surveys. *Journal of Official Statistics, 22*(2), 191–210.

Kam, C., Risavy, S. D., & Perunovic, W. E. (2015). Using over-claiming technique to probe social desirability ratings of personality items: A validity examination. *Personality and Individual Differences, 74*, 177–181.

Liu, M., & Cernat, A. (2018). Item-by-item versus matrix questions: A web survey experiment. *Social Science Computer Review, 36*(6), 690–706. https://doi.org/10.1177/0894439316674459

Nisbett, R. E., & Wilson, T. D. (1977). Telling more than we can know: Verbal reports on mental processes. *Psychological Review, 84*(3), 231.

Paulhus, D. L., Harms, P. D., Bruce, M. N., & Lysy, D. C. (2003). The over-claiming technique: Measuring self-enhancement independent of ability. *Journal of Personality and Social Psychology, 84*(4), 890–904.

Toepoel, V., Das, M., & Van Soest, A. (2009). Design of web questionnaires: The effects of the number of items per screen. *Field Methods, 21*(2), 200–213.

Tourangeau, R., Couper, M. P., & Conrad, F. (2004). Spacing, position, and order: Interpretive heuristics for visual features of survey questions. *Public Opinion Quarterly, 68*(3), 368–393.

Willits, F. K., & Saltiel, J. (1995). Question order effects on subjective measures of quality of life. *Rural Sociology, 60*(4), 654–665.

Yerkes, R. M. (1921). *Psychological examining in the United States army* (Vol. 15). US Government Printing Office.

Further Reading

Cialdini, R. B. (2006). *Influence: The psychology of persuasion* (revised ed.). Harper Business.

- Cialdini's book *Influence*, originally published in 1984 and revised in 2006, summarizes decades of empirical research on the science and art of persuasion, both by him and others. Written for the popular press, it is an accessible introduction to persuasion techniques that anyone can benefit from. It is a little outdated now but is still regarded as one of a very small set of trustworthy, science-based self-help books.

Dillman, D. A., Smyth, J. D., & Christian, L. M. (2014). *Internet, phone, mail, and mixed-mode surveys: The tailored design method.* Wiley.

- Although originally intended for more of a sociological audience, Dillman and colleagues wrote what is now often considered the definitive guidebook for conducting survey research. If you see yourself surveying organizations for a living, you should read this book cover to cover.

Meade, A. W., & Craig, S. B. (2012). Identifying careless responses in survey data. *Psychological Methods, 17*(3), 437–455.

- As Meade himself wrote earlier in the chapter you just read, this article has become one of the most foundational works for the detection of careless responding. It outlines several approaches and compares their success both conceptually and empirically.

Podsakoff, P. M., MacKenzie, S. B., Lee, J. Y., & Podsakoff, N. P. (2003). Common method biases in behavioral research: A critical review of the literature and recommended remedies. *Journal of Applied Psychology, 88*(5), 879–903.
  • Podsakoff and colleagues' 2003 study opened the eyes of many I-O psychologists as to just how important a problem common method variance can be. In short, it can influence results in unexpected ways, it is difficult to meaningfully test for, and it can completely undercut the validity of conclusions drawn from studies that rely entirely on questionnaires.

Questions to Think About

1. What are the strengths and weaknesses of using electronic surveys?
2. Assume you want to assess your peers' attitudes toward their graduate program. Create three Likert-type items and three semantic differential items to assess this construct.
3. What is cognitive load? How can researchers measure the cognitive load of a survey, and what are effective strategies for reducing cognitive load?
4. Describe assimilation and contrast effects. Provide an example of each.
5. Describe two ways to ensure a good survey response rate.
6. Describe the three kinds of undesirable survey responses discussed in this chapter. What are effective strategies for screening these responses out?

Key Terms

• gender
• in outlier analysis, identification of a specific percentile at which scores are considered problematic, at which point scores are replaced with the percentile cutoff
• interactive voice response (IVR)
• low effort respondents
• manipulation check
• matrix
• mixed methods survey
• optimal performance test
• order effect
• overclaiming technique
• personal identifiable information (PII)
• priming effect
• race
• sex
• skip logic
• Web Content Accessibility Guidelines (WCAG)

Chapter 10

Creating a Rating Scale That Reflects a Construct

Learning Objectives

After reading this chapter, you will be able to:

1. Explain why rating scales are used to measure constructs
2. Distinguish between formative and reflective measures of constructs
3. Follow a step-by-step process for high-quality scale development
4. Distinguish between different types of scales
5. Apply good developmental practices to scale development

Chapter Content

As explained in Chapter 7, test validity – the degree to which a measure actually measures what you think it does – is a key concern. To maximize the chances that the measure you develop will in fact be valid, researchers have published quite literally thousands of articles, chapters, and entire books providing guidelines, tips, and techniques about measure development. We say this to emphasize to you that reading this chapter alone will not be enough for you to know 100% of the ins and outs of measure development; however, it will give you a good foundation on which to build that knowledge. For that reason, the end of this chapter contains references to many additional resources that we recommend reading once you're comfortable with the basics presented here. We'll also be focusing here on **rating scales**, which is just one type of measure but is likely the most common type of measure you'll run into as an I-O psychologist. Rating scales are represents a specific type of data collection

The reason that measure development is so complicated is the result of one fact that tends to surprise people: we can never be 100% confident that any construct we want to measure is actually the one being measured by any particular measurement instrument. In short, there is no such thing as a "valid test." Instead, validity of measures is a concept that is judged in terms of *strength of evidence*. For any particular research study where we need to measure a construct, we must decide instead if there is *sufficient evidence* to support using any particular measure of it, knowing that we might be wrong. We must decide if that measure is "good enough" for our intended use of it, using the types of validity evidence introduced in Chapter 7.

DOI: 10.4324/9781315167473-13

You might think this is unique to psychology and its inherently fuzzy constructs, but that's not true. Even something as seemingly objective as distance (a construct) can be mismeasured. For example, a handheld ruler cannot give you precision to the nanometer. Instead, we make a "good enough" judgment, such as "one millimeter is as much precision as we need for this project." If you don't need to know distance in nanometers, you don't need a measurement instrument that precise, and a ruler will serve that role just fine.

With psychological constructs, this is more difficult, because the relationship between a construct and its measures is not as self-evident. You can look at a ruler and easily judge, because you have been intimately familiar with the idea of both distance and rulers since a very young age, "this measures distance." In psychological construct measurement, when reviewing questions, this becomes decidedly more difficult.

So what sort and how much validity evidence do you need to decide that your measure is "good enough"? What do you actually *do* to ensure you have enough evidence for other people to trust measures you've developed? Answering those questions is the purpose of this chapter.

The Assumptions Behind Reflective Measures

As described in Chapter 7, reflective measurement and formative measurement entail different underlying assumptions about the nature of constructs and the relationships between constructs and measures. The focus of this chapter will be on building high-quality multi-item reflective measures, specifically. To recap, the basic assumption behind a reflective approach to measurement is that constructs exist independently of your attempt to measure them. For example, even if I never ask you to fill out a conscientiousness questionnaire, you still *have a particular level of conscientiousness*, and your "true score" on conscientiousness causes conscientiousness-related behaviors. Those behaviors *reflect* the construct.

Meaningful reflective measurement thus only occurs when you, as the researcher, create a situation where a person's true score on the target construct *causes* differences in something you're measuring. We would only conclude that items designed to measure conscientiousness do in fact measure conscientiousness if those questions cause people

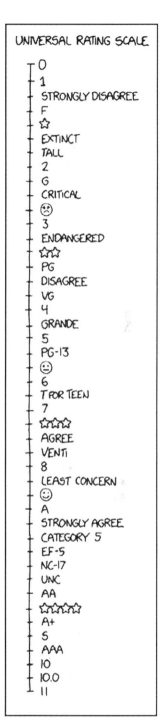

Courtesy xkcd.com.

high in conscientiousness to respond differently than people low in conscientiousness. With a different level of conscientiousness, a person would *therefore* have a different score on the measure.

It's important that you pay attention to how the word "cause" was used in that last paragraph. This is another example of counterfactual thinking as we introduced in Chapter 8. You probably already think counterfactually about your own life when you wonder, "What would be happening now if I had made a different decision earlier?" You now just need to get in the habit of thinking this way about rating scales. To set up a counterfactual, just fill in the following sentence: "If only X had been different, Y would have been different too."

We can do this explicitly with our previous example. "If the person that completed this scale (or item) had a higher level of conscientiousness, they would have responded more positively to my questions." If you can't say that, then you don't have a high-quality reflective measure.

Don't Assume Constructs Exist

As a psychologist-in-training, you need to be warned that you are certain to bring a particular bias to scale development and construct specification. That bias, as described by Brick et al. (2022), is based on an idea called **illusory essence**. Specifically, people trained in the philosophical traditions of psychology tend to assume things have innate, objective, fundamental essences. For example, in the case of the psychological trait, conscientiousness, we psychologists tend to assume that a person has a fundamental essence within them called conscientiousness which causes them to behave in particular ways that we can observe and measure. Although there is intuitive appeal to this idea, it's important to realize that there is no empirical evidence for such an essence of conscientiousness. It's purely an assumption we make when developing reflective scales, most directly driven by a philosophy of science rooted in realism. It is also plausible that conscientiousness is an illusion, something we believe happens because it seems like a logical explanation to our flawed human brains for patterns of behavior we have observed both with our eyes and in data. For now, it's okay to assume such essences exist, but remember that it is just that – an assumption – and be careful not to apply that assumption automatically in the future without critical reflection.

Why We're Ignoring Formative Measures in This Chapter

As described in Chapter 7, formative measurement can be conceptualized as the opposite of reflective: in a formative measurement model, measures cause (i.e., form) constructs. The existence and use of formative measures is an area of significant controversy. Some researchers do not even believe that formative measurement is possible and that current implementations are little more than statistical sleight of hand. A prime example of a formative construct – one that theoretically does not exist unless you measure it – is socioeconomic status (SES). SES cannot be measured reflectively because SES does not exist unless we measure a few things – usually income, parent's income, education, parent's education and a variety of similar concepts – and then call them, as a group, "SES."

This leaves us with two options. First, we could conclude that SES is not a construct, and some researchers do argue this. Second, we could invent a concept called formative measurement and call it a construct anyway.

A reasonable criticism of formative measurement is that constructs are only formative when you haven't put enough thought into them being reflective. For example, you could measure income, parent's income, education, and parent's education individually and reflectively, and then use all of them in a statistical model as direct predictors of whatever you wanted to predict. In this approach, you might conclude that you no longer need SES, since you have all of its parts.

A reasonable counter to that view is that is that researchers utilizing formative measures aren't interested in the individual predictors; instead, they want to know about the *shared* impact of all of those dimensions together in order to understand what aspects of outcomes are caused by "SES" and what aspects are uniquely caused by individual pieces of SES.

Even with these disagreements, what everyone can agree on is that the distinction between formative and reflective measurement is not an empirical one. Or in other words, you should definitely *not* try both approaches given a particular dataset and see which way works better. This is a theory-driven decision alone; it must follow from your expertise and professional judgment.

Formative Measurement

For more detail on why formative measurement may be risky, see the following paper:

Edwards, J. (2010). The fallacy of formative measurement. *Organizational Research Methods,* *14*, 370–388.

A Brief Primer on Confirmatory Factor Analysis

One of the most useful tools in the reflective measure development toolkit is **confirmatory factor analysis (CFA)**, a predecessor to and close cousin of structural equation modeling. CFA is commonly used to provide construct validity evidence in the form of "evidence supporting the internal structure of the test" described in Chapter 7. The reason a CFA can provide this sort of evidence is that it closely reflects what you do with a CFA: you propose a theoretical model of internal structure and then assess how well the data you collected **fit** this proposed model. An example of a CFA analysis appears in Figure 10.1. Once again, there's not enough space in this book to teach you the full complexity of CFA, especially mathematically, but some basic understanding of how to interpret them will do you a world of good when trying to understand journal articles. Importantly, more statistics are returned from a CFA than we'll discuss here, but the ones we'll talk about here are most important for scale development.

You can determine what the researchers actually *measured* versus what they believe *caused* their measures by the use of circles and rectangles. In Chapter 2, we introduced these in the context of path diagrams as *constructs* and *operational definitions*, respectively. In the context of CFAs, and from here forward in this book, we'll use slightly different, broader terms in relation to path diagrams. Constructs are just one example of a **latent variable**, whereas operational definitions are one example of an **indicator**. The reason for this change

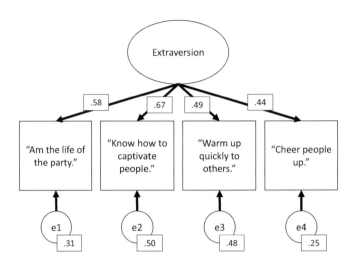

Figure 10.1 Confirmatory factor analysis path diagram of a four-item extraversion measure with standardized parameter estimates.

Standardized Versus Unstandardized Estimates

If you want to interpret path diagrams, be careful about whether standardized or unstandardized coefficients are provided. The examples discussed here are all about *standardized* model estimates, which means that numbers have been adjusted for increased interpretability. For example, in an unstandardized model, item residuals are no longer interpretable as proportion of unique variance and factor loadings are no longer interpretable as correlations. So be careful to check first which type of numbers you're looking at before interpreting them as instructed here.

---

will be more obvious in just a moment. Just as with the more specific terms, *constructs* and *operational definitions,* all latent variables are unmeasured, theoretical concepts whereas all indicators are numbers provided by the researcher, usually as the result of data collection. Thus, this CFA involves four indicators (which are in reality a four-item scale) and five latent variables that caused responses on those indicators. In some CFA diagrams, the lower four circles are omitted to save space, sometimes appearing as unattached lines or possibly even being omitted entirely, but that doesn't imply they weren't modeled.

So what are these item-specific latent variables? These are called disturbance or **uniqueness** terms and they are used as latent representations of the **residual variance of each item**. In a CFA, they indicate the amount of variance in each item that was not explained by the latent variable specified. When you're looking at a **standardized** CFA path diagram, they are in fact proportions and interpretable as such. In this example, 1 − .31 = .69 = 69%, so 69% of the variance in "Am the life of the party" was caused by extraversion and the remaining (the residual) 31% was "unique," without an identified cause. From looking at this path diagram, you can see that between 50% and 75% of each item can be explained by extraversion. For psychological scales, you generally want these uniqueness terms to be less than 50%. An item with more than 50% uniqueness is more greatly affected by constructs other than the one you're trying to measure!

There are also numbers on the arrows leading between extraversion and each item. These are called **factor loadings**. When standardized, they can be interpreted as the correlation between the item and the latent variable that you have theorized to cause it. In this case, the correlation between extraversion and responses to "Am the life of the party" is .58. In general, you want factor loadings to be pretty high, at least .50 but less than .90. Anything outside those bounds requires more investigation but is not necessarily a problem. As an example, if you discover a standardized factor loading of 1.0, it suggests that you may not need any other items, because that item measures the construct perfectly!

Several additional numbers designed to assess fit are also often reported alongside path diagrams called **fit indices**. Fit indices reflect the degree to which the data match your theoretical model, but they each involve different assumptions and somewhat different comparisons. Complete interpretation of fit indices is beyond the scope of this textbook, but Table 10.1 provides a commonly cited set of guidelines for both common fit indices and the other numbers described previously.

Importantly, in all of the previous cases, the interpretation provided relies upon the use of "standardized" estimates. Much as correlations are much easier to interpret than covariances because correlations are standardized covariances, standardized parameter estimates in CFA aid in their meaningful interpretation. You should generally default to interpreting standardized estimates unless you have a particular reason to look at unstandardized.

Table 10.1 Traditional CFA fit indices plus typical cutoffs for acceptable fit

	"Marginal" fit threshold	Relevant literature
Estimates		
Uniqueness (standardized)	< .50	Bagozzi and Yi (1988)
Factor loading (standardized)	> .50 and < .95	
Composite reliability (CR)	> .60	
Average variance explained (AVE)	> .50	
Absolute fit indices		
p-value from χ^2 (chi-squared)	> .05	Bagozzi and Yi (1988)
χ^2/df	Uninterpretable; do not use	Gefen et al. (2000)
Relative fit indices		
GFI or AGFI	Uninterpretable; do not use	Sharma et al. (2005)
Root mean-square error of approximation (RMSEA)	< .06, or lack of statistical significance (confidence interval overlaps or nearly overlaps zero)	Browne and Cudeck (1993) MacCallum et al. (1996) Hu and Bentler (1999)
Comparative fit (CFI)	> .96	Hu and Bentler (1999)
Tucker-Lewis (or non-normed fit) (TLI or NNFI)	> .95	
Standardized root mean-square residual (SRMR or "standardized RMR")	< .08	

Note. When sample size is less than 250, Hu and Bentler (1999) recommended focusing upon CFI and SRMR in combination, because they state RMSEA and TLI are overly conservative with small sample sizes.

Fit Indices

For more details on the calculation and interpretation of fit indices, see David Kenny's webpage on the topic, which is actually updated fairly regularly despite its internet-of-the-1990s appearance: http://davidakenny.net/cm/fit.htm

For more details on the development of fit indices and why they can be controversial, see:

Bollen, K. A., & Long, J. S. (1992). Tests for structural equation models: Introduction. *Sociological Methods & Research*, *21*, 123–131.

For a more recent approach to fit indices, see the R package *dynamic* and accompanying paper:

McNeish, D., & Wolf, M. G. (2023). Dynamic fit index cutoffs for confirmatory factor analysis models. *Psychological Methods*, *28*.

So what results in poor fit? This is a common area of confusion for people trying to understand CFA (and its cousin, structural equation modeling). In CFA, misfit is caused by paths that you specify as "zero" not actually being zero. In Figure 10.1, there are six of these paths – the intercorrelations amongst the residuals. To help you understand, these are depicted explicitly in Figure 10.2.

Understanding the difference between Figures 10.1 and 10.2 is the key to understanding fit. Remember that both are theoretical models and fit captures the degree to which the data reflect those theoretical models. That means the Figure 10.1 is stating a set of assumptions: the item variances are not related to each other *except* through the shared cause of extraversion. To the extent that this is not true, data fitted with the CFA in Figure 10.1 will fit more poorly.

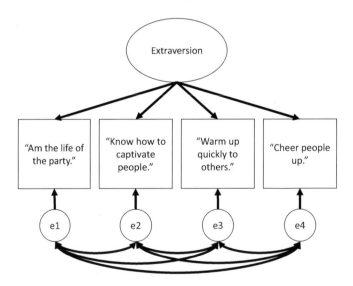

Figure 10.2 A perfectly fitting CFA with all item residual correlations freed.

This is a useful diagnostic tool. Remember that the key to classical test theory is this formula: $X = T + e$. We apply this formula in the measurement context to refer to items; a person's true score on a construct is equal to the mean of their item responses because we can assume that error averages to zero across items (i.e., unsystematic error). In other words, the only thing in common between the causes of responses to each item is the causal force of the target construct across all of them. If there are residual correlations between items in a CFA, *this is no longer true*. Instead, there is *systematic* error in our measurement and the things possible assuming classical test theory can no longer be assumed. This means we cannot use other statistical procedures on such a measure with any confidence, because we cannot be sure what the scale is measuring: the construct (true score) or the systematic error.

To understand what impact this has on measurement in real studies, let's imagine that Figure 10.3 represents the "true model" for this measure. Specifically, there is a relationship between item 1 and item 2. This might be signified in a CFA by either freeing the path between the residuals on items 1 and 2 or by misfit (if that path were not freed and should have been).

Practically speaking, what does this mean? The most likely explanation is that there is an unknown, external construct influencing both of these items. Instead of what is displayed in Figure 10.3, perhaps what is really going on is what is depicted in Figure 10.4.

There's no way to know from data alone what causes correlated item residuals, so I've guessed at the name of a new construct in Figure 10.4: party personality! Perhaps people with party personalities are more likely to respond positively to both "am the life of the party" and "know how to captivate people," independently of their level of extraversion, and this is what's causing the correlation between item residuals. When we account for party personality by modeling, the correlation between item residuals disappears.

Why is this a problem? Let's imagine you try to predict answers to a criterion question: "Did you go to a party in the last week?" with the intent of determining the relationship between extraversion and party attendance. You calculate an average of the four items and then correlate it with party attendance. There's a relationship! Unfortunately, you have no

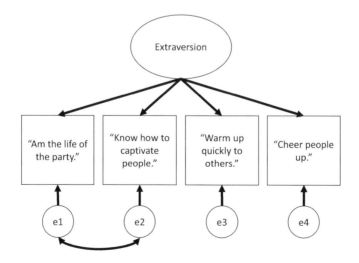

Figure 10.3 A four-item extraversion scale with two correlated uniqueness terms.

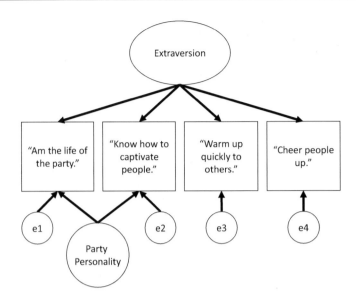

Figure 10.4 A four-item scale in which two items are also caused by an external unintended construct.

way to know if it's because extraversion and party attendance are correlated or if, instead, it's because party and party attendance are correlated. There's no way to separate them in this analysis! That's because the systematic error introduced by mismeasurement is *still contained within the mean score*. Because of this, we should never have tried using mean scores from this scale in the first place, because if this was happening, the CFA depicted way back in Figure 10.1 *would not have fit well*.

That's why misfit is so important when diagnosing a measure. If the measure had been developed appropriately originally, this item residual correlation would not have been in the final scale, and you could be confident (all else held equal) that your extraversion measure was really an extraversion measure. This example is a little silly, but hopefully it demonstrates to you why ensuring your items are uncorrelated is so important and also how a CFA can help you diagnose whether a scale of high quality or not.

How to Create a Trustworthy Psychological Rating Scale

As mentioned earlier, we will focus on rating scales here. There are many types and variations of rating scales, but all ratings scales require a person to make judgments about individual prompts and then assign ratings which are mapped onto numbers. Some rating scales are text; others are graphical. Some rating scales are about the person completing the scale, whereas others ask about other people. But in all of these contexts, the ratings are mapped onto numbers and then somehow combined, such as through summation or by calculating a mean score.

Like many of the development processes used in I-O psychology, scale development is done iteratively, returning to earlier stages depending on what happens in later stages. But putting in your due diligence and thinking carefully at earlier stages definitely reduces the

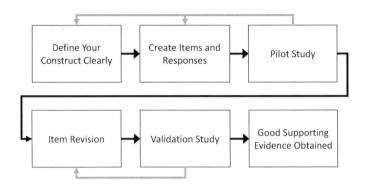

Figure 10.5 Steps to scale development.

number of times you'll likely need to do so. The steps involved in scale development appear in Figure 10.5.

Step 1: Define Your Construct Clearly

Your construct definition is the first and most important step of scale development. Your construct definition provides a roadmap for decisions you will make in all later stages. If you are making a scale for an existing construct, this definition should be derived from all existing research literature on that construct, relying upon your judgment as a subject matter expert (or preferably, your entire team's) to develop it. If you are trying to create a brand-new construct, this is much more difficult, but common approaches involve conducting qualitative research studies to gather information from subject matter experts.

For example, the goal of the research studies reported by Landers and Callan (2014) was to develop scales assessing "beneficial" and "harmful" employee social media behaviors while at work. The first step of scale development was therefore to figure out what behaviors people engage in on social media while at work; thus a qualitative study was conducted gathering that information, and a content analysis was done to sort those behaviors into categories, which then became the target constructs for scale development.

Several concepts introduced in Chapter 7 about conceptualizing constructs apply directly in this step. Be sure to establish a firm theoretical foundation for your construct. Don't assume because you've never heard of someone studying a construct that no one else has. They might have studied it under a name you haven't imagined; in this way, beware the jingle-jangle fallacy.

If you don't develop good construct definitions, you will regret it in all of the steps that follow. Take your time, do it right, and be confident in your definition before moving on.

Step 2: Create Items and Responses

Once again, the basic measurement concepts introduced in Chapter 7 apply when writing multi-item scales. Item construction is still done based on the expertise of subject matter experts, which in most cases is you. Crafting a high-quality item is a complex process, and you will write a lot of bad items in pursuit of good ones. In fact, a good rule to live by is that you shouldn't assume any item you've written is a good item until you have data in hand supporting it.

The shift to a multi-question format, all targeted at a single construct, does create some additional concerns related to **scaling**, which refers to the specific scoring strategy for multi-question quantitative construct measures, particularly related to how scores across items are combined. Scoring is sometimes numeric, sometimes text, and sometimes both. Typically, items on psychological scales have five or seven **anchors**, where anchors are the verbal descriptions that correspond to numerical ratings. Good anchors are both **exhaustive** and **mutually exclusive**.

Early in the scale development literature, a lot of attention was paid toward the specific format of these anchors. For example, the effects of a variety of **graphic rating scales** were explored in paper and pencil formats, such as the endorsement of anchors by making checkmarks, drawing Xs, placing ticks, circling smiley faces, and so on. A very short summary of this research is: usually, it doesn't matter. Thus, these days, for most purposes, scale developers have generally settled upon numbers and/or text anchors.

The most common response format today is called a **Likert ("LICK-urt")-type scale**, after the researcher who made them popular, Dr. Rensis Likert. Most people mispronounce Likert with a long "i" sound, so don't be surprised if you hear it either way.

Effective Likert-type items typically possess two qualities: symmetry and balance. Symmetry means that the items contain the same number of positive and negative positions. Balance means that the distance between each position is the same. Likert-type scales also assume that the unidimensional construct being assessed can be represented linearly, along a straight line from low to high, and that the anchors can be represented as numbers, even if they are presented as text. We also generally assume interval level scale of measurement. Likert-*type* scales differ from Likert scales in that true Likert scale development involves verifying these assumptions empirically as described by Likert (1932). Further, Likert only promoted this idea with symmetric "agreement" scales, such as those ranging from Strongly Disagree to Strongly Agree. The term "Likert-type scaling" is used as a broader term to refer to items that resemble Likert scales, including those with different response options, different text prompts, and no empirical verification of internal-like scale of measurement.

Because of this, Likert-type scales can be a bit controversial in some circles. One reason they are so popular is that the interval-level scale of measurement assumption allows the numbers that the scale produces to be used in analyses that examine variances and covariances. The treatment of Likert-type scale scores as interval thus enables power statistical analyses that can't be as easily applied to ordinal or nominal scales. But the assumption of interval-level measurement suggests that the gaps between anchors are roughly equally distanced, psychologically speaking – in other words, that the distance between 1 and 2 is roughly as much "more" of the trait as the distance between 2 and 3. Yet this isn't always a reasonable assumption. During scale development, you should assess this by looking for a mean scale score near the middle of your scale's range (e.g., if 1 to 5, near a 2.5) and a normal distribution of scores surrounding it. If either of those isn't true, you might need to redraft your items and/or revisit your scale anchors.

Table 10.2 contains a few examples of Likert-type scaling.

Table 10.2 Examples of 5-point Likert-type scales and common approaches to response coding

5	4	3	2	1
1	2	3	4	5
−2	−1	0	1	2
Strongly Disagree	Disagree	Neither Agree or Disagree	Agree	Strongly Agree
Never	Occasionally	Sometimes	Often	Very Often
Poor	Fair	Average	Good	Excellent

Given the popularity of Likert scales in the social sciences, there is plenty of research outlining the components of an effective Likert-type item. Among the most common guidelines are the following, as discussed by Crocker and Algina (2008):

1. Put statements or questions in the present tense.
2. Do not include statements that are factual or able of being interpreted as factual.
3. Avoid statements that can have more than one interpretation.
4. Avoid statements that are likely to be endorsed by everyone or no one.
5. Try to have an almost equal number of statements expressing positive and negative feelings.
6. Statements should be short, rarely exceeding 20 words.
7. Each statement should be a proper grammatical sentence.
8. Statements containing universals such as *all, always, none,* and *never* often introduce ambiguity and should be avoided.
9. Avoid use of indefinite qualifiers such as *only, just, merely, many, few,* or *seldom.*
10. Whenever possible, statements should be in simple sentences rather than complex or compound sentences. Avoid sentences that contain "*if*" or "*because*" clauses.
11. Use vocabulary that can be understood easily by respondents.
12. Avoid use of negatives such as *none, not,* and *never.*

Researchers often debate about the appropriate number of response options to include for Likert-type items. A study by Dawes (2008) investigated this, finding that 5- and 7-point scales produced the same mean scores after appropriate rescaling. He also found, however, that 10-point scales tended to produce slightly lower mean scores than the 5- and 7-point options after rescaling. Other data characteristics such as skewness were similar regardless of the number of response options. We encourage survey researchers to use the more common 5- or 7-point scaling options, unless they have a clear reason to use an alternative number.

Importantly, don't assume that a Likert-type rating scale is the only or even the best option to measure a particular construct, especially if that scale is not psychological in nature. Likert-type scales are popular due to their extreme flexibility in being arguably appropriate for a wide range of constructs, but there are other meaningful options to explore, depending upon your goals for research and practice using that scale.

Should I include a midpoint in my Likert-type scale?

Midpoint refers to the "center" response option, typically representing neutrality, in a Likert-type scale. Likert-type scales with odd numbers of items (e.g., 5, 7) will have a midpoint, whereas even numbers of items (e.g., 4, 6) will not have a midpoint. The choice here is a somewhat controversial issue.

To understand the controversy, consider why people might endorse a midpoint. On one hand, a person may respond with the neutral option because they are truly neutral or undecided. If you don't include a midpoint, creating what can be referred to as a **binary forced choice scale**, participants may be required to endorse a response that they don't believe represents their (truly neutral) opinion or leave the question blank. On the other hand, the inclusion of a midpoint may encourage respondents who don't want to appear opinionated or to be wrong to endorse that midpoint in a way that does not reflect their true construct standing.

On balance, we recommend the inclusion of midpoints, but the correct answer likely varies depending upon your particular research and practice needs. For an accessible exploration of these issues in much greater detail, see Chyung et al. (2017).

DICHOTOMOUS SCALES

Dichotomous and Likert-type scales are quite similar, differing primarily in the number of response options given to participants, as dichotomous items only have two responses, like true/false or yes/no, and are typically coded numerically as either 0/1 or –1/+1, which brings implications for scale of measurement. A clear advantage of dichotomous scales is that they are easy to interpret; respondents can only answer in two ways. Whereas Likert-type scales often allow individuals to select a "neutral" or "neither agree nor disagree" option, dichotomous items always force individuals to pick a side. This can help overcome the **central tendency bias**, which is common among individuals who wish to avoid being perceived as having extremist views.

Scales with "correct" answers, such as knowledge and ability tests, may be dichotomously scales but appear multiple choice. For example, consider the following question:

Which scale of measurement requires the most assumptions?

a. Ratio
b. Interval
c. Ordinal
d. Nominal

Although this question has four possible answers, it is dichotomous. Most likely, answering (a) would result in a score of "1," representing "correct," and answering (b), (c), or (d) would result in a score of "0," representing "incorrect." Across multiple questions, this would create a measure with ratio scale of measurement, since the average of all the 0/1 scores would create a proportion of correct answers out of all possible answers. Be careful not to assume scale of measurement or scaling approach more broadly based upon the textual appearance of a question alone – it always depends on the scoring that will be applied after data are collected and how well that scoring reflects construct standing.

GRAPHIC RATING SCALES

We can get creative about the ways we ask people to respond to items. For example, rather than asking them to click a number between 1 and 5 that indicates their level of agreement with a statement, we can ask them to indicate that number in a more graphic way. Most survey hosting sites allow users to ask questions using a slider, as shown in Figure 10.6.

Although this is still fundamentally a Likert-type scale, the use of a slider may be more engaging than merely clicking numbers. Most survey hosting sites have engaging response formats that are well suited for certain kinds of items. For example, you may wish to ask respondents to rate the speed of something by asking them to place a needle on a speedometer, or you may ask them to assign a letter grade from A to F to assess the quality of something. These graphic response options may seem inconsequential, but they can go a long way in giving your respondents a positive experience. When used appropriately, these response options also benefit you as the researcher. For example, some data may require you to show content that cannot easily be described with text – it would be easier to show respondents an company's logo than to describe it to them. Or you may be working with a sample of respondents who have inadequate reading abilities to complete a text survey. In such cases, there are plenty of rating scales that use universally understood emoticons in addition to or in place of text responses, as shown in Figure 10.7.

SEMANTIC DIFFERENTIAL SCALES

Semantic differential scales measure individuals' subjective attitudes about a certain concept with the use of adjectives. Respondents are first presented with an object or idea, and then they are then shown a pair of adjectives with opposite meanings, making this another approach to forced choice scaling. They must then indicate where, on a continuum of one

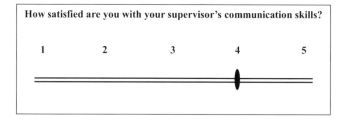

Figure 10.6 Slider-based graphic rating scale item.

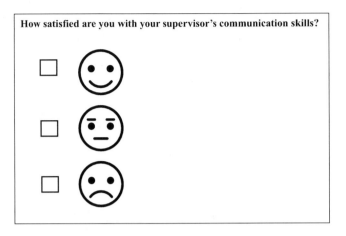

Figure 10.7 Face-based graphic rating scale item.

adjective to the other, they feel that the characteristic of interest lies. For example, consider the following three scales all applied to the same focal concept:

Robots
Useless   _____   Useful
Dangerous _____   Safe
Dumb   _____   Smart

One study compared responses to Likert-type and semantic differential scales regarding positive psychological constructs. Investigating resilience as their focal construct, they found that the factor structure of semantic differential scale version fit the data better than the Likert-type version (Friborg et al., 2006). This, they argued, was because respondents were less likely to exhibit an **acquiescence bias**. Also known as the "yes bias," the acquiescence bias describes the tendency of respondents to respond positively to any question they are asked. Semantic differential scales use a wide variety of adjectives to assess attitudes, and as a result they place a greater cognitive demand on respondents. However, this cognitive demand may be worthwhile if we suspect respondents would otherwise lazily "agree" to Likert-type items.

GUTTMAN SCALES

Also known as **cumulative scales**, **Guttman scales** require respondents to indicate whether they endorse a series of items. The items themselves are ordered so that they increase in intensity. Louis Guttman originally developed these scales for students, so an appropriate introductory example is mathematics. When thinking about the mathematical operations that children master, they generally follow the following sequence: counting to addition to subtraction to multiplication to division. That is, if you can subtract, you probably know how to add. And if you can divide, you probably know how to count, add, and so on.

The same logic applies to attitude and personality items, such that if you agree with whatever statement is included in item 4, you probably also agree with the statements in items 1,

2, and 3. These kinds of items are excellent for establishing a one-dimensional continuum for a construct you hope to measure. Consider the following hypothetical example, which assesses attitudes towards disabled workers.

_____I would be comfortable if a disabled worker joined my community.
_____I would be comfortable if a disabled worker joined my organization.
_____I would be comfortable if a disabled worker joined my department.

Anyone who endorses the third item would logically endorse the first two items. There may be a few exceptions to this rule, which can be observed in a process called a **scalogram analysis.** This analysis helps survey researchers identify which items most closely follow the cumulative scale outlined by Guttman. A clear disadvantage of Guttman scales is that they can be difficult to produce, which explains why they are rarely used by contemporary survey researchers. In situations where attitudes or behaviors can be represented in a stepwise fashion, however, this item type has the added benefit of being more one-dimensional than Likert-type scales often are.

BEHAVIORALLY ANCHORED RATING SCALES

Another approach to scaling that appears with some frequency in I-O psychology is the **behaviorally anchored rating scale** (BARS; see Smith & Kendall, 1963), especially in the context of performance appraisal. In short, a BARS replaces or supplements text anchors (like Agree or Disagree) with examples of observed behaviors written in text. The goal of such anchors is to encourage calibration between raters in terms of what specific scale points represent. When constructs are behavioral in nature, the use of BARS can improve reliability and thus the validity of ratings made, at the trade of much greater costs for scale development, since the behavioral anchors need to be developed and validated separately.

AVOIDING RESPONSE BIASES

We have already briefly introduced a couple of **response biases**, which refer to the cognitive shortcuts that respondents might take, either intentionally or not, when responding to questionnaires. There are many such biases. We list some of the most common here, which you should consider when developing both individual items and larger scales:

* *Acquiescence and **dissent bias*.** Respondents often don't want to appear negative, so most people tend to endorse positive responses, like Yes or Agree, more often than negative ones, like No or Disagree. A smaller set of people engage in dissent bias by doing the opposite.
* *Social desirability bias.* Respondents tend to think of themselves in positive terms and can be reluctant to admit to behaviors or thoughts that are socially undesirable. For example, a person who responds with an Agree to "I like meeting new people" is unlikely to respond with a Disagree with "I don't like meeting new people." They are more likely to respond neutrally.
* *Neutrality (or central tendency) **bias*.** This bias refers to a cognitive shortcut taken by respondents by avoiding taking a strong stance on any question, such as by responding mostly with Neutral and the occasional Agree or Disagree on a 5-point Likert-type scale.

- **Extreme response bias.** This bias refers to a different cognitive shortcut, taken by avoiding nuanced views on questions. A person engaging in this bias will make a dichotomous judgment about each question regardless of scaling, such as by responding entirely with Strongly Disagree and Strongly Agree on a 5-point Likert-type scale.
- **Demand bias** (*sometimes* **demand characteristics bias**). Although this is also a threat to internal validity related to study design, it also applies to scale responses in that a respondent may infer what hypothesis you are testing and try to answer in a way that helps you support it. If you administer a questionnaire about workplace theft and integrity, some respondents may fudge their answers a bit based on what they think you are trying to conclude.
- *Insufficient effort (or careless response bias).* Respondents often want to minimize effort expended on completing your questionnaire or study. This can manifest in a lot of different ways but often involves **straightlining**, such as responding "Agree" to every question or simply not reading questions very carefully before answering. Meade and Craig (2012) an in-depth discussion of detection methods to minimize the effects of this kind of bias, and we covered it in more detail in Chapter 9.

Importantly, response biases cannot be avoided entirely, but you can take steps to minimize them. For example, acquiescence and social desirability biases can be minimized by taking care not to write questions with obviously "good" and "bad" response options. Neutrality, extreme response, and low effort biases can be minimized by not over-taxing respondents, such as with unnecessarily long scales. Demand bias can be minimized by avoiding **telegraphing** the intent of the scales, such as by administering only two questionnaires with an obvious conceptual connection.

Despite these recommendations, there are ultimately no "rules" for avoiding response bias. It is up to you, as the researcher, to empathize with your respondents, imagine what they will be thinking and feeling at every stage of data collection, and make changes as feasible to minimize the effects of these biases.

Step 3: Pilot Study

Now that we've got some questions to ask and scales to be rated, what do we do with them? This occurs in two phases.

In the first phase, the **alpha test**. Ask people outside of your team, preferably people who could theoretically fulfill the role of "reviewer" on a manuscript where you introduce this scale, to take a look at your items. Do they make sense? Do they seem to measure what you claim them to measure? It's important to do this because it's fairly easy for your team to get trapped in circular thinking: you spent a lot of time writing these, so they must be good, right? Don't fall into this trap. Get an external review before you bother running your full pilot study. This step also serves as an initial assessment of content-related validation evidence for your new scale.

That brings us to the second phase, the **beta test**, or more traditionally, a **pilot study**. Once you are confident that your items are "good enough to be tested," you'll want to randomly sample the population that you want to use this scale with in the future and administer them all of your items. If you are developing a scale to be used with managers, that means you would be *best* off finding managers to test it with. Failing that, you would want to find a population as similar as possible to your target population and use that instead, using good sampling techniques, as discussed in Chapter 4.

Once you've identified a population to sample, the next problem is one of quantity. How many people do you need for your initial data collection effort? This is also a matter of significant disagreement in the literature, in part because the answer to this question depends on several factors, such as the magnitude of your factor loadings. Since you don't know the magnitude of your factor loadings and item intercorrelations yet, you must rely on rules of thumb. For simplicity, we recommend at least either 150 participants or 20 participants per item (e.g., if you were testing 20 items, 400 participants as a minimum), whichever is larger. It is generally not a good idea to try to test multiple constructs simultaneously unless it is a single, multidimensional construct, in which case you would consider all items uniquely (e.g., if you developed 10 items per dimension across 3 dimensions, 600 participants would be a good lower bound). Having said that, more participants is always better, because it gives you greater precision, increasing the chances that your findings will replicate in your next sample.

In practice, authors often get away with fewer than this when publishing papers, but that often just kicks the problem down the road to later authors trying to figure out why your scale doesn't work as advertised. Do your own housekeeping, and you'll do good science. Additionally, if you skip steps for the sake of speed, perhaps because you have a thesis or dissertation you need this scale for, you'll just be kicking the can down the road to yourself, and you don't want that either.

Step 4: Item Revision

Once you have data in hand, you need to decide which items to keep, which items to eliminate, and which items to modify. This is done with two types of analyses that do slightly different things.

The first type of analysis that you'll do is that of **dimension extraction**. Dimension extraction refers to a group of data-driven approaches that attempt to identify shared causes among groups of variables. Put another way, it is a way to determine the most probable latent variables causing the data you have without specifying your own theoretical model, as you do with CFA. There are two major types commonly used in I-O which are closely related: **exploratory factor analysis (EFA)**, sometimes called common factor analysis or principal axis factoring, and **principal components analysis (PCA)**. Both analyses, most of the time, will lead you to the same answer. Situations where they won't are generally when you have a very large number of items. For example, if you try dimension extraction with 100 items, EFA and PCA may lead you to different conclusions. But in those cases, you'd be better off running multiple pilot studies in sequence anyway or cutting down the number of items you're testing ahead of time.

You will need to make several decisions when conducting either EFA or PCA:

1. *How many dimensions do I extract?* Both EFA and PCA will attempt to allocate 100% of the variance in your variables to a specific number of dimensions that you specify. Neither produces this number automatically, so you need to specify it. For scale development, the simplest option is using the **Kaiser criterion**, which refers to the extraction of any dimension for which the Eigenvalue is greater than 1. The Kaiser criterion is usually a safe choice because it tends to over-prescribe factors; you end up with more than probably actually exist, which is useful diagnostically. If you were actually using EFA or PCA to determine the number of factors in your items in a theoretically meaningful way, you

probably would not use it, because the Kaiser criterion is flawed as a scientific indicator of dimensionality; it's only good as a rule of thumb. In scale development, we are only targeting one dimension with one set of questions, so any number of dimensions more than 1 is a problem to be solved, not a theoretically interesting conclusion, which makes this a safe choice. If you were trying to identify multiple subscales within a higher-order construct, you would probably instead use **parallel analysis**, which involves simulating random data with the same general shape as the data you collected and then comparing Eigenvalues between an EFA/PCA conducted on the random data with an EFA/PCA conducted on your collected data.

2. *How do I rotate the solution?* Rotation in factor analysis is similar to standardization in CFA; its only purpose is to increase interpretability. Since we are trying to interpret our results, you should definitely rotate. But there are so many options: so which way? Because you have written questions with the intent of measuring a single construct, that means any "bad" questions likely still measure your intended construct fairly well; they just measure other constructs too. Your purpose here is to distinguish between items that measure your intended construct "cleanly" versus those that don't. That means you should use an **oblique rotation**, which allows extracted factors to correlate with each other (in contrast to an **orthogonal rotation**, which doesn't). Common oblique rotation techniques are direct oblimin and promax.

3. *Which table do I interpret?* Once you've conducted your obliquely rotated PCA or EFA, you should end up with two tables that you might want to interpret: a **pattern matrix** and a **structure matrix**. Each row of the pattern matrix can be interpreted like a set of standardized regression weights; it tells you how strongly each factor predicts each item relevant to all other factors. The structure matrix is more straightforward; it tells you the correlation between the item and each factor score. In general, you'll focus on the structure matrix, although the pattern matrix is sometimes informative. Another closely related statistic is the **item-total correlation**, which refers to the correlation between each item and the mean score of the scale; whereas a structure matrix compares items to latent factors, item-total correlations compare items to their own mean.

Once you understand how to interpret the output you're seeing, the next task is to *make decisions about items*. Much like item generation, there's a bit of art to this, because you need to balance several factors. Not only should you pay attention to the data itself, but you also need to remember the item content. To illustrate why, consider the following group of four Likert-type conscientiousness items:

1. I regularly clean up my room.
2. I regularly clean up my workspace.
3. I regularly clean up after myself.
4. I always fulfill my obligations.

If you conducted a study with these four items, you would certainly find that the first three items hang together much more strongly than the fourth. However, the reason for this is that there is probably a hidden, omitted cause that is not what we want to measure: a preference for cleaning. Data-driven approaches don't care what you're *trying* to measure; they only extract factors based on the data given to them. If you followed the data alone, you might eliminate item 4 based upon results from the structure matrix. Given the item content, however, you would *not* want to do that, because it means you're now probably measuring something other than conscientiousness. This is an example of a **linguistic trap**, where commonalities in language are leading you to think that constructs are being measured, but in reality, you're picking up on language features shared across items. This is also a source of *common method variance*, as described in Chapter 9. So always keep the item content in mind, and think carefully about why you're seeing the values you're seeing. It's not so simple as, "this number is low, so get rid of the item."

So step by step, what do you actually do at this stage? We find it useful to break down the process into a few typical steps.

1. *Make easy decisions first.* Assuming all went as expected, the first factor in your structure matrix should be the strongest, and unless you're quite terrible at writing questions, it likely represents the construct you're after. That means you can scan the first column for extremely low factor loadings (<.3) and eliminate all of those items. Then rerun your EFA/PCA. Next, eliminate items that have **crossloadings** higher than their primary factor loadings, one at a time. Crossloadings occur when an item reflects multiple factors simultaneously. If you have a crossloading higher than your first-factor loading, get rid of that item, because it measures something else better than it measures your focal construct. However, be sure to rerun your EFA/PCA between each item elimination.

2. *Re-evaluate dimensionality.* Does your EFA/PCA only identify one factor? If you are identifying multiple factors, are you getting dramatically more variance extracted from your first factor than your second (e.g., 80% versus 5%)? If you answered yes to either question, you likely have a unidimensional scale and can skip the next step. If no, you need to diagnose why you've ended up with more than one factor through content review of items within and across factors. If your goal is to develop a single unidimensional scale, understanding and addressing multidimensionality in your developmental sample is a critical step. Don't go much further until you're confident your scale is unidimensional.

3. *Make hard decisions carefully, and one item at a time.* Every item that you eliminate changes the data that are being analyzed by the EFA/PCA, so you should only remove one item at a time as you go. Look at cross-loadings, look at the item content, and figure out what the "worst" items are, one at a time – ones with relatively low loadings or high crossloadings. Each time you re-run, check to see if the number of extracted dimensions has dropped to one or two. If you have two dimensions but a lot of items left, keep eliminating items until you have only one. Once you reach one of these two thresholds, you can move forward.

4. *Evaluate scale length.* How many items do you have left? If you have fewer than 4, you have a problem. You probably need to draft new items and re-run your pilot study but could be worse than that. If, for example, you started with 20 and ended up with 3, it probably signifies a larger-scale problem; the most common cause is that your construct definition was not quite specific enough and needs to be reworked. If so, return to that step and start over. If you have at least 4 items and they all load onto (essentially) one factor, with little cross-loading, you have a prototype scale.

5. *Evaluate reliability.* Calculate a **coefficient alpha** (roughly speaking, the average inter-item correlation among your items) or preferably **coefficient omega** (roughly speaking, the average item-total correlation among your items) on your scale to get a sense of its internal consistency reliability. Values over 0.70 are generally considered a bare minimum, and over 0.80 or 0.90 is much preferred. If reliability is too low, assuming you've

done the preceding steps correctly, you now have a good set of unidimensional items but *not enough of them*. You should look carefully at that list of items and try to figure out why they hang together so well. Then write more items like that and return to the previous scale development step. But be careful not to get caught in linguistic traps like the one described earlier.

Why Do I Have So Many Crossloadings?

In scale development, crossloadings occur when two items on your scale correlate with each other in a way that isn't explained by the shared cause of their primary factor. Technically speaking, this is how the problem of correlated residual item variances shows up in an EFA/PCA. If you find you have a lot of crossloadings, it's probably because you wrote a lot of items using a similar writing strategy without realizing that's what you were doing.

Let's reconsider the linguistic trap example. If those 3 cleaning-oriented items had been assessed along with 20 other non-cleaning-oriented items, a "cleaning" factor likely would have emerged in an EFA/PCA. Following the instructions given here, you would likely end up retaining one of those three items, and it would probably be the one with the highest primary factor loading. The reason this happens is that once you eliminate two of the three cleaning items, the topic of cleaning only appears once, so cleaning-related language changes from systematic error (i.e., multiple items talking about cleaning that hang together) into unsystematic error (i.e., random item variation in relation to all other items).

Step 5: Validation Study

After the previous step, you should now be reasonably confident that you have a set of items that are reliable and unidimensional. However, there's always still a possibility that you capitalized on chance variation in your sample when you made your item elimination decisions. To test this, you will conduct a new study using your final scale items, but instead of analyzing it with an EFA, you'll analyze it with a CFA and a sample size of at least 250. Once you have conducted your CFA, you can analyze it using the same standards discussed at the beginning of the chapter; with uncorrelated item residuals, you should have acceptable values for your factor loadings, uniqueness terms, composite reliability, average variance explained, and fit indices, using the standards shown in Table 10.1.

Remember that meeting these thresholds is not proof that your scale is "good." Instead, it simply means that your scale has reached a minimum level of confidence for use and further study: you have created "good supporting evidence" supporting the internal structure of your measure, another type of validation evidence.

If your measure fails one or more of these standards, you need to figure out why. If the standards are only slightly off from the thresholds in Table 10.1, don't panic. This is probably due to chance variation and nothing to worry about. However, if it's performing substantially differently unexpectedly, you need to try to figure out why. Did you change your sampling technique? Did the final items end up being more similar to each other, and this became more obvious when they were asked in sequence? Did asking those items in sequence cause people to process them differently? These and more possibilities need to be investigated, possibly with additional studies.

Once you have completed a validation study that you're happy with, you might also consider **norming** the scores obtained on that measure by administering it to a meaningful **normative sample**. Populations to be used for normative samples are generally identified because they are deemed useful for some specific application of the test. For example, an I-O practitioner might norm a scale separately for applicants to low and high complexity jobs to enable separate comparisons to "average low complexity applicants" and "average high complexity applicants." This ultimately means meaningfully identifying relevant samples (see Chapter 4) and administering your new scale to them.

A related concept, standardization, refers to the process of converting raw scores into standardized scores, which are simply raw scores transformed into some more meaningfully interpretable set of numbers through simple mathematics. For example, let's imagine you create an IQ test, and in a normed sample, you found a mean of 15.37 and a standard deviation of 1.2. Classic IQ tests are normed such that the mean is 100 and the standard deviation is 15; on a classic IQ test, you could for example immediately determine that the score of a person achieving 130 on such a test scored 2 standard deviations above the normative sample mean. To convert scores from your sample into the M = 100/SD = 15 standardization scheme, simply convert the score with this formula: $x_{std} = (x_{raw} - M_{raw})/SD_{raw} \times SD_{std} + M_{std}$. In our example, a score of 16 would become $x_{std} = (16–15.37)/1.2 \times 15 + 100 = 107.875$. Another common kind of standardization is the **T-score** (not to be confused with "t-statistic"), which is normed with a mean of 50 and a standard deviation of 10.

The key to meaningful norming and standardization is therefore the identification of a meaningful normative sample to serve as the basis for this sort of conversion. Without such a sample, both norming and standardization are nothing more than marketing techniques. For example, re-expressing your new IQ test on the same M = 100/SD = 15 system as classic IQ tests does not influence the validity of your scale whatsoever; it only makes it look more credible to people who don't know any better.

How to Identify a Trustworthy Psychological Scale

Given all of the steps described here, identification of a trustworthy psychological scale is easy; is there a paper somewhere that describes all of these steps, and is it cited in the one you're reading? If not, what evidence is available? Do you trust it?

Importantly, reliability alone is not sufficient. Many researchers think that a coefficient alpha of .7 or higher is sufficient evidence by itself for scale quality. Unfortunately, for reasons explained much better by Cortina (1993), scale length can increase alpha even in the presence of multidimensionality. Unfortunately, many – and perhaps most – scales in psychology were not well developed and likely assess multiple constructs, using this thinking. When you use such a scale in your own research, you take a risk that it will not perform well. We do not recommend it. Remember back in Chapter 2 when we discussed how more "basic" questions need to be answered confidently before more complex ones can even be attempted. Measurement is almost the most basic question you can ask. Without good measurement, you have no idea what any results based upon those measures actually mean.

Furthermore, using coefficient omega is only a partial solution to this problem. Although omega assesses the general factor saturation of a test, it does not assess the degree to which any secondary factors are problematic. This is only possible in EFA/PCA or CFA, where you can examine individual item diagnostics. If a scale you are developing evidences correlated item residuals, it needs to be fixed before that scale is released, regardless of the level of omega (or alpha).

Another issue that many researchers forget is that reliability is a property of a scale-by-respondent interaction and not a property of the scale itself. To illustrate, a scale that demonstrates high reliability in one context, like college students completing it for extra credit, may not demonstrate high reliability in another context, like job applicants completing it as a part of a job application. If the respondents in pilot testing or validation engage in meaningfully different response processes than the respondents you eventually want to administer it to, those original reliability estimates may not be relevant. Always be careful to ensure that development processes occurred with respondents engaging in similar response processes to the respondents you ultimately want to administer the scale to.

Finally, we feel it's critical to remind you here to review Chapter 7, where we discussed the five kinds of evidence that should be used to support arguments about construct validity. As a reminder, they are:

- Evidence based on test content
- Evidence based on response processes
- Evidence based on internal structure
- Evidence based on relations to other variables
- Evidence based on the consequences of test use

Each of these categories represents a specific perspective from which to view the singular question of: "does this measure what I think it measures?" The broader the evidence is across types, and the better the research designs are creating that evidence, the more confident you can be. But expressed this way, it should be obvious that "validation" never truly ends. Every new study that utilizes a scale becomes a new piece of validity evidence in support of or undermining the validity of that scale. There is never a point where we can say "validation is complete." We can only say "the evidence is good enough that I trust our use of this scale for this study."

With each new study, ask yourself: did you get similar measurement quality in this new population? When circumstances changed? If not, why? Each study becomes part of a measure's validation history, and you should remember to consult that history, too. If you rely on the original development paper alone, you may miss something important. Even worse, if you just assume it was well developed without tracking down its history, just because it's been used in published research since then, you're taking a big risk.

What If an Existing Scale Is Close but Not Close Enough?

Sometimes, we find a scale that's very close to what we want, but not quite good enough. Perhaps we want to change a few words or phrases. Perhaps we want to drop an item we don't think will work for our population, or perhaps we want to add an item to get at a different dimension of the construct that we think is important for our population. Can we just change a scale, or do we need to go through this entire process from the beginning? What prior evidence can still be trusted with a revised scale?

Unfortunately, the answer is once again, "It depends." From a technical standpoint, changing *anything* about an existing scale means you have developed a new scale. There is no guarantee that anything about your new scale will still be the same. However, in practice, in most cases, it's probably not *very* different. So this has become a matter of some disagreement with few clear ways to empirically resolve it. For example, I (Richard) feel complete comfort changing referent groups in items. The Intrinsic Motivation Inventory, for example, contains items like "I enjoyed doing this activity very much." Without a second thought, I might change this scale to read "I enjoyed this game very much" or "I enjoyed participating today very much." But with more changed worse, and especially with a twist of meaning, I are more reluctant. For example, "I enjoyed playing this game very much" adds a bit of an emotional tone in the word "playing." It implies happy, fun, and carefree. And that might just change the meaning enough to be a problem, which is enough for me to be extra-thorough during analysis of the psychometric properties of that scale. And it's definitely enough for me to talk about that analysis in pre-registration and any journal-submitted manuscripts.

In the end, this is a matter of your professional judgment, which was also the conclusion of our recommended reading on the topic:

Heggestad, E. D., Scheaf, D. J., Banks, G. C., Monroe Hausfeld, M., Tonidandel, S., & Williams, E. B. (2019). Scale adaptation in organizational science research: A review and best-practice recommendations. *Journal of Management*, *45*(6), 2596–2627.

References

Bagozzi, R. P., & Yi, Y. (1988). On the evaluation of structural equation models. *Journal of the Academy of Marketing Science*, *16*, 74–94.

Brick, C., Hood, B., Ekroll, V., & De-Wit, L. (2022). Illusory essences: A bias holding back theorizing in psychological science. *Perspectives on Psychological Science*, *17*(2), 491–506.

Browne, M. W., & Cudeck, R. (1993). Alternative ways of assessing model fit. In K. A. Bollen & J. S. Long (Eds.), *Testing structural equation models* (pp. 136–162). Sage.

Chyung, S. Y. (Yonnie), Roberts, K., Swanson, I., & Hankinson, A. (2017). Evidence-based survey design: The use of a midpoint on the Likert scale. *Performance Improvement*, *56*(10), 15–23.

Cortina, J. M. (1993). What is coefficient alpha? An examination of theory and applications. *Journal of Applied Psychology*, *78*, 98–104.

Crocker, L., & Algina, J. (2008). Chapter 7 – Procedures for estimating reliability. In *Introduction to classical and modern test theory*.

Dawes, J. (2008). Do data characteristics change according to the number of scale points used? An experiment using 5-point, 7-point and 10-point scales. *International Journal of Market Research*, *50*(1), 61–104.

Friborg, O., Martinussen, M., & Rosenvinge, J. H. (2006). Likert-based vs. semantic differential-based scorings of positive psychological constructs: A psychometric comparison of two versions of a scale measuring resilience. *Personality and Individual Differences*, *40*(5), 873–884.

Gefen, D., Straub, D., & Boudreau, M. C. (2000). Structural equation modeling and regression: Guidelines for research practice. *Communications of the Association for Information Systems*, *4*(1), 7.

Heggestad, E. D., Scheaf, D. J., Banks, G. C., Monroe Hausfeld, M., Tonidandel, S., & Williams, E. B. (2019). Scale adaptation in organizational science research: A review and best-practice recommendations. *Journal of Management*, *45*(6), 2596–2627.

Hu, L. T., & Bentler, P. M. (1999). Cutoff criteria for fit indexes in covariance structure analysis: Conventional criteria versus new alternatives. *Structural Equation Modeling: A Multidisciplinary Journal*, 6(1), 1–55.

Landers, R. N., & Callan, R. C. (2014). Validation of the beneficial and harmful work-related social media behavioral taxonomies: Development of the work-related social media questionnaire (WSMQ). *Social Science Computer Review*, 32, 628–646.

Likert, R. (1932). A technique for the measurement of attitudes. *Archives of Psychology*, 22(140), 55.

MacCallum, R. C., Browne, M. W., & Sugawara, H. M. (1996). Power analysis and determination of sample size for covariance structure modeling. *Psychological Methods*, 1(2), 130.

Meade, A. W., & Craig, S. B. (2012). Identifying careless responses in survey data. *Psychological Methods*, 17(3), 437.

Sharma, S., Mukherjee, S., Kumar, A., & Dillon, W. R. (2005). A simulation study to investigate the use of cutoff values for assessing model fit in covariance structure models. *Journal of Business Research*, 58(7), 935–943.

Smith, P. C., & Kendall, L. M. (1963). Retranslation of expectations: An approach to the construction of unambiguous anchors for rating scales. *Journal of Applied Psychology*, 47(2), 149.

Further Reading

Bollen, K. A., & Long, J. S. (1993). Tests for structural equation models: Introduction. *Sociological Methods & Research*, 21, 123–131.

- Bollen and Long, after publishing a foundational textbook on SEM in 1992, organized a special issue of this journal covering testing SEM models. If you find yourself frequently trying to choose or interpret fit indices, whether for the purpose of scale development or SEM, take a look at this article and the special issue it introduces to understand the full complexity and many pitfalls associated with using simple universal cutoffs for these indices.

Edwards, J. (2010). The fallacy of formative measurement. *Organizational Research Methods*, 14, 370–388.

- Edwards lays bare the fundamental conceptual challenges associated with formative measurement. If you find yourself frequently trying to understand composite formative indices, like socioeconomic status, check out this paper to understand why trying to apply a formative measurement model will probably raise some eyebrows.

Heggestad, E. D., Scheaf, D. J., Banks, G. C., Monroe Hausfeld, M., Tonidandel, S., & Williams, E. B. (2019). Scale adaptation in organizational science research: A review and best-practice recommendations. *Journal of Management*, 45(6), 2596–2627.

- Heggestad and colleagues explore one of the most common problems for organizational researchers in both academia and practice: adapting scales. To understand the problem, they take a multifaceted approach, including a general study of adapted scale descriptions in past research, a more in-depth study of six specific scales commonly adapted, and a study of journal editorial board members and psychometricians to assess their perspectives on scale adaptation.

Hinkin, T. R. (1995). A review of scale development practices in the study of organizations. *Journal of Management*, 21(5), 967–988.

- Hinkin provides a state-of-the-art and practice how-to guide for scale development for 1995. Although it's a bit old at this point, it remains surprisingly full of best practices that remain today. Although you shouldn't rely on it alone, you may find it interesting to see just how little has changed in "best practices" for scale development over the decades.

Questions to Think About

1. Why is it controversial to create a rating scale for a formative construct?
2. What is fit, how is it assessed, and why is it important for diagnosing a measure?
3. Describe the six steps to scale development discussed in this chapter.
4. Consider that you created a rating scale to measure the satisfaction of workers at a manufacturing plant. You create a 10-item scale, with items such as "I am content with my working conditions." The items use a 1–7 Likert-type scale, where 1 represents "Strongly disagree" and 7 represents "Strongly agree." Describe the kinds of conclusions we can and cannot draw using responses to these items.
5. What is a factor loading? What do cross loadings tell us, and how can we address them?
6. Compare and contrast confirmatory factor analysis (CFA) and exploratory factor analysis (EFA). In what situations might you use each?

Key Terms

- factor loading
- fit
- fit index (or indices)
- graphic rating scale
- Guttman scales
- illusory essence
- indicator
- item-total correlation
- Kaiser criterion
- latent variable
- Likert-type scale
- linguistic trap
- midpoint
- mutually exclusive
- normative sample
- norming
- oblique rotation
- orthogonal rotation
- parallel analysis
- pattern matrix
- pilot study
- principal components analysis (PCA)
- rating scale
- residual variance of an item
- scaling
- scalogram analysis
- semantic differential scale
- standardization
- straightlining
- structure matrix
- T-score
- telegraphing
- uniqueness

## Chapter 11

Cleaning Data Without Hacking Them

Learning Objectives

1. Explain the stakes for your career associated with improper data cleaning procedures
2. Identify decisions in your own research that might lie in the garden of forking paths
3. Explain how open science practices can help safeguard your career and increase the trustworthiness of your research
4. Utilize codebooks, logbooks, alpha testing, beta testing, and pre-registration to safeguard against poor-quality data
5. Use outlier and influential case detection, careless and insufficient effort responding detection, and missingness handling to improve the quality of your collected data

In the APS flagship journal *Psychological Science* in 2010, researchers Dana Carney, Amy Cuddy, and Andy Yap presented a study in which 42 research participants were randomly assigned to either hold a "power pose" in which they were to position themselves expansively and with open limbs in an expression of "power" or to pose with closed arms or clasped hands. After posing, the researchers measured levels of the hormones testosterone and cortisol, as well as self-reported "feelings of power" and risk tolerance, concluding rather provocatively that "a person can, by assuming two simple 1-min poses, embody power and instantly become more powerful."

From a media perspective, this study looks pretty phenomenal: immediate real-world impact, actionable results, and provocative headlines. The implications for this intervention as a way to improve workplace outcomes were significant and attractive. However, this research became somewhat of a poster child for poorly conducted research and badly cleaned data, a key study at the epicenter of the **replication crisis**. The small sample size notwithstanding, it came to light several years after publication that some of the data cleaning was a bit questionable. In the later words of Dana Carney, lead author on the original paper:

Source line: Image by Freepiks.

"I do not believe that 'power pose' effects are real. . . . The data are real. The sample size is tiny. The data are flimsy. The effects are small and barely there in many cases. Initially, the primary test of the DV of interest was risk-taking. We ran subjects in chunks and checked

DOI: 10.4324/9781315167473-14

the effect along the way. It was something like 25 subjects run, then 10, then 7, then 5. Back then this did not seem like *p*-hacking" (Carney, 2016).

We recommend reading Dr. Carney's (2016) comments in full, but the short of it is that the study didn't have a strong research design to begin with, and afterward the data were massaged to create a compelling story for journal reviewers, which ultimately converted a mildly disappointing research result into a massive and cross-disciplinary problem. Fallout from the case, both from academic and popular press critics, ultimately led to Amy Cuddy exiting her tenure-track academic career, in part likely because she continued to defend the study's findings after these comments were shared and after numerous failed replication studies, after she managed to secure a speaking role for the TED conference on the topic, and after she began what is presumably a lucrative speaking career on power posing. Importantly, Dr. Carney was not nearly so directly affected, as she admitted to the mistakes given new knowledge and new scrutiny, an important lesson for reasons beyond data cleaning.

The full details of this case are outside the scope of this text, although you are encouraged to Google it, with particularly informative discussions by Gelman and Fund (2016) and Peters (2016). We describe it here to emphasize that the stakes for quality data cleaning processes can be quite high indeed. Careers have been broken on data that were cleaned inappropriately. Careers have been made for those pointing out the poor practices. But more importantly, such practices are often credited as the cause of the replication crisis, which might be described as the sudden realization by many scientists that a potentially very large portion of our research literature does not contain generalizable knowledge.

Given those stakes, it is particularly important for you, as an I-O psychologist, to develop a personal understanding of what data cleaning is, why it's important to get it right, and how to approach it correctly. It is not nearly so simple as following a single set of data cleaning rules. Instead, it is about deeply embracing a healthy philosophical approach to and relationship with data, to understand why data might be "dirty" and what can reasonably be done to clean them. A critical realization, for example, is that failing to sufficiently clean data can be just as problematic as cleaning too liberally. Using your developed understanding, you will be prepared to make decisions in often ambiguous situations to make the most ethical decisions you can, to ensure the integrity of the conclusions you draw, whether for academic publishing or practical research within organizations.

Research as a Series of Seemingly Trivial Decisions

Although there are numerous conceptual frameworks for understanding decision-making during data cleaning, one of the most compelling is the **garden of forking paths**, a concept popularized by Gelman and Loken (2013, 2014). The garden of forking paths refers to the myriad decisions that you make during the data cleaning and analytic process, all targeted at a singular goal: an interesting or desirable result for your research. Even if your goal is not to engage in dishonest behavior or especially outright fraud, every little decision you make is regardless still firmly pointed at that outcome.

Sometimes these little decisions are obvious and unquestionable, like realizing that the undergraduate research assistant that you thought was paying attention while coding has entered values into your spreadsheets that are quite literally impossible. Sometimes these decisions are a little problematic, such as the listwise deletion of influential cases or the transformation of a skewed variable because the data didn't quite "look right." And sometimes these decisions are more obviously a big problem, such as dropping different cases when $p = .051$ until the result turns out the way you'd hoped.

There is frankly no way for us to give you examples of every possible **questionable research practice** that one could engage in. To illustrate, John et al. (2012) asked this set of questions of researchers, each intended to reflect a QRP:

1. In a paper, failing to report all of a study's dependent measures
2. Deciding whether to collect more data after looking to see whether the results were significant
3. In a paper, failing to report all of a study's conditions
4. Stopping collecting data earlier than planned because one found the result that one had been looking for
5. In a paper, 'rounding off' a p value (e.g., reporting that a p value of .054 is less than .05)
6. In a paper, selectively reporting studies that 'worked'
7. Deciding whether to exclude data after looking at the impact of doing so on the results
8. In a paper, reporting an unexpected finding as having been predicted from the start
9. In a paper, claiming the results are unaffected by demographic variables (e.g., gender) when one is actually unsure (or knows that they do)
10. Falsifying data

Although this might appear on first glance to be a reasonable list, one needs look no further than Fiedler and Schwarz (2016) to find a lengthy list of criticisms. For example, they criticized item #1 as potentially

> not reporting subsidiary results of a post-experimental interview, results of irrelevant extra analyses broken down by demographic variables, invariance test for monotonic transformations, or conscientious checks on reliability, scale level, factor structures, or an endless list of variables generated in computer simulations.
>
> (p. 46)

But wait – wouldn't failing to report "extra analyses" indeed potentially be a QRP?

This is really the challenge. QRP is a socially constructed concept. There are no rules. There is only the general opinion and as-much-consensus-as-possible agreement between researchers as to what is acceptable and not. Beyond this problem, it's a moving target. Today's normal practice, as Dana Carney lamented, is tomorrow's QRP. And today's QRP may be discovered not to be so bad after all.

In fact, within this list, we only identified two types of problems that are universally decried, and we'd go so far as to say these aren't QRPs – they are simply, ethically, morally wrong. The first of these is outright lying. #8 is an example of this; if you conducted an exploratory study but wrote it up with the claim that it was confirmatory, this is an outright lie. It is not questionable. It is wrong. The second of these is **fraud**, a willful and explicit attempt to mislead. Complete **data fabrication** is the worst kind of fraud, as it does not necessarily bear any relationship whatsoever to reality. However, fraud can occur in much more subtle ways, such as stating that a cited paper makes a bulletproof claim that it does not in fact make.

The remaining QRPs in this list fall instead in a third category: **omissions**, the act of leaving out a relevant piece of information from a manuscript. For example, if a researcher runs a four-cell between-subjects experiment but then only reports the results from three of those conditions but makes no claim as to the total number of cells in which data were collected, there is no lie, yet there is an omission, and potentially a very important one. Yet there are reasons that this omission could be reasonable; for example, the researchers might have reasoned that they weren't sure if their manipulation even fundamentally worked, so they ran an extra condition without the bells and whistles of their "full design," just to double-check that the stimulus materials they were using did what they believed. Then, they decided not to write up that "extra condition" in their study, because they could see no way to include it that would not confuse reviewers.

Is such an "extra condition" a problem? Maybe, maybe not. And that's what makes true QRPs so problematic. For true QRPs, there is an argument both ways, that the practice is both harmful and helpful. It's not outright lying or fraud, but neither is it clearly a "good decision." The specific nature of that decision ends up being highly situational specific, which is why there are so few "rules" about this sort of thing.

How to Not p-Hack and Ruin Your Career

Engagement in QRPs in the context of statistical significance testing is sometimes referred to as *p*-hacking, which more directly refers to those QRPs that are intended to reduce an observed *p*-value. As discussed in Chapter 12, there is a lot of reviewer expectation inappropriately placed on statistical significant results in many scientific fields, I-O psychology included, which creates a lot of external pressure on researchers to push that *p*-value below its .05 threshold through both questionable and outright fraudulent practices.

There are few specific rules for what constitutes *p*-hacking and what doesn't except in cases of outright fraud. One practice that leans a bit more toward the fraud side is **hypothesizing after results are known (HARKing)**, which refers to a practice in which researchers throw a lot of statistical significance tests at a dataset and then write papers about whichever tests were significant, pretending that those hypotheses were part of their plan their whole time. But instead of trying to follow rules for *avoiding* *p*-hacking, you are much better off approaching this from the opposite direction, by "doing good" instead of "avoiding bad": practice **open science**.

Although we'll revisit this idea in Chapter 14 when discussing how to communicate research to others, a few open science concepts are relevant here. Open science does not refer to any particular set of practices but rather the end goal of those practices: maximally transparent and accessible scientific research (van der Zee & Reich, 2018).

Perhaps you can already guess the solution: if every analysis you conduct, if every bit of data cleaning you execute is transparently documented, and you make that **documentation** accessible to both reviewers and all eventual readers of your paper, it's difficult for someone to reasonably accuse you of *p*-hacking. At worst, you were just incompetent! But frankly, that's a lot better than being a fraud.

In the remainder of this chapter, we'll describe a variety of common scenarios that you are likely to face relevant to data cleaning during the execution of research, highlighting where decisions might be controversial so that you can make an informed decision about what to do. However, it cannot be overemphasized that these are not rules, and that for every decision, you need to carefully consider the specific nature of your particular dataset. Above all, be transparent about your reasoning, if not in your papers then at least in your analytic documentation (more on code documentation will come in Chapter 14).

Preparatory Data Cleaning

Broadly speaking, data cleaning really involves two stages of work: 1) preparatory practices, before data collection that increase the chances that you'll end up with clean data and 2) corrective practices that address problems that you didn't anticipate or couldn't prevent. As the old saying goes, "An ounce of prevention is worth a pound of cure." Obviously, it's preferable to prepare so well that little to no cleaning is necessary, but in the real world, there's no way to prevent the need for corrective practices entirely due to the inherently messy nature of data collection involving real people. That doesn't mean we shouldn't try.

Creating a Paper Trail: Codebooks and Data Dictionaries

The most important type of documentation that you should create for every research study is a **codebook**, also called a **data dictionary**. A study's codebook contains sufficient documentation to allow a person completely naive to your research study to understand precisely what generated every **feature** of your eventually collected dataset, which serves as not only a formal record of your study but also as a way to check the integrity of your data collection both before and after it occurs.

You can think of features as the columns in your dataset. Features include both **data**, which refers to primary information collected about the person completing the study, and **metadata**, which refers to secondary information collected in reference to how data were collected. For example, if you ask participants to respond with 200 words to an open-ended prompt, the actual response would be considered data and the amount of time they took to write it (if you collect this information) is an example of metadata.

This generally means the inclusion of at least the following specific pieces of information for each feature you collect, a sample of which appears in Table 11.1:

1. ***Feature identifiers***. You should aim to use single-phrase (no spaces) item identifiers and keep these identifiers as consistent as possible both across features and across formats and record these identifiers in your codebook. For example, if you want to name a feature BigFive_E1 to represent the first item in an extraversion scale within a Big Five personality inventory, you should keep this pattern in all features that reference Big Five items, and you should keep this general naming convention (i.e., **camel-case** overall measure reference [BigFive] followed by an underscore [_] followed by an initial to represent scale [E] followed by a single-digit number [1]) across your entire codebook, and you should use these same names when importing data into your analytic program.
2. *Metadata cross-referencing*. If this feature is metadata collected in relation to a specific scale or item, write the item identifier (or indicate a range). For data, leave this blank. This will make it easier to sort out metadata later when just trying to get a simple list of everything participants saw and also help you tie specific metadata back to the specific items they were collected on.
3. *Item order*. For data, include a non-repeating list of numbers reflecting the order that people saw the prompts, starting with 1. If you use a branching survey, ensure this order is always accurate no matter which branch respondents saw. Do not ever repeat numbers.

Table 11.1 Example codebook for four-item survey

Feature ID	Meta	Ord	Type	Values	Description	Prompt	Coding
ipip_e1		1	Num	1:5,99	IPIP 10-item Extraversion Item 1	Am the life of the party.	(1) Strongly Disagree (2) Disagree (3) Neither (4) Agree (5) Strongly Agree (99) Choose not to answer
ipip_e2		2	Num	1:5,99	IPIP 10-item Extraversion Item 2	Feel comfortable around people.	( ) [Left blank] (1) Strongly Disagree (2) Disagree (3) Neither (4) Agree (5) Strongly Agree (99) Choose not to answer
ipip_e3		3	Num	1:5,99	IPIP 10-item Extraversion Item 6	Don't talk a lot.	( ) [Left blank] (1) Strongly Disagree (2) Disagree (3) Neither (4) Agree (5) Strongly Agree (99) Choose not to answer
ipip_et	ipip_e	N/A	Num	Times	Time to complete ipip_e items	(not visible)	( ) [Left blank] [time in milliseconds]
gender_1		4	Num	1,0	Gender checkbox (respondent selects all that apply)	Please indicate your gender among the options below: Female	(1) Female (0) [Not endorsed]
gender_2		4	Num	1,0	Gender checkbox (respondent selects all that apply)	Please indicate your gender among the options below: Male	(1) Male (0) [Not endorsed]
gender_3		4	Num	1,0	Gender checkbox (respondent selects all that apply)	Please indicate your gender among the options below: Transgender	(1) Transgender (0) [Not endorsed]
gender_4		4	Num	1,0	Gender checkbox (respondent selects all that apply)	Please indicate your gender among the options below: Other	(1) Other (0) [Not endorsed]

Note. Some fields were omitted for space. In your own codebooks, which should be digital in Excel, Google Sheets, or some other spreadsheeting program, be sure to include all fields.

4. *Branch identifiers*. If you use branching surveys, where subsets of respondents may see different items than other subsets, you should include one column in your codebook for each branching option, to clearly indicate which branch or which respondents to whom the item was visible.
5. *Variable type*. Is this numeric or text? Something else?
6. *Values range*. If numeric, what is the range of acceptable values? Integers, decimals, negatives? If text, what limits should exist on the specific content of that text? If reverse coded, how?
7. *Description*. A one-sentence or less plain language description of what the feature represents.
8. *Prompt text*. If this feature reflects an item displayed to the respondent, what is the text of that item?
9. *Coding*. If this feature is a multiple choice item, what options are visible to respondents? If the multiple choice options are being coded as numbers, what is the coding scheme? If numeric, what do numbers represent? If text, what does the text represent (if anything?) Always write the exact options, letter for letter. Always clearly indicate which text is visible to respondents and which is not. In Figure 11.1, brackets indicate that the text given was not visible.

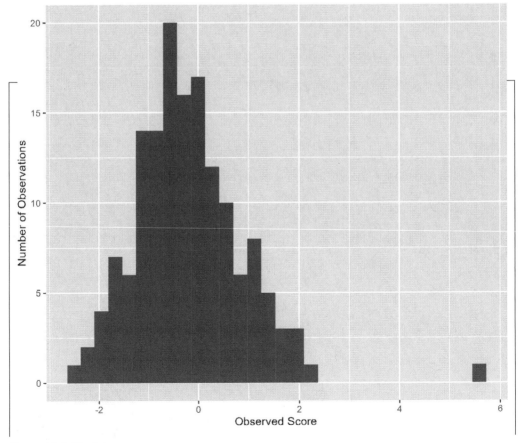

Figure 11.1 Outlying case.

10. *Source.* If this item is from a published scale, what is the citation to that scale? If not, where did it come from? Is it calculated from other data? Was it generated by a system, and if so, how?

11. *Notes.* Is there anything else unusual about this feature that is not written down in another field?

Feature Naming Conventions

We don't necessarily endorse any particular naming convention for features, because naming conventions are best when they reflect a chosen **style guide** for the statistical language that will be used for analysis.

If you use R as your analytic platform of choice, you might adopt the tidyverse style guide (https://style.tidyverse.org/index.html) which states all variables names should be entirely made of lowercase letters, numbers, and underscores. This implies feature names in our example like bigfive_e1 or bigfive_e_1 or big5_e1.

If you use Python as your analytic platform of choice, you might adopt the *pythonic* naming conventions given by the Python Software Foundation (www.python.org/dev/peps/pep-0008/). These standards mostly just emphasize choosing a naming convention and sticking with it (suggesting, e.g., lower_case_with_undersores, UPPER_CASE_WITH_UNDERSCORES, CamelCase, and mixedCase) but avoiding certain specific names.

If you use SPSS (I'm sorry for your loss), you will be constrained by the language itself: up to 32 characters, no spaces, no periods or underscores at the end, and no SPSS reserved keywords (like AND, BY, LE, LT, or WITH). Beyond that, you can do whatever you want.

If you use Excel or another spreadsheet program, it's lawless out there. Do whatever you want, but still be consistent about it!

As you advance further in your career, also consider writing your own lab or work-group style guide. Any time you work with other people on datasets and/or code, having a consistent language to communicate in never hurts. For example, all employees at Google are expected to follow naming conventions in the Google style guide (https://google.github.io/styleguide/pyguide.html#s3.16-naming).

Automation of Data Collection

Any data collection that can be automated or verified should be automated or verified. This might seem obvious upon first glance, but often people don't realize it until after data collection is complete.

For example, let's imagine that you wanted to collect the first day of employment for each respondent to your assessment on a digital assessment using questionnaire administration software. On first blush, you might think that the easiest approach is simply to use a text box to ask for this date. However, if you did so, you'd quickly discover that people use a wide range of possible formats for dates, such as "February 12, 2019", "12-Feb-2019", or "I think it was February a couple of years ago?" By using a text box, you've inadvertently created a later data cleaning nightmare. Thus, converting this text box into three separate dropdown boxes – for month, day, and year – will dramatically increase the chance that you'll end up with clean data.

Automation is even better; if you can automatically grab information without the respondent needing to input it manually, you'll be in an even better position. One of the most common places that needs automation is the entry of Amazon Mechanical Turk or Prolific user ids as a means of tracking participation. These identifiers are highly prone to incorrect typing and incorrect copy/pasting, which just creates headaches for you later. Fortunately, there are also techniques to automatically include those identifiers in your dataset without the user every needing to type them. The precise approach varies by software and by service, so as an example, we'll just walk through one of your author's (Richard) favorite combinations: data collection with Qualtrics with participants from Prolific.

The key in this situation is to determine 1) how can Prolific IDs be sent out of Prolific and 2) how can arbitrary data be collected by Qualtrics from outside of Qualtrics. In this case, it's only a few steps:

1. When setting up a Prolific job, once you paste your Qualtrics link into Prolific, select the option to use "URL parameters." This will add an expression that looks like &PRO-LIFIC_PID={{%PROLIFIC_PID%%}} at the end of your study link.
2. In Qualtrics, add an Embedded Data item in the survey flow called PROLIFIC_PID, to match the variable name being sent by Prolific.

That's it! You're done! Two simple steps to avoid a non-zero number of emails about people's work not being credited correctly to their accounts. Always be on the lookout for ways to automatically record data like this, to remove human error from data collection, to reduce the need for cleaning later to fix those human errors.

Alpha and Beta Testing

The terms alpha testing and beta testing which we briefly introduced in Chapter 10 when discussing scale development come from the software development industry and quality assurance practices. We use the terms here because the process is the same, and they serve as an easy-to-understand framework to improve your research design. In research, much like software development, you must **engineer** a solution to a problem, in this case study materials to adequately address your research question. The materials you develop initially for your study are *probably fine*, but they are almost certainly not the best they could be. The only way to figure out what to fix is to test, observe, fix, and repeat.

Additionally, these procedures don't apply only to digital research. Although it is common to use or at least heavily integrate computerized data collection into modern I-O research, these techniques apply equally well to completely analog data collection as well as hybrid data collection, such as when some aspects of a study are done live and in-person and others are done via computer.

During alpha testing, you complete the study you've designed yourself, in the role of a participant, and later ask colleagues within your research team to do so. All alpha testing occurs before any "real" participants see your study. This type of testing helps you to understand what the *experience* of participating in your study is like before bringing innocent participants into the mix. It helps you empathize, to understand where your study procedure is not doing what you think it's doing. You should engage in three specific types of alpha testing, asking several specific questions during alpha testing:

1. First, you will engage in **acceptance testing** in which your goal is to ensure that the system you've created is initially acceptable in terms of your goals for it. To do this, you will complete the entire study from start to finish, exactly as a participant would experience it. This includes any condition assignments, email notifications, payment steps, etc. Literally everything. As you go, enter responses as if you were a legitimate participant and either use screengrabs (such as using Greenshot: https://getgreenshot.org) or write down your responses to literally every question. On this run, ask:

   - Does every image, every video, and every bit of text match up with your vision for what a participant should experience in your study?
   - Did any parts not work like you expected? If so, change them and restart the experience from the beginning. Don't jump to the part you fixed, because you can't always predict what else broke as a result of your fix.
   - Once you have completed the study, download all datasets and put them together. If using R or Python (we hope you are), go ahead and write the code needed to merge the datasets and observe if there are any problems doing so. For example, are you saving participant identifiers in the same formats across sources? Now is the time to fix such problems.
   - Cross-check your screengrabs or written log of your responses against the data you collected. They should be identical. If they aren't, you have something else to fix.
   - Cross-check your screengrabs with your codebook. Is everything exactly correct? If not, fix it now.
   - Once you've completed acceptance testing on the initial study, repeat the process for all possible branches. For example, if there are questions that might lead a respondent down different paths depending upon their answers, you need to test *every* path to ensure that it shows exactly what it is supposed to show. Do not skip this step!

2. After completing acceptance testing, you will complete **usability** and **functional testing.** For this step, ask people in your research lab, other graduate students, friends, and naive colleagues to also complete your study from start to finish. For this stage of testing, choose people who don't know how your study works or perhaps even what you are studying. If you have branches, assign them to complete the study in different ways, for example, by instructing them to respond particular ways on the questions you know will trigger branch assignments.

   - For functional testing, have each person write down their answers, or better yet, assign a response strategy. Asking such people to make screengrabs of every response is probably a bit too much of an ask, so instead ask some people to complete the study honestly and others to use a pattern (e.g., by responding 1 2 3 4 5 4 3 2 1 on multiple choice items).
   - For usability testing, prepare your alpha testers with instructions that ask them to write down their observations, like: "As you complete the study, write down any aspect of the experience that you find unclear or confusing. Also, we'd appreciate you letting us know if you spot any typos or graphics glitches."
   - If your study is digital and remote, try to get alpha testers with a wide range of computing systems to ensure you have a sample, for example, of desktops, laptops, tablets,

and smartphones, across Windows, Mac, and Linux systems or various ages. You won't be able to find every possible combination, but try to get a sample reasonable representative of the technology your respondents will be using.

3. Once you are done fixing "typical" problems, the final step of alpha testing is hunting for "unusual" problems, in what is called **ad-hoc testing** or "red-teaming". In ad-hoc testing, either you or the people you previously asked to help complete the study again with the explicit purpose of breaking it. Appropriate ad-hoc testing varies by project, but here are some potential strategies to get you started. Most of these are for digital collection, especially in a web browser, but you'll get the general idea:

- Try using back and forward buttons at inappropriate times.
- Try refreshing the page randomly.
- Try entering inappropriate text data in text fields (e.g., numbers for words, words for numbers).
- Try randomly changing information in the address bar.
- Try copying the web address from an early part of the study and going to that page at a later part of the study.
- Try leaving things blank that are required to proceed.
- Any time the page tells you that you can't do something (e.g., "you must answer this to proceed"), try to find a way around the warning.
- Try closing the page entirely and restarting with the invitation link from the beginning.
- Try pausing any videos or sounds that play.
- Try to bypass videos and sounds (e.g., by clicking through without listening/watching).

Once you've completed acceptance, usability, functional, and ad hoc testing, it's time to begin your beta test. Ideally, at this stage, your study is in fact *done*. Beta testing is really just a way to be absolutely sure of this with authentic participants, because you won't be able to test certain aspects of your study that are unique to participating authentically. For example, if you were conducting a study using Prolific as a data source, you won't be able to test the accurate transfer of the Prolific Participant ID numbers into your study during alpha testing.

To do this kind of small-scale test, simply run your post-alpha study in its final form with a small group of real participants – usually 5 to 10. Check that you can pay everyone, that your datasets still can be stitched together as before, that there aren't any holes in your datasets, that you don't receive 5 to 10 complaint emails, and so on. In this way, you'll be as sure as you can be than when you run the study with hundreds of people, things should work the way you expect.

Syntax and Code Reuse

One of the best ways to ensure that you can test your research questions and hypotheses with the data you collect is to write your analytic code ahead of time using alpha data, or if your alpha data are inappropriate for some reason (e.g., lack of variance, an unrealistic covariance matrix), using simulated data. In addition to being more confident that your analyses will actually run when you want them to, you won't need to scramble under time pressure to write that code after data have been collected, which is otherwise what usually ends up happening.

One thing to constantly consider as you create analytic code is how to write that code so that it can be reused in future analytic projects. Code that has been vetted by multiple people, reused in multiple projects, and is checked and updated frequently is more likely to be bug-free than code you write ad-hoc to meet a particular project analytic requirement. Well-considered bug-free code saves times and creates fewer data cleaning headaches later.

Always try to think of your future self, trying to understand and/or re-implement the code you're writing now. Don't just pity them for the choices you are making now; make your future self's job easier by doing a little extra work today.

Pre-Registration

Once you have a working study, with a complete codebook, prepped logbook, completed alpha- and beta-testing, and prepared syntax for analysis, you should **pre-register** your final study design and analytic plan. The term *pre-registration* is actually very general, referring to the filing of some kind of plan about your study with a trusted pre-registration filing authority, typically a data collection plan and/or analytic plan, which might even include analytic code, before you do any of the things your plan contains.

Filing a pre-registration does not itself ensure clean data; instead, pre-registration serves a few broader purposes related to the clean data your study produces and their interpretation:

1. It forces you, as the study designer, to work out all of the details of your data collection and analytic strategy in advance, at least to the extent possible. Researcher often intend to do this, or even think they've done this, whereas they've really skipped a few steps. By writing it down and formalizing it, you must work through details you might otherwise have missed. Ideally, this plan is a plan for attaining clean data.
2. It provides a blueprint for you, as the study designer, to follow later, to discourage wandering down forking paths.
3. It declares these specific details with a public authority to provide assurance to anyone reading your research later that you did not in fact wander – or if you did, that you declared your intention to do so in your pre-registration, encouraging your results to be viewed through the correct interpretive lens.

There are downsides to pre-registration if you aren't careful, including:

1. If you haven't really completely thought through your study, you may pre-register something that was not optimal for the data you ended up collecting. This is unfortunately something that you will best learn through experience. The lesson to be learned in such situations is not to stop pre-registering your research but instead to think more carefully about your plan before filing it.
2. You may legitimately encounter surprises that require a different approach to data collection or analysis that was not within the scope of your pre-registration. Once again, the lesson is not that pre-registration was a mistake, but that being transparent about changes made to that pre-registration is vital for good science. Deviation from a pre-registered plan is not by itself a sign of a problem with the research, as long as the deviation is clearly documented and described, so that a consumer of research can judge for themselves if the change was warranted and what effect it might have had on study results.

Pre-registration documents themselves take many different forms, and you should choose one appropriate to your project. The most common in I-O psychology research are the University of Pennsylvania's AsPredicted (https://aspredicted.org) and the Center for Open Science's Open Science Framework (OSF; https://osf.io; see https://osf.io/zab38/wiki/home/ for pre-registration templates). Whereas AsPredicted is more singularly focused upon pre-registration, OSF provides a broad range of tools to help you share your research more effectively.

We'll revisit both philosophical and technical details related to pre-registration in much greater detail in our discussion of sharing results (Chapter 14) and recommend you check them out before pre-registering your own research.

Pre-Registration Does Not Imply Trustworthy Research

Just as pre-registration alone does not ensure clean data in your own research, it also does not signal the quality of research you are reading. Do not assume an existing pre-registration means a study is trustworthy and generalizable. A pre-registration is a recorded plan of data collection and/or analysis; nothing more, nothing less. If the pre-registered plan was unideal for the study, the study analysis and results remain unideal after the analysis has taken place. And even if the plan was ideal, sometimes people that pre-register don't follow their own filed plans and don't even mention this in their papers! It's up to you as the consumer of such research to check that the pre-registered plan was in fact reasonable, that the authors did what they said they would do, and that any deviations from that plan were justified and justifiable according to your own professional judgment. We'll revisit this concept in Chapter 14 in our discussion of manuscript development and sharing.

Corrective Data Cleaning

With so much preparation, you might think that you have created a bulwark against low-quality data. And although you have certainly created a strong initial defense, people are hard to predict, things are going to go wrong, and these issues are going to harm your ability to analyze your data. Thus, our next question concerns corrective practices: once you have a quality problem with collected data, what can you do about it?

Ideally, you should plan in advance for which corrective practices you will engage in and what lines must be crossed to trigger them. Thus, this section in some ways serves as advice about what to write in your pre-registration. However, you are likely to encounter problems outside the scope of what we can reasonably cover here. In such cases, we can only make the same call we made before: reason through it careful and be completely transparent about what you did.

Having said that, there are three areas of data cleaning that people must commonly deal with in most I-O human subjects research: outliers and influential cases, careless and insufficient effort responders, and missingness. As such, we'll dive a bit more deeply into specific practices in each of these categories, so that you can make a reasoned judgment for both your pre-registration and when you inevitably run into problems for which you have not pre-registered.

Outliers and Influential Cases

Outliers are improbable data given a particular data-generated mechanism. That's a fancy way of saying "this score seems unlikely to be due to a natural event given the other scores I've collected." We think of cases as outliers because they are suspicious; we imagine a certain cause for the score pattern we see and don't believe that the case we're looking at has the same causes. An example of a **univariate outlier** appears in Figure 11.1.

In this example, there is what appears to be a normally distributed variable centered around a score of zero, and a case off on its own with a value of 5.5. When looking at this figure, most people have an immediate reaction of "there must be something wrong with that 5.5." This is called a univariate outlier because it is outlying on only a single variable. However, cases can be **multivariate outliers** as well, as shown in Figure 11.2.

In this example, there are two outliers to consider more carefully. The case at [–1.5, 1.5] is not a univariate outlier on either Variable 1 or Variable 2, because it is within the ordinary range of scores that we see on each variable individually. If we were to draw a histogram of Variable 1 and a histogram of Variable 2, we'd see nothing unusual about this case in either. Thus, where it is unusual is in the combination of those scores; it clearly falls far outside the pattern shown among the other cases, suggesting it is a multivariate outlier though not a univariate outlier.

The second outlier worth considering is the score close to [–3, –3]. This score is the lowest value on both Variable 1 and Variable 2, suggesting it might be a univariate outlier on

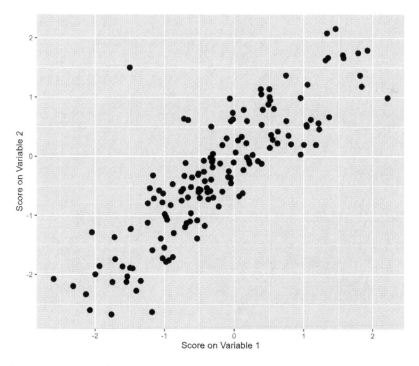

Figure 11.2 Scatterplot illustrating multivariate outliers and influential cases.

Variable 1, a univariate outlier on Variable 2, and a multivariate outlier on both all at the same time.

If a regression analysis were conducted here, for example regressing Variable 2 on Variable 1, both of these cases would have an outsized influence on the regression weights obtained. Whereas the [–1.5, 1.5] case would have more impact decreasing the coefficient associated with the regression line than all of the clustered cases, the [–3, –3] case would have more impact increasing it. In this way, both of these might be labeled **influential cases**.

To this point, we've been diagnosing outlyingness by sight. Although this is a good way to get a general sense of the prevalence of outlyingness in your dataset, it is subject to those human biases we want to escape in the garden of forking paths. It's easy, looking at either of these figures, to conclude that there is something unusual about these cases. But real data are rarely so well behaved, even in terms of outlyingness. To illustrate, look at Figure 11.3 and decide where the outliers are.

Is Variable 1 at –3 outlying? What about Variable 2 at +4? What about [–3, –4]? Each of these cases is debatable based upon a visual inspection alone, and this is precisely the problem. Eliminating outlying cases purely based upon such calls is ripe with p-hacking potential, which means we should endeavor to avoid it as your primary outlier detection technique.

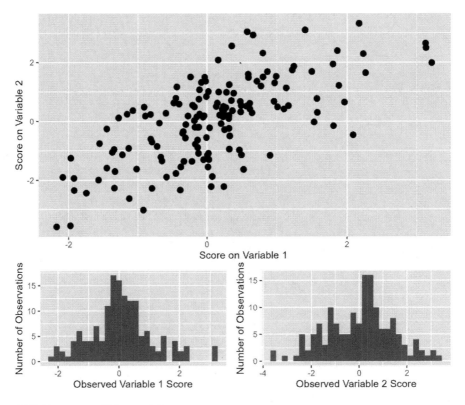

Figure 11.3 Test yourself for outlyingness.

Importantly, visual inspection should not be abandoned altogether. As in Figure 11.1, sometimes outlyingness is so extreme that it points to another, identifiable problem. For example, upon observing that case being so far out of spec, you would revisit the original data collection materials and hunt for an obvious cause, such as miscoding, reversed digits on a chart, or some other such researcher mistake. In such cases, scores can be corrected with little risk. But what do we do for the edge cases, where there's an argument to be made for both outlyingness and typicality? And once we identify the outliers, what do we do with them?

There is fortunately a relatively small set of mainstream outlier detection techniques to consider when looking at normally distributed data. They are:

1. Using a technique referred to as **Tukey's (1977) fences**, univariate outliers may be defined as scores beyond 1.5 times the interquartile range (IQR), which is itself defined as the distance between the first quartile (25% of cases are smaller than this value) and the third quarter (75% of cases are smaller than this value). For example, if the mean was 0, the first quartile was –0.5, and the third quartile was +1 = 0.5, the IQR would be +0.5 – (–0.5) = 1 and scores 1.5 × 1 = 1.5 points beyond those quartiles (i.e., –0.5 – 1.5 = –2 and 0.5 + 1.5 = 2) would be considered outliers. These points also correspond to the ends of the "whiskers" on a standard boxplot. Tukey also considered 3.0 as the line at which "far out" outliers occurred. There is no consensus on which of these numbers is "better" in any particular situation.

2. Univariate outliers may be defined as z-scores beyond 2.5. Or 3.0. Or 3.5. Or 4.0. As a reminder, z-scores are standardized scores and represent the number of standard deviations away from the mean that a score is. A z-score of –3 is 3 standard deviations below the mean. There is no generally agreed-upon distance to define outlyingness this way.

3. Multivariate outliers may be defined using **Mahalanobis distances** (D_M) and then either looking for univariate outlying scores among those D_M using either of the previous univariate techniques (IQR or z-scores) or by identifying statistically significant D_M. A Mahalanobis distance is a way of quantifying how unusual a score is in a multivariate space. Looking back to Figure 11.2, you can imagine a D_M reflecting to what degree each point is unusual (versus each score individual), as in the two cases we visually identified, in relation to all other possible points. The wonder of D_M is that it can be calculated for any number of variables, far more than we could possibly visualize. The calculation of D_M requires some matrix algebra to do it by hand, so we'll skip demonstrating it here. But in short, a D_M is calculated for each case in your dataset, to determine how outlying it is.

4. Influential cases may be defined using **Cook's distance** (D_C), which quantifies the degree to which predicted y scores are influenced by the exclusion of cases by re-running the regression with and without each case, and weighting this by the case's leverage (i.e., the degree to which the regression line differs between models with and without that case). Thus, much like with D_M, a D_C is calculated for each case in your dataset given a particular regression analysis, to determine how influential it is. A case may be considered influential when D_C is outlying, per one of the univariate outlyingness tests described previously, including from visualization. Additionally, values of .5 or 1 are sometimes considered cutoffs for "influence." Larger scores indicate greater influence.

5. Influential cases may be defined using **difference in fits (DFFITS)**, which roughly speaking quantifies the degree to which predicted *y* scores are influenced by the exclusion of cases by re-running the regression with and without each case. D_C and DFFITS are conceptually and computationally very similar, which means they tend to be highly correlated. The main conceptual differences are that D_C is calculated using squared differences (i.e., larger scores indicate greater influence) whereas DFFITS is not (i.e., scores further from zero, either negative or positive, indicate greater influence), and the weighting strategy for leverages are slightly different (although not usually in a meaningful way).

Outlier Detection Using R

The use of R makes the detection of outliers and influential cases with all of these strategies quite easy. As usual, remember to *install.packages()* any libraries you don't already have installed. For this demo, we'll use the BFI dataset within the *psych* package:

```
library(tidyverse)     # for data manipulation
library(psych)         # for the dataset
library(modi)          # for Mahalanobis distances with missing values
data(bfi)

# shows "1" and "2" are outlying by the interquartile method in a boxplot
ggplot(bfi, aes(x=A5)) + geom_boxplot()
# calculate Tukey's fences directly
A5_25q <- quantile(bfi$A5, .25, na.rm=T)   # determine 1st quartile (25%)
A5_75q <- quantile(bfi$A5, .75, na.rm=T)   # determine 3rd quartile (75%)
A5_IQR <- IQR(bfi$A5, na.rm=T)             # determine interquartile range
lower <- A5_25q - 1.5 * A5_IQR             # lower fence
upper <- A5_75q + 1.5 * A5_IQR             # upper fence
filter(bfi, A5 < lower | A5 > upper) %>% nrow   # count outliers beyond fences


# convert to z scores and look at result
bfi <- mutate(bfi, A5z = scale(A5))            # create z scores
ggplot(bfi, aes(x=A5z)) + geom_histogram()     # create histogram of z scores


# calculate Mahalanobis D values across agreeableness items with missing
    values
agree_df <- select(bfi, A1:A5)          # select only agreeablness items
agree_df$mahal <- MDmiss(agree_df,      # place mahalanobis d values in dataset
            colMeans(agree_df, na.rm=T),
            cov(agree_df, use="pairwise")
)
agree_df$mahal_p <- pchisq(agree_df$mahal,  # place p-values in dataset too
            df=4,
            lower.tail=F
)
```

```
ggplot(agree_df, aes(x=mahal)) +          # visualize mahalanobis d
      geom_histogram()
ggplot(agree_df, aes(x=mahal_p)) +        # visualize mahalanobis d p-values < .25
      geom_histogram() +
      xlim(c(0, .25))
filter(agree_df, mahal_p < .05) %>% nrow  # count cases that are significant

# calculate Cook's D and DFFITS values for a given regression analysis
regression_df <- drop_na(agree_df)        # listwise deletion for
                                            simplicity of example
model <- lm(A5 ~ A1 + A2 + A3 + A4,       # our old friend, regression
      data=regression_df
)
regression_df <- bind_cols(regression_df, # add influence measures to
                                            dataset
            as_tibble(influence.measures(model)$infmat))
ggplot(regression_df, aes(x=dffit)) +     # visualize DFFITS
      geom_histogram()
ggplot(regression_df, aes(x=cook.d)) +    # visualize Cook's distances
      geom_histogram()
cor(regression_df$dffit^2,                # correlation between influence
                                            metrics
      regression_df$cook.d
)
```

If you noticed in this list of outlier and influential case detection strategies that there seem to be myriad standards and no clear indication of which is "best," you have made an astute observation. This is absolutely correct. There is no single agreed-upon way to detect either outliers or influential cases. In most labs, outlier and influence case handling is something passed down through academic advising heritage. Your advisor did it, so you do it too. To be honest, this isn't usually bad as a starting point, as the finer points of outlier handling are not usually mission-critical, but as you mature as a researcher, you should endeavor to figure out why your advisor does what they do and see if you agree with it. And if you don't agree, figure out what makes sense to you.

What you absolutely should not do is frequently change your outlier and influential case handling strategy between studies, as this is likely to signal *p*-hacking. It suggests that you run your analyses, and if you don't like the results, you fiddle with your outlier handling until the study comes out with the result you want. So don't do that. Identify what strategy makes the most sense to you and stick with it in most of your studies. And even better, pre-register those strategies every time, just to make your defense of reasonable outlier handling bulletproof.

For further reading on outliers and influential cases, see:

Roth, P. L., & Switzer, F. S. (2002). Outliers and influential cases: Handling those discordant contaminated maverick rogues. In S. Rogelberg (Ed.), *Handbook of research methods in industrial and organizational psychology* (pp. 297–309). Blackwell.

Careless or Insufficient Effort Responding

Careless responding and insufficient effort responding (IER), introduced in Chapter 9, refer to the same general phenomenon: people participate in your research and don't appear to put any effort in. This is distinct from problematic response strategies, such as central tendency bias (see Chapter 10). Those strategies still reflect the authentic response of the respondent; for example, if a person responds with all 3s, 4s, and 5s on a 7-point scale because they are hesitant to respond to extreme values, that hesitance is a legitimate part of their response strategy. Carelessness and IER, on the other hand, reflect nothing – they just add noise to your data, and such noise can bias your results (e.g., if low effort covaries with a construct you are studying) or simply make it more difficult to draw valid conclusions from your own research due to increased sample size requirements associated with greater error.

Much like with detecting outliers and influential cases, there are myriad detection strategies for detecting IER and there is no clear "best" option. However, what is clear from the IER research literature is that using multiple detection strategies is important, because people are careless in different ways, and carelessness also varies even over the course of a single response. For example, if your study takes 30 minutes of a person's time, they might stop paying attention for only the middle 10 minutes, or even on a single measure they find uninteresting. If you base your IER detection only upon aggregate study-wide measures, you might not flag such a person.

So what strategies can be used? Here's a list:

1. *Time*. Completing a study too quickly (e.g., rushing through it) or too slowly (e.g., taking a break in the middle). Time-based outliers can be calculated study-wise or for individual sections of a study to determine carelessness.
2. *Bogus items*. A bogus item is one with a pre-determined response if a person is paying attention, which has zero room for error. For example, "1 + 2 =" is a bogus item, as is "I am currently living on the planet Saturn." Bogus items can be risky, because some respondents who *are* paying attention will sometimes endorse bogus items because they think doing so is funny (and frankly, as in the Saturn case, it sort of is). If you want to use bogus items, you'll want to place them throughout your study, roughly every 50 questions, and you'll want to write them so that they appear similar to the other questions that surround them. Remember that the point is to catch people not paying attention, not to force them to think hard.
3. *Instructed response items*. An instructed response item, as discussed in Chapter 9, is one that literally instructs the respondent to respond in a particular way. For example, "Respond 'strongly agree' to this question.' Directed response items are a relatively uncontroversial way to flag IER but again should be placed throughout the study, in the middle of big blocks of items, and roughly every 50 questions.
4. *Psychometric antonyms and synonyms*. Another approach to flagging IER is an approach in which correlations are calculated among all items pairs after data collection is complete to identify item pairs that are particularly strongly positively or negatively correlated (Meade & Craig, 2012, suggest beyond +/– .60). Using those pairs, calculate the within-person correlations among the positive items and among the negative items. Univariate outlyingness on either metric suggests IER. Although there is value to this approach, it

requires the inclusion of multiple features likely to be correlated beyond +/– .60, which means it is not applicable to many research designs.

5. *LongString*. A longstring value refers to the maximum number of sequential responses with the same value at a single data collection point, usually defined as a visible page in a web browser, and comes in many variations. Two of the most common are maximum and mean. For example, a person who respond "strongly disagree" to 8 questions in a row on a page with 10 questions on it and then to 9 questions in a row on the next page with 10 questions on it would have a maximum longstring of 9 and an average longstring of 8.5. If your study has different numbers of questions on different pages, you should calculate longstring as a proportion instead (e.g., 80% and 90% in the previous examples), as otherwise pages with more items on them will be weighted more heavily in mean longstring calculations.

6. *Intraindividual response variability (IRV)*. IRV refers to the standard deviation across a series of consecutively administered items with similar response profiles (e.g., personality assessment items on a 5-point scale). It is conceptually very similar to longstring but detects patterns than longstring cannot (e.g., 1 2 1 2 1 2 1 2 would show a longstring of 1 but probably outlying low IRV).

7. *Multivariate outlyingness*. As you might guess, this refers to the use of Mahalanobis distances as an indicator of IER. The logic here is that multivariate outlyingness across an entire dataset suggests a respondent didn't respond in a similar pattern to any other respondent, and the most likely reason for such inconsistency across so many individually measured variables is IER.

8. *Self-reported data quality*. One way to assess IER is, at the end of materials, simply ask the respondent if they engaged in high-quality practices. For example, Meade and Craig (2012) provide 9 items to measure "self-reported diligence," with items like "I carefully read every survey item." and "I probably should have been more careful during this survey." No matter what specific prompt you use, it is important to indicate that the person's study credit, pay, or other outcomes won't be affected by their answer to such questions.

9. *Single-item direct questioning*. Finally, one can assess IER with an emotional plea of the following flavor: "We're scientists. We're trying to make society better. It really hurts us if we include data in our research from people who didn't put in any effort. How much effort did you put in?" on a scale from "almost none" to "a lot." Ok, so don't use that *exact* prompt, but you get the idea – you're trying to make the careless folks feel guilty and admit to their carelessness. Another common variation is: "In your opinion, should we include your response when we analyze the results of this study?" Much as with self-reported data quality measures, respondents should be assured their responses won't affect earned credit, pay, or other desirable outcomes.

Across all of these techniques, there are two major methods to flag specific cases, and you should choose between these based upon your judgment:

1. *Assume anyone flagged is engaging in IER*. In some of these cases, there may be reason to believe that a particular metric is 100% reliable in reflecting carelessness. For example, if you require participants to read 2000 words, any respondent finishing your study in

less than 60 seconds is definitely engaging in IER. In such cases, you might decide on a particular hard cutoff for IER metrics, to flag someone as definite IER. Just be careful to explain the specific rationale for such cutoffs.

2. *Look for univariate outliers in IER metrics by any of the methods discussed earlier.* If no hard cutoff can be made conceptually, you can look for cases visually, flag cases outside of Tukey's fences, or you can set specific z-score cutoffs. There are no special rules for outlyingness among these metrics.

3. *Some combination of these.* There are few "rules" in data cleaning in part because the unique combination of measures and stimuli you use can lead to unique interactions in terms of experienced problems. Given that, you might have some metrics that have clear arguments for a priori flags and others that might not, and this still might vary by study. Again, above all, use a combination that makes sense, pre-register your plan, and describe how you deviate from your plan in your final write-up, either in the paper itself or in online supplementary material.

For further reading in careless and insufficient effort responding, see:

Meade, A. W., & Craig, S. B. (2012). Identifying careless responses in survey data. *Psychological Methods, 17,* 437–455.

My Approach to Carelessness

Like everyone else, your authors each use their own idiosyncratic approaches to detecting carelessness but try to be consistent about it across all of their research. One of your authors, Richard, generally includes directed response items, calculates proportional longstring, assesses multivariate outlyingness, and uses a single-item self-report data quality measure. For each participant, he looks for visual indicators of outlyingness and sets a cutoff if there is an obvious one. Within each participant, for each cutoff reached, they get one (1) carelessness point. Next, he adds the carelessness points together to get an overall carelessness score, which he in turn visualizes and looks for univariate outliers. This is a relatively conservative approach, as it doesn't usually flag many people as outlying across multiple metrics, and when the approach does flag a lot of people, those people are no longer outliers, so they are not considered IERs. For example, if across 500 respondents, 100 are flagged once and 50 are flagged twice, he will usually listwise delete the 50 but not the 100. If across 500 respondents, 50 are flagged once, and 5 are flagged twice, he will usually listwise delete all 55. He bases this on a mostly arbitrary heuristic that "5 to 15% of respondents are probably engaging in IER in any given data collection." But he takes this approach in almost every study he does, which at least makes it consistent. He also only does any of this after appropriate alpha and beta testing using primary panel data; in organizational datasets, or more broadly when analyzing data collected by others where he had little or no control over data collection techniques, he is generally a bit more conservative in terms of flagging cases.

IER Detection Using R

IER detection varies by approach. Some require computation and some are just descriptive. To illustrate the methods requiring computation, we'll use the same BFI dataset as before, and we'll pretend the entire questionnaire was assessed in the order it appears in the dataset. We'll also pretend it was given on two pages, 10 items on the first page and 15 items on the second. We'll also get rid of all cases with missing values to make the example a bit easier to follow:

```
library(psych)
library(tidyverse)
library(careless)
careless_df <- select(bfi, A1:O5) %>% drop_na
indicators_df <- tibble(
       # Psychometric synonyms and antonyms, slightly relaxed critical value
       psychsyn = psychsyn(careless_df, critval = .5),
       psychant = psychant(careless_df, critval = .5),

       # Longstring per page, proportional per page, and maximums
       longstring_page1 = careless_df %>% select(A1:C5) %>% longstring(),
       longstring_page2 = careless_df %>% select(E1:O5) %>% longstring(),
       longstring_page1_prop = longstring_page1 / 10,
       longstring_page2_prop = longstring_page2 / 15,
       longstring_max = pmax(longstring_page1, longstring_page2),
       # Intra-individual response variability and Mahalanobis distances
       longstring_prop_max=pmax(longstring_page1_prop, longstring_page2_prop),
       irv = irv(careless_df, split=TRUE, num.split=3),
       mahad = mahad(careless_df)
) %>%
       # Mean proportional longstring (separate due to tidy row-wise processing)
       rowwise() %>%
       mutate(longstring_prop_avg =
              mean(c(longstring_page1_prop, longstring_page2_prop)))
```

Missing Data

Missing data pose numerous problems during data cleaning. On one hand, a single missing value will halt many analyses that require it. For example, if you are regressing job performance on 15 potential predictors of job performance, any case missing even one of those values cannot be included. Thus there is a significant motivation to avoid this problem in order to maximize your usable sample size. On the other hand, the only way to address a missing value is to replace it with another number, one that you didn't actually collect, which can be risky in terms of the trustworthiness of your study's results. As a result, addressing missingness, just as with outliers, influential cases, and careless responders, is fairly subjective and lacks clear "correct" answers.

Unlike the previous issues we've explored, missingness itself is not a judgment call. Either the score exists or it does not. The problem instead is determining the *reason for* and *extent of* missingness, as that decision drives what follow-up is most appropriate. Similar to the other corrective practices, you will need to exercise your professional judgment to identify these aspects of missingness and decide what to do about it. The principal way to classify

First, we can classify missingness by cause and the relationship of that cause to study variables:

1. **Missing completely at random (MCAR).** This type of missingness has occurred when completely random chance factors cause missingness. For example, if every participant in your study flipped a coin before choosing whether to participate or not, and only participated if the coin turned up heads, assuming all coins were fair, your collected data would exhibit MCAR. Similarly, if you were concerned about the length of your survey and randomly assigned each half of your participants to complete one half of the items, their missing data would also be MCAR. As you might have noticed, MCAR is conceptually similar to random assignment. As such, it is also extremely uncommon in the wild. Typically, people skip questions for some *reason*. And if there is a reason, it's probably not MCAR.

2. **Missing at random (MAR)** or **ignorable missingness.** Justifying MAR is often the goal of missingness analysis, because concluding MAR justifies the use of a variety of analyses and adjustments to correct for it. MAR occurs when missingness is correlated with population values of variables contained within your dataset and when controlling for those variables leaves only data that are MCAR. For example, let's imagine you are evaluating a leadership training and development program for which you asked for volunteers to participate. As part of this study, you administered an extraversion questionnaire, because you anticipated that more extraverted people would be more likely to volunteer for your program. Sure enough, the mean extraversion score for your training is lower than the mean extraversion score for your organization. This has a variety of undesirable effects; for example, any correlation with extraversion in your observed data (and any relationship with any variable itself correlated with extraversion) will be attenuated (i.e., systematically smaller than its population value, or alternatively: "downwardly biased"). However, because you know the mean score that extraversion *should* have been, you can rescale it so that this value equals zero and then enter extraversion as a control variable in those analyses, allowing for the recovery of population values. In this way, controlling for extraversion addressed its missingness and produces more unbiased estimates of other effects related to it.

3. **Missing not at random (MNAR).** As you read that last example, you might have thought: "But wait a minute. How do we know extraversion was the cause of volunteerism? What if there was something else in addition to extraversion that we didn't know about?" This is MNAR territory. When people choose not to participate in your training in the real world, you probably won't know exactly why, which means missingness will be confounded with variables you are interested in measuring. Such data are MNAR, which is the most problematic among the three types of missingness, because there is a possibility for that missingness

effect to covary with the effects you are studying, yet it is impossible to diagnose just how big that missingness effect actually is. Its true score is unknown. In general, good research design is intended to prevent or at least discourage MNAR as much as possible.

The primary challenge with missingness, as you might have guessed, is that there's no way to actually verify the reason that data are missing. You must instead make a judgment call, and that judgment call will be based upon a few additional factors. Specifically, you should also consider the extent and importance of the missingness, regardless of its cause:

1. *Criterion missingness.* This is the most problematic way for missingness to occur. Historically, missingness researchers argued that you should never replace a missing criterion score (i.e., the outcome or dependent variable in your analysis) with a value you did not actually collect. Most analyses we use in I-O are based upon the general linear model, like regression or analysis of variance, which are designed around the idea of creating the best possible formula to predict a criterion. Thus, if you use predictor information to guess at the criterion value and then replace the missing criterion value with that guess, you can upwardly bias inferential test results if the data are not truly MAR or MCAR; in other words, you may observe statistical significance that is unjustified by your data. By assuming MAR, you may walk in a problematic direction in the garden of forking paths. However, this issue is not as clear cut as it might seem. One common approach to address criterion missingness, as we'll explore later, is deleting the entire case from the dataset. Yet this is not risk-free; you potentially throw out a lot of useful information and may bias observed effects through overzealous cleaning. In short, criterion missingness is not a clear-cut issue, and if you have extensive criterion missingness, we recommend reading Newman (2014) for more a more detailed treatment of this issue.

2. *Within-scale predictor missingness.* In contrast, within-scale predictor missingness is one of the easiest types of missingness to address. Within psychological scales, missingness sometimes occurs on individual items. However, because items within scales are all designed to address the same construct, and assuming that the scale was designed and tested according to the assumptions of classical test theory, a person skipping a small proportion of items is not so problematic. For example, imagine you have given a 10-item extraversion scale, and someone skips question #8. It's a reasonable assumption that something unique to question #8, and not unique to extraversion, caused the person to skip that question. Thus, missingness in this situation is generally assumed to be MAR.

3. *Scale-wise predictor missingness.* This type of missingness, which refers to missingness among most or all indicators of construct, is the most complicated to deal with. For example, let's imagine you gave that 10-item extraversion scale and someone skipped #1–#8, providing only two answers. Those two answers by definition will provide much less information and therefore a much less stable estimate of extraversion, making it less clear what to do with the result. Although this is still ultimately a judgment call, a common cutoff that has emerged is what we'll call **the 75% rule** – if 75% of scores within a scale are available, the scale score (after utilizing the specific cleaning strategies we will discuss later in this chapter) is usable. If it's less than 75%, it probably isn't.

For further reading on missingness, see:

Graham, J. W., Cumsille, P. E., and Elek-Fisk, E. (2003). Methods for handling missing data. In J. A. Schinka & W. F. Velicer (Eds.), *Handbook of psychology* (Vol. 2, pp. 87–114). John Wiley & Sons.

A Statistical Test for MCAR

Little (1988) introduced a statistical test for MCAR in multivariate data. The general idea is certainly an attractive one: run **Little's MCAR test**, and if it's statistically significant, you have evidence against MCAR. If you conclude that you do have MCAR, this knowledge simplifies your potential responses to missingness, as MCAR is assumed in many of the most straightforward data cleaning strategies. If you conclude you do not have MCAR, you must either have MAR or NMAR, so figuring out which it is should be your next step – and there's no test for that.

Cleaning Strategies

If you're now thinking, "If deciding data need to be corrected somehow is so subjective, surely what you do in response to all of these decisions is subjective too," well then you're starting to get the hang of data cleaning. Just as in detection, there is no single approved strategy for what to do with outlying, influential, low-effort, or missing cases. The safest thing you can do is articulate in your pre-registration a well-reasoned cleaning strategy or specific cleaning steps that you will take, selected among the following typical approaches as appropriate for your data, research questions, hypotheses, and particular data cleaning challenge.

CLEANING OUTLIERS AND INFLUENTIAL CASES

Outliers and influential cases are among the oldest identified data challenges in this list, and the techniques to address them are well-established. Despite this, there is little agreement on the "ideal" approach. As with all cleaning strategies, use your judgment.

- *Do nothing*. Perhaps the *easiest* strategy to address outlying and influential cases is simply to ignore the problem. This is also in some ways the most conservative choice as it reflects an axiom many people endorse: "the data are the data." In general, not "fiddling" with your data is seen as a safe choice. The risk with this approach is that outlyingness and influence, if due to non-random factors, could bias your effects either up or down.
- **Listwise deletion.** In the case of high influence or multivariate outlyingness, you might have a conceptual case to simply delete the case from your dataset, referred to as listwise deletion. Unfortunately, most outlyingness and influential cases are more ambiguous in their cause, and listwise is a very blunt instrument. Don't use it unless you are certain it's justified, and even then rarely.
- **Trimming.** Trimming refers to the replacement of outlying values in a dataset with values that are not outlying. For example, a 2% trimmed mean listwise deletes all scores exceeding the 2nd and 98th percentiles but at the analytic stage. Whereas an overall listwise

deletion strategy eliminates the cases from your dataset entirely, trimming excludes cases on an analysis-by-analysis basis. Regardless, it is still a blunt instrument; use with caution.

- **Winsorization.** Similar to trimming, Winsorization (named after one of its creators, Charles Winsor) identifies a specific percentile at which scores are considered problematic. However, instead of deleting them, they are replaced with the percentile cutoff. For example, 96% Winsorization involves the same scores as a 2% trimmed mean but handles then differently. Where the trimmed mean deletes cases, Winsorizing replaces scores above the 98th percentile with the score observed at the 98th percentile, and scores below the 2nd percentile are replaced with the 2nd percentile observed score. In this way, the original sample size is maintained but any analyses using these scores will be more robust to outliers. Winsorization to address outliers is also a generally uncontroversial approach, as long as the Winsorization is not very extreme (e.g., no less than 95%) and the data are normal.

CLEANING CARELESSNESS AND IER

When addressing IER, you are faced with a decision between considering only the parts of a person's data in which IER occurs to be problematic or to consider the entire case to be problematic. Broadly speaking, making individual, case-by-case decisions about the inclusion of particular variables from particular people probably opens a garden of forking paths you don't want to tread. Thus, we recommend generally approaching IER as a case-by-case problem rather than diving within cases. So what do you do with problematic cases?

- *Do nothing.* As with outliers, one can choose to ignore careless responders and proceed without cleaning their data. However, we view this as the riskier option; carelessness can wreak absolute havoc with your estimates in both directions, creating unexpected confounds and biasing effects in either direction. If you're interested in construct representations and their covariances – and if you're doing I-O research, you almost certainly are – you don't want carelessness to influence your effects. Thus, this approach wholesale is not recommended.
- *Listwise deletion.* Much like with outliers, careless responders should only be listwise deleted when cases are clearly and unambiguously problematic. For example, if a case's longstring is equal to the total number of items asked, that is, they responded with a "3" to literally every question, including the directed response and bogus items, that case should unambiguously be listwise deleted. In general, we recommend listwise deletion as your primary strategy to deal with IER, but recommend you be relatively conservative about it. For a worked example, see the earlier box entitled "Our Approach to Carelessness."
- *Score conversion to missingness.* Although we don't recommend it, if you did take a variable-by-variable approach to careless responding, one strategy to deal with those variables you suspect to be carelessly completed is to change those values to missing data. We only mention it here to explicitly recommend against it; this just compounds IER problems with missingness problems, which provides little empirical rationale for any decision you might make. As much as possible, don't walk in the garden!

CLEANING MISSINGNESS

Of all the corrective practices, missingness still has the most active research literature due largely to the commonness of missing data in "big data." In such datasets, sometimes 90%+ of the data in every case is missing, yet decisions need to be made about those cases. As a result, the approaches to address missingness presented here are much more volatile than in other situations. We give you a list of approaches that are "common" but this should in no way be considered an exhaustive list.

- *Listwise deletion*. For missingness, the question of listwise deletion is a little different than in the other two cases: is so much data missing that the case is unusable and unsalvageable? This should be considered a "final option" after all other potential approaches have been considered and explored, especially the ones we outline in the following.
- *Pairwise deletion*. People unhappy with listwise deletion sometimes suggest pairwise deletion as a replacement strategy, which is essentially listwise deletion on an analysis-by-analysis basis. The most clear sign of a pairwise deletion strategy to address missingness is a correlation matrix with different sample sizes across cells that vary by a few cases – most likely, each correlation is based upon a unique dataset. The main problem with pairwise deletion is as just stated – it is essentially listwise deletion with a twist! Thus it shares almost all of the same drawbacks. Again, this should only be used if there is a particular compelling rationale, and even then rarely.
- *Score ignorance*. In the case of within-scale predictor missingness, a common approach is simply to calculate the scale mean score without including missing items. For example, if someone skipped #8 on a 10-question scale, their mean would be calculated out of 9 scores. In general, we don't recommend this approach, because it throws away useful information unnecessarily.
- *Use a modeling approach that has its own missing data handling technique*. The most common of these is full information maximum likelihood (FIML) estimation, a technique for estimating parameter values when using structural equation modeling. These techniques tend to
- *Imputation*. Broadly speaking, imputation refers to the generation of predicted values for missing scores on the basis of statistical modeling. In other words, the remainder of the dataset that is not missing is used to predict scores that are missing, using techniques of varying sophistication. People often apply the 75% Rule to imputation, only imputing values for cases where this criterion is met. There are several common approaches to imputation, and the following list contains only a subset of them, but they are the ones you'll likely hear the most about:

  - **Median imputation.** The simplest approach, this replaces missing values with the across-all-cases median of that variable. Although this is fast to implement, its major downside is that it ignores correlations between items, and median imputation can still create an upward or downward bias in any calculations that involve that variable's mean. For categorical data, modal imputation is sometimes used instead.
  - **Single imputation.** One family of techniques for imputation involves the use of individual predicted values to replace missing ones. The core idea can be described quite simply: regress a variable with missing values on all other variables and use the resulting predictive formula to generate missing values. There are many variations on

imputation by regression to address specific problems with specific versions of the analysis. The simplest case, using ordinary least squares regression, is not generally a good choice, because so many of its assumptions will be violated that the predicted scores will be from a model so overfitted that those scores are no longer useful. Additionally, by calculating imputations one variable at a time, problems tend to compound upon each other. This problem is directly addressed in multiple imputation approaches.

- **Multiple imputation** via expectation-maximization or imputation-posterior methods. One key weakness of single imputation methods is that they don't consider the full dataset when making missing value predictions, making each variable's missing value imputation independent of what is done on other variables. To address this, as well as many of the other issues raised previously, multiple imputation generates missing values on a dataset-wide basis, using one of several different techniques to generate all missing values simultaneously, then repeats that analysis several times and reports on variations across the imputed versions. Because multiple imputation relies upon bootstrapping, which uses randomness as part of its data generation procedure, each imputed dataset is randomly different in its imputed values from other datasets using the same procedure. As a result, researchers using multiple imputation tend to take one of two approaches. First and more robustly, they might generate multiple imputed datasets (typically somewhere between 5 and 50), run all of their analyses on all of those datasets, and then combine the results from their analyses across all of those tests, which is called **pooling**. Second and less robustly (but much conceptually simpler) is to generate multiple imputed datasets, place them sequentially in a new datafile, then run your analysis on the resulting dataset, which is called **stacking**. This in effect weights your analysis by imputed dataset, since each case is now represented multiple times in your analysis. This approach biases and inflates standard errors, discards information about the differences between imputed datasets, and can't be used with categorical variables, but it does produce accurate parameter estimates. Importantly, multiple imputation techniques generally require multivariate normality.

- **Multivariate imputation by chained equations (MICE)**. MICE is a specific, complex multiple imputation technique for imputing missing values based on a long series of studies by Stef van Buuren and Groothuis-Oudshoorn (2011). If you want to use it, we recommend studying van Burren's work in much greater detail; we include it here just to demonstrate its flexibility and momentarily to provide you with sample code. Importantly, as you move into more complex forms of missing values imputation, there is a quickly growing number of settings for imputation that change the imputation values that you end up with. You should understand exactly what all of those settings do before committing to any particular imputation strategy to ensure you are setting them correctly. The primary disadvantage to MICE is its speed; even modestly sized datasets will take some time to impute.

- **k-nearest-neighbors (kNN)** or **random forests imputation**. kNN and random forests are machine learning techniques that can be used to make predictions of multivariate missing data, using the rest of the variables in the dataset as predictors and the variable showing missingness as the criterion. These techniques are actually variations on single-variable single imputation, as each variable is imputed one at a time; however, the use of machine learning overcomes some problems associated with single imputation by ordinary least square regression related to assumptions violations (which these machine learning techniques are generally robust to). Machine-learning-based single imputation is generally considered the "good enough" option in data science circles, considering its dramatically greater speed than multiple imputation, especially with "big data," but increased accuracy beyond traditional single imputation approaches. Additionally, kNN and random forests don't require multivariate normality, which is generally needed for accurate multiple imputation.

Quantifying and Handling Missingness Using R

In this demonstration, we'll show you how to detect and handle missingness. The most complicated issues arise here related to imputation. Because new approaches to imputation are appearing with some regularity, new R libraries also keep appearing. For simplicity, we provide a demonstration of only the techniques we've listed previously. However, you should consider for yourself if these techniques make the most sense to you given your project requirements and then ensure you always pre-register your intent to use that technique. Once again, we'll use the BFI dataset from *psych*, but this time, we'll take a look at all of the BFI items.

```
library(psych)
library(tidyverse)
missing_df <- select(bfi, A1:O5)

# How many cases have some missingness?
nrow(missing_df) - sum(complete.cases(missing_df))

# How much missingness is there overall and within each scale?
for_listwise_df <- missing_df
for_listwise_df$missingAll <- rowSums(is.na(for_listwise_df))
for_listwise_df$missingA <- rowSums(is.na(select(for_listwise_df,A1:A5)))
for_listwise_df$missingC<-rowSums(is.na(select(for_listwise_df,C1:C5)))
for_listwise_df$missingE<-rowSums(is.na(select(for_listwise_df,E1:E5)))
for_listwise_df$missingN<-rowSums(is.na(select(for_listwise_df,N1:N5)))
for_listwise_df$missingO<-rowSums(is.na(select(for_listwise_df,O1:O5)))
table(for_listwise_df$missingAll)
table(for_listwise_df$missingA)
table(for_listwise_df$missingC)
table(for_listwise_df$missingE)
table(for_listwise_df$missingN)
table(for_listwise_df$missingO)

# Listwise deletion using 75% rule
listwise_df <- filter(for_listwise_df, missingA < 2, missingC < 2,
                      missingE < 2, missingN < 2, missingO < 2)
nrow(for_listwise_df) - nrow(listwise_df) # cases deleted

# Scale ignorance
ignored_df <- missing_df %>%
```

```
  rowwise() %>%
  mutate(A.mean = mean(c_across(A1:A5), na.rm=T),  # notice use of na.rm to
         C.mean = mean(c_across(C1:C5), na.rm=T),  # ignore missing
                                              values
         E.mean = mean(c_across(E1:E5), na.rm=T),
         N.mean = mean(c_across(N1:N5), na.rm=T),
         O.mean = mean(c_across(O1:O5), na.rm=T))
# Median imputation
library(caret)
imputed_median_df <-
  predict(
    preProcess(missing_df, "medianImpute"),
    missing_df)
nrow(missing_df) - sum(complete.cases(missing_df))

# Multiple imputation via bootstrapped expectation maximization
library(Amelia)
library(Zelig)
amelia_results <- amelia(missing_df, m=5)          # creates 5 imputed
                                                     datasets
EM_imputed_df <- amelia_results$imputations[[1]]   # extract the first to
                                                     look at
zelig(A1 ~ A2 + A3 + A4,                            # regression with
                                                     pooled MI

      model="ls",
      data=EM_imputed_df)

# Multivariate imputation by chained equations (MICE)
library(mice)
mice_results <- mice(missing_df, m=5)              # creates 5 imputed
                                                     datasets
mice_imputed_df <- complete(mice_results, 1)       # extract the first
                                                     to look at
mice_stacked_df <- complete(mice_results, .        # stacked MI
                            "long")
mice_reg_stacked <- lm(A1 ~ A2 + A3 + A4,          # regression with
                                                     stacked MI data

                       data=mice_stacked_df)
summary(mice_reg_stacked)                          # ignore  p-values,
                                                     SEs, etc
mice_reg_pooled <- with(mice_results,              # regression with
                        lm(A1 ~ A2 + A3 + A4))       pooled MI
summary(pool(mice_reg_pooled))

# Single imputation using kNN
library(caret)
imputed_knn_df <-
  predict(
```

```
    preProcess(missing_df, "knnImpute"),          # note kNN will
                                                    standardize data

    missing_df)

# Single imputation using random forests
library(missRanger)
imputed_ranger_df <- missRanger(missing_df)
```

Putting It All Together

So that's a lot, right? Data cleaning can involve literally hundreds of little decisions, which is why most people end up inheriting their data cleaning practices from their advisors. To aid you in your journey to develop data cleaning procedures that make sense to you, what follows is a summary of the steps we take in each study related to data cleaning for experimental or correlational studies. If you are conducting archival research, such as on organizational data, some of these steps won't apply quite the same way, but the general order of steps is the same.

1. Create your study design and all materials. Include bogus items and directed response items, if you'll be using them for IER detection.
2. Develop an a priori handling strategy for outliers, influential cases, IER, and missingness given the guidelines in this chapter.
3. Create a draft codebook, and also a logbook if in-person data collection will occur.
4. Do an initial check through all materials to see if anything can be automated or simplified before testing begins.
5. Begin systematic alpha testing yourself. Try literally every button, every page, every click. Every everything. Take notes and make changes. Then test again. Update the codebook with every change. Download the alpha dataset and compare with notes. After you're happy with your own testing, invite other people to complete your study. Instruct them to take meaningful data as relevant to the study. Cross-check with actual collected data. Refine the codebook. Refine other study materials to make instructions clearer.
6. When happy with alpha testing, conduct beta testing – just the first 10 participants. Don't analyze the data for hypothesis tests. Just be sure everything is *working*. Do numbers appear in all the places they are supposed to appear? Does text? Did anyone email you angrily to complain? If you're collecting a very large dataset (e.g., 500+), also consider repeating this test at $N = 50$, but only to check for univariate and multivariate normality. Don't run any meaningful analysis related to your hypotheses or research questions until your planned samples size is collected.
7. Once happy with beta testing, file your pre-registration with all of your final materials and procedures etched in stone. The goal at this point is to set things up so that you will not need to deviate from your pre-registered plan from this point forward. If you aren't confident it's ready, don't proceed.
8. With pre-registration filed, run your study! Collect all of your data! It's a research-o-rama!

9. Once all data have been collected, listwise delete people from your dataset who did not actually complete the study. If they didn't reach the end, we generally interpret that as a withdrawal of consent. Don't even look at people's data who withdrew consent. Also listwise delete people who weren't qualified (e.g., if they were under your age limit or failed some other inclusion criterion).

10. Implement your careless responding detection and handling strategy. Always do this first, because outliers, influential cases, and missingness handlings will all be affected by the inclusion of data that appears complete but is actually flawed. After this stage, you should only have people who completed your study and put in the minimum effort needed to do so in your dataset (see the boxes titled, "Our Approaches to Carelessness" and "IER Detection Using R").

11. Implement your missingness strategy next. After this point, you should have people who completed your study, put in the minimum effort, and imputed or otherwise addressed missing values across your dataset. We generally default to pooled MICE (see the box titled, "Quantifying and Handling Missingness in R"), mostly because its implementation of pooling in R is less clunky than Amelia's. If you're a little lucky, you may even have perfect representation of all scores across all cases after this stage (i.e., if you were able to reasonably and technically impute all missing values), which makes things much easier at the analytic and reporting stages of your project. Don't force it though; stick to your plan. Don't miss the forest for the trees.

12. Implement your univariate and multivariate outlier handling strategy. We generally take the "do nothing" approach at this stage, except for earlier use of Mahalanobis distances for IER detection. Our plan usually involves a visual inspection, and unless things look catastrophic (i.e., enough for you to think "maybe I should just throw out these data without analyzing them and try again"), we leave the data alone.

13. Now you're ready to analyze your data (according to your pre-registered analytic plan!). Importantly, *don't go back to prior steps unless you majorly messed something up*. Remember that the purpose of this careful ordering of steps is to not only prevent you from heading into the garden of forking paths but to prevent even the temptation of doing so. Make a well-considered plan and stick to it as much as possible. For every deviation, report it clearly and transparently. For more on transparent reporting, we'll be revisiting these open science concepts in our discussion of sharing research with others in Chapter 14.

References

Carney, D. (2016). *My position on "power poses"*. https://faculty.haas.berkeley.edu/dana_carney/pdf_my%20position%20on%20power%20poses.pdf

Fiedler, K., & Schwarz, N. (2016). Questionable research practices revisited. *Social Psychological and Personality Science, 7*(1), 45–52.

Gelman, A., & Fund, K. (2016, January 19). The power of the "power pose". *Slate*. https://slate.com/technology/2016/01/amy-cuddys-power-pose-research-is-the-latest-example-of-scientific-over-reach.html

Gelman, A., & Loken, E. (2013). *The garden of forking paths: Why multiple comparisons can be a problem, even when there is no "fishing expedition" or "p-hacking" and the research hypothesis was posited ahead of time*. https://osf.io/n3axs/download

Gelman, A., & Loken, E. (2014). The statistical crisis in science: Data-dependent analysis. A "garden of forking paths", explains why many statistically significant comparisons don't hold up. *American Scientist, 102*(6).

John, L. K., Loewenstein, G., & Prelec, D. (2012). Measuring the prevalence of questionable research practices with incentives for truth telling. *Psychological Science, 23*(5), 524–532.

Little, R. J. A. (1988). A test of missing completely at random for multivariate data with missing values. *Journal of the American Statistical Association, 83*(404), 1198–1202. https://doi.org/10.2307/229 0157

Newman, D. A. (2014). Missing data: Five practical guidelines. *Organizational Research Methods, 17,* 372–411.

Peters, M. (2016, October 1). "Power poses" co-author: "I do not believe the effects are real". *NPR.* www.npr.org/2016/10/01/496093672/power-poses-co-author-i-do-not-believe-the-effects-are-real

van Buuren, S., & Groothuis-Oudshoorn, K. (2011). MICE: Multivariate imputation by chained equations in R. *Journal of Statistical Software, 45*(1), 1–67. https://doi.org/10.18637/jss.v045.i03

van der Zee, T., & Reich, J. (2018). Open education science. *AERA Open, 4*(3), 1–15.

Further Reading

Unlike the content in previous chapters, there are extremely diverse perspectives on what kinds of cleaning are acceptable and which represent fundamental mistakes and QRPs. As a result, in this chapter, we will simply present some of the papers we've found most thought provoking and helpful to our own research here. We share an illustrative quote from each to help you decide if you want to dive deeper.

General Recommendations

- Aguinis, H., Hill, N. S., & Bailey, J. R. (2021). Best practices in data collection and preparation: Recommendations for reviewers, editors, and authors. *Organizational Research Methods, 24,* 678–693.
    - "Insufficient methodological transparency is a detriment to practice as well. Namely, untrustworthy methodology is an insuperable barrier to using the findings and conclusions to drive policy changes or inform good managerial practices" (p. 679).
- Behrens, J. T. (1997). Principles and procedures of exploratory data analysis. *Psychological Methods, 2,* 131–160.
    - "In EDA, the goal is not to draw conclusions regarding guilt and innocence but rather to investigate the actors, generate hunches, and provide preliminary evidence. EDA is more like an interrogation in which clean and corrupted stories are told, whereas CDA is testimony regarding evidence that fits carefully laid-out trial procedures" (p. 133).
- DeSimone, J. A., & Harms, P. D. (2018). Dirty data: The effects of screening respondents who provide low-quality data in survey research. *Journal of Business and Psychology, 33*(5), 559–577.
    - "Kyle and Jane respond without considering the content of the items. Kate and Henry respond in accordance with their beliefs about how the questions will be scored and used. All four participants seem unconcerned with providing responses that accurately reflect their self-perceptions of character strengths. . . . Should Dr. Smith use the data provided by Kyle, Jane, Kate, and Henry?" (p. 560).
- Smith, P., Budzeika, K., Edwards, N., Johnson, S., & Bearse, L. (1986). Guidelines for clean data: Detection of common mistakes. *Journal of Applied Psychology, 71,* 457–460.
    - "Anticipate Murphy's Law. The suggested guidelines are intended to circumvent the inevitability of disaster (i.e., "Whatever can go wrong will, and at the worst possible moment.") The suggested

methods for the detection of errors are listed in Table 1. Their use, together with participation and planning in the research, and proper labeling and storing of data, may avoid common mistakes in the handling of data" (p. 460).

Missing Data

- Graham, J. W. (2009). Missing data analysis: Making it work in the real world. *Annual Review of Psychology, 60*, 549–576.
  - "Try to move away from the fear of missing data and attrition. Situations will occur in which missing data and attrition will affect your research conclusions in an undesirable way. But don't fear that eventuality. Embrace the knowledge that you will be more confident in your research conclusions, either way. Don't see this possible situation as a reason not to understand missing data issues. Focus instead on the idea that your new knowledge means that when your research conclusions are desirable, you needn't have the fear that you got away with something. Rather, you can go ahead with the cautious optimism that your study really did work" (p. 573).
- Schlomer, G. L., Bauman, S., & Card, N. A. (2010). Best practices for missing data management in counseling psychology. *Journal of Counseling Psychology, 57*(1), 1–10.
  - "The scientist–practitioner model is the foundation upon which training and practice are constructed. If science is to accurately inform practice, it must not ignore such an important element of good science as accounting for the missing data that is so commonly found in research. Just as researchers routinely screen and clean their data prior to analysis and gather descriptive data about their samples, they should make missing data analysis part of the systematic first steps in data analysis" (p. 8).
- Parent, M. C. (2013). Handling item-level missing data: Simpler is just as good. *The Counseling Psychologist, 41*(4), 568–600.
  - "There have been calls for the use of sophisticated and complex methods to handle missing data (Schlomer et al., 2010). Such calls are perhaps spurred on by advances in computational power and software accessibility that enable analyses that may have taken hours of dedicated mainframe time in the past to now be completed in seconds on a personal computer. Calls . . . are encouraging insomuch as they speak to the importance of, and the eagerness of researchers to use, the best available nascent methodologies. However, there is a potential limitation if these complex methods are not necessary" (p. 569).

Questions to Think About

1. Why is data cleaning so controversial? How will you navigate this controversy in your own research?
2. How will you tell the difference between when you've undercleaned versus overcleaned your data?
3. What general steps can you take a) before and b) after data collection to ensure you end up with clean data?
4. What information should you keep in a codebook? Why?
5. Does pre-registration prevent poor-quality research from being published? Why or why not?
6. How can careless responding be detected? Which methods will you use?
7. A researcher collects data on the effects of a goal setting intervention in an authentic organization in which small groups discussions were organized weekly so that teams could check in with each other and decide on the next week's goals. But after

collecting all the data, she notices some irregularities – some data are missing for one group, after the third (of four) weeks of the program. She inquires with the company and learns that in the fourth meeting, everyone got very angry about some aspect of the discussion. There were raised voices and a lot of threats. Afterward, the company decided to shut that group down. But you still do have partial data for their group, collected during the first three meetings. They were in the experimental group. What would you do here, and why?

Key Terms

- 75% rule (in missingness analysis)
- acceptance testing
- ad-hoc testing
- bogus item
- camel case
- codebook
- Cook's distance
- data
- data dictionary
- data fabrication
- difference in fits (DFITS)
- documentation
- engineer
- feature
- feature identifiers
- fraud
- functional testing
- garden of forking paths
- hypothesizing after results are known (HARK)
- ignorable missingness
- imputation
- influential cases
- intraindividual response variability (IRV)
- k-nearest-neighbors (kNN) imputation
- listwise deletion
- Little's MCAR test
- LongString
- Mahalanobis distance
- median imputation
- metadata
- missing at random (MAR)
- missing completely at random (MCAR)
- missing not at random (MNAR)
- multiple imputation
- multivariate imputation by chained equations (MICE)
- multivariate outlier
- omission
- open science
- outlier
- p-hacking
- pairwise deletion
- pooling
- pre-registration
- psychometric synonyms and antonyms
- questionable research practice (QRP)
- random forests imputation
- replication crisis
- single imputation
- stacking
- style guide
- trimming
- Tukey's (1977) fences
- univariate outlier
- usability

Part IV

Advanced Topics

Null Hypothesis Significance Testing and Reasonable Alternatives

Learning Objectives

After reading this chapter, learners will be able to:

1. Describe and critique the assumptions of null hypothesis significance testing
2. Calculate p-values and effect sizes
3. Conduct a power analysis
4. Contrast NHST with alternatives such as Bayesianism, data mining, and machine learning

In March 2019, three researchers decided to stage a revolt. They published a commentary in the super-prestigious journal, *Nature*, titled "Retire Statistical Significance" (Amrhein et al., 2019), accompanied by a list of 854 co-signers across 52 countries. Their argument was that p-values are ruining science, ruining logic, and causing us to miss important discoveries. The authors' concern was that real-world meaningful effects were being ignored because they were not associated with statistical significance.

On the other hand, the widely beloved quantitative psychologist Greg Hancock frequently tells a story about listening to a presentation from animal scientists who were testing out new eye drops for cows. They gave the eye drops to three cows, and then kept three cows as a control and concluded that since none of the three cows developed side effects, the eye drops were safe. He found this conclusion highly questionable because there is no way that a small sample of six cows could have generated statistically significant results.

So, what is the essence of the issue at hand? What are p-values and statistical significance, and do we need them?

As one of the so-called inexact sciences, I-O psychology research will always rely on probabilistic reasoning to draw conclusions. Put another way, for reasons discussed in Chapter 1, we tend not to make claims about definite truth, but probable truth. What is most likely to be true given all available evidence and reasoning?

As you've seen across previous chapters, the strength of claims about truth has a lot to do with how you have designed your study and collected your evidence. Commonly, underlying all of these choices for many I-O psychologists is a way of thinking called **null hypothesis significance testing (NHST)**. NHST is a particular logical setup that allows researchers to make probabilistic claims about truth.

DOI: 10.4324/9781315167473-16

Right up front, we need to emphasize that NHST is one of the most misunderstood and misused concepts in research methods. If you took an undergraduate statistics course, we're willing to bet that you have some understanding of the phrase "$p < .05$" that isn't totally correct. We also need to emphasize that NHST is only one way of thinking about probability. In this chapter, we will introduce and analyze the components of NHST and then offer some alternatives that can be more precise and more descriptive.

As you consider the discussion in this chapter, always keep this goal in mind: we employ probabilistic reasoning to extrapolate beyond the data we have in front of us to make a guess about what might be true elsewhere. We want to make generalizable claims, as discussed in Chapter 8. Any system of statistical inference you use must be used in service of that goal. It should never be used as a way to simply check a box and claim, "my research finding is real and important."

The History of NHST

NHST has a long and controversial history. In the early 20th century, Ronald Fisher developed many of the basic concepts and techniques of NHST, including the null hypothesis, the test statistic, and the p-value, as well as several specific tools for conducting NHST, including analysis of variance and the t-test. He believed that NHST could be used to make objective decisions about the significance of research findings, and he advocated for its widespread use in scientific research.

Fisher's ideas were not universally accepted, however, and many statisticians and scientists criticized NHST for its limitations and potential for misuse. One of the main criticisms of NHST is that it is based on a binary decision-making framework (i.e., reject or fail to reject the null hypothesis), which they suspected would lead to oversimplified interpretations of research findings. That prediction has come true; conclusions related to NHST in many research literatures, including I-O, are often inaccurately drawn. Others criticized Fisher and his work based on his interest applying it to genetics and human variation in intelligence, especially his personal associations with the eugenics movement. Despite issues with both the substance of Fisher's ideas and his personal views, NHST became and remains the dominant statistical paradigm in quantitative psychology research.

For readers who want to learn more about this period of history and the views of Fisher, we recommend this summary:

Bodmer, W., Bailey, R. A., Charlesworth, B., Eyre-Walker, A., Farewell, V., Mead, A., & Senn, S. (2021). The outstanding scientist, R. A. Fisher: His views on eugenics and race. *Heredity*, *126*, 565–576. https://doi.org/10.1038/s41437-020-00394-6

The Earth Is Round ($p < .05$): The Logic of NHST

The title of this section is the same as the title of a famous paper by legendary methodologist Jacob Cohen, in which he argued that the traditional threshold of $p < .05$ for statistical significance was arbitrary and not based on a solid scientific foundation. He advocated for a greater emphasis on effect sizes, confidence intervals, and meta-analysis, which he believed would provide a more accurate and meaningful way to assess the evidence for or against a particular hypothesis. He wrote:

> Consider the following: A colleague approaches me with a statistical problem. He believes that a generally rare disease does not exist at all in a given population, hence Ho: P = 0.

He draws a more or less random sample of 30 cases from this population and finds that one of the cases has the disease, hence p = 1/30 = .033. He is not sure how to test Ho, chi-square with Yates's (1951) correction or the Fisher exact test, and wonders whether he has enough power. Would you believe it? And would you believe that if he tried to publish this result without a significance test, one or more reviewers might complain? It could happen.

(p. 997)

Cohen's argument is that samples, distributions, and inferential tests are not needed in this case–some research questions are structured in a way that does not require NHST logic. In his example, a single instance of the disease disproves the idea that the disease doesn't exist. Yet it self-evidently exists, simply because a case was observed, absent any statistical test.

In some cases, research questions concern the existence of a phenomenon in a population. For example, you might ask, "are there any female narcissist CEOs?" When phrased this way, a single instance of a female narcissist CEO is sufficient to answer the question definitively: yes. Once a single positive case is identified, no number of negative cases will undo that finding and statistical inference is not needed. Similarly, a question that is phrased in the form "all X are Y" can be disproven with a single case of X that is not Y. We (Tara and Richard) have not seen any research questions of this form in the I-O psychology literature lately; I-Os generally heavily emphasize statistical inference. But we'd be excited to see a creative thinker ask a research question of this nature, relying on logical inference instead of statistical inference.

In I-O practice, automatically leaning toward statistical inference as your primary tool for decision-making can be misleading for executives or even harmful for employees. For example, imagine you are asked by your CEO to determine if people are dissatisfied with their jobs. You run a study collecting job satisfaction data from every employee in the company, $N = 30$. You find a mean of 3.1 on a 5-point scale, meaning that the average response is slightly above "neither satisfied nor dissatisfied." You run a directional one-sample t-test comparing 3.1 to 2 (mean score of "dissatisfied") and fail to reject the null hypothesis, concluding "people are not dissatisfied." However, this is a flatly incorrect conclusion for two reasons. First, an inferential test in this situation is unnecessary, because you just collected data from the entire population; you now know the satisfaction level of every employee in the company. Second, even a single item with a score below 3 suggests that at least one employee is dissatisfied about something, and that's what the CEO asked you to investigate – not statistical significance.

Cases like this are rare in I-O research and practice. In most cases, we ask questions about the strength of relationships or the effects of interventions on populations we don't have access to. When we can only sample from a population (recall Chapter 4) yet want to make conclusions about that population, we need some kind of inference. If we use NHST, we particularly need to know if we have sampled a large enough number of people to make a high-quality inference. This requires an understanding of distributions, which we review next.

A Refresher on Distributions

A **distribution** is a shorthand way we describe the shape and spread of a dataset or population. Using 5-point Likert scale data, we might expect to see any of the kinds of distributions in Figure 12.1, which are:

- Rectangular: equal numbers of each response category
- Normal: Peak in the middle with symmetrically decreasing numbers of more extreme responses

- Inverse normal: Valley in the middle with symmetrically increasing numbers of more extreme responses
- Skewed: Peak at high or low end with gradually decreasing numbers moving away from that end
- Bimodal: Two peaks with lower frequencies between the peaks
- Irregular: Some other shape besides the ones described previously

Although the y-axis in these distributions reflect case counts (e.g., 5 indicates 5 cases), we can also express these numbers as proportions of total sample size (e.g., 5 of 16 cases = .31). In that format, the sum of all the displayed proportions will always equal 1, because 100% of cases are represented in the distribution. If we were selecting a case at random from the irregular distribution shown in Figure 12.1 (bottom-right), there is therefore a 5/16 = 31% chance of drawing a 1, a 4/16 = 25% chance of drawing a 2, a 2/16 = 13% chance of drawing a 3, a 4/16 = 25% chance of drawing a 4, and a 1/16 = 6% chance of drawing a 5.31 + 25 + 13 + 25 + 6 = 100, as expected.

When we draw a line connecting such probabilities as shown in Figure 12.2, the shaded area underneath it is referred to as the **area under the curve**. In a rectangular distribution, the area under each point is 20% of the whole area, so the probability of observing any particular response is 20%. When the distribution is made of discrete values, like in this example, the area under the curve at any one point is easy to conceptualize.

It is slightly more difficult to apply this to distributions that represent continuous data, because each observed value (e.g., 3.15) may be unique; it is no longer helpful to count such values. So instead of talking about particular values, we can talk about ranges of values. In the continuous distribution in Figure 12.2, the proportion of the overall distribution occupied by the darker shaded region to the right represents the probability of obtaining a score of *9 or above*.

Normal distributions have several useful properties that make them central to NHST. Most importantly, the probabilities associated with a normal distribution are always the same regardless of the original data used to create the distribution. In Figure 12.3, you can

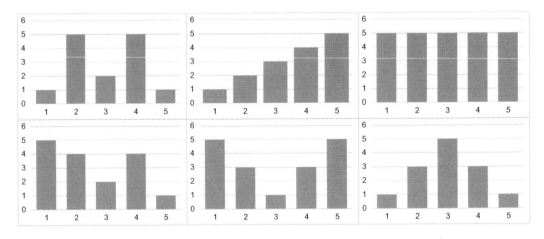

Figure 12.1 Distributions; clockwise from top-right: rectangular, normal, inverse normal, irregular, bimodal, skewed.

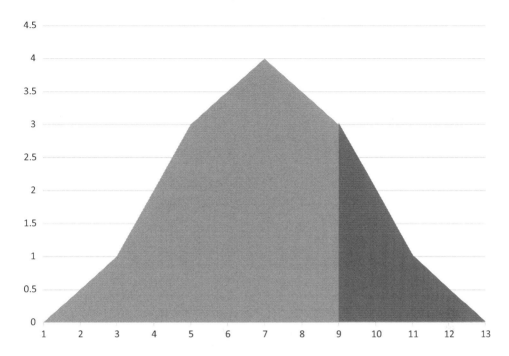

Figure 12.2 An (approximately) normal distribution.

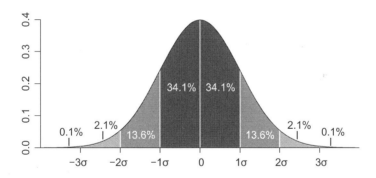

Figure 12.3 Areas under the curve for a normal distribution of IQ scores (mean = 100, sd = 15).

see these probabilities superimposed onto a normal distribution of IQ scores (mean = 100, SD = 15). In this case, you can infer that the probability of having an IQ over 100 is 50%, and the probability of having an IQ over 130 is 2.5%.

The logic of NHST rests on how these probabilities are observed after sampling a population, which is described by the **central limit theorem**, one of the most central concepts in statistical theory. The most important implications of this theorem for NHST are that if we were to sample a population an infinite number of times, 1) the mean of the resulting **sampling distribution** (i.e., the distribution of sample means) should be equal to the population mean, and 2) regardless of the distribution of the original data, the sampling distribution should approximate a normal distribution. NHST assumes this to be true, regardless of what the sample data actually look like and regardless of what the shape the sampling distribution actually is. This is a necessary assumption in NHST logic, because we cannot actually collect infinite samples. By making this assumption, we can estimate the probability of a particular sample mean being drawn from a particular sampling distribution, which is called a p-value.

With this statistical background in mind, we can start engaging in some hypothetical thinking. We cannot observe a sampling distribution, but we can imagine it fairly precisely, given a few assumptions. For instance, we know because of the central limit theorem that the standard deviation of a sampling distribution should be equal to the standard deviation of a sample drawn from it divided by the square root of $N - 1$. Thus, measuring the standard deviation of a sample allows us to estimate the standard deviation of the (population) sampling distribution. This number is also called the **standard error**.

Now let's imagine a population distribution with a mean of 100, like the one shown in Figure 12.3. When we collect a sample of $N = 30$ from this population, we find a sample mean of 102.79 and a standard deviation of 15. This allows us to estimate the standard error at $15/\text{sqrt}(30 - 1) = 2.79$. If we assume the sampling distribution is normally distributed, as suggested by the central limit theorem, we can now map our observation of 102.79 onto a specific probability using the probabilities illustrated in Figure 12.2. In this case, 102.79 is exactly 1 standard error greater than 100. Thus, $13.6 + 2.1 + 0.1 = 15.8\%$ of sample means are greater or equal to 102.79 in the sampling distribution.

In psychology research using NHST, we use this logic to ask a question about whether a particular relationship or effect exists. In more specific terms, we ask if that relationship or effect is zero or not zero. For example, we might believe that a training intervention we created has a non-zero effect. In this case, we imagine a world in which the population d-value effect was zero ($\Delta = 0$), which we call the **null hypothesis**, and then we calculate the probability that our study's observed effect size would have been sampled from that population. For example, a p-value of .20 suggests that in a world where all training interventions have no effect, 20% of training interventions would have still found an effect as large as the one we found in our study, due to chance alone (or, put another way, 20% of sample means under the curve of the sampling distribution are greater than the observed sample mean).

Thus, the null hypothesis at the center of all NHST states that the population parameter you are interested in, whether it's a correlation, mean, different score, or whatever else, is *precisely* zero. When you report a p-value, you are reporting the likelihood of observing your sample statistic if that null hypothesis were true.

Consider this example. You measure the salaries of 10 men and women working at TNT Corp, a company that has many employees but keeps terrible records. The data we have are shown in Table 12.1.

What you want to know is: is there a salary gap between the genders in this organization? To put this into the language of null hypothesis significance testing, I instead ask myself: if there were no salary gap in the organization overall (i.e., the population), how likely is it that I would have observed a gap as big or bigger as I did in this sample of 10 people?

Note that in order for this logic to make sense, the 10 people have to be representative of the overall organization, as discussed in Chapter 4. If I selected the 10 newest employees, or the 10 tallest, or the 10 who were most willing to answer my questions, I do not have a representative sample, and the assumptions underlying NHST are not met. The sample I collect must be a random draw from the population I want to know about.

Table 12.1 Example salary and gender data

Employee	Gender	Salary (in thousands)
1	F	83
2	F	88
3	F	51
4	F	57
5	F	80
6	M	75
7	M	76
8	M	91
9	M	102
10	M	101

Additionally, there must be a good reason to believe that the null hypothesis is a reasonable baseline – specifically, we must be willing to say if the population value is anything other than exactly zero, we therefore reject the null and embrace the alternative, that the population value is not zero. In our example, if the gender gap in salary in the population was $1, the "correct" conclusion to NHST would be to reject the null hypothesis, even if a $1 gender pay gap was not **practically significant**. Thus, a rejected null, also referred to as **statistical significance**, does not speak to the importance or practicality of an observed effect. It only speaks to probability given the complex network of assumptions explained here.

To dive deeper, we will next look at how to actually calculate *p*-values. This is a good time for a reminder, though. All the calculations in the world aren't worth anything if you aren't thinking about what the numbers mean. The purpose of the next section is not to teach you how to calculate – it's to teach you how to think, reason, and interpret. Don't fall into the trap of plugging numbers into your computer and reporting the results without asking yourself, "what am I really saying here?"

Common Misinterpretations of *p*-values

P-values are one of the most commonly misinterpreted statistics across all sciences. Consider the following lists of facts any time you try to interpret a *p*-value, both in your own research and in papers you're reading.

1. A *p*-value is the probability that a sample statistic or one more extreme could have been drawn from the distribution implied by an assumed null hypothesis.
2. A *p*-value is not the probability that the null hypothesis is true.
3. A *p*-value below .05 does not imply that an effect is "significant," because statistical significance and practical significance are different. Always specify what kind of significance you are talking about.
4. A *p*-value does not indicate the size or importance of an effect. A small *p*-value can be associated with a small effect, and a large *p*-value can be associated with a large effect.

5. A p-value cannot confirm a null hypothesis; you can only reject a null. When rejecting the null, you assume the alternative to the null must be true. But this is still an assumption.
6. A p-value is not more objective than any other statistic. A lot of assumptions and values go into a p-value.
7. Smaller p-values do not imply stronger evidence or larger effects than larger p-values.
8. Smaller p-values do not imply that a finding is more replicable than larger p-values.
9. p-values cannot be meaningfully compared to each other in isolation.
10. p-values alone should never be used to make decisions about hypotheses.

Calculating p-values

To illustrate the calculation of p-values, we'll do so in one of the simplest statistical tests common to psychology: an independent-samples t-test. For a more complete discussion of calculation and the peculiarities of specific tests, we recommend you consult a statistics textbook.

In the case of the data shown in Table 12.1, we might believe that population mean salaries for men and women are different and want to test this belief using the data collected. Using the logic of NHST, we first establish our null hypothesis, stated as Ho: The population mean salary for men equals the population mean salary for women, or $\mu1 = \mu2$. To test that the population means are different with our sample data, we follow a series of known steps to conduct an independent-samples t-test:

1. Calculate the mean and variance of each sample
2. Estimate the population variance (i.e., if we assume in the null hypothesis that the two samples are drawn from the same population, each is an independent estimate of the variance of that population)
3. Estimate the standard error of the difference between the means
4. Express the distance between the sample means in terms of how many standard errors apart they are, better known as a **t-statistic**

Typically, these steps are done for you when selecting the "t-test" button if you are using SPSS, Excel, or some other point-and-click analytic program. The underlying mathematics, however, are not complex and can also easily be done by hand. Going through the mathematics also help makes it more obvious what assumptions are being made. In this case:

1. Mean M = 71.8, var M = 276.7
   Mean F = 89, var F = 170.5
2. Pooled variance = (276.7 + 170.5)/2 = 223.6
3. Standard error M = 223.6/5 = 44.72
   Standard error F = 223.6/5 = 44.72
   Standard error of difference = sqrt(44.72 + 44.72) = 9.46
4. Mean difference = 89–71.8 = 17.2
   Mean difference in standard error of the difference units = t = 17.2/9.46 = 1.8

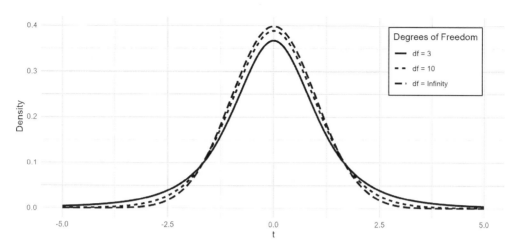

Figure 12.4 t-distributions.

The resulting t-statistic corresponds to a location on a sampling distribution, which is assumed to be normally distributed due to the central limit theorem. Unlike the standard normal distribution shown in Figure 12.3, t-distributions have thicker tails when sample sizes are smaller.

Once the t-statistic is calculated, the next step is to use integral calculus to calculate the area under the curve that is equal to or more extreme than the value of 1.8. We would hazard a guess that despite probably having calculated some t-tests and *p*-values before, you've probably never done this yourself. This is common in psychology graduate programs. Instead, we use software programs to do this calculus and determine the associated probability. In the era before software programs could do this quickly and easily, you needed to look up reference values in a table created by someone who did that calculus by hand. In this era, however, you should just remember that the *p*-value you get back from the software is the area under the curve of a region of a sampling distribution.

In our salary example, the resulting *p*-value is .053. This is above the threshold of .05 that people typically use to make accept/reject decisions for the null hypothesis in psychology, so most would at this point conclude that we cannot reject the null hypothesis and cannot conclude that men and women have different average salaries. We *should not* however conclude that men and women's salaries are the same in the population; a *p*-value cannot tell us that.

Interpreting *p*-Values in the Context of a Study

When a *p*-value is small, we interpret this to mean that "if the population mean was really zero, this score would be unlikely. So, it probably isn't zero." When we make this inference though, we understand that we might be wrong. Saying that something is unlikely doesn't mean that it is impossible. In fact it is definitely possible and will happen some percentage of the time. In an ideal world without *p*-hacking or QRPs, your willingness to accept this kind of error is something you control, conventionally set in psychology at 5%. We accept this possibility and accept that our conclusion might be wrong. We can be wrong in two ways:

A **Type I error** means that we have observed something that would be unlikely if the null was true, leading us to conclude the null isn't true. But the null actually is true. We have mistakenly identified a nonexistent effect. We set our willingness to accept a Type I error before running our study by picking an acceptable **Type I error rate**, which is commonly called **alpha** and conventionally set to .05 in psychological research.

A **Type II error** means that we have observed something that would be fairly likely if the null is true, so we accepted the null as true, but the null is actually false. We have missed a real effect. We set our willingness to accept a Type II error before running our study by picking an acceptable level of **power**, which is 1 – the **Type II error rate**, which is commonly called **beta** and conventionally set to .80, .90, or .95 in psychological research.

So which is worse, Type 1 or Type 2 error? The answer to this question depends entirely on what kind of effect you are looking for and what the consequences of your test will be. Let's say I'm looking to find out if a new, more expensive training program leads to better learning outcomes, and I make a Type 2 error. In reality the new program works better but I think it doesn't. My "cost" here is in missed opportunities for my employees to learn. On the other hand, if I make a Type 1 error – I conclude that the new program is better but they are really equal – my cost is wasted money on a new program that isn't any better than the old one. Which of these is worse? It depends entirely on the organization's tolerance for risk and waste.

Power

Throughout this book, we have emphasized the ways that seemingly "objective" analyses rely on researcher judgment. The estimation of power for NHST is another one of these ways that researchers make their best guess and then wrap that guess in numbers. The goal of power analysis is to set the probability of finding a significant effect, assuming one exists, before collecting any data. In other words, greater power means a lower probability of making a Type II error. This likelihood depends on the parameter being estimated, the type of statistical test in question, the size of the population, the size and variability of the sample, and the size of the true effect.

The tricky thing about power is that if you knew with confidence all the numbers you need to meaningfully calculate it, you wouldn't need any statistical tests at all, because you would already know the answer to your research question. Thus, setting power for a particular study is always best on estimation – your best guesses about the effect or effects that you are looking for.

Power and Type I error rate are represented visually in Figure 12.5. It is easiest to understand this figure by always remembering that only one of these distributions can be a true representation of the population distribution. Both cannot be relevant to a particular statistical test simultaneously, yet we don't know which is the correct one to reference, because we don't know what's going on in the population except via samples. Thus we always plan research as if either could be true.

The distribution on the left is the null distribution we've been discussing. If the null distribution is the true reflection of reality, there are only two valid conclusions: 1) a correct failure to reject the null when the p-value is observed greater than alpha, or 2) an incorrect rejection of the null when the p-value is observed less than alpha, which is a Type I error.

To the right of this distribution is a hypothetical distribution of the **alternative hypothesis,** which is the population sampling distribution that a parameter must have been drawn

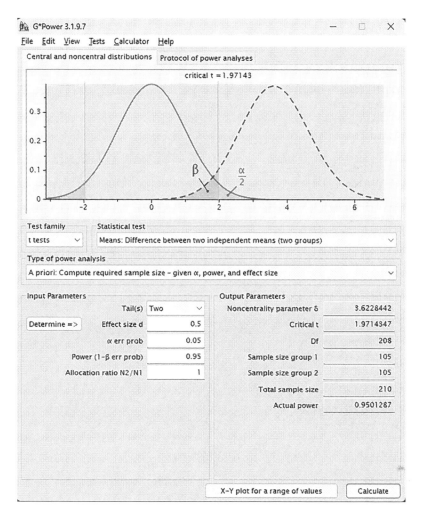

Figure 12.5 The interrelationship between power (β) and Type I error rate (α).

from if the null was *not* true. If the alternative distribution is true, there are only two valid conclusions: 1) an incorrect failure to reject the null when the *p*-value is observed greater than alpha, which is Type II error, or 2) a correct rejection of the null when the *p*-value is observed less than alpha.

In this image you can see that power will be greater if the distributions for the null and alternative hypotheses are further away from each other, which happens when the effect is larger. Power also depends on the shape and spread of the distribution. Power will also be greater when alpha is set to a larger value; you are less likely to find an effect at $\alpha = .001$ than when $\alpha = .05$. Thus these estimates become inputs to a **power analysis**.

Power analyses can be conducted before data collection begins, called **a priori power analysis**, to determine the needed sample size when you are planning your research. You can also conduct power analysis after the fact, post hoc, which is especially needed if you did not find significance and you want to estimate whether this finding is likely to be Type II error or a true lack of effect.

The more complicated the analytic approach, the more complicated the power analysis will be. As a starting point, we recommend **G*Power** as the preferred software to conduct a priori power analyses for basic analyses. G*Power is open-source and can be downloaded free from the G*Power website, www.psychologie.hhu.de/arbeitsgruppen/allgemeine-psychologie-und-arbeitspsychologie/gpower

An example of the G*Power interface is shown in Figure 12.6. In this example, power is being estimated for an independent-samples t-test. I have set alpha to .05 and power to .95. I have also estimated a true effect size of .5 standard deviations between the two population means. After pressing Calculate, the values in the "Output Parameters" are calculated and appear.

This output says that a sample of 210 people is needed to achieve 95% power, assuming a true difference of half a standard deviation between population means. As noted earlier, 95% is on the high end of set power in psychology; if we change power to .8, the required sample size decreases to 128. As you can see in Figure 12.7, a sample of 1000 people would still only have 40% power if the effect size was small, at $d = 0.1$. But a larger effect, $d = 0.5$, would likely be detected with fewer than 200 people.

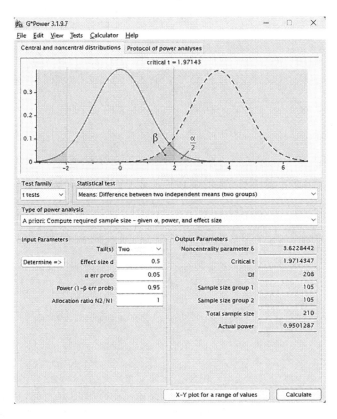

Figure 12.6 Basic G*Power analysis.

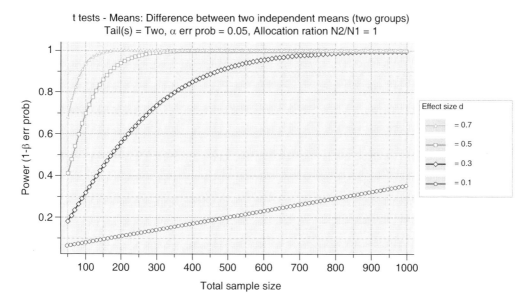

Figure 12.7 Power of an independent-samples t-test as a function of sample size and effect size when $a = .05$.

The most difficult part of power analysis is estimating how large of an effect size you should estimate. If you already knew the population value of the effect size you were studying, you would not need to collect data to study it. So instead, effect size for power analysis is always an educated guess. If you've done previous research on the same effect you're studying now, you might use the mean observed effect size across your prior research. If not, you might look at other researchers who've studied the same effect. If researchers have only previously studied *similar* effects, you might use those instead. Lacking anything better, you might even use benchmarks (see the inset later in this chapter titled "Effect Size Benchmarks").

The more uncertainty you have about the effect size you're trying to measure, the more strongly we recommend that you estimate power based on a range of different sources, and then choose a sample size based on a holistic judgment about all of the estimates you put together. In the previous example, I might have reason to think that the effect is somewhere between .3 and .7. As long as .3 is a reasonable lower bound, I can see that a sample size of approximately 350 would give me at least 80% power. This is the kind of reasoning often necessary in power analysis.

Power analysis gets more complicated as tests become more complicated. Every NHST test you conduct needs its own power analysis if you want to do things the right way. G*Power has preset menu functions for X2, F, and t-tests. More sophisticated power analyses require Monte Carlo simulations. A variety of R packages and apps now exist to assist with these analyses. For example, pwrSEM can be used to estimate power for SEM analyses. More detail about this package can be found here:

Wang, Y. A., & Rhemtulla, M. (2021). Power analysis for parameter estimation in structural equation modeling: A discussion and tutorial. *Advances in Methods and Practices in Psychological Science*, *4*(1). https://doi.org/10.1177/2515245920918253

Confidence Intervals

In a wonderful and rare example of researchers having a sense of humor, Richard Morey and his colleagues opened their 2015 paper about confidence intervals with a quote from the movie *Princess Bride*: "You keep using that word. I do not think it means what you think it means." So what are confidence intervals and what do most people think they mean?

Confidence intervals are based on NHST philosophy. A confidence interval assumes a sampling distribution around a sample estimate of a parameter and reports a range of plausible sample values given that parameter. For example, if you observed in a sample a correlation of .3 with a 95% confidence interval of [.2, .4], this tells you that if the true score correlation (ρ) were really .3, 95% of samples of same size as the one you collected would observe correlations between .2 and .4.

Much like NHST concepts broadly, confidence intervals are commonly misinterpreted. It is not accurate to say "I'm 95% confident that the true parameter is in this confidence interval." Researchers often try to use the width of an interval to make a claim about the precision of their estimate, but this is only half-true. Smaller confidence intervals are associated with larger sample sizes and therefore greater precision, but this does not imply that the value at the center of the confidence interval is truly a good estimate of a population parameter. Because confidence intervals are based in NHST logic, the claims you can make with a confidence interval are no different than those you can make with a *p*-value.

This means you should always be cautious when you hear the admitted common phrase, "we have 95% confidence that . . ." This phrase is a shorthand for something much more specific that is often not what the researchers imply: "Assuming our sample estimate is a perfect reflection of the population parameter, 95% of samples of the same size as ours, the same population, and the same research design would result in observed values within this range."

Confusion about confidence intervals is common. If you want to read more about this issue and see some examples of researchers engaging in spirited debate, read the following three papers:

- Morey, R. D., Hoekstra, R., Rouder, J. N., Lee, M. D., & Wagenmakers, E. J. (2015). The fallacy of placing confidence in confidence intervals. *Psychonomic Bulletin & Review*. https://learnbayes.org/papers/confidenceIntervalsFallacy/index.html
- Miller, J., & Ulrich, R. (2015). Interpreting confidence intervals: A comment on Hoekstra et al. (2014). *Psychonomic Bulletin & Review*, 23.
- Morey, R. D., Hoekstra, R., Rouder, J. N., & Wagenmakers, E. (2016). Continued misinterpretation of confidence intervals: response to Miller and Ulrich. *Psychonomic Bulletin & Review*, 23, 131–140. https://doi.org/10.3758/s13423-015-0955-8

Alternatives to NHST

Whenever you encounter NHST in research, be careful to revisit what such results actually tell us. It poses a single question: in a hypothetical world where a true effect is zero, would we expect to see an observed effect like the one we observed? An example for which this kind of inference is useful might be in interpreting the weather. Let's say it's a hot summer day. The temperature is 5 degrees above normal for this area. You say "gosh, I guess this is good evidence for climate change. The temperature is higher." Your skeptical friend, though, says in response, "5 degrees is normal fluctuation. I don't think this is beyond what would be normally expected assuming there is no climate change."

In this case, the null hypothesis is that there is no effect – no climate change. The NHST approach can determine whether a 5 degree fluctuation is big enough to be sufficiently unusual and noteworthy under those conditions. In this example, 1) the null hypothesis is interesting, 2) the pattern and distribution of temperature is well established, and 3) the point estimate of what the actual temperature change is less interesting than whether a change happened at all.

Do these conditions also apply for the kinds of questions that I-O psychologists really care about? In most cases, probably not. Take the first point: that the null hypothesis is actually interesting. In the social sciences, there are very few true zero effects. Most measurements we take will have some trivial correlations with each other.

For example, imagine any pair of personality traits. At all. Do you expect that if we were to somehow be able to measure every human being on Earth, that every was or ever will be, on those traits, that the true relationship between these traits would be equal to exactly zero? Given the weight of evidence psychology has collected so far, we can say with near-certainty that it is not. Almost every such population correlation is greater than zero, to some degree.

So to ask the question, "in a world where the true relationship between Trait X and Trait Y is zero, how likely is it that I'd observe a correlation of .15?" is fairly pointless. The associated p-value does not tell us anything we didn't know before we calculated it. We already know with near-certainty that the real relationship is not equal to zero. What we actually want to know is, *how big is the relationship? How much does this relationship matter? Is the change I've observed real? Will it happen again if I repeat my test under different conditions or with different people? Does it matter to organizational outcomes? Should it change the way we make decisions about people in organizations? Will it matter in the organization I'm trying to help right now?*

NHST, by design, will never tell us the answer to those questions. Yet we commonly apply it as if it will. Luckily, there is a better way. Several better ways in fact.

Effect Sizes

Most new researchers actually want to know how big an effect is. That is, they want to generate a quantitative estimate of **effect size**. Many measures of effect size exist, which are described in the following. Effect sizes are related to but distinct from statistical significance; larger population effects, all else equal, are more likely to be detected as statistically significant than smaller effects. However, a statistically significant finding alone does not imply a particular size of effect, nor does a large or small effect imply statistical significance.

There are three major types of effect sizes that you are likely to see: 1) those that summarize differences between groups, 2) those that summarize relationships between variables, and 3) probabilities or ratios of probabilities.

To understand the first type, imagine that you are studying selection. You want to know if hiring left-handed salespeople is a good idea, so you conduct a validation study, and you measure handedness and sales performance in dollars per month. Dollars is the unit of interest, and it is inherently meaningful and interpretable to the organization. Finding out that handedness is significantly related to sales is not sufficient – you'd want to know how many dollars more a left-handed person could be expected to bring in. The **mean difference** you observe between left- and right-handed people is an effect size summarizing the difference between these groups. If you find out that the mean difference is only 10 dollars per month, you'd probably decide that it isn't worth the cost of implementing this new measure into the selection system, regardless of statistical significance. You would instead conclude that the effect was not *practically significant*.

Mean differences are usually **unstandardized**, which means they are expressed in terms of the original measurement. In the previous example, the difference was measured in dollars. In contrast, **Cohen's *d*** is a type of standardized mean difference, meaning that the mean difference has been contextualized to make it comparable to other mean differences contextualized the same way. In the case of Cohen's *d*, this standardization involves expressing the unstandardized mean difference in standard deviation units.

To calculate Cohen's *d*, the following formula is used:

$$d = (\text{Mean1} - \text{Mean2})/\text{SD}$$

In the handedness example, let's use the following data:

Left-Hand mean sales in dollars:	$100,000
Right-Hand mean sales in dollars:	$99,000
Standard deviation of sales in dollars:	$10,000

To calculate Cohen's *d*:

$$d = (100,000–99,000)/10,000 = 1000/10000 = .1$$

If you were to put a Cohen's *d* value into a sentence, you might say "Left-handed people perform at one-tenth of one standard deviation greater than right-handed people, which translates to about $1000 more yearly on average."

The second major type of effect size is one that summarizes correlationships between variables. Although there are unstandardized effect sizes of this type, they are uncommon. Instead, the most common in I-O psychology is a standardized effect called a correlation coefficient (often shortened to simply "correlation"). There are many types of correlations with the most common in I-O being Pearson's *r*. However, there are many, many others, including Spearman's rho, tetrachoric correlations, polychoric correlations, phi coefficients, and intraclass correlations. Each of these effect sizes (and many others) is intended to summarize the magnitude of a relationship between two or more variables given certain rules and assumptions. For example, a Pearson's *r* summarizes the linear relationship between two continuous variables of interval or ratio level scale of measurement (see Chapter 7), whereas a Spearman's rho summarizes the linear relationship between two ordinal variables re-expressed as ranks. Because every effect size measure of this type brings different assumptions, you should be sure to learn the differences between the most common in your particular subdomain of I-O to know when to use each.

The third major type of effect size is a probability or a ratio of probabilities. We don't often encounter this kind of effect size in I-O except in a few specific contexts – the most common are when predicting low-frequency high-importance events like turnover or theft. We'll revisit all three types of effect size estimates, including this last type, in a bit more detail in Chapter 13's discussion of how effect sizes are meta-analyzed.

The choice of a meaningful effect size to describe a particular effect is an important one. One of the most obvious situations for this is the relationship between smoking and mortality. This correlation has been estimated as somewhere between .14 and .29 (Darden et al., 2018), which doesn't sound like a big effect at all. When converted to a Cohen's *d*, that range becomes 0.28 to 0.62 standard deviations, which gives a little bit better picture of importance. But when expressed as an unstandardized effect, we can see that smoking is associated with 4.3- to 9.3-year shorter lifespan. Expressed at another level of analysis, smoking is associated with 480,000 deaths per year in the United States alone. Although you are most likely not studying death as an I-O researcher, you should not underestimate the importance of reporting decisions like these – they can dramatically change the implications of your research.

Effect Size Benchmarks

Because numbers like .1 are difficult to contextualize on their own (is that big? How big should it be?" Various efforts over the years have attempted to create **effect size benchmarks**. Famed methodologist Jacob Cohen, offered rough benchmarks claiming that when looking at *d*-statistics, .2 can be considered a "small" effect, and .5 a "big" effect. We understand why such benchmarks are tempting. The motivation to contextualize an effect size with an adjective is probably why NHST is so dominant in the first place – it feels more authoritative somehow to say this is a "big" effect and cite Cohen. We recommend that you don't do this. Cohen's original intent stating these numbers was not to create a permanent, authoritative statement about meaningful effect sizes across all of social science and for all time. Although that's how they have been applied, they are not meaningful when used this way. This is because the "bigness" of an effect depends completely on what you are measuring and what similar studies in your area tend to find (see the smoking example in the main text).

Most of the phenomena we study are complex and multidetermined, meaning the effect on any one stimulus or intervention will be small. It would be naive to expect, for example, that I could have a "big" effect on a person's long-term career success with a 10-minute intervention. In this case, a "small" effect is still important and interesting. The bigness of an effect should be compared to similar studies of similar phenomena instead of global generic adjectives.

In a landmark initiative, Frank Bosco and his colleagues set out to do something really useful for the field of I-O psychology. Their project, called MetaBUS (https://metabus.org), empirically aggregated over one hundred thousand effect sizes from published research in I-O psychology journals. They then made this information available to the research community. By creating this database, the MetaBUS team made it possible to contextualize findings from a single study by comparing it to other studies of similar phenomena, using similar methods. Although using benchmarks from Meta-BUS is probably more useful than the old Cohen standards, you still need to carefully justify why the particular benchmarks you choose are the best choices for interpreting your conclusions.

Recommendations for how to use effect sizes:

1. Report them prominently
2. Use large samples to get more precise estimates
3. Use unstandardized effect sizes when they are interpretable
4. Contextualize all effect sizes with meaningful benchmarks
5. Collect meaningful measures in the first place
6. Avoid labeling things "small" and "large" without justification beyond benchmarks

Bayes' Theorem

Effect sizes can be used to add context to NHST findings, and many researchers argue using them in tandem to describe both statistical and practical significance. This is less common in the next alternative to NHST that we'll explore, due to a much larger philosophical difference between the two sides, a debate commonly referred to as **frequentism versus Bayesianism**. Frequentism refers to a fundamental assumption of NHST that the frequency of observation across a large sample trends toward an objective truth about a population. In reality, truth is probably quite a bit more complicated in most of the situations we commonly study.

By now, you've learned what p-values are NOT– they are not expressions of how likely something is. Sometimes, you do actually want to know how likely something will be in the future. NHST may not help you very much in this situation, because it assumes that the frequency of observation in the past is a perfect representation of future probability, aside from random noise. If that assumption is unsafe, you need something different.

Bayesianism could be the system you need instead. Maybe you've heard the old expression, "where there's smoke, there's fire." This is technically a claim about the *probability of current fire* given that you have *observed current smoke*. In I-O, a similar expression might be "where there's low job satisfaction, there's turnover." (Not quite as catchy, granted). Imagine we wanted to know whether low job satisfaction (A) was likely after we visited a company and learned that they have high turnover (B). In the logic language of Bayesianism, we can rewrite this question as:

- How often does A happen, given that B happened? What is P(A|B)?
  How often do people turn over, given that satisfaction is low? What is P(HighTurnover|Low Satisfaction)

This **conditional probability** can be calculated with three other pieces of information:

- How likely A is on its own? What is P(A)?
  How often do people turn over? What is P(HighTurnover)?
- How likely B is on its own? What is P(B)?
  How often do people have low satisfaction? What is P(LowSatisfaction)?
- How often does B happen given that A happens? What is P(B|A)?
  How often do people have low satisfaction, given that they turn over? What is P(LowSatisfaction|HighTurnover)?

These four terms are the foundation of Bayes' theorem, as shown in Figure 12.8.

Let's look at two variables, job satisfaction and turnover, and express them in terms of overall and joint probabilities. From Table 12.2, we could for example conclude that 10% of all organizations have high job satisfaction AND high turnover, which is called a **joint probability**. Next, we can calculate **marginal probabilities** of high/medium/low job satisfaction overall by adding across the row, and high/low turnover by adding down the columns, as also shown in Table 12.2. From this table, we can conclude that the overall probability of high job satisfaction is .3, and the overall probability of high turnover is .6. The joint probability of high job satisfaction and high turnover is .1.

Next we can calculate conditional probabilities, which in this case address this question: What is the probability of high, medium, or low JS given high turnover?

P(HighSatisfaction | HighTurnover) = .1/.6 = .17
P(MedSatisfaction | HighTurnover) = .1/.6 = .17
P(LowSatisfaction | HighTurnover) = .4/.6 = .68

We can also calculate conditional probabilities for high or low turnover given high JS:

P(HighTurnover | HighSatisfaction) = .1/.3 = .33
P(LowTurnover | High Satisfaction) =: .2/.3 = .67

In reference to Bayes' theorem (Figure 12.9), we can now see that 1) the marginal probability, P(LowSatisfaction), equals .5; 2) the marginal probability, P(HighTurnover), is .6; and 3) the conditional probability, P(HighTurnover | LowSatisfaction) is .5. Plugging these values into Bayes' theorem, we are able to calculate the **posterior probability** that we were originally after:

$$P(A|B) = .5 \times .5 / .6 = .42.$$

$$P(A \mid B) = \frac{P(A)P(B \mid A)}{P(A)}$$

Figure 12.8 Bayes' theorem.

Table 12.2 Contingency table of turnover versus job satisfaction probabilities, plus marginal probabilities

	High turnover	Low turnover	JS marginal probabilities
High JS	.1	.2	**.3**
Medium JS	.1	.1	**.2**
Low JS	.4	.1	**.5**
Turnover marginal probabilities	**.6**	**.4**	

Thus, there is a 42% chance in this organization that a person with low job satisfaction will turn over. Importantly, this is slightly larger than the observed (frequentist) probability of 40%. These numbers can be quite different, as we will explore next, and the Bayesian estimate is likely to be closer to the population truth.

Avoiding Misleading Conclusions With Bayes

Let's look at some examples to illustrate why Bayesianism produces more accurate estimates than frequentist approaches in this type of situation. Imagine we are developing a test to screen for narcissists as part of a leadership selection battery. The test is 95% sensitive and 95% specific, which means that the test will produce 95% true positive results for narcissists and 95% true negative results for non-narcissists. Five percent of narcissists will be miscategorized as non-narcissists, and 5% of non-narcissists will be miscategorized as narcissists.

We also know that 10% of the applicant population are narcissists based on traditional questionnaire-based research methods. So what is the probability that any randomly selected leader with a positive result is actually a narcissist?

Wrong answer: 95%. It is tempting to say "the test is 95% sensitive, so it is probably true that a person who has a positive result is a narcissist." This answer is wrong because it neglects base rate. Only 10% of people in the population are narcissists. A randomly selected person from the population has only a 10% chance of being a narcissist. Our best guess for the person with the positive test needs to incorporate this information. We can do this with Bayes' theorem, just like before.

For example, if 1000 individuals are tested, there are expected to be 900 non-narcissists and 100 narcissists. From the 900 non-narcissists, $0.05 \times 900 \simeq 45$ false positives are expected. From the 100 narcissists, $0.95 \times 100 \approx 95$ true positives are expected. Out of 140 positive results, only 95 are genuine! So for someone with a positive result, there is only a 67% chance that they are indeed a narcissist.

What if the population base rate was even smaller, say, 1%? In that case, if 1000 individuals are tested, there would be expected to be 990 non-narcissists and 10 narcissists. From the 990 non-narcissists, $0.05 \times 990 \simeq 49$ false positives are expected. From the 10 narcissists, $0.95 \times 10 \approx 1$ true positives are expected. Out of 50 positive results, only 1 is genuine! So for someone with a positive result, there would only be a 2% chance that they are indeed a narcissist.

The initial guess based on the population, 1%, is called the **prior probability**, or commonly just the **prior**. After a positive test, the probability estimate moves from the prior of 1% to the posterior of 2%.

The beauty of Bayes is that it allows us to update our beliefs and use what we already know to be true to make better estimates about what we don't know. Modern recommender systems and machine learning commonly use Bayesian reasoning to make better predictions. If I type "Behrend" into a search engine, Google can use what it already knows about me to guess that I want search results about Tara Behrend, the I-O psychologist, and will take me to her university website. Someone who lives in Erie, Pennsylvania, who searches for "Behrend" will probably be directed to the website for Penn State University Behrend Campus instead. The search algorithm takes into account both the overall popularity of those two sites (a prior), and also my past search behavior (also a prior) and what I am likely to be interested in (a prior too!), and makes a guess about what I most likely want (the posterior). In this way, familiar analytic frameworks like regression can be applied within a Bayesian framework by establishing priors for each parameter, calculating posteriors as new data are collected, and using those posteriors to inform new priors in future analyses.

Calculating Bayes Factors

A common way that Bayesian estimates are applied to hypothesis testing is with **Bayes factors**, which are ratios of likelihoods of observing the data you observed based upon two competing models. Some researchers mimic NHST when setting up this kind of analysis, such as by setting a null hypothesis as the model to be compared with a specific alternative. For example, imagine that you are interested in the effect of work from home policies on experienced job stress. You might set up the following:

- H0 (null): Establishing a work from home policy harms or increases job stress.
- H1 (alternative): Establishing a work from home policy reduces job stress.

After collecting data, two conditional probabilities can be calculated:

- P(Data|H0) – the probability that the data would be observed if the null were true
- P(Data|H1) – the probability that the data would be observed if the alternative were true

Using Bayes' theorem twice, we can calculate posterior probabilities associated with both of these hypotheses. The ratio of these posteriors (i.e., P(Data|H1)/P(Data|H0) is a Bayes factor. Bayes factors, usually represented with K, are commonly interpreted in terms of **Jeffreys' scale**, proposed by Harold Jeffreys (1939). Although there are many ways Jeffreys' scale has been operationalized and reinterpreted over the years, the most common interpretation is that $K > 3.2$ constitutes evidence in favor of the alternative; that is, H1 must be at least 3 times as likely as H0 to accept H1 (Kass & Raftery, 1995).

Importantly, this ratio is just as arbitrary as the $\alpha = .05$ standard and the "small/medium/large" effect size standards. Like those, it is something that a researcher with deep expertise in the specifics of the statistical method published many years ago, toward the beginning of the technique's consideration by a broader group of researchers, to help those new researchers figure out how to adopt it with much less expertise. Much as in those situations, careful reasoning is necessary; you should not automatically assume $K > 3.2$ is "real" any more than you accept the other two. Always think carefully about what applies in your particular situation.

Data Mining

One of your authors, Richard, is a proud graduate of the University of Minnesota. Despite that association, I (Tara) would never accuse him of **dust bowl empiricism**, a close relative to data mining. *Dust bowl empiricism* is a term you may have heard used to disparagingly refer to the analysis of data absent theory-building, most closely associated with a particular period of our history.

In the mid-20th century, psychologists were going through a phase. The phase, like all phases, was a reaction to what came before: highly interpretive and subjective methods of generating insight, with Freudian thought at the center. The "dust bowl empiricists" reacted by insisting that the observations were all that mattered. Guessing an unobservable meaning underlying the data was, in their opinion, unscientific. The logical consequence was to emphasize research questions that were strictly empirical and focused only on observed relationships, without worrying at all about what the observations *meant*. Thus, the quality of conclusions from such research were criticized as empty of any intellectual nutrition – much like the Dust Bowl of the 1930s, when a stretch of land centering on the United States' Kansas, Oklahoma, and Texas were hit by drought so intense that few crops could grow, regardless of the skill of the farmer.

In I-O psychology, and specifically in the case of employee selection, the term *dust bowl empiricism* was commonly used to criticize biodata inventories that asked questions to predict job performance absent any compelling reason for observed relationships. If people who liked making paper airplanes ended up being better engineers, why ask why! Just start measuring paper airplane aptitude. Much of this work was done by simply hunting for significant *p*-values.

Since this time, almost all areas of psychology, including I-O, have moved toward post-positivism, which as discussed in Chapter 1 emphasizes the lens of human interpretation and meaning-making in research design, analysis, and interpretation. Yet we still see the specter of dust bowl empiricism research today, such as in research mining trace data from social media, biometric monitors, and other devices for statistically significant patterns around which papers can be written. All of this activity, new and old, is nothing more than a fancy fishing expedition, driven by the hunt for significant *p*-values.

This era of I-O psychology is commonly what people think of when considering **data mining**, which refers to the systematic quantitative exploration of datasets to discover patterns and new insights. Although they can use similar tools, they come from very different philosophical traditions, which changes the way researchers approach and discuss them. Whereas dust bowl empiricism elevated the importance of *p*-values over theory, using the *p*-values to suggest that various relationships existed or did not exist, data mining done well does not use *p*-values at all. Instead, the goal of data mining is generally to either develop new theory on the basis of exploration (i.e., inductive research; see Chapter 2) or to contextualize existing theory given collected data to solve a specific problem (i.e., abductive research).

The key to effective data mining is to admit this, recognize the biases it brings, and consider this throughout the analytic process. A very basic example of data mining in the abductive tradition might look something like this:

1. An organization becomes aware of some incidents between employees that suggest some pressing issues related to systemic racism and sexism. Specifically, white men are being promoted at a higher rate than everyone else, and no one is quite sure why.
2. As the resident I-O at this organization, you decide to measure a broad collection of DEI-related variables during the next employee pulse survey. From your review of the research literature, you determine that there are around a dozen common correlates of promotion decision-making, but you aren't sure which apply in this particular situation. So you measure them all among those making promotion decisions.
3. You create a correlation matrix between demographic variables and promotion decisions made within your company, and by looking carefully at it, you discover that white men and white women are much more likely to decide to promote white men than everyone else.

4. Based on those results, you decide to collect new data from white men and white women about their decision-making processes during promotions.

In each stage of this process, you collected a wide variety of data with no specific analysis in mind, as would be necessary in a deductive NHST approach. Instead, you approached this research as a problem to be solved. You acted as a detective, using research methods as your magnifying glass and investigations notebook.

There is nothing wrong with this kind of research, either in practice or in academic journals. In fact, if you are tackling an important, interesting problem, it is probably more useful to real-world decision making and new theory than most published NHST-centric studies, which tend to be more derivative and less novel because of the deductive approach inherent to the approach.

The only problem with data mining is when people lie about it. If you create and execute an abductive data mining study, you should not post hoc pretend it was a deductive study and write about all the hypotheses you tested. Doing so is a QRP and possibly even fraud. Instead, you didn't test any hypotheses – and that's okay. Posing hypotheses does not imply good research, nor does the absence of hypotheses imply bad research. A good data mining study requires you ask good questions, use rigorous and thoughtful methods to investigate them, and draw honest conclusions based on the relative strengths and limitations of the approach you chose – just like every other method we've discussed in this book.

Machine Learning and Artificial Intelligence

Artificial intelligence (AI) is one of the hottest topics in organizations right now, both inside and outside the I-O context. AI is a bit of a weasel word, because it can be used to mean just about anything. Most fundamentally, AI refers to any task without a single well-defined path from start to finish that a human could normally do that can now be done by a computer.

For example, a robot that always picks up a car door handle from a stack of car door handles that is always the same and welds it to a car door from a stack of car doors that is always the same, then moves the newly assembled door into a pile that is always the same is not AI. This is because the robot is simply replicating the same series of movements over and over again without anything resembling reasoning or cognition. Instead, it is simply repeating a **mechanistic process**. You can see this most obviously when something goes wrong – if that door handle or door are even slightly in the wrong place, the robot will likely fail. It can do nothing other than repeat the process it has been programmed to repeat.

AI, in contrast, can react. If that same robot was able to use cameras to identify where the next door and door handle was, compare the images it receives against an image database of "good" and "bad" parts, and then asks its human supervisor for next steps when it concludes it has been given a low-quality handle to weld, we are now more in AI territory. In this example, the robot is mimicking human reasoning by considering a novel object and trying to "decide" what to do with it.

AI is not always so complex, however. As an I-O psychologist, you have probably by now run a regression analysis – this is a specific type of AI increasingly common in I-O psychology called **machine learning**. It is called this because by providing your computer with data, your computer is able to make predictions in new datasets it has never seen before on the basis of the data it has received. For example, if you provide a dataset to SPSS or R and use it to calculate a regression line of $Y = 2x + 1$, your computer can now also apply that formula in a new dataset to make new predictions. It is in this sense that your computer has "learned."

Machine learning, much like data mining, does not generally involve hypothesis testing the way NHST approaches it. But unlike both data mining and NHST, machine learning methods generally do not prioritize meaning for the coefficients they estimate. Instead, they often sacrifice meaning for better out-of-sample predictive accuracy. This tradeoff is commonly referred to as **prediction versus explanation** (Yarkoni & Westfall, 2017). The social sciences have historically focused on explanation, such as via thoughtful research design with the purpose of determine the effects of carefully defined experimental interventions or the use of advanced quantitative techniques to better understand the networks of causal relationships in complex models. Consider the following examples to illustrate the distinction:

1. *Explanation:* A researcher is interested in the effects of supervisor behaviors on turnover. They carefully measure known antecedents based on existing literature and select a few demographic variables they believe to be important. They collect these data and create a structural equation model explaining how much each factor is likely to influence turnover, alongside theoretical explanations as to why this pattern of effects was observed. In doing so, they better understand the explanatory value of several key variables so as to drive future decision-making in turnover reduction interventions.
2. *Prediction:* A researcher is interested in the effect of supervisor behaviors on turnover. They collect every possible variable from HR datasets that they can find related to the way that supervisors interact with their direct reports. They use a variety of machine learning techniques to maximize the predictive accuracy of the model they create. This model creates highly accurate predictions of who is likely to turn over within the next 6 months.

When prioritizing prediction over explanation, a lot of new kinds of analyses become possible that are not within a NHST framework, including:

1. Computer vision, which involves prediction from images and videos. Computer vision projects involve first converting the source material into a dataset, such as by converting a 1920 × 1080-pixel image into 2.1 million pixels of color, and then converting each of those 2.1 million pixels into three color channel variables: red, green, and blue. Thus computer vision from a 1080p image starts with a 6.3-million variable dataset, which can then be used to predict other outcomes of interest, a situation where NHST is not recommended.
2. Natural language processing, which involves prediction from unstructured text. Similar to computer vision, natural language processing projects starts by first converting the source material into a dataset, such as by converting a 500-word response to an open ended text prompt into a dataset recording word frequencies, vectors of meaning, and many other types of variables. These variables can then be used to predict other outcomes of interest, much as in computer vision.
3. Auditory signal processing, which involves prediction from sound. The most common version of this for I-O is speech recognition, which allows videos to be converted into text for input into natural language processing algorithms, which in turn allows for things like the automated scoring of virtual interventions.

4. Anomaly detection, which involves predicting low-frequency events where traditional assumptions about distribution are impossible. When you're trying to predict who will engage in a physically violent act in a company where such incidents occur only once every 3 to 6 months, traditional I-O research methods and statistics are not likely to produce a useful model.

Machine learning, and the broader field of AI, are quite new to I-O. Yet tools like these are likely to transform work and the way we study work in ways that are difficult to imagine, even over the next decade. Importantly, however, AI is not inherently "better" than traditional methods. The explanation versus prediction tradeoff can create a real loss of information when AI methods are adopted instead of NHST, effect sizes, Bayesian approaches, or data mining. Current applications of AI are often not inductive, deductive, or abductive – they are instead frequently descriptive. This loss of explanation throws out meaning, yet meaning is at the very core of I-O psychology's value to both organizations and society in general.

As in almost all areas we've discussed in this book, we recommend balance. AI brings certain new innovations that will undoubtedly transform research methods and our field. At the same time, more than a century of research methods development has not become irrelevant overnight; many of the core contributions of our field remain relevant. What is unclear right now is where the balance is: the best combination of old and new. And as part of the next generation of methodologists, you share that responsibility for helping us figure out how!

References

Amrhein, V., Greenland, S., & McShane, B. (2019). Retire statistical significance. *Nature, 567*, 305–307. https://doi.org/10.1038/d41586-019-00857-9

Darden, M., Gilleskie, D. B., & Strumpf, K. (2018). Smoking and mortality: New evidence from a long panel. *International Economic Review, 59*(3), 1571–1619.

Jeffreys, H. (1939). *Theory of probability.* Oxford University Press.

Kass, R. E., & Raftery, A. E. (1995). Bayes factors. *Journal of the American Statistical Association, 90*(430), 773–795.

Yates, F. (1951). The influence of statistical methods for research workers on the development of the science of statistics. *Journal of the American Statistical Association, 46*(253), 19–34.

Further Reading

Amrhein, V., Greenland, S., & McShane, B. (2019). Retire statistical significance. *Nature, 567*, 305–307. https://doi.org/10.1038/d41586-019-00857-9

- This hotly discussed comment submitted to *Nature* started a lot of the "retire NHST" discussion in earnest. At only 3 pages, it is full of passionate pleas to stop ruining science with significance tests. Whether you agree or not, it's certainly worth the quick read.

Lakens, D. (2021). The practical alternative to the *p* value is the correctly used *p* value. *Perspectives on Psychological Science, 16*. https://doi.org/10.1177/1745691620958012

- Lakens offers a view of *p*-values suggesting that it is not the fault of the *p*-value that it is so commonly misinterpreted. He suggests *p*-values have continued value for psychology now and in the future, but that this requires we accept what *p*-values actually tell us and no more.

Oswald, F. L., Behrend, T. S., Putka, D. J., & Sinar, E. (2020). Big data in industrial-organizational psychology and human resource management: Forward progress for organizational research and practice. *Annual Review of Organizational Psychology and Organizational Behavior, 7*, 505–533.

- Oswald and colleagues provide a big picture view of the challenges for I-O psychology when branching out into the analysis of large, unstructured datasets, highlighting the need for changes in how I-Os understand data infrastructure, as well as the need to develop new coding, analytic, and visualization skills. They also discuss some of the challenges applying existing I-O approaches to such datasets.

Wasserstein, R. L., & Lazar, N. A. (2016). The ASA statement on *p*-values: Context, process, and purpose. *The American Statistician*, *70*(2), 129–133.

- One of the earliest and most influential works in the debate about NHST was a 3-page statement released in 2016 by the American Statistical Association calling for reduced reliance on *p*-values due to consistent misuse and misinterpretation. In this article, Wassertein and Lazar provide a lot more context and discussion about this controversial policy document.

Yarkoni, T., & Westfall, J. (2017). Choosing prediction over explanation in psychology: Lessons from machine learning. *Perspectives on Psychological Science*, *12*(6), 1100–1122.

- Yarkoni and Westfall are often credited with introducing the value of machine learning to the mainstream of psychology. Although machine learning was commonly used well before this article, it brought the underlying philosophical conflicts into starker relief for a much broader audience. If you are interested in how machine learning can be best integrated into psychology, this is a great place to start.

Questions to Think About

1. What are the core assumptions of NHST?
2. Are the null hypotheses tested in your research area usually meaningful or arbitrary?
3. Does our field's reliance on *p*-values for NHST ultimately help or harm scientific progress?
4. What approach will you default to when first considering a new research question or hypothesis? Why do you default to that?
5. What is the best way to consider effect sizes in relation to NHST? Should they replace or supplement NHST approaches?
6. What is preventing you from applying Bayesian methods in your current research projects? How could you get over these barriers?
7. Are there any areas of your research where a data mining or machine learning approach might be better than the research that's been conducted recently? What would be better in such research? What would be worse?

Key Terms

- a priori power analysis
- alpha (in NHST)
- alternative hypothesis
- anomaly detection
- area under the curve
- artificial intelligence
- auditory signal processing
- Bayes factor
- Bayes' theorem
- Bayesianism
- beta (in NHST)
- central limit theorem
- Cohen's *d*
- computer vision
- conditional probability
- confidence interval
- data mining
- dust bowl empiricism
- effect size
- effect size benchmarks
- frequentism versus Bayesianism
- G*Power

- Jeffreys' scale
- joint probability
- machine learning
- marginal probability
- mean difference
- mechanistic process
- null hypothesis
- null hypothesis significance testing (NHST)
- p-value
- posterior probability
- power
- power analysis
- practically significant
- prediction versus explanation
- prior probability
- sampling distribution
- standard error
- statistically significant
- t-statistic
- Type 1 error
- Type 2 error
- Type I error rate
- Type II error rate
- unstandardized

## Chapter 13

Understanding and Executing Meta-Analyses

Learning Objectives

1. Apply the mathematical foundations of meta-analysis to understand meta-analytic results
2. Recognize common artifacts that bias the conclusions of individual studies
3. Compare common meta-analytic approaches and the effects of adopting them
4. Conduct a meta-analysis
5. Evaluate the relative strengths and weaknesses of meta-analyses with different design decisions
6. Consider all the ways meta-analytic results can be misleading due to the garden of forking paths

Meta-analysis has become one of the most trusted methods for the quantitative synthesis of research results across multiple studies. When published, meta-analyses tend to be highly cited and frequently referenced as authoritative statements about bodies of literature, specific theories, and specific construct relationships. They have largely replaced narrative review as a research method, an approach historically taken in which researchers simply wrote about all the research they could find on a topic and drew conclusions as they saw reasonable without collecting new evidence or running additional analyses. Meta-analysts are quick to point out that a narrative review cannot help but be biased towards the pet theories of those who conducted it, and there are numerous examples of multiple narrative reviews published around the same time on the same topic reaching opposing conclusions. Meta-analysis promises objectivity – a fair evaluation of all available evidence to reach the most meaningful conclusions. Meta-analyses are so well-respected as providing objective, conclusive statements on the current state of a research literature that entire journals exist in psychology devoted almost entirely to studies using meta-analytic methods. Most visibly, the highly respected journal *Psychological Bulletin* went from almost 100% narrative reviews to almost 100% meta-analyses over only a few decades.

Meta-analysis *can* achieve this vision. They *can* be significantly better than the sum of their parts, contributing meaningfully to a research literature beyond what the original studies could do individually. But they don't always succeed at this vision, and when this happens, it is actively damaging. Specifically, a poorly conducted meta-analysis, because of its elevated place among other types of evidence in the minds of many, can mislead and misdirect future researchers for decades. For example, a researcher will have a much easier time

DOI: 10.4324/9781315167473-17

MANY META-ANALYSIS STUDIES INCLUDE
THE PHRASE "WE SEARCHED MEDLINE,
EMBASE, AND COCHRANE FOR STUDIES..."

THIS HAS LED TO META-META-ANALYSES
COMPARING META-ANALYSIS METHODS.
e.g. M SAMPSON (2003), PL ROYLE (2005)
E LEE (2011), AR LEMESHOW (2005)

WE PERFORMED A META-META-META-ANALYSIS
OF THESE META-META-ANALYSES.

METHODS: WE SEARCHED MEDLINE, EMBASE,
AND COCHRANE FOR THE PHRASE "WE SEARCHED
MEDLINE, EMBASE, AND COCHRANE FOR THE
PHRASE "WE SEARCHED MEDLINE, EMBASE, AND

LIFE GOAL #28: GET A PAPER REJECTED
WITH THE COMMENT "TOO META"

Figure 13.1 "Life goal #29 is to get enough of them rejected that I can publish a comparative analysis of the rejection letters." Courtesy xkcd.com.

publishing a paper showing Theory X is *not* supported if no meta-analysis on that theory already exists. If a meta-analysis does exist supporting Theory X, that researcher will have a more difficult time finding a publication home for that paper; reviewers tend to assume that past meta-analyses are "right" and anything contradicting them must be unusual, unrepresentative, or just plain wrong.

Much as we've recommended to you in previous chapters, you should develop a more sophisticated view than this common one. Each meta-analysis has unique strengths and weaknesses that affect its internal validity and generalizability, just like every other primary study we discussed in Chapter 8. This means you need to evaluate every meta-analysis on its own merits, by scrutinizing the decisions that were made that led to the stated conclusions. Perhaps most importantly, you must realize that meta-analysis is one of the most *subjective* quantitative methods used in I-O psychology due to the sheer volume of judgment calls that must be made in their planning, execution, and interpretation. And meta-analysts vary greatly in the amount of effort they put into actively managing this subjectivity.

In this chapter, we'll explore how to both understand existing meta-analytic research and how to conduct your own, with a particular emphasis on the many decisions that must be made along the way.

The Modern Role of Narrative Review

Although narrative review is no longer common as a *research method*, it is still extremely common as a writing technique and communications tool. For example, the introductory section of a meta-analytic research article is itself a narrative review, a necessary step to justify that the meta-analysis is needed, that the research questions and hypotheses tested are worth the time and effort to test, and that the reader should care enough to keep reading. We also see narrative review commonly used in review articles, such as those found in the *Annual Review of Organizational Psychology and Organizational Behavior*, the goal of which is to summarize the current state of a theory, hypothesis, or literature rather than propose new hypotheses or research questions. There are also journals devoted entirely to papers proposing new theory without ever testing what is proposed, such as the *Academy of Management Review*. In this sense, narrative review is extremely common; the important things to remember are that 1) narrative review alone is insufficient to support a hypothesis and 2) narrative review can be biased in ways that are difficult to detect.

There is also a variation on the research method version of narrative review popularized since 1993 by the **Cochrane Collaboration** as the best way to understand health and medical intervention called systematic review. Cochrane even developed a centralized online database, the Cochrane Database of Systematic Reviews, which holds over 7500 reviews, all at the standards prescribed by Cochrane. Originally, systematic reviews were narrative reviews following strict rules intended to reduce researcher bias; these days, systematic reviews usually contain meta-analyses as a component of the approach.

Fundamentals of Meta-Analysis

Why do we need meta-analysis in the first place? Isn't primary research good enough to draw conclusions about theory?

As you've seen throughout this book, there are many decisions to make about research design. Each research design decision that you make shapes the internal validity and generalizability of your results. Meta-analysis allows us to study these decisions systematically by qualitatively categorizing and quantitatively summarizing differences between such studies based upon these design-level decisions. For example, Researcher A might usually study a phenomenon with experimental designs whereas Researcher B might usually study a phenomenon with correlational designs. The impact of this decision can be studied explicitly using meta-analytic methods to compare the observed relationship when studied with experimental versus correlational designs.

In Chapter 13, we discussed why null hypothesis significance testing can be misleading. It does not tell us what we want it to tell us, and what it does tell us is often not useful, at least by itself, to drawing meaningful conclusions about theory. All a significant p-value can tell us is that the particular population estimate we're looking at, whether a correlation or mean or whatever else, is unlikely to have occurred given certain assumptions. If those assumptions are not meaningful, neither is the p-value.

Unfortunately, many researchers incorrectly try to interpret p-values as support for a tested hypothesis, claiming things like "two studies found significant effects and one didn't; thus, the evidence is stronger for the hypothesis being true." This is a flatly incorrect interpretation. This approach, called **vote counting**, rests on an invalid interpretation of p-values. In the best case scenario, where all research has been strictly held to high methodological standards without any p-hacking or other QRPs, vote counts will be correlated with but not necessarily indicative of the truth of a hypothesis, making it a poor choice. Nevertheless, it remains a common approach in many research literatures outside of I-O psychology where methods fluency tends to be a bit lower. More subtly, it is also the method most commonly used in narrative reviews; even if they never explicitly count the studies they are summarizing, it is common to use significance as a proxy for truth. This is not correct, and you should not do this.

One example that I (Richard) am very familiar with, because it was closely related to the subject of my doctoral dissertation, was the early study of differences between face-to-face and distance education, a literature on which I later conducted difference scores meta-analyses. Most educational research of that time period (and honestly, still today) incorporated sample sizes that were far too small to meaningfully interpret the results of NHST given the expected effect sizes studied. One case that I recall was a between-subjects quasi-experiment examining 14 students split into two classrooms – one face-to-face and one in a correspondence course. Assuming no other interpretive challenges with the research (and there were many, as I recall), finding a statistically significant difference would require an observed effect of roughly $d = 1.2$ standard deviations or greater with two groups of seven research participants. This is an absolutely enormous effect size for educational or psychological research, should not have been a reasonable expectation for the researchers, and is a good sign that those researchers neither understood NHST nor attempted anything resembling a power analysis. Yet that study appeared in published educational research literature – with a non-significant result. As that research literature grew, more studies were added, of highly variable quality, some finding significance and others not, eventually leading to a book by Russell (1999) titled *The No Significant Difference Phenomenon*, which cataloged 355 studies of in-person versus correspondence-based education, in effect vote-counting its way to its conclusions about the effectiveness of distance education. A better interpretation of this entire research literature would have been, "most existing research was badly designed."

Fixed Versus Random Effect Modeling

An important concept in meta-analysis is the choice between fixed and random-effects modeling. **Fixed effects modeling** refers to the assumption that there is a single true population value to describe a particular relationship of interest. A sampling distribution can then be drawn around this value for any given sample size, which is visualized in Figure 13.2. For example, if we were studying the relationship between general cognitive ability and job

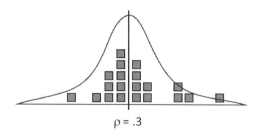

$\rho = .3$

Figure 13.2 Assumptions of a fixed effects model; there is one population of study estimates from which each study is drawn at random.

performance, using fixed effects modeling assumes that there is just one true relationship between these two constructs and that everything else is noise. If this relationship was estimated at $\rho = .3$, use of a fixed effects model would imply that $.3 \times .3 = 9\%$ of the variance in job performance is always explained by general cognitive ability, regardless of organizational context, regardless of job type, and regardless of any other moderating variable. If you were to conduct a study in your own organization and found $\rho = .25$, the fixed effect assumptions would necessarily imply that your estimate was below the population estimate due to random factors. Perhaps you'll hire more people and the relationship will be closer to .3 next time.

As you can see, using fixed effect modeling requires some very strong assumptions that are in most cases probably not met. If we don't feel we can make those assumptions, we turn to **random effects modeling**, which instead assumes that there is an overall population distribution from which subpopulations are drawn, and it is from these subpopulations in turn that samples are drawn, as visualized in Figure 13.3. For example, if the overall relationship was estimated at $\rho = .3$, a random effects model asserts that 9% of the variance in job performance is *on average* explained by general cognitive ability *across* organizational context, job type, and other moderating variables. Each moderator, in turn, reflects a subpopulation. Perhaps in this case, the .35 was drawn from a subpopulation with "moderately high job complexity" and the .25 from a subpopulation with "moderately low job complexity." If you were to conduct your own study of this relationship in the context of a high complexity job, you'd expect to be drawing from the subpopulation with $\rho = .35$ – not the other two.

As you will see in the following sections, the decision between fixed or random effects modeling in meta-analysis can have some big consequences.

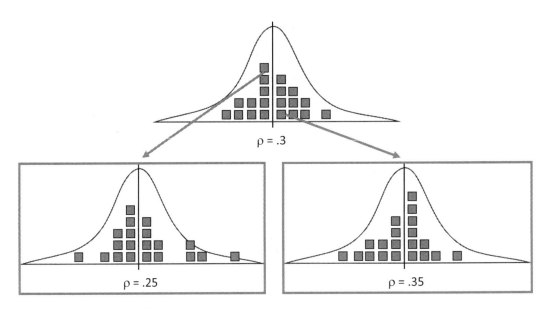

Figure 13.3 Assumptions of a random effects model; there is one population of study estimates from which subpopulations are sampled, and each study in turn samples from a subpopulation of study estimates.

Point Estimates

Meta-analysts tend to focus more on effect size estimates than NHST (see Chapter 12). In some forms of meta-analysis that we will discuss, NHST for any reason is explicitly discouraged. In others, it is used in limited ways to test certain assumptions. But all meta-analyses embrace the idea that some kind of **weighted effect size** is the best way to estimate relationships across studies. **Weighting** is used to make high-quality effect size estimates more influential on the overall meta-analytic estimate than low-quality effect size estimates, although there is disagreement between meta-analytic approaches as to what specific kind of weighting is the best.

These weighted effect sizes come in three major forms: covariances, difference scores, and **odds ratios**.

- Covariances are more commonly studied using the coefficient of determination, R^2. If we wanted to estimate the relationship between conscientiousness and job performance, we would be studying a (standardized) covariance.
- Difference scores are most commonly studied using a standardized estimate, like Cohen's *d* (see Chapter 13) or **Hedges' g,** which is Cohen's *d* corrected for small sample size bias. In some cases, where there is a natural metric for the difference (e.g., a meta-analysis of studies predicting return on investment in dollars), the estimate can be meta-analyzed in its original unstandardized form. If we wanted to estimate the effect of a team building intervention on perceptions of supervisory support, we would be studying a difference score.
- Odds ratios are ratios of probabilities. For example, in I-O psychology, a common probability studied as an outcome is attrition risk. Imagine, for example, that a study found that 50% of employees with poor supervisor relationships left the organization within 6 months whereas only 25% of employees with good supervisor relationships left the organization within 6 months. We can summarize this difference with an odds ratio like this one: there is 2 times the risk of attrition for employees with poor relationships than employees with good ones.

The primary result of a meta-analysis in I-O psychology is usually a **point estimate** in one of these three forms, along with a variety of other information related to it. Covariances are by a wide margin the most common, because most I-O psychology research is correlational. Difference scores are common in subdomains where interventions are studied experimentally, especially training and development. Odds ratios are common in subdomains where outcomes tend to be dichotomous, such as the study of attrition.

Meta-Analysis, Meta-Analyses, and Meta-Analysts, Oh My

A common point of confusion for people beginning in meta-analysis is understanding precisely what each very slight variation of the word "meta-analysis" actually refers to. Here's a handy guide:

- *Meta-analysis*. Meta-analysis is a specific mathematical process by which a single weighted effect size estimate is calculated, along with associated diagnostic and summary statistics.

- *Meta-analyze.* When you conduct a meta-analysis, you are meta-analyzing.
- *Meta-analyses.* The plural of meta-analysis. A single research paper incorporating meta-analysis usually contains more than one and often dozens of meta-analyses.
- *Meta-analytic.* Because a research paper can contains any number of meta-analyses, it is easier to simply refer to it as incorporating meta-analytic research methods. It is also common to see "meta-analytic work," "meta-analytic studies," and many other variations.
- *Meta-analyst.* A person who does meta-analyses! Soon, that will include you.
- *All together now.* In her meta-analytic research, the meta-analyst meta-analyzed her data in a series of meta-analyses.

Interval Estimates

All of the estimates described in the previous section are called point estimates, because they summarize the observed effects in a research literature with a single, best estimate. We can also estimate the magnitude of an effect with an **interval estimate** that provides a range of plausible values for the effect.

There are two major kinds of interval estimates, one of which you are already familiar with from Chapter 12 and probably from a statistics course: the confidence interval. Confidence intervals are close cousins of NHST in that they carry identical assumptions about the underlying distributions of data from which they are drawn, as detailed in Chapter 12. In the meta-analytic context, confidence intervals have the same basic interpretation with a few important differences. Here's an example:

- In a primary study, a sample correlation of 0.5 (i.e., a point estimate of a population correlation) is observed. This is based upon a collected dataset of 250 *people.* Using standard calculations, we determine the 95% confidence interval around this correlation to range from 0.401 to 0.588. This suggests that *if* the population correlation is 0.5, we'd expect 95% of research studies conducted the same way to find sample correlations between 0.401 and 0.588.5% of studies would find estimates outside this interval.
- In a meta-analysis, a weighted mean correlation of 0.5 (i.e., a point estimate of a population correlation) is observed by aggregated across *studies.* This is based on 250 *studies.* Using standard calculations, we determine the 95% confidence interval around this correlation to range from 0.401 to 0.588. This suggests that *if* the population correlation is 0.5, we'd expect 95% of research studies conducted the same way to find sample correlations between 0.401 and 0.588.5% of studies would find estimates outside this interval.

They look the same, right? The main difference is in the underlying datasets – one containing people and the other containing study estimates. But because of that difference, the specific pair of findings previously is very unlikely. But why?

The key is in the statement "95% of research studies conducted the same way." In each case, we must assume a population exists that we are drawing from. In the primary study case, this population is a single research study. We can imagine a population of research studies that look exactly like this one – *direct replications*, as we discuss in Chapter 14. A confidence interval in this context assumes a hypothetical population of direct replications.

This can make sense in the context of fixed effects meta-analysis, because that approach assumes there is a single population effect of interest – any variation due to study design choices, moderators, and so on are all asserted to be noise. Thus a confidence interval in a fixed effects analysis gives us a direct indication of how accurately we are able to measure that single population effect estimate.

In case of random effects meta analysis, the population is a lot more complicated – it contains myriad subpopulations. Can we reasonably assume that the particular studies included in this meta-analysis are a *random sample* drawn from all possible research study designs with all possible moderators? If we have already decided on a random effects approach, probably not. We already are admitting that there are multiple subpopulations hiding within our collected research studies. If these subpopulations were not sampled randomly, the resulting sampling distribution is lumpy and unpredictable. And for all the challenges with primary study and fixed effects confidence intervals, this makes the interpretation of meta-analytic confidence intervals nearly impossible. For this reason, guidelines for random effects meta-analytic methods often explicitly discourage even bothering with computing meta-analytic confidence intervals, as we will see in the following.

Random effects meta-analytic methods do, however, embrace the other type of interval estimate, the **credibility interval**. Credibility intervals are much simpler conceptually than confidence intervals; they describe the range of plausible point estimates for a new sample given the observed point estimates. For example, if we were to meta-analyze 100 studies and found them to fall in the shape of a normal distribution, we would be able to apply the standard z-score to percentile conversion – we'd expect 64% of point estimates to fall between –1 and +1 standard deviation, 95% to fall between –2 and +2 standard deviations, and 99.7% to fall between –3 and +3 standard deviations from the population mean. Thus, a 95% credibility interval would be the effect estimate found at –2 and +2 standard deviations.

For reasons that I've never been able to understand, meta-analysts have embraced the 80% credibility interval as the "standard" interval typically reported in published research. This corresponds to an interval of –1.28 and +1.28 standard deviations. Sometimes meta-analysts will instead report 90% **credibility value**, which refers to the point estimate at which 90% of point estimates are larger. Thus, a 90% credibility value is the same as the lower bound of an 80% credibility interval and is found at –1.28 standard deviations among the study estimates you collected.

We will walk through hand calculation of both a confidence interval and credibility interval later in this chapter – it will be easier than you expect.

Artifact Corrections

The quality of meta-analytic research depends on the quality of the estimates that are included in it. Put another way, a meta-analysis will be biased if the studies it contains are biased. We've talked about this issue at the study level in many previous chapters; for example, in Chapter 8, we discussed how demand characteristics can cause research participants to do what they perceive the researcher wants them to do instead of what they would naturally do. In an experiment, this would usually increase observed effect size by moving the experimental mean further away from the control group mean. If this study were included in a meta-analysis, it would bias meta-analytic estimates of that effect upward; the mean difference would appear larger than it truly is.

The effects of many biases, like this one, cannot be measured easily. But there is a family of biases called **artifacts** that can be understood mathematically. Whereas demand characteristics can bias effect estimates in many difficult-to-measure ways, artifacts are usually more predictable. Specifically, if you know what artifacts apply in a particular meta-analytic context, and if you know the mathematical implications of those artifacts, you could estimate what the true effect *would have been* if the artifacts had not been present. (Think of this a bit like a counterfactual in the sense explained in Chapter 8.)

Meta-analysts call this kind of estimation **correction**, because the general idea is that we are able to "correct" observed estimates from past research to get better estimates of population- and construct-level values. In short, the thinking is that if we know artifacts were present in past research, and if our goal is to maximize accuracy of population estimates, we should always correct for known artifacts to maximize accuracy. Artifacts always make observed estimates smaller than true values, so the downward biasing effect of artifacts is commonly referred to as attenuation, which is the same kind of attenuation we discussed in Chapter 4.

I-O psychologists Frank Schmidt and Jack Hunter (2014) are commonly associated with artifact corrections due to their relatively extreme view that more aggressive corrections are almost always justifiable. In their foundational book on meta-analysis, which we will discuss at length in the following, they listed several common artifacts:

1. Sampling error
2. Unreliability
3. Artificial dichotomization
4. Range restriction
5. Imperfect construct validity
6. Reporting errors
7. Extraneous factors

In each of these cases, an observed relationship is likely to be smaller than the true relationship due to the presence of that artifact. To illustrate, consider the following scenario: a meta-analyst is interested in the effect of DEI training on gender climate. Here are possible artifacts in the same order:

1. In essentially all research, study validities will vary from their population values due to sampling error, and this attenuation can be corrected.
2. DEI training is measured perfectly because it's an intervention, so no correction is needed here. However, gender climate is usually measured with less than perfect reliability, so we could correct for unreliability in this variable.
3. DEI training is an intervention, so that's a natural dichotomy and needs no correction. Gender climate, however, could be measured with many different kinds of scales. Perhaps in some cases it is measured with a simple question: "Is gender climate better now? Yes or No." In these cases, the true effect on gender climate is likely attenuated.
4. If only a subset of people in each organization received DEI training, and the reason for their selection was related to the success of the training, they were likely range restricted (refer back to Chapter 4). Perhaps the population consisted only of volunteers for DEI training; this would suggest range restriction corrections in the first variable. Perhaps

also people who did not like the gender climate left the organization before the study was conducted; this would suggest further range restriction corrections in the second variable.

5. Is the DEI training used in the research literature representative of all DEI training that organizations could use? If not, there may be attenuation due to construct validity problems. Are the gender climate measures completely lacking contamination and deficiency problems (see Chapter 7)? If not, there may be attenuation here too.

6. Do you expect that every number on every form was written without error? No computer glitches? No accidental altering of even one cell of data in a spreadsheet? If not, there could be attenuation here too.

7. Is there absolutely anything else that could cause misestimation? Correct for it too!

As you can see, Hunter and Schmidt were very liberal in their recommendations to correct for attenuation from as many identifiable sources as possible. And this is where things get a bit controversial. Hunter and Schmidt would argue that because we can never truly know all of the artifacts present in research, erring on the side of **overcorrection** is really no overcorrection at all – it just means we're closer to where we would have been if the research had been conducted to better reflect true score relationships. But other researchers advise caution, suggesting that although meta-analysis can "make lemonade out of lemons" (Köhler et al., 2015, pp. 355–356), overcorrection is just that – too much of a good thing.

As we'll see in the next section, the philosophies underlying different meta-analytic frameworks drive a lot of decision-making along the path to a completed meta-analysis. Hunter and Schmidt put a lot of emphasis on corrections; others, less so. It's up to you to decide which framework makes the assumptions that you are most comfortable with.

Controversial Correction

There is no topic in meta-analysis as controversial as the appropriateness of various corrections. To illustrate, consider the title of LeBreton et al.'s (2014) paper regarding criterion reliability corrections: "Corrections for criterion reliability in validity generalization: A false prophet in a land of suspended judgment." That's one of the strongest stances we've ever seen *in the title of a paper*.

The underlying issue in this area relates all the way back to Chapter 1: these are differences in philosophy. On one hand, if you trust well-established theoretical models of sampling error, reliability, range restriction, and so on, and if you already rely on those theories for things like significance testing or reporting on the psychometric properties of tests, corrections like the ones discussed here are just applications of theories you already accept. On the other hand, if you believe the assumptions underlying those theoretical models are often violated, and that overcorrecting leaves you in a worse place than where you started, then corrections are not just inappropriate but actively harmful, leading us away from useful and accurate true score estimates. There is no way to demonstrate this with data, because true scores cannot ever be measured directly.

There are even a variety of middle grounds from which correcting for *some* artifacts and not for others can be considered more meaningful to test specific research questions. A common example of this is **operational validity**, which refers to estimates of the true score relationship between a predictor of job performance and job performance correcting only for unreliability in the criterion. The logic of this approach is that when a company uses a selection test for hiring, the unreliability of that test affects how well the test can predict job performance – thus, correcting for predictor unreliability gives an unrealistically optimistic picture of the true *operational* relationship between these constructs. In contrast, job performance will be affected regardless of whether or not we can measure it – thus, correcting for criterion unreliability gives us a better idea of that true operational relationship.

Thus, meta-analysts and those reading meta-analytic research often find themselves struggling with philosophical issues surrounding corrections. You should evaluate for yourself which set of assumptions make more sense to you and be prepared to justify your perspective if asked, but especially if you write a paper using meta-analytic methods.

Meta-Analytic Approaches

Differences in how we treat the interrelationship between random versus fixed effects, NHST, effect size estimate calculation, level of analysis, and artifact correction has led to several different schools of thought related to how to most meaningfully conduct meta-analyses. Some of these are more common than others. In all cases, a meta-analysis will estimate population characteristics based upon the studies it draws from. The specific path from raw data to those estimates varies quite a bit, though. Although there are many approaches to meta-analysis, we'll focus on the ones you are most likely to encounter.

Glassian Meta-Analysis

The modern popularity of meta-analysis can be traced back to Gene Glass (1976), who coined the term "meta-analysis" in his presidential address to the American Educational Research Association, expanded on paper for the first time in a highly influential article published in *Educational Researcher*. As discussed earlier in this chapter, educational research, to a somewhat greater degree than psychology, frequently suffered from extremely underpowered studies that made the interpretation of statistical significance complicated. Most research was conducted in the field with pre-existing classes and instructional settings, most often quite undersized given the complexity of research questions that researchers wanted to ask. Glass summarized the problem succinctly:

> In education, the findings are fragile; they vary in confusing irregularity across contexts, classes of subjects, and countless other factors. Where ten studies might suffice to resolve a matter in biology, ten studies on computer assisted instruction or reading may fail to show the same pattern of results twice. . . . Their meaning can no more be grasped in our traditional narrative, discursive review than one can grasp the sense of 500 test scores without the aid of techniques for organizing, depicting, and interrelating data.
>
> (pp. 3–4)

In short, the educational research literature – even in the 1970s – was in many domains already too vast, too complex, and too inconsistent to meaningfully conduct and interpret narrative reviews. Instead, Glass suggested a simple systematic and mathematical approach: collect all studies on a particular topic, calculate the average point estimate (a correlation coefficient, in Glass' original case), and interpret that instead. As more studies become available contributing to that average, researchers can be increasingly confident in the generalizability of the estimate.

From this foundation, Glass and those building upon his work established many of the fundamentals of meta-analysis still present today, such as emphasis on point estimates of effect size instead of statistical significance, weighting studies on the strength of evidence they provide, and systematically studying potential of causes of variance among study estimates. However, **Glassian meta-analysis** itself is now considered a bit outdated and rarely used, at least in its original form.

Hunter-Schmidt Meta-Analysis

Hunter-Schmidt meta-analysis, sometimes called **psychometric meta-analysis**, is the most common in I-O psychology research today, likely due both Hunter and Schmidt publishing frequently in the I-O psychology literature. In fact, their drive to develop meta-analysis stemmed largely from the theoretical challenge of **validity generalization**. In short, there used to be a pervasive belief that predictors of job performance were essentially unique to each organization employing them. This was in part caused by the relatively little agreement described by narrative reviews of the time when exploring correlation coefficients between predictors and job performance across studies, leading to the **situational specificity hypothesis**. In short, this hypothesis suggested that the correlation between employment test scores and job performance was unique in each organization and therefore that comparisons across studies would give us no useful information to shape theory about job performance and its causes. If you react to this idea by thinking, "But we know that personality, cognitive ability, etc., all have fairly consistent relationships across jobs," you have Hunter and Schmidt to thank directly for that knowledge.

At the time, Schmidt and Hunter believed situational specificity was incorrect but did not have the data or tools to demonstrate it empirically. One of their major concerns was that validation studies at that time were frequently underpowered, which made the interpretation of NHST in those studies questionable at best, adding to a general inconsistency in the literature similar to the one Glass faced. Their first major success attempting to rectify this problem was Schmidt and Hunter's (1977) paper suggesting a specific application of Bayesian statistical modeling for more accurately contrasting results across studies, which was also their first paper on the topic of validity generalization. That paper contained an error, however, in its ignorance of the effects of reliability and range restriction, an error that was fixed in Schmidt et al. (1979). You can probably already see where this is going – in 1982, based on a recommendation from Lee Cronbach, Hunter and Schmidt (1982) published a book applying the method combining their modeling approach with corrections for reliability and range restriction not only to I-O's validity generalization problem but to quantitative research more generally. Thus the Schmidt-Hunter approach was formalized, and the most recent edition of this book is still considered its authoritative how-to manual and reference guide.

In contrast to Glassian meta-analysis, the Hunter-Schmidt approach placed a heavy emphasis on corrections of the kind listed earlier in this chapter. It focuses on the creation of point estimates of effect sizes by **sample size weighting**, meaning that larger studies are more influential on the mean effect size than smaller studies, reflecting the likely smaller amount of sampling error present in larger studies. After obtaining a sample-size weighted effect estimate, Hunter-Schmidt then applies corrections to estimate the population value of that estimate, converted either a observed weighted average r into an estimate of the population correlation ρ or an observed weighted average difference score d into an estimate of the population difference score Δ. The Hunter-Schmidt method is also highly critical of fixed-effects models, suggesting they should only be used when explicitly justified, and even then suggesting that it is rarely safe to assume. Thus, Hunter-Schmidt is almost entirely associated with random-effects models, and it incorporates several concrete steps to explore population-level variation between studies when trying to assess the presence of moderators. The method also relies mostly on researcher expert judgments about effect size to determine next steps. We'll explore the Hunter-Schmidt method in detail later in this chapter.

The authoritative reference for Hunter-Schmidt meta-analysis is:

Schmidt, F. L., & Hunter, J. E. (2014). *Methods of meta-analysis: Correcting error and bias in research findings* (3rd ed.). Sage.

Hedges-Olkin Meta-Analysis

Hedges-Olkin meta-analysis is the second most common in I-O psychology, but it is almost twice as popular outside of I-O. This is likely attributable to the home discipline of each; whereas Hunter-Schmidt comes from the small, scrappy, yet incredibly important field of I-O, Larry Hedges and Ingram Olkin approached the problem of research synthesis from the perspective of education, building directly on Glass' work. Thus, even today, Hedges-Olkin is the primary meta-analytic method employed in educational research.

Although building from Glassian meta-analysis, Hedges and Olkin changed a number of key aspects of the approach. Most centrally, and quite different from Hunter-Schmidt, Hedges-Olkin meta-analysis weighted by the inverse variance of the effect size, which is calculated by dividing 1 by the variance of each correlation, which is itself determined by the correlation itself and the sample size used to measure it. For example, the inverse-variance weight for a correlation of can be calculated as shown in Figure 13.4. To understand the effect of this different weighting strategy, look at Table 13.1, which contains a comparison of weights by sample size.

As you can see in Table 13.1, across the different values of r, Hunter-Schmidt weighs a study of $N = 1000$ 100× more strongly than a study of $N = 10$, whereas Hedges-Olkin weighs that study roughly 111× more strongly. In practice, this means that bigger correlations are more influential in meta-analytic estimates than small correlations, and research from I-O has suggested that this, along with other peculiarities of Hedges-Olkin, results in biased Hedges-Olkin estimates relative to Hunter-Schmidt estimates (Hall & Brannick, 2002).

The authoritative references for Hedges-Olkin meta-analysis is:

Hedges, L. V., & Olkin, I. (1985). *Statistical methods for meta-analysis*. Academic Press.

$$\frac{N-1}{(1-r^2)^2}$$

Figure 13.4 Inverse variance of a correlation.

Table 13.1 Hunter-Schmidt and Hedges-Olkin weights comparisons for various values of r and N

	r	$N = 10$	$N = 20$	$N = 50$	$N = 100$	$N = 500$	$N = 1000$
Hunter-Schmidt	All	10	20	50	100	500	1000
Hedges-Olkin	0.1	9.2	19.4	50.0	101.0	509.1	1019.3
Hedges-Olkin	0.2	9.8	20.6	53.2	107.4	541.4	1084.0
Hedges-Olkin	0.5	16.0	33.8	87.1	176.0	887.1	1776.0

Rosenthal-Rubin Meta-Analysis

A type of meta-analysis not commonly seen in I-O research that has nevertheless contributed specific methods is the one created by Robert Rosenthal and Donald Rubin. **Rosenthal-Rubin meta-analysis** refers to the meta-analytic methods proposed by Rosenthal (1984) building upon the work of Rubin (1974). Most centrally, Rubin proposed that the best way to learn about causal phenomena was through experimentation and careful quasi-experimental design (hopefully these are familiar given this book!). Assuming a meta-analyst then starts with a collection of archival results from experiments and quasi-experiments, Rubin proposed meta-analyzing p-values to get a better sense of true causal effect among that family of studies. Although future researchers leaned a bit away from this approach and toward effect size estimation, p-value aggregation nevertheless rests at the heart of Rosenthal-Rubin methods. The major advantage to p-value aggregation beyond effect size aggregation is that p-values can be calculated, given certain assumptions, for any effect size. Because p-value aggregation is not particularly common in I-O – itself likely due to the relatively few experiments we conduct compared to other fields – we won't discuss it further here.

Rosenthal's broader contributions, on the other hand, have significantly influenced I-O meta-analytic practices. Rosenthal's (1979) core concern was that regardless of whether researchers were using narrative review, meta-analysis, or any other archival method, papers with controversial or null results tend to be suppressed in the research literature. Put another way, if you don't find support for your hypothesis, it tends to be more difficult to get your research published. Rosenthal explained that although publication is less likely with non-significant results, non-significant results do not imply that studies finding those results were badly designed. In fact, studies with null results can be significantly more rigorous in design and precise in their conclusions, such that the null result is the result of good research design practices. These two situations together create an unfortunate combination: low-quality research can be more likely to be published than high-quality research if the results are flashy enough. This is the heart of what Rosenthal called the **file drawer problem**, the consequence of too many results being shoved in the file drawer, never to be published. It is called a file drawer because many decades in the past, researchers would literally stick their papers in a file drawer never to be seen again. We now more frequently refer to this issue by its effect: **publication bias**.

To deal with this problem, when Rosenthal (1984) published his reference guide to meta-analysis, he suggested a concrete solution: the **fail-safe N**. Keeping in mind that Rosenthal-Rubin is mostly focused on p-values, the fail-safe N was conceptualized as the number of additional research studies that would need to be published with null results to make the resulting aggregated p-value non-significant. Although fail-safe N has fallen a bit out of favor these days, the idea that meta-analysts should quantify publication bias, to get a concrete sense of how trustworthy a meta-analytic result is, has stuck around. We'll cover these approaches later in this chapter.

The primary reference for Rosenthal-Rubin meta-analysis is:

Rosenthal, R. (1984). *Meta-analytic procedures for social research*. Sage Publications.

Mixed Approach Meta-Analysis and Comparing Methods

We've only covered four major approaches to meta-analysis here: Glassian, Hunter-Schmidt, Hedges-Olkin, and Rosenthal-Rubin. There are many more than this. And, importantly, although they have been presented and are often discussed as if they are coherent, formalized methods, researchers frequently mix and match components between them depending on their specific goals. For example, a researcher might prefer the focus on random-effects modeling, sample-size weighting, and approach to corrections in Hunter-Schmidt but prefer statistical significance testing for hypotheses about the presence of moderators, borrowing from Hedges-Olkin.

These differences, in *most* cases, do not dramatically affect conclusions. But they can sometimes, so it's important to recognize the differences and make philosophically consistent choices when deciding how to approach a particular research problem with meta-analysis. For example, you wouldn't want to employ *p*-values aggregation from Rosenthal-Rubin but then try to interpret variance explained statistics from Hunter-Schmidt because the two approaches rely on very different underlying assumptions about how to meaningfully aggregate data. A comparison of the biggest differences between Hunter-Schmidt and Hedges-Olkin, the two most popular in our field, appear in Table 13.2.

Walking Through a Meta-Analytic Project

Meta-analysis is somewhat unusual among common I-O research methods due to its archival nature and focus on the "previous study results" level of analysis. In short, it is the only quantitative method we commonly use that does not study people directly. As a result, it requires a host of techniques that are not seen extensively in other approaches. In this section, we'll walk through a basic Hunter-Schmidt meta-analysis, step by step. We'll use fake data to make calculations easy, but we'll use a realistic research question to ground the example in something tangible.

Our research question is this: is the dark triad (personality traits: narcissism, Machiavellianism, and subclinical psychopathy) related to counterproductive work behavior?

Table 13.2 Comparison of Hunter-Schmidt and Hedges-Olkin meta-analytic methods

	Hunter-Schmidt method	Hedges-Olkin method
Estimator	sample-size weighted	inverse-variance weighted
Population model	random-effects	mostly fixed-effects
Hypothesis tests	interpreting effect magnitudes	statistical significance
Interpretive focus	credibility intervals	confidence intervals
Moderator detection	% variance explained	Q_B significance test

Step 1: Develop a Coding Sheet

The first step to a meta-analysis is to develop a **coding sheet**, which refers to a spreadsheet containing the definitions of all key terms that will be used in the meta-analysis for use by meta-analytic raters and a specific way to rate each study. Developing the coding sheet is usually not quite so straightforward as writing down all of the variables you're interested in measuring. Instead, it requires a bit of development: write a draft, share it with your co-authors and **coders** for feedback, revise, and repeat until you all agree on an approach.

The coding sheet is central to the meta-analytic process because it reflects the **shared mental model** of the meta-analyses to be conducted between all study personnel. The need to achieve a shared mental model among co-authors should be obvious – you all need to agree on why you're doing this project and what you want to learn before actually executing the project. Coders, on the other hand, are the people that will actually be reading the primary research papers and then interpreting them for inclusion in your **meta-analytic database**. Sometimes your coders are the same as your co-authors, and sometimes they aren't. In either case, if your coders don't have the same shared mental model of key study variables, they're going to disagree more often, which will reduce the reliability of your measures, which is going to be important later.

This mindset – that you are using coders to measure characteristics of research papers – is an important one. You can and should apply all the lessons about measurement from Chapters 7, 9, and 10 to this problem. There is some "true" characteristic of the research paper that you are trying to reflect, and your coders (i.e., raters) are trying to uncover that truth. They're going to disagree to the degree that the truth is ambiguous *or* that the approach you're taking to measurement is poorly specified. You can't control the truth, but you can definitely control measurement.

A good coding sheet consists of two parts: 1) a written document that gives definitions of all variables to be coded and 2) a spreadsheet where coders actually record their individual interpretations of the papers they are reading. In our example study, we might initially come up with this list of variables of interest:

1. Narcissism
2. Machiavellianism
3. Subclinical psychopathy
4. Counterproductive work behavior

But wait! There are actually a lot of different ways to measure these three traits, and a study is probably but not necessarily going to use the same one for all three. Counterproductive work behaviors could be conceptualized as multidimensional and, depending on which framework is being used, could be measured with any of several different scales. There are also study-level concerns; although this literature is all going to be correlational, there might be important differences in population studied, sampling techniques, design, and other contextual issues. We also need to record which research paper provided each set of values in our coding sheet! We also need to get both the sample size and effect estimate for every effect of interest. So we might expand on our initial list like this:

1. Citation to article (text, APA 7 style citation)
2. Published or unpublished source? (P, UP)

3. Book chapter, journal article, dissertation, working paper, or something else? (BC, JA, DISS, WP, OTHER)
4. Correlational design or something else? (CORR, OTHER)
5. If #4 is other, what research design? (text)
6. Narcissism versus CWB correlation (*r*)
7. Sample size for #6 (whole number)
8. Notes on conversion calculations for #6 (text)
9. Machiavellianism vs CWB correlation (*r*)
10. Sample size for #9 (whole number)
11. Notes on conversion calculations for #9 (text)
12. Subclinical psychopathy vs CWB correlation (*r*)
13. Sample size for #12 (whole number)
14. Notes on conversion calculations for #12 (text)
15. Narcissism measure (text)
16. Reliability of #15 (decimal number)
17. Machiavellianism measure (text)
18. Reliability of #17 (decimal number)
19. Subclinical psychopathy measure (text)
20. Reliability of #19 (decimal number)
21. CWB measure (text)
22. CWB type (CWBI, CWBO, PRODDEV, TIMETHEFT, PROPTHEFT, OTHER)
23. If #22 is other, what was it? (text)
24. Reliability of #21 (decimal number)
25. Any potential for range restriction on any of the four focal vars? (YES, NO, NOT SURE)

Despite an interest in only four variables, this list has become quite a bit longer. You might also notice that **content codes** have been added to each line reflecting the *only* valid text to be entered into the spreadsheet after coding. And we haven't even explored if intercorrelations between these traits would be of interest, if there are other literature-specific factors that should be considered, or really any of a host of other decisions to be made.

This list must be revised until everyone is in complete agreement with both its contents and the meaning of individual components. It's also generally a good idea to write down in a sentence or two what each of the lines refers to, specifically, along with citations to any supporting literature that would help clarify the issue. And hopefully the complexity of what we'd need to do to meaningfully conduct this relatively series of meta-analyses should illustrate to you both how complicated and how subjective this process can be.

Once your team has agreed on the written coding sheet, you can convert it into a spreadsheet, like the not-complete one shown in Table 13.3 given the previous list. It will make the lives of your coders easiest if you group similar information into buckets (in this case, 1–5, 6–8, 9–11) as shown. Color-coding sections is also common. Once you have agreement on your research questions, hypotheses, and what specific information you're looking for in your meta-analyses, things get quite a bit more complicated.

Step 2: Identify Studies for Inclusion

The next step in a meta-analysis is finding source material. Everything in Step 1 was driven by your a priori assumptions and decisions about what you want to accomplish in your project. Now you need to see how well your a priori expectations actually match up to what is available in the research literature.

Table 13.3 Partial coding spreadsheet for example meta-analytic project (cols 1–11 only)

Publication info					Narcissism effect			Machiavellianism effect		
1 Cite	**2 Pub**	**3 Typ**	**4 RDe**	**5 Oth**	**6 r**	**7 N**	**8 Nts**	**9 r**	**10 N**	**11 Nts**
Janeway (1995)										
Picard (1987)										
Pike (2022)										

The first decision to be made here is setting **inclusion criteria**. You can think of these like hard rules that define the boundary conditions of your research. In the example case, you might start with relatively simple inclusion criteria:

1. Study sample must be drawn from a population in an authentic, identifiable workplace
2. Sufficient information must be available to determine at least one of the focal effect sizes (#6, #9, or #12 on the coding sheet)

This most obviously means that you'd be excluding all research conducted with students or with panel research participants. Is that really what you want? If not, you'll need to revise your inclusion criteria. Whatever you do, make this decision *explicitly*, as you'll need to later justify it in any manuscript you write about your project.

To figure out if your inclusion criteria are realistic and practical, you'll next need to actually find some studies that meet your criteria, which means first developing a **literature search strategy.** We discussed strategy a bit in Chapter 2 in relation to developing your research question originally. To be clear, you should have already done that well before this point in the meta-analytic research strategy, because that is where the research questions and hypotheses should have come from. What you should do *now* is draw from that experience to develop a more comprehensive search strategy.

The goal here is somewhat the opposite of what it was in Chapter 2. There, you wanted to identify the most useful and relevant research papers to drive your decision-making. Here, you want to develop a search strategy that is *exhaustive* given your research question. In other words, your goal is to final 100% of all research studies ever conducted that match your inclusion criteria. If that sounds like a lot of work, that's because it is.

Draw on your origins literature review strategy to develop some basic search terms and then select some search engines relevant to your research question. The same places you searched before are still appropriate now – in most cases, some combination of Google Scholar, PsycINFO, Web of Science and Scopus. Once you have that list, think carefully about what search terms you will use in each to uncover relevant research. Each is a little different.

Optimizing Your Searches

Compared to Chapter 2, you're in the big leagues now. You need to master each search engine you're using to most directly and comprehensively identify all research literature relevant to the relationships you are studying. Each search engine has its own quirks that you should investigate and learn to use. Google Scholar has a bunch, including but not limited to those appearing in Table 13.4

Table 13.4 Google Scholar power user search terms

"search phrase"	Surrounding a search in double quotes only returns matches to the exact phrase
term AND "phrase of interest"	The word AND can be used to craft a "Boolean search" requiring both terms on either side of the AND to be present
"another phrase" OR "this one"	The word OR can be used similarly to match a search term on *either* side of the OR
intitle:word	The intitle: helper only searches for words or phrases that appear in the research paper's title
author:landers	The author: helper only returns papers with authors matching this keyword (can be first, middle or last names)
source:"personnel psychology"	The source: helper only returns papers with the specified keywords in its source – this search returns both *Personnel Psychology* and *Journal of Personnel Psychology*
"search term" 2023	Just adding a specific year to your search will limit results to publications from that year

In addition to published search engines, you will need to search the **gray literature**, which refers to any publicly shared material that is not managed external to the authors by a publisher, such as a book publisher or academic journal editing process. Social media posts, such as LinkedIn posts or random webpages, can be thought of as a type of gray literature. However, content posted in such places is usually not quite detailed enough to be called gray literature in the way we mean here. Specifically, gray literature in the sense relevant to I-O research refers to complete reports on research studies to the scientific standards laid out in this book yet not (yet) published by a traditional publisher (for more on publishers, see Chapter 14).

Finding relevant gray literature can be quite difficult. Common strategies include 1) searching ProQuest directly for dissertations; 2) searching osf.io or arxiv.org for working papers and preprints; 3) searching past conference programs such as for the annual conferences of SIOP and Academy of Management followed by emails to authors who have presented on similar topics as yours; and 4) posting on social media, such as listservs and forums, asking for unpublished work meeting your inclusion criteria.

A very common strategy for finding gray literature is called **snowballing**, which refers to looking up citations in papers that you've already found. For example, a research paper on the relationship between Machiavellianism and theft probably cites a lot of papers also studying the relationship between Machiavellianism and theft, some published and some not. Since your goal is to find *every paper that has ever studied this relationship*, you need to look through them all.

This comprehensiveness-above-all goal sometimes leads meta-analysts to find themselves in strange situations. For example, Blacksmith et al. (2016) found themselves needing to collect past conference programs that had not been digitized. As a result, they made a special visit to the headquarters of the International Communication Association in Washington DC, sat down, and began sorting through paper copies on the hunt for studies meeting their inclusion criteria.

Importantly, you might find at this stage that some of the things you put on your coding sheet are not commonly reported. If they are sufficiently uncommonly reported, this may justify removing them from your coding sheet. Similarly, you might notice that a lot of researchers commonly ask and measure variables for a research question related to what you set out to do but had not originally targeted. Similarly consider in this case if you should *add* something to your coding sheet. Another change you might make at this stage is revising your inclusion criteria if you discover that you are missing an important segment of research given your existing criteria. For example, if snowballing uncovers a lot of research that looks relevant to your research question but doesn't quite match what you specified, you might need to revise. Similarly, you might need to create **exclusion criteria** if you discover you went too far in the other direction and need to systematically exclude large portions of the literature.

The goal in this task is balance. If we imagine every item in a coding sheet takes an average of 10 seconds to find in a PDF and write down, and we anticipate needing to review 500 papers, we are expecting 5000 seconds = 1.4 hours per rater per column in our coding sheet. That is a lot of time. Don't include things just because they "might be interesting." It is a common rookie meta-analyst mistake to just throw in a dozen variables that they aren't sure if they actually care about or not – which in this case would add 17 hours of work per coder, assuming they still only took 10 seconds per column. Revise your coding sheet both to meaningfully assess what you need to test your research questions and hypotheses while also being respectful of your coders' time.

Independence of Cases

A big challenge in creating a meta-analytic database is ensuring you meet the **assumption of independence**. All meta-analytic methods rest on the assumption that every effect in your database can be conceptualized as a random draw from a population of estimates of that effect. This is a tenuous assumption at the best of times in many meta-analyses. Researchers tend to use the same sorts of analyses across their studies, so including two studies by the same research team is likely to create at least a minor threat to this assumption. In fact, if there are so many papers in your meta-analytic database by a particular research team that you think your overall effect estimate might become biased, it suggests you should test *research team* as a moderator!

The more common situation where this assumption is threatened is when you collect multiple estimates of an effect from a single paper. In this case, you should be very careful to ensure that cases are independent in the literature sense, that is, that no participant is represented in more than one estimate included in your meta-analysis. There are a variety of techniques for doing this, most of which involve aggregating across the studies within the paper and including them as a single case in your final dataset. For example, if you are studying the relationship between A and B, but a researcher split their conceptualization of A into A1 and A2, you will basically need to calculate a weighted average of their estimates of A1 vs B and A2 vs B to determine the final value for inclusion in your database. Just thinking through how to best do this can take quite a lot of time.

The most difficult cases tend to occur when researchers have been salami slicing as we discuss in Chapter 14. Datasets can be reused across multiple studies, and cases may be shared in common between studies that do not seem obviously connected beyond a subtle author note or strange citation to another paper in the "Participants" section. Unfortunately there is no solution to this problem other than doing your homework to figure out if the samples did in fact overlap. The "good" news is this makes you *very* aware of the researchers conducting this and other QRPs within your research area. What you do with that information is up to you.

Step 3: Content Coding

Once you have a final list of studies for inclusion and finalized your coding sheets with that list, you are ready for your coders to dive into the literature. The basic idea here is that each coder will code some portion of your database. How much depends a bit on exactly what you're doing.

Remember that in Step 1, we conceptualized the coding sheet as a sort of construct measurement exercise. The better you did on this step in terms of construct validity (i.e., definitions are clear, all raters understand them completely, and all raters understand how this information is represented in the articles they are coding), the fewer coders you are likely to need. However, this is not a known number when you start. Assume you'll need a minimum of two raters for every variable in every case, as a starting point. Three is a bit safer.

The best tactic for determining reliability while simultaneously getting some coding done is **frame-of-reference training**. This is a type of rater training focused on developing a shared mental model of the task that your coders are all on, that is, a common frame of reference. There are many variations on this kind of training, but we suggest the following strategy:

1. Ask *all* coders to code the same five papers, based upon the same coding sheet.
2. Meet to discuss agreements and disagreements. In this meeting, the goal is for each person to share their mental model for coding and to comment on how others' models are the same or different from their own.
3. As a group, decide on the "correct" ratings for each rating where any disagreement was observed. Ensure everyone agrees. If it's difficult to reach an agreement, figure out why. It must be one of the following:

    a. Definitions are ambiguous or confusing.
    b. Rater understandings of definitions are incorrect.
    c. Articles are ambiguous or confusing in relation to definitions.
    d. Articles are ambiguous or confusing in relation to the realities of rating.

If the problem is (a) or (c), you may need to revise your rating sheet and try this rating task again. If the problem is (b), you may need to develop additional training on the definitions. If the problem is (d), you may need to develop more precise rating rules (e.g., "on column 6, if you see q r or s, always rate y").

4. Assess inter-rater agreement *on every variable*, using one of the following:

    • For nominal data, Fleiss' kappa
    • For ordinal data, Kendall's *W*
    • For internal or ratio data, intra-class correlation

5. Ask *all* coders to code an additional five papers.

6. Meet to discuss agreements and disagreements. There should be a noticeable increase in agreement, and this meeting should go much faster. If not, consider the same four possible causes as previously.
7. Assess inter-rater agreement again and compare. Values should be higher or remain high compared to the first time. In general, you want rater agreement statistics above 0.9, although as low as 0.7 is generally regarded as acceptable.
8. Determine if you have sufficient raters, and if not, how many raters you would need. This can be calculated with the following, which is a variation on the **Spearman-Brown prophecy formula**:

$$\frac{g(1-r)}{r(1-g)}N$$

where g is your "goal" reliability, r is your observed reliability, and N is your current average number of raters per case. For example, if our agreement study revealed an ICC of 0.62 with two raters per case, we could calculate necessary raters as such:

$$\frac{0.9(1-0.62)}{0.62(1-0.9)}2 = \frac{0.342}{0.062}2 = (5.5)2 = 11$$

At this point, you have a choice: 1) train and use that many raters per case, 2) change your definitions or rating materials as suggested previously and retry from the beginning, or 3) lower your reliability standards. Regardless, if you encounter this problem, it does not make sense at this point to start coding anyway, since if you ended up pursuing option (2), you'd need to ask your coders to redo a lot of work
9. Once you've achieved a good coding reliability and valid definitions for all variables, it's time to set your coders to work.

Once your coders have finished their coding, there's a final bit of preparatory work to be done. The immediate next step is to calculate final values and reliability estimates for all of your variables. This varies a bit depending on the nature of the variable:

- For nominal and ordinal data, hold a meeting with relevant coders to resolve disagreements. If you have a relatively large number of coders, you can reduce workload here by using clear modal response (e.g., if you have five coders, automatically assume the modal response is correct if agreement is four versus one; in cases of two versus three, discuss).
- For interval and ratio data, calculate averages between coders.

If any of your reliability estimates are lower than expected, you now have a bigger problem to solve. But assuming your frame-of-reference training was successful and you now have a collection of high-quality effect estimates, it's time for some math.

Step 4: Run the Meta-Analysis

You're finally ready to actually conduct the analyses at the heart of meta-analysis: deriving core point and interval estimates of the effect you are studying. In the Hunter-Schmidt method, the core concept is that observed effects are always biased downward from

Table 13.5 Example meta-analytic database

Publication info		Sample size	Observed effects (r)		Observed reliabilities (two rxx and one ryy)		
Cite	Pub	N	Narc	Mach	Narc	Mach	CWB
Janeway (1995)	P	124	.18	124	.75	.66	.60
Picard (1987)	P	100	.29	100	.80	.70	.55
Pike (2022)	UP	35	.19	35	.74	.75	.46
Kirk (1965)	P	242	.23	242	.66	.75	.58
Archer (2001)	UP	98	.13	98	.92	.61	.69
Sisko (1993)	P	77	.33	77	.77	.87	.71
Burnham (2017)	UP	366	.01	366	.70	.92	.51

Table 13.6 Results of meta-analyses of Table 13.5 example database

	k	N	Mean r	SD r	SE r	SD res	ρ	SDρ	95% CI	80% CrI
Narc versus CWB	7	1042	.205	.048	.018	.000	.309	.000	.225, .393	.309, .309
– Pub	4	543	.236	.044	.022	.000	.353	.000	.211, .494	.353, .353
– Unpub	3	499	.171	.025	.014	.000	.259	.000	.075, .444	.259, .259
Mach versus CWB	7	1042	.211	.219	.083	.205	.313	.310	.006, .620	−.133, .759
– Pub	4	543	.398	.080	.040	.033	.596	.084	.377, .815	.458, .734
– Unpub	3	499	.008	.045	.026	.000	.011	.000	−.157, .179	.011, .011

population effects by artifacts, and our primary goal is to figure out how big that bias is so that we can remove its effects from our estimates. If we reason that the observed bias explains 100% of the differences between observed correlations in our dataset, we conclude that we have very precisely estimated a fixed effect. If we don't explain all of the differences, it instead suggests that moderators of that relationship are likely in the population.

For demonstration purposes, we're going to subset down a bit from our broader example to two meta-analyses: the correlations between narcissism or Machiavellianism and counterproductive work behavior. This dataset is fake but has been constructed to illustrate two different common ways a meta-analysis can go. The data for this analysis appears in Table 13.5. Notice that we have moderator information (the Pub column), sample size, effect size estimates, and reliability estimates for each variable. The six resulting meta-analyses of this table appear in Table 13.6.

Understanding these statistics is central to accurately interpreting the results of a meta-analysis, whether it's one your read or one you conducted, so we'll cover each one:

- *k* is the number of effects included in the meta-analysis; you can see that for the publication moderator analyses, these sum to the overall *k*. That isn't usually the case though, as moderators are often not reported in all studies.
- *N* is the total number of cases included in the meta-analysis; the same summing can be done here. If the total *N* for the overall meta-analysis does not equal the sum of the moderator analysis *N*, that means some studies did not report the moderator, and you should think about why that might have happened and what influence it could have had on the estimates.

- *Mean r* is the weighted average effect among the observed effects, which in this case are correlations. If all of the included studies had equal sample sizes, this would be the same as calculating a simple arithmetic average of the effect column in Table 13.5. If sample sizes vary, larger sample sizes (in this case) will be weighted more heavily.
- *SD r* is similarly the weighted standard deviation of the observed effects. If sample sizes were the same, this would be equal to the simple standard deviation of an effect column.
- *SE r* is the estimated standard error of *Mean r*. This is calculated as *SD r* divided by the square root of *k*, just as the standard error would be calculated in a primary dataset.
- *SD res*, the **residual standard deviation**, is a bit more complicated. This value is the amount of *SD r* remaining after correcting for attenuation due to sampling error. In Table 13.6, you can see this value is .205 for the Machiavellianism versus CWB correlation, compared to .219 for the SD. This means that .219 − .205 = .014 of that observed SD was attributable to sampling error bias. If this number is zero, as is the case in several rows of this table, it suggests that the only reason observed correlations differed from one another was due to sampling error and not due to random effects. In other words, a residual variance of zero suggests that whatever is being analyzed is likely a fixed effect with no further moderators.
- ρ (rho) is our correlation coefficient corrected for all artifacts, which in this case is sampling error, predictor reliability, and criterion reliability. It could be anything, however – different studies correct correlations for different artifacts but always call the resulting number rho. Here, we can see that although the observed Machiavellianism versus CWB correlation was .211, once corrected for these three artifacts, the true score population relationship is estimated as .313. By converting these to coefficients of determination, we can see how much additional variance has been explained: $.313^2/.211^2 = 220\%$. That's a big correction.
- SDρ is the true score population standard deviation of rho. You can think of this as the standard deviation of the sample means shown in the top distribution appearing in Figure 13.3. If this number is zero, it suggests that there is no variability of effect in the population – 100% of that variation can be explained by artifacts. Thus, when SD res is zero, SDρ is also always zero.
- 95% CI is a 95% confidence interval surrounding rho. Think of this as a way to assess precision of measurement at the study level, similar to how we discussed it in Chapter 13. In that same Machiavellianism versus CWB row, we'd conclude that assuming our sample of studies of this relationship were perfectly representative of the broader population of studies of this relationship, if we could sample from that population, 95% of our estimates would fall between .006 and .620. Since that confidence interval does not overlap zero, it is also common to interpret this as a "statistically significant" result, although Hunter-Schmidt does not endorse this approach, suggesting you instead focus on effect magnitudes and especially the credibility interval.
- 80% CrI is an 80% credibility interval surrounding rho. This suggests that given the random-effects model of this value, 80% of population effects would be expected to fall between these two values. In the Machiavellianism versus CWB case, 80% of population values are expected to fall between −.133 and .759. Although this effect was statistically significant, that's a massive range, suggesting the presence of additional moderators.

Interpreting this sort of table in relation to research questions and hypotheses requires understanding the interrelationships between all of these numbers. In this case, the residual variance in the comparison of narcissism and CWB was already zero, suggesting that a fixed-effect model might be more appropriate for this relationship, which further suggests that moderators of that relationship are unlikely to be meaningful. In this case, if we had instead taken a NHST view, we'd be led to the same conclusion – the confidence intervals for the moderators overlap substantially, suggesting they are probably drawn from the same distribution and thus not meaningfully different. In the case of Machiavellianism, the credibility interval of the overall effect is huge, the moderators are statistically significantly different, and each moderator is itself significantly different from zero. This means that all evidence points to the opposite conclusion for this trait, that is, that the Machiavellianism-CWB relationship is moderated by publication status. We could further look at residual variances for the moderators, noticing the evidence that the published studies may have further moderators but that the unpublished studies likely don't.

What this should also communicate to you is the importance of sample size. Although we have a much larger number of participants contributing to these meta-analyses than any one study likely would alone, our level of analysis is still at the study level. Thus, our sample size here ranges from 3 to 7. That's quite tiny. Small meta-analyses can still be the *best* estimates we have available, but you should keep in mind that just because something is a meta-analysis doesn't mean its estimates are automatically more generalizable than the studies it draws from. Similar rules of thumb apply here as with primary research; think of $k = 20$ as a *bare minimum* to even discuss generalizability but preferably closer to a few hundred, and if the meta-analysis is complex, you'll definitely want a lot more than that.

Meta-Analysis Using R

Fortunately, meta-analysis is quite easy to do these days thanks to the *psychmeta* package in R, created by Dahlke and Wiernik (2019), two I-O psychologists, while they were graduate students. Code to run the meta-analyses in Table 13.6 appears in the following.

```
library(psychmeta)

example_df <- data.frame(
  narc_r = c(.18, .29, .19, .23, .13, .27, .18),
  mach_r = c(.31, .38, .12, .47, -.04, .33, .01),
  N = c(124, 100, 35, 242, 98, 77, 366),
  pub = c("P","P","UP","P","UP","P","UP"),
  narc_rxx = c(.75, .53, .87, .77, .91, .83, .72),
  mach_rxx = c(.66, .70, .75, .75, .61, .87, .92),
  ryy = c(.60, .55, .46, .58, .69, .71, .51)
)

summary(ma_r(
  data = example_df,
  rxyi = narc_r,
  rxx = narc_rxx,
```

```
  ryy = ryy,
  n = N,
  ma_method = "ic",
  moderators = pub
))

summary(ma_r(
  data = example_df,
  rxyi = mach_r,
  rxx = mach_rxx,
  ryy = ryy,
  n = N,
  ma_method = "ic",
  moderators = pub
))
```

Step 5: Follow-Up Theory-Relevant Analyses

Just as in primary research, our analytic goal with meta-analysis is usually to estimate one or more of three kinds of relationships: direct effects, moderation, and mediation. The way we do this, however, is a little more complex.

Direct Effects

Direct effects are relatively straightforward in that if we're interested in the relationship between A and B, we can identify a lot of research studies that measured the relationship between A and B, write down the effects they found, and then calculate a weighted effect size estimate based on what we wrote down. This is the simplest case, but it also does not really take advantage of the unique characteristics of a meta-analytic dataset.

Moderation

The most common research question asked in meta-analysis is study-level moderation. Specifically, a meta-analytic dataset allows us to systematically compare results from different groups of studies based upon different research designs (e.g., quasi-experimental versus experimental versus correlational; within-subjects versus between-subjects; students versus employees), measurement techniques (e.g., NEO-PI-R versus BFI versus TIPI for Big Five personality measurement; supervisory ratings versus objective scores for performance measurement), or really just about anything that is different among studies and could be theoretically interesting as a hypothesis or research question.

This approach allows us to test a wide range of moderators that cannot be easily tested in primary research. For many researchers, this is the primary purpose of meta-analysis. If you wanted to study the effect of between- versus within-subjects research designs in primary research, you'd need a sample of each kind of design! You'd need dozens of studies to get even a reasonable sample size! Starting from scratch, that's a tall order, but looking at studies *others* have done seems a lot more reasonable. The specific methods used for moderation tests in meta-analysis vary between approaches.

One of these, **subset analysis**, was demonstrated in the last section. Subset analysis involves splitting a meta-analytic database into pieces and reporting meta-analytic results separately based upon the split. This is most often done as a type of moderator testing. The conditions necessary to conclude that moderators are present vary dramatically by approach. The most common approach in Hunter-Schmidt is the **75% rule**. This rule of thumb rests on the assumption that researchers are rarely able to correct for all meaningful artifacts, so if at least 75% of the variance in obtained correlations is explained by artifacts, there are unlikely to be meaningful moderators in the remaining 25% – it is probably instead uncorrected artifacts. In practice, researchers tend to test whatever moderators they originally planned to test anyway regardless of the outcome of this or any statistical test.

Another common follow-up analysis for moderation is **meta-regression**, which refers to use of the entire meta-analytic database and observed effects in regression analysis. For example, in our meta-analytic database, we could regress the observed effect sizes on a dummy-coded publication status variable – essentially giving us another way to conduct subset analysis. Notably, Schmidt and Hunter (2014) don't explicitly recommend against meta-regression but do provide many pages explaining all of the disadvantages to using it and only about half a paragraph to advantages. One of the most important of the advantages is that subset analysis does not provide any obvious way to test continuous moderators – something that meta-regression can handle easily. Importantly, meta-regression is not just ordinary least squares regression – it is slightly different due to the unique role of sampling error in meta-analysis. We suggest investigating metareg() in the *meta* package in R for more guidance.

Mediation

Mediation is the most complex follow-up analytic approach for meta-analysis. As we discussed in Chapter 8, mediation in primary research is usually tested using something like PROCESS or using structural equation modeling software like *lavaan* in R or Mplus. Although we've left the mathematics of these tests to other books, it is worth briefly exploring how these kinds of tests can be done with meta-analysis, which is called **meta-analytic structural equation modeling (MASEM)**. MASEM requires you to obtain a trustworthy true-score estimate of every relationship you want to model. This gets complicated very quickly with large models. For example, imagine we wanted to test the model shown in Figure 13.5. That model implies the correlation matrix shown in Table 13.7 as input to MASEM. We'd also need good meta-analytic estimates of reliability for each of the five variables. Thus, to use

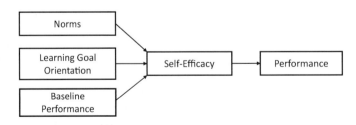

Figure 13.5 Mediational model, adapted from Mathieu and Taylor (2006).

Table 13.7 Matrix of meta-analytic rho estimates necessary to test Figure 13.5 model using MASEM

	Norms	LGO	Baseline	SE
LGO	ρ_{11}			
Baseline	ρ_{21}	ρ_{22}		
SE	ρ_{31}	ρ_{32}	ρ_{33}	
Performance	ρ_{41}	ρ_{42}	ρ_{43}	ρ_{44}

MASEM in this context, we'd need 15 meta-analytic estimates. It's unlikely we'd be able to find all of these estimates in the same research studies, so we'd be using different sets of studies from different sources for each meta-analysis before even getting to the MASEM analysis itself. And all of this for a relatively simple model. Many SEM expressions of theory are much larger.

Despite these challenges, you will still see MASEM sometimes, as it allows for tests of complex theoretical relationships that can't always be studied in primary research. Even when those models could be tested in primary research, MASEM hypothetically brings all the advantages of using meta-analytic estimates, especially greater estimate stability, better population representation, and reduced influence of sample-specific sources of variance on conclusions. If this is a technique you'd like to try, check out:

Cheung, M. W. L., & Chan, W. (2005). Meta-analytic structural equation modeling: A two-stage approach. *Psychological Methods, 10*(1), 40–64.

Related Issues to Consider

As you have probably noticed by now, meta-analysis is an area full of subjective judgments about study design, analytic approach, and interpretation. There is rarely an obvious "correct" approach to a meta-analytic problem. This combination of ambiguous guidelines and high "citeability" has caused a flood of meta-analyses to appeared across all research literatures. This should lead you to be extra cautious in evaluating them. Just as we discussed in Chapter 11 in relation to primary research, the garden of forking paths drives a lot of meta-analytic thinking.

A good illustration of this is in the approach taken to corrections. In our example, we had reliability estimates available for every scale in every study. This is quite rare in practice. In most meta-analyses, a subset of studies reported values that could be used for artifact corrections. Since we had them all available, we used a technique called **individual corrections**, an approach in which every unique effect estimate is corrected based upon the specific artifacts that the meta-analysts believe apply to it. For example, let's imagine that the meta-analysis of narcissism actually contained 50 studies, and 42 of them reported reliability. For the remaining eight, we have many options in an individual corrections approach, including 1) using the median reliability of 42 to replace the missing reliabilities, 2) imputing the missing reliabilities based on other study characteristics, 3) looking up meta-analyses of the scales used to find their mean reliabilities, 4) consulting our own past research to find realistic numbers, or 5) basically anything we can imagine doing and justifying. That's a *lot* of flexibility. For that reason, other researchers use an approach called **artifact distribution**

corrections, in which a weighted reliability estimate is used instead. But all of these decisions are fully at the discretion of the meta-analyst, which means if you're trying to understand a particular meta-analysis, it is your responsibility to figure out which approach was taken and what effect it might have had.

This problem extends also to inclusion criteria and exclusion criteria. You must decide if you agree with the reasons that the database includes the studies it does. Entire literatures can be omitted from meta-analyses in which they seem they'd be relevant, and this can be difficult to detect if you were unfamiliar with those literatures before reading the meta-analysis. This problem is sometimes described as **GIGO**, or **garbage-in/garbage-out.** In short, if the inclusion and exclusion criteria are not meaningful given the research question posed, the use of meta-analytic methods will not solve that problem. If you start with garbage studies, you'll end with garbage meta-analytic estimates. This can also create opportunities; for example, if you notice a particular research design characteristic in your literature that you believe is resulting in misleading effect estimates, that's a prime candidate for moderator analysis.

The sheer quantity of decisions in meta-analysis, some of which are never clearly documented, means that meta-analyses of the same relationships can result in different conclusions despite looking at similar literature with similar inclusion and exclusion criteria. You can imagine this a bit like there being a population of meta-analyses from which the meta-analysis you're reading (or conducting) is drawn. The random differences among those meta-analyses is referred to as **second order sampling error**, a term that presupposes that meta-analysts only differ from each other due to random factors. Investigating such a thing requires a **second order meta-analysis**, which is what it sounds like – a meta-analysis of meta-analytic estimates. Just like in meta-analysis, a second order meta-analysis tries to separate out the effects of sampling error (of the second order, in this case) and moderators. Moderators in second order meta-analyses can get quite interesting; for example, we might ask if meta-analyses created by authors working at companies with the products being meta-analyzed make systematically different conclusions from independent researchers. Hypothetically, third, fourth, or any order meta-analysis is possible, although we haven't seen one yet in mainstream I-O research. If you think this level of metameta seems a little silly, you're not alone, as suggested by Figure 13.1. Second-order meta-analysis can play an important role in I-O psychology. Higher-order, we're less sure.

A final issue to think about is how to address publication bias. As discussed earlier, methods for doing so began to be studied in earnest starting with Rosenthal's fail-safe N. Although fail-safe N is now fairly uncommon in I-O, many new methods have appeared to diagnose and handle this bias. Probably the most common is the **funnel plot**, like the one shown in Figure 13.6, which is a scatterplot comparing effect size on the x-axis with standard errors on the y-axis across a meta-analytic database. Because larger standard errors (i.e., effect estimates drawn from smaller-N studies) should generally result in more varied estimates, funnel plots should generally reveal noisier estimates when error is high (i.e., a wide spread at the high-SE side of the plot) and a more consistent estimates when error is low (i.e., a narrow spread at the low-SE side of the plot). To the extent that a funnel plot is lopsided or clustered, this could indicate publication bias. However, it could also indicate unspecified moderators/subgroups. To address this, researchers have come up with a variety of methods for statistically analyzing or adjusting funnel plots. All of this can make interpretation of funnel plots rather difficult – and, perhaps more distressing, yet another forking

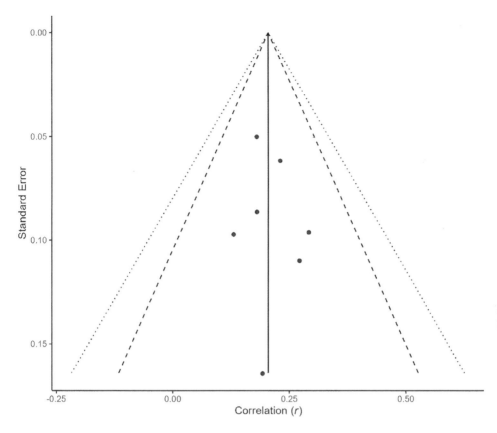

Figure 13.6 Funnel plot of individually corrected studies of narcissism from Table 13.5, created using *plot_funnel()* in *psychmeta*, with lines representing 95% and 99% confidence region levels.

path. Kepes et al. (2023) summarized the benefits and challenges associated with funnel plots, alongside several other ways to assess publication bias and is recommended reading on this issue.

Given the myriad decisions you'll either make when conducting a meta-analysis or recognize the importance of while reading a report on one, you might think to yourself – surely there's a standardized way to keep track of all of this? The good news is yes, there are two: the American Psychological Association's **Meta-Analytic Reporting Standards** (Cooper, 2010) and the **Preferred Reporting Items for Systematic Review and Meta-Analyses (PRISMA)**.

Developed by Köhler et al. (2015), PRISMA is a checklist for all of the information that should be included in a meta-analysis (or narrative review) documenting all the decisions that were made. Importantly, much like with pre-registration, PRISMA should be thought of more as a "minimum" than a comprehensive list of everything that might be relevant to interpreting a meta-analysis. For this reason, it serves as a valuable checklist when writing up results, to be sure you haven't missed anything major. You can find a PDF of the PRISMA checklist, along with many additional resources, at https://prisma-statement.org.

References

Cheung, M. W. L., & Chan, W. (2005). Meta-analytic structural equation modeling: A two-stage approach. *Psychological Methods, 10*(1), 40–64.

Cooper, H. (2010). *Research synthesis and meta-analysis: A step-by-step approach* (4th ed., Applied Social Research Methods Series, Vol. 2). Sage.

Dahlke, J. A., & Wiernik, B. M. (2019). Psychmeta: An R package for psychometric meta-analysis. *Applied Psychological Measurement, 43*(5), 415–416. https://doi.org/10.1177/0146621618795933

Glass, G. V. (1976). Primary, secondary, and meta-analysis of research. *Educational Researcher, 5*(10), 3–8.

Hall, S. M., & Brannick, M. T. (2002). Comparison of two random-effects methods of meta-analysis. *Journal of Applied Psychology, 87*, 377–389.

Hedges, L. V., & Olkin, I. (1985). *Statistical methods for meta-analysis*. Academic Press.

Hunter, J. E., & Schmidt, F. L. (1982). Meta-analysis. In Ronald K. Hambleton and Jac N. Zaal (Eds.), *Advances in educational and psychological testing: Theory and applications* (pp. 157–183). Springer Netherlands.

Kepes, S., Wang, W., & Cortina, J. M. (2023). Assessing publication bias: A 7-step user's guide with best-practice recommendations. *Journal of Business and Psychology, 38*, 957–982. https://doi.org/10.1007/s10869-022-09840-0

Köhler, T., Cortina, J. M., Kurtessis, J. N., & Gölz, M. (2015). Are we correcting correctly? Interdependence of reliabilities in meta-analysis. *Organizational Research Methods, 18*(3), 355–428.

LeBreton, J. M., Scherer, K. T., & James, L. R. (2014). Corrections for criterion reliability in validity generalization: A false prophet in a land of suspended judgment. *Industrial and Organizational Psychology: Perspectives on Science and Practice, 7*, 478–500. https://doi.org/10.1111/iops.12184

Mathieu, J. E., & Taylor, S. R. (2006). Clarifying conditions and decision points for mediational type inferences in organizational behavior. *Journal of Organizational Behavior, 27*(8), 1031–1056.

Rosenthal, R. (1979). The file drawer problem and tolerance for null results. *Psychological Bulletin, 86*(3), 638–641.

Rubin, D. B. (1974). Estimating causal effects of treatments in randomized and nonrandomized studies. *Journal of Educational Psychology, 66*(5), 688–701.

Russell, T. L. (1999). *The no significant difference phenomenon*. North Carolina State University.

Schmidt, F. L., & Hunter, J. E. (1977). Development of a general solution to the problem of validity generalization. *Journal of Applied Psychology, 62*(5), 529.

Schmidt, F. L., & Hunter, J. E. (2014). *Methods of meta-analysis: Correcting error and bias in research findings* (3rd ed.). Sage.

Schmidt, F. L., Pearlman, K., Hunter, J. E., & Shane, G. S. (1979). Further tests of the Schmidt-Hunter Bayesian validity generalization procedure. *Personnel Psychology, 32*(2), 257–281.

Further Reading

Moher, D., Shamseer, L., Clarke, M., Ghersi, D., Liberati, A., Petticrew, M., Shekelle, P., Stewart, L. A., & PRISMA-P Group. (2015). Preferred reporting items for systematic review and meta-analysis protocols (PRISMA-P). *Systematic Reviews, 4*(1).

- Moher and colleagues provide the most commonly referenced and most comprehensive list of information to include in meta-analytic reporting. Whether you're writing a manuscript incorporating meta-analytic methods or trying to understand a meta-analysis, the items in the PRISMA checklist should be at the front of your mind.

Schmidt, F. L., & Hunter, J. E. (2014). *Methods of meta-analysis: Correcting error and bias in research findings* (3rd ed.). Sage.

- Schmidt and Hunter's book on meta-analysis remains the gold standard in I-O psychologists practicing meta-analysis. If you want to run your own meta-analyses, reading this cover to cover is where you should start.

Questions to Think About

1. When is it appropriate to conduct a meta-analysis? What value can a new meta-analysis bring when another meta-analysis on the same topic has been recently published?
2. What design features of a meta-analysis will lead you to trust it? What would lead you to distrust it?
3. When do the differences between meta-analytic approaches actually matter when drawing conclusions?
4. If you were to conduct a meta-analysis, what training techniques would you use to maximize coder agreement?
5. How does the garden of forking paths influence meta-analytic results? Consider the garden as navigated by both primary researchers and meta-analysts themselves.
6. How would you handle GIGO in your research area? Moderator analysis or exclusion criteria?
7. Find a prominent, published, and well-regarded meta-analysis within an area of personal interest. Did the authors follow the PRISMA guidelines closely? If not, how does that change your opinion of the quality of the meta-analysis?

Key Terms

- 75% rule (in meta-analysis)
- artifact (in meta-analysis)
- artifact distribution corrections
- assumption of independence
- bias, publication
- Cochrane collaboration
- coders
- coding sheet
- content codes
- correction
- credibility interval
- credibility value
- exclusion criteria
- fail-safe N
- file drawer problem
- frame-of-reference training
- funnel plot
- garbage-in/garbage-out (GIGO)
- Glassian meta-analysis
- gray literature
- Hedges-Olkin meta-analysis
- Hedges' g
- Hunter-Schmidt meta-analysis
- inclusion criteria
- individual corrections
- interval estimate
- literature search strategy
- meta-analytic database
- Meta-Analytic Reporting Standards (MARS)
- meta-analytic structural equation modeling (MASEM)
- meta-regression
- model, shared mental
- modeling, fixed effects
- modeling, random effects
- odds ratio
- operational validity
- overcorrection
- point estimate
- Preferred Reporting Items for Systematic Review and Meta-Analyses (PRISMA)
- psychometric meta-analysis
- Rosenthal-Rubin meta-analysis
- sample-size weighting
- SD res
- second order meta-analysis
- second order sampling error
- situational specificity hypothesis
- snowballing
- Spearman-Brown prophecy formula
- subset analysis
- validity generalization
- vote counting
- weighted effect size
- weighting

Chapter 14

Strategies for Openly Sharing Research, Materials, and Data

Learning Objectives

1. Develop your personal goals in relation to sharing your results and conclusions
2. Pre-register your research effectively
3. Maximize the reproducibility of your research
4. Avoid cargo cult science
5. Engage in effective self-development for public speaking about research
6. Describe the publishing landscape and the politics surrounding it

If you've read the first three parts of this book (and we hope you have!), you now have a substantial chunk of the basic scientific toolkit in I-O psychology. You can, at this point, define a philosophy of science for yourself, create interesting research questions, review research literatures, select research strategies, identify samples, identify meaningful questions for qualitative research, execute and analyze qualitative research studies, measure psychological constructs, investigate causality, design effective quantitative research, build questionnaires, develop scales to good psychometric standards of reliability and validity, and clean your data in order to run useful, interesting analyses. But what comes next is arguably the most important part: sharing your results with others.

Science is a collaborative process that occurs at a distance. It is about experts convincing other experts, given the weight of evidence, that our current scientific understanding of the world (i.e., theory) should change. The bigger the claims are, the bigger the weight of evidence required.

This is already challenging within our **disciplinary silo**, which in our case refers to I-O psychologists trying to convince other I-O psychologists that their theories need updating. The fundamental challenge here is establishing that your ideas stand on the shoulders of giants (recall Chapter 5) but also accomplish something that those giants haven't accomplished already. That's a tall order. Following the guidelines and recommendations you've read about so far will help you plan a firm footing on those giants in terms of your science. But it doesn't necessarily imply that anyone will care what you have to say.

This is a tricky balancing act and leads to a lot of well-intentioned but ultimately poor advice. One of the most common is "make it a story." We know (from science!) that stories and anecdotes are generally very convincing to humans. People are more likely to believe and learn from personal anecdotes from their friends than from a professor carefully laying

DOI: 10.4324/9781315167473-18

out arguments based on evidence. And despite our training, scientists easily fall into this trap as well. So it only makes sense to make your research papers sound like anecdotes, right? Set up an important question and tell a story about the journey from your question to your methods, stop briefly in your analysis, and ultimately end up with some groundbreaking conclusion that *just makes sense* given the narrative that led up to it. The reviewers will love it, right?

And they do. Reviewers, on average, will respond better to pretty narratives tied up in a good story. But that doesn't 1) make the work they're reviewing good science, 2) suggest you should trust published research conclusions without evaluating it on its methodological merits, 3) imply that you should write this way, or 4) encourage you to do the same thing as a reviewer. There is value in a coherent research narrative explaining your logic and the process you used to reach the conclusions you provided. But, importantly, there is harm in a research narrative that misleads your audience. When you let the story become more important than the science, you have walked the wrong path.

Some researchers are extremely talented at telling good stories that other researchers enjoy hearing. This is a valuable, developed skill. Such researchers can quickly weave compelling narrative threads through their papers in a way that will make you feel like you want to trust them – but unfortunately, sometimes, these stories go a bit further than the data actually support. Armed with the knowledge in this book, we hope you will take a skeptical approach to well-written stories, appreciating them but evaluating the merit of the research on more appropriate terms. As discussed throughout this book, strength of evidence as supported through research design, thoughtful analysis, and careful interpretation, all supported by a coherent philosophical orientation toward the research, is what makes the resulting research conclusions trustworthy. You should always focus on and evaluate these features on their own merits. A good story should at most be a nice extra – and only when it legitimately worked out that way.

Knowing how to present your work so that other people can easily see its value, without overselling, is an important skill to develop in either academia (especially when trying to publish your work) or practice (especially when trying to convince executives that you found something important). A convoluted figure, like Figure 14.1, may accurately represent your data but communicate little about it to the audiences that need to hear the message. Thus, in the remainder of this chapter, we're sharing with you the lessons we've learned over

Figure 14.1 "The worst are graphs with qualitative, vaguely-labeled axes and very little actual data." Courtesy xkcd.com.

our careers in how to effectively communicate the implications of your work – without telling stories that lack substance.

Revisiting Your Identity

The first step toward effectively communicating your science is understanding your role in the scientific community, within the context of your personal values and professional identity (see Chapter 1). Then, to a degree, you can shape that perception to better meet your bigger goals.

As such, the first thing you should ask yourself is: what are my bigger goals? Common worthwhile goals include:

1. Making a positive impact in state or national policy
2. Helping individuals through your work outputs or via personal mentoring
3. Being an excellent science communicator and improving access to science
4. Achieving a work-life balance that you find satisfying and meaningful
5. Continuously learning about your topic area
6. Improving capability and access to those disadvantaged by society
7. Making the world a better place to live

Metrics you should probably pay less attention to include:

1. Getting promoted or advancing in academic rank
2. Increasing your earning potential
3. Being able to work independently
4. Being recognized by other scientists, the media, or the public
5. Networking with powerful people
6. Leaving a legacy
7. Getting published

This is not to say that keeping an eye on the second set of goals is "bad." You *should not* sacrifice your well-being for the sake of science. You *should not* be willing to accept less pay than your work is worth just because your profession is noble. But seeking increased pay and recognition above all else is a dangerous path that has led many researchers toward QRPs and bad science.

Importantly, if you primarily pursue the goals in the first list, many of the outcomes in the second list will naturally follow. Yet if you single mindedly pursue the goals in the second list, you may never achieve the goals in the first. And that's at best a waste of a career and at worst harmful to our community.

As a personal story, both of us (Tara and Richard) earned our PhDs in an era when technology was not a major part of I-O psychology research. In fact, we both routinely received feedback in those early years from editors that our work, for example examining the causal impact of moving organizational processes into virtual worlds and understanding people's response to those kinds of managerial policies in terms of attitudes and performance (we're definitely not bitter), were "not I-O psychology." We believed otherwise. And now we have found ourselves on the opposite side of all that struggle in a much better position, having achieved many of the items in the second list yet rarely having worked directly toward any of them.

So all of this is not to say that you should always prioritize the needs of the many above your own. Instead it means that you should always think about why you are doing what you're doing and be sure you have a good reason. If your work doesn't pay enough, making more money so that you do not need to worry about how to feed yourself and your family is an important and meaningful goal. But once you've met that goal, think carefully about what to prioritize next.

It's Personal

So you're reading and probably thinking to yourself, "But I *do* want to make some money!" That is perfectly fine. In our modern society, money is necessary to survive, and if you're struggling to feed yourself, you're not going to be able to do good science anyway. But you must also recognize that becoming a meaning-maker in society – the kind of person who reveals truths and helps others find a better path through this world – is both a rare privilege and a heavy responsibility. Once your needs are reasonably met, you need to look beyond yourself. This is a **moral imperative**, a value that you should internalize early and always act from, before you become so powerful and important that you forget how you got there.

This is one of the reasons why we (Richard and Tara) both get suddenly upset whenever we hear about researchers abusing these privileges. A researcher with a primary career goal of "more publications" is much more likely to abuse the trust placed in them by *p*-hacking, faking data, abusing supervisees, and many other harmful behaviors. When all that matters is $p < .05$, that's what you'll optimize your behavior on. When you let personal achievement and careerism drive your decision-making, you lose sight of the effects of your actions on others who trust you. This hurts them. It also hurts our field, and it ultimately hurts science.

This is very personal. It is about you and your choices. Yes, you. By training to become a researcher, you will become a person of importance. Your opinion and voice will increasingly carry weight as you advance in your career. You have the power and authority to use your voice responsibly to make the world a better place. Wield it well.

Communicating Your Identity

Once you have a sense of who you are within I-O psychology, why you want to be here, and what you want to accomplish while you are, you should think about how your identity is communicated to the world. This is an important issue even if you have no specific research results to share – with an I-O degree, you are responsible for representing our field well to the broader world. So how do you do that?

There are many conventional approaches. Presentations at professional meetings and conferences are common. Peer-reviewed publication of your research is often regarded as a gold standard mark of approval. But these methods are often more about communicating your work – not your identity. And yet we now find ourselves attached to a digital world where identity is front and center.

Thus, one of the most common mechanisms these days that scientists use to curate a particular public image is social media. We cannot overstate the importance of actively working to prevent social media from overwhelming your own view of yourself. Social media has a tendency to force us to view ourselves through the eyes of others, and the eyes of others are half closed on the best day. If you let the curation of an image on social media control how you present yourself, you will quickly find yourself focused on the list of goals to avoid. Instead, treat social media as a tool to be used; it is a mechanism to connect with others. It does not define you or your science. Especially in cases where you study topics that are associated with any sort of controversy, most especially if you study anything touching diversity, equity, and inclusion, the opinions of others about you can be loud and based more on their political views than on the quality of your work or ideas.

In evaluating the use of social media or any other communication tool as part of your communications strategy, you should always consider two numbers. The first of these is **return on investment**, which refers to the potential benefits you could gain as a result of investing your time, money, and other resources into something. In the context of social media, this mostly refers to the time you spend managing your social media presence and learning new software to curate it. Importantly, all investments come with **opportunity cost**, which refers to the things you *aren't* doing because you've chosen to do something else. If you are choosing to spend your time posting online at the expense of better science, you should think carefully about whether the return you get on that posting is worthwhile. Importantly, return on investment in this context is not about money. It is about what you gain after spending yourself – your time and your energy.

The second number you should consider is the **risk/reward ratio**. Any time you make an investment of your time, energy, or anything else, you take a risk. Perhaps this new research study will open new doors, or perhaps it won't work at all. Perhaps this new internship will help you develop the skills you need to develop, or perhaps you'll just end up managing coffee orders. Perhaps changing research supervisors would make your dissertation move a little more quickly, or perhaps it'll just lead to a lot of avoidable stress. In these situations and many more you will face in your career, you will struggle to predict the future. All you can (and should) do is make the best judgment and decision you can, based on your own informed opinion and the opinions of those you trust. Be sure to always take a moment to ask yourself if the risk is worth it. That doesn't mean shy away from risk – it means to always strive to understand what you are getting yourself into before you get there.

Preparing Your Results to Share

Once you have an overall communications strategy firmly in mind, it's time to prepare a specific piece of research you've conducted to be shared. There are several things to think about as you consider how, before you've written a word.

Pre-Registration and Pre-Publication Peer Review

In the 2010s, psychology suddenly but not unexpectedly (at least to methodologists) experienced what is now referred to as the replication crisis. Despite being referred to as a "crisis," it was pretty slow-moving, with a variety of small events occurring over the course of a decade. Although there had been grumbling about replication problems over many decades, a specific event triggered a much bigger response. Specifically, a well-regarded and well-respected professor emeritus at Cornell named Daryl Bem (2011) published a paper about psi, also referred to extrasensory perception, in the flagship journal of social psychology, the *Journal of Personality and Social Psychology (JPSP)*. This paper used quite common and standard experimental designs, using nine distinct samples, to demonstrate that participants possessed a precognition, that is, that they could accurately predict the future. This paper is cited in the references to this chapter, and it's a doozy. You should check it out.

As you might expect about a paper published in the flagship journal of a psychology discipline claiming to present ironclad evidence that people have extrasensory perceptions, it got a bit of a reaction from the researcher community. On a surface evaluation of Bem's results, if you ignore the fact that he was testing for clairvoyance, the study appears quite ordinary. Bem randomly assigns people to groups, finds effects when in experimental conditions, and interprets those results precisely as you might expect. But as pointed out by Wagenmakers et al. (2011) and Alcock (2011), there are some irregularities – not in the stated design but in analysis. Specifically, several observed data patterns are highly improbable, that is, suggesting that only a portion of the data that had been collected was presented in the paper, a practice called **selective reporting**, one that was pretty common among social psychologists of that time period.

Selective reporting is not necessarily dishonest. It is a QRP, like the ones we discussed in Chapter 11. There are many reasons why you might not share results of a study that failed. For example, if you discovered post hoc that none of the proctors running your study actually followed the instructions correctly, there is no reason to think those data reveal anything accurate about whatever it is that you were studying. But if you ran 20 studies and dropped the 10 with $p > .05$, that's a bit different. So although selective reporting is not by itself a perfect indicator that the story told in the research is intended to mislead, it is certainly "questionable." And as discussed by Alcock (2011), the QRPs in Bem's research did not end there. Three later failed replications of Bem's work by Ritchie et al. (2012) seemed to confirm these suspicions.

In the wake of the replication crisis, many strategies were recommended to reduce the chances that this kind of thing would happen again. One of these was pre-registration, the act of recording details about your research study in some public, permanent repository so that later researchers can put your results into the broader context of your plan. Pre-registration is not a panacea that solves problems with QRPs, but it does add a layer of protection in the form of verifiability. If a researcher pre-registers plan A but then executes plan B, they'd better explain the change somewhere in their paper. Importantly, executing plan B instead is not the problem! The only problems stem from a lack of **transparency**. By requiring preregistration, journals prevent that researcher from claiming that they had planned on plan B from the start. That may create a less compelling story in the final paper, but likely a more accurate one.

In I-O psychology, there is also some resistance to preregistration because many of our field samples occur in organizations where data are already difficult to obtain. The argument is that by requiring preregistration, journals limit what we can learn from organizational datasets. If you find yourself in this situation, we recommend a balanced approach: work with the organization to determine exactly what data they have, but before analyzing it, pre-register your research questions, hypotheses, and intended analysis. If you discover something you didn't expect, that's great – just be honest that you discovered it post-hoc while exploring the dataset and don't imply that it was what you'd planned to do all along.

Some journals, like *Journal of Business and Psychology*, pioneered a hybrid approach to preregistration called **hybrid registered reports**, or sometimes just **registered reports**, making this a type of **pre-publication peer review**. In this model, the researcher submits a proposal of research for peer review. If the editor accepts the proposal, the resulting work will almost certainly be published as long as the researchers indeed do what they proposed they would do. This removes some of the **perverse incentives** of publishing – if the quality of your "story" doesn't affect whether your paper will be published or not, there is less reason to tell anything other than the truth of what happened when you conducted the research.

In general, binary thinking about success/failure of a research question or hypothesis test (Chapter 11) feeds into this problem. In addition to being less interesting, this kind of success/failure metric has powerful effects on researcher decision-making and attention. In essence, it encourages researchers to chase significant effects to "prove their study worked." **Goodhart's law** states "When a measure becomes a target, it is no longer a good measure." This expression describes our very human tendency to game whatever system we are within. Whatever is defined as success will drive our behavior– we will do what is rewarded. When significant results and gripping stories are all anyone cares about, researchers will change their behavior in a way that is likely to lead to more significant findings and more fanciful stories.

The reality remains that preregistration is a small bandage on a large, complex, systemic problem related to harmful incentives for publishing snazzy, ground-breaking research. It probably helps, but it doesn't fix the underlying problem. As a result, we suggest striving to pre-register all of your research at a fine enough level of detail to reasonably describe what you plan to do. Just be honest. If you feel the risk/reward ratio is too low for the time it would take you to do something that is good for science but technically unnecessary, try creating a hybrid registered report instead. Neither prevents you from doing good science – they just force you to be a little more thoughtful ahead of time about how you're doing it.

What to Do With Studies Showing Unwanted Results

One of the most frustrating experiences for a researcher is when a research study doesn't "work out." What this phrase really means is that the researcher had certain expectations for the results that were not met once the data were analyzed. There are a few common causes of this situation:

1. *The study was not designed appropriately.* Sometimes, conducting research is more of a learning experience than a legitimate attempt to address a meaningful research question. For example, you might discover after collecting data that a particular scale you chose was not psychometrically valid when used to assess the intended construct in the sample you collected. Design failures like this are often irrecoverable, meaning that there is no clear path forward other than redesigning your study and trying again. In these cases, papers often end up in the file drawer, a concept we introduced in Chapter 13. Lishner (2022) provides a taxonomy of reasons papers end up in the file drawer worth checking out.

2. *The results were not analyzed appropriately.* Sometimes, your beautifully pre-registered analytic plan turns out to be inappropriate, or perhaps incomplete, relative to the actual data you collected. For example, you might not have realized ahead of time that one of your criteria was a count and therefore not normally distributed, requiring a different analysis than the one you preregistered. These types of errors can be corrected post-hoc by changing your analysis and explaining why this change was made between your preregistered analysis and actual analysis. However, the more such changes you make

mid-analysis, the more likely it is that you are overcorrecting, that is, optimizing your data cleaning procedures on the basis of the specific sample you collected. As discussed in Chapter 11, this can lead to misleading conclusions.

3. *The truth is different from what you expected.* Perhaps most commonly, reality is simply not what you predicted it would be. Perhaps you developed a theory suggesting that *y* causes *x*, but the reality is that *x* causes *y*. These studies sometimes end up in the file drawer, or sometimes researchers change their theories to match their data, which is a QRP.

Regardless of which of the three causes is actually the situation, most researchers will try to **salvage** the study upon encountering unwanted results. Salvaging refers to trying to make something useful out of a study in a way that was not originally unintended, usually by changing data cleaning or analytic strategies. In some cases, researchers might try to collect additional data.

Salvaging can be a reasonable solution. If the errors came from your predictions, judgment, and decision-making, not your theories and conclusions, then salvaging pushes the scientific consensus closer to the truth. When salvaging is transparent, this is ideally how science works; we collect data and change the way we understand the world based upon what we learn from those data.

The problem is case #3. Salvaging in this situation can lead you to conclude something that is not true, which has downstream consequences. For example, if such a work was published, future researchers would spend their time and energy trying to replicate or build on a finding that was not real. If you do this, you contribute directly to slowing down scientific progress.

The overarching challenge is that you do not know which of these three situations is the one you are in for any particular project. This is where professional judgment becomes critical. You need to work to develop a good sense of "how much is too much" when salvaging. The extremes are relatively easy. For example, in case #2, salvaging might only involve changing from ordinary least squares regression to Poisson regression. In this case, there is little controversy that a count criterion variable should not be analyzed with ordinary least squares regression, so being transparent about the change and doing the generally accepted analysis instead of the one you proposed is uncontroversial: "We mistakenly pre-registered an analysis inappropriate for the data." In case #1, your scale is not valid, but why? Perhaps you run an additional analysis and discover that of the nine items on your scale, two are performing very strangely – very little variance compared to the others. Should you throw out the two underperforming items and re-run your analysis on the remainder, or should you throw out all analyses related to that scale? Either could be fine, as long as you are transparent about what you did and have good reasons, but it is your professional judgment that will drive that decision.

This space between "obviously problematic" and "obviously acceptable" is often a gray one, and unfortunately, researchers tend to err on the side of problematic. Banks and colleagues (2016) described this problem in the management literature by comparing dissertations, which are essentially extremely detailed preregistrations, with the research studies that were actually later published based upon them. They discovered that the ratio of supported to unsupported hypotheses doubled in published research compared to unpublished versions of the same research, seemingly caused by a combination of dropping hypotheses that weren't supported, adding new hypotheses that were, reversing the direction of predictions, and various kinds of new data cleaning that were not present in the original dissertations.

Even in these cases, we don't really know if cause #1, #2, or #3 was truly at play in each situation. Dissertations sometimes get less attention from advisors than papers to be published, so it's possible that once a finer-toothed comb was applied after a dissertation defense, the paper's co-authors realized some non-controversial errors or oversights and fixed them. Perhaps overzealous reviewers suggested hypotheses or demanded material be dropped. Perhaps it was old-fashioned careerism, practices not just questionable but condemnable.

Deciding between these options, whether for your own research or the research you're reading, once again becomes a matter of your professional judgment. Just be sure to weigh the evidence yourself; don't let others make that judgment for you.

Project Repositories in the Cloud and Reproducibility

A big challenge to science is that the places where we share the results of research studies, like book chapters and journal articles, rarely contain enough space for us to communicate precisely what we did in a way that would make the studies **reproducible**. Yet reproducibility is the hallmark of good science; what we do rests on the assumption that any other scientists, with the same resources, could run an identical study to one we ran and get roughly the same result. If our study does not contain enough information for another scientist to reproduce it, this key step in the scientific method is broken.

Project repositories, such as those hosted by the Center for Open Science (https://osf.io), provide a cloud-based solution for project management and the long-term stories of materials. When you are ready to submit a manuscript for publication, you should create a Project on that website to house it. All of it. Ideally, your project includes IRB approval, all materials shown to participants, all rater training materials, all scripts, all (anonymized) data, all code that was used to analyze those data, all versions of your manuscript submitted to all potential publishers – literally *everything you have* that directly informs the conclusions you drew in your paper (e.g., if you had five drafts of those rater training materials but only included the fifth, that's the only one that affected your results, so that's the only one you should share!).

Yes, this is a tall order. But it provides a paper trail for those that come after you, so that they can build on your science with their own as effectively as possible. It prevents gatekeeping of high-quality materials within already-successful research groups. It allows future researchers to see if your analysis contains any errors, preventing your findings from staying in the research literature for decades or more, misleading generation after generation of researchers into thinking something was real that was not. And perhaps you can see from that description why "leaving a legacy" is in our "bad goal" list.

You are not your research. You merely facilitated it. If it's wrong, retract it, move on, and learn a lesson for next time. You *want* errors to be discovered. You *want* the scientific record to be corrected. That is progress. That is your purpose as a publishing researcher. Don't hide what you did just because you're afraid it wasn't perfect. No research is.

Reproducible Versus Replicable

One of the most commonly confused sets of terms in open science is reproducibility versus replicability. In short, *studies are reproducible; findings replicate.*

If you re-create precisely what another researcher did in their study, from sampling to analysis to the creation of the figures in their paper, it is reproducible. If you then collect data in that new study and get the same result, this means the study was replicable. In this way a study can be reproducible but not replicable (i.e., we can recreate what the original researcher did, but we don't get the same result) or replicable but not reproducible (i.e., we don't know precisely what the original researcher did, but when we run a study testing the same hypothesis, we get the same result).

Replication studies come in two major types, as we first introduced in Chapter 3. The first is a direct replication, which refers to another researcher conducting a perfect copy of the original research design – perhaps even with identical analyses and analytic choices. A study must be reproducible for a researcher to be able to conduct a direct replication – otherwise, they don't have enough information to design it accurately. The second is a conceptual replication, sometimes called a **generalizability study**, which tests the same hypotheses as another study but under different conditions. For example, if we found that conscientiousness predicts job performance and built a theory around it, every study that later tests that relationship is a conceptual replication of that result and a new test of that theory.

Science is built on a foundation of both direct and conceptual replications. When possible, in your own work, try to design research with a **replication and extension**. Within this approach, research replicates key findings from past theories and then extends them with new knowledge. This is often a more valuable approach for furthering our understanding of phenomenon than either replication or new theory alone, because it allows us to build something new while double-checking the existing foundation we built it on.

For more on reproducibility, see:

Munafò, M. R., Nosek, B. A., Bishop, D. V., Button, K. S., Chambers, C. D., Percie du Sert, N., Simonsohn, U., Wagenmakers, E. J., Ware, J. J., & Ioannidis, J. (2017). A manifesto for reproducible science. *Nature Human Behavior*, *1*(1), 1–9.

Curating Useful Materials

When sharing materials in an open science repository, the burden of understanding is in part on you. The materials should be **curated** in a way that it only requires a reasonable and appropriate effort to understand and reuse them for your audience. Your audience for these materials comprise three major groups: **peer reviewers**, the inspired, and *future-you*.

Future-you is probably the audience you should care most about for these materials. In most cases, you are the most likely person to need to revisit your materials a few months or years later. In most cases, you'll have a new project that references or requires something you did in an earlier project. If you curate your materials for future-you, future-you will spend a lot less time trying to piece together details they forgot.

If you do that, *the inspired* are easy. The inspired are people who read your research and thought it was inspiring, so they decided to conduct their own research based upon what you shared. The inspired already like the way you think and communicate. So when you curate materials effectively for future-you, you are also curating materials for them.

Reviewers are the trickiest. Reviewers are everyone who will formally evaluate your work. This might include thesis and dissertation committees, work supervisors, or traditional scholarly peer reviewers (we will discuss this group in much greater detail later in this chapter). In all cases, reviewers are looking for hard evidence that you actually did what you claimed in whatever you wrote about it. For example, if you said you ran a t-test on a dataset with 478 cases, they'd better be able to find a dataset with 478 cases *or* a larger dataset with some analytic code that still runs that t-test on a subset with $N = 478$.

Reviewers are in some ways the easiest for whom to curate materials. To do this effectively, simply run through every word of every description of your methods and your results, and ensure that every name of something is the same name you see throughout your materials and every number you see can be generated again using the analytic code and datasets that are provided. Put another way, you need to be able to reproduce your own analysis from scratch, given the materials you have curated.

Through this lens, curating for future-you and the inspired is more difficult, because you must imagine what future-you *might* want to do with these materials. You must forecast future needs, wants, and interests. Reviewers, on the other hand, just want to verify the past.

File Names and the Final Final Version

One of the simplest changes you can make to your existing curation practices is to start using a **file naming convention**. This refers to a template for file naming that you stick to across projects and use consistently across everything you do. If you don't define and stick to file naming conventions, you often end up with hodgepodge filenames like this one:

Manuscript FINAL_03052008_FINAL-rl-tb-2 (final).docx

As you can see here, Richard and Tara wrote a paper, which was finalized in March 05 2008, but then required a few more edits from both of us, across two versions, and those versions might or might not have happened on the first final version. Then we probably had to make further changes on the basis of reviews? Maybe this was revision 3 since there are three finals? Who knows! It's now a mystery file.

Using conventions helps avoid this problem, and you should define your own conventions to help future-you. For example, a common convention is "never use the word final in a filename." The reason for this convention is that virtually no document you ever write is truly "final," and you shouldn't pretend that it is, even if it feels nice at the time to imply, "I am done with this file that has caused me headaches for 6 months."

Another common convention is to name everything based upon what day it was last edited and who last touched it, starting with the date in an order that allows the date to be sorted. For example, it is easy to tell what happened and in what order in this series of files:

20230801 Title-tb.docx
20230801a Title-rl.docx
20230807 Title-tb.docx

20230816 Title-tb.docx
CURRENT Title-rl.docx

In this system, the CURRENT file *must be* renamed using the same convention before it gets emailed back to Tara. After that point, if either Richard or Tara edited the resulting file, it would also be named CURRENT while on their personal computers but renamed according to the rules before being emailed anywhere.

Also note that this problem can be reduced but not avoided using a **collaborative document workspace** that enables real-time simultaneous editing by multiple editors, such as Google Docs or Dropbox. You'll still have multiple versions of files to indicate various important "versions of record," such as which one was submitted to a journal. To avoid confusion, you should still stick to a file naming convention; you just won't have quite so many files to keep track of.

Converting Observed Data Into Shareable Data

Curating your project requires in part that you provide curated data. If you have permission from the people the data were collected from, such as via the consent process, you may be able to share raw data in public repositories. In general, you should always try to include language in the consent process, if necessary, to share data with other researchers. But if you don't have that permission, you need to figure out what you do have permission to share. In many cases, especially with uncontroversial and non-identifying data like questionnaire responses, you may be able to share the data as-is after **anonymization**. This refers to the systematic removal of PII from the data, like names and identification numbers. It does not necessarily involve the removal of demographic data.

Anonymization is made trickier due to the risk of **reidentification**, which refers to analyzes that people can apply to anonymized data to determine their identity even after PII have been removed. This is mostly possible through demographic data; for example, if only one 26-year-old trans man worked in the Sales department in 2006 of the organization where you collected data, anyone with access to human resources records with that information could directly link that person's identity with your publicly shared data. A few decades ago, Sweeney (1997) documented multiple cases where hundreds of thousands of people's identities were recovered from supposedly anonymous data in healthcare, marketing, and other fields. With modern machine learning based reidentification software, the problem has become only more difficult. Thus, our recommendation is not to share a demographic variable in a public database *unless* that specific demographic variable is central to your hypotheses or research questions. You need to evaluate this one variable at a time.

A common roadblock for data sharing when working with organizational data is the organization's counsel, that is, their lawyers. Many lawyers see no reason to allow a researcher to share internal, private organizational data with anyone else for any reason. To lawyers, this is simply an unnecessary risk, as such data could be hypothetically used in some way in the future to harm the organization with no direct benefit to the organization for sharing them. Traditional anonymization is often insufficient for them to feel safe. In these cases, depending upon the specific analyses you applied, you can use any of a variety of techniques called **data obfuscation**. All data obfuscation approaches involve altering a dataset to make it more difficult to tie back to original data; in this way, anonymization is a specific type of data obfuscation. A common data obfuscation approach in I-O other than anonymization is **intermediate results reporting**. The most common version of this technique is to report a covariance matrix (i.e., not a correlation matrix) along with means, standard deviations, and associated sample sizes. This allows a later researcher to recreate many common analyses, including regression, structural equation modeling, and factor analysis, without access to the original data. Doing this makes it impossible to link specific cases with real people, because specific cases are never shared. The disadvantage to obfuscation like this is that many small details about the dataset will be lost, which could lead to different results using the obfuscated dataset than the original. But if an organization will not allow you to share original anonymized data, the next best option is usually to share obfuscated results.

The most secure approach beyond anonymization is **simulation**, which in this context refers to the creation of fake data on the basis of the measured characteristics of variables in collected data. This is a method of last resort and common solution to lawyers, since no permission is required to share data that were never associated with the organization in the first place. Using simulation, the researcher can create a fake dataset based on the means, standard deviations, skewness, kurtosis, covariance matrix, and so on, as observed in the real data. Thus, anyone trying to reproduce analyses will ideally find the same results even though they are not using the real data. The disadvantage to simulation in this manner is that much as with intermediate results reporting, it is impossible to perfectly simulate absolutely all of the characteristics of the original dataset, and the more details the simulation misses, the less reproducible the study will be.

Importantly, the laws about what data you can share vary significantly around the world. In Europe, for example, there are significantly more stringent protections on data sharing than in the United States. You should consult your own IRB to determine what steps you need to take during the consent process and later to ensure legal compliance.

Metadata and Documentation

Even if you share your original data, future-you may not remember or understand what those data represented. We first introduced this challenge in Chapter 11 along with a few solutions related to documentation, which refers to both written text explanations, like codebooks, and metadata explaining the nature of the observed data.

Documentation is a general term that describes any effort made to provide context and explanation for code or data. We'll revisit this in the code context a little later in this chapter. In the data context, documentation includes, most obviously, the research papers you write about the project, whether they are published or not. Each of those papers forms a part of a written record explaining where the data came from and what they represent. However, documentation in this format is rarely if ever sufficient for a reader to fully understand what the data represent.

Metadata, which you can think of as "data about data," fill in these gaps. Metadata ideally are constructed to provide comprehensive information about precisely how each number in your dataset or text in your qualitative corpus came from, including all stimulus materials surrounding it. For example, if you administered the IPIP personality measure, you could separate information about each question into a few different pieces: 1) the construct being assessed, 2) the question being asked, 3) the response format, 4) the response options, 5) the coding strategy, 6) the names of the variables containing these responses. We might summarize this in a data dictionary similar to the one shown in Table 11.1.

There is no magic formula for what should go into a data dictionary, or how much detail to include, but you should always have one and think about what future-you would want there. In this case, you can see that the creator of this data dictionary did not feel it necessary to spell out that the codes in the fourth column represent a range from Very Inaccurate to Very Accurate with a Don't Know option. Might someone get confused about that later? If so, you should probably write something different in yours.

Creating Reproducible Code and Analyses

One of the biggest challenges for reproducible analyses is creating a **reproducible analytic pipeline** that can be executed by others on data that you collected to produce the same results and output you saw. A reproducible analytic pipeline is a step-by-step process, starting with observed data and ending with figure and table generation, that enables your research audience to completely reconstruct everything that you referenced, discussed, or wrote about how you used your data to draw conclusions.

This is substantially easier using some analytic tools than others. Most critically, you need an analytic process that relies on code. If you are just pointing and clicking to run analyses and to produce figures and tables, it will be nearly impossible to create a reproducible analytic pipeline for your work. If you use software where syntax is *optional*, like SPSS, it will be difficult but possible. If you use a **programming language** like R or Python, or other syntax-based analytic software like Mplus, you will have the easiest time. For example, Figure 14.2 contains a reproducible analytic pipeline for analysis of a hypothesis about gender differences in neuroticism on a dataset included with the psych library written for R. If you run this code right now, you'll probably get exactly the same results that I (Richard) did when I wrote it.

Figure 14.2 contains a lot of key components to a reproducible analytic pipeline that you should always include:

1. The ability to run the code, from start to finish, starting from a blank environment with no existing variables loaded and produce identical output every time
2. The creation of all figures and blocks of text containing statistical output that will appear in any published/shared materials with labels representing their final placement in the published version (e.g., Figure 1, Table 1).
3. Comments labeling sections by purpose (e.g., import, analysis, reporting)
4. Comments labeling individual lines of code with their purpose (e.g., "listwise deletion")

By reviewing the previous code block, you can spot a few things that might not have been reported in the paper, such as listwise deletion from a larger dataset. You could also recreate "Fig 1" from that analysis with different assumptions; for example, it would be fairly trivial at this point to modify the code to impute missing values and re-run all analysis to see what changes. This gives maximum flexibility to the inspired to understand what you did, why you did it, and if they should do the same thing in their research. It also communicates to reviewers that you aren't hiding QRPs.

```
### Big Five Inventory neuroticism analysis by gender
###
### Results appear in Landers, R. N. & Behrend, T.S. (2024).
### Last edited 2023-07-27
### R v.4.3.1
## Script Resources and Libraries
library(tidyverse)   # data manipulation; v.2.0.0
library(psych)       # reliability analyses; v.2.3.6
## Data Import and Cleaning
data(bfi)
bfi_tbl <- tibble(bfi) %>%
  select(N1:N5, gender) %>%              # neuroticism and gender only
  filter(complete.cases(.)) %>%          # listwise deletion
  mutate(neur = rowMeans(across(N1:N5))) # mean scores across N items
## Analysis
# Reliability
neur_reliability <- bfi_tbl %>%
  select(N1:N5) %>%
  psych::alpha()
# H1: Neuroticism differs by gender.
h1_test <- t.test(neur ~ gender, data = bfi_tbl)       ·
## Visualization
# Figure 1: Boxplots of differences in neuroticism by gender
(ggplot(bfi_tbl,
      aes(x = gender, y = neur, group = gender)) +
    geom_boxplot()) %>%
  ggsave(filename="fig1.png")
## Reporting
paste0("The reliability of the neuroticism scale met traditional standards ",
       "(α=",
       neur_reliability$total$raw_alpha,
       ").")
paste0("A t-test was used to compare neuroticism scores between genders, ",
       "which was not statistically significant t(",
       h1_test$parameter,
       ") = ",
       h1_test$statistic,
       ", p = ",
       h1_test$p.value,
       ", which compared neuroticism across genders, was not supported.")
```

Figure 14.2 Example of a reproducible analytic pipeline in R using real data.

Code documentation like this is a great first step toward a fully reproducible analytic pipeline. But it leaves one vector of non-reproducibility – the aging of software and packages. You might have noticed that Figure 14.1 contains version numbers for R and the two packages loaded. This helps future viewers of this code track down bugs and errors when running it using later software. This is a more complex problem than it initially appears; for example, the read_csv() function is loaded with tidyverse but is not actually part of the tidyverse package – if you install v.2.0.0 of tidyverse, you won't necessary have the same version of read_csv() that was used when this code was written. Instead, library(tidyverse) loads 9 different packages, each with their own version numbers.

If you want to do a *complete* job of reporting versions, you need to report every version of everything you *actually* used. In R, you can find out what is running by running the command sessionInfo(). As you will see, however, the package lists get very long very quickly. Sometimes people deal with *that* by saving the output of sessionInfo() to a text file. Another common approach is using the *checkpoint, renv,* or *groundhog* libraries, which allow you to load packages current as of a specific date. They do not, however, solve the problem of older versions of R itself. All of these approaches are fairly quick to implement but a little clunky and inconvenient in practice.

Recognizing this problem, the most comprehensive option is to use **containers**, which refer to **virtualized environments** containing a snapshot of a particular computational environment. For example, you could create a container that virtualizes a specific version of R, specific version of all loaded packages, and even contains all the same files in the same places as when you originally worked on it. The most common platform for this is Docker, which creates a fully self-contained container file that later researchers can load to recreate your original analytic environment. The major downside to Docker is complexity; although there are many tutorials, learning how to use Docker effectively will take a bit of learning.

Creating Analytic Tools and Workflows for Others

If you are already using a programming language, like R or Python, for your statistical analyses, you already benefit from countless hours spent by volunteers maintaining the packages you use. Both of these platforms have a vibrant and extensive community of people just like you making resources for others to use. Many I-O researchers have done the same. For example, in R, the *psychmeta* package was originally created by I-O graduate students, although it has grown since then. If you want to give back to the community, you could build these kinds of resources too.

Another option is to use these platforms to develop software that people with less statistical and methods expertise than you. We asked the famed I-O psychologist and methodologist, Fred Oswald, head of the Organization and Workforce Laboratory (OWL) at Rice University, about his favorite examples of this kind of software, and he provided us with three, adding: "Hopefully, you will these tools to be interesting and useful, and more broadly, perhaps you will be inspired to create new interactive tools that also serve to improve organizational research and practice."

Alexander, L., III, & Oswald, F. L. (2019). *Free adverse impact resource (FAIR).* https://orgtools. shinyapps.io/FAIR/
- Determine whether a set of employment data shows adverse impact (e.g., differences in hiring rates by race/ethnicity or gender). Adverse impact statistics are generated on a dashboard, and they recalculate in real time as you adjust the hiring scenario originally provided by the data (e.g., hire more candidates within a minority subgroup).
  Alexander, L., III, Mulfinger, E., & Oswald, F. L. (2019). *Investing in people online* (Version 2.0). https://orgtools.shinyapps.io/IIP3/
- The user enters information online about the nature of an organization (e.g., absenteeism rates, employee attitudes), and the fixed and variable costs associated with HR activities (e.g., hiring, training and development). Then, the program calculates the utility provided by those activities in dollars, as a means of communication to managers.

Mulfinger, E., Alexander, L., III, Wu, F., & Oswald, F. L. (2021). *O*NET download tool*. https://orgtools.shinyapps.io/ONETDownloadTool/

- The O*NET is an occupational database maintained by the Department of Labor, used widely by researchers and practitioners. However, the data provided reside in separate files. This tool allows researchers to request desired worker and workplace characteristics of occupations, merging the requested data into a single file.

Sharing Your Results With an Audience

Getting the results of your researchers into the hands of people outside your research team is arguably the entire purpose of scientific research. If you're a practicing researcher, you want your research to influence the decision-making of those with decision-making authority, like directory and your company's chief officers, which usually means developing a technical report or white paper plus giving a presentation on your results. If you're an academic researcher, you want your research to influence the scientific consensus, which usually means some combination of presentation at a scientific conference and publication in the same academic research literature that you've been reading and drawing from.

We're going to assume in this section that you're already at least generally familiar with the most basic ethical and process requirements of writing up your results. If any of these are unfamiliar, we recommend reading the current edition of the **Publication Manual of the American Psychological Association**, often referred to simply as the **APA Manual**. This book contains many specific, technical requirements and recommendations for sharing results, including:

- The components of an APA-style research paper
- Specific requirements for the formatting of APA-style papers, from page format to fonts
- Recommendations around writing style and grammar
- Language guidelines, including how to use bias-free language
- Table, figure, citation, and reference formatting requirements

Many learners ask themselves an obvious question at this point: why do publishers and others care about what font I use? Why does any of this matter? Isn't this just pointless gatekeeping? The short answer is: it's a little bit of gatekeeping, but it's mostly about maximizing efficiency and predictability. When someone opens up your manuscript, their goal is to figure out what new, useful, trustworthy information it contains as quickly as possible. Standardizing formatting, structure, and so on make that task easier. Thus these sorts of standards were born. It does act as a type of gatekeeping, because if you do not adhere to expected standards, no one will ever even see your work long enough to consider the substance of your contribution. At the same time, it also respects the volunteer contributions of reviewers and maximizes the digestibility of your research. Perhaps you will push back on these arbitrary disciplinary norms later in your career; for now, we recommend just learning to write in correct APA style.

Having said all that, although creating materials in a known style is an important fundamental skill, we're going to devote the rest of this chapter to much bigger – and honestly more interesting – issues to consider related to sharing your work.

For us, above all, you want to avoid **cargo cult science**. This term, coined by physicist Richard Feynman, most literally describes the cargo cults, a term used by anthropologists in the 1930s to describe tribal religious practices in New Guinea in response to the sudden, unexplained appearance of Western technology. In his words:

> In the South Seas there is a cargo cult of people. During the war they saw airplanes land with lots of good materials, and they want the same thing to happen now. So they've arranged to imitate things like runways, to put fires along the sides of the runways, to make a wooden hut for a man to sit in, with two wooden pieces on his head like headphones and bars of bamboo sticking out like antennas – he's the controller – and they wait for the airplanes to land. They're doing everything right. The form is perfect. It looks exactly the way it looked before. But it doesn't work. No airplanes land. So I call these things cargo cult science, because they follow all the apparent precepts and forms of scientific investigation, but they're missing something essential, because the planes don't land.
>
> (Feynman, 2010, p. 340)

Although this is almost certainly an oversimplified, Western-biased interpretation of what was observed in New Guinea, the basic humanity of it is relatable all over the world: when we want a specific outcome but don't quite understand how to get there, we make our best guesses as to what *might* work and try that.

This has led to a lot of peculiar approaches to sharing results in our field and elsewhere. As I-O psychology legend Paul Sackett (2021) describes it:

> I greatly value papers that present an incisive test of propositions made by a theory. But many papers do not do this. Instead they position themselves as "informed by theories X, Y, and Z, we test a set of hypotheses." I often get the sense that researchers had a set of relationships they wanted to examine and then hunted down theoretical frameworks that could be discussed in order to check the "adequate theory" box. I commonly read manuscripts with the opening few pages making a case for what the authors propose to do. Often, I react "that makes sense, and they have convinced me this is worth doing." I turn to the next section of the paper, expecting it to be a methods section, only to find that it is a theory development section – a lengthy elaboration of what has already been laid out in the intro. Only if the intro is not persuasive do I read this, to see if this section makes the case more clearly (if it does, then the intro was deficient and needs rewriting). I believe we can shorten papers substantially with little loss.
>
> (p. 15)

Humans, including scientists (despite some cases you might be skeptical about), tend to look for the most direct path from here to there – in this case, from a research idea to a publication or organizational change. The most direct path is usually a checklist, with items like "coefficient alpha must be greater than .7." It is significantly easier to take a checklist approach, mimicking scientific practices, than it is to actually engage in good science. Good science requires thinking about **wicked problems**, problems that are both ill defined and difficult to address, with many twists and turns as you better understand them. Just as wicked problems do not have easy answers, neither is there a single "correct" path from a research question to a meaningful conclusion. You must find that path for yourself for every project.

And it is that combination of expertise and thoughtfulness that will make your results meaning to whatever audience you are trying to reach. Without that thoughtfulness, you are in the cargo cult, and you really don't want to be in the cargo cult.

Assuming you embrace complexity and avoid joining the cargo cult, you next have two choices to make. First, what format are you going to share results in? Second, how can you design your materials to most appropriate to the audience those results will reach? We'll focus the remainder of this chapter on the first question, but keep in mind that both of these questions must always be considered simultaneously.

Public Speaking

The most common way to share results is public speaking. Whether in practice or academia, talking intelligently about your research is central to the scientific process. As discussed earlier in this chapter, people generally remember and trust stories more than facts. They also trust a live human being in front of them more than words on a screen. All of this means that public speaking is one of the most important ways to deliver your conclusions to an audience that needs to hear them, for whatever reason.

There are several common types of public speaking for I-O researchers. The one that looms most obviously on the horizon for a graduate student is a **thesis defense**, which can occur at the master's level, the doctoral level, or both. The specific rules for a thesis defense vary depending on your institution's rules, but they generally involve giving a presentation on your conclusions followed by a sometimes very length question-and-answer period from your **thesis committee**, who are ideally a group of both experts on the specific topic of your thesis and also experts on the general domain of your research. In practice, this doesn't always happen, but the goal gives you an idea of the purpose of a defense: you are being evaluated on your ability to meaningfully explain the purpose of your research, your methods, your analytic strategies, and your conclusions to both experts and people with a general interest.

The first half of a thesis defense is the most common public speaking context: a prepared speech, often called a **talk**. Talks are commonly somewhere between 5 minutes and an hour. Most presenters use presentation software like Microsoft PowerPoint, Apple Keynote, Google Slides, Prezi, or Canva. Within a talk like this, the general expectation is that you process through material in the same general order as you see in research papers: 1) an introduction to the general problem and justification of your research questions/hypotheses, 2) a description of the method you used to investigate those research questions/hypotheses, 3) a description of the analyses you applied and results you obtained, and 4) a discussion the meaning of those results and the implications for both future science and practice.

You should assume your time limit is a hard maximum; if you're told 12 minutes, you have precisely 720 seconds and no more. You can use a timer to keep you tightly to this limit. As a starting point, you'll probably want to devote roughly one-third of your presentation to your introduction and discussion sections, with the remaining third split between methods and results. In a 12-minute presentation, that suggests 4 minutes for the introduction, 4 minutes for the discussion, and 2 minutes each for the methods and results. As you can see, that's not a lot of time, so it's important to practice several times in front of a practice audience like other graduate students or a reluctant significant other. If you don't have an audience handy, a mirror is better than nothing; you'll feel a little awkward doing it, which is the purpose.

As you gain skill with presenting, you'll get a better sense for how long things take. Usually, graduate students underestimate how much they know and how much they have to say. Presentations at the graduate level tend to run long instead of short. But running long is just as much of a problem as running short. This is why you need to practice in front of an audience with a timer so as to better simulate the conditions of your actual presentation, where your nerves will disrupt your ability to speak at a consistent speed.

Having giving hundreds of presentations like this, we have some advice:

- *Most importantly, do not read directly from slides or notes.* It is tempting when you are nervous to give yourself a crutch of words on a page that you read out loud. However, doing this, you will never grow in skill as a presenter. Plus it just looks strange to the audience. Practice enough so that you only need to glance at bullet point notes, at most, when presenting.
- *Do not cram too much information onto a slide.* Any time you change slides, most of your attendees will read whatever you wrote there instead of listening to you. Then they'll get lost in what you're saying. Help them by not writing too much. The best approach is to use slides with only pictures or slides with no more than three to five bullet points, each containing no more than five or six words. Less is usually better than more.
- *Do not include information you do not intend to walk through completely.* One of the biggest mistakes presenting scientific results is when including results tables on a slide. If you include a full results table, you *must* walk through the *entire* table. Every column, every row. If you don't need to do that to get your point across, your entire table does not need to be in that presentation. Cut it down to what you're going to talk about directly.
- *Maintain eye contact with your audience.* Many nervous presenters struggle to look out into a room of faces. As you get more experience, you will want to try to make eye contact with individual people in your audience. This gives you useful non-verbal feedback about whether people understand what you're saying and where to change course to improve how your message is being received. When you're just starting out, however, it is fine to think of your audience as a big nameless mass that your eyes are just generally sweeping over as you speak about your research. Never look above eye-height of people sitting in the last row of the room or look below eye-height of people sitting in the first row. Beyond that, it's fine to just let your eyes get a little out of focus and sweep slowly over the room without ever actually looking at anyone in particular. But this will give the impression to your audience that you are speaking directly to them, which is what you want.
- *Use meaningful nonverbal cues.* Nonverbal cues are a tricky balancing act. Too few, and you look like a nervous robot. Too many, and you look like you can't control yourself. This is also something you won't naturally realize you're doing – you'll just use your arms and legs and body in ways that feel right in the moment without really thinking about it. You'll need to start thinking about it. The easiest way to get better at this is to watch a recording of yourself given while speaking. This will make you conscious of your own nonverbal tendencies so that you can make a decision about which of those are helpful to your message and which are distracting.
- *Employ humor you are comfortable with.* Humor is a great way to keep an audience engaged, but you should only use humor you are comfortable with. Many graduate students make the mistake of thinking that they should plant a joke somewhere in their talk

like it's a standup act. It's perfectly fine to plan something like that, but it's not *necessary*, especially if you're uncomfortable telling a joke to the audience you're speaking to.

- *Practice and pursue good feedback.* As you hopefully learned in your training and development coursework, practice is the key to skill development, and live presentation is definitely a skill to be practiced. However bad you think you are at it, practice will make it better, and everyone is capable of being an excellent presenter. Give your presentations multiple times to low-stakes audiences, like your classmates or advisor, and ask them for honest constructive feedback on your presentation skills. Record yourself in front of the mirror and critique your own performance. As long as every presentation is a little smoother and cleaner than the last, you've found a good self-development strategy.

Talks like this can be given in any context but are particularly common at **conferences**, which are gatherings of researchers for the purposes of networking and sharing research results before publication. Conferences can be targeted at researchers in academia, in practice, or both. Common national and international general audience conferences where I-O psychologists present I-O research include:

- The Society for Industrial and Organizational Psychology (SIOP) annual conference, split audience
- The SIOP Leading Edge Consortium, mostly targeting I-Os in practice
- Industrial Organizational/Organizational Behavior (IOOB), targeting I-O graduate students
- Academy of Management annual conference, Human Resources and Organizational Behavior divisions, almost exclusively academics
- European Association of Work and Organizational Psychology biennial conference, split audience

Every conference has its own specific presentation formats, so if you want to present at once, you'll need to research what those are in order to put together a good submission in response to a **call for proposals (CFP)**. For example, at the SIOP Annual Conference, you cannot submit a solo talk by itself; instead, it must be submitted as part of a thematic set of talks called a **symposium** or in one of a few other defined formats. Always study CFPs carefully to understand what is expected of you both in terms of your proposal submission and presentation requirements.

Conferences also frequently have a peculiar format for sharing your results called a **scientific poster**. Posters are prototypically what they sound like – all the information about your research is organized on an oversized large piece of paper. Size requirements vary by conference, although posters at SIOP's annual conference are typically 4 feet wide by 3 feet tall. At the conference itself, you must literally pin this giant piece of paper to a board in a presentation hall, usually with thumb tacks, during an assigned presentation period. During that period, people will wander by your poster and ask questions about it.

One of the most common question-comments given in front of a poster is something like, "So tell me about what you did here." For those people, you should have a roughly-2-minute talk prepared in the same general format as a full-blown presentation: a sentence or two each on the problem, research questions/hypotheses, methods, results, and conclusions. Practice this too, with the same guidelines as given previously.

Planning for Poster Logistics

Most graduate students have never tried to bring an awkwardly shaped object onto an airplane before, but this is a common experience for first-time conference presenters. To bring a 4-foot-wide piece of paper to a conference in another state, you're going to need a **poster tube**, which is a large plastic tube with a carrying strap. To create the poster itself, you're probably going to need to either use an on-campus "large format" printer or have it printed by a local printing services company, such as FedEx Office. Once printed, the poster gets rolled up and stuffed into the tube. On the plane, this counts as your "personal item" and can be stowed in the back of an overhead compartment.

If you want to avoid all that, consider **fabric posters**. Just as you can have a paper poster printed, you can also have it printed on fabric. There are many advantages to fabric posters, most important that you can just fold them up and put them in a suitcase alongside your clothes. There are also many stories on the internet of creative uses for fabric posters after presentation, including turning them into blankets, Halloween costumes, and clothes. The most common source for fabric posters currently is Spoonflower (https://spoonflower.com/presentation-posters). Shipping typically takes a couple of weeks, so plan ahead.

Peer Review

Regardless of where you ultimately share your written work, it's going to be reviewed and possibly **peer reviewed**. Like other terms in this chapter, we've mentioned peer review before but will now go into a bit more detail. Peer review is an area where a lot of people find a lot of frustration, as illustrated by this quote from Glass (2000), appearing in the *Journal of Systems and Software*:

> I shall skip the usual point-by-point description of every single change we made in response to the critiques. After all, it is fairly clear that your anonymous reviewers are less interested in the details of scientific procedure than in working out their personality problems and sexual frustrations by seeking some kind of demented glee in the sadistic and arbitrary exercise of tyrannical power over hapless authors like ourselves who happen to fall into their clutches. We do understand that, in view of the misanthropic psychopaths you have on your editorial board, you need to keep sending them papers, for if they were not reviewing manuscripts they would probably be out mugging little old ladies or clubbing baby seals to death. Still, from this batch of reviewers, C was clearly the most hostile, and we request that you not ask him to review this revision. Indeed, we have mailed letter bombs to four or five people we suspected of being reviewer C, so if you send the manuscript back to them, the review process could be unduly delayed.
>
> (p. 1)

Ideally, peer review involves experts in the topic of your manuscript reading it and providing constructive criticism about how to improve it. I use the word "ideally" because this is clearly not what always happens. Peer reviewers are rarely compensated for their time; they are asked by editors because they are respected, and they agree to review because they want to contribute back to their disciplines. Some respected experts do not want to contribute back to their disciplines this volunteer service like this. In these cases, the editor has little choice but to move on to somewhat less expert reviewers. These tend to be the most frustrating.

When a manuscript is deemed likely to improve the scientific discussion around its central topic, it is **accepted**. If it is not quite at that standard but is improvable, the editor may invite a **revise and resubmit**, which ideally comes with specific instructions on what needs to be changed in order to achieve acceptance. In cases where in the judgment of the editor the manuscript cannot be improved to a sufficient standard, it is **declined**. After one or more rounds of revision, you might get a **provisional acceptance**, which describes when the editor decides that they'd like to see another revision but don't intend to send it for further peer review; instead, if you do what they ask, they intend to accept it completely next time.

You might have noticed that all of those decisions are by the editor, not the peer reviewers. A common assumption by people just getting into academic publishing is that peer reviewers are the ones making the decisions about whether your manuscript is accepted or declined. But the action editor actually has unlimited authority to override the decisions of peer reviewers, and editors vary widely in how much they pay attention to reviewer complaints. For this reason, if you find yourself reviewing a paper, be sure not to say things like "I would like to accept/decline this paper" – a review does not have the ability to decide that.

Criticism is unfortunately part and parcel of academic publishing. This is a business that centers on, at least in the intent, only allowing work of the highest quality into academic discussions and work toward the scientific consensus. It is professional gatekeeping, a system designed to get the "good" research *in* and keep the "bad" research *out*. Yet as you have seen throughout this book, professional judgment has a lot of gray areas. There is rarely a "correct" way to go about research. As a result, you must work actively to divorce your own sense of identity from that of the manuscript you write and the presentations you give. Your writing and presentations are products you create, not reflections of you as a person. Peer reviewers, as hostile as they can sometimes be, are only peer reviewing because they believe in the integrity of the research area that they are reviewing for.

This is at worst an opportunity for you to grow. A bad review is neither a condemnation of your potential nor a sign that you "aren't cut out" for this kind of work. Both of us (Richard and Tara) have had our work rejected dozens of times. As we've progressed in our careers, it has happened less, because we've made an active effort to learn from these experiences and grow.

Don't elevate rejection to more than it is. If the work you created is truly bad, figure out why and don't do it next time. And if a reviewer is just a jackass, pick out the useful bits from their comments, submit your work somewhere else, and see what happens there.

Books

A book is a traditional written outlet for research. Books written by I-Os comes in several common forms:

1. **Edited volumes** involve one researcher, called the **editor**, inviting other researchers to author individual chapters. These can also be thought of as thematic collections of works by a variety of authors. If you see a CFP about writing a "chapter," it is for an edited volume.

2. Textbooks like the one you're reading now!

3. **Monographs** are fairly uncommon these days but are books written to explain a single research study or group of studies in extreme detail. A good historical example in I-O is *Assessment of Men*, a book written to describe a series of research studies conducted at the US Office of Strategic Services, predecessor to the Central Intelligence Agency, exploring how to meaningfully select high potential job candidates to become spies during World War II.

4. **Science translation** books involve research results being explained in simpler terms for non-scientist audiences. In most cases, details about method are present but tend to be a bit light in this kind of book, which is a balancing act between keeping an audience engaged and supporting your assertions with research. A good example of this approach in I-O is Steven Rogelberg's *The Surprising Science of Meetings*.

5. **Airport book** is not a specific category but rather a somewhat pejorative term used to refer to the kind of book you find in an airport. Sometimes research gets "translated" a little too hard, so to speak, creating a work with little substance but is an entertaining read for business travelers. These books tend to be better selling than the other kinds, because a bigger audience finds them interesting to read.

Books are united in very few ways, but one is that peer review tends to be somewhere between "none" and "a little." For this reason, many academic researchers do not publish their "best" work in books, instead using it primarily for science translation, reflective work, and speculative work that would not be likely to make it through peer review. This is not to say that a particular book is necessarily lower quality or less rigorous than a journal article; instead, it is safer to say that they are correlated – on average, books will contain lower quality and less rigorous work than journals. Fortunately, having read this book, you already know to evaluate every study on its own design and analytic merits rather than the location you found it.

Academic Journals

Academic journals are quite a bit more homogeneous than books. We've used the term "journal" and "publisher" throughout this book, but it's worth taking a moment to discuss them in a bit more detail – what exactly are they? In short, **academic journals** are created when academic researchers who believe in the need to have a centralized location to publish work on a specific topic manage to convince a **publisher** to fund the infrastructure necessary to support that vision. The publisher is a company that has the financial resources to pay for everything necessary to run a journal, like an editorial staff, printing, website hosting, and so on. Here are two examples:

1. The American Psychological Association wanted to be the definitive home for American psychology research, so they funded their own internal publishing arm. Their journal portfolio includes the *Journal of Applied Psychology*.

2. The European Association for Work and Organizational Psychology wanted to have a central place for European psychologists to publish high-quality work, and they convinced publisher Taylor & Francis to create the *European Journal of Work and Organizational Psychology*, which EAWOP manages.

The relationship between publisher and journal is a complicated one. In cases where a for-profit publisher manages the journal, the publisher may put pressure on the editor-in-chief to get to certain outcomes, like achieving a certain impact factor by a certain date or risk the journal being shut down. Publishers do this in pursuit of profit, which can be shockingly high (Buranyi, 2017), especially considering the army of unpaid editors, reviewers, and authors that provide them content.

Writing for a journal is arguably the single most difficult writing task you will face. The standards for clarity and rigor are never higher than in journal reviews, and both your study and your writing about your study are evaluated simultaneously during the peer review process. Like journals themselves, we've mentioned peer review a few times in this book, but it's important to really understand what peer review is intended to do versus what it actually does. Peer review is in an ideal world a constructive evaluation of research with the goal of making every piece of research as strong as possible, and once certain standards have been reached, making those results available to be considered by the scientific community. If the results are strong enough, they can become part of the scientific consensus on a topic. If the results are not strong enough, the paper will be ignored. It is with this logic that **impact factors**, which refer to the average number of citations a paper in a journal receives, are often used to evaluate journal quality.

The problem with this approach is that by creating a metric that can be easily optimized upon, people optimize upon it. Most pronounced in business schools, academics receive career rewards from publishing in high-impact factor journals, including cash rewards, which we referred to earlier in this chapter as "perverse incentives." If you pursue a career that involves academic publishing, you will certainly need to navigate this broken incentive system and make decisions for yourself about where your ethical lines in the sand are.

As an example, consider one of the most obnoxious: the **least publishable unit**. A common well-intentioned piece of advice for people graduating into academic research is to conduct a dissertation that can be split apart into as many publications as possible, a practice sometimes called **salami slicing**. Trying to identify the smallest amount of work that can result in "one publication" is the heart of pursuit of the least publishable unit. This approach, quite clearly, reflects careerism, that is, the prioritization of career outcomes over quality of science. If you're wondering why this is a problematic approach, consider what is *not* transparent when research is salami sliced. First, it is often not clearly explained in papers when portions of datasets from the same data collections efforts are reused or recombined across manuscripts. This can create greater trust in a result, that is, undue influence on the scientific consensus, by implying that replication has occurred that has not. Combined with *p*-hacking or QRPs, suddenly an entire research literature can be shifted by weighing what is really *one study* too heavily. Second, doing this prevents future researchers from seeing the interrelationships between variables collected in the study; it literally holds us back. For example, imagine a study of the Big Five personality traits and three different ways of looking at job performance. If this study were split into 1) a study of Big Five versus task performance, 2) a study of Big Five versus organization deviance, and 3) a study of Big Five versus organizational citizenship, the interrelationships between the three types of performance are never published. Perhaps there was really a halo effect in the collected sample, and the three forms of performance are actually indistinguishable – what was published as three papers was really one valid conclusion never mentioned in any of the three. This kind of behavior hurts science, and you should not engage in it.

Another challenging issue in writing academic journal articles is to determine both **authorship** and **authorship order**. This is in large part because of the incentive structures that most people who value publishing in academic journals find themselves in. Being an author is important by itself. But then, being a primary author is worth a lot more "credit" in one's career than being a secondary author, meaning there is a lot of motivation to ensure the order is accurate. This can also be uniquely confusing, because different disciplines have different standards for authorship, making generic advice you find on the internet a bit questionable.

In I-O, authorship follows a traditional social scientific model, which is roughly this:

1. Only people who contribute intellectually to the work should be recognized with authorship. A purely technical role, such as running participants or statistical analysis, is insufficient on its own to merit authorship. However, for a technician who also made an intellectual contribution, their technical contribution can be considered part of what they contributed when determining authorship order.

2. Authorship order should recognize magnitude of contribution, in reverse order. In other words, the first author, referred to as the role of **principal authorship** or in social science, **first authorship**, should be the primary driving intellectual force for the work, working your way down through remaining authors. The exception to this approach is when a graduate student leading the on-the-ground research effort with a mentor guiding them are both on the project; in these cases, the supervisor/mentor/lab director often takes the final author position, sometimes called a **senior author**. However, this should not be done if either 1) the supervisor/mentor/lab director was truly the one leading the work, in which case that person should be first, or 2) the supervisor/mentor/lab director didn't actually contribute intellectually to the project, in which case that person should not be an author at all. The American Psychological Association also produced an "Authorship Determination Scorecard" to help you figure out issues like this: www.apa.org/science/leadership/students/authorship-determination-scorecard.pdf.

3. Authorship order is ideally decided before the project begins. In this situation, each person is responsible for ensuring that they maintain the role they have been given. For example, the principal author should be doing more intellectual work than anyone else. In cases where the workload shifts around, this should always be renegotiated *explicitly*. No one should ever assume anything about authorship, and if authorship order might need changing, it should be done as soon as possible after this is known.

So Many Editors!

One of the most confusing terms in publishing is "editor," because this term is used to refer to a very general activity: editing. "Editing," without a qualifier, really just refers to someone who is not the original author empowered to change something about an author's work. In reality, there are dozens of different editorial roles, and different people have different roles. Here are a few common ones you might come across in the context of I-O:

- *Associate editors* are usually I-Os volunteering to handle incoming manuscripts to an academic journal and make decisions about publishing them. An associate editor will invite reviewers, manage the review process, make accept/reject decisions, and write decision letters.

- *Editors-in-chief* are I-Os volunteering to manage associate editors by conducting initial desk rejections and then sorting out which associate editor manages which manuscript. They also manage the relationship between the journal and the publisher itself.
- *Action editors* are the specific academic editors assigned to a particular manuscript. This could be an associate editor or the editor-in-chief. Thus, "action editor" is not a role; it's a particular assignment.
- *Managing editors* are hard to pin down, because different publishers use this term to refer to different people. A managing editor is most commonly the person assigned to a specific journal by the publisher to manage day-to-day operations, such as by coordinating with the editor-in-chief and acting as the first responder when someone emails the journal. In some journals, this person will instead be called an *editorial assistant*. In the book publishing context, managing editors are often the primary contact person at the publisher for a particular book.
- *Production editors* handle manuscripts after they have been accepted for publication. This editor emails authors directly to get final versions of documents, ask for signatures on important documents, and otherwise shepherd a manuscript through the publisher's internal system to get it into print.
- *Layout editors* and *copy editors* manage layouts and copy, respectively. Layout editors are the people who convert your manuscript into a visual format within a journal or book, whereas copy editors read your manuscript and fix spelling, grammar, and confusing language.

Generally speaking, the larger a publisher is, the more diverse and specialized the editorial staff becomes. At a very small publisher, one person might manage production, layout, and copy for a journal. At a large publisher, a different person from a pool of copy editors might be assigned to copy-edit each manuscript as it arrives. Every publisher is at least a little different.

Gray Literature

Beyond formal, traditional publications, I-Os often contribute to the gray literature, a term we introduced in Chapter 13 as a common inclusion target for meta-analysis.

In academia, gray literature appears in two major forms: **preprints** and **working papers**. Preprints are final versions of research papers submitted for publication in academic journals but have not yet been peer-reviewed. OSF, which we discussed in the context of preregistration, is a common outlet for preprints. The main reason to release a preprint is to make others aware of your research before the review process, which can take months or even years. When a research paper is not finalized for submission, that is, when you are looking for feedback on it from a community before submitting it for peer review and have posted it online, it is instead referred to as a working paper. Posting a manuscript in either format can be a bit dangerous, as academic publishers might view a posted preprint or working paper as "already published" and refuse to publish it even after successful peer review. Thus, we generally recommend that you do not share preprints and working papers publicly; instead, after acceptance to a journal, post each submitted version of your paper, including your pre-peer review manuscript and each subsequent revision, in an OSF project. This maintains a complete and public record of your work, including how it morphed during peer review. Another common strategy is to post preprints to OSF whenever they are finalized but not to make links to them publicly visible.

For practicing I-Os, gray literature appears in two other forms: **technical reports** and **white papers**. Technical reports are generally written for the purpose of exhaustively documenting some internal process at the organization. They are most commonly created in I-O psychology in talent selection, where there are often complex legal requirements related to documentation in the creation of a new assessment for hiring or promotion. Technical reports are often intended to fill this documentation role by explaining, in excruciating detail, exactly how the assessment was created and what standards were used for its development. Historically, the term "white paper" was used to refer to a publicly shared document in which a company stated its official position on some issue of importance. For example, an I-O talent selection firm might release a paper explaining the scientific literature on which its internal decision-making is based and then explain its commitment to those principles. These days, the term "white paper" is used to refer to just about any document release for external stakeholders by an organization. Commonly, this means many white papers are better thought of as sales documents, intended to provide slightly more technical detail than you'd normally find on a sales website but still carefully curated to encourage someone to buy something. If you find yourself writing either, ethics will become a major concern for you. There is some pressure, for example, not to include negative results in technical reports and not to share literally anything that could harm sales in a white paper. We encourage you to resist both of those forces. If you find yourself *reading* a technical report or white paper, remember that no peer review has occurred, and that the authors often have a motive to be a bit less than completely truthful and forthcoming. Whether you ultimately trust what is written, once again, is ultimately up to your professional judgment.

Predatory Publishers and Vanity Presses

In this world of perverse incentives, two other tricky things to look out for are **predatory publishers** and **vanity presses.**

A vanity press is a publisher that will publish just about whatever you send them as long as you give them enough money. The problem with this approach is 1) people who know it's a vanity press are not going to pay attention to literally anything published within it, and 2) once you've published it in a vanity press, it cannot be published anywhere else because the vanity press will require you sign over your copyright. Even if the research is of good quality, people will be much less likely to see it or care about it. So you need to avoid vanity presses.

Predatory publishers take this a step further by actively hunting down people they view as vulnerable and try to lure them into signing unfavorable publishing agreements. Unlike vanity presses, which at least are straightforward in what they are and offer, these are scams. A common story about a predatory publisher goes something like this:

1. The publisher spam emails 100,000 researchers with one publication in a real journal somewhere saying something like, "We need a paper submitted today! Guaranteed fast review! YOU CAN BE PUBLISHED TOMORROW!!!"

2. A small subset of authors fall for it and submit their paper to the journal. This submission process often requires signing a copyright statement saying "if accepted, the journal owns your manuscript." So these authors have now signed away their rights.
3. The journal comes back after a fake 24-hour peer-review process with the note, "Congratulations, your paper was peer reviewed successfully and has been accepted. Now please pay $6000 for the open access fee, and we will publish it."
4. The author replies, "You didn't advertise that there was a fee! I would like to withdraw my paper and submit it elsewhere."
5. The journal responds, "Too bad, we own it now."

Spotting predatory journals and vanity presses can be very difficult. The easiest way to be sure a journal is not one is if you recognize the publisher's name from journals you have read in past coursework. In I-O psychology, common authentic publishers are the American Psychological Association, Academy of Management, Elsevier, SAGE, Routledge, Springer, Taylor and Francis, and Wiley. There are also several legitimate publishers associated with universities, such as the Cambridge University Press and Oxford University Press. If the journal you want to submit to is published by any of these publishers, it is at least *not* predatory. That doesn't guarantee you'll have a good experience or that a paper published there will be respected, but at the least, they're not trying to steal your money under false pretenses. There have also been a number of high-profile **scholarly publishing stings**, which generally involve researchers submitting what they know to be fake, poor-quality manuscripts to suspected-predatory journals to see if they are accepted, and if so, to reveal them as predatory.

This situation creates several systemic problems in scholarly publishing. Most academic publishers are for-profit and make money on readers accessing the materials they own. Most predatory publishers, in contrast, are **open access**, meaning they promise to publish your paper and make it available to the public without a fee. Open access publications are not inherently predatory, but predatory publishers almost always claim to be open access. This situation has disincentivized new open access journals, because it can be difficult to tell which are which. It makes open access journals seem untrustworthy, and this discourages innovating in academic publishing – which is itself closely related to why so many traditional journal publishers make such outrageous profits off the backs of free academic labor. And the willingness of many researchers to pay open access fees at all has now incentivized some traditional publishers to be a little more accepting about lower quality work as long as someone intends to pay their open access fee.

How can you tell the difference between a predatory open-access journal and a non-predatory open-access journal? This challenge led to the creation of **Beall's List** (https://beallslist.net), a set of curated lists of publishers and journals believed to be predatory. It is called Beall's List because it was originally started by Jeffrey Beall, an American research librarian who created the first version of it in 2008 to increase awareness of predatory publishing, which at that time was a relatively new problem. Over the years, Beall's List was tested in a few ways. In a sting operation conducted by *Science*, a giant in scientific academic publishing, Bohannon (2013) submitted a fake manuscript claiming to have discovered the cure to cancer without clinical trials to 304 open access journals, including 121 from Beall's List, and he achieved an 82% acceptance rate among those 121. Beall's List is no longer maintained by Beall. In 2013, several publishers he had named in his list threatened to sue for defamation, and in 2017, Beall's website was taken down by Beall himself, due to pressure from his employer, the University of Colorado, that caused him to fear for his job (Beall, 2017). Since that time, several other people and organizations have attempted to create a similar kind of list, but most have been subsequently taken down. As of this writing, a website not created by Beall has appeared at https://beallslist.net/, but it is unclear who did create it. Ultimately, evaluating predatory journals is like many aspects of research left to your professional judgment.

The academic publishing world is a very complicated one with an entire field dedicated to studying it called "journalology." If you're going to be publishing in journals in the future, you don't need to become a journalologist, but you should learn a bit more about the politics surrounding the world you're stepping into. As a starting point, check out:

Kingsley, D. A., & Kennan, M. A. (2015). Open access: The whipping boy for problems in scholarly publishing. *Communications of the Association for Information Systems, 34*(14), 329–350.

Also consider consulting https://thinkchecksubmit.org plus the following rubric when trying to evaluate if a journal is predatory or not:

Rele, S., Kennedy, M., & Blas, N. (2017). *Journal evaluation tool* (LMU Librarian Publications & Presentations 40). https://digitalcommons.lmu.edu/librarian_pubs/40

References

Alcock, J. E. (2011). Back from the future: Parapsychology and the Bem affair. *Skeptical Inquirer, 35*(2), 31–39.

Banks, G. C., O'Boyle Jr, E. H., Pollack, J. M., White, C. D., Batchelor, J. H., Whelpley, C. E., Abston, K. A., Bennett, A. A., & Adkins, C. L. (2016). Questions about questionable research practices in the field of management: A guest commentary. *Journal of Management, 42*(1), 5–20.

Beall, J. (2017). What I learned from predatory publishers. *Biochemia Medica, 27*(2), 273–278.

Bem, D. J. (2011). Feeling the future: Experimental evidence for anomalous retroactive influences on cognition and affect. *Journal of Personality and Social Psychology, 100*(3), 407–425. https://doi.org/10.1037/a0021524

Bohannon, J. (2013). Who's afraid of peer review? *Science, 342*(6154), 60–65.

Buranyi, S. (2017, June 27). Is the staggeringly profitable business of scientific publishing bad for science? *The Guardian.* www.theguardian.com/science/2017/jun/27/profitable-business-scientific-publishing-bad-for-science

Feynman, R. P. (2010). *Surely you're joking, Mr. Feynman! Adventures of a curious character.* W. W. Norton & Company.

Kingsley, D. A., & Kennan, M. A. (2015). Open access: The whipping boy for problems in scholarly publishing. *Communications of the Association for Information Systems, 34*(14), 329–350.

Munafò, M. R., Nosek, B. A., Bishop, D. V., Button, K. S., Chambers, C. D., Percie du Sert, N., Simonsohn, U., Wagenmakers, E. J., Ware, J. J., & Ioannidis, J. (2017). A manifesto for reproducible science. *Nature Human Behaviour, 1*(1), 1–9.

Ritchie, S. J., Wiseman, R., & French, C. C. (2012). Failing the future: Three unsuccessful attempts to replicate Bem's "retroactive facilitation of recall" effect. *PLOS One, 7*(3), e33423. https://doi.org/10.1371/journal.pone.0033423

Rosenthal, R. (1984). *Meta-analytic procedures for social research.* Sage Publications.

Sackett, P. R. (2021). Reflections on a career studying individual differences in the workplace. *Annual Review of Organizational Psychology and Organizational Behavior, 8*, 1–18.

Sweeney, L. (1997). Guaranteeing anonymity when sharing medical data, the datafly system. *Proceedings, Journal of the American Medical Informatics Association*, 51–55.

Wagenmakers, E. J., Wetzels, R., Borsboom, D., & van der Maas, H. L. (2011). Why psychologists must change the way they analyze their data: The case of psi: Comment on Bem (2011). *Journal of Personality and Social Psychology, 100*(3), 426–432. https://doi.org/10.1037/a0022790

Further Reading

Bohannon, J. (2013). Who's afraid of peer review? *Science, 342*(6154), 60–65.
- One of the most well-known scholarly publishing stings was conducted by Bohannon, who sent 304 versions of a fake paper that purportedly could cure cancer, full of basic scientific illiteracy problems and poor research methods, to open-access journals. This entertaining report explains his decision making along the way as well as his results.

Campbell, R. J. (1970). On becoming a psychologist in industry: A symposium. *Personnel Psychology, 23*(2), 191–221. https://doi.org/10.1111/j.1744-6570.1970.tb01646.x
- Campbell provides a conversational snapshot into I-O psychology of old with this written re-telling of an I-O psychology symposium presented at the American Psychological Association, during a time before the Society for Industrial-Organizational Psychology, and therefore an obvious place to present I-O work, even existed. Although we here reference the editorial article, each of the articles in this special issue of Personnel Psychology gives a little window into the expectations of this time period, including what it meant to become a practicing I-O psychologist in the 1960s. If you think things are complicated now, check it out.

Feynman, R. P. (1974). *Cargo cult science: Some remarks on science, pseudoscience, and learning how to not fool yourself.* https://calteches.library.caltech.edu/51/2/CargoCult.htm
- Feynman is one of the most famous physicists because of his thoughtful, nuanced, and often critical views on scientific methods, ones he was not afraid of sharing. His arguably most famous speech was on cargo cult science, given at the 1974 commencement address at the California Institute of Technology (CalTech). It's both short and very much worth your time, full of examples, including in psychology, of how researchers can easily mislead themselves even with the best of intentions.

Glass, R. L. (2000). A letter from the frustrated author of a journal paper. *Journal of Systems and Software, 54,* 1.
- If you've ever submitted or plan to submit a paper for publication in an academic journal, you should read this one. Trust us.

Lishner, D. A. (2022). Sorting the file drawer: A typology for describing unpublished studies. *Perspectives on Psychological Science, 17*(1), 252–269.
- Lishner develops and describes a typology of 12 general reasons for researchers to leave papers in the file drawer, from statistical and methodological concerns to opposition to publication from collaborators.

Nosek, B. A., Beck, E. D., Campbell, L., Flake, J. K., Hardwicke, T. E., Mellor, D. T., van't Veer, A. E., & Vazire, S. (2019). Preregistration is hard, and worthwhile. *Trends in Cognitive Sciences, 23*(10), 815–818.
- In a short and accessible introduction to the problem, Nosek and colleagues outline the many difficulties in crafting a high-quality pre-registration, effectively summarized with this sentence: "Research is hard, and scientists are fallible." (p. 817). This group of researchers helped lead the open science charge in psychology, and this short article is certainly worth a quick read.

Questions to Think About

1. Given your current career goals, how will you choose what to present and to whom? What audiences are worth your time and effort, and how will you reach them?
2. What does pre-registration actually help with and what does it not help with? Does pre-registration guarantee high-quality research? What can go wrong?

3. What digital tools do you have access to today to maximize the reproducibility of your existing research?
4. How will you develop your public speaking skills related to your research? What concrete steps will you take next?
5. What conferences will you submit your work to and why those?
6. What harms are done when researchers salami slice? How could you own research have been affected by this kind of practice?
7. If you were asked to write content for gray literature, what standards would you apply? If there were a conflict between your own ethical standards and what your supervisor asked you to do, how would you handle it?
8. What are the most common trusted journals in your particular subject area within I-O psychology? Have you seen any vanity presses or predatory journals with work in your area? How do you know?

Key Terms

- academic journals
- accept
- airport book
- anonymization
- APA Manual
- authorship
- authorship order
- Beall's list
- call for proposals (CFP)
- cargo cult science
- collaborative document workspace
- conference
- container
- curation
- data obfuscation
- decline
- disciplinary silo
- edited volume
- editor
- fabric posters
- file naming convention
- generalizability study
- Goodhart's law
- hybrid registered reports
- impact factor
- intermediate results reporting
- least publishable unit
- monograph
- moral imperative
- open-access
- opportunity cost
- peer review, pre-publication
- peer review, traditional
- peer reviewers
- perverse incentives
- poster tube
- predatory publisher
- preprint
- programming language
- provisional accept
- Publication Manual of the American Psychological Association
- publisher
- registered report
- reidentification
- replication and extension
- reproducibility
- reproducible analytic pipeline
- return on investment
- revise and resubmit
- risk/reward ratio
- salami slicing
- salvaging
- scholarly publishing stings
- science translation
- scientific poster
- selective reporting
- senior author

- simulation
- talk
- technical report
- thesis committee
- thesis defense
- transparency (in research)

- vanity press
- virtual environment
- white paper
- wicked problem
- working paper

## Chapter 15

From Start to Finish

Guidelines and a Checklist for Conducting Research

Learning Objectives

1. Plan, execute, and share the results of a successful research study.

Success in research is only partially about having a brilliant idea. The other part of research, like in many other domains of life, is in making a careful plan, and asking yourself the right questions at each stage before moving on. It is about effective self regulation and intense attention to detail. In this chapter, we will present an overarching game plan for the practical aspects of conducting research. Most sections are elaborated upon elsewhere in the book, and we expect you to have read those other chapters; look for notations to connect you to material you don't remember clearly. The major goal of this chapter is to help you conceptualize research from start to finish – to give you a course through decision-making so that you can better see how earlier steps lead into later steps, and to use that course to create a plan that avoids wasted time and effort.

When conducting research, you always walk the garden of forking paths. Each decision may seem minor in the moment but can lead different researchers to totally different conclusions. The choices that you make about conceptualization, operationalization, manipulation, sampling, experimental design, analysis, and so on all have reverberating consequences for your conclusions. Articulating these choices makes it easier to put your study in the right context, and helps future researchers, including you, resolve discrepancies between studies. So, in this way, careful planning and documentation of your decisions better enables you to contribute to the scholarly conversation.

In addition to this nobler purpose, a good plan will help you personally. Any seasoned researcher will be able to tell you a heartbreaking story about working hard on a project for many months, only to sit down at the end and discover that an early error rendered their entire dataset unusable. For me (Tara), I am still haunted by the time that I skipped a step in the experimental procedure for the first 10 participants in my first real research project as a graduate student, making those data completely useless. Since each participant took over two hours to complete the study, those 10 people represented over 20 hours of effort over several weeks, not to mention their time and good will. Wasting participant time is unethical, in addition to being personally frustrating. And my story is the best-case scenario, because I noticed the problem and fixed it relatively early. Even worse than throwing out data is proceeding without awareness, leading to faulty and misleading conclusions.

DOI: 10.4324/9781315167473-19

Importantly, just as there is no perfect research study, there are no perfect researchers. You will make mistakes, but if you try to learn good lessons from each mistake you make, you will make fewer such mistakes as your career progresses.

To aid in this journey, we've first provided in the following some guidelines on common logic errors made throughout the research process, followed by a checklist for conducting good research. The checklist combines recommendations from across this entire book, followed by some additional big-picture recommendations related to each. Following this checklist will not prevent every mistake you could make, but we hope it will help your mistakes learn more towards "learning experiences" and away from "deep regrets."

Common Logic Errors Across Research Stages

Human thinking evolved to be efficient, reward/punishment focused, and social. These are generally good things that keep us alive and safe. Frequently these tendencies interfere, though, when we need to engage in effortful and careful thinking. Before beginning a new project, you should reflect on these and other common logical fallacies to minimize their influence on your thinking. Refer to them any time they are relevant.

Strawman. This fallacy refers to creating a false position, the straw man, to attack, misrepresenting the actual nature of a debate and making it easier to criticize. For instance, you could argue that "all previous research in this area has focused on managers and therefore is hostile to the needs of employees" in order to justify your paper's focus on employees.

Post hoc, ergo propter hoc. This is my (Tara's) favorite Latin phrase (besides *sic transit gloria mundi*, which is not relevant here), and also a very common fallacy committed by well-meaning researchers all the time. The phrase means, "after it, therefore because of it." The logic that something must be causally related because it followed in time is sloppy at best. You have learned about how to support causal claims in this book. Be on the lookout for poor causal reasoning in your interpretation and argumentation.

Begging the question. This fallacy is poorly named. "Begging the question" sounds like it means "raises the question." But it does not. It means "assuming the premise of the argument to be true while attempting to prove it." Not as catchy. But it is nonetheless a common fallacy committed by researchers. For example, saying, "I know Richard is an honest person, because he told me that he was honest." Or, "low morale isn't a problem here, and I know because we haven't received any complaints." This statement ignores the possibility that morale is so low that people are not motivated enough to submit complaints. Or that they are so afraid of retaliation that they dare not. By assuming the premise that morale is high, the statement ignores other possibilities.

Appeal to authority. We all have research heroes. When I (Tara) was in graduate school, my research heroes were people like Sara Kiesler, Jeffrey Stanton, and Diane Bailey. Anything they said was unquestioned. I also looked up to and admired the faculty in my graduate program, and believed everything they told me. A little research fangirling will not hurt anyone. However it is no basis to form an argument. I can't say "Adam Meade says that this method is the best so I am using it." Opinions are not evidence, even if they are written down. We realize that we are painting ourselves into a corner a bit with this statement, considering that this whole book is full of our opinions . . . You should listen to all our advice. Just don't use it as the base of evidence in a paper.

Naturalistic fallacy. This fallacy has to do with what we judge to be right, or "normal." It is easy to look around and observe your surroundings and come to the incorrect conclusion that the way things *are* is how they *should* be. "Of course people should have managers! Everyone has a manager!" You say. This kind of thinking is dangerous since you can easily lose sight of how your own values and lens on the world are affecting the research questions you ask. Until recently, most people were not permitted to fully participate in US society, due to their sex, or race, or religion. We now look back with great shame on those mistakes of the past. At the time, many people believed that this way of structuring society was right, because it was the way it always had been. You should be brave and ask challenging questions that do not make this assumption.

Appeal to emotion. Imagine reading a paper that started, "telework policies make it possible for parents to spend more time with their kids, ensuring that they don't miss birthdays and recitals and that their kids are happy and loved." The paper is hoping that you will have an emotional reaction to this scenario, maybe reflecting on your own family, and thus be more likely to believe that the research is worthy and important. The ability of an argument to evoke strong emotions, however, has nothing to do with its truthfulness or soundness. Telework policies may indeed improve work-life balance. But evidence, not appeals to emotion, are needed to make that case.

Cherry-picking. When you are conducting a literature review, you will definitely find that previous research is not fully in agreement on every topic (or even most topics). It may be tempting to pick out the papers that support whatever you want to say in your paper in order to support your case. That practice is called cherry-picking, and it's not okay. Your job is to accurately represent the state of knowledge on your topic. If there is a debate happening in the literature, you need to describe it, and explain why you are choosing one side or another. Cherry-picking is also used to describe a bad analysis habit that some researchers have– imagine that five of your predicted results came out the way you expected and five did not. Reporting only the successful analyses, or the successful studies, is unethical and dishonest. It's also bad logic.

Ad hominem. This term refers to criticizing a person instead of their argument. You might say "this person is a misogynist so we can't believe any of their data." Sometimes unpleasant people have good ideas. Attempting to argue a point by focusing on the person who made the point is not good logic.

Source fallacy. Related to an ad hominem argument is the source fallacy. In some ways, the source fallacy is the opposite of the appeal to authority. You might say, "that person doesn't even have kids, how can they know anything about work-family balance research?" Or maybe you disregard a person's work because you believe their politics are different from yours. On one hand, you should certainly pay attention to the source if the person's work has been called into question on ethical grounds– maybe they are a *p*-hacker, or have been misrepresenting the things people tell them in interviews. On the other hand, though, it is possible for a person you disagree with to be right. Focus on the study, the arguments, and the methods, and not on the person reporting them.

Work to recognize when you or your coauthors fall in these thinking traps. At best, they'll frustrate and slow down your research. At worst, you'll waste the time and resources of both you and others. Frequently stop, step outside yourself, and question the logic of what you doing. With that in the back of your mind, you are in a good position to get some good research started.

The Research Checklist

- **Laying the Foundation**

    - Define Your Foundational Philosophies (Chapter 1)
    - Literature Review (Chapter 2)
    - Choose an Overall Approach (Chapter 3)
    - Define a Population of Interest (Chapter 4)
    - Form Research Questions and Hypotheses (Chapter 2)
    - Identify a Target Audience (Chapter 14)
    - Review the JARS Standards (Chapter 14)

- **Planning**

    - Create a Research Plan (Chapters 2, 5, 6, 7, 8)

        - Decide Between Archival or Primary Research
        - Decide Between Measurement or Manipulation
        - Operationalize Measures and Manipulations
        - Choose a Sampling Strategy
        - Develop an Analytic Plan
        - Plan for Data Quality, Including Power Analysis

    - Discuss Project Responsibilities and Intended Authorship (Chapter 14)
    - Double Check Plan Against JARS standards (Chapter 14)

- **Preparation and Development**

    - Apply for Ethics Approval (Chapter 1)
    - Develop, Pilot Test, and Finalize Materials (Chapters 5, 6, 7, 9, 10, 11)
    - Set Up Record-Keeping and Organizational Materials (Chapters 11, 12)
    - Pre-Register (Chapters 11, 14)

        - Optional: Submit a Hybrid Registered Report

- **Execution and Analysis**

    - Collect and/or Acquire Data (Chapters 6, 8)

        - Actively Monitor Data Collection
        - Debrief and Compensate Participants

    - Data Cleaning (Chapter 11)
    - Hypothesis Tests and Investigation of Research Questions (Chapter 12)
    - Exploratory Analyses (Chapter 12)

- **Sharing and Write-up**

    - Post Open Science Documents (Chapter 11)
    - Identify and Select Meaningful Outlets (Chapter 14)
    - Outline, Write, Edit, Get and Act on Feedback (Chapters 2, 14)

        - Review the JARS Standards One Last Time

    - Submit, Revise, Resubmit (Chapter 14)
    - Promote the Work With Target Audiences (Chapter 14)

Laying the Foundation

As we have written repeatedly in this book, no amount of fancy analysis will save you if you use that analysis to answer the wrong question. The I-O psychology research community has a tendency to focus too much on the precision of our tools and the carefulness of our designs. But if you want your voice to be heard, you must ask an important, interesting, and answerable question. This is the foundation on which all other decisions are built.

Define Your Foundational Philosophies (Chapter 1): The decisions you make as you design, execute, and interpret research are ultimately based in your professional and personal values, which are themselves based heavily in philosophical orientations. It is very common for graduate students to finish their education simply accepting what their advisors and professors have told them rather than reflecting on why their advisors and professors believe the things they believe and deciding if they believe them too.

You are ready to move on when you can answer the following questions:

1. Why am I conducting this research?
2. What am I hoping to learn or accomplish as a result of conducting this research?
3. How big a role should this research take in my life? Is this a short-term interest or part of a long-term research program?
4. How will I maintain a work-life balance while pursuing this research? What parts of myself do I want to keep safe as the demands of the project increase?
5. What beliefs and philosophies am I bringing with me into this research? Could they bias me along the way?

Literature Review (Chapter 2): Next, you have to immerse yourself in the literature and become a world-class expert on your selected topic. Relative to what you might have done as an undergraduate, your goal here is to go much deeper. You should become so familiar with the various issues related to a research question that you start to ask deeper questions. For example, you will find yourself remembering the names of the people who write about your area and what their big ideas are. You will start to notice when clusters of articles express similar values and goals in their introductions.

Why does Hackett disagree with Su? What might be the underlying but unstated assumptions behind their arguments? If you agree with one side more, what kind of evidence would contribute to their argument or cast doubt on the other argument? These are the sorts of questions you will begin to ask when you are "deep enough" in a literature.

As you do that, you will start to notice gaps in the known universe of knowledge, and at that point, you're ready to form an argument for why and how the gap should be filled.

You are ready to move on when you can answer the following questions:

1. What problem am I interested in solving?
2. What is already known about this problem?
3. What has been discussed in the past 5 years about this problem? In which journals is the conversation happening? In what kind of organizations is this a real problem?
4. What is the gap that would move this conversation forward?
5. Why is it important to address this gap?
6. What other areas of literature are needed to fully understand this gap?

Choose An Overall Approach (Chapter 3): Based on your literature review, you should have a sense of how developed or mature your research area is. The first decision is whether you will take a qualitative or quantitative approach. If you choose qualitative methods, you should do so because you want to create a rich description of a phenomenon or answer questions that require a qualitative approach to generate an example of a principle. If you choose a quantitative approach, it should be because you want to make inferences about relationships or effects. Your analytic approach, then, could be either inductive or deductive. In deductive reasoning, previous theory should clearly support a particular prediction, and testing that prediction should generate some insight about the theory. In other cases, a more inductive approach is preferable. Perhaps the theory is light in this area, or two theories make competing predictions. Or you intend to take a fully exploratory approach. Either approach is fine as long as you clearly specify and defend your choice. In the past, I-O journals would insist on theory-based deductive descriptions of research, even if it was actually conducted in an exploratory way. We are personally glad to see that era coming to a close. Now, you are more free to choose the approach that makes the most scientific sense, and describe it accurately and honestly, and that is what we recommend you do.

A key lesson from this book is that no research method, no matter where it comes from or how it was developed, conclusively gives you all relevant information about a phenomenon you are studying. All have strengths and weaknesses. It is your responsibility as a researcher to understand the strengths and weaknesses of any method you use in your own research as well as any method you read about someone else using. It is tempting to choose methods that are either familiar or novel. Don't fall into either trap.

An aspect of this stage that we have not discussed in this book so far is **mixed methods**, which refers to the blending of qualitative and quantitative approaches to address a single research question (or family of research questions). This is distinct from **multimethod research**, which refers to the use of either multiple datasets or multiple studies of the same philosophical orientation (in I-O, usually multiple closely related quantitative studies labeled Study 1, Study 2, etc.) to address shared research questions within a single paper. In contrast, mixed methods traditionally refers to the use of studies adopting both philosophical approaches (recall Chapter 1) across different studies, typically sequentially, which could appear in one paper or in a series.

Creswell and Plano Clark (2017) provide very detailed descriptions of many different ways to mix your methods, and we'll highlight their highest-level categorizations here to help you understand their potential. There are many variations on each, as there is no agreed-upon way to combine information from multiple philosophical orientations, and we point you to their book for more detail.

1. **Triangulation.** Triangulation refers to the use of two or more methods to converge the same research question. The most basic triangulation design is simply to conduct one qualitative study and one quantitative study to see if the conclusions drawn from both studies agree.
2. **Embedding.** Embedded mixed methods refers to a series of studies in which one study or group of studies plays a secondary role to a primary study or group. Embedding is quite common in I-O psychology mixed methods; for example, a qualitative pilot study might be used to inform aspects of a quantitative design, such as conducting a think-aloud with an experimental stimulus video to see if participants are perceiving the video as intended.

3. **Explanation.** Explanatory mixed methods involve the initial use of quantitative research to uncover interesting or provocative results, followed by the use of a qualitative method to better understand and contextualize those findings. Explanatory mixed methods are relatively uncommon in I-O, as there is a general bias toward believing that once quantitative research has been completed, there is little new information that qualitative could add to its conclusions. We do not generally agree with this stance. In fact, one of the most valuable mixed study designs we can imagine is the use of an explanatory design to understand why an expected result didn't go the way it was planned, such as following up with participants when an effect was much smaller than expected (or put in a more cynical yet practical way: an effect was not statistically significant, and it's not clear why). More often, and to the detriment of our field, such studies are instead filed away somewhere, never to be published. We discuss this "file drawer problem" in more detail in our discussions of both meta-analysis (Chapter 13) and sharing results (Chapter 14).

4. **Exploration.** Exploratory mixed methods are the reverse of explanatory methods – qualitative research is used first to help develop research questions and hypotheses, and a quantitative study is used to test those ideas. This differs from embedded mixed methods in that there is no implied relative value between the studies; the qualitative research presents the theory and the quantitative study tests it. Both are equally important in developing a complete understanding of the theory.

Because qualitative methods tend to be inductive and quantitative methods tend to be deductive, a general strength of mixed methods is that it better enables abduction to come to some underlying truth of a problem.

You are ready to move on when you can answer the following questions:

1. Am I going to use a qualitative design, quantitative design, or some combination?
2. Does the theory in this area clearly support a particular hypothesis or only suggest more general research questions?
3. Do various theories make conflicting predictions?
4. Is it the case that a finding in either direction would be equally interesting? Or is only one kind of effect interesting? As such, will I use a deductive, inductive, or abductive approach?
5. Is this really a question that can be addressed with a single research study?

Define The Population of Interest (Chapter 4): In this step, you need to think about the people that you are trying to describe with your research. Do your predictions apply to "workers" universally defined? Across all times, settings, and units of analysis? What exactly are the meaningful differences that set your population of interest apart as worth studying? A common pitfall for beginning researchers is thinking that studying a new population is enough to make a contribution. For instance, maybe The Theory of Workiness has been tested on nurses, post office workers, and veterinarians, but not accountants. It is not good enough to say that you are making a contribution by testing the theory in accountants. You have to also specify what is different about the new sample that will generate new and useful information. Is it the level of autonomy experienced in accountants that differs? The pay level? And why would autonomy or pay level matter for the theory? That is, why do you think that the theory as it is currently understood will not generalize to accountants?

You are ready to move on when you can answer the following questions:

1. Who am I trying to make claims about?
2. Who is not included in this population, and why?
3. Why is the population I've identified theoretically interesting?
4. Do I expect that time, place, culture, or other context-level factors will be important in defining my population?

Form Research Questions and Hypotheses (Chapter 2)**:** Based on your literature review, chosen and approach, and population of interest, a set of questions should emerge. Initially, you will have too many questions. Your goal at this stage should be to narrow your focus to a small set of research questions (1 or 2) that will be at the heart of your research. From the research questions, you may or may not also pose specific predictions/hypotheses.

Put another way, you are at this stage of your research building a **model**. Although you have seen many kinds of "models" used throughout this book, the term generally refers to any simplified representation of a complex phenomenon. A model, by necessity, oversimplifies the universe to zoom in on one particular aspect of interest and describe it with relatively simple and straightforward language and rules. In this stage, you are trying to zoom in on the exact relationships or effects that we currently misunderstand enough to necessitate new research. You are identifying a gap in the current model and proposing a new model to replace it based upon your literature review. You do not know if your gap is "true" or not, and that's how you are justifying the need to collect data about it.

Remember here a famous quote by the famous statistician George E. P. Box (1979): "All models are wrong but some are useful." Box made this statement to illustrate two points that he earlier referred to as **parsimony** and **worrying selectively**. He wrote:

- *Parismony*. Since all models are wrong the scientist cannot obtain a "correct" one by excessive elaboration. On the contrary, following William of Occam he should seek an economical description of natural phenomena. Just as the ability to devise simple but evocative models is the signature of the great scientist so overelaboration and overparameterization is often the mark of mediocrity.
- *Worrying Selectively*. Since all models are wrong the scientist must be alert to what is importantly wrong. It is inappropriate to be concerned about mice when there are tigers abroad.

(Box, 1976, p. 792)

Make sure your model is useful; it should help you and other experts make sense of the world in a meaningful way that you could not before.

You are ready to move on when you can answer the following questions:

1. What are the relationships that I am interested in?
2. Do I have sufficient justification to include causal effects in my model? (if so, be prepared to choose an appropriate methodology in the following)
3. How do the various relationships and effects that I care about fit together into a coherent whole?
4. How does time play a role in my model? Do some variables precede others or do they all happen at once? Is this temporal aspect represented correctly in my model?

5. Do I think my model will hold equally well for all the people, settings, and conditions I am interested in? Or, do I need to think about moderation/conditional effects?
6. Can I justify each of my predictions with relevant, coherent, high-quality literature?

Identify a Target Audience (Chapter 12): Although you won't be writing up your results any time soon, this is a good time to look ahead toward when you will. If you're designing your research with the intent of finding a home for it in an academic journal, it's worth thinking about what the people that read that journal care about. Remember that almost any research question can be examined through almost any philosophical and disciplinary lenses. This means that to join an expert, scholarly conversation about a topic, you need to understand the topic from the perspective of the people you want to convince.

This is what makes **interdisciplinary research** so challenging; you need to meaningfully identify gaps and develop insights combining multiple disciplines in a way that is convincing to the particular gatekeepers where you will share your results. This reality is not meant to scare you away from interdisciplinary research; instead, it should highlight for you the additional challenges that interdisciplinary researchers face that siloed researchers generally do not face, despite the fact that interdisciplinary research is often more useful and important than siloed research to meaningfully solving problems. Interdisciplinary research is also more challenging that **multidisciplinary research**, which refers to researchers within different silos all working on the same project but not really combining their expertises and perspectives to joint understanding. In multidisciplinary research, we're working in the same room; in interdisciplinary research, we're a team, working together.

It is always valuable at this stage to consider the different philosophies and perspectives that will be brought to your research once it is complete. Taking a moment to consider this, and potentially to change course a bit if necessary, can save a great deal of time and effort later.

You are ready to move on when you can answer the following questions:

1. What is the end-product of this research? A journal article? A technical report? My own growth?
2. Who do I want to listen to me once this research is complete?
3. Why would that audience listen to me? What do I need to accomplish during my research so that they'll care?

Review the JARS Standards (Chapter 12): This is the first of several times that you should refer to the **Journal Article Reporting Standards (JARS)**. JARS, published by the American Psychological Association, are a set of comprehensive and useful guides to the reporting expectations in APA journals for empirical research, with different versions for quantitative, qualitative, and mixed methods research. Regardless of whether you intend to actually publish your work in an APA journal (such as the *Journal of Applied Psychology* or *Technology, Mind, and Behavior*), JARS is a beneficial reference. The reason to check now, at the foundational stage, is to make sure that you are setting yourself up to be able to provide the information required by JARS when you get to the writing stage. JARS is expansive, and contains recommendations for everything from reporting sample demographics to choosing a title.

You are ready to move on when you can answer the following questions:

1. Which version of JARS applies to my research?
2. Are there any items within the applicable JARS that should change any decisions I've already made or will make during the planning phase that comes next?

Planning Stage

Having established the conceptualization of your study, the next phase is to plan operational details and make concrete choices about methodology and broader contextual details.

Create a Research Plan (Chapters 2, 5, 6, 7, 8)**:** The majority of the planning stage is the creation of the research plan itself. After this, you will have a very clear mental picture of what will happen in your study, and you will have assembled all the materials you need to create that vision in reality. Assuming that you are collecting data from human subjects, you will know every single thing that the participant will do, in order, from the moment they learn of your study until the moment you debrief and compensate them. You will also have a clear sense of what your data will look like and how you are going to analyze it. Now is not the time to "build the plane as you fly it." Now is the time to build the plane on the ground in a hangar, and then do a bunch of little tiny test flights until you are completely confident that the plane is in good shape. And then you can maybe think about flying it.

Importantly, you should think of the research plan as a wicked problem (see Chapter 14), one in which every decision you make potentially affects the value or appropriateness of prior decisions. Although it can be quite emotionally challenging, resist the urge to stick to a questionable research plan after evidence begins to mount that it might not be the great idea you originally thought. You must embrace the idea that until you have submitted a research plan for ethics approval, every decision you have made in the research plan can be changed. Only after you have confirmed every decision is in harmony with every other decision should you finalize the plan and move forward.

Decide Between Archival or Primary Research. The first major decision you need to make is whether to collect your own data or use data that has been collected or exists already. For example, if you want to study "happiness," you can either look for a dataset that contains some measure of happiness or collect those data yourself. Or, if you decide that you will measure happiness by tracking state-level use of therapy services, you can look for published statistics that might exist already. Then your challenge is getting access to that data. You can use Google dataset search (https://datasetsearch.research.google.com/) or other resources to find potential data sources. Or, you can contact organizations or others who you think might have collected the data that you need.

You are ready to move on when you can answer the following questions:

1. Is collecting data for my chosen variables feasible, financially and practically?
2. Do existing datasets exist that might contain all the measures I am interested in?
3. For existing data, am I confident that it was collected in a trustworthy way?

Decide Between Measurement or Manipulation. If you decide on primary research, you'll need to decide whether to measure or manipulate key variables. Some variables cannot be manipulated, so the choice is made for you. A few fairly obvious examples are age, profession, intelligence, and nationality. You won't be randomly assigning anyone to be high or low in intelligence or to be raised in Sweden or Mexico. Assuming that manipulation is possible, however, you'll need to think carefully about what type of research design – experimental, quasi-experimental, or correlational – is most appropriate and also feasible for both your research question and the resources you can bring to bear. There is often a tradeoff between realism and control inherent in this choice. JARS will ask for evidence of validity for any such materials. Manipulation checks are also an important part of experimental designs: these are measures that assess whether the manipulation had its intended effect.

JARS also requires details about how participants were assigned to conditions, and whether they were aware of the manipulation. I-O psychologists tend to use many more nonexperimental or quasi-experimental designs. We suspect that this has a lot to do with the historical emphasis we have placed on creating generalizable knowledge that organizations can use in their human resource management efforts. As the field grows and evolves, we expect to see more diverse methods, including more experiments and more big data mining efforts.

You are ready to move on when you can answer the following questions:

1. Will I measure or manipulate each variable in my study?
2. If I am using manipulation (i.e., experimental design), how will I know the manipulation worked?
3. Will participants or experimenters be aware of the experimental condition they are experiencing? If so, how might that affect the results? Is **masking** possible? (*Note:* In the past, this feature of an experiment was referred to as "blind" or "double blind." You might see this language in older research.)

Operationalize Measures and Manipulations: Whether you decide to measure or manipulate, you'll need to consider operationalization, a concept we introduced in Chapter 2. Since that chapter, we have provided you with many more tools to actually create those operational definitions – the tangible ways that you will define every variable in your study for the purpose of measuring it. Your choices here are infinite and should be guided by practical realities and established precedent. In qualitative research, a manipulation operationalization might take the form of an interview. In quantitative research, a measurement operationalization might take the form of a previously-validated Likert-type scale (as discussed in Chapter 7), or a count variable of some behavior.

For instance, consider all these possible ways to quantitatively operationalize job satisfaction:

- responses to the Job Satisfaction Survey (Spector, 1994)
- response to a single-item question, "How satisfied are you with your job?"
- count of number of positive words used in company email exchanges
- instances of disciplinary action
- number of minutes spent in voluntary company social events

Some of these measures are more direct than others. Your choice might have a lot to do with what is logistically feasible for your population. If you don't have access to company emails, that is out. If your partner organization won't allow you to survey employees, those are out too. So, both scientific and practical concerns will end up being relevant in your operationalizations. But regardless of the measure you choose, since you are taking a quantitative approach, reliability and validity evidence must be established.

JARS has specific requirements about demonstrating the reliability and validity of your measures, including interrrater reliability for judgment data. Don't fall into the trap of assuming that some measures are more "objective" and therefore better. The truth is that all operationalizations of latent constructs require inferences to be made. And those inferences can be either sound or less sound. You establish the soundness of your inferences by presenting convincing reliability and validity evidence, which must itself meet the scientific standards we've laid out in this text.

In addition to measuring the variables that make up your model, you also need to think about how you will collect data about participant characteristics. JARS requires that you report on the participants' age, gender, ethnicity, socioeconomic status if relevant, and any other-context-specific characteristics. These variables don't go into your model, but they are used to contextualize your findings by describing your sample.

You are ready to move on when you can answer the following questions:

1. What is the total list of variables I need to measure in this study?
2. For each, is there an established measure I can use?
3. Do I have sufficient information about the reliability and validity of those measures?
4. What are the pros and cons of each measure over other options that are available?
5. If I need to make my own measure, how will I pilot test it before using it?

Choose a Sampling Strategy: If you are conducting primary research, the next step is to decide whom you will collect data from. Refer back to Chapter 4 for detailed information about sampling strategies. Here you need to think about the ways that sampling can affect the conclusions you draw, as well as the practical questions of how you will accomplish your sampling and whether it will have any effects on the participants. For instance, in deciding to administer a training intervention to some employees but not others, you deprive the ones who weren't chosen of a valuable development experience. Finally you need to think about whether you will introduce any validity threats by using the strategy you have chosen. Sampling will affect generalizability, and you need to be clear about which population you are actually comfortable generalizing to, given your sample. For example: if I use a snowball sample (where I send the study to a few contacts, and ask them to invite their contacts in turn), what is unusual about my friends and colleagues? What population do I think they actually represent? Many of my friends live on the East or West Coast of the US; they are highly educated; and they have excellent personalities. In this way they are probably not representative of "US Workers."

You are ready to move on when you can answer the following questions:

1. Will my strategy ensure that confounds are minimized?
2. If I'm using a nonrandom sample, can I measure and control any potential confounding variables?
3. Will my strategy be successful, practically speaking? Do I have sufficient resources and commitments from others?
4. What implications will my strategy have for the generalizability of my findings?

Develop an Analytic Plan: After your measures and manipulations have been operationalized within the context of a particular research design (e.g., experimental, quasi-experimental, correlational), you may find that your existing design decisions imply a particular analytic framework. For example, if you are conducting a correlational study involving a complex network of observed variables and want to test a theory with a lot of assumptions about causality, you're probably going to need to plan for structural equation modeling. Even so, you typically have some freedom in choosing a specific analysis that is as simple as possible while completely addressing your research questions and hypotheses, that is, a parsimonious analysis. Resist the temptation to automatically use the fanciest analysis you have heard of. Also resist the temptation to let your intended analysis drive your research questions.

Instead, choose an analysis that is robust to any particulars of your data, and appropriate for the number of cases and variables you are working with.

You are ready to move on when you can answer the following questions:

1. Which analytic framework will I use?
2. What size effect do I expect?
3. Do I have the requisite statistical skills and tools to conduct this analysis? What software or other resources do I need to do it well?

Plan for Data Quality, Including Power Analysis: Many of the ways you will establish the quality of your data can be accomplished in the analysis phase of the project; many of these approaches require that you either ask a few extra questions or enable special kinds of data tracking. For example, if you will use any attention check items (see Chapter 9), those need to be identified now. As noted in that chapter, choosing original attention checks is necessary, because most people who have taken surveys in the past have become familiar with common attention-checking tactics. This is especially, but not uniquely, true for professional survey-takers who are members of online platforms. Finally you should set a priori cutoffs for when to remove cases from your sample, if possible.

Once you have created all materials and set desired quality standards, you need to pick a sample size. If you are planning to use NHST as an analytic framework, you should conduct a power analysis as appropriate to your planned analyses. If you are planning something else, you should forecast necessary sample size as needed to reasonably draw conclusions from whatever it is you are planning to do. For example, analytic approaches incorporating machine learning algorithms often require very large sample sizes to take advantage of the advanced predictive modeling capabilities of those algorithms.

In any quantitative design, you will need to determine how much data you need in order to detect the effects you hope to find given some desired level of precision and accuracy. Recall from Chapter 12 that power analysis involves a lot of guesswork about how you think your variables will behave–how will they relate to each other, how much will they vary, etc. You may be able to turn to the literature to get information that will inform these guesses–for example, we know generally how Big 5 personality variables relate to each other, thanks to the many meta-analyses that have been conducted on those variables. Or, you may have to pull your guesses out of thin air, doing the best you can with limited knowledge. In that case, we recommend estimating power at many different levels of the parameter you are estimating– for example, you might come up with five different covariance estimates and generate estimates for five effect sizes. All those estimates can be plotted on a graph –manually or automatically like the ones G*power produces – to give you a general sense of how much data you will need.

You are ready to move on when you can answer the following questions:

1. How will I establish data quality?
2. Have I included valid data quality indicators within my materials?
3. How much data do I need to reasonably conduct planned analysis?
4. What cutoffs will I use to remove people from the sample? Are the cutoffs based on precedent or evidence?

Discuss Project Responsibilities and Intended Authorship (Chapter 14)**:** Collaborative research is rewarding, and often necessary for complex projects. As soon as more than one person is involved in a project, though, confusion and misunderstandings can arise about authorship. This is not the sort of thing that can be solved with a universal rubric, although there are some general rules of thumb we can offer. The most important thing to do is to have a conversation as early as possible with collaborators about authorship and expectations, and then to revisit the agreement periodically to ensure that people's expectations are still aligned. Ideally, you had this conversation at the inception of the project, but in real-world research, we often discover that project team members are interested in doing more or less work than they originally believed. If there is any doubt whatsoever about authorship, have a conversation about it now to set expectations for both workload during the project and recognition later.

As described in Chapter 14, authorship is a sign that someone has contributed intellectually to a project. Several journals (e.g., *Psychological Science*) now ask that author contributions to a manuscript are spelled out explicitly (e.g., "RL wrote the manuscript, TB conceptualized the project, TB and RL collected data, TB analyzed data and reviewed a draft, RL provided snacks). Even if the journal doesn't require it, writing out a statement like this can help clarify if there are any points of disagreement.

You are ready to move on when you can answer the following questions:

1. Who will be the first, second, third, and so on author?
2. What are the expectations for who will do which task, and when?
3. Are all authors in agreement about the plan and the timeline?
4. Does anyone outside the core research team (e.g., data owner, sponsor, advisor) expect authorship? If so how will you handle that?
5. Will authorship order remain the same for all research products (e.g., conference presentations and publications)?
6. Who are the non-authors who should be acknowledged with an author note in the paper?

Double Check Plan Against JARS Standards (Chapter 14): You've seen JARS mentioned a lot in this checklist, but once you've created a complete, final draft of your research plan, you should revisit it more closely, line by line, to be sure that you will be able to meet all the requirements specified there.

You are ready to move on when you can answer the following questions:

1. If my plan is enacted as designed, will I have sufficient data and other information to fulfill all JARS requirements?
2. Is there anything that could go wrong that would make fulfilling JARS requirements difficult? For example, what happens if a study proctor forgets to record data in the participant log?

Preparation and Development

Having created a plan as well as you can, you can now start taking concrete steps towards making your research really, really real. Until this point, only you and your collaborators have been involved in the planning. At this point, you will start to involve other parties who have a role to play, from the ethics review board to the pilot testers.

Apply for Ethics Approval (Chapter 1): Most large institutions, whether in academia or practice, have internal ethical boards that reviews studies to ensure that participants are treated with respect and that the risks of the study (to participants or to society at large) are outweighed by the benefits. The board is frequently, but not always, called an Institutional Review Board (IRB), and all universities, and many large corporations, have internal IRBs. Applying for IRB approval is frequently a multi-round activity, in which you propose an initial plan and the board requests changes or additional information.

In planning your study timeline, be sure to allot sufficient time for this phase. Depending on the level of risk that the IRB identifies in your study, you may also need to re-apply periodically in order to continue working with the data. Chapter 1 has more detail about IRBs and ethical considerations. You may feel that the IRB is a useless box-checking exercise, because your study doesn't involve injecting people with anything or putting them in any danger. But I-O psychology research is absolutely not risk-free for participants. A few ways you could harm your participants:

- If their data are not handled confidentially, it could be de-anonymized and used by their employer to punish them.
- You could be compensating people unfairly without realizing it.
- People could feel compelled to participate against their wishes if their employer is "encouraging" them too strongly.
- Your experiment could cause distress or discomfort.

Trust that the IRB will help you identify any such possibilities and adjust your design to minimize risk of harm.

You are ready to move on when:

1. The official ethics review body of your institution, probably the IRB, has either approved your study as proposed or identified it as exempt from further review.

Develop, Pilot Test, and Finalize Materials (Chapters 5, 6, 7, 9, 10, 11)**:** You will need many kinds of materials for your research: survey and interview instruments, focus group plans, experimental manipulations, maybe informational or background material for participants, and so on. Before you invest the effort into collecting data using these materials, you need to make sure they are going to do what you need them to do. For example:

- In the case of an interview guide, you should pre-test to determine how long the interview will probably take, whether the questions are clear and understandable, and whether they are at the right level of depth to elicit meaningful responses.
- For a survey, you want to check the expected duration and readability, and also that the technical/software aspects of the survey work correctly.
- In the case of newly designed experimental materials–things you will use to manipulate an independent variable–you need to verify that they create the response you expect them to. If I was conducting an experiment about emotions at work, I might want to induce negative or positive emotions by showing people videos clips from sad movies or happy movies. I'd want to conduct a pilot test by asking people to watch many clips and rate their level of happiness or sadness. I'd then want to choose clips that had clear happy or sad ratings and ask a new set of people to watch them, and then give those people an emotion questionnaire to see how they felt. I might learn that watching happy movie clips doesn't consistently make people feel happy, in which case I'd need to go back and rethink my plan.

In some cases, you need IRB approval for this kind of development, and in other cases, you don't. For example, if you're just giving a prototype Likert-type measure that you're developing to friends and labmates to get their reactions as you work on writing new questions, you don't need IRB approval. If you're giving your newly developed measure to independent research participants, you almost certainly do. Always be sure to check with your institution's ethics board before collecting data if you aren't 100% sure that ethics review does not apply.

You are ready to move on when you can answer the following questions:

1. Am I confident that all of my measures and manipulations are construct valid, that is, they actually represent what I need them to represent?
2. Am I confident that all of my measures and manipulation are appropriate for the population I will be using them with?
3. Would I be more confident in any of these measures or manipulations after conducting pilot testing, including acceptance testing, usability testing, functional testing, and ad-hoc testing (see Chapter 11)?

Set Up Record-Keeping and Organizational Materials (Chapters 11, 12)**:** Before you collect *any* data, get organized. It is fairly common for new researchers to assume that they will be able to remember all the important details of the project. But do your future self a big favor and don't trust anything to memory. I (Tara) have been asked to clarify details of a study procedure for a paper I published 10 years ago. I barely remembered that the study existed. But luckily for me, I had a detailed codebook to refer to so I could respond to the request. You need a few things to be organized. Chapter 11 described several tools you can use to do this, including codebooks (see Table 15.1 for another example) and participant logs (Table 15.2). A codebook is a detailed manual to all the variables in your study. Your codebook should be fully understandable by someone other than you. Imagine handing it to someone else with no explanation, along with your data, so they can make use of it. No shorthand or notes to self should be included. Treat the codebook like a public record, because if all goes well, it will be. A **participant log** is a type of data created by study proctors reporting on their actions and observations during proctoring. Both types of documents are invaluable records both during and after a study has been completed.

Table 15.1 Example codebook

Variable name	Item text	Response scale	Reversed?	Scale name	Source
Con01	I always follow the rules.	1 (strongly disagree) to 5 (strongly agree)	N	Conscientiousness	IPIP (Goldberg, 1999)
Con02	My room is a mess	1 (strongly disagree) to 5 (strongly agree)	Y	Conscientiousness	IPIP (Goldberg, 1999)
Gender	Please indicate your gender	1=male 2=female 3=other	N	Gender	new
Perf	Rate the employee's performance	1=poor 2=medium 3=excellent	N	Job Performance	new

Table 15.2 Example participant log

Date	ID	Condition: 1 = control 2 = low pay 3 = high pay	Experimenter	Notes
1/1/2024	2055	1	Jolene	Participant left early
1/1/2024	2056	2	Jolene	
1/2/2024	2057	1	Amber	Check data quality; participant seemed checked out
1/2/2024	2058	3	Amber	

Participant logs typically do not enable links between data and PII, such as participant names or email addresses. If you need identifying information for the purpose of paying or giving credit for participation, you might need a separate **compensation log**. Unless you have obtained explicit IRB approval otherwise, the ID used in the participant log should be anonymous and the only way participants are identified in other data files.

The final document you might want to create at this stage is an explanation of data and documentation organizational structure. Historically, this kind of file was named *readme. txt* but is now more generally known as a **readme file**, so that researchers would always know the first file to look at when opening an unfamiliar folder. Especially during collaborative projects, it is very easy to get lost when multiple people start adding files to the same folder. The readme file serves as a place for everyone to make notes about where files should be placed and why, so that nobody needs to rely on their or anyone else's memory. The test of whether you have done this well is to imagine handing your files to a stranger and asking them to run the analyses. Would they get the same result you did? If not, label things better.

You are ready to move on when you can answer the following questions:

1. Does every variable have an entry in the codebook?
2. Is the codebook labeled thoroughly with response scales, scale names, and sources?
3. How will I track participant assignment to conditions, completion date, and other relevant logistic details?
4. How will data be stored and organized?
5. If someone called me in 10 years with a specific question about the data would I be able to answer them?
6. Is the documentation sufficiently organized that someone other than me could retrace all my steps and come to the same conclusion in the analysis?

Pre-Register (Chapters 11, 14)**:** We are enthusiastic supporters of open science practices, and we think these practices will soon become required in more outlets. Even if they are not required, they are something we recommend strongly to make our science stronger, as described in Chapter 14. Pre-registration is one of the most straightforward aspects of open science if you have planned your study completely, as we recommend in the present chapter. A major purpose of pre-registration is to make it more difficult to go back after the data collection is done and change your hypotheses to better fit the data, or to drop data that don't cooperate. We know you would never do that. But pre-registration makes your commitment public, and gives your findings stronger credibility. There are several options for pre-registration. The idea is to publish your hypotheses and plan before you collect data, and before you know what the outcome is. As described in Chapter 11, you have two major options for pre-registration: aspredicted.org and the Open Science Framework. Neither is "better" than other, but they do ask for different information. Check out both and make a decision that best meets the needs of your project.

Optional: Submit a Hybrid Registered Report. As described in Chapter 14, several journals now include an option to publish using hybrid registered reports. In this model, a manuscript is submitted with a literature review and hypotheses, detailed methodology and analysis plans, but no results. The manuscript is reviewed for technical soundness and contribution to the literature without any regard to the conclusions, since the study has not yet been conducted. If the reviewers determine that the paper is worthwhile and technically sound, the journal will accept the paper conditionally, under the condition that the analyses are reported thoroughly and accurately according to the proposed plan (aka an **"in-principle acceptance"**). Then after you conduct the study and write up the results, you send the complete paper in, and it will be published. The guidelines from the *Journal of Business and Psychology* can be found on its webpage: https://jbp.charlotte.edu/

You are ready to move on when either:

1. You have pre-registered your study as aspredicted.org or OSF, or
2. A hybrid registered report has been accepted at the journal where this research will eventually be published.

Execution and Analysis

When all the planning is done, when all materials are developed and ready to go, and when you've gone through this list twice to make sure you are truly ready, it's time to get your hands on some data and analyze it. Sadly, some misguided researchers start with this step and try to backfill and post-hoc justify their contribution to the scientific conversation. Not only is that dishonest, but it is much harder than doing things the right way. We will assume that you have approached the serious endeavor of research with the right level of planning, transparency, and documentation, and you have set yourself up to make data collection and analysis go smoothly.

Collect and/or Acquire Data (Chapters 6, 8)**:** The distinction between collecting or acquiring data varies based on the design you have chosen. If you are using a meta-analytic approach (Chapter 13), you need to do both – first acquire the data by collecting archival primary research papers and then collect data by coding them according to a scheme you have created. If you are conducting an experiment in a lab setting, you will collect data by asking participants to proceed through a research design that you have created, recording their responses somehow. If you've decided to collect information about public behavior, for example, from social media, collecting the data might mean launching a program you've written to automatically obtain information from web sites. If you're doing an archival analysis, acquiring the data might be as simple as literally *getting* the data from someone who already has it. They might even hand it to you in a ready-to-analyze format, although it's more likely that you will have to do some work to get it into a usable format. If you're conducting interviews, you could spend months or years on this step. And, if you're using a nonexperimental survey design, getting the data might mean sending a link to an online questionnaire. As you can see, this step could take 10 seconds or 10 months.

Actively Monitor Data Collection: A common mistake during some kinds of data collection is to simply set it up and walk away. This is a surefire way to become frustrated later when you discover some of your data were not collected in the way you expected. Although we conduct alpha and beta tests (see Chapter 11) to minimize the chances that this will happen, sometimes you get surprised. For example, imagine the data collection program that worked perfectly fine during testing goes down for maintenance. You should disable the ability to start the study during that time, or you'll find yourself with partial/incomplete data and possibly some angry participants.

Importantly, this doesn't mean you should be pulling data and repeatedly test your hypotheses as you go so that you can stop data collection once you've found what you want to find. That practice is a particularly problematic QRP called **optional stopping**, which when done within the framework of NHST (see Chapter 12) violates the assumptions of NHST-related analyses. Instead, this kind of monitoring is strictly for unexpected technical and ethical issues with your research.

Debrief and Compensate Participants: In primary research studies involving **deception**, **debriefing** is always required, which involves explaining to your participants, after they have completed your study, how you deceived them. Debriefing gives you the opportunity to double-check that no participants feel like their rights were violated. If they do feel that way, participants usually have the right to remove their data from your study. Even when deception is not involved, debriefing is a public good in that informing research participants about why their participation was important is an easy way to engage in effective science communication. You should also at this point be sure all participants have been compensated in the ways they were promised.

You're ready to move on when you can answer the following question:

1. Did I collect or acquire data in the way described in my pre-registration? Did I double-check data integrity as it came in?
2. If I needed to make changes to my data collection/acquisition strategy, how will I justify those changes later?
3. Have all participants been debriefed?

Data Cleaning (Chapter 11). As described in Chapters 9 and 11, when you designed your study, you should have also identified some data quality checks and incorporated them into your design. This includes many approaches, like psychometric antonyms, attention checks, manipulation checks, and analysis of metadata. In this step, you will use those data quality indicators to clean the data. You will also create scale scores and reverse the reverse-coded items. As discussed in Chapter 11, we recommend creating new variables in your dataset for this step–in general, you should *never* edit raw data.

This step should also involve visual inspection of your data. Run descriptive statistics (min, max, mean, SD) for every variable and look for anything strange. Maybe someone reported that they are 300 years old. Maybe a variable that should have a range from 1–5 has negative values. This kind of error happens and you need to diagnose what went wrong. Participant error is one explanation, and researcher error is the other. Check your codebook and materials for misalignments or other mistakes.

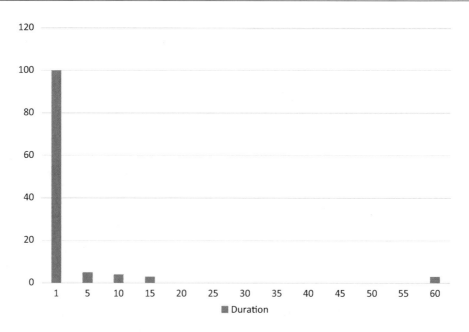

Figure 15.1 Histogram of uncleaned duration data.

Look at the variance for every item. Is there any variable with no variance? Look at a histogram for every variable. Does any variable have a distribution that doesn't make any sense? Here is a real example of a problem with a questionnaire that I (Tara) uncovered while data cleaning. My research team examined the duration of each participant's questionnaire in order to identify people who rushed through the questions without paying attention, finding a mean of 11.75 and standard deviation of 5.35. We planned to flag anyone who was drastically below average. This is what the data looked like when we first created the histogram appearing in Figure 15.1.

Unless somebody truly took 950 minutes while everyone else took less than 10 minutes, something is very wrong here. When we went back and looked at the data collection log, we found that the person had not submitted their responses after finishing; instead, a research assistant had noticed and hit "submit" only when the next participant arrived to take their questionnaire the next day. After we removed that person's time from the analysis, the mean dropped to 3.62, the standard deviation to 2.01, and the histogram became the one in Figure 15.2.

This figure makes much more sense. Now we could see that the survey took most people about 3.5 minutes, and somebody who only spent 1 minute on the survey might be rushing. We flagged those responses for further examination and continued with our data cleaning process. Without paying close attention, we would have concluded that everyone who took 3 minutes was suspicious since they were three times as fast as the average of 11.75 minutes. Note that we did not delete the 950-minute person's data– there was nothing else wrong with their responses. Only the time stamp was incorrect.

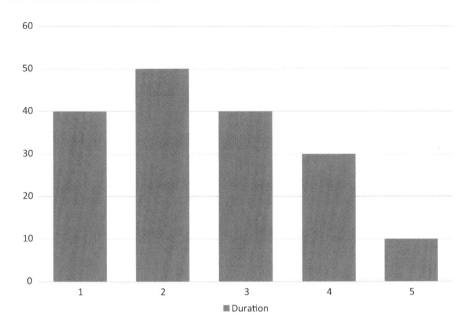

Figure 15.2 Histogram of cleaned duration data.

You're ready to move on from data cleaning when you can answer the following questions:

1. Have I visually inspected my data?
2. Have I examined all distributions and descriptive statistics to look for anomalies?
3. Have I conducted quality check analyses to identify low-effort responses where applicable?
4. Have I created a detailed log that outlines every data cleaning step I've taken so far, so someone else can reproduce my results?

Hypothesis Tests and Investigation of Research Questions (Chapter 12)**.** In quantitative designs, this step is where you will conduct the planned analyses for your hypothesis tests and research questions. You will need to do this while following the specific guidance that corresponds to each analysis being done, referring to the JARS, and following your own pre-registered analyses. No matter what kind of analysis you are doing, you must keep a careful record of everything you do and every step you take. Save all your coding syntax (see Chapter 14) and annotate it carefully. Remember that the goal should be to end up with a result that anyone else could reproduce easily, given your raw data, by following the steps you lay out.

In qualitative designs, you will begin the process of open coding and axial coding during this step. Your goal is to identify themes, interconnections, and insights by iteratively applying tags to the data you have collected, reviewing and combining tags, and capturing illustrative examples of the ideas that emerge. Keeping track of your steps is just as important in qualitative analysis as it is in quantitative analysis. You should expect to share your codebook and other metadata you generate with peer researchers who request it.

You are ready to move on when:

1. You have conducted all analyses according to your preregistration.
2. You have prepared detailed documentation of the decisions you made, all analyses, and all results.

Exploratory Analyses (Chapter 12). For many, the greatest joys of research are in discovery. We guarantee that something about your data will surprise you. The exploration phase of research is to pursue these surprises and see what you can discover about your data. It is very important to be transparent about what is happening at this stage. If you start exploring and find an interesting relationship, *do not* go back to the hypotheses and add it. If you preregistered, which you should have done, this kind of post-hoc theorizing will be impossible – which is much of the point of preregistration. Instead, treat the exploration like the mystery that it is. If you don't know why something happened, say you don't know. You can certainly offer some speculation in the discussion, but it should be very limited. It isn't appropriate to wax poetic about ideas that go beyond what your data can actually demonstrate.

You are ready to move on when you can answer the following questions:

1. What does the pattern of correlations in your study tell you? Do any further analyses seem warranted based on what you see?
2. Are open-ended comments from participants raising any interesting ideas? Can those ideas be organized into themes?
3. Can any of the effects in your study be further contextualized?
4. How will you present the results of these exploratory analyses to make it clear to the consumers of your research that they were in fact exploratory and should be treated as tentative?

Sharing and Write-Up

At last! You have finished the analysis and you are ready to share your findings with the world. For some reason, after months and years of planning a study, you'd think that this part would be easy. You've been thinking so hard about the study for so long, and the logic and beauty of your accomplishment are clear in your mind. The study is 90% done. And yet we have seen so many early researchers get to this point and then give up. It doesn't make any sense, and yet it happens all the time. Remember that this is the whole point of the research – to write it down and share it with the research community. If you struggle with writing, you could consider doing some writing work before the research is complete. For example, you could have a full introduction and literature review written up, along with a method section, before you get your data. In fact, if you are doing this research as part of a required master's thesis or doctoral dissertation, you will have to write up those sections as part of the proposal document. The following section, however, assumes that you have not written anything yet.

Post Open Science Documents (Chapter 11): Once you have finalized your analyses and are ready to construct a manuscript, presentation, or whatever is, it is time to fully document your study. If you've been following the recommendations of this checklist to this point, especially the recommendations in Chapter 11, this should be fairly straightforward: just post all of your anonymized data, logs, and other materials to OSF. If you are nervous about other researchers stealing your ideas or materials before they are published, no problem – just keep those materials private until you're ready for them to be public. But posting them at this time provides objective evidence that your study proceeded exactly as planned and explained during preregistration. Even better, if you completed pre-registration on OSF, your pre-registration and materials will be right next to each other.

You are ready to move on when you can answer the following questions:

1. Are my anonymized data and analytic code available on OSF?
2. Have I double checked that no PII has been posted?
3. Could an independent researcher fully reproduce my project's data collection or acquisition methods?
4. Could an independent researcher fully reproduce the analyses I conducted using the analytic code I have posted?
5. Could an independent researcher re-create all figures and tables that will be in my final manuscript?

Identify and Select Meaningful Outlets (Chapter 14)**:** It may seem surprising to you that you should choose an outlet before you start writing. The reason to do so is that each journal has its own style and norms and focus. There are a number of variables to consider when choosing an outlet (also covered in chapter 20). First, where is the scientific conversation on your topic happening? Which journals are publishing similar papers? Second, which journal has readers that you want to find your study? Third, and a bit less important in our opinion, you should consider things like the prestige of the journal and whether it will count for your employer if and when they measure your productivity.

Once you have one or more outlets in mind, read other articles from that outlet on similar topics and pay attention to any norms about length, scope, tone, and style. Also take this time to learn about the journal's specific policies for submissions, often referred to as **author guidelines** or **submission guidelines**. You can often find these most quickly by searching for "*name of journal* guidelines" on Google. For example, the publisher Springer (2023), which produces several prominent I-O journals, offers the following ethical guidance to authors across all of its journals:

Authors should refrain from misrepresenting research results which could damage the trust in the journal, the professionalism of scientific authorship, and ultimately the entire scientific endeavour. Maintaining integrity of the research and its presentation is helped by following the rules of good scientific practice, which include:

- The manuscript should not be submitted to more than one journal for simultaneous consideration.
- The submitted work should be original and should not have been published elsewhere in any form or language (partially or in full), unless the new work concerns an expansion of previous work. (Please provide transparency on the re-use of material to avoid the concerns about text-recycling ('self-plagiarism').
- A single study should not be split up into several parts to increase the quantity of submissions and submitted to various journals or to one journal over time (i.e. 'salami-slicing/ publishing').
- Concurrent or secondary publication is sometimes justifiable, provided certain conditions are met. Examples include: translations or a manuscript that is intended for a different group of readers.

- Results should be presented clearly, honestly, and without fabrication, falsification or inappropriate data manipulation (including image based manipulation). Authors should adhere to discipline-specific rules for acquiring, selecting and processing data.
- No data, text, or theories by others are presented as if they were the author's own ('plagiarism'). Proper acknowledgements to other works must be given (this includes material that is closely copied (near verbatim), summarized and/or paraphrased), quotation marks (to indicate words taken from another source) are used for verbatim copying of material, and permissions secured for material that is copyrighted.

You are ready to move on when you can answer the following questions:

1. What outlet or type of document(s) am I targeting?
2. What do other already-shared research products in this place usually look like?
3. Are there any specific guidelines or rules about sending something to this outlet?
4. Why am I targeting this outlet instead of others?

Outline, Write, Edit, Get and Act on Feedback (Chapters 2, 14): Now you are ready to write! We already covered the mechanics of outlining and technical writing in detail in Chapter 2, and we urge you to revisit that content. Those strategies are likely to help you no matter what you're trying to write, from presentation to journal manuscript.

For most applied research projects, your goal is probably to create a presentation, white paper, or technical report. In each of these cases, you will want to be sure to write toward the expectations of whomever you are writing for, commonly your supervisor or a client, very clearly. Be active soliciting feedback from this person; if you don't mention that you're confused about anything, they will likely assume you have no questions and will produce a flawless writeup without their intervention. Applied I-O researchers also frequently submit their research to the Annual Conference of the Society for Industrial and Organizational Psychology (SIOP), which typically has a submission deadline around October each year, with presentation some time in April or May. For many practitioners, presentation at this conference is the only time that work will be shared publicly.

For all academic research projects, and for some in practice, your goal is probably to create a presentation or a manuscript to be submitted for peer review and eventually published in academic literature. Like with practitioners, it is common for academic researchers to submit work nearing completion or recently completed to the SIOP Annual Conference, but with a slightly different goal: getting feedback before journal submission.

Whatever you are trying to write, we believe the following recommendations will serve you well. Your first step is to organize your thoughts by generating an outline. Each line of the outline should represent a paragraph in the ultimate paper. You will use this to work toward complete sentences that will be the topic sentences of each paragraph in your final paper, as explained in detail in Chapter 2. What follows is an example of an effective outline structure:

I.   (Introductory Section, not a formal heading)

    a. Training is an essential part of organizational success, but there is a shortage of high-quality trainers in the world.

    b. Nobody knows whether aliens from Mars would make good trainers.

c. There has been some research on the topic but it is inconclusive.

d. This study will experimentally test the efficacy of Martian trainers in a leadership training course.

II. Literature review

a. There are reasons to think Martians would make good trainers.

b. There are also reasons to think they might not.

c. The best theory to understand this question is the Theory of Alien Trainers (TAT).

d. The TAT points to a number of moderator variables that are worth exploring.

e. Combining the TAT with the Theory of Alien Leaders, which has not been used in a training context, will lead to new insights.

f. The first prediction is that aliens will be better able to establish rapport with trainees.

g. The second prediction is that trainees will learn more in Martian-led training programs.

h. The third prediction is that greatest learning will occur when the Martians are teaching remotely vs in-person.

i. These effects are displayed in Fig 1.

III. Method

a. Design

b. Participants

c. Procedure

IV. Results

a. Hypothesis 1 predicted that aliens would have greater rapport than humans. To test this prediction, we used a t-test. Results showed that this hypothesis was supported, $t(204) = 3.45, p = .04$, Cohen's $d = 1.5$), such that rapport in the alien conditions was higher, $M = 3.8$, $SD = .56$, than in human conditions, $M = 3.1$, $SD = .45$).

b. Repeat for H2

c. Repeat for H3.

V. Discussion

a. This study set out to study the phenomenon of Martian trainers.

b. The results were mixed, suggesting that some people may be put off by the Martians' giant bug eyes and antennae.

c. The results indicate that the TAT can be expanded to include these concepts.

d. When interpreting these results, note that the study had a limited context and scope that could be expanded in future research.

e. There are promising applications here for addressing the trainer shortage using creative extraterrestrial means.

Each line in the outline becomes a paragraph by adding supporting detail, evidence, and reasoning, so that your argument is as strong as possible. This might be done in outline form, or you might jump straight to writing paragraphs. We do, however, recommend not jumping to writing paragraphs too quickly, as you may just be delaying challenging thinking to a future you that wants to do it even less than present you does. The truth is that *writing is easy, but thinking is hard*. Creating an outline is really about organizing your thoughts so you know what you want to say. Writer's block is usually thinking block in disguise. If you outline well, writing from your completed outline is very easy.

Once you have completed a draft, you will start the editing process. It's important to detach yourself a bit as you edit; it's very common to fall in love with a particular sentence and look for a way to include it. Be merciless and ask yourself: is every sentence needed? Is it doing an important job? No matter how much work you put into a paragraph while drafting, it should always be considered a candidate for removal, if that's ultimately better for your final manuscript. We also recommend seeking advice from others at this stage, for more objective evaluation.

We are very fond of Strunk and White's (1999) *The Elements of Style*, which contains recommendations for writing that have held up well for over a century, since Strunk's first version written in 1918. We encourage you to refer to it frequently, and the foundation of many of our recommendations about writing can be found there, including the following:

- Write simply and clearly.
- Allow your ideas to speak for themselves.
- Avoid cliche and excessively metaphoric language. Tried-and-true, stumbling block, diamond in the rough, and double-edged sword are examples of cliche metaphors that muddy the water.
- "Muddy the water" is also a cliche. A more precise expression would be "make the intent more difficult to understand." Whoops.

Do not be tempted to mimic the flowery, "academic" sounding language you may have seen in other papers. To really make this point clearly, we used a generative artificial intelligence to generate some "academic-sounding" language, which appears in Table 15.3. Your goal should be to sound like a human, not an AI's caricature of a "scholar."

Table 15.3 AI-generated examples of academic language and better alternatives

Don't write:	Instead, write:
"The intricacies of human personality and its nuanced manifestations collectively give rise to a plethora of unique predilections towards disparate work environments. These intrinsic idiosyncrasies engender a multifaceted spectrum of professional preferences, underscoring the need for nuanced understanding and diversity in occupational settings. This inherent diversity in individual disposition precipitates an array of personal inclinations towards distinct modes of employment, thereby enriching the dynamism of the workforce landscape."	"People have different personalities, and those differences cause them to prefer different work environments"
"Although one may perceive the ubiquity of digital communication as the quintessential hallmark of the 21st-century human experience, it is nevertheless crucial to consider the ever-present digital divide that continues to stratify society; therefore, despite the apparent homogeneity conferred by our increasingly interconnected world, profound disparities persist, which oblige us to grapple with the multifarious dimensions of our inexorably digitized existence."	"We might assume that everyone is online now, but many people still don't have access to digital tools."
"Individuals oftentimes exhibit a propensity to inadvertently transpose negativity onto the members of their domestic circle, thereby creating an undesired cascade of emotional transference predicated upon the initial unfavorable occupational experiences."	"When people have a bad day at work, their resulting bad mood often affects their families"

Table 15.4 Common academic words, academic phrases, and metaphors to avoid

Academic-ese	Clear language
Extant literature	Literature
Ways in which	How
We argue that [argument], we contend that [argument], etc.	[argument]
Moreover	Also/and
Twofold	Two
Myriad	Lots of
Burgeoning	New/growing
There is a dearth of literature on [topic]	We don't know [fact] about [topic] (but you probably don't need to say this at all)
In this day and age, nowadays	In [year]
Few and far between	Rare
Has the potential to be able to	Can
Under the particular conditions where, in the event of	If
Double-edged sword	[list the advantages and disadvantages]
Society, modern society, people, workers, etc.	[list the specific people you are referencing]
Research shows that [fact]	[fact]
It is worth noting that [point], Importantly, [point], it is evident that [point]	[point]
X impacts Y, X is impactful on Y, etc.	Affects, relates to, correlates with
Utilize	Use
Nevertheless, however, therefore, nonetheless, though, in contrast, conversely, indeed, etc.	These are sometimes okay. Use as few as possible. Never put them at the beginning of a sentence. Never use them to make a sloppy paragraph appear more cohesive.
Nuanced	Just don't ever say nuanced. Very little in psychology is un-nuanced. Of course your points are nuanced. No need to say it.

One way that many academics try to communicate their expertise and imply in their writing that they are part of academic in-groups is to use unnecessarily confusing or convoluted language, many examples of which are shown in Table 15.4. You should try to avoid all of these. We recommend reviewing this list any time you are about to submit a paper. Once they are part of your vocabulary, it's difficult to get them out.

When you think you're done editing, edit some more. Read your paper aloud. Ask a friend to read it. Have some dictation software read it to you. Before it's done, we recommend anywhere between 10 and 50 top-to-bottom edits, preferably passed between different editors (e.g., you, an advisor, another grad student with passing interest in your topic) each pass.

Review the JARS Standards One Last Time. I bet you knew JARS was coming again! Once you've created your semi-final draft, after incorporating all feedback and changes, just before sending it off somewhere for review, be sure to check the JARS one last time, line by line, to be sure you didn't miss anything. And after you're sure – you're done writing. For now.

You are ready to move on when you can answer the following questions:

1. Have I written exactly what I wanted to say?
2. Have I written clearly and straightforwardly, and ruthlessly removed all fluff?

3. Am I hiding behind jargon or obscure language as a way of being vague when I am unsure of my argument?
4. Is every item on the JARS accounted for?

Submit, Revise, Resubmit (Chapter 14): Depending on where your work is being sent next, you can expect one of a few different things to happen. If you have written a white paper or technical report, you might get feedback from your supervisor or the eventual owner of the report, who might ask you to make revisions.

If you have submitted to a conference or journal, you probably have a long wait ahead of you due to the peer review process as explained in Chapter 14. Expect to wait at least a month to get a decision on your paper. Three to 6 months is common. More than 6 months is unusual and worth emailing the action editor to ask how it's going.

When the decision comes, you will usually get two or more sets of very detailed feedback from anonymous experts. The feedback will ideally be constructive, but it will probably sting a bit anyway. Sometimes, action editors will provide integrating comments that give you a sense of which comments they saw as most important. Sometimes they will provide additional feedback.

As described in Chapter 14, the decision itself will almost always be either an invitation to respond to the reviewers by writing a response letter and submitting a revised manuscript (a "revise and resubmit" decision) or an outright rejection. Acceptance on initial submission is exceedingly rare – at best, a once-in-a-lifetime event at respectable journals. A decline decision is ideally only made when the editor determines that the objections from reviewers cannot be resolved. Perhaps they objected to the conceptualization, or the measures, or the sample, for example.

Declines are very, very common. Top I-O psychology journals have decline rates of over 90%. Consider that everyone from junior to senior scholars submits their very best work to the top journals, and 90% of that work doesn't make the cut. So if you receive an invitation to revise your paper, you should celebrate! It is a victory. But if you get a decline, dust yourself off and regroup to submit to a different outlet. Resolve any problems that you can resolve. But also remember that a lot of the review process is imperfect. Good papers get rejected, just as bad papers get accepted – it is not a process with perfect reliability and validity. It's just the best we have right now. One set of reviewers might hate your paper and another set might love it. So don't make any attributions about yourself, your capabilities, or your potential based on a single rejection.

You are ready to move on when:

1. Your work has been declined not just from one outlet but from every outlet you can imagine it fitting in, or
2. Your work has been accepted by the audience you created it for! Hooray!

Promote the Work With Target Audiences (Chapter 14): Once your research finds a home, the last thing to do is to make sure people know about it. In the old pre-internet days, researchers would receive journals, white papers, and other important research write-ups regularly by postal service. Each one would be an exciting new opportunity to catch up on the most recent work in the field. These days, very few people read journals cover to cover; instead, they more often rely on email alerts with tables of contents, search alerts based on keywords, and word of mouth. Beyond that, research is mostly discoverable via search engines. Word of mouth is, perhaps surprisingly, is still one of the best ways to raise awareness of your work.

One important way that we create word of mouth, both now and in the ancient preinternet days, is through scientific conferences, as described in Chapter 14. Attending and presenting at appropriate conferences makes people aware of you and your work. If your work is relevant to theirs, they are much more likely to remember it and you if they met you at a conference talking about it earlier. Thus, you should always try to present your work at a conference, both to maximize awareness of your work and also to maximize other researchers' awareness of you doing work relevant to them.

You are ready to move on when . . .

1. Never. Increasing awareness and building on your own prior work will take the rest of your career – at least.

References

Box, G. E. P. (1976). Science and statistics. *Journal of the American Statistical Association*, *71*(356), 791–799.

Box, G. E. P. (1979). Robustness in the strategy of scientific model building. In R. L. Launer & G. N. Wilkinson (Eds.), *Robustness in statistics* (pp. 201–236). Academic Press. https://doi.org/10.1016/B978-0-12-438150-6.50018-2

Creswell, J. W., & Plano Clark, V. L. (2017). *Designing and conducting mixed methods research*. Sage.

Goldberg, L. R. (1999). A broad-bandwidth, public domain, personality inventory measuring the lower-level facets of several five-factor models. In I. Mervielde, I. Deary, F. De Fruyt, & F. Ostendorf (Eds.), *Personality psychology in Europe* (Vol. 7, pp. 7–28). Tilburg University Press.

Spector, P. (1994). *Job satisfaction survey*. https://paulspector.com/assessments/pauls-no-cost-assessments/job-satisfaction-survey-jss/

Springer. (2023). *Ethical responsibilities of authors*. www.springer.com/gp/editorial-policies/ethical-responsibilities-of-authors

Strunk, W., Jr., & White, E. B. (1999). *The elements of style* (4th ed.). Longman.

Further Reading

Box, G. E. P. (1976). Science and statistics. *Journal of the American Statistical Association*, *71*(356), 791–799.

- Although you might only have previously thought about Box when trying to make a Box-Cox transformation, Box was right up there with Fisher, Pearson, and other influential statisticians of the mid-20th century. This article illustrates many of his values – ones that you might consider in your own research. It's also where Box used the expression "all models are wrong" for the first time in his writing.

Strunk, W., Jr., & White, E. B. (1999). *The elements of style* (4th ed.). Longman.

- Strunk and White's classic book is often lauded as one of the best collections of concise, relevant, comprehensive, and clear advice about writing, applicable across almost all fields of study and types of writing. It's a quick read too. Check it out.

Questions to Think About

1. How will you apply the research checklist on your next project?
2. What is the research checklist missing when applied to your research area?

3. What aspects of the checklist would your advisor or coauthors consider poor advice, and why?
4. How have your past experiences, including classes you've taken and mentors you've had, influenced your own internalized research checklist?
5. What projects have you participated in or completed already that would (have) benefit(ed) from this checklist? What can be done now to make them better?

Key Terms

- ad hominem
- appeal to authority
- appeal to emotion
- author guidelines
- begging the question
- cherry-picking
- compensation log
- debriefing
- deception
- embedding
- explanation
- exploration
- in-principle acceptance
- Journal Article Reporting Standards (JARS)
- masking
- mixed methods
- model
- multimethod research
- naturalistic fallacy
- optional stopping
- parsimony
- post hoc, ergo propter hoc
- readme file
- research, interdisciplinary
- research, multidisciplinary
- source fallacy
- strawman
- submission guidelines
- triangulation
- worrying selectively

Glossary

75% rule (in meta-analysis)   a rule of thumb in Hunter-Schmidt meta-analysis suggesting that if at least 75% of the variance in obtained correlations is explained by artifacts, there are unlikely to be meaningful moderators in the remaining 25%

75% rule (in missingness analysis)   in missingness analysis, a rule of thumb that, within a scale, if fewer than 25% of scores are missing, scale scores can still be calculated without much loss of information; however, imputation should still be considered

abduce   see abduction

abduction   methods in which existing theory and new evidence are considered together and weighed against each other to inform revisions of theory

academic journals   a collection of research reports within a specific topic or domain produced and supported by a publisher, with new issues released on a regular basis

accept   after a peer review round, a decision in which a submission is permitted to be shared or published

acceptance testing   an initial test run of a system, like an experimental protocol, to ensure it meets the basic requirements outlined when it was created

action research   a collection of qualitative research methods that all assert that the people who are affected by research should be active participants in that research

ad-hoc testing   repeated exploration of a system to identify uncommon or hidden bugs that might derail results

ad hominem   a logical fallacy in which the person making an argument is criticized instead of the argument itself

advanced logic   see branching

aggregation   the conversion of data at a lower level into data at a higher level, such as by calculating teamwise averages from person-level data

airport book   a somewhat pejorative term used to refer to the kind of book you find in an airport; generally implies a lack of scientific rigor

alpha (in NHST)   see Type I error rate

alpha test   in test development or research design, refers to the first attempted data collection with research team members serving as pseudo-research participants for testing purposes

alternate forms reliability   the reliability of a psychometric measure assuming true score variance can be conceptualized as consistency between versions of a test designed to be parallel

alternative hypothesis   a hypothesis that is assumed to be true if the null hypothesis is demonstrated to be unlikely

anchoring effect (in bias)   a cognitive bias that occurs when we use information in the environment as a conceptual starting place for making a guess about something we don't know

anchoring effect (in internal validity threats)   an internal validity threat that refers to a participant holding a perspective or idea in their mind due to earlier test content when answering later content; may result in assimilation or contrast

anchors   in scale construction, refers to the verbal descriptions corresponding to numerical ratings; sometimes refers to the ratings themselves

annotated bibliography   a list of citations organized by subtopic that addresses aspects of your research question, with each citation accompanied by a text description

anomaly detection   prediction of low-frequency events where traditional assumptions about distribution are impossible

anonymity   when informants for research are not identifiable to anyone

anonymization   a type of data obfuscation in which observed data are altered to make them anonymous by removing PII (and possibly other variables); see anonymity and confidentiality

APA code   the professional ethics standards of the American Psychological Association

APA Manual   see Publication Manual of the American Psychological Association

appeal to authority   a logical fallacy in which an argument is made on the basis of the identity of the person who made it

appeal to emotion   a logical fallacy in which emotional and affective weight is used to argue for the validity of a point or position

appearing moderate   an internal validity threat that refers to a participant choosing not to share their truly held, more extreme views; may result in assimilation

application   consideration of how your findings can inform practical problems faced in society

a priori power analysis   an estimate of the necessary sample size for a targeted level of power given assumed effect sizes to be observed later

archival methods   see archival research

archival research   the use of primary research data someone else collected

area under the curve   when a sampling distribution is drawn as a density plot, the proportion of space under the line, which corresponds to probability of drawing such data

artifact (in meta-analysis)   in meta-analysis, a quantifiable bias in a meta-analytic point or interval estimate

artifact (in qualitative research)   any physical object related to a research participant that gives information about a psychological or cultural phenomenon of interest

artifact distribution corrections   in meta-analysis, the correction of a group of observed effect sizes for artifacts based upon an assumed distribution of artifact effects

artificial intelligence   any task without a single well-defined path from start to finish that a human could normally do that can now be done by a computer

artificial intelligence (for literature search)   in the context of research paper searches, a predictive model that responses to your questions by finding the most likely text predicted to follow whatever text you provided it

assimilation   the process by which a participant's responses become more similar with greater exposure to a test; contrast with contrast

assumption of independence   in meta-analysis, the requirement for each effect size included to represent data collected without any dependency on other included effect sizes

attention checks   questions asked to assess if a participant is paying attention

attenuation   the reduction in observed covariance resulting from range restriction

auditory signal processing   the conversion of audio into variables to be used in other analyses, most frequently machine learning

author guidelines   see submission guidelines

authorship   in psychology, reflects an intellectual contribution to the research resulting in a particular report or manuscript

authorship order   the order in which authors appear in research bylines; in psychology, usually in descending order of contribution except in the case of final authors

axial coding   the process of converting codes into meaningful themes (or broader codes)

axioms   the values and assumptions that researchers hold as self-evident

bag-of-words tokenization   the conversion of unstructured text into word or phrase counts for use in quantitative analyses

Bayes factor   a ratios of likelihoods of observing the data based upon two competing models

Bayesianism   analyses based upon Bayes' theorem

Bayes' theorem   a mathematical formula for the prediction of a future event given past events

Beall's list   one of the earliest lists of predatory publishers

begging the question   a logical fallacy in which the premise of an argument is assumed to be true while attempting to prove it

behaviorally anchored rating scale (BARS)   a scale that replaces response options on a rated scale with descriptions of behaviors

Belmont Report   a proposal of professional ethics developed in 1978 in the United States

beneficence   a principle from the Belmont Report stating that researchers should always strive to maximize benefits and minimize harm

beta (in NHST)   see Type II error rate

beta test   in test development or research design, refers to the second attempted data collection, done with the target population

between-persons design   a research design in which people are compared to each other

bias (in qualitative research)   any instance of personal values or ideas being inserted into research findings without being acknowledged as such

bias, acquiescence   a response bias in which participants respond positively to any question they are asked

bias, central tendency   a response bias in which participants try to avoid revealing extreme stances by sticking to the middle of a scale, such as answering all 2–4 on a scale ranging from 1–5

bias, cognitive   a bias resulting from human susceptibility to suggestion and reconstruction when it comes to memory

bias, common method   a bias that makes variables appear more strongly correlated than they really are due to shared measurement methods

bias, confirmation   a common result of expectation bias in which a person seeks information that confirms their expectation

bias, cultural   a bias resulting from a person's background, including personal history and past experience

bias, demand   a response bias in which participants respond to demand characteristics

bias, demand characteristics   see demand bias

bias, dissent   a response bias in which participants respond negative to all questions

bias, epistemological   within objectivism or constructivism, any systematic difference between individual understanding and truth

bias, evidential   the degree to which research results from well-designed validation studies support an argument for the test validity

bias, expectation   a cognitive bias that occurs when our expectations lead to our interpretation instead of the reality we observe

bias, extreme response   a response bias in which participants make a dichotomous judgment to each question and respond consistently with that judgment

bias, measurement   error in measurement attributable to systematic external causes

bias, neutrality   see central tendency bias

bias, predictive   a common way to evaluate test fairness, done by determining if test scores predict outcomes equally well for members of different socially defined groups

bias, publication   the result of the tendency for published research to contain more positive results and larger effects in comparison to unpublished research, also called the fire drawer problem; effects are generally larger than would be expected when publication bias is present; may refer to the magnitude of this bias in meta-analytic estimates

bias, response   the cognitive shortcuts that respondents might take, either intentionally or not, when responding to questionnaires

bias, social desirability   a response bias in which participants respond in ways that they believe are socially acceptable

bigram   a two-word token

binary forced choice scale   a scale that forced participants to have an opinion in order to response, even if their true opinion is neutral

bogus item   see attention check item

bots   in research, refers to computer programs that appear to participate in research but do not reflect authentic participation by humans

branching   when a questionnaire shows different questions to different people adaptively based upon previous responses

burnout   a psychological state in which work is always accompanied by a feeling of anxiety or dread

call for proposals (CFP)   a document distributed by the organizers of a conference outlining requirements for submissions; will be evaluated for inclusion

camel case   a method of writing feature identifiers by including meaningful capital letters in the middle, such as SupSupport1

careerism   optimizing decision-making in research to maximize career-related outcomes instead of conducting high-quality science

careless respondents   people who do not pay adequate attention or expend adequate cognitive resources to provide data that reflects their true responses if paying attention

cargo cult science   popularized by Richard Feynman, refers to practices that mimic good scientific practice without underlying understanding

carryover effect   an internal validity threat that refers to a participant recalling information from a prior question and using that information to response; may result in assimilation

case study an in-depth exploration of some phenomenon, such as a person, and organization, or an event

causal effect estimation research with the purpose of determining the amount of impact on some outcome resulting from a change; often relies on experimentation

cause a stimulus that comes first in a chain of events and can be linked to subsequent events as an explanation for those events

central limit theorem a statistical concept on which NHST relies; if we were to sample a population an infinite number of times, 1) the mean of the resulting sampling distribution should be equal to the population mean, and 2) regardless of the distribution of the original data, the sampling distribution should approximate a normal distribution

cherry-picking a logical fallacy in which information that supports an argument is used and information that is contrary is ignored or suppressed

classical test theory in psychometrics, the assumption that observed scores comprise the combination of true scores and error, as well as the consequences of that assumption for measurement; contrast with item response theory

cluster sampling probability sampling at random among predefined groups at the group level

Cochrane Collaboration a British non-profit organization dedicated to higher quality, evidence-based insights for medicine and medical practice

codebook documentation that allows a person completely naive to your research study to understand precisely what generated every feature of your dataset

coders in meta-analysis, a common term for raters

codes classifications made by the observer based upon what was observed that relate to themes

coding sheet in meta-analysis, a spreadsheet containing the definitions of all key terms that will be used in the meta-analysis for use by meta-analytic raters and a specific way to rate each study

coefficient alpha see Cronbach's alpha

coefficient omega approximately the average item-total correlation among items, used as a measure of reliability

cognitive load in research methods, refers to the cognitive burden placed on a research participant over the course of participation

Cohen's *d* a standardized mean difference, expressed in standard deviation units; for example, $d = 1$ implies that the mean score in one group is 1 standard deviation higher than the mean score of another

collaborative document workspace a web-based platform for real-time simultaneous viewing and editing of files among collaborators

Collaborative Institutional Training Initiative (CITI) an organization that puts together ethics training for researchers; a common requirement of IRBs around the world

Committee for the Advancement of Professional Ethics (CAPE) a committee within the Society for Industrial and Organizational Psychology dedicated to providing guidance and support in ethical dilemmas faced by I-O psychologists

Common Rule US Federal Regulations Title 45 Part 46 that describes the rules that federal agencies and academic institutions must follow when conducting human subjects research

compensation log a tracking document used to ensure research participants are compensated as promised during informed consent; should be kept separate from other documents to increase confidentiality/anonymity

completeness in qualitative research, refers to the extent of reporting

computational linguistics a discipline dedicated to understanding the structure and purpose of language using computer-enabled techniques

computer vision machine learning that uses variables derived from images as predictors

conceptual replication replication with the purpose of testing the same hypothesis or research question as in prior research; other features may be changed

condition in experimentation, a specific version of an experiment; all treatment groups and the control group are within independent experimental conditions

conditional effect see moderator and interaction

conditional probability the probability that an event will occur given that another event has already occurred

conference in the research context, refers to a gathering, either in-person or virtually, of professionals to present and discuss research

confidence interval an interval estimate providing the expected range of sample values given a particular population parameter and sample size used to draw from that population

confidentiality when informants for the research are not personally identifiable to anyone except the researcher

confirmatory factor analysis (CFA) a statistical technique used to investigate the internal structure of multiple indicators of the same construct

confirmatory research in contrast to exploratory research, research with the purpose of testing existing hypotheses

confound occurs when the effect of one variable cannot be meaningfully separated from the effect of another variable

conjecture a proposed statement about reality, to be falsified in post-positivism

consent form a formal document outlining major aspects of informed consent shared directly with research participants; often signed to indicate acknowledgement

construct a "constructed" concept; something that cannot be measured but nevertheless has meaning; example: personality traits, cognitive ability, philosophies

construct contamination occurs when a measure reflects additional constructs beyond the desired or claimed construct

construct deficiency occurs when a measure does not reflect the entire breadth of the desired or claimed construct

construct validity the degree to which observed scores reflect intended true scores

construct, formative a theoretical model of a construct asserting that indicators create constructs; in path models, observed variables point to constructs; contrast with reflective construct

construct, reflective a theoretical model of a construct asserting that constructs cause indicators of those constructs; in path models, constructs point to observed variables; contrast with formative construct

constructivism an epistemological framework asserting that knowledge is both individually and socially constructed, combining elements of objectivism and subjectivism

container a virtualized environment containing a snapshot of a particular computational environment

contamination see construct contamination

content analysis a generic term for interpreting unstructured data, usually text, into meaningful categories; this term refers to different specific approaches depending on the broader approach chosen

content codes in meta-analysis, the specific words or numbers used to rated specific variables

context features surrounding research that could affect the conclusions drawn from it; in qualitative research, understanding context is usually a goal; in quantitative research, minimizing bias due to context is usually a goal

contrast the process by which a participant's responses become more differentiated with greater exposure to a test; contrast with assimilation

contribution an abstract way of referring to how much impact your study results could have on the thinking of scholars in your areas

control (in experimentation) in experimentation, the version of a manipulation that researchers have defined as the baseline; contrast with treatment

control (in research design) creating a situation so that alternative explanations for the patterns you see can be ruled out

control group an experimental group defined as a control

convenience sampling sampling in which no specific probabilistic mechanism is used

Cook's distance a metric to quantify the degree to which a case is influential in a regression (or related) analysis

correction in meta-analysis, the adjustment of point estimates to account for predicted effects of artifacts

counterfactual a way to understand causality by asking "if x has been different in the past, would y be different now?"

covary any well-measured variable will have some high scores and some low scores; the more differences there are like this, the more variance that variable contains; when the variance in one variable is related to the variance in another (e.g., if people with high scores on one tend to have high scores on the other), they are said to covary

credibility interval in meta-analysis, a type of interval estimate that describes a plausible range of subpopulation parameters within a random effects model, commonly reported at the 80% level

credibility value in meta-analysis, a point estimate describing the value at which some expected proportion of subpopulation estimates is likely to be greater, commonly reported at the 90% level, which is equivalent to the lower bound of an 80% credibility interval

criterion a variable predicted by the values of other variables; does not imply causality; contrast with predictor

critical incidents an especially salient episode of good or bad performance that reveals an underlying assumption about what causes success or failure

Cronbach's alpha the most common metric assessing internal consistency reliability, which expresses it in terms of covariance to variance ratio among items and is roughly equivalent to the average inter-item correlation among items

cross-classified data multilevel data in which group membership is not nested; members may belong to multiple groups

cross-level design a research design in which between-persons and within-person effects are studied simultaneously

crossloadings in exploratory factor analysis, refers to items that have strong relationships with multiple extracted factors/constructs

cumulative scales see Guttman scales

curated database a collection of citations and related information describing existing scientific research literature, curated by some professional organization

curation the systematic and purposeful shaping of materials to maximize later value to people looking at or referencing them

curvilinearity having the property of a curved line

dark side of goal-setting unintended consequences of creating highly motivating goals

data primary information collected about the person completing the study (or whatever level of analysis)

data dictionary see codebook

data fabrication the most extreme kind of fraud in which nonexistent data are faked

data mining the systematic quantitative exploration of datasets to discover patterns and new insights

data obfuscation altering a dataset to make it more difficult to tie back to original data

debriefing explaining to research participants additional detail about their participation after it has finished; often done when studies involve deception

deception lying to research participants

Declaration of Helsinki the inspiration for the Common Rule, itself an update of the Nuremberg code

decline after a peer review round, a decision in which a submission will no longer be considered for sharing or publication

deduce see deduction

deduction methods in which a theory is presented and evidence is collected to support or falsify that theory

deficiency see construct deficiency

Delphi study a qualitative research method designed to allow each participant's voice to contribute to the discussion and prevent a single powerful voice or perspective from dominating conclusions; has specific defined steps

demand characteristics an internal validity threat that refers to the clues that an experimenter might give off that hint to participants about what is expected of them

dependent variable (DV) a variable measured/observed by a researcher

description see descriptive research

descriptive research research with the purpose of understanding the nature of something

design thinking a series of steps popularized by the Stanford Design School originally to apply lessons from social science to the development of effective technologies as people really use them

dichotomous having two possible values; often coded 0 or 1

dictionary in natural language processing, datasets containing lists of lemmas and associated values, such as for sentiment analysis

dictionary form see lemma

difference in fits (DFITS) a metric to quantify the degree to which a case is influential by quantifying the degree to which predicted y scores are influenced by the exclusion of cases by re-running the regression with and without each case

differential item functioning (DIF) in item response theory, occurs when item parameters vary as a function of something other than a person's theta

difficulty in classical test theory, the proportion of correct answers on a test; in item response theory, the proportion of correct answers on an item

diffusion of treatment an internal validity threat that refers to situations in which participants become aware how they are being treated differently from others within a research study, which causes them to change their behavior

digital observation a type of observational method in which behavior is observed digitally, such as through digital trace data

dimension extraction in test development, refers to analyses conducted with the intent of identifying previously unknown latent constructs

direct effect a causal relationship between two variables without mediation

direct range restriction range restriction that occurs when groups are range restricted on the basis of a variable being measured

direct replication replication that is exact; everything from the prior study is re-created as well as possible

directed responding see instructed responding

disciplinary silo refers to the tendency for people trained within a discipline to mostly talk to other people within their discipline instead of all those relevant to the problems their research addresses

documentation in research, refers to the documents and other records you put together to help both your future self and later external parties to understand why you made decisions along the garden of forking paths and what consequences those decisions might have had

dominance response process in item response theory, describes a linear relationship between a trait and the response to a measure

double-barreled items questions that are phrased in such a way that a participant might have more than one answer to it

Dunning-Kruger effect a concept that those who know very little about a topic have more confidence in their abilities than those who know a lot; research suggests it is not quite as severe an effect as most people believe

dust bowl empiricism the analysis of data without reference or regard to theory

edited volume a book containing scholarly writing from many different authors

editor a person who organizes, evaluates, or otherwise handles submitted reports and manuscripts

effect size the magnitude of an effect, such as the amount of change from an experimental intervention or the amount of covariance in a relationship

effect size benchmarks common reference points used to interpret the magnitude of an effect size relative to other effect sizes; the most useful benchmarks are highly contextualized

embeddedness a sense of being connected to a community, which can help with feelings of imposter syndrome

embedding an approach to mixed methods in which a series of studies in which one study or group of studies plays a secondary role to a primary study or group

empirical study a research study designed to collect and interpret data

empiricism   a philosophical framework from antiquity asserting that data are the best way to inform knowledge

engineer   often contrasted with science, refers to an iterative approach to problem solving, with the goal of creating a product, such as software

epistemology   the study of epistemological frameworks

epistemological framework   a belief system about the way knowledge is created

equality of opportunity to succeed   a common way to define fairness, done in terms of whether people from different socially defined groups have the same flexibility and freedom to act and achieve

equality of outcomes   a common way to define fairness, done in terms of whether people from different socially defined groups receive the same scores or other outcomes

error   difference between true score and observed score; can be subdivided into different types and sources

ethics   a key consideration for research related to how personal and professional ethics will be applied when planning research

ethnicity   a social construct used to categorize people across and within races; has different structure and contents around the world

ethnography   a qualitative research method that provides a very detailed, very rich account of a cultural phenomenon requiring researchers to establish and maintain long-term relationships with the subjects of their research

evidence   data collected systematically with the purpose of testing a research question and its associated interpretation, if done to current professional standards

evidence based on internal structure   according to the Standards under the unitary view of test validity, evidence supporting a test validity argument by demonstrating that the interrelationships between items or observations within a measure are interrelated as would be theoretically expected

evidence based on relations to other variables   according to the Standards under the unitary view of test validity, evidence supporting a test validity argument by demonstrating that the measure is related to other measures as would be expected from theory, usually considered in terms of both concurrent (i.e., correlations without regard to time) and predictive (i.e., temporally bound, causal effects) evidence; also usually conceptualized in terms of convergence and discrimination

evidence based on response processes   according to the Standards under the unitary view of test validity, evidence supporting a test validity argument by demonstrating that people responding to the test engage in cognitive or other psychological processes as expected given the theoretical nature of the construct being measured

evidence based on test content   according to the Standards under the unitary view of test validity, evidence supporting a test validity argument by demonstrating that the content of the test matches what experts would judge as appropriate

evidence based on the consequences of test use   according to the Standards under the unitary view of test validity, evidence supporting a test validity argument by demonstrating that decision-making using test scores results in the outcomes theoretically expected

exclusion criteria   in meta-analysis, the conditions that, when met, prevents a study from being useful for meta-analysis despite meeting inclusion criteria

exhaustive   in scaling, refers to the selection of all reasonable options for response to a question; a desirable quality of a scale

experiment   see experimentation

experimentation   a type of research design in which a situation is created that holds as many variables constant as possible so as to better understand the effect of specific variables of interest

explanation   an approach to mixed methods in which the initial quantitative research is used to uncover interesting or provocative results, followed by the use of a qualitative method to better understand and contextualize those findings

exploration   an approach to mixed methods in which qualitative research is used first to help develop research questions and hypotheses, and a quantitative study is used to test those ideas

exploratory factor analysis (EFA)   in test development, used to identify latent constructs within a dataset containing unknown constructs; assumes constructs are measured with error; contrast with principal components analysis

exploratory research   in contrast to confirmatory research, research designed to examine a research question from multiple angles; embraces unexpected results

external validity   how well a treatment effect (i.e., the result of an intervention) observed in a study would replicate either in the population from which the sample was drawn from ("generalizing to") or in related populations ("generalizing across"); compare to generalizability

fabric posters   a scientific poster printed onto fabric, which makes it easier to transport long distances

facet   in generalizability theory, a source of variation that affects reliability

factor loading   in confirmatory factor analysis, the covariance (or correlation, if standardized) between an item and its associated latent variable

factorial design   a research design in which all possible combinations of between-persons and within-person conditions are studied at once

fail-safe *N*   in meta-analysis, an estimate of the number of new cases with null results necessary to be published to reduce an effect size estimates below some desirable level

fairness, test   a social concept, based in goals and values in a society, describing whether outcomes for a person are justified

falsification   the primary analytic tool of post-positivism that asserts the only way to build knowledge is to present a conjecture and then attempt to prove it false

feasibility   a key consideration for research related to how realistically it can be conducted given available resources

feature   when referring to data, any variable calculated or used in any way

feature identifiers   short alphanumeric codes used to label variables; often shorthand for the original label, such as "E1" for the first item in an extraversion scale

field research   research conducted in any setting other than a controlled setting created by a researcher

fighting a war on two fronts   an idiomatic expression that refers to Germany fighting on both its eastern and western borders during World War II, effectively splitting its resources; in research, refers to situations where you too narrowly split your own scientific goals

file drawer problem   the tendency for replication research and research with undesirable results to be published less often than research with novel findings and desirable results

file naming convention   a technique for file curation in which standardized patterns are used for naming files

fit   how reasonably data could have been drawn from a given model

fit index (or indices)   in confirmatory factor analysis, a metric used to assess fit; split into relative and absolute types

focus group   in qualitative research, asking questions to multiple interviewees in a group where interviewees can react to one another

frame-of-reference training   a type of rater training focused on developing a shared mental model of the task that your coders are all on, that is, a common frame of reference

fraud   in research, a willful and explicit attempt to mislead in reporting research results

frequentism versus Bayesianism   a term used to refer to the debate between NHST-based methods and Bayesian methods

functional testing   a test run of a system, like an experimental protocol, to ensure that users can do everything they need to do in order to complete the protocol

funnel plot   a visualization used to determine the extent of publication bias in a meta-analytic estimate

G*Power   open-source software that can be used to conduct power analysis for many common, basic analyses

gap   missing evidence or unconsidered perspectives in current theory; often filling a gap is the purpose of research

garbage-in/garbage-out (GIGO)   in secondary research, refers to low-quality conclusions being drawn from low-quality research

garden of forking paths   the myriad decisions that you make during the data cleaning and analytic process

gatekeeping   the enforcement of professional practices, standards, and other expectation with the purpose of excluding people or ideas that a community does not want allowed in

gender   a social construct used to categorize people, correlated but not perfectly with the presence of primary sex characteristics; has different structure and contents around the world

generalizability (in research design)   the degree to which observed patterns or explanations can be expected to hold across other situations

generalizability study   see conceptual replication

generalizability theory (G-theory)   an alternative conceptualization of reliability focusing on identifying specific sources of variation, called facets, among a given set of scores

Glassian meta-analysis   a meta-analytic method focusing on calculating the average effect size across a research literature; considered outdated

Goodhart's law   "When a measure becomes a target, it is no longer a good measure," which describes our very human tendency to game whatever system we are within

Google Scholar   a search engine that indexes the internet for anything that looks sort of like a research paper; not a curated database

graphic rating scale   in scaling, refers to response options that are graphical instead of text

gray literature   any publicly shared material that is not managed external to the authors by a publisher, such as a book publisher or academic journal editing process

grounded theory   a prescribed set of procedures for the inductive generation of theory from data originally proposed in the mid-20th century by Glaser and Strauss (2017)

growth mindset   see mastery orientation

Guttman scales a scale type that requires respondents to indicate whether they endorse a series of increasingly intense items

Hedges' g a Cohen's *d* corrected for small sample bias; will be approximately equal to Cohen's *d* when sample size is large

Hedges-Olkin meta-analysis a meta-analytic method focusing on calculating the inverse-variance weighted effect size across a research literature and using statistical significance tests for examining moderation

history an internal validity threat that refers to events external to a research design that may nevertheless influence results

homogeneous a term used to refer to populations where interindividual differences are relatively small

Hunter-Schmidt meta-analysis a meta-analytic method focusing on calculating the sample-size weighted effect size across a research literature and aggressively correcting for artifacts

hybrid registered reports pre-registration at a journal; generally involves submitting a research plan to a journal and some degree of guarantee of publication if that plan is followed regardless of how the results turn out

hypothesis a precisely stated testable proposition (within a postpositivistic research framework)

hypothesize the act of creating a hypothesis

hypothesizing after results are known (HARK) a questionable research practice in which researchers throw a lot of statistical significance tests at a dataset and then write papers about whichever tests were significant

ideal point response process in item response theory, describes a specific point along the continuum of possible responses as indicative of strongest standing on a trait

identity formation the process by which you come to understand your own personal identity within the larger professional and interpersonal world in which you live and work

ignorable missingness see missing at random

illusory essence a tendency by people trained in the philosophical traditions of psychology tend to assume things have innate, objective fundamental essences

impact factor the average number of citations a paper in a journal receives

imposter syndrome the belief that you are unqualified for an opportunity or position that you are clearly qualified for according to external observers (especially those that selected you for that purpose)

imputation the generation of predicted values for missing scores on the basis of statistical modeling

inclusion criteria in meta-analysis, the conditions that must be met for a research study to be included in a meta-analytic database

incremental research research that fills a small gap in understanding, with the purpose of getting the scientific consensus just a bit closer to truth

independent variable (IV) a variable manipulated by a researcher; used to define conditions

indicator observed data intended to reflect a construct

indirect effect a causal relationship between two variables through a mediating variable or variables

indirect range restriction　range restriction that occurs when groups are range restricted on the basis of a variable correlated with a variable being measured

individual corrections　in meta-analysis, the correction of each observed effect size for the artifacts expected in each study, individually

induce　see induction

induction　methods in which evidence is collected and theory is developed based upon observed patterns in evidence

inference　a logical conclusion based on evidence

influential cases　unusual cases that create bias in regression coefficients or other analyses; might not be outliers

inform theory　an expression used to describe research that improves theory using evidence

informed consent　an endless process that when followed implies that every participant in a research study know exactly what they will be asked to do before they are asked to do it; what information they will be asked to provide; what will happen to their responses; who will have access to their responses; who will know their identity; how they will be compensated, if at all; and that they have the right to refuse to participate at any time without any negative consequences

in-principle acceptance　when a hybrid registered report is accepted, suggesting that as long as the research plan outlined in the report is executed, the final paper will be accepted regardless of study outcome

institutional review board　an independent body within a US federal agency, academic institution, or other entity that interprets the Common Rule to provide ethical oversight to research within an institution

instructed responding　an attention check question in which a participant is directly told to respond in a particular way

integration　a term used to describe the careful combination of elements or components of multiple theories

interaction　statistically, occurs when the combination of specific levels of two or more variables creates an outcome that would not be expected from the effect of those variables by themselves

interactive voice response (IVR)　when a researcher verbally asks questions to a respondent over the phone, or leaves prerecorded messages to which a respondent answers, verbally or via a keypad

intermediate results reporting　a type of data obfuscation in which researchers share partially analyzed data, such as a covariance matrix, instead of raw data

internal consistency reliability　the reliability of a psychometric measure assuming true score variance can be conceptualized as consistency among the items on a multi-item measure

internal validity threat　in research design, refers to the potential for a confound

inter-rater reliability　the reliability of a psychometric measure assuming true score variance can be conceptualized as consistent among multiple scores used to describe a single rating target

interrupted time-series design　a quasi-experimental research design in which data are collected over an extended period of time, both before and after the introduction of an intervention or treatment (the "interruption")

interval　a scale of measurement in which labels have meaning, order, and equal distances between them

interval estimate   two values provided as a plausible range for a population parameter given varying assumptions

interview   dialogue between two people, commonly used in qualitative research

intraindividual response variability (IRV)   a method of assessing careless responding by calculating the standard deviation across a series of consecutively administered items with similar response profiles

introduction to the introduction   in scientific papers, the text from the start up until the beginning of the first labeled section

introspection   the process by which people tell themselves stories about the explanations for events in their lives to better understand themselves

item characteristic curve   in item response theory, a mathematical function describing the relationship between theta and probability of a correct response

item information   in item response theory, the amount of precision an item has when discriminating between people which varies across the latent trait (i.e., across difficulties)

item response theory (IRT)   an alternative to classical test theory focusing on the diagnosticity of individual items on a test for measurement, as well as the consequences of focusing on items for measurement; contrast with classical test theory

item-total correlation   the correlation between an item's observed scores with the sum or average score across all items intended to measure the same construct, including the item being examined

jangle   a tendency for researchers to consider two constructs different because they have different names

jargon   high-complexity and uncommon words used in formal research to refer to complex ideas in few words; often abused for the purpose of gatekeeping

Jeffreys' scale   a proposed evaluative standard for Bayes factors suggesting $K > 3.2$ favors the alternative hypothesis

jingle   a tendency for researchers to consider two constructs the same because they have similar names

jingle-jangle fallacy   a term used to describe both jingle and jangle challenges associated with construct specification

joint probability   the probability that two conditions will be true at the same time

Journal Article Reporting Standards (JARS)   a set of standards for writing up research results created by the American Psychological Association

justice   a principle from the Belmont Report stating that researchers should always treat others fairly

Kaiser criterion   a traditional cutoff used in exploratory factor analysis to determine how many factors to extract, defined as an Eigenvalue of 1

k-nearest-neighbors (kNN) imputation   a machine learning technique commonly used for single imputation

knowledge   a collection of justified true beliefs

lab versus field   a classic debate in I-O psychology pitting the pros and cons of laboratory research (usually college students) against field research (usually workers in organizations); an outdated distinction

latent variable   the representation of a construct in confirmatory factor analysis; defined as the regression of an imagined value given a series of observed indicators

leading question   in qualitative research, a question that gives the respondent a cue about how the researcher wants them to respond

least publishable unit a pejorative term for the practice of identifying the smallest possible aspect of a research project that is able to be published

lemma the root form of a given word; for example, "eat" is the lemma for "eating," "eats," and "ate"

lemmatization the conversion of a word into its lemma for use as a token

level in research design, refers to each point at which independent observations can be made without nesting, such as the person level, team level, or organization level

level of analysis whenever data exist at multiple levels (such as when nested), the level at which analysis will be conducted

Lewinian spiral a concept in action research describing the cyclical process of planning, action, and fact-finding

Likert-type scale a common method of assessing psychological traits in which multiple questions are asked about the same construct, each with a common set of response options, typically between 5 and 7, and most frequently including the items Strongly Disagree, Disagree, Neither, Agree, and Strongly Agree

Linguistic Inquiry and Word Count (LIWC) a dictionary-based approach developed by Pennebaker et al. (2001) commonly used in psychological research for sentiment analysis

linguistic trap a bias introduced in scale development in which commonalities in language lead you to think that a construct is being measured, but the reality is that shared language features are leading to the observed pattern

listwise deletion in missingness analysis, the removal of all cases with any missingness

literature search strategy the specific techniques used to identify research reports relevant to a particular research question (in literature review) or inclusion criterion (in meta-analysis)

Little's MCAR test a statistical test for missingness completely at random

logical positivism a philosophical framework associated with David Hume and Immanual Kant asserting the necessity of verification to establish truth

LongString a method of assessing careless responding by examining how many times responses are repeated across a case

low-effort respondents see careless respondents

machine learning any analysis conducted via computer in which the computer uses existing data to generate predictions in future, unseen data

Mahalanobis distance a metric calculated to determine each case's multivariate outlyingness

manipulation in experimentation, features of an experiment that are controlled systematically by a researcher to examine their causal effects

manipulation check a question asked to assess if a participant remembers key features of the condition they were in

manipulation strength the intensity of the causal effect of the treatment; greater manipulation strength is likely to result in greater changes in a dependent variable

manual transcription the process by which a researcher types out a transcript

marginal probability the probability that a condition will be true within the constraints of another condition

masking practices that reduce or eliminate participant or researcher awareness of which conditions participants are in at a point where such knowledge could change participant behavior

mastery orientation   in contrast to performance goal orientation, a trait describing a persistent attitude a person brings across contexts in which they believe that success means learning something you didn't know before, not simply doing well on objective markers of success like grades

matrix   a questionnaire design in which questions are listed in rows and response options in columns, intended to minimize repeated text when response options are repeated

maturation   an internal validity threat that refers to history effects related to the passage of time

mean difference   a common unstandardized effect size comparing group means

meaning-making   the process by which a person understands their own experiences

measure   a specific tool developed for the purpose of measurement

measurement   in psychology, the operationalization of constructs; more broadly, the application of numbers to some idea in order to speak about that idea in terms of precise quantity

mechanistic process   any task with a single set of steps taken from start to finish

median imputation   the replacement of missing values with the across-all-cases median of each variable

mediation   the process by which a variable influences another through an intermediate third variable

mediator   a variable in the middle of a mediation, caused by an antecedent and causing an outcome or criterion

meta-analysis   a quantitative secondary research method that involves calculating weighted effect size estimates across previously conducted research studies (see Chapter 13)

meta-analytic database   the collection of research results to be coded in meta-analysis

Meta-Analytic Reporting Standards (MARS)   a set of standards for meta-analysis created by the American Psychological Association

meta-analytic structural equation modeling (MASEM)   a framework for using meta-analytic effect size estimates in mediation analysis

metacognitive skill   skill at thinking about your own thinking; self-reflection about your own cognition

metadata   secondary information collected in reference to how data were collected

meta-regression   use of the entire meta-analytic database and observed effects in regression analysis

midpoint   in scaling, refers to a neutral or neither option

mind map   a particular approach to visualizing schemata

missing at random (MAR)   data where missingness is correlated with population values of variables contained within your dataset, and when controlling for those variables leaves only data that are missing completely at random

missing completely at random (MCAR)   data that are missing due to solely random chance factors

missing not at random (MNAR)   data where missingness does not meet the requirements of MCAR or MAR

mixed methods   the blending of qualitative and quantitative research methods to address a single research question

mixed methods survey   a survey conducted via multiple media, such as paper and electronic, simultaneously

model   any simplified representation of a complex phenomenon

model, hypothetico-deductive   a deductive decision-making framework in which hypotheses are deduced from existing theory

model, partial credit   in item response theory, a type of polytomous model that identifies the probabilities associated with responses varying in their degrees of correctness

model, polytomous   in item response theory, describes models of items and tests without correct answers

model, scientist-practitioner   a concept of education and practice in which methods, goals, and perspectives of those conducting basic research with those applying research in practice

model, shared mental   a conceptual understanding and structure for a specific body of knowledge in common between multiple people

modeling, fixed effects   modeling built upon the assumption that there is a single true population value to describe a particular relationship of interest; contrast with random effects modeling

modeling, random effects   modeling built upon the assumption that there is an overall population distribution from which subpopulations are drawn, and it is from these subpopulations in turn that samples are drawn; contrast with fixed effects modeling

moderation by person   research exploring how a relationship or effect differs depending on the characteristics of the people involved

moderation by situation   research exploring how a relationship or effect differs depending on the situation in which it occurs

moderator   a construct that is theorized to affect how other constructs are related to each other

modern test theory   see item response theory

monograph   a book about a specific study or series of studies, in significant detail

monotonicity   in item response theory, describes an item characteristic curve in which greater difficulty is always associated with higher theta

moral imperative   a personal, ethical principle that drives your behavior across situations

motivate   when hypothesizing, refers to using arguments and evidence to support a proposed hypothesis or research question

multilevel data   observed data that exist at multiple levels

multimethod research   the use of either multiple datasets or multiple studies of the same philosophical orientation

multiple imputation   a family of techniques for imputation involving generating multiple predictions of missing values, running analyses on multiple imputed datasets, and then examining consistency across those analyses via pooling

multiple rater reliability   see inter-rater reliability

multivariate imputation by chained equations (MICE)   a complex multiple imputation technique for imputing missing values based on a long series of studies by Stef van Buuren (2011)

multivariate outlier   an outlier in terms of a case being unusual relative to the expected shape of a relationship between two or more variables

mutually exclusive   in scaling, refers to response options that do not overlap; a desirable quality of a scale

named theories theories that have become sufficiently well-known so as to have a specific name that most researchers refer to them using, such as goal-setting theory

narrative review a secondary research method in which previously gathered literature is gathered and re-interpreted in aggregate

natural language processing a generic term for the use of computers to process text, whether for the interpretation of existing text or the generation of new text

naturalistic fallacy a logical fallacy in which the way things currently are is treated as the way things should be

naturalistic observation when observation is conducted directly and in-person without interference

naturalistic research see naturalistic observation

nesting in research design, refers to levels wholly contained within other levels

n-gram a generic term for tokens that combine n words

nominal a scale of measurement in which labels have meaning

non-experimental research designs in which researchers do not manipulate any variables

normal science a term popularized by Thomas Kuhn describing a period in which a scientific discipline agrees on its basic philosophy of science

normative sample the sample chosen for norming

norming re-calculating scores in terms of a reference group or desired score pattern (usually in terms of mean and standard deviation)

null hypothesis a distribution assumed and tested against in NHST

null hypothesis significance testing (NHST) a particular approach to statistical testing that requires defining a null hypothesis and examining how probable observed data are given that assumption

Nuremburg Code the set of research ethics developed in response to atrocities committed in the name of science during World War II

n-way design see factorial design

objectivism an epistemological framework asserting that knowledge of reality comes from reality itself

oblique rotation in exploratory factor analysis, a technique to increase the interpretability of extracted factor loadings that allows extracted factors to correlate with each other; contrast with orthogonal rotation

observation any method in which a researcher watches behaviors of interest as they naturally occur in some context and interprets what they observe

observational methods a non-experimental research design where observers watch research participants make observations

observed score the actual value of a variable as measured; contrast with true score

odds ratio a ratio of probabilities; interpreted as how much more probable one probability is than another

omission a questionable research practice describing information that is not technically required for reporting but which if not omitted, might lead reviewers or other research consumers to come to different conclusions about the research conducted

online panels a common source of convenience samples; often crowdworkers who have volunteered to participate in research studies for pay

ontological stance a belief system about the nature of reality

ontology the philosophical field that studies the nature of ontological stances

open science   a collection of practices intended to maximize reproducibility, replicability, and transparency in research; something you should do

open-access   research published such that it is available to the public with no fee

operational definitions   a measurement of a construct; commonly numeric values or text

operational validity   in meta-analysis, estimates of the true score relationship between a predictor of job performance and job performance correcting only for unreliability in the criterion

operationalization   see operational definition

opportunity cost   the opportunities that you cannot pursue because you are spending your time and effort on something else

optimal performance test   a test that assess an individuals' aptitude or achievement in a given domain; items have correct answers

optional stopping   a questionable research practice in which researchers analyze results until they look good; explicitly forbidden by the underlying logic of NHST

order effect   an internal validity threat that refers to the order of items on a questionnaire influencing how people respond independently of construct standing

ordinal   a scale of measurement in which labels have meaning and order

orthogonal rotation   in exploratory factor analysis, a technique to increase the interpretability of extracted factor loadings that allows extracted factors to correlate with each other; contrast with oblique rotation

outlier   improbable data given a particular data-generated mechanism

overclaiming technique   asking questions to detect the tendency of fakers to claim that they have knowledge about something that does not exist

overcorrection   in meta-analysis, correction that leads to more optimistic point or interval estimates than can be reasonably justified

pairwise deletion   in missingness analysis, the removal of cases only from analyses where those variables are used

paradigm shift   a term popularized by Thomas Kuhn describing a major shift in philosophy of science by an entire scientific discipline

parallel analysis   in exploratory factor analysis, the comparison of factor analysis conducted on random data to identify a better cutoff for determining how many factors to extract than the Kaiser criterion

parameters   estimated values for populations, like means (mu), standard deviation (sigma), and correlation (rho)

parsimony   the description of a complex phenomenon as completely but briefly as possible

part-of-speech tagging   a technique used in bag-of-words tokenization in which part of speech is defined as a key aspect of a token

path diagram   a precise statement of theory, represented with ovals, boxes, and arrows, indicating interrelationships between constructs and their operationalizations

pattern matrix   in exploratory factor analysis, output that tells you how strongly each factor predicts each item relevant to all other factors

peer review, pre-publication   a variety of approaches in which research reports are peer reviewed before or instead of being reviewed in the context of submission to a traditional journal outlet

peer review, traditional   after a research report is submitted to a conference or journal, peer reviewers evaluate that submission for inclusion according to professional standards and their own judgment

peer reviewers   people with expertise in the subject matter of a research paper asked to provide a formal critique of that paper

performance goal orientation   in contrast to mastery orientation, a trait describing a persistent attitude a person brings across contexts in which they believe success means achieving specific performance goals

personal ethics   guidelines you develop for yourself, building on professional ethics but going further in line with your personal values

personal identifiable information (PII)   data collected that can be used to specifically identify a particular participant

perverse incentives   social and career pressures to engage in questionable research practices

p-hacking   a group of questionable research practices conducted with the goal of creating smaller p-values

phenomenology   the explicit study of subjective experience, with a long history starting with philosophers like Jean-Paul Sartre who were interested in the study of consciousness with a fundamental goal of describing how people engage in meaning-making

philosophical movement   a general term for how a group of researchers in the past applied their ontologies and epistemologies to form a standard, agreed-upon approach for research

philosophy of science   a philosophical movement purporting to define what science is, what qualifies as scientific research, and the purpose of science

philosophy of social science   a philosophy of science specific to social science

pilot study   in test development or research design, any study used to develop better materials rather than test hypotheses or research questions; also see beta test

point estimate   a single value provided as the best guess as to a population parameter, based upon a sample or samples

pooling   the combination of results to reach consensus conclusions in multiple imputation

population   the group of people, team, organizations, or any other unit that you decide to understand using your research

positionality   the social and political context that informs your identity, and in turn, how your identity affects your understanding and interactions with the subject matter you are researching

positivism   a 19th-century philosophical movement associated with Auguste Comte asserting that knowledge stems from what we experience through our human sense

post hoc, ergo propter hoc   a logical fallacy in which cause is attributed to something solely because it occurs later in time

poster tube   a cardboard tube designed to enable the transport of paper scientific posters long distances

posterior probability   the probability that an event will occur in the future given data

post-positivism   a philosophical movement associated with Karl Popper and Thomas Kuhn asserting that it is impossible to verify truth; only falsification leads to knowledge

power   the probability that a researcher will reject the null hypothesis assuming the null hypothesis is false, equal to 1 minus beta

power analysis   any analysis of the value of power, conducted either before or after data have been collected

practically significant   a research finding with implications for changing practice

practice effect   an upward bias in observed scores after multiple completions of a test

predatory publisher   a vanity press that hides the fact it is a vanity press so as to extort money from researchers

prediction   a common goal of quantitative research to create accurate forecasts of the future

prediction versus explanation   a term used to contrast research with a goal of maximizing prediction with research with a goal of maximizing theoretical explanation

predictor   a variable used to predict the value of another variable; does not imply causality; contrast with criterion

Preferred Reporting Items for Systematic Review and Meta-Analyses (PRISMA)   a checklist for all of the information that should be included in a meta-analysis (or narrative review) documenting all the decisions that were made developed by Moher et al. (2015)

preprint   final versions of research papers submitted for publication in academic journals but have not yet been peer-reviewed

preprocessing   the process of changing raw unstructured text to make it more suitable for tokenization (or other analytic processes)

pre-registration   the formal submission of a document outlining planned research design and analysis to a generally accepted repository or journal

primary research   research in which you collect and interpret data on the subjects of your research questions

priming effect   an internal validity threat that refers to a researcher's actions or choices making a participant aware or ready to behave in a certain way later; may result in assimilation or contrast

principal components analysis (PCA)   in test development, used to identify latent constructs within a dataset containing unknown constructs; assumes constructs are measured without error; contrast with exploratory factor analysis

prior probability   the assumed probability that an event will occur in the future before new data are collected

probability sampling   the careful specification of a population of interest and the selection of a subset of that population based upon meaningful probabilities

probing   in qualitative research, refers to researchers asking additional follow-up questions during data collection to get more detail or clarification

process   in writing, the idiosyncratic way each person approaches the act of writing

professional ethics   guidelines developed by consensus outlining what is appropriate and inappropriate behavior for professionals, often moral in nature

professional judgment   bringing together your personal values and ethics, professional standards and ethics, personal experience and expertise, and anything else relevant about you or your background, to make high-quality decisions about research; good professional judgment requires investing in yourself

programming language   a set of vocabulary, syntax, and other rules for creating computer algorithms; can be conceptualized as a way to provide computers with instructions and direction

provisional accept   after a peer review round, a revise and resubmit decision but with some assurance that a complete round of peer review is unlikely after resubmission; implies only an editor or organizer will evaluate the revised submission

psychometric meta-analysis see Hunter-Schmidt meta-analysis

psychometric synonyms and antonyms a method of assessing careless responding by examining consistency between items intended to be identical or polar opposites

psychometrics a subdiscipline within psychology focusing on the measurement of psychological constructs

PsycINFO a curated database of psychology related research maintained by the American Psychological Association

Publication Manual of the American Psychological Association a standardized set of rules for writing, citing, referencing and more produced by the American Psychological Association to standardize reporting within psychology and other fields

publisher an organization responsible for the logistical, procedural, and technological aspects of running a journal or producing books

pure applied research research for the purpose of solving a specific problem

pure basic research research for the purpose of advancing a basic understanding of the world for its own sake

p-value the probability of a particular sample mean being drawn from a particular sampling distribution

Q-grid a pyramid shaped visual aid used in Q-methodology

Q-methodology see Q-sort method

Q-sample see Q-set

Q-set a collection of opinion statements to be rated and/or ranked into a Q-grid

Q-sort method the "systematic study of subjectivity" (Brown, 1993) that asks participants to rank-order opinion statements to rate a Q-set using a Q-grid

qualitative research in contrast to quantitative research, research focused on deep understanding and narrative description; typically involves collection of unstructured data and tends to be more exploratory

quantitative research in contrast to qualitative research, research focused on careful measurement and precision to capture information about constructs; typically relies on statistics

quasi-experimentation non-experimental research designs comparing groups without strict experimental control

questionable research practice (QRP) research design and analytic decisions made that are not universally "good" or "bad" but with the potential to create misleading or fraudulent results

questionable research practices (QRP) decisions of unclear purpose and consequence; may create bias

questionnaire a standardized series of questions asked to research participants, usually on paper or a web-based form

race a social construct used to categorize people; has different structure and contents around the world, although some aspects are more common across cultures than others

random assignment the placement of research participants into conditions completely at random so that the only difference between people across conditions is due to the manipulated independent variable

random forests imputation a machine learning technique commonly used for single imputation

random sampling probability sampling completely at random

random selection see random sampling

random variable   a variable with imperfect measurement in which error occurs at random

range restriction   a possible consequence of convenience sampling; occurs when the ranges of variables are narrower in samples than in the populations they are intended to represent

rating scale   a series of questions intended to measure the same construct at a higher level of reliability and validity than possible with a single question; usually for psychological constructs

ratio   a scale of measurement in which labels have meaning, order, equal distance between them, and a meaningful zero that reflects absence

readme file   any text document providing context, metadata, or other information intended to be the first file a person looks at when opening an unfamiliar folder or directory

realism   any ontological stance that asserts there is a single true reality; contrast with relativism

reflexivity   the extent to which unexamined assumptions about the researcher's own beliefs and biases that might have ultimately suppressed and concealed more than they presented and revealed

registered report   see hybrid registered report

regression discontinuity design   a quasi-experimental research design in which the researcher selects a threshold or cutoff point that determines who is eligible to receive the treatment or intervention and compares change across groups

regression to the mean   the tendency for extreme scores in observed data to become less extreme after repeated testing; do not confuse with the statistical test called regression

reidentification   the process of reconstructing the identity of a research participant from anonymous or anonymized data

relationship estimation   research with the purpose of determining the correlationship between two or more constructs when measured; often relies on observation

relativism   any ontological stance that asserts reality exists for each person observing it; contrast with realism

reliability   in psychometrics, the proportion of observed score variance attributable to true score variance (i.e., the relative contribution of T and e to X)

replicate-and-extent   a research strategy combining replication with novel research goals

replication   re-creating someone else's research to provide additional data or context for the generalizability of that research

replication and extension   describes research with two goals, 1) to replicate a past research finding, such as a specific hypothesis test, and 2) once replicated, to test something new related to the subject of replication

replication crisis   a recent paradigm shift in psychology and other fields resulting in increased attention to the robustness and replicability of research results

representativeness   the degree to which a sample's characteristics are the same as a population's

reproducibility   the degree to which a naive researcher can use available materials, instructions, and writings about a study to re-create its methods precisely; contrast with replication

reproducible analytic pipeline   a coding technique to maximize reproducibility that involves writing code such that it always starts with raw data as input and produces output comprising all major research results, including all reported statistics, tables, and figures

rescope changing the breadth or depth of research questions and hypotheses to avoid fighting a war on two fronts

research the subject of this book; a systematic approach for deeply understanding a particular topic to the standards of a professional discipline

research design a generic term for decision-making about control and generalizability for a specific research study, but often used to refer to the specific approach taken to collect data

research methods the specific tools and techniques used for research

research question a specific, clearly-stated question that describes the goals of a specific research project

research, extant if research has already been conducted, it is extant. all research, except research you are imagining, is extant; in most cases, "extant" is an unnecessary clarification

research, interdisciplinary research in which perspectives from multiple disciplines are integrated to reach a more complete understanding of a problem of phenomenon

research, multidisciplinary research in which researchers from multiple disciplines all work together to collect data but work independently in theoretical development, analysis, and interpretation

residual variance of an item in confirmatory factor analysis, the amount of variance in each item that was not explained by the latent variable specified

respect for persons a principle from the Belmont Report stating that researchers should respect others regardless of their identities and behave in a way that is free of prejudice

retrieval-practice effect the theoretical foundation of the testing effect; describes how humans learn from practicing remembering things

return on investment a ratio of benefits to costs; ideally considers benefits to society, to research, and to yourself together to societal, research, and personal costs; should be high

reverse causality refers to theoretical explanations that are reversed from the true causal order

revise and resubmit after a peer-review round, a decision in which a submission is determined not to be ready for acceptance, but acceptance may be possible after a resubmission with changes

revolutionary science a term popularized by Thomas Kuhn describing a period in which the basic philosophy of science in a scientific disciplines is being challenged

rigor taking care and caution to ensure that the conclusions of your research are justified by the evidence you've collected

risk/reward ratio a ratio of risk to benefits

Rosenthal-Rubin meta-analysis a meta-analytic method focusing on aggregating p-values across studies; generally should not be used

salami slicing the identification and pursuit of least publishable units

salvaging refers to the process of figuring out how to publish the results of a study after the study does not go as expected

sample the group of people you research with the intent of drawing conclusions about the population from which they are drawn

sample-size weighting in meta-analysis, the calculation of a weighted effect size by multiplying each effect size estimate by its associated sample size, calculating the average, and dividing by the total sample size

sampling the process by which a sample is drawn from a population

sampling distribution   the distribution of sample means expected when drawing infinitely from a given population at a consistent sample size

saturation   a term referring to the point in qualitative research at which point no new theoretical information is being uncovered through additional data collection

scale of measurement   the assumed mathematical relationship between the response the numbers used to represent various answers to a question and construct standing

scaling   the specific scoring strategy for multi-question quantitative construct measures, particularly related to how scores across items are combined

scalogram analysis   an analytic techniques used with Guttman scales to evaluate if response options are truly in increasing order of intensity

schema   the mental organization system you use to keep information organized

schemata   plural or schema

scholarly publishing stings   an organized effort to collect evidence supporting the claim that a particular publisher is a vanity press or predatory publisher

science translation   a book intended to share the results and implications of scientific research with non-scientists

scientific consensus   how a substantial majority of researchers currently understands a phenomenon; current theory

scientific poster   a large piece of paper or fabric attached to a rigid display board at a conference that explains a research study

Scopus   a database of research papers curated by Elsevier

SD res   the amount of SD r remaining after correcting for attenuation due to sampling error in psychometric meta-analysis

second order meta-analysis   a meta-analysis of meta-analytic estimates

second order sampling error   random differences between meta-analytic estimates of the same effect

secondary research   research in which you collect and interpret previously gathered primary research data and results

selection   an internal validity threat that refers to systematic differences between the people joining your research and the population you intended to study

selective reporting   a questionable research practice in which researchers report only results that support their desired narrative

self-fulfilling prophecy   a common outcome of confirmation bias; by pursuing confirmation of a firmly held belief, you may create the reality of that belief

semantic differential scale   a scale that measures individuals' subjective attitudes about a certain concept with the use of paired adjectives

senior author   in psychology, the final author of a research paper when that final author is the mentor or supervisor of the first author

sensemaking   an application of meaning-making in management meant to uncover the ways that people make sense of events through introspection, commonly associated with Karl Weick

sentiment analysis   the quantification of text in terms of its emotional content or context

sex   historically, defined as a biological trait in psychology; in practice, it has been more often defined by whatever was written on a participant's birth certificate; in present day, used less often and replaced with gender

share variance   see covary

signals   subtle cues about expectations

Simpson's paradox   when multilevel data are analyzed at an inappropriate level of analysis, describes how observed relationships can appear reversed under certain circumstances

simulation   in data obfuscation, when researchers create fake data that mimics the properties of the original dataset, typically in terms of means, standard deviations, distributional characteristics, ranges, and variable interrelationships

single imputation   a family of techniques for imputation involving the use of individual predicted values to replace missing ones

single-N research   see single-subject research

single-subject research   a class of research designs in which a sample consists of only one person (or team or organization)

situational specificity hypothesis   in the validity generalization debate, the argument that validity estimates should only be considered valid for the organization in which they were collected

skip logic   see branching

snowballing   in meta-analysis, identifying new research reports for inclusion by examining the reference lists of research already collected in a meta-analytic database

Soloman 4-group design   a research design in which participants are randomly split into four groups, systematically varying the presence of a pre-test and an intervention as between-subjects effects, to isolate the effects of pre-testing and the intervention itself

source fallacy   a logical fallacy in which the validity of an argument is derived from the credibility of the person who made it

Spearman-Brown prophecy formula   a mathematical formula for predicting the necessary number of raters to reach a desirable level of reliability given additional raters drawn from the same population as existing raters

split-half reliability   the reliability of a psychometric measure assuming true score variance can be conceptualized as consistency between two arbitrarily defined halves of a complete test

spurious   used to describe relationships that appear plausibly causal but are not causal in reality

stacking   the combination of datasets using multiple imputation

stand on the shoulders of giants   an expression used to describe how all new science rests and relies on the foundation of science that came before it

standard error   the standard deviation of a sampling distribution

standardization   in confirmatory factor analysis, the re-expression of estimated values on easier-to-understand metrics

Standards, The   a common short name for the Standards for Educational and Psychological Testing, a document produced by the American Psychological Association, the American Educational Research Association, and the National Committee for Measurement in Education, intended to create standards for psychometrics

statistically significant   a p-value less than the Type I error rate for a particular null hypothesis

stemming   a technique used to make bag-of-words tokenization more meaningful by removing common word suffixes when lemmatization is not possible or feasible

straightlining   a response pattern commonly observed when participants are exhibiting careless responding; often characterized by all responses being the same regardless of underlying content

stratified random sampling   probability sampling at random within predefined groups of interest, to produce specific proportional representation of those groups

stratum   a group defined for stratified random sampling

strawman   a logical fallacy in which a false position, the straw man, is stated and attacked, misrepresenting the actual nature of a debate and making it easier to criticize

structure   the standardization of materials to be used in research; intended to reduce bias

structure matrix   in exploratory factor analysis, output that tells you the correlation between each item and factor score

style guide   a document that outlines standardized ways to record data, write code, or create other documentation; research groups ideally have their own

subject matter experts (SMEs)   people with identified expertise in something you want to understand

subjectivism   an epistemological framework asserting that knowledge of reality comes through exploration of that reality by the person creating it

submission guidelines   the lists of rules and expectations released by an academic journal or book publisher for consideration for publication

subset analysis   splitting a meta-analytic database into pieces and reporting meta-analytic results separately based upon the split

survey   the administration of questionnaires to a sample drawn from a population of interest in which respondents are asked to produce measurements on the variables we want to measure; contrast with questionnaire

systematic review   a qualitative secondary research method that builds upon narrative review with structured guidelines and rules, to improve quality of conclusions drawn; popularized by the Cochrane Collaboration

talk   in the context of presentation, refers to a standalone formal presentation of research results, often given at a conference

tautology   an assertion that cannot be tested

technical report   a research report written for the purpose of exhaustively documenting some internal process at the organization

technical writing   a highly structured way of writing common in scientific reporting; generally structured around writing assertions or arguments followed by evidence, on a paragraph-by-paragraph basis; the most central purpose of technical writing is being complete, not conversational and easy-to-read; these things are nice but secondary

telegraphing   occurs when researchers unintentionally create demand characteristics

test validity   see construct validity

testing   an internal validity threat that refers to changes in behavior caused by the act of completing a test

test-retest reliability   the reliability of a psychometric measure assuming true score variance can be conceptualized as consistency over time or administrations

theory   one of the most abused words in I-O psychology; refers to the current, generally agreed upon, scientific understanding of a phenomenon of interest

thesis committee   a group of people evaluating a person giving a thesis defense; rules for who can be on a committee vary greatly by institution

thesis defense   typically, a formal presentation and question-and-answer session used to evaluate a specific piece of research conducted for career progression at the postgraduate level; typically a defense of either a master's thesis or doctoral dissertation

theta   in item response theory, refers to true scores on the construct intended to be measured

third variable problem   a common challenge in research where an unmeasured or unknown variable has exerted causal influence on observed variables

tinkering   research driven purely by curiosity and improvisation

token   a variable representing the number of times a meaningful word unit is used; can be word counts or something more complicated

topic sentence   in technical writing, a concise and complete sentence summarizing a major point to be made in the paragraph that follows

transformational research   research with the potential to change researchers' minds, create new paradigms, or radically shift thinking

transparency (in qualitative research)   the degree to which research presents sufficient information for an outsider to assess with some confidence whether the analyses were carried out honestly and whether they support the conclusions

transparency (in research)   the degree to which a researcher makes their decisions, context, and other information apparently and accessible to consumers of their research

treatment   in experimentation, a version of a manipulation in which researchers have changed something in relation to some baseline; contrast with control

treatment group   an experimental group defined by its treatment

triangulation   an approach to mixed methods in which two or more methods are used to converge on the same research question

trigram   a three-word token

trimming   in outlier analysis, the replacement of cases with extreme values with less extreme values

trinitarian view of test validity   a conceptualization of test validity splitting test validity into "construct," "criterion" and "content" types; now considered outdated; contrast with the unitary view of test validity

true score   the hypothetical value of a variable if measured without error; contrast with observed score

T-score   a standardized score with a mean of 50 and standard deviation of 10

t-statistic   the distance between two means, or a mean and an assumed value, in standard error units

Tukey's (1977) fences   a technique for identifying univariate outliers relying on interquartile range

Type I error   occurs when the null hypothesis is true but a researcher concludes it is false

Type II error   occurs when the null hypothesis is false but a research concludes it is true

Type I error rate   the probability a researcher is willing to accept that a Type I error occurs, which should be set before research is conducted and is usually .05

Type II error rate   the probability a researcher is willing to accept that a Type II error occurs, which is set indirectly by setting power before research is conducted

unbiased, epistemologically   when your personal beliefs and values do not influence the substance of your research results

unequal control groups design   a quasi-experimental research design in which intact, existing groups are treated differently and compared

uniqueness   see residual variance of an item

unitary view of test validity   a conceptualization of test validity treating test validity as a single concept, emphasizing the collection of diverse evidence supporting an argument in support of it

units, treatments, observations, settings (UTOS)   four common categorizations of generalizability threats proposed by Cook and Campbell

univariate outlier   an outlier in terms of a case being unusual relative to the expected distribution of that variable

unstandardized   expressed in terms of the original unit of measurement

usability   the degree to which a system is intuitive to use by end users

useful abstraction of reality   see theory

use-inspired basic research   research for the purpose of generating a basic understanding of the world while simultaneously solving practical problems; also called Pasteur's quadrant

validation study   a research study designed to create evidence supporting a construct validity argument

validity   a property of inference that refers to its truthfulness or usefulness; defined in different ways in different contexts

validity (in qualitative research)   coherence and care placed into designing methods that will reach meaningful conclusions

validity generalization   a classic theoretical problem in I-O psychology questioning whether the results of validation studies in one organization can be reasonably generalized to other organizations

validity study   see validation study

validity, internal   in research design, refers to the choices made to maximize confidence in causal conclusions

vanity press   a publisher that will publish just about whatever you send them as long as you give them enough money

verification principle   a concept from logical positivism asserting that a statement must be empirically testable to reasonable build knowledge; otherwise, it is tautological

virtual environment   a simulated computing environment within another computer environment

vote counting   a quantitative secondary research method that involves counting statistically significant results; should not be used

waitlist control design   a research design in which everyone receives the treatment, but some people receive it right away and some receive it later

Web Content Accessibility Guidelines (WCAG)   a document managed by the World Wide Web Consortium (W3C) that provides guidance on how to maximize accessibility in web content

Web of Science   a database of research papers curated by Reuters

weighted effect size   an effect size calculated by averaging effect sizes across previous research, more strongly considering effect size estimates that provide higher quality information

weighting   giving greater influence in an estimate to some contributors than others

white paper historically, a publicly shared document in which a company stated its official position on some issue of importance; today, more likely to be a sales document with lots of science words

wicked problem problems that are both ill defined and difficult to address, with many twists and turns as you better understand them

Winsorization identifies a specific percentile at which scores are considered problematic. However, instead of deleting them, they are replaced with the percentile cutoff

within-person design a research design in which people are compared to themselves, often at different time points or under different contexts

word counts the number of times a word is used in a case of unstructured text

working paper like a preprint, but intended for prepublication peer review

worrying selectively paying attention to important problems with research

writer's block a psychological state in which a person finds it difficult to write

Yerkes-Dodson law a concept that describes how each person has an ideal level of stress that pushes them to perform but does not inhibit their performance

Yule-Simpson effect see Simpson's paradox

Index

Note: Page numbers in *italics* indicate a figure and page numbers in **bold** indicate a table on the corresponding page.

75% rule 352, 421

abduction 421
abductive methods 32
abstract concepts 150
abstractions of reality 30
academic journals 381–384, 421
academic language 416–417
academic research 36
acceptance testing 271, 421
acquiescence bias 251
action editors 384
action research 112–113, 421
ad-hoc testing 272, 421
ad hominem 421
advanced logic *see* branching
age and accent strength, relationship between *183*, 183–184
aggregation 196, 421
airport books 381, 421
alpha test 270–272, 421
alternate forms reliability 156–157, 421
alternative hypothesis 308, 421
American Psychological Association 16–17, 40, 355, 374, 381, 383, 386
analytic plan development 402–403
anchoring effects 129, 222, 422
anchors 246, 422
annotated bibliography 422
anomaly detection 323, 422
anonymity 422
anonymization 369–370, 422
answerability 38
APA *see* American Psychological Association
APA code 17, 422
appeal: to authority 422; to emotion 422
appearing moderate 222, 422
applicant reactions theory 64

approach selection 396–397
archival methods 203
archival qualitative data sources 117–118
archival research 93, 400, 422
area under curve 422
artifact 125; distribution corrections 353–354, 422; in meta-analysis 422; in qualitative research 422
artificial intelligence (AI) 40, 321–323, 422
assimilation 221, 422
associate editors 383–384
assumption of independence 422
attention check questions 231
attention checks 423
attenuation 84, 423
audience selection 47
auditory signal processing 323, 423
authorship 383, 423
authorship order 423
automation of data collection 269–270
axial coding 138, 423
axioms 423

bag-of-words tokenization 139, **141**, **142**, 423
BARS *see* behaviorally anchored rating scale
Bayes factor 319, 423
Bayesianism 423
Bayes' theorem 316–319, 423
Beall's list 386, 423
"begging the question" 392, 423
behaviorally anchored rating scale 423
behavioral traces, online and offline 127
Belmont Report 17, 423
beneficence 423
beta test 272, 423
between-persons designs 197–198
bias: acquiescence 423; central tendency 423; cognitive 128–132, 423; common method

423; confirmation 423; cultural 423; demand 423; dissent 424; epistemological 424; evidential 424; expectation 424; extreme response 424; measurement 424; mitigating 131–132; predictive 424; publication 424; in qualitative research 423; response 424; social desirability 424
bigram 141, 424
binary forced choice scale 248, 424
bogus items 280
books 380–381
bots 424
branch identifiers 268
branching 225–226, 424
burnout 13, 424

call for proposals 378, 424
CAPE *see* Committee for the Advancement of Professional Ethics
careerism 18–19, 424
carelessness 282
careless respondents 231–233, 424
careless responding 282
careless response bias 252
cargo cult science 375–376, 424
carryover effects 222, 424
case studies 105–108, 424
causal effects: between construct and operational definition *59*; estimation 57–58, 425; with experiments, isolating 191–200
causal inference 182
causality 182
causal questions 184
causal relationships, path diagram of 29–30, *30*
causal theories, testing 206; direct effects and moderation 206–207; mediation and indirect effects 207–208
causation *vs.* correlation 182, *182*
causes and effects 181–182
Center for Open Science 366
central limit theorem 303, 425
CEOs, case study of 106–107
CFA *see* confirmatory factor analysis
CFP *see* call for proposals
checking and JARS standards 404
chemistry, realist and objectivist approach to 8
cherry-picking 425
CIT *see* Collaborative Institutional Training Initiative
citation rates 36
classical test theory 425; assumptions about latent variables 153–154, 165; based approach to measurement 154–156, 165; G-theory 163–164; model *166*; reliability 155–156
cleary model 161

cluster sampling 82, 425
Cochrane Collaboration 328, 425
codebook 406, 425
codes 425
coding sheet 425
coefficient omega 425
cognitive biases 128; anchoring effects 129; expectation bias 129–130, *130*; in interview context 130–131
cognitive load 226, 425
Cohen's *d* 314, 425
collaborative document workspace 369, 425
Collaborative Institutional Training Initiative 425
collect leads 42–43
college student samples 88–89
Committee for the Advancement of Professional Ethics 17, 425
common logic errors: ad hominem 393; appeal to authority 392; appeal to emotion 393; "begging the question" 392; cherry-picking 393; naturalistic fallacy 393; post hoc, ergo propter hoc 392; source fallacy 393; strawman 392
common method bias 221
Common Rule 16–17, 425
compensation log 407, 425
completeness 425
completion time, techniques to estimate 226–227
computational linguistics 139, 426
computer-based tracking 201
computer vision 322, 426
conceptual replication 73, 426
conditional effect 60
conditional probability 316–317, 426
conferences 378
confidence intervals 312, 426
confidentiality 426
confirmatory factor analysis 239–244, 426; fit indices 241, **241**; of four-item extraversion measure 240, *240*; indicators 240; with item residual correlations *242*
confirmatory research 426
confounds **90**
conjecture 9, 426
conscientiousness 237–238
consensus 38
consent form 114, 426
construct and operational definition: causal effect between *59*; in path diagram *57*
constructivism 6–7, 426
construct 29–30, 237, 426; contamination 426; deficiency 426; definition of 150; depicted with path diagram notation *56*; formative 426; formative *vs.* reflective 162–163; measurement challenges 150–153; and

operational definitions of theory 30–31; reflective 426; specification, bias to 238; validity 10, 157–158, 426
content analysis 138, 427
content codes 342, 427
content validity 158
context, aspects of *192*
contextual variables 202
contingency table **317**
contrast effects 221
contribution 70
control: in experimentation 427; group 193, 427; in research design 427
convenience sample types, sampling strategy between **90**
convenience sampling 427; common types of 88–89; direct range restriction 83–85, *84*; endogeneity 86–88; indirect range restriction 85–86, *86*; representativeness concerns 83; single-subject designs and samples 89–91
Cook's distance 277, 427
correction 334–335
corrective data cleaning 274; careless responding 282; influential cases 276–279; insufficient effort responding 282–283; missing data problems during 283–286; outliers 275–279; steps 292–293
corrective data cleaning strategies: carelessness and IER 287; missingness 288–292; outliers and influential cases 286–287
correlation: *vs.* causation 182, *182*; inverse variance of *338*; between leaders and followers **184**, 184–185
counterfactuals 182, 427
counterfactual thinking 238
counterproductive work behavior 341, 348
covariances 331
covary 427
credibility interval 333, 427
credibility value 333, 427
criterion deficiency and contamination 160
criterion missingness 285
criterion validity 158
critical incidents 124, 427
Cronbach's alpha 157, 427
cross-classified data 200, 427
cross-level design 198–200, *199*, 427
crossloadings 255–256, 428
cross-tabulation 12, **12**
CTT *see* classical test theory
cultural biases 131
cumulative scales *see* Guttman scales
curated database 428
curated materials 367–368
curation 428

curvilinearity 428
curvilinear relationship 177

dark matter writing 117
dark side of goal-setting 18, 428
databases 40
data cleaning 409–411
data cleaning procedures 262–263; frameworks for understanding decision-making during 263; garden of forking paths and 263–265; importance of 263; *see also* corrective data cleaning; preparatory data cleaning
data collection: and acquisition 408–409; automation of 269–270
data dictionary *see* codebook
data fabrication 264, 428
data mining 319–321, 428
data obfuscation 370, 428
data quality 403
data sources, archival qualitative 117–118
debriefing 428
deception 428
Declaration of Helsinki 16, 428
deductive methods 32
Delphi studies 135–136, 428
demand bias 252
demand characteristics 428
demographic items 215–217
dependent variables 193, 428
descriptive research 428
design thinking 112–113, *113*, 428
DFITS *see* difference in fits
dichotomous scoring 220
dictionaries 143
DIF *see* differential item functioning
difference in fits 278, 428
difference scores 331
differential item functioning 177–178, 428
diffusion of treatment 429
digital observation 203, 429
digital traces 127
dimension extraction 253, 429
directed responding 231
direct effects 206–207, 351, 429
direct range restriction 83–85, *84*, 429
direct replication 72–73, 429
disciplinary silo 429
dissent bias 251
distributions 301–302
documentation 429
dominance response process 177, 429
double-barreled items 219, 429
Dunning-Kruger effect 14, *14* 429
dust bowl empiricism 319–320, 429
DVs *see* dependent variables

ecological validity 158
editing process 416
"editor" in publishing 383–384
editors-in-chief 384
EFA *see* exploratory factor analysis
effect size 313–316, 429; benchmarks 315, 429; recommendations to use 316
electronic surveying: branching 225–226; types of 224–225
Elsevier 41
email-based surveys 224–225
embedded mixed methods 396
embeddedness 13, 429
"emotional content" 143
empiricism 8, 429
endogeneity 86–88
epistemological framework 430
epistemology 6–7, 430
equality: of opportunity to succeed 161, 430; of outcome 430; of outcomes 160
error 154
ethical research 16; personal ethics 18–19; professional ethics 16–18
ethics 16, 38–39, 71–72, 430; in sampling 93; in survey design 223–224
ethics of qualitative research 113–117, **116**; anonymity 115; bias 115; completeness 115–116; confidentiality 115; informed consent 114–115; reflexivity 117
ethnicity 216, 430
ethnography 109–111, 430
evidence 29, 159–160, 207, 430; based on internal structure 430; based on relations to other variable 430; based on response processes 430; based on test content 430; based on the consequences of test use 430; broad categories of 159–160; consideration for theory 31–32; to create theory 32–33; types of 31
exclusion criteria 345, 430
expectation bias 129–130, *130*
experimental design: between-persons designs 197–198; choosing 195; controls and treatments 192–193; cross-level designs 198–199, *199*; demand characteristics 186; dependent variables 193; describing 199; diffusion of treatment 188; generalizability threats 188–191; history 186; independent variables 193; level of analysis 195–199; manipulation strength 194; maturation 187; random assignment 193–194; regression to mean 187; selection 188; testing 187; within-person designs 198
experimentation 185, 430
explanatory mixed methods 397
exploratory analyses 412

exploratory factor analysis 253–254, 431
exploratory mixed method 397
exploratory research 431
"extant" research: definition of 37; making decisions about 35–36
external validity 188–190, 431
extreme response bias 252
eye tracking data, heat map visualization of *127*

fabric posters 379, 431
facets 164, 431
factorial design 199, 431
factor loading 241, 431
fail-safe *N* 339
fairness, test 160–162, 431
fakers 233
falsification 431
feasibility 71
feature identifiers 266, 431
feature naming conventions 269
field research 431
field studies 200–208; archival methods 203; causal theories, testing 206–208; contextual variables 202; field experiments 203–204; observational methods 202–203; quasi-experimental design 204–206; quasi-experiments 203–204; survey-based methods 202
file drawer problem 339, 431
file names and last version 368–369
file naming convention 431
financial rewards 229
fit indices 241–242, 431
five-way interaction 61
focal research question development 45–46
focus groups 124, 432
formative construct 162–163
formative measurement 237–239
formative model of job satisfaction *162*
four-way interaction 61
frame-of-reference training 346, 432
fraud 264
frequentism *vs.* Bayesianism 316, 432
frivolous research 18
functional testing 432
funnel plot 354–355, *355*, 432

gaps in research literature 34–35, 54
garbage-in/garbage-out 354, 432
garden of forking paths 263, 432
gatekeeping 33–34, 432
gender: bias at work 196, **196**; and sexuality 216–217
generalizability: in research design 432; study 367; threats 188–191
generalizability theory 163–164, 432

Glassian meta-analysis 336–337, 432
goal orientation, in research literature review 28–29
goal-setting theory 64
goals for literature review 29–37; decisions about "extant" research 35–37; evidence consideration 31–32; gap filling 34–35; theory creation 32–33; theory understanding 29–31
Goodhart's law 364, 432
Google Scholar 40, 432
Google Scholar power user search terms **344**
G*Power 310, 432
graphic rating scale 246, 432
gray literature 344, 384–385, 432
Greek characters 58
grounded theory 108–109, 432
growth mindset, concept of 15
G-theory *see* generalizability theory
Guttman scales 432

heat map visualization of eye tracking data *127*
Hedges' g 331, 432
Hedges-Olkin meta-analysis 338–339, *340*, 432
higher-level observations **196**
homogeneous sample 132
human subjects research: research ethics for 16–17
Hunter-Schmidt meta-analysis 337–338, *340*, 433
hybrid registered reports 363, 433
hypothesis 32, 433; development 45–46; tests 411–412
hypothesizing after results are known 265, 433
hypothetico-deductive model 32

ICC *see* item characteristic curve
ideal point response process 177, 433
identity: communication 361–362; formation 20–23, 433
IER *see* insufficient effort responding
IER detection 283
illusory essence 238, 433
IM *see* impression management
imposter syndrome 13, 15, 433
imprecise language problem 151
impression management **109**
imputation 288–289, 433
inclusion criteria 343, 433
incremental research 433
independence of cases 345
independent-samples t-test 306–307
independent variable 193, 433
indirect effects 207–208, 433
indirect range restriction 85–86, *86*, 433
individual corrections 353, 433

induction 33
inductive approach 108
inductive integration of flux capacitor 33
inductive methods 32
inferences 158
influential cases 286–287, 434
informed consent 434
inform theory 32, 434
in-principle acceptance 434
institutional review boards 16–18, 114, 404–405, 434
instructed responding 231, 434
instructed response items 280
insufficient effort responding 282
intended authorship 403–404
interaction 60
interaction structuring 134–136
interactive voice response 225, 434
intermediate results reporting 370, 434
internal consistency 157
internal consistency reliability 434
internal structure, evidence based on 159
"internal validity" 10
internal validity threats 186–188, 434; cross-level designs to reduce 199–200; demand characteristics 186; diffusion of treatment 188; history 186; maturation 187; regression to mean 187; selection 188; testing 187
internet observation 126–127
inter-rater reliability 434
interrupted time-series 204
interrupted time-series design 434
interval estimate 434
interval-level measure 155
interview: cognitive biases in context of 130–131
interviewers: impression management applied by 108–109, *109*; impressions theory **110**
interview questions: structure in 131–132
interviews 122–124
intraindividual response variability 281, 435
introduction, outlining and writing 46–47
introduction to introduction 48–49
introduction to the introduction 435
introspection 111, 435
intrusion of privacy 30
Inverse variance of correlation *338*
I-O psychology *5*, 31; action research 112–113; case studies 105–108; epistemologies 6–7; ethics 17; ethnography 109–111; framework for conducting 9–10; grounded theory 108–109; issues affecting 17; ontology 4–6; phenomenology 111–112; philosophical movements 7–10; validity of claims made by 9
IRBs *see* institutional review boards

IRT *see* item response theory
IRV *see* intraindividual response variability
item characteristic curve 167, 435; with high
    discrimination *169*; with low discrimination
    168; negatively skewed *172*; points of
    inflection and 169; probability of endorsing
    correct response *173*; for three items 170,
    171; for two items 169–170, *170*
item information 173, 435
item information curves (IICs), bell-shaped
    distribution of 173–174, *174*
item order 266
item response theory 435; basics of 165–167;
    models *167*, 172–173; parameters,
    demonstration of 167–172; reliability in
    173–175; uses of 177–178; vocational
    interests survey 175–177
item-total correlation 254, 435
item types of survey: demographic items
    215–217; item construction 219–221;
    optimal performance items 218–219
IV *see* independent variable

jangle 435
JAP *see* Journal of Applied Psychology
jargon 33
JARS *see* Journal Article Reporting Standards
Jeffreys' scale 435
jingle-jangle fallacy 151, 435
job interview literature 131–132
joint probability 317, 435
Journal Article Reporting Standards 417–418,
    435; checking and 404; review 399
Journal of Applied Psychology 101, **102**
justice 435

Kaiser criterion 253, 435
k-nearest-neighbors 289–290, 435
knowledge 4; method for creating 8–9; and
    positivism 8

lab *versus* field problem 76–79, 78–79, 435
"ladder of causation" 182
latent variable 435
leader-member exchange theory 64
leadership style, case study of 107
leading question 123
leads, collection of 42–43
learning orientation 28–29
least publishable unit 435
lemma 141, 435
lemmatization 141, 436
level of analysis 195–199, 436
Lewinian spiral 112, *112*, 436
Lewin, Kurt 112
Likert-type scale 436

Likert ("LICK-urt")-type scale 246–248
Linguistic Inquiry and Word Count 143, 436
linguistic trap 255, 436
listwise deletion 286–288, 436
literature review *see* research literature review
Little's MCAR test 436
logical positivism 8–9, 436
logic of falsification 9
longstring 281, 436
low-effort respondents 231–233, 436
lower-level observations **196**

Machiavellianism 341, 348–350
machine learning 321–323, 436
Mahalanobis distance 277, 436
managing editors 384
manipulation 436; check 231, 436; strength
    194, 436
manual transcription 136, 436
marginal probability 317, 436
MARS *see* Meta-Analytic Reporting Standards
MASEM *see* meta-analytic structural equation
    modeling
masking 436
mastery orientation 15, 436
materials for research 405–406
matrix 437
maturation 437
MCAR *see* missing completely at random
mean difference 313–314, 437
meaning-making 111, 437
measure development 237
measurement 211; based on samples of behavior
    151–152; bias 154, 161; challenges for
    constructs 150–153; essence of 149; and
    evidence 159–160; fairness 160–162;
    interval scale of 155; nominal scale of 154;
    numbers 149–150; ordinal scale of 155; or
    manipulation 400–401; potential ways for
    150; ratio scale of 155; reliability 155–157;
    research questions 57; subject to error 152;
    units of 152; universally accepted 150–151;
    validity 157–158; *see also* questionnaires
mechanistic process 321, 437
median imputation 288, 437
mediation 61–63, 352–353, 437; analyses
    208; direct and indirect effects 63, *63*; with
    experimental antecedent *208*; indirect effect
    62, *62*; and indirect effects 207–208; and
    moderation, differences between 63–64
mediator 61–62
"me-search" 23
meta-analysis 69, 326–327, 437; artifact
    corrections 333–335; artifact distribution
    corrections 353–354; fixed effects modeling
    329–330; funnel plot 354–355, *355*;

garbage-in/garbage-out 354; importance of 328–329; individual corrections 353; interval estimates 332–333; point estimates 331; random effects modeling 330, 333; related issues to consider 353–355; second order meta-analysis 354; second order sampling error 354; shared mental model of 341; using R 350–351; variation of 331–332
meta-analytic approaches: Glassian meta-analysis 336–337; Hedges-Olkin meta-analysis 338–339; Hunter-Schmidt meta-analysis 337–338; mixed approach meta-analysis and comparing methods 340; Rosenthal-Rubin meta-analysis 339–340
meta-analytic database 341, **348**, 437
meta-analytic project 340; coding sheet development 341–342, *343*; content coding 346–347; finding source material 342–346; follow-up theory-relevant analyses 351–353; interpretation of results 348–350; running meta-analysis 347–351
Meta-Analytic Reporting Standards 355, 437
meta-analytic structural equation modeling 352–353, 437
metacognition 14
metacognitive skill 437
metadata 437
metadata cross-referencing 266
meta-regression 352, 437
"method-mindedness" 53–54, 57
MICE *see* multivariate imputation by chained equations
midpoint 248
missing at random 437
missing completely at random 437
missing data problems: criterion missingness 285; missing at random 284; missing completely at random 284, 285; missing not at random 284–285; scale-wise predictor missingness 285; within-scale predictor missingness 285
missingness: quantifying and handling using R 290–292; score conversion to 287
missing not at random 437
mixed approach meta-analysis and comparing methods 340
mixed methods 396, 437; research 68, 437; survey 224, 437
mobile surveys 225
modeling: fixed effects 438; meta-analytic structural equation 352–353; psychological variable 61; random effects 438
models: cleary 161; formative *162*; hypothetic-deductive 437; monotonic IRT 172; partial credit 172, 437; polytomous 438; polytomous IRT 172–173, 175–177; reflective *162*;

scientist-practitioner 438; shared mental 341, 438; social scientific 383
moderation: direct effects and 206–207; follow-up analysis for 351; and mediation, differences between 63–64; of moderation 61; by person 61, 438; by person, path diagram notation of *62*; by situation *60*, 60–61, 438; u-shaped relationship 208
moderator 60
modern test theory *see* item response theory
monographs 381, 438
monotonic IRT models 172
moral imperative 438
motivation 15, 49, 61–62
multilevel data 196, 200, 438
multimethod research 396, 438
multiple imputation 289, 438
multiple questions, asking 64–66
multiple rater reliability *see* inter-rater reliability
multiple rater (or inter-rater) reliability 157
multivariate imputation by chained equations 289, 438
multivariate outliers 277, 438
multivariate outlyingness 281

named theories 64, 438
narcissism 341, 348–350, *355*
narrative review 68–69, 327–328, 438
naturalistic fallacy 439
naturalistic observation 125, 439
naturalistic research *see* naturalistic observation; observational methods
natural language processing 139–142, 322, 438
natural sciences 8
"negative emotional reaction" 65
negative feedback 15
negative reinforcement 229
nesting 191, 439
neutrality bias 251
n-gram 141, 439
NHST *see* null hypothesis significance testing
NLP *see* natural language processing
nominal-level measure 154
normal distributions 302–303
normal science 9, 439
normative sample 439
norming 439
notes, taking 42–43
null hypothesis 304, 439
null hypothesis significance testing 299, 328–329, 439; artificial intelligence and 321–323; Bayes' theorem and 316–319; confidence intervals 312; data mining and 319–321; effect size and 313–316; history of 300; logic of 300–305; machine learning and 321–323; power for 308–311

numbers 149–150
Nuremburg Code 16, 439
n-way design 199

objectivism 439
objectivist epistemology 6
oblique rotation 254, 439
observation 125–128; higher-level **196**; lower-
    level **196**
observational methods 202–203, 439
observed score 154, 439
odds ratio 331, 439
omission 264, 439
omitted variables bias 86–88
online and offline behavioral traces 127
online panels 88, 89, 439
ontological stance 4–6, 5
ontology 439
open-access 386, 439
open coding of research data *138*
open science 265, 439
open-space office designs 107
operational definitions 29, 439
operationalization 401–402
operational validity 336, 439
opportunity cost 362, 440
optimal performance test 218–219, 440
optional stopping 440
order effects 440; anchoring effects 222;
    appearing moderate 222; assimilation 221;
    carryover effects 222; contrast 221; guidelines
    related to 223; priming effects 222
ordinal-level measure 155
organizational behavior 31
organizational materials 406–407
organizational samples 88–89
organizational surveys 233–234
orthogonal rotation 254, 440
outlets 413–414
outlier 440; cleaning strategies 286–287;
    detection techniques 277–278; and
    influential cases. 276, 278; multivariate 277;
    time-based 280; univariate 277
outlier detection: Tukey's (1977) fence for 277;
    using R 278–279
outlying case **268**
outlyingness 276, 277
overclaiming technique 233, 440
overcommitment 18
overconfidence 15
overcorrection 335, 440

pairwise deletion 288, 440
papers, reading 42–43
paper writing theory 49
paper writing training 49

paradigm shift 9, 440
parallel analysis 254, 440
parameters 77
parsimony 440
partial coding spreadsheet *343*
partial credit model 172
participant log 406, 407
part-of-speech tagging 141, 440
path diagram 29–30, *30*, *64*, 64–65, 440;
    cheat sheet *66*; construct and its operational
    definition in *57*, *59*; construct depicted with
    56; mediation (direct and indirect effects)
    in *63*; mediation (indirect effect only) in *62*;
    moderation by person in *62*; moderation by
    situation in *60*; theory of relationship *60*
pattern matrix 254
PCA *see* principal components analysis
peer review 379; pre-publication 362–364, 440;
    traditional 440
peer reviewers 367–368, 440
performance goal orientation 28–29, 440
personal ethics 18–19, 441
personal identifiable information 223, 441
person-environment (P-E) fit 163
perverse incentives 363–364, 441
p-hacking 265, 441
phenomenology 111–112, 441
philosophical foundations of research:
    epistemologies 6–7; importance of
    understanding 4; ontology 4–6; philosophical
    movements 7–10
philosophical movement 7–10, 441
philosophy of science 8, 441
philosophy of social science 8, 441
PII *see* personal identifiable information
point estimate 441
polytomous IRT models 172–173, 175–177
pooling 289, 441
population: access to 78; cluster sampling
    82; convenience sampling 86–91; making
    decision about 77; parameters 77–78;
    random sampling 80; representative 77; and
    samples 77–78; selection of 76; stratified
    random sampling 80–82
population of interest 397–398
positionality 72, 441
Position Analysis Questionnaire 57
positive reinforcements 229
positivism 8, 441
posterior probability 317, 441
poster tube 441
post hoc, ergo propter hoc 441
post open science documents 412–413
post-positivism 9, 441
power analysis 308–311, 403, 441
practicality 39

predatory publishers 385–387, 441
prediction 100
prediction *vs.* explanation 322, 441
predictive bias 161
predictor 441
Preferred Reporting Items for Systematic Review and Meta-Analyses 355, 442
preparatory data cleaning: alpha testing 270–272; automation of data collection 269–270; beta testing 272; codebooks and data dictionaries 266–267; corrective practices 266; before data collection 266; feature naming conventions 269; pre-registration 272–274; syntax and code reuse 272–273
preprints 384–385
preprocessing 141, 442
pre-publication peer review 362–363
pre-registration 272–274, 362–363, 407–408, 442
presentations 377–378
primary research 67–68, 400, 442
priming effects 222
principal components analysis 253–254, 442
priori power analysis 309, 422
prior probability 318, 442
PRISMA *see* Preferred Reporting Items for Systematic Review and Meta-Analyses
probabilistic justification 4–5
probabilistic reasoning 299
probability sampling 80–82, 442
procedural justice 30
PROCESS macro 208
production editors 384
professional ethics 16–18, 442
professional judgment 107, 442
programming language 442
project repositories 366
project responsibilities 403–404
promotion among audience 418–419
provisional accept 442
pseudo-guessing parameter 170–171
psychological construct *see* construct
psychological variable modeling 61
psychometric antonyms and synonyms 280–281
psychometric meta-analysis *see* Hunter-Schmidt meta-analysis
psychometrics 150, 442
psychometric synonyms and antonyms 442
PsycINFO 40, 442
publication bias 92, 339
Publication Manual of the American Psychological Association 442
public speaking 376–379
publishers 41, 442
publishing venue 47

pure applied research 12, 443
pure basic research 12, 443
p-value 300, 328, 443; calculation of 305–306; in context of study 307–308; definition of 304; misinterpretations of 305–306

QDR *see* qualitative data repository
Q-grid 135, *135*, 443
Q-methodology *see* Q-sort method
QRP *see* questionable research practice
Q sample 135
Q-set 443
Q-sort method 135, 443
qualitative and quantitative research approaches 57
qualitative data analysis: natural language processing 139–142; thematic analysis 137–138
qualitative data repository 117–118
qualitative methods, types of 121; artifact analysis 125; criteria for choosing 128; focus groups 124; interviews 122–124; observation 125–128
qualitative papers 113
qualitative research 56, 67–68, 99–100, 443; definition of 101, 103–104; ethics of 113–117; examples of 101; history of 101; subjectivity and objectivity 104; valid/good 105
qualitative research approaches 105, **106**; action research 112–113; case studies 105–108; ethnography 109–111; grounded theory 108–109; phenomenology 111–112
qualitative study planning: interaction structuring 134–136; sample size 132–133; script creation 134; writing good questions 133–134
quantitative research 56, 67–68, 103, 443
quasi-experimental design: interrupted time-series 204; regression discontinuity 204–205, *205*; unequal control group field experiments 205–206
quasi-experimentation 443
questionable research practice 72, 264–265, 443
question-and-answer session 134
questionnaire 151, 211, 443; completion time, techniques to estimate 226–227; look and feel, selecting 224–228; question spacing 227–228; response rates 228–230; screening out bad responses to 230–233; *vs.* survey 211; visual elements 228
questionnaires, development of: ethics in 223–224; item construction 219–220; item type selection for 215–217; optimal performance items 218–219; order effects

to consider for 221–223; risk areas and pitfalls to consider for 220–221; scale of measurement, identifying 214–215; writing research questions 211–214
questions, writing good 133–134, 211–214

race 216, 443
random assignment 193–195, 443
random forests imputation 290, 443
random sampling 80, 194, 443
random selection 194
random variable 153, 443
range restriction 83–86, 443
rating scale 237–238, 443; avoiding response biases 251–252; behaviorally anchored rating scales 251; confirmatory factor analysis and 239–244; development of 244–247, 252–257; dichotomous scales 248–249; formative measures and 238–239; graphic rating scales 249; Guttman scales 250–251; identification of 257–258; reflective measures and 237–238; semantic differential scales 249–250; types and variations of 244
ratio-level measure 155
readme file 407, 443
realism 5–6, 444
realist and objectivist approach 8–9
recommendations for writing 416
recordings, transcribing 136–137
record-keeping 406–407
reflective constructs 162–163
reflective measurement, assumption behind 237–238
reflective model of job satisfaction 162
reflexivity 72, 444
registered reports 363
regression discontinuity design 204–205, 205, 444
regression to the mean 444
reidentification 444
relationship estimation 59, 444
relativism 6, 444
reliability 155–157, 444; alternate forms 156–157, 421; internal consistency 434; inter-rater 434; in IRT 173–175; multiple rater (or inter-rater) 157; split-half 157, 447; test-retest 156, 448
replicate-and-extend research strategy 73, 444
replication: crisis 262, 444; and extension 367, 444; as research strategy 72–73
representative 77
representativeness 77
representativeness concerns 83
reproducibility 366–367, 444
reproducible analytic pipeline 444
rescope 55, 444

research 3; activities classified as 11; data, open coding of 138; definition of 10–11; extant 445; interdisciplinary 445; methods 10; multidisciplinary 445; role in professional life 11–16; values about 3–4
research and experimental development (R&D) 10
research approach for research question 66–69
research, checklist for laying foundation of 394; approach selection 396–397; foundational philosophies 395; JARS standards review 399; literature review 395; population of interest 397–398; research questions and hypotheses 398–399; target audience 399
research design 181–182, 185, 263, 444; control 185; demand characteristics 186; diffusion of treatment 188; generalizability 185; generalizability threats 188–191; history 186; internal validity threats 186–188; maturation 187; misconception 201; regression to mean 187; selection 188; testing 187; UTOS perspective 189–191
research execution and analysis checklist: data cleaning 409–411; data collection and acquisition 408–409; exploratory analyses 412; hypothesis tests 411–412; investigation of research questions 411–412
research literature: filling gaps in 34–35; search strategy 343–344, 436
research literature review 27, 53, 395; challenge in 33; empirical research 54–55; goal orientation in 28–29; research question types 55–66
research literature review goals 29–37; decisions about "extant" research 35–37; evidence consideration 31–32; gap filling 34–35; theory creation 32–33; theory understanding 29–31
research literature review strategy 37, 37–47; artificial intelligence for 40; collect leads, and take notes 42–43; focal research question development 45–46; hypothesis development 45–46; introduction, outlining and writing 46–47; papers, reading 42–43; research questions for 37–39; schema development 43–45; search terms development for 39–41; titles and abstracts, reading 41–42
research methods 444
research orientation 12
research performance score 53
research plan checklist: analytic plan development 402–403; archival or primary research 400; checking and JARS standards 404; data quality 403; intended authorship 403–404; measurement or manipulation 400–401; operationalization 401–402; power analysis 403; project responsibilities 403–404; sampling strategy selection 402

research preparation and development checklist:
 IRB approval 404–405; materials for research
 405–406; organizational materials 406–407;
 pre-register 407–408; record-keeping
 406–407
research questions 28, 53–54, **55**, 55–66,
 184, 444; and approach, selecting 69–72;
 asking multiple 64–66; characteristics of
 37–38; examples of 38–39; how 61–63;
 and hypotheses 398–399; investigation of
 411–412; research approach for 66–69; what
 56–59; which 59–61
research result sharing: challenges of 358–359;
 narratives for 359
research result sharing strategies 359; analytic
 tools and workflows 373–374; with
 audience 374–387; common goals 360–361;
 curating useful materials 367–368; identity
 communication 361–362; metadata and
 documentation 370–371; peer-reviewed
 publication 361; pre-publication peer
 review 363–364; pre-registration 362–363;
 presentations 361; project repositories 366;
 reproducibility 366–367; reproducible
 code and analyses 371–373; shareable
 data 369–370; social media 362–363; for
 unwanted results 364–366
research sharing and write-up checklist 412;
 academic language 416–417; editing process
 416; JARS standards 417–418; outlets
 413–414; outlining 414–415; post open
 science documents 412–413; promotion
 among audience 418–419; recommendations
 for writing 416; reviewing 417; submit, revise,
 resubmit 418; technical writing 414–415
research strategy, replication as 72–73
residual variance 240, 445
respect for persons 445
respondents' time 226
response biases 251–252
response processes, evidence based on 159
response rates to surveys 228–230
result preparation 362–374; analytic tools
 and workflows 373–374; curated materials
 367–369; metadata and documentation
 370–371; pre-registration and pre-publication
 peer review 362–364; project repositories
 366; reproducibility 366–367; reproducible
 code and analyses 371–373; shareable data
 369–370; unwanted results 364–366
result sharing with audience 374–375; academic
 journals 381–384; books for 380–381; gray
 literature 384–385; peculiar approaches to
 375; peer review 379; predatory publishers
 and vanity presses 385–387; public speaking
 376–379

retrieval-practice effect 187, 445
return on investment 362, 445
reverse causality 183, 445
reviewing 417
revise and resubmit 445
revolutionary science 9, 445
rigor 100, 445
risk/reward ratio 362
Rosenthal-Rubin meta-analysis 445

salami slicing 382, 445
saliency 228–229
salvaging 445
samples: and populations 77–78; and single-
 subject designs 89–91
sample size: qualitative study planning
 132–133; weighting 338, 445
sampling 76, 445; approach to 82; cluster 82;
 concerns 91–93; distribution 303–304, 445;
 ethics in 93; probability 80–82; random 80;
 strategies for I-O psychology research 76–77;
 strategy between convenience sample types
 90; strategy selection 402; stratified random
 80–82
sampling lab *versus* field 78–79
scale development, bias to 238
scale of measurement 154–155, 214–215, **215**,
 445
scale-wise predictor missingness 285
scaling 246, 445
scalogram analysis 446
scatterplot *197*
schema 43–45, 446
scholarly publishing stings 386, 446
science as collaborative process 358
science translation 381, 446
scientific consensus 38, 446
scientific method 8
scientific poster 378–379, 446
scientific writing *see* technical writing
Scopus 40, 446
score conversion to missingness 287
score ignorance 288
screening procedures for undesirable responses
 230–233
script creation 134
search engine optimization 343–344
search terms, development of 39–41
secondary data, sampling concerns with 93
secondary research 68–69, 91, 446
second order meta-analysis 354, 446
second order sampling error 354, 446
selective reporting 363, 446
self-efficacy, debate on 197–198
self-fulfilling prophecies 130, 446
self-reported data quality 281–282

semantic differential scale 446
sensemaking 111, 446
sentiment analysis 142, 446
sex 446
shareable data 369–370
shared mental model 341
signals 130
Simpson's paradox 196, *197*, *198*, 446
simulation 370, 446
single imputation 288–289, 447
single-item direct questioning 281
single-subject designs and samples 89–91
single-subject research 447
SIOP *see* Society for Industrial and
    Organizational Psychology
situational specificity hypothesis 337, 447
skeleton outline writing 47–48
skip logic *see* branching
SMEs *see* subject matter experts
snowballing 344, 447
social desirability bias 251
social media 362–363
social scientific model 383
social scientific research methods 9
Society for Industrial and Organizational
    Psychology 16
socioeconomic status 238–239
Solomon 4-group design 199–200, 447
source fallacy 447
Spearman-Brown prophecy formula 347, 447
Specialized interview techniques 123–124
split-half reliability 157, 447
spurious relationship 183
stacking 289
standard error 304, 447
standardization 153, 447
standardized *vs.* unstandardized estimates 240
standards 153, 447; *see also* Journal Article
    Reporting Standards
stand on the shoulders of giants 447
statistically significant 447
statistical significance 305
stemming 141, 447
straightlining 252, 447
stratified random sampling 80–82, 447
stratum 447
strength of evidence 359
stress, Yerkes-Dodson law 15–16
structure matrix 254, 448
study-level moderation 351
style guide 448
subclinical psychopathy 341
subjectivism 448
subject matter experts 56, 448
submission guidelines 448
subset analysis 352, 448

success, meaning of 15
summary outline creation 48–50
supporting points, adding 50
survey 448; codebook for **267**; *vs.* questionnaire
    211; vocabulary decision 211
survey-based methods 202
symposium 378
syntax and code reuse 272–273
systematic review 91–92, 448

talks 376–378
target audience 399
tautology 448
t-distributions 307
technical reports 385, 448
technical writing 46, 414–415, 448; adding
    supporting points 50; audience selection
    47; plan to write 47; publishing venue 47;
    skeleton outline writing 47–48; summary
    outline creation 48–50; topic sentences
    49–50
telegraphing 448
telephone surveys 225
test content, evidence based on 159
test information curve *175*
test-retest reliability 156, 448
test use, evidence based on consequences of
    159–160
test validity *see* construct, validity
text analysis strategies *139*, **140**
thematic analysis 137–138
theory: aspects of 29–30; considering evidence
    31–32; constructs and operational definitions
    30–31; understanding 29–31; using evidence
    to create 32–33
thesis committee 376, 448
thesis defense 376, 448
third variable problem 448
time-based outliers 280
tinkering 12, 448
titles and abstracts, reading 41–42
topic sentences 47, 49–50, 449
tracking during training 194–195
transformational research 449
transparency 30, 363, 449
treatment group 193
triangulation 396, 449
trigram 141, 449
trimming 286–287, 449
trinitarian view of test validity 158, 449
true score 154
T-score 449
t-statistic 306
Tukey's (1977) fences 449
type I error 449
type II error 308, 449

type I error rate 308, 309, 449
type II error rate 449

undesirable responses, screening procedures for 230–233
unequal control group field experiments 205–206
unequal control groups design 449
unitary approach 159
unitary view of test validity 158, 449
units, treatments, observations, settings 449
univariate outliers 277, 449
unrepresentative respondents 230–231
unwanted results, studies showing 364–366
usability and functional testing 271–272
use-inspired basic research 12, 450
u-shaped relationship 208
UTOS *see* units, treatments, observations, settings
"UTOS" acronym 189–191

validation study 450
validity 157–158, 185–186, 450; definition of 10; generalization 43, 337; internal 450; of measures 237; types of 10
values about research 19–21
vanity presses 441, 450
variance 59
verbatim headings 48–49
verification principle 8, 450

video observation 125–126
virtual environment 450
virtual reality and learning 192–193
vocabulary decision 211
vocational interests survey 175–177
vote counting 328, 450

waitlist control design 195, 450
WCAG *see* Web Content Accessibility Guidelines
web-based surveys 224–225
Web Content Accessibility Guidelines 225, 450
Web of Science 40, 450
weighted effect size 331, 450
weighting 331, 450
what research question 56–59
which research question 59–61
white papers 385, 450
wicked problems 375, 450
wildland firefighters, ethnography of 111
Winsorization 287, 450
within-person design 198, 450
within-scale predictor missingness 285–286
working papers 384–385, 451
workplace outcomes 262
writer's block 46, 451

Yerkes-Dodson law *15*, 15–16, 451
Yule-Simpson effect *see* Simpson's paradox

Made in United States
Orlando, FL
26 August 2025

64332107R00262